Reading Becomes
a Necessity of Life

Reading Becomes a Necessity of Life

Material and Cultural Life
in Rural New England, 1780–1835

William J. Gilmore

The University of Tennessee Press
Knoxville

Publication of this book has been aided by a grant from the American Council of
Learned Societies from funds provided by the Andrew W. Mellon Foundation.

The paper in this book meets the minimum requirements of the American National
Standard for Permanence of Paper for Printed Library Materials. ∞   The binding
materials have been chosen for strength and durability.

Frontispiece: *The Holy Family*. Engraving by Isaac Eddy. *The Holy Bible: Containing the
Old and New Testaments* . . . (Windsor, 1812). New Testament, opposite title page.
Courtesy, Vermont Historical Society. The Holy Family bridged the world of the Israelites
and Upper Valley rural life. Opposite the New Testament title page, Isaac Eddy of
Weathersfield presents John the Baptist, Mary, infant Jesus, and Joseph as an ordinary
farm family. In the background, a homestead and a meeting house link family, religion,
and farm life in a sanctified set of enduring values amid economic, social, and cultural
transformation.

Library of Congress Cataloging in Publication Data

Gilmore, William J., 1945-
   Reading becomes a necessity of life : material and cultural life
   in rural New England, 1780–1835 / by William J. Gilmore – 1st ed.
     p.   cm.
   Bibliography: p.
   Includes index.
   ISBN 0-87049-586-0 (cloth: alk. cloth)
   ISBN 0-87049-768-5 (pbk.: alk. paper)
   1. Books and reading—New England—History—19th century.
   2. Books and reading—New England—History—18th century. 3. New
England—Intellectual life. 4. New England—Economic conditions.
5. Literacy—New England—History. I. Title.
ZI003.N4G54   1989
028'.9'0974–DC19   88–10692   CIP

In memory of my first great teacher,
Edward G. Roddy, Jr., of Merrimack College;
for Merrill D. Peterson, my second great teacher;
and for Lisa, who ensures a life of surprises.

Contents

Preface [xvii]

Acknowledgments [xxiii]

Introduction [1]

Chapter 1   "Competence Among the Rocks": Continuity and
Change in Rural New England,
1760–1835 [17]

Reading Becomes a Necessity of Life:
The Broad Context of North Atlantic Civilization [18]

The Study Area and the Scale of Generalization [27]

Reading Instruction in Rural New England,
1780–1830, and Its Conservative Intent [34]

Toward the Intellectual Emancipation
of American Women [42]

Part I   **Material and Cultural Foundations** [51]

Chapter 2   The Commercialization of Rural Life,
1760–1835 [53]

The Commercialization of Rural New England,
1760–1835 [54]

Understandings of Economic Life
in Windsor District, 1760–1835 [60]

Commercialization, Stage One, 1760–95:
The Settlement Era [70]

Commercialization, Stage Two, 1795–1815:
The Rise of a Commercial Society and Economy [84]

Commercialization, Stage Three, 1815–35:
The Commercialization of Daily Life   [98]

Conclusions   [110]

Chapter 3   The Foundations of Participation
             in Rural New England Culture, 1760–1835   [114]

Upper Valley Cultural Expression:
The Place of Print Communications   [114]

Trends in the Acquisition of Elementary Literacy
in the Upper Valley   [118]

Agents of Literacy—Family and District School   [121]

Elementary Literacy—Pace and Motives   [127]

The Uses of Literacy and the History of Knowledge
in the Upper Valley   [130]

Chapter 4   The Human Habitats of Rural New England,
             1780–1835: Sets of Conditions Shaping
             Participation in Cultural Life   [135]

A Network of Human Habitats
as an Organizing Conception   [137]

Description of the Human Habitats
of Windsor District, 1760–1835   [141]

History of the Network of Human Habitats,
1760–1835   [148]

Key Characteristics of the Network
of Human Habitats   [149]

Part II   Print Communications and Cultural Exchange   [155]

Chapter 5   The Communication System and
             the Book Trade in Rural New England:
             The Upper Valley, 1778–1835   [157]

Contact Points and the Life Cycle of Printed Objects   [157]

The Circulation System for Print Culture
in the Upper Valley, 1778–1835   [163]

Dissemination: Zones of Access to Print Culture
in the Upper Valley   [178]

Chapter 6   Upper Valley Vehicles of Print Communicatons
             and the World of Popular Sellers, 1778–1830   [189]

	Print Vehicles	[190]
	Printed Matter Published in the Upper Valley, 1778–1830	[195]
	The World of Popular Sellers in the Upper Valley: Collective Cultural Trends, 1805–30	[204]
	Popular Sellers and the Life Cycle	[217]
Part III	**Family Foundations**	[223]
Chapter 7	Varieties of Family Life: The Material Anchors of Knowledge in Windsor District, 1780–1830	[225]
	The Family as the Foundation of Collective Existence	[225]
	Household, Wealth, Work, and Public Position, 1780–1830	[227]
	Windsor District Society and the American Northeast, 1760–1830	[240]
	Wealth and Holdings of Printed Matter	[247]
Chapter 8	Deep Structure and Rural New England *Mentalités*: Reading and the Family Circle, 1780–1835	[254]
	Family and Bible: The Center of Reading Activity in Windsor District, 1780–1835	[254]
	Family Libraries: Kinds of Works Retained and Reading Habits	[264]
	Windsor District Family Libraries: Incidence and Size	[269]
	Family Libraries: Windsor District and Rural America, 1700–1850	[273]
	Types of Family Libraries in Windsor District Through 1830	[277]
Part IV	***Mentalités*: Intellectual Reservoirs and Their Replenishment**	[283]
Chapter 9	Mending and Rebirth: Human Habitats, Reading Communities, and *Mentalités*, 1780–1830	[285]
	Continuity and Change in the Upper Valley Network of Human Habitats	[285]
	Complexity in the Reading Experience: Libraries, Texts, Interests, and Meanings	[288]

Cultural Life in the Hardscrabble Human Habitat [292]

Cultural Life in the
Self-Sufficient Farmstead Human Habitat [301]

Cultural Life in the
Self-Sufficient Hamlet Human Habitat [311]

Cultural Life in the
Fortunate Farmstead Human Habitat [320]

Cultural Life in the
Fortunate Village Human Habitat [329]

Chapter 10   The Dawn of a "Modern Age":
Historical Conclusions and
Public Policy Implications [344]

The Dawn of a "Modern Age"
in Rural New England, 1780–1835 [346]

The Commercialization of Economic, Social,
and Cultural Life, and the Creation of an
Early Modern Rural Infrastructure [352]

The Emergence of an Age of Reading in America [354]

Rural Pluralism and Cultural Diversity [359]

A Shift in the Meanings of Human Happiness [361]

Public Policy Implications: History and the Study
of Context [364]

Appendix 1   Print Culture and Evidence for Other Forms
of Cultural Expression [377]

Appendix 2   Windsor District Human Habitats, 1780–1835:
Interrelationships among Primary Factors [384]

Appendix 3   The Upper Valley Occupational System,
1780–1835 [396]

Appendix 4   Inventories, Spine Titles, and Family Libraries,
1787–1835 [402]

Appendix 5   Snuff and an "Electrikl Machine":
A Scholar in the Wilderness [410]

Notes [415]

Abbreviations [481]

Bibliography [483]

Index [515]

Illustrations

Plates

The Holy Family. The Holy Bible.   Frontispiece

Oxen Hauling a Sled on Clinton Gilbert's Farm,
Woodstock, Vermont   [3]

Threshing Grain, Waitsfield, Washington County,
Vermont.   [24]

Pilgrim's Dream. [John Bunyan]. *The Christian Pilgrim.*   [36]

Fiftieth Anniversary Banquet (1885)
of Black River Academy, Ludlow, Vermont.   [46]

Louisa's Retirement. John Bennett.
Letters to a Young Lady.   [48]

Federal Money. Daniel Adams, *The Scholar's Arithmetic.*   [58]

Country General Store Stock on Hand.   [94]

Tyson Furnace, Plymouth, Vermont.   [99]

Alvin Fisher. *Corn Husking Frolic,* 1828–29.   [105]

Windsor, Vermont: Armory and Machine Shop in the
Mid-nineteenth Century.   [111]

Family Scene with Newspaper. Albert Alden
Proof Book. 1840. Engraved by David C. Johnston.   [117]

Schoolhouse Exterior. Plymouth, Vermont.   [125]

Schoolhouse Interior. Waitsfield, Vermont.   [126]

Angier March Bookstore. Newburyport.   [159]

Ebenezer Larkin Bookstore. Boston   [173]

Plates, continued

Peddler James Fisk, Jr., of Burlington, Vermont. [177]

The Heavenly Nine. David Claypoole Johnston, 1828. [191]

The Angel with the Book. The Holy Bible. [211]

Pro Patria. George Washington.
[John Corry]. *Biographical Memoirs.* [213]

Squire Thornhill Carrying off Olivia. Oliver Goldsmith.
The Vicar of Wakefield. [214]

Freemason's Heart. Broadside. [215]

Frontispiece. George Fisher. *[American] Instructor.* [218]

Plymouth Ponds from the South, Plymouth, Vermont. [229]

Search the Scriptures. Albert Alden, "Scriptures." [258]

Farmhouse in Winter. Randolph, Orange County,
Vermont. [293]

Lovejoy Broad Brook Farm in Winter, South Royalton,
Vermont. [303]

Anon. *View of Cavendish, Vermont, c.1825.* [313]

Albert Bierstadt. *Ascutney Mountain, Vermont,
from Claremont, New Hampshire* (1862). [321]

Anon. *Windsor Village from Cornish Hills.* [331]

Figures

1–1 New England and the Upper Valley, c.1830 [28]

1–2 Windsor District, 1787–1835 [30]

2–1 Windsor District Community Size and Geography
of Settlement, 1790 and 1800 [71]

2–2a Upper Connecticut River Valley Market Centers, 1790 [75]

2–2b Upper Connecticut River Valley Market Centers, 1800 [76]

2–3 Windsor District Economic Locales, 1780–1835 [78]

2–4 Upper Connecticut River Valley Press, 1783–1800 [86]

2–5 Vermont Journal Post–Rider Delivery Points, 1800 [87]

Figures, continued

2–6   Windsor District Community Size
      and Geography of Settlement, 1810 and 1830   [90]

2–7   Upper Connecticut River Valley Press, 1801–15   [91]

2–8   Upper Connecticut River Valley Market Centers, 1810 [92]

2–9   Upper Connecticut River Valley Market Centers, 1830 [101]

4–1   Windsor District Human Habitats, 1787–1830   [139]

5–1   Upper Valley Permanent Print Centers, 1787–1830   [166]

5–2   Upper Valley Auxiliary Print Centers Through 1830   [168]

5–3   Upper Valley Bookstore Locations Through 1830   [172]

5–4   Upper Valley Newspaper Locations Through 1830   [174]

5–5   Upper Valley Differential Access Zones, 1820–30   [179]

5–6   Upper Valley Full Access Zone, 1820–30   [180]

5–7   Windsor District Travel Distances, c.1810   [183]

5–8   Windsor District Zones of Access
      and Communication System, 1800   [185]

5–9   Windsor District Zones of Access
      and Communication System, 1825   [186]

6–1   Places of Publication with Ten or More Editions
      for Sale in Windsor District, 1805–30   [204]

Graphs

3–1   Elementary Literacy for Windsor District Townships,
      1761–1830: Deed Signatures   [122]

3–2   Elementary Literacy, Windsor District, Vermont,
      1787–1830: Will Makers and Witnesses   [123]

6–1   Vermont Imprints, 1778–1820   [197]

8–1   Windsor District Inventories: Proportions with a
      Family Library at Death of Head of Household,
      1787–1836   [271]

8–2   Windsor District Inventories:
      Average and Median Number of Volumes
      per Family Library, 1787–1830   [272]

Tables

1–1   Windsor District Population, 1770–1840   [32]

2–1   Windsor District Family Libraries, 1787–1830:
Most Widely Read Authors and Works   [64–67]

3–1   Male and Female Elementary Literacy in the
Upper Valley, 1760–1851   [120]

3–2   Elementary Literacy for Deeds:
Windsor District Communities, 1760–1830   [121]

4–1   Windsor District, Vermont, Human Habitats, 1787–1830   [142]

4–2   Windsor District Wealth,
by Communications Access Zone, 1787–1830   [143]

4–3   Patterns of Family Library Retention and Estimates
for 1830 by Human Habitats   [151]

5–1   Upper Valley Vermont Counties—
Print Center Record Through 1830   [164]

5–2   Upper Valley New Hampshire Counties—
Print Center Record Through 1830   [165]

5–3   Seasonal Pattern for Upper Valley Advertisements:
Month Advertisement of Books First Appeared,
1802–30   [170]

6–1   Proportion of U.S. Households Subscribing to a
Newspaper, 1780–1830   [194]

6–2   The Structure of Knowledge Employed in Analysis of
Sales and Retention Records, 1787–1830   [206–7]

6–3   Largest Twenty-Five Categories of Popular Sellers in
Windsor District, 1802–30   [209]

7–1   Windsor District Occupational Data, 1787–1830   [230]

7–2   The Occupational Structure of the
Upper Connecticut River Valley, 1787–1830   [243]

7–3   Comparative Economic Class Structure,
Windsor District, 1760–1830   [246]

7–4   Family Libraries and Wealth Levels,
Windsor District, 1787–1830   [250]

8–1   Size of Windsor District Family Libraries, 1787–1830   [273]

Tables, continued

8–2	Composite Size of Family Libraries, Windsor District, 1787–1830	[276]
8–3	Family Libraries, by Type of Library: Windsor District, 1787–1830	[278]
9–1	Hardscrabble Family Libraries	[296]
9–2	Self-Sufficient Farmstead Family Libraries	[305]
9–3	Self-Sufficient Hamlet Family Libraries	[315]
9–4	Fortunate Farmstead Family Libraries	[325]
9–5	Fortunate Village Family Libraries	[335]
9–6	Fortunate Village Reading Interests	[336]
10–1	Windsor District Basic *Mentalités*, 1780–1830	[347]
App. 1–1	Estimated Crafts and Arts Makers, Windsor, Vermont, 1815	[381]
App. 2–1	Participation in Print Culture, by Community Type and Communications Access Zone: Windsor District, 1787–1830	[387]
App. 2–2	Windsor District Wealth, by Township, 1787–1830	[389]
App. 2–3	Windsor District Family Library Size, by Primary Occupation, 1787–1830	[391]
App. 2–4	Windsor District Occupations, by Access Zone, 1787–1830	[394]
App. 3–1	Occupational Systems for Preindustrial America	[399]
App. 4–1	Share of Population and Share of Inventories for Windsor District Townships, 1787–1830	[406]
App. 5–1	Leverett Family Library	[412–13]
N–1	Share of Windsor District Families Participating in Market Exchange	[434]
N–2	Wealth of Artisan Households at Inventory	[453]
N–3	Hardscrabble Libraries, 1787–1830	[462]
N–4	Self-Sufficient Farmstead Libraries: Comparative Size	[463]
N–5	Self-Sufficient Farmstead Libraries, 1787–1830	[464]

N–6   Self-Sufficient Hamlet Family Libraries and Participation
       in Lending Libraries   [465]

N–7   Fortunate Farmstead Family Libraries:
       Comparative Size   [467]

N–8   Fortunate Farmstead Libraries and Participation
       in Lending Libraries by Size of Library   [468]

N–9   Fortunate Farmstead Libraries and Participation
       in Lending Libraries, 1787–1830   [469]

N–10   Fortunate Village Libraries, 1787–1830   [470]

N–11   Fortunate Village Libraries and Participation
       in Lending Libraries by Size of Library   [471]

Preface

DESCRIPTION OF A PALACE IN A VALLEY
Ye who listen with credulity to the whispers of fancy, and pursue
with eagerness the phantoms of hope; who expect that age will
perform the promises of youth, and that the deficiencies of the
present day will be supplied by the morrow; attend to the history
of Rasselas, Prince of Abissinia.

—Samuel Johnson
The History of Rasselas, Prince of Abissinia

I grew up during the 1940s and 1950s in Lawrence, Massachusetts, a decaying
industrial city. Several decades of economic depression and its insularity had
fostered in the "immigrant city" a distinctively vulturine outlook, to which no
Lawrencian was immune. In the early 1980s, for example, a book contended
that Lawrence had the worst quality of life among 276 American cities studied.
The mayor of Lawrence reacted by making disparaging comparisons with two
nearby cities, concluding that Lawrence should rank no lower than 274th.

But somehow life seemed okay in my territory next to the railroad tracks
in South Lawrence during the post–World War II era. My memories included
many happy ones: jumping boxcars which passed my house on their way
to Lowell or Haverhill; shooting rats and catching carp in the Merrimack
River; continually fixing up and then proudly displaying five-color cars; and,
most typically, "hanging out" and harassing passing motorists. Many of my
friends and I were raised to believe that life could be much worse, could in
fact be permeated rather than just streaked with desperation. A set of neighbors in the three-tenement building next door had no running water. But I
also knew that I did not live in paradise. Like many Massachusetts kids from
industrial cities, I grew up thinking that the Vermont border was the entrance
to paradise. For many of us, Vermont was the Garden of Eden.

You can imagine my surprise in college when I learned that many Vermonters living through the crisp rural beginnings of modern industrial society had
become disillusioned and embittered about their lives amid the sumptuous

Green Mountains. Vermont's "dark, leafy beauty"[1] and plentiful factory goods had not been enough to ensure happiness. As rural Vermonters learned that their lives were intertwined with those of Americans from other regions, and that they had to share the benefits of economic and cultural change with them, they became despondent. How could anyone be that spoiled and ungrateful, I wondered. If people could accept life in a Lawrence working-class neighborhood, where a Sunday afternoon treat meant picking through cuttings of human hair and other garbage up and down back alleys, then why not amid the pristine beauty of Vermont? My utter puzzlement led to this study. I think I have begun to learn how disillusionment with life could emerge in rural northwestern New England by the 1830s, and what this tells us about human happiness and its complex relationship to life's most basic circumstances.

Much of twentieth century culture teaches us that human beings in the modern West, while far better off materially than people in previous civilizations, have been far less happy and fulfilled. Disenchantment cuts across race, gender, economic status, social class, and outlook on life. Why, despite the gains in material comfort and security that have accompanied modernity, has the level of human happiness declined?

Earlier societies, to be sure, offered few people a choice between material comfort and immaterial spiritual pleasures. Heaven was the only society imaginable that could provide sufficient necessities and luxuries for large numbers to achieve happiness, and entry to heaven was severely restricted. Aside from visions of salvation, private fantasy offered the only escape from material privation.

With the emergence of the modern world, vastly expanded opportunities for personal material pleasure became available for the first time in human history. Many (not all) Americans now have all the material comforts that humanity has ever imagined. Striving to achieve and lauding private accumulation, many of us pursue a narrowly defined quest for material comfort at the expense of deep-seated values rooted in a life of principle. Most community needs and public policy considerations have been excluded from our personal calculus.

One dominant message is transmitted by modern culture, in music and literature, philosophy and painting: an exclusive life goal of purely material achievement is profoundly inadequate to express the essence of what it is to be human. Our modernity has been reached on the backs of African slaves and through the theft of lands and lifetimes from Native Americans. We have pursued material happiness by exploiting human beings elsewhere on our planet. The toll in ruined lives, brutality, and death has been awesome. Between 1945 and 1975, at the peak of its power as a nation, America achieved two earthshaking goals: to leave the planet's atmosphere and reach the moon, and to realize the ability to end human history through nuclear destruction. Both achievements are materialistic to the core; each carries with it a profoundly spiritual warning to everyone on the planet. We now know—and in their best moments some early modern Americans suspected—that modernity is an inherently unsettling and often profoundly unsatisfying state. We must create a better balance between physical comfort and mental and spiritual satisfaction. And Americans must participate much more actively in this worldwide search for alternative accommodations to modernity.

As a citizen of an increasingly international electronic civilization and as an historian, I believe that the choices made—and those discarded—in the formation of modern civilization require serious analysis, aimed at gaining historical perspective and understanding and applying them to the choices presented by contemporary life. Once awakened to the historical realities of our national origins and heritage, we may begin to act more responsibly in the present. We are in desperate need of the quality of historical wisdom previous generations of American leaders relied upon in comprehending the larger world and in formulating public policy. Over the past decade the narrowest forms of flag waving and perfectionist civics have all too often substituted for a realistic appraisal of America's history. We do not need another "new" history, nor do we need a "conservative New Realism"; we need a more fundamental historical realism.[2] This new historical realism can help us shape a future fulfilling our best promise as a vibrant, varied multiracial and multicultural people.

This personal assessment is not motivated by longing for an earlier era. In fact, I believe that those who pretend that we can return to simpler times pose great danger to our survival. Oversimplifying the past is worse than ignoring it altogether. Rather, we must examine the texture of life in the past in as accurate a manner as possible, not to inhabit the past but to learn from it. At its best, history expands our view of human complexity and provides alternatives to our own narrow ways of living and thinking. History would be a trivial pursuit were it not morally instructive. In an age of antiquarianism and nostalgia, when slogans and packaging have replaced concern with principles, it is time for historians to renew their traditional task of drawing ethical inferences from evidence. Historically, this has been the great value of the art of history. It is time for all citizens of the earth to begin renegotiating the premises upon which modern life is based. In this pursuit, knowledge of the history of America within transatlantic civilization has a central role to play.

My broad objective, which I share with many other historians taking a fresh look at early American, British, and European experience, is to enrich thinking about alternative ways to live fuller, more humane lives. How and why did we enter upon our present course? Which paths did we choose and which did we leave untraveled? Applying historical wisdom means reassessing the dawn of modernity, reevaluating it to enrich current public policy formulation. It may be hoped that concrete changes will occur in time to outpace forces portending our collective destruction.

To gain some perspective on our current predicament I have chosen to return to the eve and the early morning of industrial civilization. My central aim is to learn how the American version of modern civilization began to influence the lives of the overwhelming majority of rural Americans. The unusual beginnings of rural modernity in northwestern New England raise new questions about modernity's present course and future prospects. The complete cycle of rural civilization this book describes has little to do with urbanization or large-scale industrialization, the two factors most frequently cited in the creation of the modern world. No cities or large factories arose in northwestern New England. Yet the degree and kinds of change in rural belief and behavior in the fifty years following the Revolution were as great as those alleged in the most extreme forms of modernization theory. This is a profound puzzle and demands that we rethink the relationship between modernization and the process of historical change. If we cannot understand the dynamics of change in an important transformative era, how can history claim to be valuable in shaping public policy in the contemporary world, as fundamental change once again envelops us?

Yet numerous public policy questions cry out for historical commentary. For example, is today's communications revolution fundamentally altering the texture of life, or are its effects considerably more modest than many believe? To what extent does a revolution in the technology of communications necessarily change world views? What exactly is a society's infrastructure, and how do its diverse elements interact to shape the ratio of continuity to change, in cultural as well as in material aspects of life? By offering a different perspective on the role of knowledge and material life in the first half century of the American Republic, this book enriches our understanding of several key contemporary public policy issues.

This study is the second installment of a long-term investigation of the origins of contemporary civilization in relation to contemporary life. The first installment, which also focused on New England's Upper Connecticut River Valley, analyzed the expansion of elementary literacy and the foundations of cultural participation in a new mass culture based on the printed and written word.[3] Extending that analysis, this book asks a very broad question: how and why did early Americans let go of their traditional web of community life, sometimes actively choosing to do so, sometimes passively allowing it to slip away, and often simply being swept up in the birth of the modern world?

I seek to disentangle and clarify, for rural New Englanders living between the 1760s and mid-1830s, the complex interrelationships among survival, livelihood, and the life of the mind and heart. Interaction among material and cultural conditions begins with the basic necessities of life. By 1830, a cumulative fund of knowledge increasingly derived from printed matter had become as much a part of daily life in rural New England as food, shelter, or clothing.

This book studies the earliest known example of a transformation all rural societies have undergone as they became "modern." The lessons our study holds are relevant to most nations inhabiting the earth. The historical problem is: how much can we learn about the interaction of stability and change in rural existence?

It is time for us to take a fresh look at the history of cultural life in America, and specifically at the history of knowledge in the emergence of early modern America. Recent events in Iran, Iraq, Israel, Lebanon, Northern Ireland, South Africa, Nicaragua, Libya, and America demonstrate that a detailed understanding of what people believe about the world is at least as central to understanding their actions as any other factor.

Detailed evidence about what early Americans believed about the world survives for the era in which reading became a necessity of life for the first time in the history of the rural West. Common people's reading and cultural participation—understood as part of the concrete conditions of their daily lives—offer, within limits, an understanding of their underlying *mentalités*, their collective ways of thinking and feeling. Rural New Englanders searched for happiness during a pivotal transformative era in North Atlantic civilization. In seeking to understand their lives, their world, and their search, this study reconstructs for the first time a substantial portion of the material and cultural life of an entire population, residents of half of a rural county in northwestern New England during the early national era. Attention centers on the emergence of two widely literate rural generations, the interaction of commercial economy and mass culture in their rural forest society, and the overall structure of their several *mentalités*.[4]

Reading Becomes a Necessity of Life is neither revisionist history nor liberal history. In its attempt to return to the fundamentals of material and cultural life during a critical period of the American past, and to consider their complex interrelationships, it may be perceived as radical history. But the historical tradition it exemplifies has existed for centuries. This tradition is premised on the belief that historical insights are essential to understanding how the world works. I assume that we must comprehend the historical mix of—in Melville's terms—necessity, human choice, and chance, if we are to survive into the next century.[5]

Acknowledgments

This book began as the introductory section of a paper on contemporary perceptions of the life cycle in rural New England, presented at the Shelby Cullom Davis Center for Historical Studies Seminar of Princeton University in December 1977. In attempting to explain why some clusters of ideas reached most of the population, whereas others reached much more limited audiences, I had written an essay in what has since been termed the history of the book trade. The reception this part of the paper received encouraged me to think more carefully about the relationship between cultural and material life in the rise of a mass culture of the printed word.

I have been blessed with more than my fair share of even-tempered and immensely patient librarians; museum, manuscript, and rare book curators; conservators; genealogists; township and court clerks; institutional archivists; out-of-print book dealers; volunteer staff; and administrators of research libraries and museums.

The unsurpassed collections of the American Antiquarian Society (AAS) made this book possible. The research required a lengthy identification of the most accurate text for each work read in Windsor District, 1780–1830, plus analysis (including full reading) of each work—some 1,200 titles in 5,630 volumes. An important part of the process entailed compiling and analyzing available Upper Valley written and printed contemporary opinion about each work. Marcus McCorison, Director of the AAS, and his superb staff have made my research there a joy.

I am grateful for a 1979–80 research fellowship from the National Endowment for the Humanities, and for several research grants and a Fall 1983 sabbatical from Stockton State College, awarded through its Research and Professional Development Committee. Both periods were spent in the Great Hall at the AAS. During these residencies, John Hench helped with the administrative details so essential to productive research. Bill Joyce, then Curator of Manuscripts, and his assistant and successor, Kathleen Major, directed my explorations in the book trades and other collections and listened to my early ideas about print culture in rural New England. Gigi Bumgardner, Andrew

Mellon Curator of Graphic Arts, has been unfailingly helpful in answering questions about visual life and broadsides in early America, finding difficult-to-locate items, suggesting leads, and arranging for many of the photographs. Her former assistant, Judy Larson, shared her vast knowledge of American visual life as well as listening to my early ideas. The Circulation staff, including former Head of Circulation Nancy Burkett; present Head of Circulation Keith Arbour; Melissa Caldwell; and especially Marie E. Lamoreaux, located and trucked thousands of volumes for me during a decade and indulged me as I worked at cracking the spine binder's code essential to understanding print culture in the period. Dick Anders was enormously helpful on almanacs and several other aspects of the book trade. Joyce Tracy, Curator of Newspapers, and her assistant, Dennis Laurie, have searched out and carted several hundred volumes of newspapers since 1978. Kenneth Desautels has shared his knowledge of the technical aspects of rare books, manuscripts, and paper. Carol Alexander, former Curator of Broadsides, called my attention to pertinent items. Jeri Stolk, former Assistant Editor of AAS publications, offered much valuable, editorial advice on an early draft. Finally, many other AAS staff have also provided valuable assistance.

The help of Stanley Shapiro of the Readex Corporation's AAS office, in searching out rare issues of newspapers and filming these and many manuscripts, in sharing his knowledge, and in listening to my attempts to interpret what I was learning is gratefully acknowledged. Stanley's assistant, Philip Lampe, himself a historian of Vermont political culture, kindly shared his data and rich knowledge of Windsor District political behavior, elections into the 1840s, and early Vermont newspapers. Through AAS I met Robinson Murray III, also an NEH Research Fellow, 1979–80, who shared his extensive files on New Hampshire imprints through 1820 and offered advice on many complex issues. The persons who have followed this book most closely, however, are research scholars and friends, Elizabeth Reilly and Randolph Roth. I am most grateful for their knowledge and honest judgment.

A second institution that has provided enormous assistance continuously since the late 1970s is the Vermont Historical Society (VHS). The entire staff helped me at every turn, especially Laura Abbott, former Librarian; the present Librarian Reidun Nuquist; Robert Malvern, who lugged hundreds of manuscript boxes and account book ledgers and then photocopied endlessly; Barney Bloom, who has continued Robert's quality assistance; Edward Hoyt, who freely shared his great knowledge of Vermont history; Mary Pat Brigham who provided valuable help with visuals and many other sources; and Loriman Brigham, whose cataloguing of the VHS manuscript holdings made my research possible. Lizzari Photographic Company helpfully reproduced many of the VHS pictures. Every trip to the VHS entailed substantial research at several other Vermont research collections in Montpelier. Essential help has been provided by D. Gregory Sanford, Vermont State Archivist, friend, and fellow historian. Vivien Bryant formerly of the Vermont State Library provided valuable advice on Vermont newspapers by mail and in person.

Windsor District residents and local historical societies have assisted my research in many ways. Laura Alexander, former Reading Town Clerk and Postmistress, and member of the Reading Historical Society, helped with Reading sources as did Erroll Locke. They both helped provide me an opportunity to present findings about inland townships and their material and cultural development at the 1983 annual meeting of the Reading Historical Society. In 1984 Dr. Leroy Wardner, President of the Wardner Family Genealogical Society of Windsor and Reading, helped me understand one of Windsor District's most influential and varied families and provided an occasion in Weathersfield to discuss the role of families in Windsor District. Valuable research assistance has also been provided at the West Windsor Historical Society under the guidance of Mary Fenn, the Windsor Public Library, the Springfield Art and Historical Museum, and many present residents throughout Windsor District. The staffs of Dartmouth College's Archives, Rare Books, and Manuscripts Divisions, especially University Archivist Kenneth Cramer, and Curator of Manuscripts Phillip N. Cronenwelt, have provided much assistance.

I have received extremely valuable assistance from John Buechner; from J. Kevin Graffagnino, Director of Special Collections, University of Vermont, Burlington; Etta Falkner and Jack Larkin at the Research Center, Old Sturbridge Village, Sturbridge, Massachusetts; and Thomas Camden, New Hampshire Historical Society, Concord. Through the prompt assistance of A. John Yacavoni and his most efficient staff at the Vermont Public Records Division, I was able to obtain virtually any local or state public record known to exist. The Center for Research on Vermont offered several kinds of help, including a research seminar arranged by the staff assistant, Kristin Peterson-Ishaq, in which I was able to take a broad look at my findings and their implications. Kind assistance was also provided by the New England Historical and Genealogical Society.

Considerable research was conducted at home, thanks largely to the preservation efforts of the Genealogical Society of the Church of Jesus Christ of Latter-Day Saints. It has microfilmed most of the local, district, and county records of Vermont and New Hampshire, including wills, inventories, deeds, and township records.

Stockton State College Library's Reference and Interlibrary Loan staffs did a splendid job in difficult circumstances for ten years. My colleague Richard Elmore has freely shared his vast knowledge of early modern French history, and has been unfailingly supportive. I am very grateful to John and Wendy Sinton, good friends, colleagues, and strong supporters of my work for fifteen years. I owe much to many wonderful people whom I first met as Stockton students and who have listened to me pose the broad framework of this study. Several have made valuable contributions through discussions, the quality of their own work, their research assistance, and their maintenance of aspects of my research and bibliographical system. All Windsor District Public Records wills, inventories, and estate settlements, 1787–1830, were checked three times, and I am most appreciative of the efforts of my trusted research assistant, 1981–83, Anne Fairweather, and her predecessor, Christal Springer. I thank Ray Morgenweck, who wrote an excellent seminar paper on Windsor District family libraries, 1831–40, Timothy McManimon, and Jay Felsberg.

My second "local" library base over the past decade has been Princeton University's Firestone Library; to its staff I am most grateful. I owe much to dozens of other research libraries, here and in England, that have been unfailingly generous in making copies of rare books, pamphlets, almanacs, broadsides, periodical and newspaper files, and manuscripts, and in responding promptly to calls to check the binding, spine title, and provenance of particular rare texts. Invaluable for my work with texts has been Terry Belanger and Donald Farren's course on descriptive bibliography in the Rare Book School, Columbia University, which I attended in summer 1985. I have just returned from applying what I learned there in a seminar, in public lectures, and in an exhibit on the Book Trade at Thammasat University, Bangkok, Thailand, 1986–1987, on a Fulbright Fellowship.

An earlier draft of this book was scoured by Marcia Brubeck of the Guilford Group; her suggestions were most helpful. I am most grateful to Mavis Bryant, formerly Editor at the University of Tennessee Press, who has encouraged me for several years and copyedited the entire manuscript. Cynthia Maude-Gembler was indispensable in encouraging me to see this project through to completion and has been a valued friend. Without their guidance I would have gone back to research and put this project aside. Lee Campbell Sioles, Managing Editor, and Dariel Mayer, Design and Production Manager, of the University of Tennessee Press have been very helpful and encouraging. The maps and figures for this book, as for my last, were prepared by Patricia Coleman-Weeks, Head of Graphics at Stockton State College, whose superb artistry is greatly appreciated. Nancy Messina typed most of the early drafts of this book very quickly and with great patience; and Virginia Burkley, my secretary and close family friend, has helped me in a thousand ways, including typing.

Work and love have made this book possible. The late Ed Roddy of Merrimack College was my first great teacher and a good friend for twenty-two years. Ed showed me how to be a historian. My second great teacher, Merrill D. Peterson of the University of Virginia, gave me an ideal to strive for and convinced me that I needed to discipline my interest in history. Both enjoyed their own work immensely and by allowing me to be their research assistant showed me how to work. My good friend and mentor for a decade, Silvan

S. Tomkins, discussed nearly every aspect of my findings. All of my knowledge of microcomputers I owe to Kenneth Tompkins, Professor of Literature at Stockton and a family friend, who introduced me to my faithful Zenith Z-161 and helped me customize it to my needs; to Microsoft's *The Word* which has for the past five years assisted my work enormously at every step; and to Peter Rinearson for sound advice on indexing.

Without the patient and persistent attention of Harvey Graff, the principal reader for several years, the book would never have been completed. I am forever in his debt as one is to a much respected patron in Thailand.

Lisa Lehne-Gilmore has been my best friend, a wonderful companion, and my wife. Lisa, our sons Abraham and Liam, our foster daughter Chanise Rhoades, and other foster children who have shared our home have taught me much about love and communication.

Reading Becomes
a Necessity of Life

Introduction

The New Englander has excellent points, but is restless in body and mind, always scheming, always in motion, never satisfied with what he has, and always seeking to make all the world like himself. . . . He is philanthropic, but makes his philanthropy his excuse for meddling with everybody else's business as if it were his own. . . . He has his use in the community, but a whole nation composed of such would be shortlived. . . . The Puritan is a reformer by nature, but he never understands the true law of progress, and never has the patience to wait till the reform he wishes for can be practically effected.

— Orestes Brownson, "Liberalism and Progress,"
Brownson's Quarterly Review (1864)

Residents of the Upper Connecticut River Valley, on the rural fringes of transatlantic society, participated in a remarkable set of developments between 1780 and 1835. They created a new kind of rural society, distinguished both by the widespread commercialization of public life and by the creation of a novel communications environment based on the regular use of printed and written texts to learn about themselves, their communities, and the broader world. These occurrences changed forever the material and cultural bases of daily rural existence.

Reading Becomes a Necessity of Life is a book about the extraordinary lives and minds of ordinary people. Each November, huddled on hilltops or secluded in isolated valleys, the forest dwellers of Vermont and New Hampshire hunkered down to face the silent, seemingly endless northern winter. Gradually they were frozen into their homesteads, where they would remain for over a third of the year. The bleakness of the Vermont climate, with its starkly contrasting grey-white and dark green, was deceptive, however. As it drove rural New Englanders "to home," nature's harshness brought their souls to life with the "white heat of vital piety" and with schemes of secular glory. By crackling fires on stone hearths, ten thousand imaginations danced in frenzy and then nestled in warm, airy inner kingdoms of possibility and bliss. In the half century following the American Revolution, most Upper Connecticut River Valley residents neither froze to death nor committed suicide during the long winter; they worked, and they also read, mused, and talked with one another. Then they emerged from their forced hibernation with hearts full of springtime promise.

This book evokes the vitality and diversity of everyday life in a rural world in transition, and analyzes how New Englanders in the early national era sought to understand their lives and their world. Our subjects are the inhabitants of the Upper Connecticut River Valley, the most rural area of New England in the Early Republic. These people—30,000 in 1775 and 183,000 by 1830—lived in a landscape of dark foliage, impressive vistas, and dramatic changes in weather from morning to early evening. Seasonal shifts made radical impacts on Upper Valley life. The Vermont winter produced a special variety of cabin fever: literate obsession. Those possessed by it later founded religions and utopias, invented gadgets, prophesied industrial strife, became president, or lost their minds.

This book puts forward a new understanding of the coming of the modern world to rural society. It broadens our understanding of four layers of daily life in the first heavily commercialized rural society to participate actively in a new mass culture of reading and writing. Each layer centered around relationships between material and cultural life, and encompassed both population-wide patterns and more diverse funds of collective experience. The layers are: economic and cultural foundations (chapters 2 through 4); communications and cultural foundations (chapters 5 and 6); family foundations of cultural participation (chapters 7 and 8); and continuity and change across five rural *mentalités* (chapter 9). We conclude with public policy implications, drawn from a comparison between the first generations seeing the emergence of a new rural order of life within a mass culture of the printed word, and the first generations living in a world of electronic communications and an emerging international electronic culture.

The first chapter begins with a discussion of the comparative historical importance of the Upper Valley within North Atlantic civilization between 1760 and 1835. The second part of the chapter describes the geography and the rugged rural texture of existence in the Upper Valley and especially Vermont's Windsor District. The Upper Valley was a coherent, representative social, geographical, and cultural subregion within the American Northeast until the 1840s. Windsor District, consisting of eleven townships forming southern Windsor County, Vermont, encompassed all of the diversity existing within the Upper Valley. During the first half century after America became a nation, these eleven townships evolved a new form of rural commerce and culture. Chapter 1 ends with a description of the role of reading and learning within the broader history of rural New England mental processes, perception, and consciousness.

Oxen Hauling a Sled on Clinton Gilbert's Farm, Woodstock, Vermont. Courtesy, Vermont Historical Society.

Especially during five months of bone-chilling Vermont and New Hampshire winter, farmstead environs were marked both by their stark beauty and their intense loneliness. "Hunkered down," inhabitants alternated between small group pleasures and quiet isolation.

The traditional necessities of life are explored in chapter 2: food, shelter, and clothing, as provided by the farming and grazing, commercial, and industrial sectors of an agricultural economy. The main theme is the impact of commercialization on the agricultural character of daily existence in 1760–1830; by 1815, commercialization had been accepted in its essentials by a majority of residents. Residents' varying perceptions of changing economic life are explored, as well as the material changes themselves.

Next, chapter 3 discusses the implications of commercialization for cultural participation. How did material and social conditions affect acquisition of the literacy skills necessary for active participation in print culture? Discussion of literacy's leading agencies, the family and the school, and the most prominent uses of literacy in daily life extends the argument of my earlier study, that reading did become a necessity of life in the years between 1780 and 1835, as part of the spread of rural commercialization and its interaction with a new environment of print communications. The resulting growth of lifelong reading, evidenced by subscriptions to and purchases of printed matter and memberships in lending libraries, eventually changed the fabric of rural experience. By the early 1830s the mental outlook of a sizable minority of Upper Valley residents was no longer shaped primarily by tradition.

Chapter 4 argues that the way Upper Valley residents carried on their daily lives varied substantially with different combinations of material and cultural conditions. Major aspects of daily life interacted in varying ways across Windsor District, producing five distinct human habitats. The conception of human habitats is defined, and the key characteristics of each of five living situations are delineated. To understand the impact on daily life of differences among human habitats we must study the diffusion of knowledge throughout the rural New England countryside.

Chapter 5 analyzes the evolution of the book trade, and the new communications environment it helped to create, through the early 1830s. The life cycle of printed objects, the circulation network and major institutions for all forms of printed and written matter, and the different zones of access emerging within the new communications environment are the major topics analyzed. Chapter 6 then looks carefully at the substance of print culture: at the several printed media in which knowledge circulated and at the best-selling works, locally printed as well as imported. Analysis of the content of popular sellers reveals important culture-wide trends shaping all rural *mentalités*.

It is also valuable to look carefully at differences within the population. Different *mentalités* are approached in their deepest, most stable form through analysis of family life and the private libraries rural families retained. For this reason, chapter 7 discusses the differing material anchors of daily life for each major element of the total population. Wealth, occupations and work experiences, and placement within the scale of prestige and public position in Windsor District society helped shape residents' ability to participate in public life and in print culture. Which social groups adapted most rapidly to change, which resisted, and, in both cases, how and why?

Differing levels and kinds of such participation are indicated in the composition of family libraries, the most important source available for reconstructing the mentalities of early Americans. Chapter 8 studies all family libraries extant for residents of Windsor District's eleven townships, 1780–1830. The major finding of chapter 8 is that the types and contents of family libraries indeed varied greatly.

Chapter 9 deepens our understanding of rural variety by analyzing the actual diversity of rural *mentalités* across Windsor District's five human habitats. The reading habits of just under 400 mostly ordinary families were reconstructed from their private libraries supplemented by evidence of participation in lending libraries and patterns of newspaper circulation. The discussion is set in the context of the dawn of rural commercial and early industrial society throughout the North Atlantic, 1780–1835.

The conclusion takes a broader and more measured look at the Upper Valley's new order of rural existence, its place within the Early Republic, and its relationship to the coming of the modern world and to changes in civilization in our own day.

At some time in the nineteenth century, virtually every rural society in the West underwent the fundamental economic, cultural, and social changes described here. All three dimensions of change appeared earlier in the Upper Valley than in other rural areas of the American Northeast, precisely because the valley's society was newly created. Between 1780 and 1835 the proliferation of novel means of production, distribution, and consumption of goods, services, and ideas irrevocably altered the texture of everyday life and the web of rural community. Supplementing farming and grazing, the rural New England landscape was crisscrossed by an extensive market system and dotted with rural factories relying mostly on water-powered laborsaving machinery. Overall, assimilation of change progressed gradually. But the rate of assimilation varied dramatically within this rural environment.

The residents of the Upper Valley in the Revolutionary era and the Early Republic comprised the first two widely and actively literate rural generations in North Atlantic civilization. Most of its male and female residents in 1780–1835, above the bottom 10 to 20 percent of society by wealth, acquired the ability to read and write (elementary literacy), usually during childhood or youth, and then sustained lifelong learning using printed and written forms of communication. In the wake of the American Revolution, a large share of families developed reading interests in several secular dimensions of life as well as in traditional sacred subjects. Upper Valley residents craved utilitarian and imaginative forms of knowledge about the broader world they inhabited, even as they strove to be counted among those destined for eternal bliss.

Schoolbooks forged links connecting sacred and secular, practical and fictive worlds of knowledge. During the formative years when literacy was inculcated, children and adolescents mastered reading, writing, and calculating to various degrees of skill. But they also learned much else: to accept and relish a God who created them and their world; to believe in their ability to grow in moral and religious knowledge; thereby to develop a conscience; to know the continents, the countries of the world, their forms of government, and the leading characteristics of each such form; to function in their own community; and to apply numerical skills to commercial life. Young people assimilated the structure and texture of many imaginative worlds. Students learned to construct and deconstruct sentences and paragraphs, to describe the world in ever more precise words, and to write letters. Such was the normal range of subjects emphasized in the rural New England homes and district schools where the young of the post-revolutionary decades acquired turnpike tickets to the new highways of printed and written knowledge. These were the broad foundations of cultural participation upon which lifelong learning was built.

In the era 1780–1835, the first widely literate rural generation in northwestern New England lived through adulthood and old age and raised even more actively literate sons and daughters. This extraordinary period in Western civilization included the American, French, and Industrial Revolutions. These were crucial decades in the rapid expansion of commercial capitalism throughout rural New England; in the first, rural phase of the Industrial Revolution; and in the creation of a new mass culture centered on the printed and written word. The accelerating pace of change, challenging centuries-old continuities and affecting many realms of daily life, makes this era especially intriguing. The interaction of material with cultural conditions in a situation of major transformation can teach us much about change in today's civilization and about central questions of social theory. What are the components of rural infrastructure? How does change begin and work its way throughout a society? At what pace and in which ways? How does a society adjust to new mixes of change and continuity? And what constitutes real gain and loss in human happiness?

There was a strikingly close, yet exceedingly complex, relationship between cultural and material conditions of life among Upper Valley residents in 1780–1835; both were partly transformed by commercial and early industrial capitalism and by the new communications environment shaping and being shaped by these changes. Historians, stressing the close fit, have more often affirmed than detailed the complexity of this process of transformation in rural life at the dawn of modernity. This study returns to the realities underlying materialist and idealist formulations of the problem. Using their valuable insights, we examine some of the leading factors in the transformation of the whole of life. The uses Upper Valley residents made of commerce and culture were many, varied, and often unexpected. They learned the heritage of the Western cultural tradition, and no-one told them not to take it seriously. Their efforts to comprehend and interpret it for their own ends were often unique and sometimes partial, literal, or just confused. Not all families shared in the rapidly expanding mode of communication embodied in printed and written matter, and among those who did, wide differences existed in the kind and quality of participation. No persuasive social theory exists to predict how this transformation in basic material and cultural conditions of life might have been expected to affect different groups within a single society.[1]

We wish to learn how the vast expansion of printed and written means of communications after 1783 reshaped how Upper Valley residents learned about the broader world and how they used their new knowledge in daily life. How was their knowledge of the world acquired in 1780? What changes occurred by 1835? Which groups did these changes reach, in what sequence, under what conditions, and to what effect? As part of a broader transformation leading to a modern civilization, mass literacy based on the printed word carried the seeds of cultural explosion, material change, and personal turmoil and triumph.

Historians have faced special difficulties in learning about the lives of ordinary people—how they carried on their daily existence, how they learned about their world, what they knew and believed about it, and to what ends they used their knowledge. When historians have probed, they have (often brilliantly) studied scattered shards which, upon close inspection, proved quite atypical.[2] In early America people's knowledge of the world and involvement in various movements and group activities was neither evenly nor randomly distributed. Care in generalizing from partial studies is essential.

Life circumstances, material and cultural, helped to direct people's interests, experience, and public engagement in complicated ways. This volume is a history of infrastructure, a term which we will understand broadly as including both cultural and material factors. In this book, interaction among eight dimensions of rural infrastructure affecting the family and the household—the latter being the basic unit of collective experience—is examined in detail. These eight determinants are: (1) the type of local community setting and ecology (village, hamlet, or farmstead) and the specific history of their development; (2) placement within the region's transportation and communications network and, accordingly, the unit's level of access to the broader world and to knowledge of that world; (3) family situation in a rural economy, including work rhythms, occupations, family size, and age distribution; (4) expanding participation within the public market economy; (5) the range of wealth and its use and dispersion in real and personal property and in social prestige and public position; (6) elementary literacy; (7) the incidence, size, and character of family libraries; and (8) the variety of rural *mentalités*. By *mentalités* we mean compounds of knowledge, emotions, and actions, or, as Frank Manuel put it, "what was 'thinkable' in a human collective at a given moment of time."[3]

Changes in rural infrastructure entailed interactions among these (and other) essential elements of the complex story of how the modern world began. The most rapidly changing aspects of life included the many habits surrounding the production, purchase, and consumption of material goods; social relations; and *mentalités*. Several key changes are delineated: growth of a new communications environment, increase in the significance of access to knowledge, the transformation of the everyday life environment from one that was continuous to one characterized by novelty and changing commercial and cultural relations, the rise of an ideal of keeping intellectually up-to-date, the emergence of new forms of community, the power of a family to shape a world view, complex intertwined forces of knowledge and circumstance, and forms of inequality.

After the Revolution both sacred and secular funds of information available to rural families exploded. The most prominent new realms of intellectual activity built on the "knowledge from distant climes" conveyed in imaginative works such as novels, poetry, histories, and travel accounts. The impact was profound. Rural residents, inhabiting a remote area thousands of miles from the vibrant centers of European civilization, began to keep up with many aspects of life there, initially seen through British cultural lenses. Ironically, these life-shattering changes in the texture of rural life throughout North Atlantic civilization occurred first and most rapidly on its far fringes—in Sweden, Scotland, and the American Northeast.

In each of the Upper Valley's five human habitats, daily life between 1780 and 1835 had been bound by local geography and ecology to an extent unknown in our world of instantaneous communication. Before the era of the telegraph, differences among rural human habitats were vast. Beginning with the telegraph in the 1840s, electronic communications came to annihilate time and space and so also geographical limitations on the diffusion of knowledge.[4]

This book details the ways in which the eight material and cultural factors listed above combined to form the five distinct rural human habitats, also called "living situations." Within each, a different *mentalité* thrived, setting a distinctive cultural tone. In each habitat some families diverged from the dominant range of cultural and material concerns, but their numbers were small. Other factors, especially religious and political affiliation and participation, were also important in shaping critical areas of human thought and action. Here we focus on the fundamental structures of rural life, the broadest foundations of individual choice and affiliative behavior. Human habitats and the reading communities they supported offer a new way to study the variety within rural life.

Each living situation was formed by different combinations of the material and cultural conditions that shaped the texture of life for all residents of the Upper Valley. Consequently, all five human habitats both shared certain characteristics of rural existence and differed in the mix of factors and in their weighting. Any single habitat had a core of knowledge about the world, consisting of information, opinion, beliefs, values, and emotions, which it held in common with the other four habitats. Contemporaries termed this core the "wisdom of the ages." But each habitat also contained vastly different and unique pools of specialized knowledge and activities which were sometimes incongruent with the common core. These pools led to special interests and involvements.

My main objective is to explore what has until recently remained a relatively forgotten, and certainly minor, era in rural life within North Atlantic civilization—the first half century of American nationhood. This transitional period fostered a different, infinitely more complex rural economy and culture than has typically been described. Much traditional history, if it does not ignore the relationship between material and cultural dimensions of life, either polarizes the two or asserts the primacy of one over the other. This study, in contrast, follows important new directions charted by the work of Natalie Zemon Davis, Robert Darnton, David Cressy, Rhys Isaac, and others.[5]

The premise of *Reading Becomes a Necessity of Life* is that cultural and material strands of life are part of the same tapestry. As we realize more clearly that ideas about reality may exist independently of what we are able to recover and identify as past reality, then we can begin to understand the rich complexity of the relationship between material and cultural dimensions of existence. As an important example, let us look at the relationship between the actual growth of a market economy in the Upper Valley; and awareness and lack of awareness, understandings and misunderstandings, of that growth at the time, which helped shape economic thought and action (see chapter 2).

Between the 1760s and the mid-1830s the Upper Valley moved through a full cycle of rural social development: settlement, stability, peak maturity and decline. This cycle provides the framework for understanding rural life in the Early Republic. As well, nearly all rural societies went through a basic process of expanding cultural awareness during the nineteenth century. Gradually localism, seen as cultural isolation, dissolved; distant and local worlds became integrated; and more regular, richer doses of regional, national, and international events, situations, and movements made an impact on local ways of life. Underlying these developments was intensified awareness of change as a constant element of everyday life.

Ironically, stunning success at carving a rich forest society out of a wilderness in the Upper Valley did not produce contentment. By the late 1830s disenchantment was widespread among Upper Valley residents. As they bitterly lamented local economic decline and cultural stagnation and decay, people elsewhere in rural America who encountered their complaints often responded with disbelief and disgust. It was easy to view discontent as evidence of "Yankee rapacity." But the particulars that underlay the Upper Valley residents' sudden disillusionment and gloomy forecasts reveal the complexity of the new order of rural life. By 1832 the first signs of a slowdown in expansion were evident. Early railroad schemes and projects aimed at transforming the "dark rolling Connecticut [River]" into the "channel of a cheap, safe, regular and expeditious communication between its extensive valley and the seaboard" had failed. Expansion elsewhere in America was widely perceived as negatively affecting Upper Valley life. People feared that the area would be left behind and then come to be ruled by distant interests. Such worries attest to a radical alteration of consciousness, based on the assumption of close integration of economic and intellectual life from Vermont to Georgia.[6]

Among the most influential rural observers of commerce and culture throughout America were newspaper editors. The major weekly in southern Windsor County in the 1830s, the *Vermont Republican and Journal*, was edited by Simeon Ide, a National Republican and later Whig. Naturally enough, Ide reserved an extra measure of criticism for the policies of the Jackson administration. Even if we discount Ide's rhetoric, however, we must attend fully to his novel belief, emerging in 1833–34, that a long era of prosperity and cultural importance was ending abruptly. In an era where no township gave Jacksonian candidates even a third of the vote, Ide expressed sentiments predominant there.[7]

In a critique of Jackson's tariff policies in March 1833, the first Windsor District editorial raising doubts about rural New England's future, Ide expressed fear that the South was attempting to "break up" New England's industry and "lay waste her resources." He quoted a North Carolinian traveler who wondered whether "the prosperity of this people" was "the hot-bed production of an artificial system" or "the result of a long-continued toil, of an industry that never tired, of an economy that never slept." Over the next several years this question was much debated, for it revived older republican fears about the relations between commerce and luxury.[8] An editorial in April 1833, answered the North Carolinian's question: despite "our hard, sterile, and inhospitable soil . . . patience, toil, and industry" had created the "happiness, industry, and prosperity" presently enjoyed. A week later Ide declared that any comparison between competing regions clearly demonstrated that New England represented "the true sources of national wealth . . . our institutions, our colleges, and our schools, our morals and our habits." Rather than a contrivance, commercial success was the natural extension of sound morality, education, and industry. These formed the bases of rural New England's "republican notions."

By the end of 1833 Ide had begun to see trouble everywhere. He worried that the growth of western marketing of breadstuffs in Windsor County portended a loss of economic independence unless local production increased. By February 1834, Ide had added scarcity of money to his expanding list of woes. Later in February, Ide pushed his analysis a step further. For the past twenty years, "the cup of national prosperity has been filled to overflowing . . . Why is it, then," in the cities "and in our villages . . . that we now only hear cries of discontent and distress . . . that we continually hear of the ruin of our merchants, of the distress of the mechanics and workingmen, of the utter prostration of business"? While Ide's specific villain was the administration, his main concern was "a true sense" of danger to rural New England's way of life.[9]

Ide believed that he represented nearly all major occupational groups in his area: farmers, mechanics, manufacturers, merchants, and other businessmen. Partly as a result of his editorials, "public indignation" intensified; in early

March 1834, the *Republican and Journal* carried reports of local meetings of citizens. By early April, Ide believed that several factors were more fundamental than Andrew Jackson's policies in blocking economic expansion. These included Windsor County's "interior position," which precluded maritime pursuits; the "coldness of their climate," which disallowed staple crops; and the poor soil, which "affords a competence for its inhabitants" only after much "patient industry." Most disconcerting was a heightened realization of the limits imposed by the county's unfavorable placement within the transatlantic transportation and communications network. For a year Ide had editorialized about the changing import of rural New England's geographical position and about a major shift in perceptions of economic health and illness. He concluded that a "derangement of business" was leading to the ruin of trade and hence to the ruin of several merchants, to social and cultural stagnation and its attendant evils, and to considerable "discontent and distress."[10]

In the eyes of many of its residents, the Upper Valley was being disregarded and forgotten and its fate determined by distant, often hostile commercial and cultural interests. Local control of life was threatened. Grave doubts about the Upper Valley's future suggested that the basis of its way of life—sound morality, education, and industry—was endangered. Their increased knowledge of the world had borne bitter fruit, as Upper Valley residents came to understand more clearly how they fit into the broader commercial and cultural network of the Northeast. The Upper Valley was becoming a commercial and cultural backwater, and no amount of individual or group effort could change its residents' collective fate.

In an 1840 pamphlet combatting one of the most pessimistic reactions to social change, the Millerite movement, Abel Tompkins lamented, "Why, then, do we labor to scatter in Israel and divide in Jacob? Why all these false prophets, these ringleaders, and founders of new orders? Whence is this strange fire? Better by far that we go back, and do our first works; for, in endeavoring to do greater things than our fathers, we have only rent the garment of Christ, and cast lots for his vesture."[11] With benefit of hindsight, this book contrasts the actual process of change with contemporary belief that Upper Valley residents lived amid an unfolding tragedy. The first two generations of Upper Valley residents were perceived by contemporaries as morally significant protagonists whose boundless, passionate ambition had established a new rural agricultural society marked by widespread commercial and cultural participation in North Atlantic civilization. The story of Upper Valley life through 1840 revolves around an ideal rural Christian yeomanry, on land new to them if not to its original inhabitants (or to those who knew better than to settle there), and expecting to live in a fine middling station. Here perhaps we can identify hubris, the "quality of self-confident greatness which makes for heroic virtue," as a tragic flaw in Upper Valley character.[12]

By the late 1830s, however, ambition had been overwhelmed by the kind of unforeseen limitations that forever bind human aspirations: relentless commercial and cultural transformation had rendered the Upper Valley a "burnt-over" economic area, at best a way-station on the road to more recently settled areas. A just people apparently had brought misfortune on itself, not by vice or depravity but by its naive confidence in endlessly expanding opportunity. In a tragedy, the reversal of fortunes comes as a great surprise to the protagonist, and the end result often is not total ruin but profound disappointment, disillusionment, and bitterness. By 1840 all of these sentiments were evident in the Upper Valley's public press and in private letters.[13]

In an important respect, Simeon Ide's perspective on Upper Valley life was accurate. Upper Valley settlement and social development duplicated southern New England's commercialization. Eking out an agricultural existence in the Upper Valley proved far more difficult than most emigrants had anticipated—the climate far harsher, the soil poorer, and the landscape more variegated, limiting the possibility of large-scale commercial farming. By 1800 commercialization and a new communications environment were being eagerly embraced. With this acceptance, the material and cultural transformation of rural life came to be widely perceived as a godsend. The years 1800–1830 demarcate a golden age of possibility in the Upper Valley, based, its residents believed, on a strong conscience, widespread elementary education, and a highly disciplined spirit of industry.

In the mid-1820s anxiety first surfaced in public dialogue, with a few individuals such as Orestes Brownson showing a prophetic disillusionment. Within another decade it became clear to most Windsor District newspaper readers that the wave of economic expansion was passing them by. The continuation of prosperity was in jeopardy; prosperity itself came to be perceived as a perilous ideal. The increasingly avid reading engaged in by so many families was proving to be a subtle curse, for the first actively reading rural society in the Western world learned weekly in rural newspapers about distant changes affecting its life.

By the mid-1830s it had become demoralizing to read about expansion and success elsewhere. The knowledge that others' gain meant one's own relative loss was the enduring result of fervent participation in commercialization and in transatlantic culture. As long as local material and cultural isolation prevailed, it had been easy enough for families to believe that they controlled their own destinies. But fruitless efforts to create linkages with fast-evolving southern New England transportation and communications networks had accelerated Upper Valley residents' awareness of their declining position. By the late 1830s readers were well aware that their livelihoods depended on an increasingly integrated regional market economy that covered much of the Northeast and tied into transatlantic economic life. It was logical that so many Upper

Valley residents should clutch their Bibles, psalm and hymn books, and devotional works so closely, while they read more and more secular works. In the drama unfolding in northwestern New England during the first decades of the nineteenth century, Baxter's *The Saints' Everlasting Rest* and similar treatises took on a new set of meanings. New World Israelites had ample reason to worry about the earthly consequences of migration to a new promised land. Small wonder, then, that *A Pilgrim's Progress*, *Robinson Crusoe*, *Paradise Lost*, and *The Vicar of Wakefield* remained among their most popular fictional reading matter.

The tragedy began when rural southern New England seemed overcrowded by the mid-eighteenth century. With the spread of communications in southern New England, a major exodus to northern New England commenced. From the outset, southern New Englanders sought to duplicate in the Upper Valley the integuments of the life they had lived in a considerably more temperate climate. Commercial and cultural institutions were established alongside those furthering farming and grazing. In a tragedy the struggle against fate often entails high irony. Many rural New England community leaders felt great pride in having created a new rural social order characterized by commercial prosperity and a cultural ideal of "currency" and "modernness." Initially, the pride appeared fully justified. Between 1780 and 1835, two generations of Upper Valley residents came to believe that their area was a significant terminus for New England economic and cultural development; the initial roads and turnpikes carrying commerce and culture led straight into the heart of rural northwestern New England. Even before the mid-1820s, however, there were portents of gloom: cholera epidemics, 1807–15; terrible summer weather in 1816, including snow and killing frost; a growing exodus thereafter; the sudden termination of Walpole as a print center in 1817, after a quarter century of apparent stability. An important message was conveyed: continued expansion was not inevitable.[14]

By the late 1830s, a sizable share of all Windsor District residents had become acutely aware both of the severe limits on agricultural, commercial, and cultural progress in the Upper Valley climate, and of the ironies accompanying continued commercial and cultural participation in transatlantic civilization. After 1825, except in a few large villages, Upper Valley growth had all but stopped. What had been a terminus was now a way-station on the westward route away from a withering appendage. Shortly after 1825, the vibrancy of commerce and culture in the Northeast began to shortcircuit the Upper Valley, pushing directly westward from Boston to Worcester and Springfield and on to Albany one hundred miles to the south. Stagnation and decline, bitterness and resentment were widespread by the early 1840s. The same phenomenon was occurring simultaneously elsewhere in the Northeast, as Whitney Cross and others have demonstrated. The roads and waterways that had brought prosperity to the Upper Valley until 1830 were taking it away, replacing the flow of emigrants with regular news of commerce and culture that seemed to be increasing everywhere but at home. Knowledge from "distant climes" had played a cruel trick on a fervent but deluded people in a harsh land.[15]

Much of the Upper Valley had completed a two-and-a-half-generation cycle, from initial migration and settlement beginning in the 1760s, through commercial and cultural expansion in 1785–1825, to stagnation thereafter, with steady, severe decline in all but a handful of townships. The establishment and apparent stabilization of a sizable rural society had seemed a triumphant march of undiluted progress at first. The novelty of another prominent factor had blinded many area residents to the fast-approaching limits of economic and cultural growth. The penetration of the market economy throughout all but the most isolated uplands of the Upper Valley had been accompanied by a vast expansion in the volume and variety of reading matter eagerly devoured by a growing majority of all families. After 1815 a large proportion of the Upper Valley population had a range of choice in goods, services, and knowledge previously unheard of in a rural society. Emerging far to the north of the centers of American life, the Upper Valley was devoted to individualism's blinding impulse to learn, to accumulate, and then to explore further. A middle-class ideal, a beautiful if awe-inspiring environment, an army of sturdy yeoman and artisan families, fewer commerce and trading families, a share of professionals, and a vigorous cultural life connecting the Upper Valley to Boston and New York, London and Europe—all united to promise unending freedom and growth.

From the outset, however, individual choices were more limited than they seemed. At first overwhelmed by the particulars of commerce and culture, Upper Valley residents gradually took serious notice of the broader connections between their economic and cultural prosperity and regional, national, and international developments. By the time they did, in the mid-1820s, organized efforts to maintain prominence in trade routes were already doomed.[16]

It is symptomatic of the broad diffusion of commerce and culture that the Upper Valley's major prophet of early industrial society, Orestes Brownson (1803–76), was neither born nor raised in one of the Upper Valley's village centers of change. Instead he grew to maturity in the foothills of the Green Mountains, a two-day ride from local commercial and cultural centers. Nonetheless, he began learning of the distant world at age nine, when his stepparents subscribed to a local weekly to follow the course of the War of 1812. Brownson's interest in transatlantic cultural and material transformation continued unabated over the next sixty years. Around 1820 he apprenticed to a printer, establishing his vocation; he was to become publicist and editor of over two dozen newspapers and periodicals. By the mid-1820s Brownson sensed, and thereafter tracked and regularly commented on, the emerging problems of rural and, later, urban industrial society in his home region and throughout the North Atlantic. Brownson left the Upper Valley for good in 1834, just about the time that Simeon Ide and others began to suggest that the area was heading for ruin.

Between the 1760s and the early 1830s most residents of the Upper Valley lived amid promise and optimism, far removed from the disillusionment that accumulated after 1830 and under which succeeding generations dwelled. Along with more detailed knowledge about life on earth and more refined perspectives on future rewards in an afterlife came the slowly dawning realization of how little Upper Valley residents controlled their earthly fate. The death of traditional localism in commerce, social relations, and culture was a devastating blow to many residents. During the Early Republic widespread awareness of the connections between local and distant societies was a phenomenon new to rural life. It was also a distinguishing mark of a broader consciousness which Upper Valley residents themselves termed modern.[17]

Such heightened awareness elicited complicated intellectual and emotional responses. More detailed knowledge of geography, politics and government, economics, and social relations, and of their interconnections, followed from an assumption that what was happening elsewhere in the North Atlantic was relevant to life in the Upper Valley. This was doubly ironic because knowledge of the real world was accompanied by a noteworthy exploration of speculative, dream, and fantasy realms. Printed matter not only brought information about strange and fantastic worlds; it also transmitted views from mysterious and intriguingly different human hearts. Reading enriched awareness of the ambiguities inherent in human development and personality traits. As a result of their reading, some rural New Englanders broke through their provincialism — the most virulent of all American cultural characteristics — and broadened their comprehension of human individuality, diversity, and universality. At the same time they became painfully aware of their actual position and decreasing role within the far larger transformation of all of North Atlantic civilization. The roots of alienation lie deeper in "modern life" than we have imagined. They are embedded in the transformation of everyday life which this book describes.

Chapter 1

"Competence Among the Rocks": Continuity and Change in Rural New England, 1760–1835

It was a period [1800–1840] of marvelous intellectual activity, in which the human mind was seeking, on the one hand, universal truths and laws, and on the other, under new forms, the subjection of nature to the wants of man.

—Sewall Cutting, "Historical Address," *Centennial Memorial of Windsor, Vermont, July 4, 1876*

Writers concerned with the early American Republic often avoid explicit large-scale generalizations about societal transformation, instead identifying several separate economic and social processes under way between 1790 and the 1840s: urbanization, the growth of a national market, and the spread of the factory system. Such descriptions, however, presuppose a direct two-stage transition between a premodern, preindustrial world and a modern, industrial one.[1] Nearly all accounts agree that the half century following the American Revolution was a troubled transitional period preceding a distinctive era of major change, the economic takeoff and cultural explosion of 1830–60.[2]

In fact, between 1780 and 1835 a series of profound but subtle material and cultural changes altered the way life was lived in rural society. Considered collectively, these changes afford a new basis for understanding the coming of the modern world. Two interrelated factors were indispensable in reshaping the texture of rural material and cultural life. Though neither necessarily would have led to urbanization or industrialism, both paved the way for a modern society.

The first factor was the creation of a new regional communications environment in the American Northeast, based on printed and written texts. Their proliferation between 1780 and 1835 led to a vast transformation in the forms of cultural exchange, as residents of the Upper Valley read more regularly and participated ever more actively in cultural life. Within North Atlantic civilization, America was one of the most rural societies, and rural New England one of America's most rural provinces. Therefore, what needs explaining is north-western New England's cultural richness and diversity despite its rural character and apparent geographcial isolation.

The second factor reshaping rural life was the commercialization of material and social existence as the Upper Valley became enmeshed in a regional market economy linked to the transatlantic commercial world.

Even in an area as recently settled as the Upper Connecticut River Valley, these two forces heralded the end of rural localism and isolation from commercial and cultural events occurring in distant places. Local influences, traditionally powerful, did not disappear but were seriously weakened by the challenge of new habits of commercial and cultural exchange and by heightened contemporary awareness of their meaning and impact. Both commercialization and the creation of a new cultural environment helped to shape a novel and increasingly modern order of life in rural New England. These twin changes, which were massive, were distinct from the social processes controlling proto-industrialization, industrialization, urbanization, and modernization which historians usually identify as the bases of fundamental change in this era.

Changes in commerce and culture had many implications for daily existence. None was more significant, however, than the emergence of reading as a necessity of life for an ever larger share of rural inhabitants in each North Atlantic country. In my research laboratory, a part of northwestern New England on the far fringes of American life, by the mid-1820s reading had become a necessity of life for at least three-quarters of all families. The conscious pursuit of lifelong learning was the most visible sign of this development, a pursuit that often dramatically increased rural residents' knowledge of the world while facilitating their adaptation to change.[3]

How and why did the "relish for reading" (as Roy Wiles has termed it) progress so rapidly and reach so deeply in an apparently isolated backwater rural society? To answer this question we must first consider the position of the Upper Valley within the North Atlantic world in the period 1760–1835.

Reading Becomes a Necessity of Life:
The Broad Context of North Atlantic Civilization

By the mid-1820s, native commentators assessing the progress of American civilization since the Revolution were identifying a new factor as the single most momentous characteristic of the age. It heralded a fourth great revolution, in addition to the American, French, and Industrial Revolutions. Speaking in 1825 when the cornerstone of the Bunker Hill monument was laid, Daniel Webster noted the creation of a new communications environment, terming his era an "age of knowledge" and citing "the general progress of knowledge" throughout

Europe and America as one of the most significant events of the 1775–1825 period. Webster observed:

> Such has been the improvement . . . above all, in liberal ideas and the general spirit of the age . . . that the whole world seems changed. [It] peculiarly marks the character of the . . . North Atlantic community of nations [that they make] a common progress like vessels on a common tide, propelled by the gales at different rates, according to their several structures and management, but all moved forward by one mighty current, strong enough to bear onward whatever does not sink beneath it.

The key to this "one mighty current" was the development of a "community of opinions and knowledge amongst men in different nations existing in a degree heretofore unknown." The "Republic of Letters" had greatly expanded, in Webster's view. As a result, in the mid-1820s "a great chord of sentiment and feeling runs through two continents and vibrates over both. . . . Knowledge has, in our time, triumphed, and is triumphing over distance," language barriers, habits, and prejudices. This was the central development of the age: "the diffusion of knowledge, so astonishing in the last half-century."[4]

Webster's assessment of the profound impact of the diffusion of knowledge was extended a year later by Joseph Story in a Phi Beta Kappa discourse delivered less than five miles away, at Cambridge. The happiness "of whole communities" had been affected by "direct or silent changes forced by . . . subtler occurrences . . . into the very structure of society." These "will be read with far deeper emotions in their effects upon future ages" than other historical trends, Story remarked. Chief among the results of these silent changes was the establishment of a new and mighty empire, the empire of public opinion, and "the operation of what Lord Bacon has characterized almost as supreme power, the power of knowledge, working its way to universality, and interposing checks upon government and people, by means gentle and decisive, which have never before been fully felt, and are even now, perhaps, incapable of being fully comprehended."

What subtler occurrences could possibly match the impact of the American Revolution, the conquest of the continent "to the Rocky Mountains," the French Revolution, or the series of revolutions in South America? Essentially there were two, Story contended. Each "has worked deepest in all the [other] changes of the age." First was "the general diffusion of knowledge. This is emphatically the age of reading." It used to be that learning was "the accomplishment of those in the higher orders" and middle classes of society, and that reading was "the privilege of the few"; in this generation it had become "the possession of the many." Reading "now radiates in all directions," chiefly because of the freedom and particularly the "cheapness" of the press. Contributing factors included the spread of schooling, "that liberal commerce, which connects by golden chains the interests of mankind," and the "spirit of inquiry" awakened by Protestantism.

The second subtle occurrence followed from the first. In Story's estimation, the general diffusion of knowledge had created a "universal love and power of reading": books and other print items were eagerly awaited. As a result, "scarcely is a work of real merit dry from the English Press, before it wings its way to both the Indies and America." Keen interest in the latest publications had ushered in a momentous shift in attitudes toward knowledge. "With such a demand for books," Story remarked, and "with such facilities of intercourse, it is no wonder that reading should cease to be a mere luxury, and should be classed among the necessaries of life."[5]

Webster and Story both spoke near Boston, one of the three leading centers of the American book trade in the mid-1820s, and as elite members of eastern Massachusetts' urban society. Were their assessments about the diffusion of print culture accurate? The present investigation concludes that in 1825 their judgments were exact for rural New England, even its most isolated northwestern quadrant.[6]

The half century following the 1783 Peace at Paris marked the first age of mass literacy. An extensive communications network and a new series of cultural forms began to enter the homes of most families. These cultural forms were diffused through books and other reading matter with the expansion of elementary literacy and the continuation of reading activity throughout the life cycle.[7]

One of the signal developments of the century 1760–1860, throughout the Western world, was the rapid expansion of print and written culture to many more social groups. By the phrase "print and written culture," we mean knowledge about self and the world received and transmitted by means of the alphabet preserved on paper in print or handwriting. For several hundred years regular reading had remained largely the preserve of the elite and a small proportion of the middle classes. By 1750, however, in Great Britain, Germany, and to a lesser extent France, and after 1775 throughout all Western civilization, the reading public expanded substantially to include rural and urban "middling sort" wealth and occupational groups. Moreover, the variety of reading matter grew enormously. By 1760 regular reading, and sometimes writing as well, had spread from the upper classes to the urban middle classes in several countries. Diffusion was widest in England, next widest in Scotland and America, and closely followed by France and Germany. Literacy was almost universal in Sweden by 1760, but popular reading matter there appears to have been largely confined to religious tracts and guides to daily living.[8] Home instruction and elementary and academy schooling expanded considerably in nearly every country in the last half of the eighteenth century and first half of the nineteenth. The acquisition and maintenance of literacy skills led to more regular perusal of books, pamphlets, almanacs, broadsides, and, to a lesser extent, newspapers and periodicals. Recent scholarship suggests that in most countries novels, travel narratives, schoolbooks, periodicals, and newspapers joined traditional fare, which included secular almanacs and pamphlet-sized stories and tales, as well as Bibles, prayer books, hymnals, psalm books, sermons, and devotional treatises.[9]

The rise of more regular reading in the century after 1760 was influenced by material and cultural conditions that varied from country to country and region to region.[10] Because the nature of the transformation remained essentially the same everywhere, however, there were some system-wide changes between 1760 and 1860.

At least six interrelated changes may be identified: (1) a sharp rise in elementary literacy, the foundation of active participation in print and written culture; (2) a dramatic increase in enrollment at the lowest level of schooling, crucial to literacy's growth except where families or parishes formally assumed the burden of inculcating basic skills (as, for example, in Sweden); (3) greater interaction between religion, with its promise of an afterworld as an effective guide to daily life, and rising interest in secular existence on earth; (4) proliferation of land and water transportation networks that expanded services and distributed new or differently produced commodities throughout rural areas; (5) faster and deeper penetration of the international market economy into rural life, paralleled by growing awareness of this social process and its implications; and (6) comparable expansion of the communications network, so that many types of printed objects and the mail began to permeate rural areas.

Elementary literacy spread at varying rates, as did the availability of different types of reading matter, once the skills of reading, writing, and numeracy had been acquired. Moreover, people quickly developed tastes for reading matter different from that used in teaching literacy skills. Among the first generation of Upper Valley settlers who had migrated from Connecticut and Massachusetts, home and district school environments alike fostered strong, lasting interest in both heaven and earth – in future salvation and in leading a prosperous life in the meantime.[11]

The ecology of rural life offered substantial resistance to the spread of print culture. Progress before 1760 had been very slow except in Sweden. The mechanics of life in rural areas simply did not encourage wide diffusion of reading and writing before the late eighteenth century. Mass literacy emerged in such areas throughout the North Atlantic only after rural life itself had begun to change, not radically but noticeably, prior to both the infiltration of the Industrial Revolution and the urbanization of the countryside. The two key local institutional developments were the initial penetration of the market economy, commercial social relations, and cultural consumption into the countryside (the first commerical goods available for sale included several varieties of printed matter); and the broadening of opportunities for schooling and education at home, especially in villages and thereafter in scores of satellite hamlets.

Once commerce, home education, and basic schooling had become firmly established in a rural area, elementary literacy spread rapidly. In the Upper Valley general stores—selling at least a limited range of printed matter—and summer and winter district schools typically emerged in unison. But in many townships of the Upper Valley hinterland, the intensification of home education and neighborhood schooling often preceded the establishment of local businesses. This latter order of precedence occurred only in the most isolated, recently settled areas that were influenced from a distance by townships with villages where a richer mix of commercial and educational institutions had already begun to develop. Thus, commerce and basic schooling developed in unison until only the most remote townships lacked both; at that point either one could enter first and the other would not be far behind. Home education and neighborhood schooling, supplemented by the printed items available at local general stores, encouraged the relish for reading. The establishment of a solid foundation of commerce and education in rural precincts, entailing both material and cultural development, subsequently accelerated the pace of change throughout rural life.[12]

It is important to understand the extreme rurality of America among North Atlantic nations through 1830. The Netherlands had proceeded most rapidly toward larger-scale population concentration: by 1800, 30% of its population lived in cities of more than 10,000 people. The population of England and Wales was 21% urban. These two countries were followed by Scotland, Spain, Belgium, and Portugal, with between 13% and 17%, and by another group of countries, including France, Denmark, Ireland, and Prussia, with between 7% and 11% urban. The thinnest urban populations were in Austria (4.3%), the United States (3.8%), and Russia (3.7%). Thus America was thirteenth among the fourteen leading nations.[13] Moreover, most countries had at least one populous "national" city. London led the list of western cities in 1800, with 880,000 residents. Another 350,000 English men and women were scattered among Leeds (53,000); Bristol (64,000); Birmingham (74,000); Liverpool (78,000); and Manchester (84,000). In comparison, New York City, the largest city in America in 1800, had just 60,000 inhabitants.[14]

By the end of the early national era, in 1830, America still stood only twelfth in urban population, with 6.7%. Not until 1850 did America advance significantly, to eighth with 12%, far behind the Netherlands (29%), Scotland (32%), and England and Wales combined (40%). New York City showed dramatic growth with nearly 200,000 inhabitants, by 1830. Baltimore and Philadelphia came next, with 80,000 each, followed by Boston's 61,000. In the same year, however, London had 1.5 million residents, and Liverpool and Glasgow slightly outdistanced New York with 202,000 each. Manchester, Birmingham, and Ed-

America very rural

inburgh each had between 145,000 and 182,000 residents. Although New York was becoming a national center of commerce and culture, by 1830 it had only attained the size of one of Great Britain's large provincial cities.[15]

In view of America's comparative level of social development, it is extraordinary that the first two widely literate, actively reading rural generations in the Western world should have emerged there. In rural New England's least settled area, the Upper Valley, on which this book focuses, widespread literacy among both males and females first appeared in large villages, which were marketing centers for rural culture by the 1780s. No township numbered even 3,000 inhabitants until the late 1820s, and the largest village before the 1830s contained about 1,500. This area was far from any sizable city, it was land-locked and mountainous, and its transportation facilities were at the mercy of a harsh climate.[16]

That a fringe area as remote as the Upper Valley developed widespread literacy and a mass culture based on reading and writing as early as it did casts a new light on rural life and its relationship to urban change. In the Upper Valley we may observe closely, in all its variety, the transformation that literacy accompanied. By "mass culture" we mean that a consistently available set of vehicles for communicating information and ideas reaches the vast majority of the population. By 1815, then, in the rural American Northeast, the first truly new rural mass culture in two millennia had emerged. Moreover, the peculiar nature of printed matter permitted local beliefs and values to thrive alongside ideas and sentiments shared throughout the Western world.

For the ordinary men and women who constituted the vast majority of humanity, the traditional five senses were now supplemented by a wholly new act. In its complex interaction of eyes, ears, mouth, and touch, the magical sixth sense of reading afforded a major new way to learn about the world. Print was a very special, complex medium that offered a particularly powerful new mode of apprehending the world. Among all uses of the senses, reading alone brought the learner knowledge from afar on a regular basis and at will. It alone could reach beyond the traditional, near limits of the five senses, and bring the distant world to the attention of myriad local readers, altering their traditional learning about the world.

The range of rural life experience expanded greatly between 1760 and 1830. While there were no sizable population centers, the Upper Valley did spawn eighteen small but powerfully generative rural townships with populations between 2,000 and 3,000, each township with a village of between 500 and 1,500 inhabitants. In addition, satellite hamlets emerged in many other townships along the major transportation routes between villages. All villages and nearly every hamlet contained a general store, that most critical local agent of transatlantic commerce and culture. Additionally, a few well-placed, competitively successful rural villages included as part of their infrastructure the central in-

Threshing Grain, Waitsfield, Washington County, Vermont. Courtesy, Vermont Historical Society.

Even in the best of weather, farmstead living mixed plenty and abundance with hard work in a terrain of ridges and rocks. "Changing works" and other forms of shared activity were essential to livelihood.

Upper Valley with the seaports to the south and east and so with the whole stitution of the expanding print culture: a print center with postal service. A print center may be defined as a multiple-function cultural institution including printing, publishing, bookselling, and advertising. The center also established distinctive shipping routes and distribution systems for printed matter imported into the area, a weekly newspaper, sometimes a periodical or a lending library, and often an attached post office (see chapter 5). The eighteen largest Upper Valley villages influenced material and cultural life in all townships within a two-day ride, i.e., in four to twelve townships surrounding each village, depending on terrain, weather, and roads. Within the Upper Valley, villages and hamlets by 1815 formed a grid embracing about 80 percent of the rural population.

Distinctive, decentralized sets of agents of both commerce and culture simultaneously generated printed matter containing information and opinion and transmitted it to most families in one of the least urban societies in the entire Western world. As a result, the same general cultural phenomenon that was spreading throughout cities and large towns in Great Britain and Europe during the period 1760–1830 affected the rural American population as well.[17] Upper Valley rural villages and hamlets were linked together by a local and regional transportation and communications network that in turn united the

North Atlantic. Not all families chose to participate in the new rural world, of course, nor were all families affected equally. Participation varied greatly during the first age of reading in the rural areas of the American Northeast. Family libraries surviving from 1787–1830 in Windsor District, Vermont, held from 1 to 909 volumes.

America had only recently been settled, lay at a great distance from all North Atlantic centers of power and ideas, and was markedly rural throughout the early national era. Fears of barbarism were frequently voiced by American and foreign observers. Thus it seems amazing that the total audience of readers, and especially female readers, particularly in a forest society on the northwestern fringe of an extremely rural land, grew so large so quickly.[18]

America's distinctiveness within the transatlantic community may be explained partly by the peculiarity of its position near the western fringe of the North Atlantic. From at least the early eighteenth century onward, distance did not entail cultural isolation in the American Northeast. As in the cases of Sweden and Scotland, position on or near the periphery of transatlantic life spurred Americans to a new kind of involvement, a novel form of cultural connectedness, and gave them a potent motive for keeping abreast of "knowledge from distant climes." American productions never constituted the bulk of reading matter in the Upper Valley. A far greater share—nearly 75 percent of all reading matter through the mid-1820s—consisted of British and, to a lesser extent, European works. In the case of America, cultural curiosity, stimulated by distance, combined with several other factors. Population growth accelerated after 1730, and as the independent nation began to thrive, a volatile, pluralistic racial and cultural heritage developed. Distance, rurality, and the Republic's newness conspired to intensify demand for knowledge and "intelligence," a favored term.

Within the Northeast, scared and secular reading increased steadily in the decades after 1730, tapping into two major intellectual movements of the eighteenth century. One, the Great Awakening, mainly involved the sacred domain. The other included the sequence of secular events that began with the French and Indian War and proceeded through the Revolutionary War, the founding of a national polity, and the creation of state governments. Between 1730 and 1780, when both the road to personal salvation and the basis of the polity were at stake, reading acts and occasions multiplied. At first gradually, a new activity—reading to keep up with the times—came to be accepted as a common occurrence. The diffusion of the reading habit throughout the rural areas of the Northeast was most pronounced, however, in the half century following the Revolution, when it became a necessity of life.

The nation's continued widespread participation in print culture was not assured after the Paris peace treaty that ended the Revolution. True, the habit of reading had become ingrained in many urban and village families, but that had been in response to earthshaking sacred and secular events. It was not inevitable, for example, that novels should gain popularity in the Upper Valley between 1780 and 1830. Although they were the rage among middle-class urban residents of Germany, France, and England by the 1760s, very few were available for purchase, borrowing, or even browsing in Windsor District before the late 1790s. Even interest in events occurring in distant lands was minimal immediately after the Revolution. Between 1784 and early 1787, the leading Upper Valley newspaper, the Windsor *Vermont Journal*, frequently complained that there were too few important events to report. Curiosity about the news reasserted itself during Shays' Rebellion and especially during the Constitutional Convention and the ratification process. But it was the establishment of the federal government in America and the French Revolution that ushered in a long period of sustained interest in both American and transatlantic events. The 1790–1830 period also brought an ever broader and richer selection of reading matter to the attention of Upper Valley residents.[19]

In the rural Western world, a relish for reading and its entertainment, enchantment, and practical value had never previously penetrated very widely. The habit of reading, which spread through virtually the entire population of the Upper Valley between 1780 and 1835, made everyday life in the American Northeast during the Early Republic an utter anomaly. In rural areas beyond the American Northeast, widespread regular reading evolved more gradually during the nineteenth century.[20]

The print vehicles that residents of North Atlantic societies most frequently chose to read in 1730–1830 varied from country to country. In rural northwestern New England, almanacs, broadsides, books, and pamphlets, including the Bible, prayer books, hymnals, psalm books, devotional works, and schoolbooks, were the print vehicles most frequently read in the 1780s. By the late 1790s novels, travel narratives, geographies, and histories had been added to the list. Within another decade rural weekly newspapers had become central in Upper Valley reading. Periodical reading was mostly restricted to quite wealthy families until the 1820s. By contrast, in Germany after 1760, the novel was primary, followed by periodicals and travel books. In France the small book and many varieties of pamphlets were dominant; clandestine publications were a consequential part of reading fare. In Great Britain, books, pamphlets, periodicals, and newspapers were the staples.[21]

The newspaper's rise to prominence heralded a further development in reading. Not only was this most versatile vehicle rich with "knowledge from distant climes" and information about local commerce and culture; it also advertised and shamelessly reprinted material first published elsewhere. Furthermore, newspapers were the most secular of all print forms. Their readers were consequently most likely those whose thirst for knowledge extended to many secular subjects. Very soon, in historical terms—by the second half of the nine-teenth century at the latest—a mass culture based on print became prevalent in several other rural areas of the Western world: Scotland, southern England, north and central France, all but southernmost Germany, Sweden, Norway, Finland, and the United States South and West.

The first signs of mass culture were unpredictable in their effects on daily life in the hills and valleys of landlocked rural Vermont and New Hampshire. Change was no longer assimilated slowly, at an almost geological pace, but arrived in rural New England households weekly, with mechanical precision. The expansion of knowledge in fresh, naïve minds fostered great anxiety but also inspired intense curiosity and self-confidence. By the late 1830s this mass culture had given rise to a series of peculiarly American cultural forms. An ideal of intellectual currency as an essential element of "modern life" had even generated a full-fledged critique of the direction being taken by contemporary commercial and early industrial capitalism.

Many cultural leaders, including a host of self-appointed prophets of prog-ress and doom, stepped forward. Joseph Smith found handwritten golden tab-lets proclaiming a new order of life on earth. William Miller prophesied the end of the world on the basis of calculations made using his Bible. Orestes Brownson predicted many aspects of early industrial society from his vantage point as a rural printer and editor. Horace Greeley and scores of other reform-ers supported a wide array of small and a few broad-ranging remedies for social ills, including intentional communities and other social experiments. These in-dividuals and groups, together with a much larger share of readers wishing to preserve their traditional values and beliefs, formed the first two widely lit-erate rural generations in the Western world.[22]

The Study Area and the Scale of Generalization

One of the key problems in history today is how to create research designs which pay careful attention to the scale of generalization. This concern is the legacy of the "new social history." By varying our scope, depending on the problem and available evidence, we may learn much about rural New England life in the half century following independence.[23] In this area, rural commerce and the emergence of a mass culture based on the diffusion of printed matter created conditions within which the spread of manufacturing came to be per-ceived as desirable and so was actively encouraged by members of a new type of early modern rural society.[24]

As Raymond Gastil has noted, "*one* approach to a cultural analysis of the United States is a regional approach that goes beyond assumptions of general national uniformity."[25] For more intensive analysis, I have chosen New Eng-

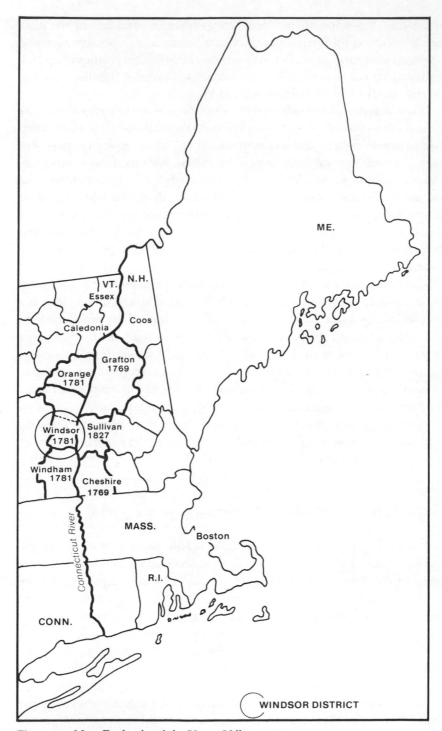

Figure 1-1: New England and the Upper Valley, c. 1830

land as a distinct region within the Northeast. Particularly when differentiated further into subregional units for more detailed analysis, the region permits a depth of research impossible in a broader study. The subregional geographical unit is the largest effective unit for two of my main purposes: first, to grasp the full workings of the transportation and communications networks in the rural countryside; and second, to follow the actual flow of commerce, and especially the book trade, along every channel through which it reached any group of residents, no matter how isolated their living situation. Because I wished to avoid the special case of seacoast life and to find an area away from, and thus influenced only indirectly by, rapid urban growth and the first wave of factory production in America, I chose the inland Upper Valley, a representative frontier and postsettlement subregional unit in the early national era (see figure 1–1).[26] The Upper Valley subregion encompassed the five settled counties of New Hampshire and Vermont bordering the Connecticut River. (There were eight in 1830. By then Sullivan County, New Hampshire, had split off from Grafton County, and was formally organized [1827], and Caledonia and Essex Counties in Vermont were moving beyond an initial settlement stage of social development.) Today the Upper Valley accounts for about a fifth of the land of Vermont and New Hampshire; in the early national era it constituted a third of the settled land. To combine comprehensiveness with precision of analysis, I also chose a smaller ecological unit, Windsor District, Vermont—the eleven townships comprising southern Windsor County (see figure 1–2). This multiple-focus approach attempts to overcome both the generality of studies focusing on an entire nation and the narrowness of single-township studies.

Part of the expanding New England frontier, the Upper Valley was settled in the Revolutionary era and the first decades of the new nation by southern New Englanders. Kinship ties to southern New England remained strong throughout the settlement era and afterward. Central Massachusetts provided sizable numbers of migrants to the Upper Valley, but central Connecticut was the largest contributor. In fact, during the Revolutionary War, Vermont was frequently called New Connecticut. The Upper Valley was a largely self-contained social, economic, political, and geographical subregion.[27] Basic settlement first moved along its central river corridor from Massachusetts and Connecticut, advancing after 1800 further northward, into more mountainous terrain. The natural landscape of the Upper Valley is a never-ending sequence of hills and valleys that gradually slope upward on either side of the Connecticut River basin. On the east, the White Mountains and their southern trailers formed a partial barrier, isolating much of the northern valley from the remainder of New Hampshire. On the west, the Green Mountains split the state of Vermont in two, leaving the valley counties only tenuously connected to the western half of the state. To the north, the narrowing of the

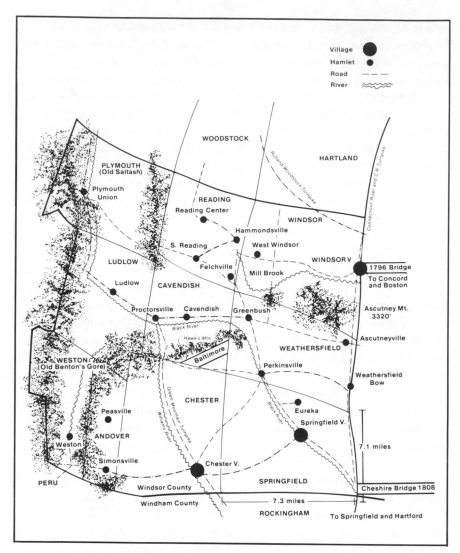

Figure 1–2: Windsor District, 1787–1835

Connecticut River, which prohibited transportation by large vessels, and the steady encroachment of the mountains on both sides of the river, also constituted a temporary barrier. As a result, substantial settlement of the northernmost counties in each state awaited the Peace of Ghent. In short, the Upper Valley was relatively enclosed, though by no means isolated, through 1830.[28]

As Upper Valley society expanded, ties with the rest of the Northeast grew apace, proceeding by land and water routes. The villages were affected first, then the hamlets, and last the most isolated countryside precincts. Links to the west ran through Rutland to the western side of Vermont and New York State. Communications and trade were somewhat limited in this direction and went mostly one way, as migrants and travelers headed westward. Connections to the east and south were much stronger. The main overland route eastward within the Upper Valley after 1795 passed from Windsor to Concord and then on to Boston. The river and post roads led south to Hartford and New Haven, southwest to Albany and southeast to Worcester and then Boston. From any of these terminal cities, London was but a long boat ride. Commodities, communications, and individuals selling services moved continuously along each of the pathways.

The spread of literacy and regular reading throughout the Upper Valley in the half century following independence bound a growing share of all families ever closer to life in Boston, New York, and Philadelphia in America and London, Edinburgh, and Paris in Europe. A single description of a new Leeds invention was read by residents of Leeds, London, New York, Hartford, and Windsor within the same eight-month period during 1790. Most poor families, and a group of farm families in isloated communities such as Plymouth Kingdom in the foothills of the Green Mountains on the western fringe of Windsor County, remained unable to participate actively in commerce or print culture until the 1820s. Some people in these two groups remained illiterate; others read only sacred works, preferring not to learn about events elsewhere in the North Atlantic world. Still, some Plymouth Kingdom families read books and pamphlets obtained from general stores, from peddlers, and even from traveling authors, and by 1815 subscribed to a rural newspaper. By these means they too obtained a varied, if selective, picture of life throughout the known world.[29]

Between 1780 and 1830, each of the Upper Valley counties was settling into a more stable pattern of rural life. Grazing, subsistence farming, and small-scale commercial farming dominated the economy. Some artisan and semi-skilled labor was available, as were professional services. Many rural factories existed, along with eighteen bustling commercial villages, most of them featuring clusters of stores and other businesses, several social and cultural institutions, and at least a few professionals. Three distinct types of living arrangements had evolved in the Upper Valley by the early 1780s: villages, hamlets, and township farmsteads. After 1800, a series of factory villages also emerged, each intensively engaged in rural manufacturing processes with machinery powered by rivers and streams. By the late 1820s, several Upper Valley counties had reached or were approaching their nineteenth-century peak in population; after several decades of steady growth, all but one had leveled off. There were no cities in the Upper Valley before 1830. The largest population center was Windsor, a village of 1,200–1,500 inhabitants in the early 1820s, in a township with a peak population (in 1830) of 3,094 (see table 1–1).

While the Upper Valley is a manageable geographical unit for analytical purposes, it included several different kinds of communities and living situa-

Table 1–1: Windsor District Population, 1770–1840

Township	1770	1790	1800	1810	1820	1830	1840⁴
Andover	—	275	622²	957²	1,000	977	878
			126%*	54%	4%	-2%	-10%
Baltimore	—	—	174	207	204	179	155
				19%	-1%	-12%	-13%
Cavendish	—	491	921	1,297	1,551	1,486	1,427
			88%	41%	20%	-4%	-4%
Chester	152¹	981	1,880	2,370	2,493	2,291	2,305
			92%	26%	5%	-8%	1%
Ludlow	—	179	409	877	1,144	1,125	1,363
			128%	114%	30%	2%	21%
Plymouth (formerly Saltash)	—	106	495	834	1,112	1,237	1,417
			367%	69%	33%	11%	15%
Reading	—	747	1,128	1,565	1,603	1,392	1,363
			51%	39%	2%	-13%	-2%
Springfield	141¹	1,097	2,038³	2,556	2,702	2,736	2,625
			86%	25%	6%	1%	-4%
Weathersfield	20¹	1,146	1,946	2,115	2,301	2,223	2,002
			70%	9%	6%	-3%	-10%
Weston	—	—²	[c. 400]²	629	890	972	1,032
				57%	42%	9%	6%
Windsor	c.250⁴	1,542	2,214	2,757	2,956	3,094	2,744
			44%	25%	7%	5%	-11%
Totals		6,564	12,227	16,164	17,956	17,712	17,311
			86%	32%	11%	-1%	-2%

*Figure below population is percent of increase.

Source: Unless noted, U.S. Census Schedules, 1790–1840.

[1] Child, *Gazetteer*, 115 (Chester); 224 (Springfield); 244 (Weathersfield).

[2] The U.S. Census lists Andover (including Weston) at 1,022. Weston was part of Andover till 1797 and still counted as such in the 1800 census. Local histories of both townships provide the figures used here.

[3] Hubbard, *Springfield*: 2,032 (85%).

[4] Zadock Thompson, *History of Vermont* (Burlington, 1842), 209–10.

[5] John Hayward, *A Gazeteer of Vermont* (Boston, 1849), 145–50.

tions. The three long-settled Vermont counties of Windham, Windsor, and Orange, encompassing 2,448 square miles, had been divided into fifty-seven townships by 1830. The three New Hampshire counties—Cheshire, Grafton, and Sullivan—that had been formed by 1827 accounted for 2,434 square miles, divided into seventy-three townships.[30] Within this subregion, I chose a smaller but representative ecological unit of analysis, the southern half of Windsor County, Vermont, because of the diversity of its community types, economic activity, and cultural life. Known to contemporaries as Windsor District, this—and not the county—was the official legal unit for local life. With an eighth of the population and an eleventh of the land in the Upper Valley, Windsor District's eleven townships contained all the major types of living situations found within the entire Upper Valley.[31]

Great cultural diversity was an enduring reality in rural New England.[32] Differential access to print and written matter led to vastly different levels of cultural participation. Windsor District will be analyzed in detail to understand patterns generally applicable throughout the Upper Valley. By this method of research, we may follow the flow of material and cultural change throughout all types of communities, occupations, wealth levels, household sizes and types, placements in the communications network of the area, and living situations.[33]

Within Windsor District, I have attempted to study, for all male and female family members and long-term residents of households: the essential circumstances of material and cultural life; particular gender roles, including differences between males and females in personality development, cultural values, and beliefs; and characteristics, roles, and attitudes males and females shared. This book studies those life experiences where men and women were more similar than divergent in their participation, and other dimensions of life where the evidence available does not permit us to distinguish by gender. Gender differences have been studied as fully as the evidence permits, and in detail with respect to literacy rates and trends, reading patterns by stages of life, and participation (or its absence) in institutions of public culture and in the initial intellectual emancipation of rural women. As in all areas of history, we must be careful not blithely to assume that role prescriptions imply the actualities of experience. This is a critical research question.[34]

Until about 1795, the Upper Valley was not extraordinary among rural societies in North Atlantic civilization. In terms of the categories defined by James Henretta, it included the early and late settlement and rural maturation phases of American social and economic development.[35] These terms, however, fail to capture the impact of events that pervaded and transformed rural life by the 1820s, altering the entire ecology of people, natural resources, physical and cultural technology, and the distribution of that technology. Remaining farmland in the more sparsely settled townships of each county was now being titled to settlers, and many hamlets were growing rapidly. A few villages had become stagnant, but many others were expanding significantly. And what used to be regarded as the purely urban process of industrialization was also growing rapidly in these rural areas.[36]

As noted above, neither the Upper Valley as a whole nor most of Windsor District remained isolated from the rest of the North Atlantic world. The broad transformation we follow delineates the earliest encroachment of changes eventually to permeate all of North Atlantic rural life. An agricultural population prepared for, and adapted and responded to, the ever more rapid changes in commerce, factories, and cities; the specialization of work and leisure; and the centralization of bureaucracy occurring throughout the North Atlantic world.

The study of the outer transformation of American life between the Revolution and the late nineteenth century has begun in earnest. The late Herbert Gutman lamented that the pace and course of modernization in factory and city to date had not been subjected to a persuasive synthesis; undoubtedly his challenge will spawn intensified efforts to create such a synthesis over the next decade.[37] But as such scholarship proceeds we must also study the inner transformation that led the way into the modern world, and begin to analyze the relationship between the two types of change. The present study begins at the beginning, with the people who lived as adults in rural New England in 1780–1835. These two generations experienced a material and cultural earthquake of magnitude sufficient to transform a forest society and its inhabitants. In this era most Americans lived thoroughly rural lives, while new institutions, businesses, information, and channels of communication infiltrated the countryside. To understand how the Great Transformation affected the mass of ordinary people, we must consider how their basic beliefs and values were acquired, shaped and reshaped, and used in daily life.

Reading Instruction in Rural New England, 1780–1830, and Its Conservative Intent

Much of this study concerns texts and their uses. It is, therefore, essential to understand the prevailing methods of reading instruction and the reading habits and uses of knowledge that children and youth acquired during the historical period under consideration. Along with new kinds of reading matter entering the Upper Valley after 1790 came novel ways of learning and new attitudes about the uses of knowledge. That these alternatives to traditional literacy had made significant headway by about 1810 is all the more remarkable in light of the power of middle to late eighteenth century pedagogy.

Although reading is often discussed as if it were a skill acquired universally and uniformly, it too has a history.[38] And its intended objectives and its meaning as an act have changed throughout time. Reading can be a strong defender of tradition or an agent of change. The role of reading instruction in instilling a conservative outlook in rural New England children and youth, males and females, is an intricate but essential subject. We must ask, What did reading instruction entail? Specifically, did rural New Englanders see differences among various vehicles of cultural expression—paintings and tavern signs, printed and written matter, music—in the messages carried and the way each mode of expression conveyed its meanings? And was expansion of an individual's fund of knowledge about the world an inevitable concomitant of the alphabet on paper? Reading *might* be a liberating experience, teaching the reader new ways of thinking and feeling, but did it *have* to be? What were the uses of print culture in the lives of people who farmed and grazed? Did differences between men's and women's lives increase or decrease as reading spread? Were changes in patterns of thought and feeling typical and even expected goals of reading?[39]

Potentially liberating uses of reading were largely ignored by rural New England reading instructors throughout the eighteenth and early nineteenth centuries because these teachers had utter confidence that those who controlled early learning processes controlled the life of the mind. Where anxiety did exist, it was directed toward fiction, especially novels, which were assumed to be both widely read and dangerous. Apart from this assault on fiction, and a small amount of criticism aimed at clandestine and pornographic works, reading was not only tolerated but actively encouraged. Indeed, criticism amounted to a minor, if shrill and persistent, note amid widespread, highly articulated concern with reading. Literacy was promoted as a way of sustaining the new nation in its perilous republican experiment and as a means of insuring individual salvation and a "Bible Commonwealth" by the inculcation of enduring Christian values and behavior. Most secular and religious leaders pursued the linked creation of an enlightened, "informed" citizenry and a phalanx of knowledgeable Christians. Educators agreed that a New World society of Christian republicans could not be sustained without sacred and secular knowledge. Republicanism and Protestantism thrived when literate participants actively engaged in lifelong learning. In the minds of proponents of reading, the twin goals of reading outweighed any fears about the influence that the reading habit might eventually exert on the lower classes; the dominant method of reading instruction in the Early Republic allayed most observers' misgivings until the process had gone too far to stop it. In retrospect it seems clear that institutionalized literacy had, as a major unintended consequence, the creation of a mass culture based on a vast variety of printed and written matter available to men and increasingly to women as well.[40]

As we begin to unravel the complexities of Upper Valley rural life, we must understand not only the material history of communications in early America, emphasizing printing office practices, labor relations, and the economics and technology of the book trade;[41] but also the cultural history of communications, including methods of reading instruction, reading acts, situations, and experiences; and also the history of readers' perceptions of the media of print (and other forms of) communications. Our own era's assumptions are often anachronistic, when applied to the past. Most rural New Englanders did not make a connection between the messages they received and the particular media involved, whether these were books, periodicals, almanacs, oral discourse,

Pilgrim's Dream. [John Bunyan], *The Christian Pilgrim* (Windsor, 1811). Courtesy, Vermont Historical Society.

The most popular religious fable of the era in the Upper Valley, Bunyan's *The Christian Pilgrim* presents an ideal of Christian morality widely accepted as "wisdom of the ages." In the frontispiece, Pilgrim dreams of what he may face in life "walking through the spacious wilderness of the world."

visual objects, dance, instrumental music, singing, writing, or reading. Except within a narrow group of professionals, different media were rarely discussed as embodying distinct modes of expression. In terms of late twentieth century conventions, most rural New Englanders of the day were partially media-blind.[42]

Conservative educators reinforced this trend by stressing the stability and continuity of intellectual traditions worth perpetuating; from their perspective, the goals of citizenship and salvation did not include challenges of whatever form to society's institutions or values. Whichever medium generated a worthwhile idea, the message would emanate from the same broad fund of knowledge—the wisdom of the ages. In retrospect, in the wake of the American Revolution and in view of the radical changes in the diffusion of reading matter then under way throughout the North Atlantic, this attitude appears extremely naïve. Nevertheless it was the dominant opinion. The particular form in which ideas were expressed received little consideration until after 1815, when it was far too late to curb the general thirst for reading and the great variety of reading matter available.

Noah Webster believed that the goal of education was neither personal liberation nor intellectual growth, but the preservation and transmission of the wisdom of the ages. In the hands of the most popular author of reading instruction manuals during the Early Republic, reading acts became a series of elaborate tribalized confirmation rites. From the first learning experiences in home and school, and Dennis Rusche has noted, "imitative learning played an important role in preparing the child for life in a world of fixed forms and ideas."[43] The primary goal of early education was not to instill in the child information about the world or to provoke a challenge to society's basic institutions, but to inaugurate the assimilation of a universe of previous "wisdom." Through about 1825, this educational philosophy prevailed in nearly all Upper Valley schools offering basic education, imparting a peculiar flavor to cultural life in the Early Republic and heightening the tension between tradition and innovation. It was in this context that plans, radical in their effects, were implemented to achieve a profoundly conservative end: the education of all white American women as "Republican mothers."[44]

Webster and his imitators taught boys and girls to read through an extremely conservative technique: the "pronouncing-form method," which was dominant until the mid-1820s. "Oral recitation" was stressed because, as Webster put it, "children learn the language by the ear."[45] Reading instruction was natural, using children's existing ability to talk and listen. Typically, a group of young people ranging in age from five to eighteen years gathered in a single-room district schoolhouse in the Upper Valley, where they began learning to read by sounding out letters, syllables, words, and sentences. The technique formed habits that strongly supported tradition rather than change. In one rural schoolhouse whose instructor was teaching from Webster's speller:

The schoolmaster would begin by selecting and correctly pronouncing a word from the speller. Then the students, sometimes singly but often in chorus, would respond. Without reference to the text, they would recite the letters of each syllable, pausing to pronounce the syllable, and then . . . proceed to the next syllable, until the whole word had been spelled and pronounced from memory. The schoolmaster with a sharp ear could detect those who had recited poorly or incorrectly. After . . . correction and reprimand, the class would start again with the next word. The whole procedure could take on a rhythm not unlike a chant. Sometimes the recitation would be based on individual competition. Each student vied with the others to see who could . . . stand at the head of the class. For variety the children would be directed to the short reading selections interspersed among the tables. Many of these selections were delightful fables or brief stories about children. . . . Webster believed that this interchange between reciting words and reading easy selections provided enough variety to maintain the interest of the child.[46]

The pronouncing-form mode of reading instruction had several important implications for the history of knowledge and its acquisition and maintenance. First, because people learned to read by speaking aloud, whereby they listened with the mind's ear, the skill was probably acquired far more rapidly than many scholars of reading instruction have assumed.[47] Residents of the Upper Valley were not used to the written word. The achievement of mass literacy for the first generation of future American citizens meant gradually moving beyond the confines of a culture with an inherently oral style of learning about the world. Webster confirmed a longstanding and eminently sensible assumption: reading was "a recreation of the author's conversation," so it should be taught by building on the experience in talking and listening, singing and chanting, that a child brought to school. Precisely because a child's life in the Early Republic was rooted in oral modes of communication, reading instruction began by pronouncing letters, syllables, words, and sentences aloud. It proceeded from the known to the unknown.

Contemporary cultural conditions have not been taken into account by many critics of Webster's modest adaptation of earlier methods of reading instruction. Rusche, however, properly notes that Webster's approach was not just "alphabetic" or, in Jennifer Monaghan's term, a "spelling-for-reading" method. The pronouncing-form method centered on the pronunciation of written words. Webster organized elementary reading instruction "to prepare the child to pronounce correctly any word he might meet in print." Far from being a random collection, in Webster's speller each sound, syllable, and word served as a type, preparing the novice for other, similar-sounding words to be encountered eventually. The link between Webster's speller and his dictionary was that of part to whole, the same relationship that he identified between early education and future cultural participation; the latter was a natural extension of the former.[48]

As boys and girls progressed in reading within Upper Valley homes and district schools, using primers, spellers, and eventually "readers," they repeatedly recited sentences encapsulating conventional wisdom about the world. They early assimilated the helpful wisdom that "reading is talking from a book." Rather than being a wholly new skill, reading started with familiar learning procedures and only gradually added to them. Regarded and taught as a mode of speaking, the habit of reading developed as an extension of the spoken word. As discussed by Rolf Engelsing for Germany and David Hall for early America, intensive reading matter and styles of reading represented a continuum with speaking and singing because they were perceived as "an oral activity aimed at a correct rehearsal of an author's speech as set down in written form."[49]

The chief implication of this sort of reading instruction for the cultural history of the Early Republic is not just that oral and reading skills were conflated, but also that the substance of oral and print culture were, from the earliest years of an individual's life, indissolubly linked. The initial fund of knowledge acquired in reading instruction blended easily with information and opinion garnered from talking, listening, singing, and chanting throughout childhood and early youth. As prevailing assumptions about the nature of learning blurred distinctions between modes of cultural expression, they weakened the bases for traditional distinctions between oral and print culture.

The long-term result of such reading instruction was that Upper Valley residents too readily accepted the authority of the printed word, any printed word. Moreover, once an individual became literate and continued the habit of reading, he or she could not easily be restricted to intensive reading styles and traditional subject matter. This was a major unintended consequence of the pronouncing-form method of reading instruction. As their reading tastes began to expand, Upper Valley residents were irresistibly drawn to new knowledge, especially knowledge of current events in the distant world. Beginning in the 1790s, rural weekly newspapers, with their balance of older and newer forms of knowledge, were readily accepted in households far removed from the cities providing so much of the newspaper's content. Regular installments of news from distant parts and information about local commerce ensured that newspapers, of all print media, became the greatest catalyst to cultural and material change throughout rural New England.

As newspapers and other alternative forms of reading matter spread, determined but futile opposition to the diffusion of some forms of new knowledge did coalesce. Supporters of widespread education were among the most outspoken critics of the novel, arguing that it encouraged a new private reading style and so fostered alternatives to the wisdom of the ages, the basic value system underpinning reading instruction. The world depicted in the wisdom of the ages was a known, stable place; the world presented in novels was an invented realm within which the fate of even an ordinary individual might and often did change dramatically. In the novel, chance and free will actively opposed determinism and eternity. Detractors regarded fiction not as lacking reality but as showcasing false and dangerously enticing alternative realities. Fiction could induce licentiousness and vice. Novels represented potential fissures in the world of wisdom. The reading of novels, as Cathy Davidson argues, was often considered a subversive activity; novels appealed directly to the imagination and thereby, according to their castigators, subverted all the normal structures of authority that governed behavior. The popularity of novels and criticism of them grew in tandem. Rev. Samuel Miller, in his 1803 *Retrospect of the Eighteenth Century*, made the most sweeping attack. Novel reading "dissipated the mind," begat "a dislike to more solid and instructive reading," and excited "a greater fondness for the productions of imagination and fancy than for the sober reasoning of the practical investigations of wisdom." Precisely because the whole point of reading was "the practical investigations of wisdom," novel reading was segregated by its critics from other reading situations and acts.[50]

At least initially in the Early Republic, the prevailing method of instruction inculcated strong habits of conformity in belief. It did so partly by the practice of reading aloud and partly by the blatant attempt at behavioral control that was associated with teaching of elocution in later education. The key assumption of the elocutionists was that reading aloud and public speaking were related processes of reenactment, of talking from a text that recounted an oral discourse. Just as reading was perceived as recreating an author's words in written form, as if he/she were *talking* to the reader, elocution instruction was perceived as guiding the student to recreate the precise emotions of the original speaker. The teacher sought to enhance an accurate recreation of the original oration by training the student to guide the listener to the proper emotional response through display of accurate physical gestures for each emotion conveyed.

In both reading aloud and elocution, the "passions" were to be repressed; only acceptable "emotions" were encouraged. Webster, Blair, Scott, and others engaged in a massive effort to dictate the proper manner of articulating sounds and so to shape audience response to knowledge. Both reading aloud and elocution directed the emotions in accordance with the pronouncing-form pedagogical strategy for structuring the intellect; the emphasis remained on learning the wisdom of the ages by ear. Conformity in behavior was the ultimate aim of conformity in reading style. In the Upper Valley, persuading the reader of the author's intended meaning through oral reading retained great popularity through 1830. Reading newspapers aloud was an especially important adaptation of this style of reading to a newly prominent vehicle of communication.[51]

The difficulty with this strategy was that the content of many popular new forms of reading matter undermined this long-term goal. The cultural battle over reading in rural New England had nothing to do with the desirability of making elementary literacy universal; instead the controversy concerned the kinds of knowledge that were acceptable. Small wonder that novelists, and especially early American fiction writers, nearly always contended in their prefaces that their tales were founded on fact, were in fact "histories," and supported traditional morality! Their shrewd stratagem helped secure a vast audience of new readers—youth who had been taught to read partly by reading moral tales and histories.

In the first rural age of reading, the interpenetration of oral and printed cultural forms, along with other cultural forms, was assumed to be almost complete. The learning process in part reflected the way in which readers perceived the mix of media that transmitted knowledge. Upper Valley residents regularly combined and blended several media that we view as distinct and separate. At the same time they defined and described those modes with which they were most familiar.[52]

Daniel Mason of Cavendish, Vermont, was learning to write as a youngster during the 1790s. He was not told by his teacher that the medium of writing was a separate form of expression. Rather, he was instructed to copy again and again the sentence, "A rapid and uniform handwriting is a speaking picture." Mason had mastered the basic cultural skills of talking, listening, and visualizing; writing was taught as a natural extension of these familiar modes. Writing would supplement previously assimilated ways of knowing.[53]

Soon after a pupil had begun spelling, reading, elementary numeracy, and writing—usually within the second month of a district school term—snippets of poetry appeared in reading selections. Most Upper Valley children learned from readers such as *Easy Lessons in Reading*. In its pages New Englander Joshua Leavitt admonished his audience to "take pains to read the poetry and not to *sing* it." Poetry must be distinguished from the familiar hymns and psalms sung on Sunday. Now the lesson was a more complex one—that not all activities were identical, even if they appeared to be. A poem might resemble a hymn on the printed page, but it differed in that a poem was primarily intended to be read rather than sung. Once again, the instructional method shaped understanding of the communication act by moving from the familiar to the unfamiliar.[54]

✳ Such assumptions about the relationship between one medium and others lasted into adulthood, reinforcing at every step the subtle interpenetration of cultural modes. New England public discourse abounds with examples. For an 1826 meeting of the Franklin Typographical Society, Thomas Green Fessenden, raised in Walpole, New Hampshire, prepared a poem to read. As if he had failed Leavitt's lesson, Fessenden termed it a "hymn" to the art of printing. He then went on to congratulate the assembled group because "the world at length had learn'd to prize, the *art of speaking to the eyes.*" The blending of imagery was further confirmed in Fessenden's statement that printed items were "silent heralds."[55]

By the mid-1820s an alternative whole-word method of reading instruction, the "reading-for-comprehension" method, blossomed. Silent reading, "by the mind's eye" rather than through the mind's ear, quickly gained a first cousin in the mental arithmetic movement. Samuel Goodrich's popular *Child's Arithmetic* urged "teaching beginning arithmetic with tangible objects like counters and bead frames," abandoning the recitation of rules and formulas. The use of concrete objects as an aid in solving problems involving abstract numbers led at more advanced levels to "arithmetic done in the mind, without pencil and paper." Warren Colburn in 1821 termed this method "intellectual arithmetic"; by the late 1820s it was challenging traditional methods in popularity.[56]

As we have seen, then, the habit of reading spread rapidly and reached deeply in rural society because it built on the dominant forms of Upper Valley cultural life. A fairly uniform set of practices introduced male and female readers to the wisdom of the ages. Conservative aims guided a consistent approach that produced solid traditionalsim in the substance of reading, in reading styles, and in the uses of knowledge. A generation passed before many new readers jettisoned Webster's cultural lenses. Some readers, however, did so almost immediately.

Toward the Intellectual Emancipation of American Women

Beginning in the 1780s, educational opportunity for both males and females expanded substantially in the American Northeast, buttressed by the widespread assumption that to remain prosperous, a republic required a well-educated and virtuous citizenry. Before the Revolution some wealthy males had traditionally been educated beyond the district school level; women had not. The Early Republic now heard commentary on female roles and functions, which "merged almost imperceptibly" into discussion of the proper scope of education for women. Within a generation, the effects of the emerging mass culture on women's intellectual development were dramatic.[57]

Opinion concerning the proper content, scope, and purposes of female education varied broadly.[58] Invoking republican theory, many commentators expressed fears of luxury and its inevitable degeneration into vice, attacked fashion as "an emblem of superficiality and dependence," and sought more republican purposes in the education of women.[59] Republican mothers, raising virtuous citizens, would counteract the effects of spreading commercialization, with its potential for degenerating into luxury and vice. By no means all writers about women, let alone the majority of the American population, thought reform in women's education was necessary or desirable. One of the most popular works in Windsor District, reaching far beyond lawyers' households, was Blackstone's *Commentaries on the Laws of England*. Its position codified the reigning opinion in many homes. In marriage,

> those chattels, which belonged formerly to the wife, are by act of law vested in the husband, . . . with the same degree of property and with the same powers, as the wife, when sole, had over them. . . . This depends entirely on the notion of an unity of person between the husband and the wife; it being held that they are one person in law, so that the very being and existence of the woman is suspended during the coverture, or entirely merged and incorporated in that of the husband.

People felt since woman was coveted, there was no use for her to be intellectual

Blackstone's position supported the assumption that, in Linda Kerber's words, "the shelter of coverture seemed to make sophisticated learning of little use to a woman." This view undergirded all discussions of changing roles, and advocates of greater education for women struggled against widespread resistance.[60]

Among writers countenancing at least some reform in women's education, the most typical position was that of republican motherhood, as conceptualized by Kerber. Mary Beth Norton has shown that the experience of the war years had enlarged women's actual role in the home. This experience strengthened arguments, beginning in the 1780s, that education would, as Kerber put it, "enable women to function more effectively within their traditional sphere." Direct political participation in the "privileges and duties of male citizens of the republic" beyond the domestic sphere was occasionally advocated, but only in a small minority of all Upper Valley commentary through the 1820s. Benjamin Rush, fairly widely read in Windsor District, held that women should assist men "in instructing their sons in the principles of liberty and government." A graduate of Susannah Rowson's rural Massachusetts academy summed up this position: a woman "skilled in every useful art, who practices every domestic virtue . . . may . . . inspire her brothers, her husband, or her sons, with such a love of virtue . . . that future heroes or statesmen shall *exaltingly declare, 'it is to my mother I owe this elevation.'*" Kerber concludes: "A pivotal political role was assigned to the least political inhabitants of the republic. . . . Women had the power to direct the moral development of the male citizens of the republic," and "motherhood was discussed almost as if it were a fourth branch of government." Moreover, as Norton notes, the "first major breach in the conventional feminine role," teaching school, was justified as a "logical extension" of motherhood.[61]

The new cultural role for women that emerged with the creation of the American Republic entailed significant though limited responsibility; it was nothing less than the development of moral fiber and civic virtue. The push for expansion in women's learning, based on increasingly widespread literacy, more regular attendance at district schools, and rising academy attendance, urged a conservative reform, a version of training in the wisdom of the ages for women. The idea meshed well with the contemporary assumption that childhood as a distinct stage of life had one major purpose: the formation of a sound conscience.[62]

The new attitude emerging in the 1780s was conservative, if viewed within the full range of possible attitudes toward women's roles, but it represented a substantial advance over previous attitudes. Behavior was another matter entirely, however. In and of itself, the ideology of republican motherhood implied no need for fundamental change. But republican motherhood led to several unintended consequences of great importance. The movement opened a new era in women's possibilities, an era which will only be concluded with the achievement of full equity within American life.

✕The cultural transformation began in the 1780s. By the late 1830s it had resulted in substantial if uneven change: dramatic alteration in women's lifelong learning and range of cultural participation; a substantial shift in women's attitudes toward their roles in American life; and minimal widening of male perspectives on women and their place in American public life. The ideology of republican motherhood permitted women to increase their reading and their knowledge of the world, so as to better raise their sons as active republican citizens; and to participate more actively in several dimensions of printed and written communication. Reading led ever greater numbers of women to intellectual emancipation and the desire for equity in more and more areas of American life. As women learned, they took positions on issues of the day and thereby became involved in more forms of cultural activity. To be sure, they were still severely constricted, especially in legal standing and direct political participation. Against great resistance, women—like men—increasingly broke free of traditional constraints on uses of knowledge and on ways of living.

How did this process of cultural growth occur in Windsor District?[63] First, between 1785 and 1810, district schools within each township began to include women students on a regular basis, first in summer schools and then in winter schools. Sunday schools also regularly included women students as soon as such schools emerged in Windsor District, around 1815. Academy training for women in the district progressed more slowly. In the 1780s and 1790s, before the rise of local academies, academies in the region advertised for Windsor District students. At least one, Moor's academy at Hanover, accepted "Young Ladies" in 1791, and separate instruction was not mentioned in its advertisement.

Within Windsor District itself, no evidence has been uncovered that the first academy, at Cavendish, accepted women during its known years of operation, 1792–95 and 1813–19. The second academy, the Windsor Grammar School, founded in 1802 at Windsor village and later renamed the Windsor Scientific and Literary Institution and the Windsor High School, did accept females, at least at first (1802–05). Once a Windsor Female Academy opened in 1814, also in Windsor village, women were no longer mentioned in advertisements of the Windsor Grammar School and were apparently not accepted. By 1830, the latter school existed "for the benefit of youth in acquiring a classical education," though it maintained three divisions—English, Classical, and Scientific Learning. Regular lectures were conducted in "Geology, Mineralogy, and Natural and Experimental Philosophy."

The Windsor Female Academy maintained classes between 1814 and 1820, did not open in 1821, was rechartered in 1822, and continued in operation through the early 1830s. By 1827, the name had changed to Mrs. A.M. Wells's Academy for Young Ladies, an "infant seminary for young ladies." Pupils had the "privilege of attending gratis the Botanical, Chemical, and other lectures to be delivered by the Principal of the [all-male] Windsor High School." By 1830 substantial improvement had been achieved in the status of women's education. A separate local academy for women was now actively supported by the major area newspaper, the *Vermont Republican and Journal*. An editorial that year noted that Wells had "upwards of 40 pupils at the close of her last term" and was expanding to make room for more. The editor proclaimed it, with two teachers, no longer "an *experiment*," but "firmly and permanently established." By August 1830 compositions exhibited at the Wells academy graduation were being reprinted.

Other academies also emerged in Windsor and elsewhere in the district, including a Windsor Stenography School, located in Windsor village, which in 1821 offered "stenography or Short-Hand writing" to men and women. The Columbian Academy, founded in 1826, was apparently shortlived and made no mention of women.

Chester too had an academy in 1814–30. No mention of women was made at first, but by the late 1820s a "Female Department" was advertised, under the charge of a woman. It held two sessions yearly, each consisting of two twelve-week quarters (forty-eight weeks per year in all). Instruction included "Common English Branches—Grammar, Geography, and Arithmetic; Latin and Greek languages; Higher English branches; Drawing, Painting and Ornamental Needle Work; Courses of Lectures on Natural Philosophy, Chemistry, and Botany." In addition, a "Select Library of Miscellaneous Books is connected with the school." Inland, the Reverend Samuel Loveland's Ministerial Training Center for Universalist males opened in Reading in 1823 and continued at least into the late 1820s. Finally, Ludlow opened the Black River Academy for men and women in 1834.

There were related educational institutions, as well. The Windsor Dancing Academy, opened for "Ladies and Gentlemen" in 1810, continued sporadically for several years. A Windsor Debating Society, opened in 1828, made no mention of women's attending its meetings. From 1810 through 1830 three Vermont

Fiftieth Anniversary Banquet (1885) of Black River Academy, Ludlow, Vermont.
Courtesy, Vermont Historical Society.

By the mid-1820s Windsor District academy training was reaching both genders
and appealing to middle class and lower middle class students. Within a decade,
academy training had spread far into the countryside, to Ludlow.

colleges advertised regularly in Windsor District: Dartmouth, Middlebury,
and the University of Vermont. All accepted only men. Near Windsor District, at Ryegate, "a boarding school for young ladies" was open in 1813. In 1830,
the Northfield [Mass.] Academy of Useful Knowledge advertised in Windsor
Distrtict: "For the next two terms, at least, young ladies will be admitted, and
can receive instruction in such languages and sciences as they may desire." Instruction for women was separate, and they were promised the opportunity
to board in good families.

Thus, between 1792 and 1830, regular educational oppoortunities existed at
the academy and college levels for men living within Windsor District. Women
were mainly limited to gender-segregated instruction, usually conducted in
separate facilities if not in wholly distinct institutions. The only known mixed
academy level instruction regularly conducted was at Windsor in 1802–1805
and at Ludlow beginning in the mid-1830s. Joint attendance at lecture series
did occur fairly regularly at Windsor after 1815. Segregated academy instruction for women was available in Windsor District at Windsor village from
1814, and at Chester village in the late 1820s and perhaps earlier. Other gender-
segregated academy instruction was available for women residents of the district to the north of Windsor District in 1813 and to the south a decade and

a half later. At Hanover women were admitted, presumably to a mixed-gender academy, in the early 1790s.

The proliferation of elementary and academy level educational institutions in the Upper Valley, and their inclusion of increasing numbers of young women, led to one of the central developments of the nineteenth century: increasing intellectual emancipation of ordinary American women. Beginning in the 1780s, lists of reading areas appropriate for women expanded far beyond reading, writing, arithmetic, and traditional sacred fare. Furthermore, in a war of lists, the appropriateness for women of particular branches on the tree of knowledge was debated for decades.[64] Increasingly, lists of acceptable subjects included grammar, rhetoric, and composition; "figures and bookkeeping," because women could expect to be "'the stewards and guardians of their husbands' property,' and executrices of their husbands' wills"; geometry; nursing and cooking; belles-lettres; religion and sacred history, "the first principles of natural philosophy;" geography; and secular history, mentioned as an antidote to novel reading, which was assumed to be occurring widely. Geography and history were presumed essential for "a general intercourse with the world." By the early 1820s several of the sciences, led by chemistry, botany, and astronomy, had been added. The practice of keeping journals and commonplace books spread and frequently formed part of academy level instruction. Music, "drawing, painting, embroidery, and tambour work" were also regularly mentioned. Changes in reading habits and in the contours of women's intellectual interests in the years 1787–1830 sank deep roots which have sustained women's intellectual emancipation ever since. As late as 1765, not even lip service was being paid to women's education.[65]

As advocacy of female education spread further in the years 1825–50, and especially where it included academy level training, it emphasized "a certain sexual destiny," encouraging mostly middle- and upper-class women, as Nancy Cott puts it, "to understand gender as the essential determinant of their lives." The gender segregation of most academy level instruction for women in Windsor District through 1830 supports this finding. The extent to which assumptions about gender served to "dissolve class and regional lines in the process," as Cott contends, is unclear in northwestern New England because very few poor or lower middle-class women could afford to attend academies through 1830. We can state with greater certainty, however, that the improvement of women's educational opportunities at the district and academy levels had the unintended effect of broadening women's intellectual interests, cultural participation, and public roles. As we shall see, what most women actually learned about the world was in great part determined by another, more historically specific complex of factors: the human habitats and reading communities shaping daily experiences.[66]

It is important not to underestimate the serious, continuing limitations on

Louisa's Retirement. Frontispiece engraving by J.J. Plocher. John Bennett, *Letters to a Young Lady,* 7th ed. (Philadelphia, 1818). Courtesy, American Antiquarian Society.

The ideal of women as active readers was furthered by books with lists of reading recommendations. Louisa's "studies are her *pleasure*," Bennett tells the reader. "One day, I found her in [the garden]. . . . A shady arbour in the middle, catching through a beautiful vista the spire of the village church, invited to meditation and to repose." Louisa was not reading a novel but rather Burke's *Essays on the Beautiful and Sublime.*

women in the Early Republic. Nevertheless, the lengthening list of subject areas actually read by women in 1780–1835, considerably broader than the lengthening list of "approved subjects," attests to the existence of a powerful set of opportunities for the intellectual emancipation of rural New England women. With the expansion of their educational roles in American society in 1785–1835, true liberation of rural female intellectual interests commenced for the first time in the Western world.[67] This was a crucial step along a very long road of advancement. The enlarged reading experience of rural New England women left its original rationale far behind, creating by the 1820s a generation of women who subsequently participated ever more actively in rural New England's cultural life. Less and less was the substance of printed matter read and retained likely to differ according to gender. In the Early Republic, private libraries were truly family libraries.

After 1815, increased attention to women's roles and female education under the banner of republican motherhood fostered two trends. One was expansive. As their knowledge of the world amplified, the distinction between women's indirect role as shapers of the rising generation of republican males and women's direct cultural participation narrowed and began to dissolve. Female participation in antebellum reform included both gender-specific and mixed-gender activities. The second direction in the evolution of women's roles was a constraining one. The cult of domesticity and the doctrine of the "spheres" sought to root American ideology in a set of gender-based cultural values which would keep women from all participation in public life.

One of the earliest examples of wider female participation in local intellectual organizations was seen in the lyceum movement. As early as 1830, the Montpelier Lyceum counted 185 members: "Gentlemen, 102 – Ladies, 83." Notices for the Windsor Lyceum later that year invited "the ladies and gentlemen of the place." Lecture series held at Windsor and Chester at that time were regularly touted as "full of interest and of great practical utility to almost every class of society," including women; one advertisement referred to "a Course of Lectures on Chemistry." Later in the century, Windsor District sustained rural women's reading clubs. For instance, the Proctorsville [Cavendish] Reading Club, composed of four young single women and eleven married women in 1876–77, and four and eight respectively in 1877–78, met weekly from early October through late March. At each meeting two women read in succession from a common reading book, then two other women read selections from other works. Held at homes of the members, the "reading and criticism" periods ran from 7 to 9 p.m. Criticisms were "to be made freely by all members without fear or favor." Among the works read were inspirational histories; biographies, including a *Life of Mrs. John Adams* and Theodore Tilton's *Life of Elizabeth Cady Stanton*; poems, including works by Longfellow; short stories, including Hawthorne's *Twice Told Tales*; and novels.[68]

As Norton notes, "the first generation of educated female Americans" included "teachers, missionaries, authors, and the early leaders of such nineteenth century reform movements as abolitionism and women's rights." Moreover, as Cott aptly concludes, sharing "a collective destiny" led increasing numbers of ordinary women to "sense that they might shape that destiny with their own minds and hands." It is no wonder that by the late 1820s Frances Wright triggered such violent reactions throughout the American Northeast. She symbolized nearly all of the dangers latent in women's intellectual development.[69]

Part I
Material and Cultural Foundations

Chapter 2

The Commercialization of Rural Life, 1760–1835

So the fortunes of culture were closely bound up with wider
economic fortunes. But the production of books was also tied to
economic and social geography.

— Henri-Jean Martin, "Printing"

The pronouncing-form method of reading instruction dominated Upper Valley child education until the 1820s. Vermont presses alone published at least twenty-seven editions of Webster's *The American Speller* between 1787 and 1820.[1] It and its competitors sought to perpetuate the wisdom of the ages, instilling in the rising generation an idealized form of the rural world view of their parents. Prepared for a socially stable rural life centered around the duties of salvation and republican citizenship, including republican motherhood, Upper Valley youngsters possessed an acquired resistance to material and cultural change.[2]

During the period 1780–1835, however, New England — and the transatlantic civilization with which it was ever more closely entwined — witnessed shattering upheavals and many subtler cumulative changes that permanently altered daily routines. By the mid-1820s nearly every commentator was suggesting that change itself had already become an essential feature of American life. Although traditional assumptions about the world were still invoked, they tended to be stated and then left standing, as speakers and their listeners went on to assess the effects of change on American life. The commentators' instincts were exactly on target. In the half century after 1775, the emergence of a heavily commercialized rural economy and the creation of a new communications environment enabled a growing majority of all families to participate in public culture. The rapid proliferation of rural weekly newspapers demonstrates a major link between citizens' relish for reading and the expanding capitalism. Being the first truly new basis of mass culture since the evolution of speech, the spread of reading was as powerful a catalyst of economic change in rural culture as the steam engine was in the printing process.

Chapter 2 recaptures and analyzes economic life as a whole—thought and action—throughout a long cycle of social development, from the settlement of the Upper Valley in the 1760s until initial recognition of a slowdown in economic and social progress in the mid-1830s. The social and cultural history of economic life are interwoven here: household and domestic production; capitalism and market relations; and a rural, decentralized Industrial Revolution in New England through 1835.[3]

Commercialization, the first of two profound sets of changes in rural life, began in the economic sphere and extended into social and cultural relations. Farming and commerce, virtue and vice, self-sufficiency and the latest "knowledge from distant climes" were regular topics of public discourse in the half century following the Revolution. Just as families pursued a livelihood in the effort to survive economically, they also participated in "a vast commerce of ideas," as Daniel Webster phrased it.[4] In 1760 Windsor District was a pioneer-stage rural society centered on settled agriculture—farming plus some grazing. By 1835 commercial transactions and rural factory goods had become integral parts of a new but still rural agricultural lifestyle. The new order of life also included regular reading and thereby allowed a large share of all Upper Valley families to participate in a new form of mass culture.

The Commercialization of Rural New England, 1760–1835

The commercialization of rural New England entailed a series of broad, interconnected economic, social, and cultural processes. Commercialization was not the primary reason for the rise of elementary literacy, nor was spreading literacy the leading cause of commercialization. The two ran parallel, coincided, and interrelated. Spreading literacy enabled larger numbers of families to subscribe to a weekly newspaper and thus to follow and engage in market activity on a regular basis. By publishing advertisements, "intelligence," and letters, newspapers helped to regularize commercial exchange. In turn, spreading commerce led to improved transportation and communications networks, increasing newspaper circulation and making available locally a greater number and variety of school texts, histories, novels, and dozens of other types of reading matter. As printed matter became more widely available, it spread literacy and intensified the relish for reading. Commerce and culture were synergistic.

In addition to new patterns of consumption, the commercialization of the Upper Valley established new patterns of production and distribution. When, by the early 1830s, Windsor District completed a long cycle of commercialization, both material and cultural life had been deeply affected. Not all Windsor District families participated in commercial life by 1835, of course. Our best estimate from a survey of all extant estate inventories and Windsor District account books is that about three-quarters of them did so. By the late 1820s, the vast majority of all families—nearly all except the poorest 20 percent—purchased some goods and services from local businesses each year. As estate inventories demonstrate, the fruits of commerce filled the homes of Windsor District residents. Word of the latest products accounted for one-fifth to one-third of the contents of most rural weeklies and advertising was crucial to every newspaper's solvency. Moreover, the legitimacy of commerce, its vices and virtues, were essential topics in all dialogue about the future of America's republican experiment. Since less than one-fifth of all families—only a tiny share of the population—had regularly engaged in commerce in 1780, the commercialization occurring over the next fifty years constituted a radical transformation of life.[5]

Between 1760 and 1835 rural New England was in transition from a very low to a very high level of commercial exchange for an agricultural society. E.J. Hobsbawm has noted that in Europe by the 1830s the "creation of a mechanized factory system" produced goods in "vast quantities and at such rapidly diminishing cost as to be no longer dependent on existing demand but to create" markets based on production and supply. The widespread commercialization of agriculture and the steady expansion of wage labor in Europe created conditions in which production and the social organization of productive relations came to dominate life. The process was evident in longer-settled areas of the American Northeast by the mid-1820s, but during the 1760–1835 era in the Upper Valley, economic life centered not on "a distinctive mode of production," but on consumption of goods obtained from several distinct modes of production.[6]

Domestic or household production constituted only one dimension of economic activity in a sprawling, complex middle stage of political economy between feudalism and full-fledged industrial capitalism. Domestic production included two distinct forms of economic exchange: subsistence production and "simple commodity production." The latter type entailed production mainly be means of family labor, supplemented occasionally by seasonal hired labor; small-scale surpluses of commodities exchanged primarily in local markets; and the purchase of a small but growing number of commodities from stores and shops in local markets. An initial rural, decentralized stage of the Industrial Revolution contributed to a commercial revolution distinguishing this second stage of political economy in rural New England. By 1815, nearly a half century of expansion in the Upper Valley commercial sector had produced a market-dominated rural economy. This shift occurred before any large-scale local factories developed and before any sizable share of workers had engaged in wage labor.[7]

Between 1760 and 1835, production, distribution, and consumption were all at issue in a pivotal struggle for control of economic life all across North Atlantic civilization. Agriculture remained the most prominent economic activity in rural New England through 1835. As a result, family-centered homestead production and consumption offer the starting point for any understanding of economic life there. The circumstances of production in rural New England, both on the farm and elsewhere, encompassed countless false starts, many quick failures, and relatively few long-term successes through 1835. The reason in part related to the ecology of rural life and its decidedly premodern hazards, accidents, limitations, and rapidly changing circumstances. Preindustrial tools were often unreliable and afforded no sustained mastery over nature. The weather was fickle, and much depended on the course of events in the natural world between the first serious thaw, marking the onset of preparations for planting, and the initial hard frost, announcing the end of the production cycle.

Production, distribution, and consumption were unequal partners in rural New England economic life until the mid-1830s. The circumstances of production were exceptionally variable, as we have seen. The earliest factories were most notable for their initiation of a radical divorce of production from consumption. All commodities had to be stored, but storage proved especially difficult for goods that had to be distributed elsewhere. Distribution networks developed slowly in the Upper Valley, inhibiting the growth of large market centers until the late 1790s. As the most stable of the three processes, consumption, relatively fixed, was the senior partner. Consumption was not the passive result of external production and distribution circumstances. Through 1810, most production and consumption occurred on the homestead, and the local distribution network for surpluses was primary. As a result, life proceeded on a foundation of consumption needs and schedules. Most farmers who produced more wheat than was needed for homestead consumption traded the surplus locally for other necessary goods or for money or credit to purchase them. A general store waited for its customers and hoped that, if and when they came, its stock would be adequate to supply their wants. The many store failures attest to these establishments' difficulties in adjusting to rural consumption patterns. Through 1810 the primary locus of consumption, the homestead, was thus also the center of a large (though declining) share of production activity.

By the 1780s, families were using goods and services other than those produced on the homestead. One method of acquiring them was the pervasive system of "changing works" with one's neighbors.[8] A second means of doing so depended upon the stock at village and hamlet stores. These stores relied on production and distribution patterns in the vicinity and in more distant areas. The most important indirect supplier of consumable goods was the general store; by the late 1790s a truly stable group of such stores, offering a great array of goods produced far from the Upper Valley, had evolved to serve the needs of Windsor District residents. Stability and longevity in more specialized product lines took about another decade.[9]

Not one but two kinds of markets affected the lives of Upper Valley residents in the years 1760–1835. One was local, the other international. In Windsor District, competition intensified between a consumption-driven local economic sector and a long-distance, production-driven international economic sector. Interaction between local and long-distance production, distribution, and local consumption steadily increased as distribution routes improved. The weekly newspaper, the fastest-expanding means of communication in the Early Republic, was crucial to the enlargement of commerce. It offered all businesses a brand new way of getting local feedback through direct appeals to consumers to reshape their personal consumption habits. The newspaper brought specific knowledge of goods and services to potential customers, and merchants learned quickly that advertising offered a potent alternative to neighborhood-based exchange relationships. By the 1820s, production had significantly reshaped consumption patterns and had begun to dominate all economic arrangements. Changes in exchange practices deeply affected social relations.

The local market consisted of a group of five to eight contiguous townships that together represented an economic locale; this market was based on local production and consumption of goods, services, and labor and encompassed storage and short-distance distribution within its perimeter. Money, including cash and notes of several types, played a dual role, as a direct means of exchange and as in indirect, uniform standard of equivalence. The most popular arithmetic schoolbook in Windsor District, Daniel Adams's *The Scholar's Arithmetic* (1801), instructed two generations of Upper Valley children and youth in both uses of money. Adams taught the young the "rules essentially necessary for every person to fit and qualify them for the transaction of business," including interest, bookkeeping, notes of exchange, and all the ways of converting old lawful money into federal money. These subjects were taught immediately after the four basic rules of arithmetic. Shortly thereafter the indirect uses of money were taught.[10]

The exchange of all goods and services through village and hamlet general stores, specialty shops, and professional (doctors and lawyers) offices from 1760 to 1835 involved determining the monetary equivalent both of the goods or services secured by an individual, and of the payment, whether in goods, services, or labor. Direct, immediate exchange and credit were the two most typical forms of payment. Although the store, shop, or professional office was the initiator, Windsor District residents actively participated in a complex exchange system based on money (coinage, bank notes, informal notes, and so forth) as the leading standard of value. The system included sales and barter of local farm crops and other products, of artisan services, and of home- and factory-produced goods. Other parties in the transaction might be residents of one's

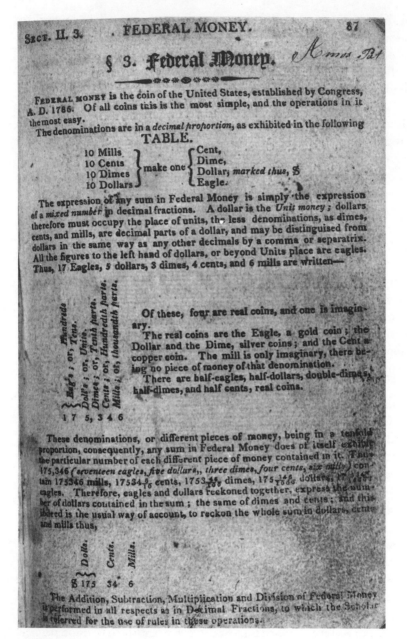

Federal Money. Daniel Adams. *The Scholar's Arithmetic,* 6th ed. (Keene, N.H., 1810), 87. Courtesy, American Antiquarian Society.

The emergence of an abstract set of skills to master commerce and currency, encouraging a calculating spirit, was essential to rural New Englanders' basic education. Numeracy was a key element in literacy training, as seen in the lesson on Federal Money from the most popular arithmetic text in Windsor District.

township, or people elsewhere within a small group of contiguous townships. The scale was small at first, but after the Revolution, trade grew rapidly.[11]

A second market, international in organization, also affected the lives of Windsor District residents. It developed over several centuries, encompassing a complex web of social and economic connections that spanned the North Atlantic.[12] Products traveled from London and elsewhere to Philadelphia, New York, and Boston. Some of these products, plus other products, were transported to Worcester, Concord, and Springfield (where a few more products were added) and then on to the Upper Valley. From the first, Windsor's general stores stocked local and Upper Valley goods, but also products from India, England, the West Indies, and all regions of America.[13]

Both the North-Callender thesis concerning the development of an inter-regional flow of goods and Bidwell's analysis of rural economy assume, incorrectly for the Upper Valley at least, that each local township was a self-enclosed unit and that production for external markets adequately reflected the township's commercial participation. Unless residents of a township produced for and hence traded directly with distant markets on major regional land and water arteries, in other words, they are assumed to have grown little or no true cash crop and to have engaged in no other significant commerce. This assumption is a serious weakness in economic analyses that focus on production versus consumption. In fact, in the Upper Valley, local commercial agriculture and a local market in its products and in other goods and services were extremely widespread by 1810; fifty-nine stores, shops, and factories operated within fifteen of Windsor County's twenty-two townships. Windsor and the other thirty Upper Valley villages formed the intersections of a vast and varied local and long-distance market network. Mick Reed has discovered considerable evidence of this phenomenon in rural England as well.[14]

The signal development in commercial exchange in the half century after the Revolution was the convergence of local and long-distance markets, as land and water trade routes expanded throughout rural New England. Once Windsor District businesses came regularly to function as local nodes of a trans-atlantic system of commerce, many of the resources of the total system were brought to bear on the consumption patterns of the rural family. The stock of the Walpole, New Hampshire, bookstore is a good example. In 1808 the shelves of this typical village bookstore held 31,280 specified volumes plus another several thousand which were undifferentiated. Fewer than a sixth of the nearly 1,500 titles, amounting to about a third of all copies, were printed in the Upper Valley. The vast majority were shipped in from twenty-three other nodes in a long-distance market supply network that stretched from Portland, Maine, south to Baltimore, northwest to Albany, and up to Burlington, Vermont. A small number of copies of about fifty different works from this supply had been printed in Europe.[15]

Understandings of Economic Life in Windsor District, 1760–1835

Windsor District residents began as children to learn techniques of planting and tending crops, orchards, and gardens designed to produce rich harvests. They also learned that many natural and human circumstances could intervene to yield poor crops. Each unfolding spring, summer, and fall reshaped the plans of the previous winter, and the old plans were revised during the succeeding winter. Inevitably idealistic, rational planning and actual grubby practice intersected during the cold days of late March. A similar process occurred as Windsor District residents learned how the larger economy *should* function and how it worked in practice. First at home and later in district schools, they learned what was just and acceptable and what was dangerous and best avoided. Through the experience of daily life, they learned how the world worked.

People frequently talked, and regularly read and wrote, about economic life. Discussions of the subject had two broad themes: first, the relationship of the individual to society, and second, the proper role of commerce and commercial wealth in life, i.e., the extent to which it contributed to the public good. By the 1780s, several leading strains of contemporary thought were influential in the Upper Valley. The major transatlantic views of agriculture, commerce, and industry had been assimilated and were applied to daily life during this period.[16]

Between 1760 and 1815, five clusters of ideas, each representing a transatlantic intellectual viewpoint concerning economic life, influenced Windsor District residents' intellectual assumptions about economic activity and its proper place in life. They included Mandevillian social theory, Christian pietistic moralism, benevolist ethics, mercantilist and Modern Whig economic thought, and Tory and radical strains of opposition political economy. Each tradition had its favorite targets and issues. Together they comprised the active intellectual context, in the form of available reading matter, within which Windsor District residents approached economic life.

The most extreme position and that to which all others responded was the satirical view expressed by Bernard Mandeville in *The Fable of the Bees*. In this work, a society of bees remained prosperous only so long as they were unscrupulous; their moral reformation left them in economic ruin. According to Mandeville, self-denial was incompatible with prosperity. The ultimate deception was to follow the course of virtue, subordinating self-interest to the supposed interests of society. For Mandeville private interest was the essential and only social glue. Acquisitive appetites must determine civil society's direction and its ends. Mandeville's fable was not itself widely read in Windsor District, in full or excerpted form, but his arguments constantly recurred as a standing challenge in Upper Valley discussions of economy and society.[17]

A second powerful position reached conclusions diametrically opposed to those of Mandeville. J.E. Crowley refers to its advocates as the Christian pietist-moralists. Baxter, Allestree, and other major figures in Windsor District devotional and theological reading contended that Mandevillian selfishness was the source of all evil, sin, and unhappiness in a world of Manichaean starkness. This world and its inhabitants were inherently evil; individual interests inevitably included an "inordinate Love of the Carnal self." Proponents of this perspective determinedly opposed riches and luxury—indeed, all forms of worldliness. Securing the best chance for salvation was the only important goal of life on earth. Secular, self-interested participation and sacred pietistic abstinence stood at opposite poles, as far as worldly gain was concerned.[18]

Between the extremes of Mandeville and the pietist-moralist tracts, three moderate positions about the role of individuals in society and the role of commerce in daily life gained currency after 1760. The benevolent ethics of Shaftesbury, Adam Smith, and the American Samuel Hopkins, all read by Windsor District residents, offered a generally positive assessment of economic development. As Crowley has observed, "The benevolists articulated an ethic which presented self-love as a motivation of work and social relations generally, and held that virtue, considered as a matter of public duty, was harmonious with a rational self-interest." For the benevolists, the public good and self-interest were not inherently in conflict and could be quite compatible. Selfishness was castigated and was sharply distinguished from self-interest.[19]

Closely related to benevolist ethics was mercantilist and Modern Whig political economy. Mercantilism applied narrow standards of usefulness and the social utility of public action, disallowing any sizable role for moral evaluations. Its specific subject matter was the market: economic production and distribution. Consumption, and particularly its effects on individuals, was downplayed. Commerce and market relations were assumed to be perfectly legitimate and mostly benign in their effects. Properly conducted, economic activity wedded private interests to the public good. In Windsor District public thought, Hamilton, Coxe, and Matthew Carey were major American proponents of this popular view.[20]

Tory and Radical strands of British opposition political thought represented still another position. Bolingbroke and his Tory associates and supporters contended that money and trade had, in the words of Crowley, "become the basis of social relations, replacing public virtue, honor, family, and friendship." The results of widespread trade increased wealth divisions very sharply. Commerce was "inevitably the agent of corruption because the accumulation of wealth enabled people to indulge their irrationality in luxury." The critique of the Commonwealthmen was similar, stressing in addition the need for a moderate balance between agriculture and commerce.[21]

Contemporary opinion about economic activity and its role in life was rich and complex. Windsor District residents drew on these five intellectual traditions to adapt their discussions to the Windsor District environment, just as a particular theater's design subtly frames the performance of a play. The specific material and cultural conditions of a rural society undergoing rapid commercialization and the spread of lifelong learning directed reading and public discourse along some paths and away from others. To complicate matters, the impact of a specific intellectual position was often greater than the verifiable incidence of copies and excerpts of works advocating it. Any analysis of the history of the book must be cautious; as with Mandeville's *Fable*, while the text may be barely visible by all quantitative measures of its contemporary distribution, the argument itself, and hence the work's implicit presence, was everywhere.[22]

Between 1780 and 1835, in Windsor District minds two competing life goals often struggled: salvation and a new secular aim—individual and collective prosperity here on earth. In 1780 the most important and the highest attainable form of human happiness was neither an agrarian nor a commercial paradise, but salvation. The world was considered a testing ground for faith in and dedication to a future state of endless joy: eternal life in heaven. Wide-ranging private religious exercises, publicly sanctioned shared worship, and benevolent institutions—all were squarely dedicated to preparation for heaven. Sunday was sacred regardless of the season or the fluctuating demands of agriculture. Many families hewed to the Christian pietist-moralist tradition and remained as aloof as possible from commerce. They stressed a life of Christian self-denial and abstinence and viewed almost all commercial exchange and excessive individual wealth as evil. The lure of commerce led the proportion of such adherents to decline seriously between 1780 and 1830, from a solid majority to a small but committed minority drawn mainly from the Baptists, Methodists, Universalists, Christians, sternly Calvinist Congregationalists and Presbyterians, and, of course, the religious independents.

Among the most popular works read and retained in Windsor District family libraries through 1830, and excerpted and commented on in newspapers, a small but very influential group of seven works reinforced the ethic of salvation and self-denial. Among these seven were five of the twelve most popular volumes: Bibles (and New Testaments), Watts' *Psalms* and his *Hymns and Spiritual Songs*, and the writings of Flavel and Baxter and Wesley (see table 2–1 throughout). Families that adhered to the Christian pietist-moralist position often kept only sacred reading matter. Published essays and letters by individuals who read more widely quoted from many of the most prominent works evaluating Britain's financial revolution only to illustrate the evils of commercial life.

Families that held a traditional sacred view of life as preparation for eternity came primarily from two Windsor District social groups. The first principally lived deep in the countryside beyond the four villages of Windsor District (see figure 1–2). Their world view and their daily life experience in the farming and grazing areas of Plymouth, Ludlow, Weston, Andover, Reading, and Baltimore, inland from the Connecticut River and major turnpike transportation, yielded only slowly, if at all, to small-scale commercial exchange. The second group consisted of the poorest village and hamlet residents. Accounting for perhaps a fifth of the population as late as 1830, these two groups of families were strongholds of the ethic of salvation and self-denial.[23]

Most other Windsor District families, especially residents of the four villages, the dozen or so hamlets, and the farmsteads near them, accepted individual and collective prosperity as legitimate life goals in addition to salvation. Prosperity on earth was embraced and defended as rational self-interested action, in commentary about secular, material happiness. Several versions of earthly prosperity contended for attention. Commercial growth was the most important dynamic economic reality of the early national era; nearly all commentaries about economic life focused on its pros and cons. What constituted virtue? And what constituted vice? These were essential questions framing public discourse, and they were themselves being rephrased to fit changing reality. After the Revolution, virtue came to be seen as insuring "to the mass of the people the enjoyment of substantial comforts, . . . allow[ing] them to be rational beings, and men, instead of mere drudges, and beasts of burden." The key issue was the sort and degree of earthly happiness and the appropriate means of attaining it.[24]

Among the increasing majority of Windsor District residents who accepted prosperity as a legitimate life goal, three major positions thrived. These included an active embrace of commerce, often including manufacturing and some aspects of Britain's earlier financial revolution; an ambivalent acceptance of the growing power of commerce in a society perceived as still firmly agricultural; and an often virulent agrarianism which included opposition to many of the effects of commerce. All positions except that of the Hamiltonian Federalists denounced the British financial revolution and the pace of economic change there in the eighteenth century. As E. James Ferguson has persuasively demonstrated, criticism of the tenor of British economic, social, and moral life "expressed internalized values that transcended political affiliation." The funding system, wage labor, tenancy, public credit, stock jobbing, control of international markets, mercantile ethics, corruption, luxury, and rule by a moneyed aristocracy all received widespread criticism. England specifically was painted as a detestable Mandevillian paradise. The net effect on the American dialogue regarding the virtues and vices of commercial life was ironic. As commerce spread throughout rural America, its role in life was more easily accepted precisely because its presence seemed so minimal in comparison with the pervasive image of a thoroughly corrupt Britain.[25]

Specific current information also reshaped longstanding beliefs. All con-

Table 2–1: Windsor District Family Libraries, 1787–1830:
Most Widely Read Authors and Works *

	No. of Works[1]	Percent of Families with a Library Retaining This Work
1. Bibles (full Bibles and separate New Testaments	520	74
Full Bibles alone[2]	330	66
New Testaments	30	7.6
Scott (*Family Bible*, 4–6 vol. eds.)	27	7
2. Webster, N. (*American Spelling Book*—c. 40; *Compendious Dictionary*—c. 5; Misc.—5)	50	12.6
3. Watts (*Psalms of David*—15; *Hymns and Spiritual Songs*—12; Misc. in 5 other fields—20)	47	12
4. Morse (*American Universal Geography*, 2 vols.—20, abridged versions—3; *Universal Gazetteer*[3]—14, abridged versions—3; Misc.—5)	45	11
5. *Laws and Statutes of Vermont*	42	10
6. Perry (*Royal Standard English Dictionary*)	31	8
7. Murray (*English Reader*[4]—11; *English Grammar*—11)	22	5.6
8. Whitelaw (*Maps of Vermont*)[5]	20	5
9. Doddridge (*Rise and Progress of Religion*—4; *Family Expositor*—4; Misc.—10)	18	4.5
10. Pike (*System of Arithmetic*)	16	4
11. Flavel (*Works*—4; *Token for Mourners*—5; *Treatise on Keeping the Heart*—4; *Touchstone of Sincerity*—3)	16	4
12. Adams (*Scholar's Arithmetic*)	15	3.8
13. Blackstone (*Commentaries*, 4 vols.)[6]	15	3.8
14. Virgil (various eds. of *Works*)	14	3.5
15. Bingham's (*American Preceptor*—8; *Columbian Orator*—3; Misc.—2)	13	3.3
16. Simmons (*Gentleman's Law Magazine*)	13	3.3
17. *Book of Common Prayer* and variations	12	3
18. Johnson (*Dictionary*—7, usually abridged version; Misc.—5)	12	3
19. Blair (*Lectures on Rhetoric and Belles Lettres*)	12	3
20. Hervey (*Meditations and Contemplations*—10; *Theron and Aspasio*—2)	12	3
21. Paley (*Principles of Moral and Political Philosophy*—4; *Evidences of Christianity*—3; Misc.—5)	12	3
22. Williams (*Natural and Civil History of Vermont*—9; *Sketches of War*—2)	11	2.8
23. Stewart** (*Elements of the Philosophy of the Human Mind*—5; Misc.—6)	11	2.8

continued

	No. of Works[1]	Percent of Families with a Library Retaining This Work
24. Robertson (*Charles V*–4; *History of America*–3; *History of Scotland*–3; Misc.–1)	11	2.8
25. Chipman (*Reports and Dissertations*–7; Misc.–4)	11	2.8
26. Edwards (*Works*; several works)	10	2.5
27. Baxter (*Saints Everlasting Rest*–7; *Call to the Unconverted*–3)	10	2.5
28. Adams, Hannah (*View of Religion*–5; *History of New England*–3; Misc.–2)	10	2.5
29. Fisher, *Young Man's Best Companion*[7]	c. 10	2.5
30. Scott, Sir Walter (several works)	9	2.3
31. Buchan, *Domestic Medicine*	9	2.3
32. Homer (*Odyssey*–5; *Iliad*–3 [Pope tr.])	8	2
33. Bunyan (*Pilgrim's Progress*–6; *Heavenly Footman*–2)	8	2
34. Chalmers** (theology and science)	8	2
35. Walker (*Critical Pronouncing Dictionary*)	8	2
36. Banks (*Peter the Great*–7; Misc.–1)	8	2
37. [Sanders] (*History of the Indian Wars*)	8	2
38. Maps of the U.S.	8	2
39. Franklin (*Autobiography*–6; *Works*–2)	8	2
40. Cummings (*Intro. to Ancient and Modern Geography*–5; *Atlas*–3)	8	2
41. Cicero (various *Works*)	8	2
42. Young (*Night Thoughts*–4; Misc.–3)	7	1.8
43. Dickinson, *Compendium of the Bible*	7	1.8
44. Niles** (several works)	7	1.8
45. Booth** (several works)	7	1.8
46. Bailey (*Key to the English Language*)	7	1.8
47. Quincy (*American Medical Lexicon*)	7	1.8
48. Guthrie (*New Geographical Grammar*–4; *Universal Geography*–3)	7	1.8
49. Clarke (*Intro. to the Making of Latin*)	7	1.8
50. Washington (*Farewell Address*)	7	1.8
51. Cowper (*Task*–4; *Works*–3)	7	1.8
52. Goldsmith (*Vicar of Wakefield*–6; *Citizen of the World*–1)	7	1.8
53. Espinasse (*Digest of Laws of Nisi Prius*)	7	1.8
54. Powell (*Essay Upon Law of Contracts*)	7	1.8
55. Wesley (*Sermons*–3; *Primitive Physician*–2; Misc.–2)	7	1.8
56. Hubbard (*American Reader*–6; Misc.–1)	7	1.8

continued

	No. of Works[1]	Percent of Families with a Library Retaining This Work
57. Macgowan (*Life of Joseph*)	6	1.5
58. Foster (*Critical and Candid Examination*)	6	1.5
59. *American State Papers and Public Documents, 1801–15*	6	1.5
60. Swift, Zephaniah (*System of the Laws of Connecticut*)	6	1.5
61. Goodrich (*History of the United States*)	6	1.5
62. *The Hive* (a reader)	6	1.5
63. Staniford (*Art of Reading*)	6	1.5
64. Perrin**(various French grammars)	6	1.5
65. Colburn**(various works)	6	1.5
66. Sterne (several works)	6	1.5
67. Locke (*Essays on Human Understanding*—4; Misc.—2)	6	1.5
68. Bigland (*View of the World*—4; *Letters*—2)	6	1.5
69. Smith, Elias (various Universalist works)	6	1.5
70. Buchanan (*Christian Researches*—4; Misc.—2)	6	1.5
71. Cheselden (*Anatomy of the Human Body*)	5	1.3
72. Weems (*Washington*)	5	1.3
73. *Dunham's Masonick Register*	5	1.3
74. Lathrop (*Farmer's Library*)	5	1.3
75. Care**(*English Liberties*)	5	1.3
76. Lesage (*Gil Blas*)	5	1.3
77. Gilbert (*Law of Evidence*)	5	1.3
78. The Websters (*Clerk's Magazine*)	5	1.3
79. Mason (*Remains*—3; *Self Knowledge*—2)	5	1.3
80. Pope (*Essays*—3; *Works*—2)[8]	5	1.3
81. Chauncy (*Seasonable Thoughts*—2; Misc.—3)	5	1.3
82. Winchester (*Universal Restoration*—4)	5	1.3
83. Beattie**(various works)	5	1.3
84. Barlow (*Vision of Columbus*—4; *Columbus*—1)	5	1.3
85. Thomson (*Seasons*—4; *Works*—1)	5	1.3
86. Law (*Serious Call*—4)	5	1.3
87. Rowe (*Devout Exercises*)	4	1
88. Venn (*Complete Duty of Man*)	4	1
89. *Village Harmony*	4	1
90. Bennett (*Letters to a Young Lady*)	4	1
91. Josephus (*Works*)	4	1
92. *American Baptist Magazine and Missionary Intelligencer* (4 runs)	4	1
93. Porter (*Narrative of Campaign in Russia*)	4	1

continued

	No. of Works[1]	Percent of Families with a Library Retaining This Work
94. Preston (*Wonders of Creation*)	4	1
95. Rees (*Cyclopaedia*)[9]	4	1
96. Horace (various editions of *Works*)	4	1
97. Carey (*Olive Branch*)[10]	4	1
98. Scott (*Lessons in Elocution*)	4	1
99. Hedge (*Elements of Logic*)	4	1
100. Jones (*Essays on the Law of Bailments*)	4	1
101. Jacob (*Law Dictionary*)	4	1
102. Peake (*Compendium of the Law of Evidence*)	4	1
103. Cowper (*Report of the Cases*)	4	1
104. Kyd (*Treatise of the Law of Bills of Exchange*)	4	1
105. *U.S. Laws and Statutes*	4	1
106. Backus (*Digest of Laws . . . Sheriff*)	4	1
107. Hall (*Disorders of the Digestive System*)	4	1
108. Lathrop (theology)	4	1
109. Ferguson**(*Astronomy*—various works)	4	1
110. Byron (various works)	4	1
111. Milton (*Paradise Lost*—3; *Regained*—1)	4	1
112. Shakespeare (*Plays and Poems*)	4	1
113. *Letter Writer* (2 very similar works)	4	1
114. Chambaud**(several works on the French language)	4	1

* For full citation of each work, see bibliography.

**Over 50 percent of the copies are from one library, usually that of the John Leverett family.

[1] Works, rather than volumes, are used here. For example, a five-volume edition of Josephus counts as one work. Hence, the number of volumes is often larger than the number of works. All percentages reflect the share of families with at least one work of this description. Thus 66 percent of the families with a library owned a full Bible.

[2] Excludes Scott, *Family Bibles.*

[3] Volume 2 of the *Universal Gazetteer* was coauthored with Elijah Parish.

[4] Includes two copies of *Sequel to the English Reader.*

[5] Many of the unspecified maps were also by Whitelaw, so the total is undoubtedly larger.

[6] This includes two libraries with an edition of Christian's *Notes* as a supplement.

[7] Many other works listed *Companion*, otherwise unspecified.

[8] See also No. 32 above for translation of Homer.

[9] Includes two copies, each of which was part of an Encyclopedia library.

[10] There were several different editions of this work; see the bibliography.

temporary positions on the role of commerce in life were shaped by an increasing amount of concrete knowledge about the spread of commerce throughout America. Rural newspapers were the principal local vehicle for the transmission of such information. In addition to reporting the rising level of commerce each week, product by product and service by service, rural weeklies consistently advocated commerce as an essential ingredient of economic life. Furthermore, more than half of the most popular 100 works in 400 surviving Windsor District family libraries also advocated a commercial society. As a result, Windsor District residents encountered positive views of a commercial republic at almost every turn.

Advocates of the first of the three major Windsor District positions regarding economic life agreed to all but the most immoderate emphasis on the benefits of commerce. This version of political and moral economy was most explicitly avowed by local Hamiltonians and moderate Federalists as well as by some moderate Madisonian Republicans. They assumed that every civilization passed through a series of stages. Helpless infancy, characterized by "the rudeness of aboriginal simplicity," was a negative standard against which all progress was measured. Commerce marked a more advanced stage, linking the passions, material self-interest, and the public good in a new secular trinity. Hume, Hobbes, Blackstone, Hamilton, Carey, Walsh, Coxe, and a host of "Modern Whigs," Walpoleans in sentiment, buttressed this strongly pro-commerce position. In fact, a large share of the reading matter perused by families in our villages, hamlets, and nearby farmsteads bristled with positive assessments of commercial activity. Newspapers took the lead, supported by fully two-fifths of the most popular hundred books in family libraries, including ten of the most popular twenty-five works. Weathersfield township, the Windsor District stronghold of Federalism, and Windsor, Chester, Cavendish, and Springfield contained important groups of families whose libraries reveal their solid support for a commercial republic. As far as we can tell, few of these families were Jeffersonian in politics.[26]

As a normal part of basic district schooling, Windsor District young people learned in arithmetic study about commercial exchange, including the view that the commercial world was as natural as air and water.[27] Works in many other areas of knowledge included commentaries on the benefits of the commercial stage of civilization in the North Atlantic world. All the most popular maps, geographies, and atlases gave prominent attention to both local and distant commerce and to descriptions of commercial life and its products. Morse led the way with his schoolbook geographies and gazetteers; also popular were geographies and atlases by Cummings and Guthrie, and Whitelaw's several maps of Vermont. The largest number of popular works supporting commerce discussed aspects of law and government.[28] Two of the three most popular works of political economy were Federalist and also procommerce. Finally, in addition to these forty works, there were several hundred works of lesser popularity that advocated the benefits of a commercial society.[29]

The second major Windsor District position on economic life encompassed an ambivalent republicanism. Its uneasy equilibrium rested on a belief that a "middle stage" of social development could be identified that combined commerce and agrarianism and adapted "the moral and social imperatives of classical republicanism to modern commercial society." As Drew McCoy has observed with respect to republican political economy generally, American society was to grow prosperous and civilized without succumbing to luxury. America could become a more advanced, commercialized society than many of what were perceived as primitive, even barbarous, republics of the past, yet could stop short of a perilous descent into Mandevillian decadence. A society dominated by agriculture but including considerable commerce and even some small-scale manufacturing was the unsteady positive ideal: it was to be pursued with diligence and industry and without avarice.[30]

Books ambivalent or mildly hostile to commercial society were numerous among Windsor District popular sellers in many fields. They accounted for about a quarter of the most widely read hundred works. Some of these works also formed the mainstay of agrarianism. Schoolbook readers usually contained several passages from writers critical of commercial society, including the Bolingboke circle and many of the later Augustan writers.[31] At least eight popular sacred works contributed further critiques of commercial society. The writings of Jefferson, Madison, John Taylor of Caroline, and several other Republican writers were kept only slightly less frequently.[32]

Agrarianism was the third major Windsor District position on political economy in the 1780–1830 period. The preeminent symbol of the agrarian tradition, concludes William Liddle, was the "sturdy yeoman farmer," who was linked with longstanding anticommercial ethical positions. Despite the growing distance between the realities of rural agriculture and the ideal of the simple yeoman, "his symbolic features," in the words of Liddle, "made of agrarianism a mostly coherent way of perceiving and understanding the world." In the agrarian tradition, "the production of commodities and the capacity to produce commodities," especially farming but also mining, lumbering, and fishing, were the "true source of the nation's wealth." Trade—especially foreign trade—was suspect. Luxury born of commerce was a negative standard; as one writer observed, "luxury always destroys, and never builds." Two groups of works frequently retained by Windsor District families advocated agrarianism: Virgil, Cicero, and Horace, all three widely read, and several of the most popular British writers of the middle and late eighteenth century, including Goldsmith, Thomson, Cowper, Hervey, and Young. Works by all of these authors were also excerpted in schoolbook readers.[33]

The majority of Windsor District residents was not at all isolated with regard to information and opinion about economic life in the North Atlantic. Reading and discussion offered an extremely wide range of opinion. Before about 1810 it was heavily weighted toward agricultural life and small-scale commercial exchange. Especially after 1800, detailed knowledge about, and advocacy of, small-scale commercial activity was widespread. The steady diet of reading matter from the Augustan age in Britain, beginning with schoolbook readers, however, reinforced a conservative agrarianism even among many rural Federalists. Ironically, the writers who shaped Windsor District residents' image of Great Britain as being in the throes of Mandevillian decay were mainly British. The results were complex. Throughout their adult lives, Windsor District residents nourished either a traditional sacred view that opposed any sustained concern with the world of commerce and trade or took one of the three secular positions about the role of commerce in life. Changes in beliefs were frequent, and there were variations and subtle combinations. Intensified contact with the North Atlantic print communications network by no means insured that the Upper Valley picture of the distant world was accurate or up to date.[34]

Commercialization, Stage One, 1760–95: The Settlement Era

The economic order of Windsor District changed dramatically between 1760 and 1830, both from the historian's perspective and in the eyes of most people who were over the age of forty in the 1820s. Especially after about 1810, the extent and effects of change were constant themes in public discussion. Economic understanding and misunderstanding of commercialization provoked considerable controversy carried on within the intellectual frameworks and lines of argument just described. Presidential and state level elections and other public events helped crystallize discussion and reflection. Not all Upper Valley families engaged in dialogue, of course. Some ignored economic change; some remained oblivious to it. Many spent their time learning about new products, services, and occurrences rather than debating commerce's merits. For many residents the local workings of commercial exchange became as normal an ingredient of daily life as agriculture by 1815; nevertheless, many ignored or only haltingly accepted as legitimate the international market in which they participated. Only after 1815 did intensified participation in commerce allay doubts about its effects on morality.

Our initial reference point is the character of economic life in the Upper Valley, and particularly in Windsor District, shortly after the American Revolution. Just under 1,150 families (6,564 individuals) inhabited the eleven townships that composed Windsor District, Vermont, in 1790. Virtually all of them had migrated there within the previous three decades, coming up the valley from Connecticut and Massachusetts (see figure 2–1).[35] Settlement within Wind-

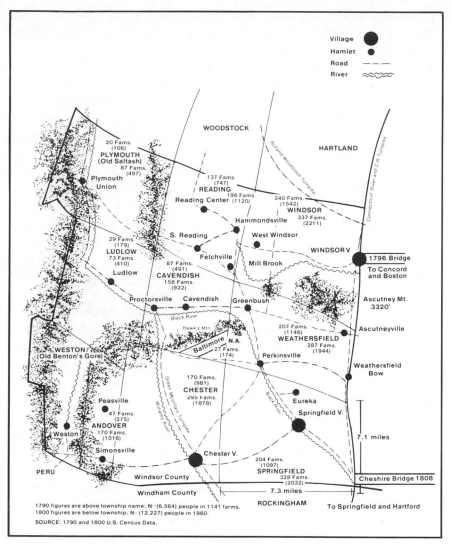

Figure 2–1: Windsor District Community Size and Geography of Settlement, 1790 and 1800

sor District at first hugged the Connecticut River, the main transportation artery, as much as possible. Windsor was the largest township in 1790; it also contained the main village in the district. Growing somewhat more slowly were Weathersfield and Springfield, also on the river, and Chester, the only other village, located on the major route inland. Cavendish and Reading, the other two communities not deep in the Green Mountains, had populations between a third and a half the size of Windsor's, followed by the four, and soon to be five, barely settled mountain townships. As one moved away from the farming communities and into the Green Mountains, a smaller share of households contained full families: females above the age of fifteen became considerably scarcer.[36]

A subtle ecology was at work when parts of rural New England were chosen for settlement before the Industrial Revolution. The quality of farming and grazing acreage was important but was not the primary consideration. Ability to remain in proximity to established land and water transportation routes connecting the district to the outside world was the leading determinant of settlement patterns. Migrants to the frontier often sought to move near the end of the tether connecting them to more settled areas, but rarely went beyond it into true wilderness isolation. Connections with family and kin in southern New England weighed heavily with many settlers of New Connecticut. Consequently, most early Windsor District residents chose to live along the best available roads and rivers, those by which they had initially reached Windsor District. In fact, some of the finest farmland and pasturage was located in the mountainous tier of townships. Although the area had been explored, it remained thinly settled. Venturing further into the Vermont forest presented too daunting a prospect for all but a tenth of District residents through 1790. The proportions of settlement and relative ease of transportation outside the Upper Valley changed very slowly over the first thirty years (1760–90). Even as late as 1830 (see table 1–1), the rank ordering of population among townships was virtually the same as it had been in 1790. Windsor remained first. Its rapid growth stifled Weathersfield, causing it to drop from second to fourth and enabling Springfield and Chester each to rise one notch. Reading and Cavendish still held fifth and sixth place, and the foothills communities remained at the bottom.

At first, commerce was not the chief reason for settlement near leading transportation routes. No more than a quarter of all early emigrants (1760–80) had participated fairly regularly in commerce and trade in Massachusetts and Connecticut. Most Windsor District settlers, as we know from Charles Grant's work on Kent, Connecticut, and Donald Smith's massive study of the origins of early Vermonters, brought with them experience only of a household and neighborhood barter economy. These families were shifting a farming and grazing life to an apparently similar set of surroundings in the Connecticut River Valley far to the north.[37]

As settlement expanded in Windsor District, a few small villages were founded. There some residents chose to establish businesses, extending to their new homes more dimensions of the regional trade network to which they were accustomed. As communities grew in the Revolutionary era, residents voted in town meetings to add to Windsor District's fledgling local transportation network.[38] Enough of the leadership of nonmountainous townships sought economic expansion to permit the establishment of a reasonably complex land

and water transportation and communications network by 1795. Small in numbers but substantial in their impact, entrepreneurial residents not only increased their own opportunities for trade but also influenced further settlement and areas of population concentration. The establishment of stores, shops, a printing office, and a post office in a village during the pioneering stage of settlement created a magnet for future emigrants. A post office and printing facilities also permitted a regular flow of letters and printed matter, reinforcing ties between Windsor District and southern New England and apprising increasing numbers of local residents of the progress of public life elsewhere in America and overseas.

Agriculture remained the basis of life. Most Windsor District yeomen, husbandmen, and tenant farm families—a sizable majority of the population—engaged in a broad range of activities that satisfied a substantial proportion of their food, shelter, and clothing needs. In addition to maintaining grassy areas for pasture, most farms grew Indian corn, wheat and rye, and barley or flax. Numerous field and garden vegetables were also cultivated, especially root vegetables such as potatoes, turnips, parsnips, and onions. The apple was the staple fruit. A herb garden supplied many items important in food preparation. Uncultivated land nurtured nuts and wild berries, maple trees for sugar, and animals, including deer, small game, various types of birds, and the ever-present ducks and geese. Streams and rivers carried rich complements of fish. Livestock was also found on virtually every farm, particularly hogs, chickens, horses, cows and bulls, sheep (especially after 1800), and occasionally turkeys. Then, too, there was the woodlot, which needed regular tending.[39]

In the first stage of commercialization within the Upper Valley, 1760–95, the dominant farming economy was primarily a face-to-face agricultural and barter-exchange system involving family, neighbors, and kin. Specialization was kept to a fairly low level; great versatility and diversity of production was a requirement in newly settled forest society. As Brissot de Warville noted about rural Massachusetts in 1788, "almost all the houses are inhabited by men who are both cultivators and artisans." From the outset, some necessary commodities were made on the farm; other goods and services were bartered for locally; and still others were purchased at general stores, small mills, and shops. By the mid-1780s, a modest variety of reading matter was also available for purchase within Windsor District.[40]

While the household, or domestic, mode of production remained dominant during Windsor District's settlement era, the basis of economic existence in the district, like everything else in life, cannot be understood in a vacuum. A small market sector had been established throughout the Upper Connecticut River Valley by the time of the Revolution; the founding of the *Vermont Journal* at Windsor in 1783 was crucial to further commercial expansion. It is impossible to grasp the full character of economic life without looking beyond the lineal family, kinship patterns, and household production to the growing network of economic activities, institutions, and relationships among people related not by blood but solely by business. Substantial general stores and smaller, more specialized shops, extensive law and medical practices, turnpike companies, incorporated lending libraries, business and financial partnerships, large land speculation ventures, and manufactories all came into prominence within the Upper Valley by 1800. These business connections were jointly owned or shared, mostly with individuals not directly linked in family lineage. Soon thereafter regional and local banking facilities emerged. As soon as evidence is available, in the 1780s, almost all families in the top fifth of household heads by wealth held "real property" shares in one or more of the above enterprises, regularly amounting to 10 to 15 percent of their estates. By the beginning decades of the nineteenth century these holdings frequently amounted to a third of the total estate of lawyer, merchant, and manufacturing families. All of these economic connections combined to strengthen the web of economic community in Windsor District, and throughout the other nine local legal districts of the Upper Valley, in the least developed economic area of New England in 1780–1830.[41]

The Upper Valley family remained the basic unit of agricultural production and property transmission in the narrow sense through 1830. In capital formation, however, and in the total picture of production, distribution, and consumption, the economic system of the American Northeast encompassed far more than family-based agriculture. By the mid-1780s, a primitive but effective transportation and communications network along the spine of the Upper Valley (see figures 2–2a and 2–2b) linked marketing center villages and their nearby hinterlands, from Haverhill in the north to Brattleboro, just over the Massachusetts border. Connected to the larger market networks of Massachusetts and Connecticut, the Upper Valley was therefore part of the North Atlantic trading community, as Vermonters writing in the area's rural weeklies were well aware. "Vermont, tho' inland in its situation, is sufficiently accessible by water, on the rivers and lakes, to be amply supplied with foreign commodities, and for vending their own produce," commented "Viator" in the Rutland, Vermont, *Farmer's Library* in 1793. The writer sharply distinguished the villages which formed the integuments of this system from cities: "No capital town, with its luxuries and vices, will poison the taste and morals of the people." Viator's description of the emerging rural market economy is typical of many. It also gave evidence of an emerging Vermont perspective on political economy and its consequences.[42]

If the "lineal family not the conjugal unit and certainly not the unattached individual . . . thus stood at the center of economic and social existence in northern agricultural society in preindustrial America," as James Henretta concludes, then by the 1780s a thicket of economic institutions within each of

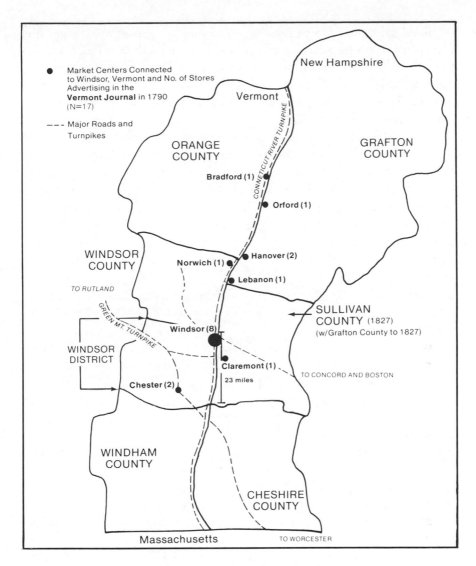

Figure 2–2a: Upper Connecticut River Valley Market Centers, 1790

a series of economic locales had begun to envelop lineal families. Local geography shaped an economic locale, nurturing the local market economy within its bounds. With an effective radius of one to two full days' travel time, the transportation and communications circuit embracing each economic locale provided steadily improving conditions for local travel and a connection to the larger regional and international market network. An economic locale served as the locus of production, distribution, and consumption, providing most of the goods and services needed for daily existence.[43]

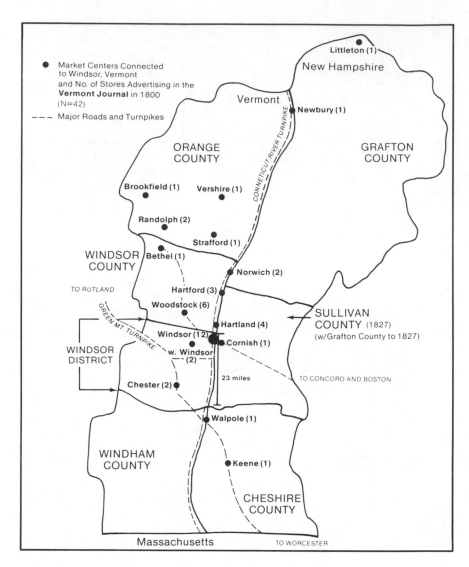

Figure 2–2b: Upper Connecticut River Valley Market Centers, 1800

By the 1780s Windsor District encompassed two economic locales (see figure 2–3), one centered in Windsor village and the other to the south, centered in Chester village.[44] The two locales were separated geographically, and users generally preferred the nearer marketing center. Chester and Windsor villages thus functioned as northerly and southerly economic magnets for the whole district. All known stores within Windsor District in 1790 were located either in or near Windsor or Chester villages. In all cases, a family's decision to trade at one center or the other entailed a calculation of travel distance and conditions, and a reckoning of the importance of the products and services to be secured and exchanged. Geography, placement within the transportation network, and a sufficiently settled hinterland determined the locations of successful village centers within Upper Valley economic locales. Nevertheless, protovillages and smaller hamlets that were seeking village status competed continuously. Hamlets were as often the remnants of failed attempts to establish villages as they were haphazard clusterings of rural, nonfarmstead artisan shops and manufactories.

Extended families and other residents interacted within economic locales, but the picture in 1790 was more complicated than it at first appears. The full economy consisted of a closely knit series of five levels: the family and household unit, kinship networks, the neighborhood, the township, and the economic locale. Different economic and social activities took place at each level, and the system's chief characteristic was the interpenetration of all five levels. Moreover, the direction in which economic life had been heading since 1760 was toward greater interaction and larger scale and, as the scale increased, toward more formalized relationships. A diminishing share of purchases involved family and kin; a growing share involved unrelated but necessary "others."

By 1800, virtually all estates valued at more than $250 carried a series of nonfamily financial obligations (notes and book accounts) that usually expanded as wealth and material possessions increased. Even a modest "self-sufficient" farmstead in the $300–$1,000 range had four to twelve liens and debts, with an average of seven or eight. In addition, as early as the 1780s, many of the notes were interest bearing. The proportion was at least a third by 1800 and a half by 1815. By 1790 many businesses had begun threatening delinquent accounts, and some had begun filing suits to recover debts.[45]

Notes and book accounts were not the only regular economic transactions to extend economic ties beyond the family unit. Shared ownership and leasing, its less egalitarian cousin, mostly involved kin, neighbors, and acquaintances living elsewhere within an economic locale. Both were becoming more frequent in Windsor District by the late 1790s. Artisans shared their tools and equipment, manufacturers their buildings, supplies, and machines, and merchants their firms, stores, and furnishings. Farmlands, woodlands, and wild acreage were shared by farmers. On a broader scale, shares (or portions) were sold on a restricted, purchaser-acceptable basis by banks, turnpike companies, factories, and lending libraries.[46] Bartering and "changing works" represented a fourth aspect of economic interdependence among families within each neighborhood, community, and economic locale. Susan Geib has thoroughly analyzed, in the case of Brookfield, Massachusetts, the changing works that appeared in labor exchanges, notes payable in services to be rendered at some future date, and agreements that animals returned were to be of the same kind and quality as those borrowed.[47]

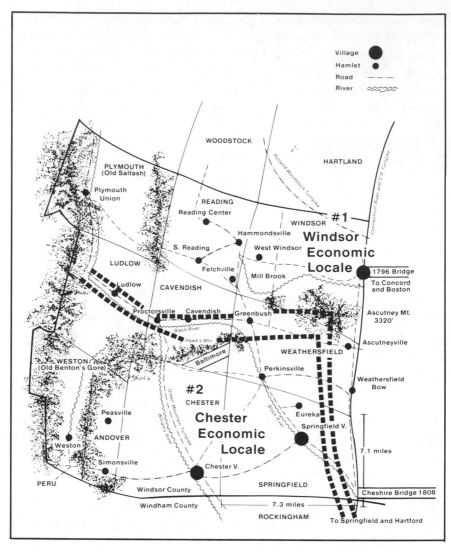

Figure 2–3: Windsor District Economic Locales, 1780–1835

Most of the seventeen stores and artisan shops which made goods and services available to Windsor District residents in 1790 advertised in the single rural weekly published in Windsor County, the Windsor *Vermont Journal*. Between a fifth and a half of the *Journal*'s total space, depending on the season, was devoted to business advertisements and notices. In the newspaper's pages, residents learned about products and services available in Windsor and Chester villages. Other pieces, letters, and even poems described and commented on economic life in the district and beyond. Perhaps two-fifths of all district households (460) subscribed to the *Journal* in 1790, a higher share in Windsor and

Chester townships than elsewhere. Post rider routes indicate that very few families who lived at a distance from the main transportation routes were likely to subscribe. It is not yet possible to specify early readership with greater accuracy. The rural weekly in 1790 was both the crucial vehicle of knowledge about an emerging market economy, extending the reach of that economy: one of the most important products of the market; and one of the initial regular commodity purchases made by Windsor District families.[48]

During 1790 the following Upper Valley stores and artisan shops sought customers through the *Vermont Journal*:

Windsor, Vt.: 4 general stores; 2 saddleries; 1 blacksmith shop; 1 print center (printing office, newspaper, bookstore)
Chester, Vt.: 2 general stores
Claremont, N.H.: 1 general store
Lebanon, N.H.: 1 general store
Norwich, Vt.: 1 general store
Hanover, N.H.: 1 general store; 1 saddlery
Orford, N.H.: 1 general store
Bradford, Vt.: 1 tanning and currying business

At a minimum, the eleven stores and artisan shops in Windsor and Chester, Vermont, and in Claremont, New Hampshire, just across the river, sought customers directly among Windsor District residents.[49]

Samuel Porter's Chester general store, opened in the late 1780s, illustrates typical operating procedures. It was middle sized among the seven firms that advertised. Porter and his colleagues stressed connections to the regional and transatlantic market. Virtually every advertisement noted that a new stock of "English, West-Indian, European, and Irish goods suitable for the season" had just arrived "by the last ships from Europe" or elsewhere. No fewer than 101 different items were advertised in notices geared to the agricultural cycle. Once or twice a year, usually in the late fall after harvest—and if a second advertisement, then in the succeeding summer—stores and other businesses would list recently arrived items plus some of their steady stock.[50]

The range of products offered for sale within Windsor District itself was quite broad for this early date. Food available in quantity included salted beef and fish, twin staples, plus a range of prominent spices and condiments: chocolate; honey, sugar, and molasses; raisins; Lisbon lemons; nutmegs; other spices; and salt. To drink there were coffees and teas; New England and West India rums and spirits; sherry; brandy; and Malaga wine. Brimstone, a sulphur-based preservative for wine and some foods, was also available. With just a small garden plot, which was almost universally available, and a place to bake, a growing share of families could live in villages, dependent for survival upon local and long-distance food production.

Basic materials for building were on hand, but among finishing materials, only nails, paints and linseed oil, and window glass six by eight inches or seven by nine inches were available. Although rough-cut wood was plentiful, no fancier boards or other forms of lumber could be obtained locally in 1790. In contrast, a wide variety of houseware, hardware, and small farm implements were in stock, including sickles, scythes, rock salt, chalk, various small tools, steel for edged tools, cuttoes, and powder and shot. There were all sorts of glass, crockery, and hollow ware; tallow and candles; tin and pewter ware; brass kettles and teapots "of all kinds and sizes"; and soap-making and washing materials. Drugs and medicines were also plentiful.

Some ready-made "clothes" were available, as well as shoes and hats, but cloth was offered in the greatest variety: half of 101 items available at Porter's general store consisted of an ample stock of woven cloth and myriad accessories. Additionally, pens, paper of several kinds, a full range of blanks and forms, a modest variety of "blank books" for journals and record keeping, and a variety of printed items were for sale at Spooner's printing office and bookstore. Stationery was sold there and in at least one general store; no store advertised any other printed items, however, apart from Bibles, the *Journal* itself, almanacs, the *State Laws of Vermont* for the year, a volume containing the Constitution and its amendments, and a chapbook edition of a moral treatise, *The Christian Oeconomy*. Beginning in the late 1790s, Spooner's own publication of printed works steadily expanded, as did imports from other presses throughout the Northeast.[51]

Rounding out the range of products and services available were saddlery and harnesses, and facilities for the repair and maintenance of carriages, sleighs, and other small vehicles. There was a blacksmith shop and shoemaker, and carpenters' tools. Windsor District also had several taverns, and Windsor had hotels. Doctors and lawyers were scarce, but a few of each were available in village and farmstead locations in both Windsor and Chester townships. The area had several small mills and manufactories, including gristmills and sawmills, a brewery in Weathersfield, and a cloth factory just across the river in Claremont, New Hampshire. Several articles in the *Journal* attested to a minor interest in "the progress of manufacturers" and in new techniques. The only notice for workers emanating from outside Windsor District came from Ira Allen, who sought thirty "young men" to raft and transport boards from Colchester, Vermont, on Lake Champlain to Quebec. They could, if they wished, help in clearing land and erecting an ironworks at Colchester upon their return the following spring and summer.[52]

As the supply of available goods and services grew, rural forms of payment expanded accordingly. In their research on the rural Northeast, 1780–1860, Michael Merrill and Christopher Clark both stressed the general shortage of cash and alleged that it was absent in most cases even from general store payment systems. In their view, the absence of cash was not "simply the product of necessity—the shortage of cash, perhaps," in Clark's words, but rather formed part of the whole precapitalist or early capitalist cultural and social ethic. Need ruled and not "the demand of production for profit in the marketplace." Emphasizing Marx's distinction between use value and exchange value, Merrill argues that the domestic mode of production did not involve "commodity relations" with accepted exchange value rules, because "need rather than price" dominated economic relations. Clark concludes that "a deeper cultural attachment to kinship and neighborhood ties and to a spirit of mutual cooperation was at the center of a distinct culture" which "generated its own values, of cooperation, of work-swapping, of household integrity and family advancement that were to be influential throughout the early period of capitalist development."[53]

The evidence of Porter's and the other seven general stores supports Merrill's and Clark's contentions regarding the character of household production in the Upper Valley. It also shows that Merrill and Clark seriously underestimated the spread of commerical exchange.[54] By the 1790s, rural economic life was becoming measurably more complex than our current emphasis on a lack of cash would suggest. Of the eleven general stores, five artisan shops, and one print center that advertised in the *Journal* during 1790, only Porter and Thomas Chandler II, the other Chester storekeeper, failed to mention cash as a form of payment.[55] Cash was accepted, was often openly welcomed, and was specifically listed by three-quarters of all stores and artisan shops that advertised in Windsor District. That cash formed an important part of the economic system in one of the least mature areas of New England economically is confirmed by a second series of "exchange," or buyers', notices. Advertisements by nine of eleven such businesses offered cash in payment; most offered only cash. Thus, of twenty-four separate businesses of all types that were advertising in the *Journal* during 1790, twenty (83 percent) listed cash as an acceptable form of payment. In 75 percent of these businesses, no distinction in value was made between cash and commodities as forms of payment.[56]

The payment situation in 1790 was even more complex. The Norwich general store of Peter Olcott and Sons accepted "PRODUCE of all kinds . . . likewise, Vermont STATE MONEY, Windsor and Orange COUNTY ORDERS, IRON, ASHES, SALTS OF LYE, AND last of all CASH." Here and in several other cases we see that money was perceived as a second exchange-value arrangement and was distinct from cash.[57] Historically accurate definitions of the term "cash" are far narrower than has been assumed. The three most widely owned dictionaries in Windsor District before 1800, two of them British, define cash identically as "money," specifically "ready money" carried on one's person. "Ready money" in all three dictionaries was restricted to "metal coined for public use," meaning the "uses of commerce." "Currency" was the broad contemporary term encompassing all forms of on-the-spot payment, coins and paper alike.

Emphasizing the concept of exchange value, "currency" also meant "the rate at which any thing is vulgarly valued." In Webster's 1806 dictionary, the definition of currency had expanded to include "paper passing for, and established as, current money." "Money" expanded in meaning to become a synonym for currency as paper and other forms of bills and notes proliferated in the late 1790s. Later, in 1828, Webster's *American Dictionary* codified changing practice: "since the institution of banks," money now "denotes also bank notes equivalent to money." Both terms were far broader than "cash."[58]

Since cash was but one subset of currency (or money), then, the presence or absence of cash tells us little about the use of currency and therefore little about the actual extent of commodity relations. Currency and money, integral to the rural economic system by the 1790s, were always acceptable forms of payment to stores and shops. Among all forms of currency, cash was usually acceptable and was only occasionally the least welcome form of payment.

The payment system in Upper Valley businesses was a mixture of barter, work, cash, and other forms of currency. Cash was employed on a regular basis in nearly all of the businesses. Customers were free to make payments in barter or in the commercial medium of exchange of their choice. This flexibility enabled all families to participate, but with varying degrees of intimacy and regularity. To contend that even in the initial period of settlement the rural New England economy functioned largely without "cash," however, is to mistake the situation within an as-yet-undetermined proportion of households for events in the rural economy as a whole. By the 1790s, exchange-value commodity relations were deeply rooted in one of the least commercialized rural areas in the American Northeast.[59]

With regard to commodities available within Windsor District in 1790, no distinction was yet made between goods produced within households (locally or at a distance) and those produced in factories (locally or at a distance). The actual relationship between household production and the market economy was complicated. Some commodities imported into Windsor District were made at home elsewhere, and some were made in shops and factories. The same was true for goods produced locally. Upper Valley residents distinguished products by their place, not their mode, of production. Items were advertised as American-produced goods (and were often not distinguished further) or as coming from England, the West Indies, Europe, Ireland, India, or Persia. Commercial activity in northwestern rural New England had already become quite varied, creating a mixed economy. Goods were either home produced or (a far smaller part) factory produced; for payment the local economy relied on barter, changing works, and several forms of currency.

A broad focus on the modes of production, advertising, and distribution of commodities and services reveals that there was substantial market activity in Windsor District involving varied sets of buyers and sellers. Considerable agricultural production for surplus existed, and a small proportion of families engaged in intense speculation in land. Windsor District families' interest in nonagricultural enterprises was still modest but was growing. There can be little doubt about the importance of lineal family relations, but there was considerable barter, "changing works," and commodity exchange carried on beyond the bounds of family and kinship networks. Active participation in the market economy of the region had already made significant inroads into family life. Widespread market-oriented activity was most pronounced in Windsor and Chester townships, where 40 percent of the district's population was centered. There probably a thin majority of all families participated in the commercial economy in 1790. In the less commercialized hinterland of each economic locale, participation levels were far lower (about 30 percent). Thus in Windsor District as a whole, perhaps two-fifths of all families had initiated direct involvement in commercial life.

Instances of class action or class conflict existed but were relatively rare in Windsor District until after 1815, perhaps understandably in view of the youthfulness of these communities, the tiny nonfarming share of the population, and the slow growth of wage labor.[60] Nevertheless, printed sources' silence on the subject is striking. Rural economic life evidently remained so fluid in 1790 that many important class-based distinctions in belief and activity had not crystallized. Then, too, as E.P. Thompson has recently noted, it is an error to assume "that classes exist, independent of historical relationships and struggle, and that they struggle because they exist rather than coming into existence out of that struggle." Thompson concludes, "Class and class consciousness are always the last, not the first, stage in the real historical process." During the decades 1790–1830, Upper Valley residents came "to find themselves in a society structured" in ways leading to "antagonistic interest" in economic activity. In rural New England, however, as compared with England and elsewhere, other major factors, which we should regard as competing loyalties in 1790 and thereafter, limited the importance of the role that productive relations played in daily life before the mid-1820s.[61]

One factor of great consequence in daily life was the very high level of male and femal elementary literacy, defined as the ability to read reasonably well, calculate family accounts, and write a letter or journal entry. Lifelong reading was spreading rapidly, and as a result, a growing number of families was learning about the emerging market economy through a vigorous booster of economic development, the *Vermont Journal*. Its basic stance fully supported commercial activity and through advertisements the *Journal* profited directly from an increase in commodity exchange. The *Journal* gained nothing from economic self-sufficiency.[62]

The *Journal* and other vehicles of print culture helped in several important ways to diffuse much of the initial potential for class antagonism inherent in market expansion. As the basic advertising medium for stores, post offices, and other businesses, the *Journal* emphasized the positive nature of modest entrepreneurship by keeping residents regularly informed about market expansion. Providing a running record of economic transformation, the *Journal* also created a wholly new realm of thought for those beyond the professions, that came to be known as "keeping up with the world." Furthermore, the existence of a newspaper greatly increased interest and participation in rural public life within Windsor District. Virtually all early commentators wrote of the public spiritedness found in Chester, Weathersfield, and most of all, Windsor. The wider the actual participation in public life—Windsor itself was first, or second to Hanover, in establishing a whole range of economic, cultural, political, religious, and social institutions within the Upper Valley—the more noneconomic alliances undercut and diluted ties based on shared economic opportunities and hardships and attendant class consciousness.[63]

Market activity and a commodity economy increasingly based on currency had longer-term costs in terms of local webs of community, self-sufficiency, barter, and work swapping, but these, not surprisingly, were infrequently discussed before the 1820s. Many residents saw the beginning stages of the major economic transformation piecemeal, from a family-centered point of view. Market activity also expanded smoothly because stores and other businesses showed flexibility in the methods of payment they accepted. The emerging market apparatus was thus grafted onto the local barter-exchange system, and to many residents it seemed to have evolved naturally. No writer in the *Journal* during the years 1783–95 mentioned, for instance, that, if more and more shoes were imported into Windsor District, local shoemakers might eventually be forced out of business. At some point local shoemakers realized that this was so, but they did not, or perhaps were not generally allowed to, use mainstream vehicle of print communication to express their anxieties and opposition. This is a crucial subject for research in the history of newspapers.

Commercialization, Stage Two, 1795–1815:
The Rise of a Commercial Society and Economy

Compared with the Revolutionary era, the decade 1785–95 was relatively stable in the northwestern New England countryside.[64] Over the next twenty years, 1795–1815, acceleration in the spread of commercial exchange fueled a remarkable transition in economic and social life. An important new group of "middling sort" families, and even some poorer families, began regular, active market exchange. The years 1795–1815 encompassed a distinct second stage in the commercialization of the Upper Valley. Its chief characteristics were the proliferation of well-developed local markets throughout the Upper Valley; the deep penetration of commerce within each economic locale; and the expansion of local connections within regional, national, and international trading networks.

The Upper Valley population nearly doubled to just under two thousand households between 1790 and 1800. Settlement spread especially swiftly in more remote places. The mountain communities grew by 244 percent, as opposed to 86 percent for the district as a whole (see figure 2–1). Throughout Windsor District, farmland and pasturage plots accounted for most of the increase, as much of the district approached maximum agricultural settlement. While Windsor District's riverbed communities did not explode during the 1790s, they did expand rapidly (between 44 percent and 86 percent each) and upon a substantial base. Windsor village, which had been settled well before the Revolution, strained against limits imposed by inadequate transportation connections until Cornish Bridge, built in 1796, linked Windsor to Concord and Boston more securely than the older ferry service had done. During the succeeding decade Windsor alone, in a fifty-mile stretch of the Connecticut River, maintained a major bridge connection to Boston. A three-decade-long expansion began almost immediately. By 1800, Windsor had become the vibrant center of an expanding web of economic and cultural interests that multiplied connections among communities within its economic locale.[65]

Expansion and integration of Upper Valley transportation and communications in 1790–1800 caused Windsor District's commerce to grow at an even faster rate than its population. In 1790 Windsor and Keene shared the burden of newspaper service for the entire Upper Valley. By 1800 six stable weeklies, published in locations from Brattleboro to Randolph, nearly one hundred miles to the north (see figure 2–4), trebled the available information and opinion about market-oriented economic activities.[66] By reconstructing post rider routes of the weekly Windsor *Vermont Journal* in 1800, we can trace an otherwise invisible web of market connections through twenty-seven Vermont townships (see figure 2–5) blanketing Windsor County, Vermont, the eastern half of Orange County, and a few nearby communities. Each of the Upper Valley's six weeklies concentrated its circulation in a more localized zone of influence. By 1800 all six had become embedded in a regional communications and transportation grid centered at Boston.[67]

The pace of business expansion so sparked Windsor District economic growth after the bridge's completion that stores and artisan shops advertising for customers increased by 147 percent between 1790 and 1800 (from seventeen in eight townships to forty-two in seventeen townships).[68] Despite sizable immigration, the ratio of stores and shops advertising locally declined from one per seventy-one households in 1790 to one per forty-seven in 1800. In com-

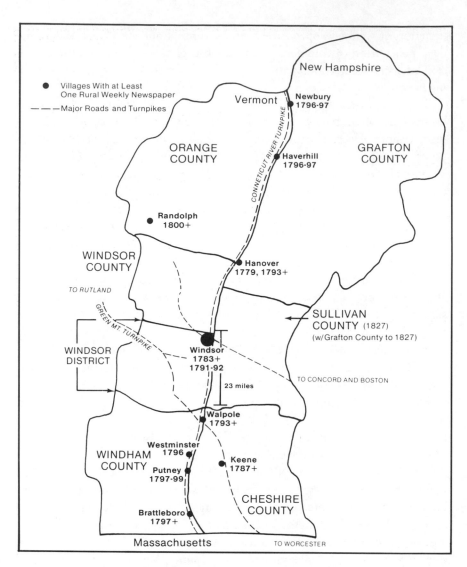

Figure 2–4: The Upper Connecticut River Valley Press, 1783–1800

merce, in rural newspaper dissemination and advertising, and in more general entrepreneurial activity, the 1790s saw substantial expansion. All three areas of economic life meshed as snugly as muscle, bone, and tendon.

In accordance with the more localized distribution of Upper Valley week-lies, Windsor County businesses seeking customers in Windsor District in 1800 accounted for three-quarters of all *Vermont Journal* advertisements:

> Windsor Township (14): 7 general stores; 1 print center; 2 saddleries; 1 shoe and boot manufactory; 2 builders; 1 blacksmith shop

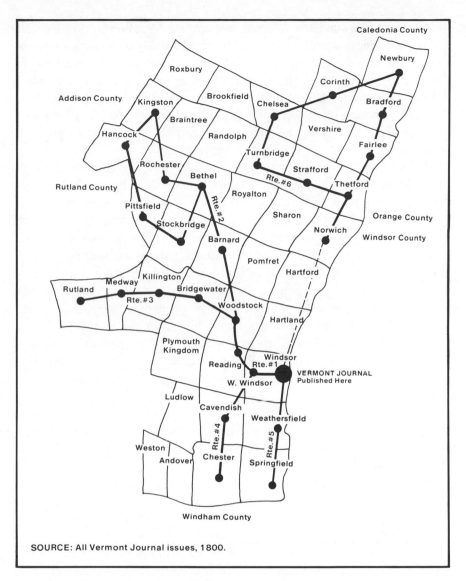

Figure 2–5: Vermont Journal Post–Rider Delivery Points, 1800

Other Windsor County and Adjacent Grafton County Townships (18): 7 general stores; 1 medical supply store (also selling books); 4 builders; 2 hatteries; 3 clothiers (factories with stores); 1 tailor's shop

Other Areas Within the Upper Valley (10): 4 general stores; 1 print center; 4 clothiers; 1 hattery

Economic growth was especially rapid in the Windsor economic locale; fully a third of all businesses were located in Windsor township itself (see figure 2–2b).[69] The number of general stores in the Windsor economic locale nearly doubled, two builders opened carpentry shops, a shoe and boot manufactory was established, and a second Windsor village print center carried on business for over a year. By 1800 business had begun to stabilize. The Windsor village stores of Isaac Green and William Leverett, both of the saddleries, and Spooner's printing office were now in their second decade. In 1801 another printing office, bookstore, and newspaper began to compete with Spooner's establishment.

The substantial spurt in market activity during the 1790s significantly broadened the proportion of Windsor District families that engaged in entrepreneurial activity, whether we consider Windsor township, the economic locale, or the district. The total share of the population engaging in transactions with stores or artisan shops increased from about two-fifths of more than 1,100 Windsor District families to about half of 2,000 families. As with population, a greater proportionate increase in new customers appeared among families living outside the village communities of Windsor and Chester (about 30 percent to about 55 percent).[70] At least one post rider route passed through ten of Windsor District's eleven townships, spreading newspaper information about commodities through much of the area by 1800. Commercial activity that supplemented household production thus penetrated farther into Windsor District's hinterland and became more frequent among those people who already participated.

Currency exchange, barter, and work swapping were all actively pursued. Cash and money payment became more frequent. Cash was mentioned as a preferred method of payment in 90 percent of all advertisements.[71] The most prominent additions to economic activities included taverns, "coffee-houses," and a "house of entertainment"; rural manufactories, especially mills combined with stores that produced and sold cloth (clothiers); and businesses engaged in printing. The rural phase of the American Industrial Revolution was gaining force by the turn of the century, well before the 1807 embargo.[72]

By 1810, both the spread and the density of commerce were altering the basic structure of Upper Valley economic life, especially in Windsor County. Household production for surplus expanded, and local and long-distance production of manufactured goods multiplied severalfold. Furthermore, the diffusion of print and written culture, with values that were overwhelmingly promanufacturing and probusiness, and somewhat proentrepreneurial, had become a decisive influence on the economic beliefs of Windsor District residents. By 1810 Windsor District was institutionally committed to local and long-distance commercial exchange as well as to early, water-powered forms of factory production. Local charters and water rights had been secured, shares had been sold, buildings had been constructed, and production had commenced. By 1810 Springfield had begun its rise to preeminence as a manufacturing center.

Twin dynamos of survival and livelihood—household production and commerical exchange—were inherently interrelated features of economic life within Windsor county, the most developed area of the Upper Valley. Their interaction powered dynamic change throughout rural agricultural society. Windsor District economic life in 1810 is best characterized as a rich blend of commerce, agriculture, and rural industry. Belief and behavior had been inseparable in this transformation. The most pronounced changes included the proliferation of a commercial, capitalist system of distribution, consumption, and currency and credit payment; the rapid diffusion of early forms of rural factory production; new distribution routes penetrating the rural New England hinterland, and extensive newspaper reading throughout all townships except those in the Green Mountain foothills.

Although Windsor District was by no means crowded, it was almost fully settled by 1810, with 2,611 families and 16,164 individuals (see figure 2–6). The net increase since 1800 remained high, at one-third. Not all communities were growing equally, however. The four townships in the foothills of the Green Mountains grew most rapidly (56 to 114 percent), as families continued to find valuable uncultivated land suitable for farming and grazing. At least one hamlet with between twelve and twenty-five households germinated within each township, and in 1809 Plymouth and Ludlow hamlets received post office status, a badge of merit awarded for their expanding commercial and cultural activity. Reading and Cavendish each grew by two-fifths, mostly in the population of five hamlets. With its fractionated village unfavorably positioned between Windsor and Springfield, and lacking a ready bridge connection to New Hampshire, the population growth of Weathersfield township had already slowed to 9 per cent.

Chester and Windsor, the townships with sizable established villages, and Springfield, in which a factory village had emerged, grew by a quarter. For all three, 1800–1810 was a major village-building decade. Road and bridge improvements complemented parallel infrastructure growth of manufactories, stores, artisan shops, public buildings, and homes. All varieties of printed objects and letters circulated on the major road and water routes. As transportation routes improved, another major element of rural infrastructure, a rich communications environment based on printed texts, spread rapidly though selectively. The connections between transportation and communications networks, village growth, and commercial and early manufactory expansion were direct and synergistic (see figure 2–7). Developments in each fed and were in turn reinforced by the others. By 1810 Chester, Springfield, and Windsor were firmly embedded in major east-west and north-south land transportation networks. Through the domination of Chester and Windsor, the district's two economic locales were beginning to resemble many long-settled southern New England areas. Within Windsor District, an increasing share of the citizenry

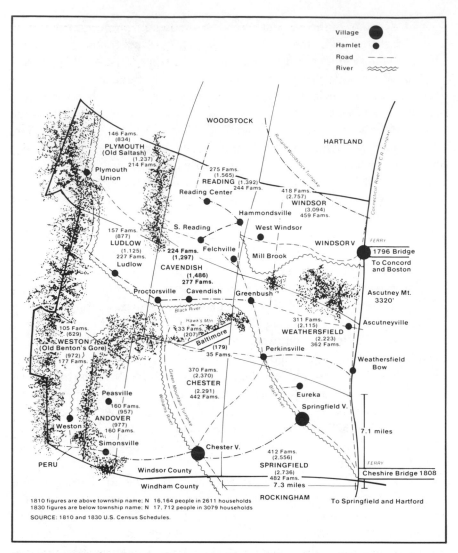

Figure 2–6: Windsor District Community Size and Geography of Settlement, 1810 and 1830

lived in hamlets and villages, eventually giving those places greater political influence. As a result, better roads were constructed, further binding the villages and hamlets together into regional commercial networks.

Commerce grew much faster than new settlement between 1800 and the onset of the War of 1812, accelerating a trend established previously. By 1810 there was a store or factory engaged in local commerce for every twenty-four households in Windsor District. Many would fail, but most were quickly replaced. By 1810 commercial exchange pervaded daily life. At least 120 stores,

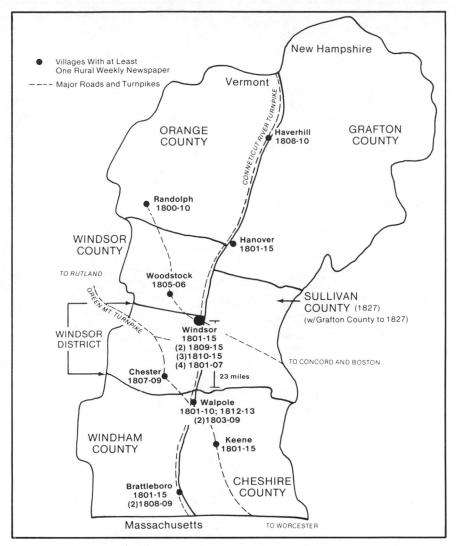

Figure 2–7: The Upper Connecticut River Valley Press, 1801–15

shops, and manufactories sought customers through the pages of Windsor District's rural weeklies, nearly triple the 42 businesses that had sought customers a decade earlier (see figure 2–8). Supplies of products being sold in Windsor District arrived from at least 45 townships in 1810, as opposed to 17 townships in 1800. The growing array of firms soliciting business from Windsor District residents directly reflected the rapid convergence of local and international markets. Business establishments invaded at least 8 of Windsor District's 11 townships, from the river valley into the foothills of the Green Mountains,

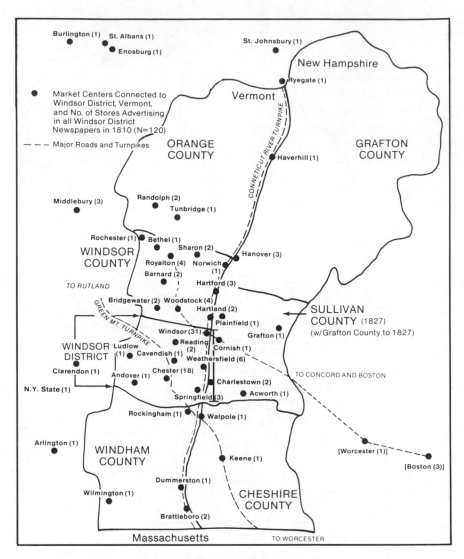

Figure 2–8: Upper Connecticut River Valley Market Centers, 1810

although not equally. These firms represented more than 70 percent of the 120 commercial enterprises that were advertising. The web of business connections that linked local and distant markets now contained many more strands.[73]

The most significant economic development of the decade 1801–1810 was the growing diversity of the 120 stores, shops, and factories seeking local customers:[74]

> Windsor Township (31): 8 general stores (including 1 general store affiliated with the Vermont State Prison); 2 clock and watch stores; 1 hardware and potware

store; 3 printing offices with bookstores, including 2 with binderies, all selling medicine; 1 independent bookstore; 2 independent binderies; 1 tailor; 1 cabinet and chairmaker; 3 taverns; 3 saddleries; 1 tannery; 1 bark mill factory; 1 shoe store; 1 shoe factory and tanyard; 1 malt house; and 1 trip hammer shop

Chester Township (18): 4 general stores; 2 other stores; 10 artisan shops, including 1 clockmaker, 2 saddleries, 3 blacksmiths, 1 wagon and chaisemaker, 1 printing office with bookstore, 1 large gristmill, and 1 large sawmill; and 2 manufactories, including 1 carding mill and a hat factory

Windsor County Beyond Windsor & Chester Townships (36): 16 general stores; 1 paper mill selling books; 10 cloth factories with stores; 1 clockmaker with store; 1 razor grinding shop; 1 tannery; 2 boot and shoe factories; 1 saddlery; 1 blacksmith shop; and 2 builders

Upper Valley Beyond Windsor County (20): 4 general stores; 2 other stores; 2 druggists; 8 printing offices with bookstores; 2 cloth factories with stores; 1 coopery; and 1 tannery

Beyond Upper Valley (15): 4 general stores; 2 other wholesale general stores; 1 druggist; 1 clothes store (wholesale); 1 tavern; 4 printing offices with bookstores; and 2 cloth factories with stores

The major effect of the spread of commerce in rural New England was profound inequality. The gulf between townships with 0 to 3 accessible businesses (averaging 1.3) and those with 4 or more firms (averaging 14.5) widened; economic, social, cultural and eventually political differences became more pronounced. A second form of inequality festered within the few communities that had many factory workers or many firms apart from stores. A small but growing number of wage-earning, laboring poor arose in Windsor and Chester. Because they lived in villages and hamlets and purchased most of the necessities of life rather than growing or making them, these working-class families depended directly upon volatile market conditions. By the early 1820s Windsor, Chester, and Woodstock just to the north were ripe for appeals to class consciousness, and class conflict first arose in these three townships. For many citizens in each village and its immediate environs, survival and the need to earn a livelihood took precedence over religious and other special interests. By the late 1820s many of them had aligned with workingmen's political groups.[75]

A total of 104 firms served Windsor District households directly; however, commerce was very unevenly spread within the district. Plymouth, Weston, and tiny Baltimore, all in mountainous areas, still had no identifiable stores, shops, or factories. These were minimum-access townships, composing a very limited zone of, at best, indirect commercial exchange. The remaining four hinterland townships (Andover, Ludlow, Reading, and Cavendish) together contained just 5 hamlet stores and shops in 1810. They formed a partial-access zone of commercial exchange. The four townships with active villages constituted a third, full-access zone. Accounting for 59 percent of the district's pop-

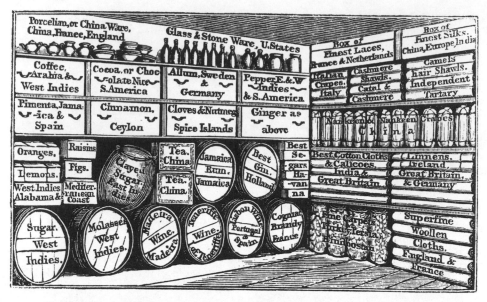

Country General Store Stock on Hand. Anonymous wood engraving from Emma Willard, *Geography for Beginners* (Hartford, 1826). Courtesy, American Antiquarian Society.

Just as knowledge from distant climes spread through the New England countryside, so too did commodities from around the world. By 1810 they filled the bins of the larger rural general stores in New Hampshire and Vermont Valley villages and hamlets.

ulation, they contained 92 percent (58 of 63) of the district's stores, shops, and factories, most of them in Windsor and Chester.[76]

As businesses grew in numbers, their diversity increased. There were basically four types of firms in 1810: general stores (38), more specialized stores and firms (37), artisan shops—rarely with a store (23), and manufactories—often with a store (22)—for a total of 120. Most Windsor District residents' initial experience with commercial exchange involved the all-purpose general store, the most pervasive business in rural New England. By 1810 twenty-three such stores sought customers within Windsor District and contiguous communities. An accessible general store existed for every 127 Windsor District families in 1810, and half the stores were more than seven years old.[77] By 1810 general stores were usually large-scale businesses, each with several hundred families and individuals maintaining credit accounts.[78] Next in size and volume among stores were the bookstores attached to printing and publishing facilities. A total of five sought customers in Windsor and Chester. Altogether nineteen printing-related facilities sought retail or wholesale business in Windsor District. Slightly less widespread in their appeal were more specialized druggists (three) and clock and watch stores attached to clockmakers (four). Finally, there were four known taverns, three of them in Windsor. The professionals in business in 1810 included several lawyers, mainly residing in Windsor, Chester, and Weathersfield, and doctors in these and at least three other Windsor District townships. The year 1810 also saw the organization of the first state-wide medical society.[79]

Artisan shops in Windsor District in 1810 were many and varied. In addition to a group of small local sawmills and gristmills in nearly every township, twenty-three shops sought customers more actively in Windsor District, including saddleries (six); blacksmith shops (three); tanneries (three); tailor shops (two); builders (two); a malt house for barley, and a cabinet and chair maker's shop in Windsor; a wagon and chaise maker's shop in Chester; and a razor-grinding shop in Weathersfield.[80]

Manufactories were dominated by the clothing industry. Ten Windsor County woolen and cotton cloth factories and clothiers were active; most had stores attached. Cloth was woven, dyed, dressed (fulled and pressed) for nearly all clothing purposes. An assortment of yarn and thread could also be purchased. Reading and Weathersfield led the way in Windsor District manufactories. Windsor and two contiguous townships held a carding mill, a hat factory, three boot and shoe factories, a bark mill factory, a paper mill, and a trip hammer shop.[81]

In the rural payment system, the increasing spread of paper and other forms of currency payment marked the decade 1800–1810. Among twenty-four general stores specifying the manner of payment in 1810, just one accepted produce as the sole form of payment. On the other hand, an eighth of the general stores accepted only currency.[82] This was an increasingly prevalent pattern. By 1815, a small majority of all firms accepted no country produce as on-the-spot payment. Surplus farm products were still acceptable as payment of book account debts by regular customers. Frequently mentioned farm products included "Beef, Butter, Cheese, Flax, Flax-Seed, Wheat, Rye, Corn, Oats, Peas, Beans, and Potatoes," "Rags, Bees Wax Boards, Shingles, Tow Cloth, Woolen Flannel," "Salts of Lye or Ashes," "Clover and Herbs, Grass Seed, Pork, Lard, Tallow," "Geese Feathers," and "Fox, Mink and Sable" pelts. The forty-nine stores and shops specifying these agricultural products attest to the emergence of a very sizable local commodities exchange market involving both barter and currency trade, with payment on the spot and by credit.[83]

In 1810 cash was second among preferred forms of payment, the first being not produce but Vermont paper money. No fewer than 80 percent of all stores that described methods of payment specified paper money. Coinage and Vermont paper money were fully welcome and were in fact the preferred forms of payment. The most interesting development in the rural payment system in the period 1795–1815 was the addition of the term "or short and approved Credit" to advertisements noting payment by "Cash, Wheat, [and] Butter."

Hardly any notices in 1790 mentioned this method of payment, whereas 57 percent of general store notices for 1800 did so and 65 percent of those for 1810. Credit payment (as opposed to on-the-spot cash or produce) had been normal for decades down the valley in Connecticut. With more than 1,500 new families migrating to Windsor District in 1790–1810, shopkeepers found themselves faced with novel worries: Would the new settlers move on? Could they be trusted to pay as much as twelve months or three years later? Would they remain in their initial township or nearby that long? Windsor District and area businesses began to offer "short and approved Credit" selectively. As Caldwell and Hubbards' general store put it: "No person need apply for Credit unless he brings good recommendations."[84]

During the years 1795–1815, Upper Valley shops and stores rapidly adjusted to the realities of high migration rates and more dispersed settlement. In the process, form of payment ceased to be an issue, while the timing and conditions of on-the-spot payment, versus more formalized credit methods, greatly increased in significance. The presence of an increasing number of relative strangers meant that store owners had to be selective in establishing a credit relationship with customers.[85]

We do not yet have a precise count of the families who participated in Windsor District commercial production, distribution, and consumption in 1810. Sharp differences in levels of market activity across Windsor District resulted from varying access to businesses via the local transportation and communications network. In the 1795–1815 decades, residents of Windsor and Plymouth Kingdom townships, separated by thirty miles of mostly poor and circuitous roads, stood at opposite extremes with respect to market access. The proliferating local rural weeklies regularly communicated some information about the market across the economic, social, and cultural gulf. I estimate from all available evidence that by 1810, nearly two-thirds of all Windsor District families engaged in market exchange. In the four townships with villages, approximately 75 percent of all families participated, while in the other seven more sparsely settled townships, about 55 percent of all families made purchases.[86]

The commercialization of Windsor District economic life was evident in many other important changes between 1795 and 1815. First of all, change in the collective value structure of Windsor District families quickened. In 1810 at least a small majority of all Windsor District households were subscribing to a rural weekly. In doing so, these families attended an informal adult education school dedicated to spreading current information and opinion about local and distant commercial affairs and about transatlantic public life. Weekly reading gradually dissolved most of the lingering opposition to commerce among the most publicly active elements of the population. Rural newspapers reflected the full complexity of this process. Pieces critical of one or another specific aspect of commercial life persisted, but wholesale opposition to com-

merce had waned by 1810. Well before a "spirit of gain" took hold, a more positive reorientation occurred in basic attitudes toward a commercial economy
and society.[87]

Each year Windsor District rural weeklies included a flood of pieces concerning manufacturing and marketplace values. The progress of manufactures
was now a major topic. Several dozen pieces appeared in 1810 alone. Merino
sheep raising; manufacturing advances in New York State, Philadelphia, western Pennsylvania, and Manchester, England; and European mining were prominent topics. Secretary of the Treasury Albert Gallatin in 1810 made a "Report
on Domestic Manufactures" that was reprinted in full in the *Vermont Journal*.
Nearly all pieces about manufacturing were favorable. Not all poems, letters,
essays, and stories about economic life advocated manufacturing and commerce, but a sizable majority did. Articles on the conditions of commerce elsewhere in the North Atlantic were frequently reprinted. In addition there were
moralistic obituaries on important local business leaders, such as a report on
the funeral of Jonathan Chase, the "active, industrious, and enterprising" moving spirit behind the Cornish Bridge.[88] These articles were supplemented by
original and reprinted essays and poems favoring commercial involvement.
The values of saving time and of frugality, economy, punctuality, reason, and
industry were constantly lauded, and there were several critiques of idleness
and wealth. Science, including technical discussions of agriculture and nature
(for example, minerals and springs), patents and their possibilities, and the
character of the "Yankee" were all topics of regular discussion.[89]

At least one editor's support was not unqualified. Alden Spooner's *Vermont
Journal* between 1795 and 1815 regularly criticized greater intolerance of debtors
and two other aspects of commercial exchange: the proliferation of professionals and the corrupting effects of life in distant cities. These last two issues were
intertwined in the minds of Upper Valley residents. Aside from perfunctory
notices of meetings, services, medical lectures at Dartmouth, and the opening
of Joseph Gallup's combined medical practice, bookstore, and drugstore, most
newspaper contributions were negative toward "Law, Physic and Divinity."[90]

A local market had spread widely but unevenly throughout the Upper Valley by 1815. In this second stage of commercialization, participation reached
a growing majority of all households. Moreover, an expanding number of families were able, for the first time in this rural agricultural society, to live permanently in villages, relying on stores and shops for most of their necessities,
which now included not only food, drink, shelter, and clothing but also, increasingly, printed matter. Attitudes toward the commercialization of life remained
mixed, but positive assessments were becoming more prevalent, particularly
because of the regular barrage from rural newspapers. A large majority of all
families engaged in agricultural pursuits, and about a third of all families still
did not participate in commercial life. Yet, far earlier than has previously been

suspected, and even in the forest society of northwestern New England, the overall balance in the activities of daily life was shifting rapidly from agriculture to a new and strikingly rich blend of farming and grazing, commercial exchange, and rural manufacturing.

Commercialization, Stage Three, 1815–35: The Commercialization of Daily Life

A heavily commercial economy became a dominant feature of daily life between 1795 and 1815. Nevertheless, as we have seen, many families initially had been wary of participating. In the course of reading about commerce and making purchases, however, they eventually had to come to terms with their profound historical ambivalence about commerce. For many, commerce still involved temptation. Questions of vice and virtue, and of harm and benefit to the nation, persisted in discussions of political economy. Only in the aftermath of the War of 1812 did these issues recede.

The visibility and activity generated by the 104 stores, shops, and factories that served Windsor District residents in 1810 spawned a new agenda of issues and problems. A third stage of commercialization emerged in the midst of this activity, in 1815–35. Its essence was the commercialization of cultural and social relations. As the economic basis of community continued to expand during the two decades surrounding the American Republic's silver anniversary, changes in the organization, substance, and style of daily life in the Upper Valley appeared everywhere. These changes forged a new order of rural existence.

Our media-saturated age has vastly underestimated the impact of the mass media in previous eras. Historians suffer from the same bias, acting as if the late twentieth century had invented sophisticated communications. In fact, one of the three or four essential breakthroughs in the long history of human communications first occurred in the rural American Northeast in the period 1780–1835. For only the second time in human history, a new rural mass culture formed. This one, based on regular reading and writing as interrelated means of communicating information, opinion, values, and beliefs, complemented talking and listening face to face. The permeation of a rural society by print and written communications before the Industrial Revolution and apart from urbanization contradicts the core assumptions made in materialist versions of modernization. Between 1780 and 1835 Upper Valley residents were active agents in a process of commercialization and rural industrialization that had profound effects on their economic, social, and cultural relations.[91]

Agriculture was still understood as the basis of rural life throughout the Upper Valley in the years 1815–35, but commerce was increasingly assumed to be the distinguishing characteristic of economic life in New England. Despite

Tyson Furnace, Plymouth, Vermont. Attributed to Myron Dimmick, n.d. Oil on canvas (51x76.4 cm). Courtesy, Vermont Historical Society.

Early Copper smelting was carried on at several Upper Valley sites by the 1820s, and here at Plymouth in the early 1830s.

expansion of commercial agriculture, attention to farming had been waning in Upper Valley weekly newspapers since about 1800, especially in the Windsor District weeklies.[92] Replacing farming as the focus of discussions of economic life was a far richer brew of commercial news and advertisements supporting several new forms of livelihood. These included more intensive grazing, particularly of sheep; trade in goods and services, with currency as the basis of credit and payment; banking and finance; manufacturing and mining; and the application of technology to create useful labor-saving machinery. Fascination with new methods and sites of production, new means of distribution, and hundreds of new consumption possibilities became very widespread. These changes eventually increased the share of the labor force that toiled for wages as factory workers, clerks, loaders, and other helpers. Commercial exchange shaped a far livelier and more contentious commercial and early rural industrial society, economy, and culture in 1815–35.

As we have seen, extensive commercial expansion was directly related to earlier increases in population density. Both processes continued after 1815. Windsor District's overall population grew slowly until the late 1820s; by then the flow of outmigrants equaled local population increase plus a dwindling stream of new settlers. Between 1810 and 1820 the village and hamlet population of the four townships engaging in sizable commerce grew modestly (only 5–7 percent), adding to an already full base of farming in each township (see figure 2–6 and table 1–1). The population of the other three long-settled farming and grazing communities—Andover, Baltimore, and Reading—leveled off or declined. Initial settlement continued in the three newest townships leading into the Green Mountains: Ludlow grew 30 percent; Plymouth 33 percent; and Weston 42 percent. Cavendish, through which the main road to two of these townships passed, grew by 20 percent, a sizable amount. During the next decade, 1820–30, very modest growth continued only in the village and hamlet population of Windsor (5 percent) and in hinterland Weston and Plymouth (9 and 11 percent, respectively). This decade marked the end of growth in long-settled agricultural townships (Andover lost 2 percent, Cavendish 4 percent, and Baltimore and Reading each 13 percent). In the 1830s, only the Green Mountain townships avoided net population loss of between 2 percent and 11 percent, and only Springfield village avoided stagnation and initial rural decline.[93]

The basic land and water transportation network serving Windsor District was in place by 1810.[94] Subsequent integration of transportation and communications throughout the American Northeast strengthened Upper Valley ties to a massive regional network that ran from Portland to Baltimore and from there to Buffalo, Burlington, and Canada. Over this network traveled countless products for sale in Upper Valley stores and shops, including a large volume of reading matter. A powerful visible symbol of this merger of local and regional market and communications networks was the establishment in the 1820s of two regional stagecoach lines: the Boston and Keene Telegraph and Dispatch Line, connecting with Chester three times per week, and the Pioneer Line from Albany to Buffalo, connecting with Windsor daily except Sunday.[95]

From the critical increases in population density, expansion of transportation and communications routes, and extensive literacy, we may conclude that Windsor District's forest society reached its rural zenith in the first third of the nineteenth century. Two generations of settlement had created a vibrant, diversified agricultural, commercial, and early industrial economy and society. From 1805 to 1835, between 9,800 and 10,300 people in 1,500 to 1,650 households occupied four village townships from Windsor to Chester. These townships formed a triangular zone of very active commercial and cultural exchange. The other seven sparsely settled farming and grazing communities, sustaining between 1,100 and 1,350 families, were influenced by life in Windsor and the other villages. Rough terrain and generally poor east-west travel, however, maintained a transportation and communications barrier that limited regular participation in village-centered commercial life and culture.[96]

Continuing a trend begun in the 1790s, the number and range of firms participating in the local market in 1810–30 grew much more rapidly than the

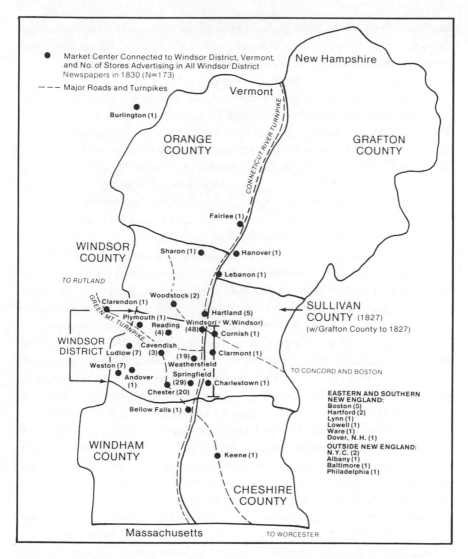

Figure 2–9: Upper Connecticut River Valley Market Centers, 1830

Windsor District population (see figure 2–9). While population rose just 10 percent in 1810–30, the number of businesses expanded 44 percent (from 120 to 173). By 1830 commerce had become so enmeshed in rural life that a store, shop, or factory existed for every eighteen households in the district.

By 1830, it should be noted, firms advertising for trade had so increased their pool of consumers that they catered to a geographical area only one fourth as large as that served in 1810. Expansion in businesses other than general stores outdistanced the population increase, 72 percent to 10 percent. Artisan shops and manufactories doubled, 1810–30, from 23 to 44; taverns and specialty stores and shops increased by 40 percent, from 22 to 46; and more specialized stores and firms increased from 37 to 51. Within Windsor District proper, general stores increased from nineteen in 1810 to twenty-six in 1830.[97]

Two key patterns in advertising products and services dominant in 1810 further intensified through 1830: a greater proportion of firms was located in Windsor District or nearby, and a related increase occurred in distant regional firms wholesaling to Windsor District businesses (18 from beyond the Upper Valley and 8 more from Upper Valley townships beyond Windsor County—totalling 15 percent).[98] Nearly all 173 businesses advertising in the Windsor District press in 1830 were serving primarily local residents. Two-fifths were located in Windsor (48) and Chester townships (20); and nearly half—46 percent—were located in other Windsor County townships (79).[99]

Entry-level market participation spread throughout the hinterland of Windsor District after 1810. The number of commercial ventures in the seven Windsor District agricultural townships without villages rose sharply (from five in 1810 to twenty-three in 1830), and their share of all firms nearly tripled (from 5 percent to 14 percent). By 1830, most residents of the seven agricultural townships, above the poorest 20 percent of families, participated in commercial exchange. Familiarity with the commercial world and at least minimal consumption of commodities had become a normal part of Upper Valley family experience by the late 1820s. Nearly all inland townships contained at least one stable general store, and several contained a few shops and a factory or two.

While the hinterland of Windsor District entered the commercial exchange economy, the general level of involvement, even in 1830, was still less than that of the village townships a quarter century earlier. In fact, between about 1800 and 1830, much more intensive commercial involvement by village residents caused their lifestyles to diverge rapidly from those of hinterland residents. The four village townships doubled the numbers of firms they contained, from 59 in 1810 to 116 in 1830. Their share of all businesses rose from one-half to two-thirds. The payment and credit system discussed earlier was strengthened by the founding in 1817 of the Bank of Windsor, a branch of the Vermont State Bank. Altogether, nearly 75 percent of all Windsor District families participated annually in some form of commercial exchange in 1830. At least 80 percent of all village township families were involved, plus about 65 percent from the other seven townships. By 1830 the most pronounced difference in the two groups was not in the incidence of at least minimal participation, but in its frequency and variety. In 1830 there was a dramatic difference between living in a hinterland township with an average of three businesses and living in a village community with an average of twenty-nine firms. In nearly every area of commercial exchange, widely unequal access was a basic characteristic within rural life in the first third of the nineteenth century. We need an entirely different way of describing vast differences in participation among living situations within rural commercial societies (see chapter 4).[100]

Between about 1805 and 1835, a new order of rural economic, social and, especially, cultural life was evolving in Windsor District. By 1810, major economic, social, political, religious, and technological changes were under way that directly affected residents of Windsor, Chester, Springfield, and Weathersfield villages and of farmsteads nearby. By the 1820s, the new order of rural life had spread into hinterland hamlets. Reading and writing facilitated its diffusion. By about 1810, the entire edifice of commercial life relied increasingly on one of its own components: the print center with its concentration of printing, publishing, newspaper distribution, and bookselling. By 1810 print centers and post offices had joined district schools and academies as central institutions in a new cultural environment. More regular reading and writing formed the substance of a communications network drawing a large majority of Windsor District's 3,100 households into several new kinds of cultural participation. A major new development in rural life was thus occurring here as throughout the Western world.[101]

Affiliative behavior in rural northwestern New England in 1815 was already deeply affected by commercialization. The proliferation of print culture suffused all aspects of rural participation in public life, gradually giving rise to multiple memberships and collective affiliations. To understand the phenomenon we must look at some of the most familiar developments in early national America, such as antebellum reform, in a slightly different light. More specifically, we must consider how changes in affiliative behavior in a heavily commercialized economy affected cultural relations, and how cultural relations altered daily life.

Printed and written communications fostered vastly increased involvement in public life in Windsor District. Particularly noteworthy was the phenomenon of specific issue petitions, often signed by large numbers of citizens in one or more townships.[102] A more complex interaction between printed and written matter and cultural relations involved joining voluntary organizations. At least seven broad types of "associations" were active locally in the late 1820s.[103] Cultural "societies" included two Windsor District debating clubs, a music society, a theater group, a lyceum, several organized lecture series, and at least ten lending libraries. Educational societies included neighborhood and township district school committees, academy and high school boards, and more temporary writing and penmanship, French, and finishing schools. A third type of association encompassed all active political groups, representing National Republicans, Antimasons, Jacksonians, and Workingmen.[104] Fourth, there were at least two dozen religious societies affiliated with nine different religious denominations active in 1830. All were Protestant. Allied with several denominations was a growing system of Sunday schools.[105]

A fifth variety of association consisted of local branches, and local members in regional branches, of several score of benevolent and humanitarian reform societies, ranging from the Masonic Order and fledgling Antimasonic groups to the Windsor County Temperance Society, Bible Society, and Sunday School Union. A sixth type of organization included an elaborate set of social clubs and militia units. Finally, a number of groups dedicated to material advantage and economic security were active and meeting in 1830. There were shareholder societies for the Windsor Bank and for various bridges, turnpikes, and factories, a Windsor County Farmers' and Mechanics' Association, an area medical society, and a Fire Insurance Company (a Springfield-based shareholder organization). These seven sets of organizations collectively encompassed many of the common concerns most actively pursued in Windsor District after 1815.

The seven leading types of Windsor District voluntary societies were essential elements in rural cultural life, especially after 1815. They assumed such importance because of the increasing role of printed and written communications, which established and sustained such organizations by disseminating notices of their meetings and word of their beliefs and activities. The formation and spread of so many new types of voluntary societies reshaped daily life. Nearly every organized group came to rely on printed matter to communicate with present members and to attract new ones. As a result, an even larger share of Windsor District families became involved in public life, drawn into broader networks of affiliation beyond kin and neighborhood. Multiple affiliation became a normal occurrence.

Change in the texture of cultural life was also evident in many informal and formal public gatherings that had arisen in the first years of Windsor District settlement: quilting and flax-scutching bees, house building, corn husking and other postharvest frolics, tavern and hotel gatherings, general socializing and visiting, Fourth of July celebrations, weddings and funerals, religious society meetings, and political party meetings. Throughout the early settlement era, printed and written communications played a minor role in local public life. Beginning in the 1790s, however, upcoming public activities were announced to a growing newspaper readership throughout Windsor District. Thereafter, the printed word gradually became an indispensable part of information-dissemination, preservation, and social action by nearly all organized groups. Many traditional gatherings, including taverns and hotels and religious and political meetings, became far more print oriented. Reading even became a frequent occurrence at bees and other social gatherings. The penetration of printed and written forms of communication throughout Windsor District life during the early national era, even into traditional rituals of agricultural society, was one major effect of commercialization on cultural life.

A special feature of printed matter was its ability to transmit knowledge into the family circle. Participants in voluntary societies created countless new links between family life and public culture,[106] as residents embraced scores

Corn Husking Frolic. Alvin Fisher, 1828–29. Oil on panel (27¾x24¼ in.). M. and M. Karolik Collection of American Paintings, 1815–1865. Courtesy, Museum of Fine Arts, Boston.

Several rural collective occasions centered about agriculture; one of the most popular was the corn husking frolic.

of special religious, social, political, medical, and intellectual causes, in addition to their advocacy of economic change. An American spirit of "joining" intensified within a very new rural cultural atmosphere. While it segmented society into scores of interest groups, it also created new, more geographically extensive bonds of affiliation based on vertical, special-interest unity rather than horizontal, class-based unity. The result was that many new strands were added to an increasingly intricate web of public community. Moreover, family, kin, and neighborhood bonds were as often strengthened as weakened. Daily life in rural northwestern New England in 1790–1830 was marked by greater involvement in an expanding series of overlapping intellectual communities, on the part of a larger share of all families, especially those living in or near a village or hamlet. Most of these affiliative bonds ironically blurred class-based visions of life and social relations.[107]

Beyond specific issue petitions and associations, general society-wide consideration of the effects of economic change represented another major area of cultural involvement. After 1810, values consonant with marketplace production and consumption—frugality, economy, planning, industry, useful employment, and punctuality—were all regularly described and advocated in rural newspapers.[108] Not surprisingly in view of the character of rural newspapers and their financing, most commentary also supported materialism, acquisitiveness, and a spirit of accumulation.[109] The power of marketplace formulations may be seen in advice to families on economic matters. As an excerpt from Timothy Dwight's *Sermons* put it, parents should teach their children "to fill up their time with useful employments, to methodize it, that it may be thus filled up; and feel that the loss of time, the neglect of talents and the waste of property, are all serious violations of their duty to God." Children raised by Dwight's advice eventually learned "a rational principle of economy: . . . waste no time, or money, or property." Idleness was the worst evil, and a "spirit of gain" took hold among many families.[110]

The most pointed example of the new entrepreneurial tone of the era was the opening of a lottery office, "The People's Mint," in Windsor during January 1830. Z.B. Glazier's sole aim was to keep "constantly for sale, Tickets in most of the popular Lotteries in the United States." Lotteries were appropriately called "schemes." Advertisements often displayed an ancient symbol of the richness of the New World—two female angels with cornucopias. An attached poem specifically appealed to the unlucky solid citizen, the aged, the unfortunate, and the failing. Interest in lotteries developed in a cultural context marked by a sustained challenge to traditional republican and Protestant values, which had stressed the moral dangers inherent in commercial activity.[111]

Between about 1805 and 1835, Windsor District residents commented on a series of new topics and issues surrounding the role of commerce in life. The leading new topic of discussion in 1830 in both Windsor papers, the *Repub-*

lican and Journal and the *Chronicle*, was the need to upgrade the network of transportation and communications connecting the Upper Valley with other parts of the Northeast. The worst fate for the Upper Valley, argued scores of observers, was to be left behind in the regional integration of economic life. The widening of the Connecticut River, the start of steamboat service between Hartford, Connecticut, and Barnet, Vermont, and the laying of a rail line between Boston and Lake Champlain were much discussed by distinct groups of advocates of enhanced trade and "communication." Related topics were canal development and the use of steamboats elsewhere in the country. Fairly regular reports of steamboat explosions around the country inspired doubts about their safety, but a greater number of pieces described striking advances in steamboat and rail travel here and in England.[112]

Manufacturing and mining formed a second frequently discussed subject. Citizens closely followed both American and British industrial developments. Science, technology, inventions other than the steamboat and railroad, and the resulting specialization in work skills formed yet a third important topical area. A new "spirit of Fact," presenting aspects of the physical world divorced from all spiritual and moral contexts, permeated public dialogue in the 1820s. Chemistry and physics were its favored forms of expression. The two local newspapers were also filled with news and some essays about regional trade, finances, markets (including monthly reports of prices current at Boston), banks and banking, the Sabbath mail controversy, and the Vermont State Prison's production system and retail store.[113]

As a new order of rural life developed in Windsor District, two attitudes toward it emerged, one largely positive toward rural life and the other predominantly negative. For convenience I shall refer to them as "the entrepreneurial ethos" and "the new rural critique of commercial society." The entrepreneurial ethos strongly endorsed a mixed-sector exchange system (farming and grazing, commerce, and manufacturing) based on currency and credit payment. Frugality, saving, and economy were advocated as essential living skills. Speed, accuracy, and currency in the circulation of knowledge were much prized. Order, uniformity, regularity, promptness, and timeliness in business dealings were consistently lauded. Temperance was frequently stressed as a capstone ideal.[114] By the late 1810s, the entrepreneurial ethos was being diffused throughout the villages and nearby farmsteads, and with spreading newspaper circulation was moving through the hinterland hamlets of rural New England, and on into inland farming and grazing areas.

Countering this assessment was a rural critique of commercial and early industrial society. It emerged as a dialogue about the effects of a heavily commercialized economy on particular social and economic groups, especially "mechanics" and "the laboring classes."[115] In the *Republican and Journal* during 1830, general interest in the "mechanick question" was considerable, averaging a piece a week. Two pictures of the typical mechanic took shape. The first, kindhearted picture assumed that hard labor kept most mechanics ill informed but that otherwise they were an important contributing force in American society as long as they stayed away from organized political action, intemperance, infidelity, and freethought.[116] An alternative picture ridiculed and dismissed mechanics and other members of the laboring classes as ignorant, lazy (rather than industrious), poor because they spent idle time in drinking and infidelity, and certainly incompetent to engage in serious political participation. Mechanics were also alleged to be enamored of atheism and freethought.[117]

The rural debate over the role of mechanics and the laboring classes in Jacksonian society was a major intellectual development because it concerned the new order and because it addressed the place of new and potentially troublesome groups in rural life. Still perceived as a fairly small minority in 1830, mechanics and the laboring classes were the first groups of white male adult Americans for whom toil did not bring land, the traditional reward of an agricultural society. Few of the old agrarian pieties appeared to apply to mechanics and other members of the laboring classes. Public discourse only offered them practical consolation: that they were part of a major economic and social transformation, that it incorporated many facets of life, and that they must accept their fate.

The state of American life was a profoundly political topic by the late 1820s. The early writings of Orestes Brownson reveal a newer second current of more radical views prevalent among some of "the laboring classes."[118] Brownson, who was born and raised in Windsor County, had himself been a day laborer and then an apprentice and journeyman printer as a young man in 1815–25. In a series of essays and letters published during 1830, Brownson proclaimed that the condition of the laboring classes, including "farmers, mechanicks, and workingmen," should be central in any consideration of rural economy and society. Brownson wished to create a new sense of community, "entwined with the cords of fraternal affection" and premised on "the greatest happiness of the greatness numbers." His specific aim was equality in the apportionment of the material benefits of life. For Brownson, equality meant "one laboring no more for another than that other labors for him." For Brownson government was not the most critical locus of necessary changes; Americans held too much confidence in the power of government. From his perspective, the form of government was less important than its effects on the laboring classes. Presently, far too much power was claimed by "a monied aristocracy," and "a few monopolists," specifically a motley collection of lawyers, "stockjobbers," "priests," "authors," and officials of government.[119] For this reason, Brownson's specific proposals centered on changes in the legal system.[120] Brownson's perspective was a slightly more coherent form of the views of the Woodstock Workingmen's Society and the *Working-Man's Gazette*, established in 1830.[121]

The extent to which most local mechanics and members of the laboring classes were aware of the emerging critique of a new rural commercial and early industrial society remains unclear.[122] Aside from a few publications with limited circulation, most available reading matter contained no serious critiques of the new order of commercial life. We do not know what inferences about their economic situation mechanics and members of the laboring classes drew from their own lived experience. We do know that, by the mid-1820s, class-based social action was spreading within Windsor District. But we also know that at least two other sets of circumstances intervened to limit class-based analysis and action. First, many members of Windsor District society were engaged in other kinds of affiliative behavior and turned their attention to other matters which deflected interest in class-based affiliations. Second, the real economic advances of the 1820s and early 1830s led most farmers, artisans, and laborers to expect that the further spread of trade, industry, and commercial farming and grazing would soon raise their standard of living. Before the mid-1830s, the mirage of unlimited economic growth arrested the advance of class-based analysis. Only with the economic downturn of the mid-1830s did mainstream public opinion shift to a far more pessimistic outlook about the economic future of the Upper Valley. By the late 1830s, a severe depression increased open discussion of class relations in the public press.[123]

Perceptions of class differences were growing in the Early Republic and almost inevitably became widespread after 1815.[124] Perceptions were not tantamount to action, however. Class-based activities were only one of several kinds of public involvement born of the widening habits of reading and writing. Each organization created a distinctive pattern of affiliative behavior, forging bonds of affinity among families and individuals who otherwise might have remained strangers. The rural weeklies and soon the religious press functioned as a quasi-public, society-wide bulletin board, informing readers of several new types of public community.[125] As a result, a series of distinctive living situations or human habitats arose within rural society. In each living situation an interrelated cluster of interest and participation thrived. These are the building blocks of a new history of rural economic life. A broad conception is essential because unity around economic interests was frequently blunted by competing religious, political, intellectual, social, and geographical interests.

The transformation of rural New England society in 1780–1835, entailing far more complex interaction between material and cultural conditions of life than the centuries preceding or following this era, offers a fascinating laboratory for research extending but also modifying earlier Marxist formulations. In periods of civilization-wide transformation, like that in which rural New

Englanders lived after the Revolution, materialism is weakest as a comprehensive theory of history.[126]

Conclusions

The basic material and cultural ecology in Windsor District was transformed in the last third of the eighteenth century and the first third of the nineteenth century. The growth of the market sector of the economy, especially after 1795, year by year made available greater quantities of a larger variety of products (including printed matter) and touched a greater share of homestead material and cultural needs. The political economy of an earlier republican order, along with its range of understandings, was fading as commercialization raised a series of novel issues. These latter included the direction of economic growth; the nature of commercial economy, society, and culture; and the effects on various groups of living in a fully commercialized rural world marked by widespread lifelong learning. Between 1780 and 1810, the material conditions of life changed far more rapidly than shared understanding of them. Older republican formulations were stretched and stretched again to encompass the changing economy of the Early Republic.[127] Thereafter cultural discussion progressed rapidly, catching up with, and in some areas surging ahead of, the material realities in question. In a historiographical context, both sets of changes, material and cultural, occurred earlier and progressed much further in the forest society of rural northwestern New England than previously has been assumed.[128]

Participation in commercial exchange and the several new forms of community it created helped to integrate major societal institutions—family, neighborhood, township, economic locale, and region. No household was compelled to engage in commerce, though the cost of resistance rose each year.[129] Far cheaper prices, a constant supply of better-quality goods, and the seduction of "fashion" captured many rural adherents.[130] After 1800, basic improvements in farm implements and tools for general use came rapidly: iron ploughs, iron lock coulters, shovels made entirely from iron, scythes, hay and manure forks, cheese presses, churns, cradles, and sleighs with metal runners.[131] Commerce yielded debits as well as credits, but contemporaries found it far more difficult to comprehend slow losses than fast gains. Between 1760 and 1810, the Upper Valley farmstead was characterized by enormous diversity, and its inhabitants by their striking versatility. Intensification of commerce gradually increased specialization of work skills. As crops and other goods produced in the household became less acceptable as direct forms of payment, families were often forced to produce some salable commodity. Once it had been established, the currency and credit economy steadily tightened its grip.[132]

Participation in commercial exchange constituted one of the three or four

Windsor, Vermont: Armory and Machine Shop in the Mid-nineteenth Century.
Stereoview. Courtesy of Special Collections, University of Vermont Library,
Burlington, Vermont.

By the late 1820s machine shops had developed at Windsor and by the early 1840s
Windsor District was a center of machine tooling.

broadest ways of reinvigorating community life during the half century following the Revolution. Economic advancement was widely touted as a major
route of escape from idleness and evil ways. As a result, material accumulation
made rapid progress as a society-wide ideal. Acquisitiveness, felt as a constant
lack, and the need for more material goods grew, along with their offspring,
anxiety. These traits had their greatest impact in the third stage of commercialization, which occurred between 1815 and 1835. But the road from steady
maintenance—an ideal epitomized by the concept of "mending"—to constant
acquisitiveness had been constructed during the three decades after the Revolu-

tion. By the late 1810s an entrepreneurial ethos, marked by regular commercial exchange and an increasingly acquisitive spirit, emerged as a basic personality trait in Upper Valley families.[133]

The economy of rural New England presented an immensely complex picture between 1760 and 1835. Farms and families were only two among several important parts of a rich scene. By 1810, a "fundamental and permanent alteration" in the basic structure of "preindustrial society" was well under way in the Upper Valley and was especially pronounced in Windsor District.[134] Daily life was vastly transformed in the process. In the economic sphere, integration occurred within a wide range of institutions linked to local and international markets through a regional network of transportation and communications. This network provided the foundation for a commercially based printed and written information system that accelerated the diffusion of knowledge throughout villages, hamlets, and their environs, and deep into the hinterland of Windsor District.

Paralleling commercialization, which helped create a new economic and social order in the years 1780–1835, was the changing network of communications, the other equally fundamental aspect of a great transformation within rural life. The highly prized ideal of citizen awareness—defined by the speed, accuracy, regularity, and currency of one's knowledge about the world—was one of its main effects. This forward-looking, process-oriented attitude was geared as much to change as to continuity. By the early 1830s, perceptions of the widely unequal distribution of the new order's benefits had fostered serious opposition to the main direction of economic, social, and political change. Print culture had described differences in wealth, power, and culture in greater detail and rendered them much more visible.

The commercialization of rural society and the enrichment of the communications network also created many competing patterns of affiliation based on interests other than class unity. The emergence of reading as a necessity of life, of lifelong learning, and of a relish for knowledge diminished solidarity among economic and social groups sharing similar material conditions of life. The use of print and written communications led to a rich tapestry of multiple affiliations and provided new ways to escape problems via inward voyages.

Fierce competition for the minds, hearts, and actions of Windsor District residents marked the years between 1825 and 1850.[135] Many individuals sought human happiness chiefly in pursuits unrelated to restructuring rural economic, social, and political relations. In a communications environment overflowing with choices for participation, attention was easily diverted from economic issues in this new generation. Only in times of economic crisis would class unity become strong enough to arrest the dispersion of interest. Deflection of time and energy away from material survival and livelihood and into multiple religious, social, political, and cultural interests was a leading characteristic of the new rural world of the early nineteenth century. Materialist approaches to the history of this era deal persuasively with occurrences in the province of their chief interest. Transformation in other dimensions of life can no longer be ignored or minimized; they too were essential elements in rural infrastructure. Material and cultural life were intimately entwined in creating a rich new rural world.

Chapter 3

The Foundations of Participation
in Rural New England Culture, 1760–1835

By the same system [learning to read, and write, and keep
accounts], too, they acquire a thirst after knowledge (we do not
allude particularly to their importunity in questioning strangers).
— *Philadelphia Analectic Magazine* (1817)

Upper Valley Cultural Expression:
The Place of Print Communications

Between 1760 and 1835, as we have seen, commercial exchange networks deeply
affected the course of daily life. To further understand the relationships between material conditions and cultural life, we must first consider the incidence and bases of participation in print culture.[1]

During the Early Republic six distinct but occasionally overlapping forms
of public cultural expression existed in the Upper Valley. Each was linked with
a specific set of communications skills: (1) printed matter, utilizing the skill of
reading; (2) oral expression, which involved talking, listening, understanding,
and, for some people, the further skill of public speaking; (3) visual expression,
focused on seeing, patterning, and comprehending, and, for some people, the
skill of making and creating visual objects entailing conscious human design
as an important aspect; (4) music and singing; (5) written forms of expression,
resulting from development of the skill of writing beyond the ability to sign
one's name and the skill of reading; and (6) theater and dance. By adulthood,
nearly all residents possessed a sufficient combination of the six sets of cultural
skills to participate at least indirectly in several dimensions of expression, so
that they lived richer lives.[2]

Because we live in a media-rich age, historians of print and written literacy
often have underestimated the breadth of human communications ability in
past societies and so, when they have considered it at all, have also underestimated broad participation in cultural life.[3] The term "the study of the inarticu-
late" has come to be used as if the "masses" in question either remained silent

and uncommunicative or, if they expressed themselves, communicated only feebly or explosively. The recent impact of anthropology on history has re-shaped many previous assumptions. We now know that talking and listening, singing and playing, and visualizing formed the primary ways of communicating cultural information and values throughout early America. For many historians it has come as a revelation that sophisticated knowledge of the self and the world was possible outside the Republic of Letters.[4]

Within the broad spectrum of ways in which Upper Valley residents expressed themselves and communicated with each other, the place of print culture was substantial. Writing and reading were frequently paired in daily life. Writing was a crucial source of self-expression. Reading was a great source of knowledge, new and old, for a population living in a forest society on the northwestern fringe of Anglo-American civilization. An inevitable tension existed between widely shared and more restricted kinds of cultural participation. A small core of ideas reached all families across all living situations in the Upper Valley. Even the most unique and eccentric characters and prophets of the age—the Pilgrims and Dorrilites, Joseph Smith, Orestes Brownson, and John Humphrey Noyes—initially held a broad world view in common with the Upper Valley's most ordinary, "passive" residents. All initially stood on the same foundation of beliefs and values. The rural Christian republican version of the wisdom of the ages encoded the world in a set of cultural symbols learned in childhood at home and reinforced by the Bible, hymnals, psalm books, prayer books, the *New England Primer*, Webster's *Speller*, district school readers, arithmetics, and geographies. These works reflected a fundamental stock of knowledge about this world and the next, and certain traditional interpretations of its meaning. To Lawrence Cremin, one of the most perceptive recent interpreters, there existed "an authentic American vernacular in education that proffered a popular paideia compounded of evangelical pieties, democratic hopes, and utilitarian strivings" and wrapped in a fervent nationalism.[5]

Nearly all residents of rural New England acquired this shared core of meaning primarily by talking and listening but also by singing and music, visual expression, and dance and ritual procession. Print and written media deepened their knowledge and helped to integrate it. Most residents learned their stablest values and beliefs from complex combinations of the six major media, each of which expressed the fundamental set of identifiable assumptions and values. Painters, lawyers, writers, musicians, farmers, artisans, and semiskilled laborers all incorporated this wisdom, which formed an initial common ground of language and feeling in the Early Republic. Other forms of cultural expression are discussed in appendix 1.

The core of knowledge absorbed during childhood and youth usually remained with Upper Valley residents throughout their lives. But each mode of cultural expression also contributed new knowledge and evaluations of life.

Solitary individuals expressed their peculiar visions of the stars' powers to shape human fate. Communities of learners emphasized specialized traditions of knowledge particular to a single mode of expression. Much wider communities of learners shared broad intellectual interests, themes, and creations that involved several forms of expression. Moreover, while a traditional core of knowledge and interpretation remained dominant culture-wide in 1760–1835, ever larger collections of families and individuals lived their lives and expressed themselves through intellectual traditions far removed from those in which their intellectual germination occurred. Cultural variety in oral and written forms, in visual and print media, and in dance, singing, and music was an essential characteristic of Upper Valley life in the half century following the Revolution. In fact, talking and listening, singing and playing, and visualizing have remained the primary means of sharing the human condition throughout the history of the Western world. Reading and writing altered the fund of knowledge drawn on in oral communication, and this had profound consequences for human action in the Upper Valley. Reading and writing as cultural acts, however, must always be understood to have been adjuncts to talking and listening for most human beings in early national America.[6]

Elsewhere I have studied in detail the bases of participation in print and written culture in the Upper Valley during 1760–1835. Trends were traced in the rate of acquisition of elementary literacy, defined primarily as the ability to read and calculate and to a lesser extent as the ability to write, and in the method by which literacy skills were attained, primarily at home and in district schools during childhood and youth. Like Sweden, another rural fringe area of the Western world, the American Northeast in the eighteenth century saw rapid expansion in the ability to read, from one generation to the next and by both males and females. Especially in New England, mass literacy was sustained by an ongoing program of active reading, that catered to an acquired thirst for knowledge, including "current" information. This trend represented a crucial society-wide expansion in the traditional uses of literacy skills. It apparently pushed cultural life in New England beyond the limits of the traditional culture, in contrast to the case in Sweden, where the intensive reading style, with its primary emphasis on maintaining Lutheran theology and religious practice as the sacred wisdom of the ages, continued to dominate print communications into the 1840s.[7]

By 1800 in rural northwestern New England, the overwhelming majority of both male and female adults, untouched by the process of urbanization under way to the south, had learned to read and write in their childhood or youth. The large majority of these, three-quarters to four-fifths, continued to participate in print communications throughout the remainder of their lives, circumstances permitting. By 1800 nearly two-thirds of all Windsor District families retained a family library past the death of the household head. Others

Family Scene with Newspaper. Albert Alden Proof Book. Printed version first used on masthead of the *Boston Notion*, 19 Dec. 1840. Engraved by David C. Johnston. Courtesy, American Antiquarian Society.

Appearing just below this scene of family reading are the words, "A family paper." Between 1780 and 1830 regular reading in the family circle encompassed an ever wider array of printed matter.

read serial and situation-specific printed matter that was not customarily saved for long: weekly newspapers and yearly almanacs. Equally consequential, the balance of reading matter had by 1800–1810 already shifted decisively from sacred to secular content, even leaving aside all elementary level schoolbooks and primers. In addition, the overall balance had also shifted, from printed matter customarily read in an intensive reading style and dedicated to the preservation of accepted truths, to styles that for the first time were adopted beyond elite families: reading as a means of escape and fantasy and as a way to obtain "information" and knowledge, especially about this world and its "more remote parts."[8]

Changing uses of literacy and shifts in reading habits and uses of knowledge throughout a whole society have not yet been traced in the history of cultural life.[9] This is especially the case concerning the active participation of a large share of all females. The attainment of active mass literacy introduced an ever wider readership to an infinite series of what Thoreau so aptly termed "inward voyages," some routine and others filled with adventure. Print communications were integral to the emergence of modern civilization in America and throughout the Western world. The American Northeast, 1780–1835, constituted the first rural society in which a new "sixth sense" of human understanding and communication with others[9] triumphed over the previously fixed limits imposed by geography, transportation, occupation, wealth, and sparseness of population. In particular, the degree to which women achieved and maintained literacy establishes this period as a profoundly important one for women's lives and consciousness during the next century. Growing knowledge and awareness of the way the world worked and active involvement in issues of the day comprised major advances in the consciousness of rural New England women.[10]

Trends in the Acquisition of Elementary Literacy in the Upper Valley

The *Philadelphia Analectic Magazine* surveyed the state of American intellectual life in several fields during the years following the peace at Ghent. When it reviewed "Systems of Elementary Education" in April 1817, only New England received sustained praise for the attention to basic education its residents "uniformly pursued":

> Our readers must hear for perhaps the five hundredth time—that there is scarcely an adult individual in all New England who cannot read, and write, and keep accounts. All these operations must be performed almost every day of their lives: and, among the other sources of independence, we may even enumerate this, that they are not under the continual necessity of running to others for what reading and writing and cyphering they may wish to have done. By the same system, too, they acquire a thirst after knowledge (we do not allude particularly to their importunity in questioning strangers); and in almost every considerable neighbourhood there are circulating libraries of useful books, which have been purchased conjointly by the inhabitants. But, what is perhaps of more consequence than all the rest, the sober habits of industry which some children acquire by a spirit of rivalry, and which others have beat into them by a twig of beech, give them an early determination to labour, which never after forsakes them. And when we add to all these causes the absolute necessity of working, or of starving, we shall not be at a loss to account for the intelligence and enterprise for which they are so deservedly celebrated.[11]

Elementary literacy, meaning instruction in the skills of reading, writing, and arithmetic, and the inculcation of a corresponding fund of knowledge about the world, is an essential prolegomenon to a new cultural history. Literacy patterns permit us to follow the actual spread of older or newer structures of knowledge communicated through print and written matter. For reading, writing, and arithmetic alone, among all the cultural skills possessed by rural New Englanders, do we presently have sufficient evidence to follow their acquisition and maintenance throughout most of the population. Instruction usually began at home and was then continued in other public institutions, especially schools. People living in the Upper Valley in 1760–1835 usually were neither literate nor illiterate all of their lives. Basic literacy skills usually were acquired during childhood and early youth, between the ages of four and eighteen, and then either were developed further through practice or languished through disuse.[12]

To test for the maintenance of elementary literacy throughout as many age groups beyond childhood and early youth as possible, I analyzed Upper Valley (and wherever possible Windsor District) account books, deeds, selected township petitions to the state legislature, and wills. A multiple-moment life-stage research design, intended to capture all possible variations throughout the life cycle, was employed.[13] Tables 3–1 and 3–2 summarize the findings. Among stages of life, very wide though not complete coverage of all males in adulthood and old age was achieved. For females, the sources provided evidence for only 41 percent and 44 percent of all adult women (with or without property) living in Plymouth and Cavendish during 1778–1830. A few widows had sold land; typically, wives and their husbands had done so. For the five townships where all deeds recorded in 1760–1830 were canvassed, signs or marks were located for all married females with substantial land sales. These accounted for about 40 percent of all females over the age of seventeen. Signs and marks on wills could also be located for a small proportion of additional female household heads (including some elderly females), almost none of whom was engaged in land sales and many of whom were quite poor. Not all adult and elderly females appear in the sources, but the group studied includes the largest proportion of the female population for which evidence exists beyond a single township in the American Northeast through 1830. The four categories encompass all known sources containing an extensive group of useful signs and marks of Windsor District male and female residents through 1830.[14]

The evidence makes it plain that both male and female elementary literacy rose to extraordinary heights, within the context of North Atlantic civilization, throughout the half century following the Revolution. The two most reliable sources of literacy rates are will makers and deed signers and cosigners. Among will makers, the overall male signing rate was 97 percent. For females the rate was 70 percent (see table 3–1). Among deed makers, the male signing rate was 97 percent and the female, 82 percent.

Trends in elementary literacy in 1760–1830 reveal that exceptionally high basic literacy among males (higher than 85 percent) was achieved by the mid-1770s and was sustained through 1830 in all but the most isolated, least populated, latest settled, and mountainous segments of Windsor District. Even the bottom 20 percent of the wealth structure is present, but it is thinly represented in all sources. Nevertheless, if only half of this group had acquired the

Table 3-1: Male and Female Elementary Literacy in the Upper Valley, 1760–1851

Sources (n=10,463)	Years Covered	Stages of Life Included	Coverage by Gender Males (n=9,584) Females (n=879)	Overall Literacy Rates	
				Males	Females
1. Account Book Customers of Stores and Shops (n=1,445)	1755–1851	All adulthood and old age	98.5% male (n=1,420) 1.5% female (n=21)	99.2%	76 %
2. a. Deed Signers and Cosigners (n=5,300)	1760–1830	All adulthood and some old age	87.6% males (n=4,642) 12.4% females (n=658)	96.8%	82.1%
b. Additional Deed Signers and Cosigners (n=591)	1761–1829	All adulthood and some old age	93.2% males (n=551) 6.8% females (n=40)	99.1%	95 %
3. Township Petitioners to the State Legislature (n=2,275)	1766–1830	All adulthood and some old old age	99.6% males (n=2,266) .4% females (n=9)	99.8%	88.9%
4. Will Makers and Witnesses (n=856)	1787–1830	All adulthood but weighted toward old age	82.4% males (n=705) 17.6% females (n=151)	98.4%	91.1%
a. Will Makers (n=225)			83.6% males (n=188) 16.4% females (n=37)	96.8%	70.3%
b. Witnesses (n=631)			81.9% males (n=517) 18.1% females (n=114)	99 %	96.5%

Source: Adapted from Gilmore, "Elementary Literacy."

ability to read and write, the overall adjusted male rates would still range between 85 and 89 percent. This is the minimum total male literacy rate for the entire population of Windsor District. Only twice in all sources did the male rate drop as low as 85 percent, and then it did so only for very brief periods in the most isolated communities in Windsor District. Otherwise, the rate

Table 3–2: Elementary Literacy for Deeds: Windsor District Communities, 1760–1830

Community	Females		Males	
	Number	*Percent*	*Number*	*Percent*
Windsor	270	86	1,658	98
Cavendish	147	86	937	98
Reading	127	75	1,170	96
Plymouth	55	71	481	92
Weston	59	83	396	97

Source: Adapted from Gilmore, "Elementary Literacy." Graphs 4–8.

never fell below 93 percent or, when adjusted, 85 percent. Literacy was not universal, even for males, in northwestern New England through the early national era.[15]

Female rates, while varying more than male levels (60 to 96 percent), were even more striking in the comparative context of North Atlantic civilization. In fact, as with male rates, women in the Upper Valley were second to Sweden within the North Atlantic in the achievement of literacy through 1830. If we assume that just half of the lowest 20 percent of females ranked by wealth acquired the ability to read and write, the overall adjusted female rate still reached a minimum of 58 percent by the late 1770s, 66 percent by the late 1780s, and 70 percent by the early 1790s; thereafter the rate fluctuated between 70 and 82 percent (1792–1830). According to the unadjusted rates, as indicated by detailed evidence, elementary literacy rates for Windsor District women rose from approximately three-fifths in the late 1770s to three-quarters by the late 1780s and, after considerable fluctuation between 74 and 91 percent over the next two decades (1792–1811), stabilized at an extraordinarily high level of about 85 percent for 1812–30 (see graphs 3–1 and 3–2). Female literacy rates across North Atlantic civilization, except in Sweden, were rarely more than half that rate.[16]

Agents of Literacy—Family and District School

The Upper Valley was a remarkably special rural environment well before the first stage of the Industrial Revolution had even gained a toehold in the area. In rural northwestern New England there were four primary ways to acquire elementary literacy skills during the Early Republic: through parental and peer instruction in the home during childhood; through the district school system during childhood and youth, the prevalent initiatory phase of formal

Graph 3-1: Elementary Literacy for Windsor District Townships,
1761-1830: Deed Signatures

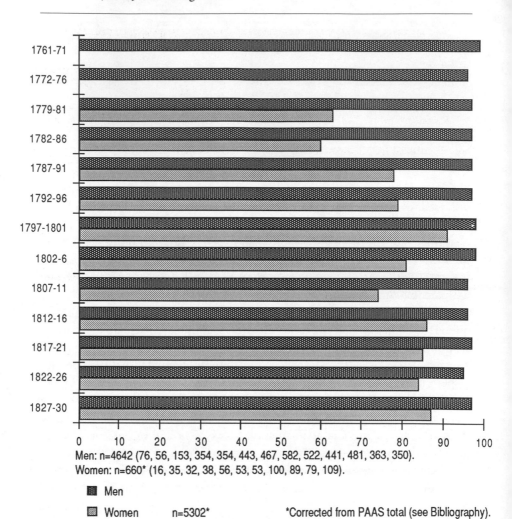

Men: n=4642 (76, 56, 153, 354, 354, 443, 467, 582, 522, 441, 481, 363, 350).
Women: n=660* (16, 35, 32, 38, 56, 53, 53, 100, 89, 79, 109).

▨ Men

▨ Women   n=5302*   *Corrected from PAAS total (see Bibliography).

enculturation throughout the Upper Valley; through the Sunday school system, once it had become established in this area shortly after 1815; and through
one or another institution or occupation affording instructional opportunities
for youth (in apprenticeships) and adults who had not acquired these skills.[17]
Not all skills were taught in each of the four situations. Home instruction usually began with singing and the basics of spelling, reading, and grammar. Its
content centered on the cultivation of conscience; after the Revolution, conscience was habitually described in metaphors drawn from the world of printing and writing (slates, impressions, engravings, imprinting, and so forth). The
Sunday school system emphasized reading (especially oral reading), together

Material and Cultural Foundations

Graph 3-2: Elementary Literacy, Windsor District, Vermont, 1787-1830: Will Makers and Witnesses

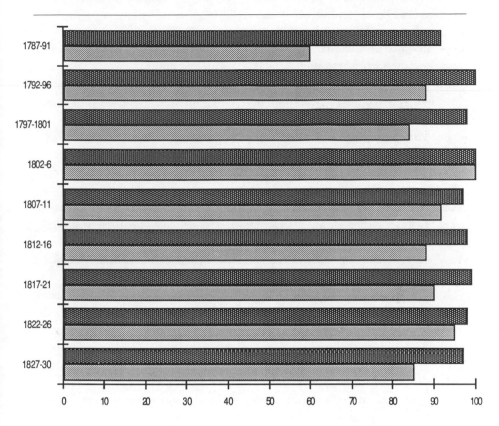

Men: n=712* (28, 33, 78*, 75, 99, 98, 120, 105, 76)
Women: n=151 (5, 9, 19, 17, 25, 18, 20, 24, 14)
Source: All wills and supporting documents, Windsor County Probate Court, Windsor District, 1787-1830.

▨ Men

▨ Women   n=863*   *Corrected from PAAS total (see Bibliography).

with memorization and rote recitation; Sunday schools normally offered no writing instruction. Adult education classes (offered at night) and occupation-based literacy were far more practical and functional in intent and results. The most popular text in both situations was George Fisher's *The Instructor, or The American Young Man's Best Companion.*[18]

Education was the childhood topic most widely discussed in the Upper Valley through 1830. Education—that is, learning that occurred between ages four and twelve or thirteen—was regarded as the central task of childhood. At home, the two most frequently used types of books for early education were the primer and the speller; in summer schools spellers dominated, and in winter schools readers were favored. Advertisements and "accounts of stock" of Upper Valley bookstores in 1780–1830 reveal that thousands of primers (the *New England Primer* and variants) and spellers (Dilworth's dominated until the mid-1790s, when Webster's overtook it) were sold every year, wholesale and retail, in each print center. Education was pursued in summer and winter schools, sometimes intermittently, and continued at home.[19]

Promotion of literacy in the rhetoric of childhood education was apparently quite effective.[20] An elaborate district school system had evolved in the Upper Valley by the 1790s. In both New Hampshire and Vermont Valley counties, schools were organized into local districts that roughly represented rural neighborhoods. Each township within Windsor District established an astounding number of neighborhood school districts (between eight and seventeen during 1770–1830); the process began fairly soon after settlement. The more detailed previous study of elementary literacy found that there was a teacher for every 100–110 inhabitants. While school attendance was entirely voluntary, a sizable majority of all parents in two rural Vermont communities, where detailed daily attendance evidence survives, sent their children to school quite regularly; two-thirds of all "scholars" attended about 80 percent of all classes.[21]

It is important to understand the process of education within the Upper Valley district school system in 1790–1830, including both the sequence in which skills were developed and the content of the lessons taught. Exactly what was learned with the acquisition of elementary literacy? Pupils first learned the fundamental ability to "read, write and keep accounts." The way in which these skills were learned, at least in rural New England, differed markedly from the English pattern discussed by Roger Schofield and other writers. Rather than reading, signing, and writing in a lengthy sequence that extended over months if not years, Upper Valley students began to learn and practice all three skills within weeks of entering the district school curriculum.

Signing one's name, written letter and word formation, oral pronunciation of letters and words, spelling, and elementary reading (first of sentences and then of short paragraphs) were introduced quickly—within 20–30 school days. Moreover, as instruction proceeded, basic grammar, writing (of what was being learned), and further reading were introduced. Arithmetic and geography were added soon thereafter, as the scope of knowledge extended beyond religion and moral maxims and tales into concern for the contemporary world. Knowledge quickly accumulated in two well-understood areas, the sacred and the secular. The wisdom of the ages and of this temporal life, as it was understood in rural New England in 1780–1830, encompassed both. From this point forward, substance and method were largely inseparable, and the level of educational attainment and skill development was a function of a complex of factors, including attendance, basic intelligence, desire to learn, perseverance, classroom atmosphere, quality of instruction, and family and community support.

Schoolhouse Exterior. Plymouth, Vermont. Courtesy, Vermont Historical Society.
   Photographed in the 1880s, this is a typical district schoolhouse of the early national era.

Although many schoolbooks were discarded, some were saved in Windsor District libraries, especially those purchased close to the date of the inventory listing. Nearly a third (29 percent, or 116 of 396) of all Windsor District family libraries contained schoolbooks. Altogether 380 such volumes were retained, 8 percent of the 4,620 specified volumes. Their quantities and variety offer a detailed map of Upper Valley schoolbook use. An Upper Valley resident through 1830, with some initial home education plus attendance in a summer school and normal attendance for at least two terms at a district winter school, would have learned more than we might guess. First, he or she would learn the skill of signing (if it had not previously been learned at home) and some general ability to write—at least enough to compose a letter. Through about

Schoolhouse Interior. Waitsfield, Vermont. Courtesy, Vermont Historical Society.
This view of an unexceptional district schoolroom, from mountainous Washington County, shows the spare environment of neighborhood elementary education.

1805, the share of families engaging in writing declined more rapidly throughout the remainder of the life cycle than did the share using reading and numerical skills. While it is presently impossible to estimate the actual proportion of the Upper Valley population through 1830 who could write, writing activity as measured by adult letter writing appears to have increased significantly between 1805 and 1830.[22]

Second were acquired a reasonable ability to read and knowledge of grammar sufficient to permit the reader to understand the family's yearly almanac, some of the contents of a rural newspaper, and other basic books and pamphlets, especially the Bible, hymnals, songbooks, devotional tracts, prayer books, schoolbooks, elementary level geographies, histories, some light fiction, poetry, short essays, and popular tracts of various sorts. These types of works were those read most frequently by the Upper Valley reading public later in life. Third, the basic stock of knowledge acquired from home and school (peers, parents, schoolbooks, and teacher) was, at the end of home and school instruction, heavily weighted toward the wisdom of the ages, but it also included some secular information about contemporary life. The mix included arithmetic, moral precepts, geography, rudimentary political economy, history, a smattering of excerpts from English and European literary classics, considerable understanding of basic Protestant religious beliefs, and a smattering of church history. As knowledge and skills progressed above this level through further reading, the proportion of the population that participated actively in print culture declined somewhat but not substantially. Since nearly two-thirds of all families with inventories kept a library in 1780–1830 and newspaper reading was increasingly widespread, it is likely that by about 1810–15 nearly three-quarters of all families included active readers.[23]

Elementary Literacy—Pace and Motives

Mass literacy and "an early reading tradition" were established in northwestern New England, which was, like Sweden, "a preindustrial, agrarian, developing country" prior to the onset of the rural phase of the Industrial Revolution. Beyond extremely high overall adjusted literacy rates for males by the mid-1770s (85 percent) and for females by the early 1790s (70 percent), Windsor District's eleven townships differed significantly in the pace at which they achieved mass literacy. To classify types of townships, I adapted several existing typologies of preindustrial American communities, e.g., Edward Cook's, and added several other factors, especially position within the communications system and relative access to print and written culture. Analyzing five of Windsor District's eleven townships in detail, I found that higher levels of elementary literacy followed directly on the heels of five interlocking developments. First was a broad-based ideological "push" (as Egil Johansson termed it) for mass literacy in the Early Republic, which was especially prevalent in New England, for example, as compared with southern New Jersey or rural Pennsylvania. Second was a clustering of population in villages and hamlets. Closely related was a quickening pace of economic life in and near these settlements, bringing with it greater concentrations of wealth and public involvement in a broader range of occupations—more transactions involving a greater proportion of all families. A fourth factor was expanded schooling. And a fifth was more concentrated distribution of a greater variety of printed and written matter, entailing wider access to writing implements and paper via the communications network and institutions relying on it, such as print centers, newspapers, district schools, and academies.[24]

From its earliest stage, commercialization—understood in the broad sense as encompassing changes in cultural and social relations as well as in economic exchange—was the most important motive for expanding literacy and maintaining it through lifelong reading. The market economy required more frequent use of elementary literacy skills (see chapter 2), but a careful look at the Windsor District pattern of spreading literacy reveals that market expansion was not the sole reason for rising literacy rates. Ideological support for extending literacy, population density, access to schooling and other institutions, and the expansion of print culture also played an important role. Rural northwestern New England was in the tightening grip of market economic activity by the early 1790s, and the establishment of district schools paralleled the spread of that activity. But in Green Mountain townships (for example, in Plymouth), local schools preceded all other factors, including local market activity.

Market transactions were regularly recorded in blotters, daybooks, and ledgers of family accounts. The spread of market activity required citizens to be reasonably educated—able to read, to calculate, and to sign their names, if not to write. Moreover, books, pamphlets, newspapers, almanacs, periodicals, sheet music, and other broadsides were among the first market commodities to circulate throughout the Upper Valley. The general spread of market exchange and the specific enticement of print commodities strongly reinforced the rise of mass literacy among both males and females.

Work (occupation), wealth, and their manifestations in economic production, consumption, and exchange also combined with community type and access to print and written communications to shape a range of living environments. Living situations in the hinterland of Windsor District diversified between 1760 and 1830, encouraging people to initiate and sustain participation in print culture. They did so by purchasing broadsides, almanacs, chapbooks, and other printed items, some of which they retained in family libraries; by borrowing reading matter both formally and informally; and by subscribing to weekly newspapers. Wherever there was a substantial lag in village and hamlet development—in transportation and communications networks and hence in access to print and written matter; in district schools; and in greater levels of market transactions and economic community—then literacy levels, especially among females, expanded more slowly.[25] Male literacy rates were very high in the first generation of settlement throughout Windsor District, as they were in southern New England, especially Connecticut and Massachusetts, which supplied Windsor District with most settlers.[26] Male rates were so high in the founding generation, 1760–90, that differences across the set of human habitats were minimal. Where lower levels of male literacy existed, however—in Plymouth and Weston—they appeared in those parts of Windsor District with living situations least favorable for farming and grazing.[27]

Complex sets of material and cultural conditions had greater impact on the progress of female literacy. With Windsor village firmly in the full-access zone but with portions of the township still in the partial-access zone, Windsor female residents attained the highest literacy rates in the district, reaching 70 percent in the early 1780s. In Cavendish, which lay within the partial-access zone but had portions of the township still in the minimal-access zone, female literacy reached the same level a decade later. Reading was more split between partial- and minimal-access zones and, though slightly more populous than Cavendish, had far smaller and less active hamlets through 1815. Reading achieved the 70 percent threshold early in the first decade of the nineteenth century, a decade later than Cavendish. Plymouth, far longer a part of the minimum-access zone and populated primarily by fairly isolated farmstead families, reached 70 percent female literacy only in the early 1820s.[28]

Weston appears to have been an anomaly, for it sustained a somewhat higher female literacy rate (80 percent) from its earliest settlement—even before it incorporated as a township in 1797. The reason may well have been one or more particular characteristics of the original female settlers, though no evidence uncovered to date sheds light on this point. Another contributing factor was that Weston was the last township in Windsor District to be settled. Its original female settlers, having remained longer in central and eastern Connecticut, where female literacy and schooling continued to expand, were more frequently literate. Moreover, Weston's first hamlet developed rapidly and contained a larger proportion of the township's tiny population than did hamlets in several other inland townships.[29]

The progress of elementary literacy in Windsor District confirms that variations in complex sets of material and cultural conditions of life contributed to the differential pace at which literacy, especially female literacy, was acquired across eleven townships. The same combinations of factors that accounted for differences in incidence, size, and content of family libraries had initially shaped differences in elementary literacy rates. Male literacy rates were generally too high throughout the district to reveal significant differences. Female rates did vary with human habitats; in more complex living situations that were further along in the process of commercialization, females became literate faster. Furthermore, the hierarchy accounts for all of the local and regional factors that scholars have recently associated with rising elementary literacy rates: more complex social development, population density, market activity, economic community, and access to print culture and its attendant institutions, especially neighborhood schools.

Finally, at the national level twin goals led to a drive for mass literacy[30] that had its effect in the Upper Valley as elsewhere in the Early Republic. Protestant ideology assumed that reading the Word was an important ingredient in the Christian's quest for salvation. And secular political philosophy assumed that an educated citizenry was vital to a healthy republican experiment.

At the heart of Upper Valley culture was the sacred world. As religions of the word and of the book, Calvinist and evangelical New England versions of Protestantism emphasized education of the individual as necessary for salvation. Two practical applications of this basic moral position developed in the

Revolutionary era. One stressed a cult of the family and domesticity and the other a specific view of human personality and the stages of life. Together they constituted a full-blown theory of human personality development: the Romantic approach to the self. Both applications favored a broad educational program beginning in the home and continuing through the district school system and on into adulthood.[31]

Paralleling this sacred push for literacy was a secular rationale that, as Soltow and Stevens have noted, "a basic literacy among the poor and a system for guaranteeing the emergence of capable political leadership were requisites to the stability and perpetuity of the American republic." Linda Kerber has recently made the additional important point that a republican education demanded the active involvement of mothers as well as fathers in the educational process. As republican mothers educated the "rising generation," they expanded their own knowledge of distant peoples and events. Further confirmation of the desirability of basic literacy came from all levels of the governmental, political, and legal systems. At the state level, for instance, both New Hampshire and Vermont had laws in force before 1800 that encouraged primary education through district schools at the neighborhood level.[32]

The Uses of Literacy and the History of Knowledge in the Upper Valley

The 1817 analysis of New England education in the *Philadelphia Analectic Magazine* accurately suggests that a drastic reorganization of daily life was rapidly reaching completion. In more than four-fifths of all Windsor District households people could read, write, calculate, and keep household accounts. In rural New England, almost all public statements before 1830 about elementary literacy, especially about reading and calculating, advocated the diffusion of these skills throughout the entire population. In large part this desire was a heritage of the long struggle for independence and for the creation of a republic. But the transformation involved much more. Once literacy had been acquired, its maintenance through continued reading was widely supported. New Englanders had gained "a thirst after knowledge," which was to be satisfied through the proliferation of lending libraries and family library collections and through widespread almanac and newspaper circulation.[33]

New Englanders were "deservedly celebrated" for "intelligence and enterprise." A definite set of values in the realm of work and social stratification guided social and economic life and were taught in district schools. "Habits of sober industry" and "an early determination to labour," both deemed necessary to survival in the harsh New England environment, were transmitted by nearly all of the schoolbooks used in Windsor District schools through 1830.

Social control was reinforced more subtly by an emphasis on acceptance of the wide differences in wealth, class, and power in the existing social order.[34]

The actual uses of literacy in the Early Republic were many and varied, as might be expected in an era when reading had come to be "counted as among the necessaries of life." Through the early 1830s reading and writing skills found several public uses. Area newspapers followed foreign affairs especially closely. Residents of the Upper Valley read about and offered public commentary regarding their republic's role within North Atlantic civilization. In government, print culture served to maintain and disseminate all official transactions. As such it was the repository of community decisionmaking, power, and legality. In the latter area, written matter also served as an official repository of contracts between individuals, apprenticeship agreements, debts and loans, and records in a wide variety of work situations. In society at large, print and written communications performed myriad functions, maintaining traditional funds of knowledge and ways of behaving. Initially the spread of reading and writing did not beget radical change in values and beliefs; quite the opposite. Consequently, the fund of knowledge initially acquired through reading and writing merely supplemented and extended oral culture, just as methods of reading instruction extended the spoken word. Overthrowing sacred or secular wisdom was a lengthy process in the Early Republic.

Nevertheless, through theological treatises and tracts, denominational meetings, and benevolent reform activity, print culture did transmit new religious beliefs and forms of action. In the secular realm as well, new information, both "knowledge from distant climes" and important regional and local information, appeared in newspapers, in almanacs, and in some books, pamphlets, and periodicals. News and ideas from distant places had always attracted the attention of the professional and business classes, but after the Revolution there was a new reason for interest. Awareness of contemporary events in Britain, on the Continent, and elsewhere in America was advocated as the duty of all citizens and also became a badge of status. Apart from the other public uses of reading, basic literacy was necessary for even minimal influence within a township; and greatly intensified involvement in community life was generally a direct result of reading, as we have seen.

Chief among many private effects of literacy was a powerful but uneven increase in the tendency toward personal freedom in expression. Greater reading of printed and written matter, including biographies, novels, travel accounts, devotional reading, accounts of sickly Christians dying young, and poetry gradually alleviated substantial pressure to conform to family, kinship, neighborhood, and community interests and opinions, and encouraged reliance on personal experience. That this freedom amounted to liberation and a form of "individualism" (in a nineteenth-century sense) for most Upper Valley residents is undeniable, but its character and extent need study. Public life had never been the only avenue to personal growth and enjoyment, but now reading enabled the individual to escape almost at will into a wonderful or terrifying secret world of fantasy. New kinds of knowledge did not immediately lead most Upper Valley readers to cast off the wisdom of the ages, but they did eventually lead most Windsor District residents to accept new ideas and material changes more rapidly and to feel a growing fascination with the contemporary world. These trends were especially pronounced among the communities of readers most advanced in the commercialization of rural life.

Print centers produced, imported, and widely advertised a broad selection of books, pamphlets, and periodicals, many of them offering new perspectives on life in North Atlantic civilization. Events occurring anywhere in that world increasingly spurred curiosity throughout its length and breadth. Fascination with Anglo-American civilization was very strong on the periphery of that civilization, in Scotland and America. As people acquired richer and more varied private funds of knowledge via family and lending libraries, individualism accelerated and attitudes and kinds of public participation among neighbors became increasingly differentiated. The rapid expansion of letter writing after 1805 complemented wider reading opportunities.

The widening uses of reading and writing by Windsor District residents in 1787–1830 were only possible because, by the 1780s, three-quarters of all families contained at least one adult (usually the head of household) who was able to read and write. By 1800 three-quarters of all families included at least one adult who actively engaged in lifelong reading. By the 1820s a large proportion of families also included at least one letter writer. In addition to cheaper and more plentiful supplies of paper and writing implements, continued migration was a real spur to letter writing. As many as half of the adults in the poorest fifth of all Upper Valley families still could not themselves read or write, but most of this small minority by 1810 nevertheless have may have been able to participate in the burgeoning world of print and written expression. Poor residents of villages and hamlets were more likely to be read to, and more often, than the poor who were isolated living deep in the hinterland of Windsor District.

The first rural age of mass reading saw frequent reading in public places because these had long been normal gathering spots in rural society. Reading, in fact, was initially learned in collective situations—at home in the family circle and in the local schoolhouse.[35] People thus frequently listened to reading aloud at home (at meals and at other family gatherings), in village and hamlet post offices, in stores, and on other public occasions, such as religious meetings. Richard Caton Woodville, William Sidney Mount, and many lesser-known genre painters attested to the regularity of public reading throughout the first half of the nineteenth century.[36]

A flood of scholarship on literacy has altered our approach to cultural life in the West. As intellectual history receded from the forefront of research in the 1960s, the study of the life of the mind turned behaviorist. For nearly two decades the acquisition of skills, and their uses, narrowly conceived, were, as research topics, preferred to the substance of intellectual life. The study of literacy, narrowly conceived, has provided valuable information about the trends, agents, pace, and motives associated with the achievement of literacy and about its uses in laying the foundations of cultural participation. Now we may proceed beyond skills and processes of learning to grasp the life of the mind and heart—the substance of human communication—and its impact on daily life. In moving forward we must reconfirm the existence of the mind, regarding it not merely as a switchboard but as both a repository for a varied and changing fund of knowledge and an active agent in the historical process of continuity and change.[37]

One way to proceed is to create a new history of knowledge (that is, information, opinion, beliefs, and values) encompassing its circulation, and its many roles, uses, and purposes in past societies. The history of knowledge includes the history of its tools and skills and their uses in a broad instrumental sense; but its main focus is the substantive history of information, opinion, beliefs, and values. Literacy skills evolved over the course of human life as a result of the changing incidence, quantity, and quality of reading and writing; and these relationships must be traced as closely as the acquisition of elementary literacy. Because of the richness of surviving evidence, the core of the history of knowledge in the Early Republic is the history of print culture and its changing reception, uses, and impact throughout life.

The key finding about the foundations of cultural participation in the Upper Valley in 1760–1830 is that these years witnessed the rise of a wholly new kind of rural mass literacy, extending to both males and females and to all major social groups (even some of the very poor). This finding highlights a development of premier importance in the long history of human communications. The rural American Northeast during the Early Republic participated in the first era in a democratization of access to knowledge, as Story and Webster recognized. But only after 1815 did the *substance* of matter actually read also spread more egalitarian values.[38]

The era 1780–1830, in which active reading first became a necessity of life in rural society, encompassed the first half century of the Age of Reading in the history of human communications. Educators, the clergy, and other advocates of an ideology of literacy in early national America played an essential role in providing ordinary people with a dramatically new way to apprehend the world. Furthermore, people could sometimes alter their lives and the world by what they learned. Cultural conformity—adherence to the wisdom of the ages—had been the chief goal in the push for mass literacy. During the half century following the Revolution, however, knowledge came to be understood in several new ways by a large majority of Upper Valley residents: as a form of power, as entertainment, as an avenue of escape, as a means of self-improvement, and as a useful tool. Intensely curious and supported by an ideology proclaiming the great value of currency in knowledge, those who could read silently and rapidly broke free of all attempts to restrict them to approved subjects and views. The rise of novel reading is only the most striking case in point. When reading became a regular part of daily life throughout much of Windsor District, the traditional balance of forces for survival, livelihood, and happiness in human life was shattered forever.

The pace at which literacy developed, and the range of uses to which it was put as reading and writing spread, varied greatly across the eleven townships of Windsor District. Did varying material and cultural conditions of life differ in their effect on the incidence of literacy? on the rate of development and the depth of basic literacy skills? on their lifelong use in obtaining knowledge about the distant world? on local participation in printed and written forms of cultural expression?

Within Windsor District there were five recognizably different living situations, each supporting a distinctive community of readers. Several factors interacted and overlapped in the creation of each. We have already seen that commercial growth and cultural participation were closely related. The dissemination of print communications fostered new standards of intellectual currency in both sacred and secular forms of knowledge. Both sets of standards were most prominent among the communities of readers most advanced in the commercialization of rural life. The relationship between outlook and commercial sophistication offers an important clue to the interaction of several major historical factors affecting individuals and families: the type of local community setting, ecology, and development; position within the Upper Valley communications network; family size, wealth, occupational situation, social status, and prestige; and participation within the market economy.

The Human Habitats of Rural New England, 1780–1835: Sets of Conditions Shaping Participation in Cultural Life

Even the . . . terms by which we distinguish the several strata of our social world, construe and interpret their contents, and determine our action in it and upon it and its action upon us . . . are predefined as . . . part of our life world which we take for granted. These terms . . . co-determine what within our culture is accepted as unquestionable, what can become questionable, and what appears as worthy of questioning. . . .

This is so because only to a very small extent does the knowledge of each individual originate from his personal experience. The overwhelming bulk of this knowledge is socially derived and transmitted to the individual in the long process of education by parents, contemporaries and predecessors. . . . All the socially derived knowledge is . . . transmitted to him as unquestionably accepted by the group, and as valid and tested. Thus it becomes an element of the form of social life, and as such forms both a common schema of interpretation of the . . . world and a means of mutual agreement and understanding.

–Alfred Schutz,
"Some Structures of the Life-World"

In reconstructing the world of everyday life in the Upper Valley, 1760–1835, we focus on the economy, the society, the general mental universe common to all rural New Englanders, and also their several more distinctive, changing funds of knowledge about the world. The goal is to unearth the foundations of material and cultural life, to provide an initial blueprint of a lost rural world and to untangle the process of change in an era of major transformation. To do so we must first delineate an organizing conception that encompasses the basic infrastructure of economic, social, and cultural life.[1]

To construe rural transformation as the urbanization of rural society, in accord with traditional conceptions of modernization, would be a mistake. No cities developed in northwestern New England, and while some institutions and agencies of existing New England urban centers increasingly influenced aspects of life in the countryside, it retained its distinctively rural agricultural foundations well into the twentieth century. The rural commercial civilization emerging during the Early Republic transformed the production, distribution, and consumption of many of life's necessities, now including printed matter. Residents of the Upper Valley were inhabitants of a republic of knowledge which was at the same time a commercial republic.[2]

Still, statements that accurately characterize the whole of the Upper Valley do not necessarily hold for each of its parts. Diversity was a watchword of the new rural order. The process by which elementary literacy skills were acquired did not vary significantly across Windsor District, but the extent of literacy's permeation did vary, especially for females. As previously noted, male rates were so high by the 1760s that significant variations across Windsor District had largely vanished. Because female rates began much lower, however, substantial variations did exist during the period 1760–1835, and these followed the commercialization of economic and social life and the spread of a new communications environment. Residents of the Upper Valley who had mastered literacy skills varied dramatically in the extent of their cultural participation using reading, calculating, and writing. Wide variations were not the result of free choice, nor were they often the product of class division. Many people were prohibited from participating in one way or another by several conditions of daily life. We must therefore consider not only the widely dispersed high rates of minimum competency but also the wide variations in cultural involvement as lifelong reading became more frequent. Variety in cultural participation was, indeed, the basis of rural commercial civilization. This chapter addresses several key questions about rural diversity: What factors noticeably shaped different levels and amounts of participation in Upper Valley print culture between 1760 and 1835? In what circumstances and on what bases did cultural participation thrive? And how much did it vary and why?

No single factor accounts for major differences in the amount and kind of participation, nor does any one set of circumstances account for the great variations in the extent of participation. Rather, we must consider several major factors and their interaction in various sets of circumstances. Differing mixes of factors existed in varying strengths within each of several distinctive living situations in Windsor District. Even age-old institutions assumed new forms. The family was especially pivotal, because it mediated the effects of all other institutions. Several new rural institutions also presented important opportunities and constraints: kinship links; the community setting (village, hamlet, or farmstead geographical neighborhood); the economic locale, including the institutional setting within which commercial exchange transpired; social class (family wealth and occupation); and the placement of the homestead within the area's transportation and communications network. Mutual, reciprocal interaction, not a dichotomy between belief and behavior, characterized rural existence.

A Network of Human Habitats as an Organizing Conception

A pressing issue facing history today is the scale of generalization. New middle-level theory is needed, a reconceptualization of sets of conditions interacting in historical causation.[3] Older formulations which gave rise to the "new history" of the 1910–40 era, then to American intellectual history in the 1940s and 1950s and to a more quantitative and behaviorist social history in 1960–80 — these no longer adequately account for the complexity of broad historical change. Rhys Isaac under the idealist banner, and Paul Johnson and James Henretta under the materialist, among others, are reformulating the relationship of material to cultural life.[4] Outside the profession, history's impact on public policy formation is minimal, precisely because its explanatory frameworks have become either rigidly idealist, materialist-behaviorist, or wholly indecisive about how change occurs in society.[5]

To capture complex interactions among several social, economic, and cultural factors, we have developed a broader, more flexible formulation of the reception, integration, and uses of knowledge in rural New England daily life.[6] Eight major factors were basic to the new rural culture that was emerging in Windsor District by the 1780s; they provide the basis for a new understanding of the life of the mind and heart in the Early Republic.[7] These factors are: wide variations in community type and environmental setting; placement within the system of transportation and communications that formed the distribution network for all commodities, including printed and written matter; expanding consumer participation within the market economy; work rhythms and occupations in conjunction with houschold size, and composition; wealth and its uses and dispersion in real and personal property; elementary literacy; the incidence, size, and character of family libraries; and the variety of rural *mentalités*. Not only were these eight factors interrelated; each factor had both material and cultural dimensions. The shifting contemporary understanding of commerce, economic exchange, and market relations was as integral to economic life as were the forms of economic behavior and trends in their development that historians have been able to reconstruct.[8]

First and foremost, all residents of the Upper Valley carried on their daily lives within a tangible human habitat. In fact, we may usefully view rural life as a network of human habitats, or living situations. We define a linked series of five distinct types of living situations and groupings of families. The concept of human habitats is especially helpful because it expresses, with a historically accurate degree of ambiguity, the interpenetration of material and cultural factors shaping participation in everyday life.

Each of the five types of human habitat discussed below contained a group of families who shared the same general mix of material and cultural circumstances of life. These included, first, a unique environmental setting and community placement within the Upper Valley, in a village or hamlet, or out on a township farmstead; second, a distinct level of access within the transportation and communications network of Windsor District; third, predominant forms of work experience and "occupations"; fourth, a particular range of wealth and material possessions; fifth, a specific mix of consumer participation in the market economy of the economic locale; sixth, some variation in literacy levels; seventh, varying incidence, size and character of family libraries; and eighth, sharp diversity in rural *mentalités*. None of the eight primary factors was determinative, nor was any single factor uniform in its effects throughout the network of living situations. Money shaped a family's involvement with print culture, for example, but, beyond the poorest fifth of society, did not usually determine it; several other factors intervened. Thus fairly poor artisans' families were more likely to participate in active and diverse ways in print culture than were considerably wealthier yeoman farm families.

There was a controlling economic, social, and cultural process within which the network of human habitats functioned. This process involved the increasing commercial and cultural integration of Windsor District into North Atlantic civilization in the half century after the Revolution. The leading elements in this integration process were commercial exchange, involving an ever larger market sphere; more centralized production and distribution of goods through larger-scale manufacturing; and a corresponding shift in knowledge resulting from the creation of a new communications environment within rural society. A fundamental shift in the importance of secular as opposed to religious knowledge emphasized life on earth and was elaborated in a quickly expanding ideal of intellectual currency.

Place was as consequential as time in defining historical change within North Atlantic civilization through 1835. Where a family lived in relation to the major factors that actively shaped daily life was critical to whether and how its members participated in the broad transformation under way throughout the North Atlantic. Awareness of change profoundly shaped the ability to participate in it or to resist its impact. Change did not wash over Upper Valley society like a tidal wave, uniformly enveloping everything in its path. Rather, like a rapidly moving summer squall, it fell more heavily here and more lightly there. Individuals and families were not free to change merely because they lived in an age of rapid transformation. Access to major social, economic, political, scientific, technological, and cultural changes, and aware-

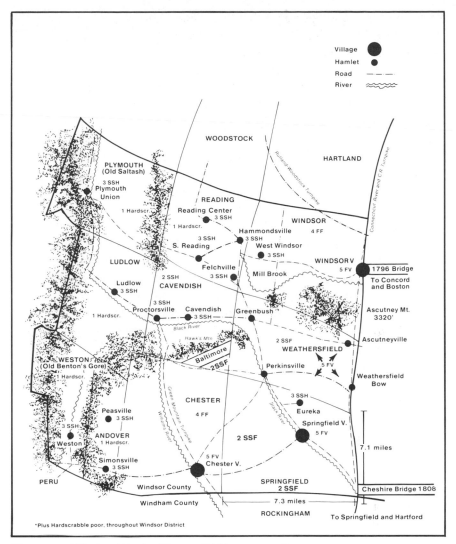

Figure 4-1: Windsor District Human Habitats, 1787–1835

ness of their progress, varied dramatically from one living situation to another. The concept of human habitats helps us understand basic patterns in access to new *mentalités* as well as new forms of livelihood.

Part of the conceptual strength of the notion of human habitats is the concreteness with which it allows us to specify relationships between material and cultural conditions. Each of the five types of human habitat consisted of three to thirteen specific places within Windsor District (see figure 4-1). The four villages constituted the "fortunate village" type of human habitat. Windsor, Chester, and the southwestern portion of Springfield farmstead areas belonged to the "fortunate farmstead" type. Thirteen hamlets fell into the "self-sufficient hamlet" subgroup; they were spread from north Springfield to West Windsor and Reading, along the Green Mountain turnpike in Cavendish, Ludlow, and Plymouth, and along the southern rim of the district in Andover and Weston townships. The "self-sufficient farmstead" form of human habitat consisted of Baltimore, Weathersfield, and Cavendish farmstead areas, and all Springfield farmsteads except those in its southwestern corner. All farmstead portions of Plymouth, Ludlow, Weston, Andover, and Reading townships, as well as the poorest families throughout Windsor District, averaging just $361 in total wealth (none had more then $700), belonged to the "hardscrabble" variety of living situation.

Altogether thirty separate human habitats existed within Windsor District, in one or another of the five types. In these five distinct living environments, different mixtures of factors helped shape five different sets of interests and ranges of views about the self and the world. Each of the thirty separate human habitats encompassed one particular cluster of material and cultural interests. Each cluster was a composite of the set of eight major factors, and each cluster shaped a more or less limited range of participation in material and cultural life, public and private. Within each type of living situation a dominant, and usually one or more variant, sets of material interests and cultural traditions thrived. Despite internal diversity in all five types of living situations, each comprised a distinctive audience for print and written expression within the Upper Valley, 1780–1835. The beliefs and values held by these audiences, who read, ruminated, and then discussed and acted on some of their beliefs, are our primary foci. The geographical site of their mental activity, while important, was only one dimension of rural life.[9]

Human habitats were connected by avenues at once physical and mental, along which tangible commodities and printed and written forms of knowledge circulated. From the perspective of social and economic history, these avenues led to the five distinct kinds of living situations. From the perspective of cultural history, the avenues helped shape five varieties of collective consciousness—which Alfred Schutz called the stock of knowledge at hand—in the late eighteenth and early nineteenth centuries. The network of human habitats constitutes a full-scale material and cultural geography for northwestern New England in the early national era.

Five distinct human habitats did not produce five completely different world views in 1780–1835 but rather shaped five *mentalités* within Windsor District. Residents of all five human habitats shared a number of fundamental beliefs and values. The instruction they received in the wisdom of the ages during childhood and youth at home and in district schools ensured that they would do so. In addition, however, each type of human habitat evolved its own interests and perspectives on the world. Families in each type of living environment participated in print culture in many distinctive ways.

There was neither one uniform cultural landscape nor an infinite variety. Each of the five human landscapes of Windsor District incorporated both unity and diversity, as did its natural environment. Human habitats in this book approximate the actual environment within which knowledge in print and written form circulated, shaping everyday life in the heart of the Upper Valley. To take an obvious instance, few isolated farming and grazing families living in Weston, Vermont, in the foothills of the Green Mountains, in 1825–35 displayed much interest in efforts to improve navigation of the Connecticut River. Several circumstances interacted to inhibit the growth of such interests. These included physical isolation within the region's transportation system, attendant subsistence and small surplus farming, the absence of bookstores and regular newspaper and periodical subscriptions, and similar impediments to the acquisition of "new" knowledge about such ventures from other sources. Distinctive reading habits and patterns issued from specific cultural interests deriving from combinations of the eight basic sets of material and cultural conditions shaping life. The position of the Upper Valley within North Atlantic civilization restricted the possibilities for survival, livelihood, and the life of the mind and heart. Inside the Upper Valley, however, a series of alternate configurations thrived.

The concept of a network of human habitats helps us comprehend specific mixes of factors motivating different rates of historical change, and the responses to them by definite groups of rural New England residents. It provides a unified field framework within which one can understand the roles of village artisan families and country-gentleman farm families, and individuals as different as Joseph Smith and William Jarvis, Orestes Brownson and Stephen Jacob. Along many dimensions of daily life, knowledge about the world showed great diversity. Print items were the most varied commodity available in the Upper Valley.

Description of the Human Habitats
of Windsor District, 1760–1835

Beginning in the 1760s with initial settlement and continuing through the late 1830s, five types of Windsor District human habitats shaped participation in both material and cultural life, from most to least active, from most to least interested in intellectual currency and events in the distant world, from most to least secular, and from broadest to narrowest in variety of reading styles and uses of knowledge (see figure 4–1 and table 4–1 throughout). Appendix 2 details the construction of the set of human habitats and the interrelationships among the major factors.[10]

The fortunate village human habitat comprised all households of the district's

Table 4–1: Windsor District, Vermont, Human Habitats, 1787–1830

	Fortunate Village	Fortunate Farmstead	Self-Sufficient Hamlet	Self-Sufficient Farmstead	Hard-scrabble
Number of Family Libraries	62	66	16	69	183
Percent of Total Libraries	16	17	4	17	46
Number of Print Items (n=5,630)	2,248	1,848	229	650	656
Percent of All Print Items	40	33	4	11.5	11.5
Range in Library Size	1–403	1–909	1–85	1–57	1–38
Average Print Items Per Library	36.2	28	14.3	9.4	3.6
Median Print Items Per Library	15	7.5	7.5	5	2
Shares in Lending Libraries (and Percent)	11¹=16%	8=12%	2=13%	3=4%	2=1%
Total Wealth	$478,497	$176,841	$45,166	$224,359	$99,699
Percent of All Wealth	46.7	17.3	4.4	21.9	9.7
Average Wealth (388 cases)	$7,718	$2,720	$2,805	$3,252	$566
Primary Occupations (n=385)²	62	66	16	68	173
Professions	19	4	3	7	0
Commerce and Trade	25	4	7	6	3
Manufacture	3	0	3	1	0
Artisan	14	5	3	3	25
Gentleman Farm	0	13	0	12	0
Yeoman Farm	0	38	0	36	78
Tenant Farm	0	2	0	2	44
Semi-skilled Laborer	1	0	0	1	23

¹ One family with two shares.
² No occupational information in 11 of the 396 cases. See ch. 4 and appendixes 2 and 3 for explication.

four substantial villages—Windsor, Chester, Weathersfield, and Springfield—with $700 or more in total wealth, the effective poverty level. Below this level Windsor District families still participated in print culture, but, as we shall see below, less frequently and in a far more traditional and restricted way. These four villages were the main trading and wholesaling centers for southern Windsor County and its environs. Windsor and Chester were also the centers of their respective economic locales. All four villages were in the top quarter of the thirty Windsor District living situations by wealth and accounted for nearly half of all wealth among families with private libraries through 1830 (see

Table 4-2: Windsor District Wealth, by Communications Access Zone, 1787–1830 *

	Number of Households (n=386)	Total Wealth	Average Wealth
Full Access Zone	172 (45%)	$ 651,829	$ 3,790
Windsor Township	[78]	[$ 248,303]	[$ 3,183]
Village	38	$ 174,561	$4,594
Farmstead	40	$ 73,742	$ 1,843
Chester Township	[69]	[$ 233,701]	[$ 3,386]
Village	20	$ 140,679	$ 7,034
Farmstead	49	$ 93,022	$ 1,898
Springfield Village	13	$ 89,019	$6,848
Weathersfield Village	12	$ 80,806	$ 6,734
Partial Access Zone	129 (33%)	$ 226,621	$ 1,757
Weathersfield Farmstead	44	$ 61,454	$ 1,397
Springfield Farmstead	39	$ 76,447	$1,960
Ludlow Hamlet	2	$ 6,045	$ 3,023
Plymouth Hamlet	2	$ 2,863	$ 1,432
Cavendish Township	[31]	[$ 56,528]	[$ 1,823]
Hamlet	6	$ 10,804	$ 1,801
Farmstead	25	$ 45,724	$ 1,829
Reading Hamlet	11	$ 23,284	$ 2,117
Minimal Access Zone	85 (22%)	$ 110,161	$ 1,296
Plymouth Farmstead	8	$ 19,161	$ 2,395
Weston Township	12	$ 11,546	$ 962
Andover Township	11	$ 21,706	$ 1,973
Ludlow Farmstead	24	$ 30,194	$ 1,258
Reading Farmstead	30	$ 27,554	$ 918

* Zones of Access are plotted for c. 1825. See figure 5–9.
[ ] Total for Township.
  Source: All Windsor District inventories with family libraries, 1787–1830, and wealth data (n=386).

table 4–2). Because there were a few extraordinarily rich families, average wealth in the fortunate village human habitat was $7,718 per family.

Overall, professional and artisan families and families engaged in commerce and trading dominated the fortunate village human habitat, with smaller clusters of manufacturing and semiskilled laboring families. The fortunate village human habitat contained all of the printing facilities in Windsor District through 1835. Windsor village was both the heart of Windsor District's print communications system and the most important print center in the Upper Valley. Families living in Windsor District villages profited immensely from these circumstances; the sixty-two fortunate village households in our study group averaged thirty-six volumes of books, pamphlets, and periodicals per family library. A sixth of the libraries contained two-fifths of all books retained in the district. In all addition measures, including range of library size, median volumes per library, and shares in lending libraries, "fortunate" was an understatement.[11]

The fortunate farmstead human habitat included all families with $700 or more in total wealth living on farmstead land in the central village townships in the district—Windsor, Chester, and southwestern Springfield. Households below this level were classified in the hardscrabble human habitat. If wealth were the sole criterion, "fortunate" would be an inappropriate designation: fortunate farmstead families were fourth among the five habitats in total wealth, averaging almost a quarter less than self-sufficient farmstead families. Proximity to Windsor and Chester villages, with their commercial and cultural ties, was the single most important consideration for these farming and grazing families. Yeoman farm households dominated the fortunate farmstead occupational range, accounting for nearly three-fifths of all families. Gentleman farm families represented another fifth.

Despite their dispersed geographical locations, families living within the fortunate farmstead human habitat were handsomely rewarded for their close proximity to centers of commercial exchange, including large general stores, bookstores, and specialty stores. As a result, modest economic circumstances yielded family libraries that were not smaller but far larger than average. Fortunate farmstead total print holdings and average library size were three times higher, and the proportion of families with a share in a lending library was 3.6 times greater, than in the self-sufficient farmstead human habitat far removed from easy access to a print center. Availability to print culture was a crucial ingredient in participation. Altogether the sixty-six fortunate farmstead families (17 percent) retained print items amounting to double their proportion of all 400 families. The range of family libraries by size was enormous, and the average library, at twenty-eight volumes, was quite large. Another indication of the benefits of proximity to a village is that, despite the fact that some shares in lending libraries were passed on before the assessment, an eighth of the inventories recorded them.

The self-sufficient hamlet human habitat was the smallest of the five human habitats, encompassing residents of a dozen or more crossroads hamlets found in eight townships. All families with $700 or more in total wealth were included. As a group these hamlets mediated between the bustle of village life and the steadier pace of farmstead life; therein lay their distinctiveness. Self-sufficient hamlet families were positioned squarely within the partial-access zone of print communications, always on the largest transportation routes inland from river valley villages. Hamlets exhibited considerable variety. Cavendish and West Windsor hamlets were on major inland roadways and surrounded by farmland, whereas Weston and Reading hamlets were along reasonably well-traveled roads but in far rougher, mountainous, minimum-access farm and grazing land. Village bookstores were some distance from most hamlets, but the difference in access between residence adjacent to a major road and residence in the hills and mountains of Windsor District remains enormous even today. Newspapers, received by post rider subscription from the east, and from Rutland to the west in the cases of Ludlow and Plymouth hamlets, were regularly found in hamlet households. Befitting their diversity, hamlet families retained a wide range of private libraries, large and small, rich and meager, current and traditional.

Overall, families engaged in commerce and trading represented the largest share of hamlet occupations—just over two-fifths—with artisan, manufacturing, and professional families accounting for a fifth each. Average wealth among self-sufficient hamlet families was quite high at $2,805 per family, slightly higher than that for fortunate farmstead families. In general, wealth and occupation conspired with opportunities for some commercial exchange (mainly shops, general stores and, by the mid 1820s, a few factory stores) and placement within the communications system to boost the involvement of inland hamlet residents in rural life.

The self-sufficient farmstead human habitat included the farmstead areas of Weathersfield, Springfield (excepting its southwestern corner), Cavendish, and tiny Baltimore townships. It may be distinguished chiefly by its wealth, its excellent farm and grazing land, and its distance from villages with print center facilities, which seriously limited access to print culture. It was a long day trip to Chester or Windsor village from a self-sufficient farmstead living situation. Self-sufficient farmstead families were quite wealthy, ranking second highest among the set of human habitats, and often lived on the best farmland in the district. The category includes all families with $700 or more in total wealth; households below this level, again, are placed in the hardscrabble human habitat. The range of occupations was quite broad. Yeoman farm families dominated (53 percent), followed by gentleman farm families (18 percent) and a smattering of all others.

While sharing with the fortunate farmstead habitat a very similar pattern of primary occupations, the self-sufficient farmstead habitat differed markedly in shares in lending libraries and incidence, range, and average size of private libraries. Self-sufficient farmstead family libraries were just a third the size of those on more centrally located fortunate farmsteads. Self-sufficient farmstead families, 17 percent of all families studied, kept only 11 percent of printed objects. On all quantitative measures, but especially in the contents of family libraries, differences between these two groups of primarily agricultural families were vast. In short, the self-sufficient farmstead human habitat was just what the name implies. These families had regular dealings with nearby general stores but few contacts with distant village bookstores, so library holdings consisted more of traditional intensive reading matter. The existence of several professional and gentleman farmstead families accounts for modest library expansion beyond the normal constraints of this living situation. In such cases wealth and occupation overrode geography, community type, and location within the district's communications system.

The hardscrabble human habitat encompassed two groups of Windsor District residents — the geographically isolated, including all wealth levels and many of the newly settled; and the relatively poor, including all families with less than $700 in total wealth. They shared a powerful disadvantage: inaccessibility to many, though not all, of the fruits of print culture. Especially lacking were nearly all vehicles of communications carrying "modern intelligence."

The first group, consisting of the inland hill people, as often grazers as farmers, encompassed all residents but the hamlet dwellers in five townships — Weston and Andover to the southwest, Ludlow, and Plymouth and Reading to the north. This living situation, on the outer perimeter of the Windsor District communications network, constituted the minimal-access zone of print culture. Mail could be sent from and received in each township for the first time only in 1823 (see chapter 5, figures 5–8 and 5–9). The post office was a direct connection to the outside world and signaled a crucial advance in involvement with the broader rural world of commerce and culture.[12]

Through the mid-1820s most residents of upland farming and grazing areas also lacked access to other essential aspects of print culture — periodical and newspaper subscriptions, bookstores, and most peddlers. Consequently, available printed matter was mostly restricted to traditional steady sellers among books and pamphlets stocked by the small local general stores. The yearly almanac plus traditional intensive reading matter — Bibles and Testaments, hymnals, psalm books, spellers, a few other district-level schoolbooks, and an occasional devotional work or chapbook — constituted the entire supply of printed matter ever purchased by all but a few professional, commerce and trading, and artisan families. Private libraries among these families remained firmly entrenched in traditional wisdom at least until the mid-1820s. What is most interesting about hardscrabble families is that, while the 86 families in our first cluster participated in print culture, they remained isolated from many of the networks most active in the diffusion of print through Windsor District. Hardscrabble families mainly read earlier, traditional works which seemed foreign to an age flooded with new knowledge. It is not at all clear, however, whether they read less frequently than residents of other, allegedly more progressive human habitats, or just less extensively. Traditional approaches to knowledge and reading are as important to a full view of cultural life in the Early Republic as the more modern ideal of intellectual currency prevalent among the most active participants in cultural exchange.

The second group of 97 hardscrabble families, all with wealth less than $700, were scattered across the remainder of Windsor District. For this group, geography and access to print communications were outweighed by the con-strictions imposed by a narrow range of work experience and by relative pov-erty (a mere $361 in average total wealth). Spare circumstances characterized geographically isolated families as well. For all families in the hardscrabble liv-ing situation, average wealth was only $566, just a fifth of the $2,640 in overall wealth that was average for all Windsor District families. With 46 percent of all households, hardscrabble families possessed just a tenth of all real and per-sonal property.[13]

The situation in family library retention was almost identical for the rela-tively poor and the isolated. Just half of all hardscrabble households retained family libraries (see below). The 183 collections surviving at inventory averaged 4 volumes per library among isolated families and 3.3 volumes among the poor. Despite having 46 percent of all libraries, hardscrabble families retained just 12 percent of all printed items. In addition, only two families (1 percent) re-tained shares in lending libraries, and subscriptions to newspapers and periodi-cals were at least as rare. As we have seen, this evidence should not lead to the inference that the frequency or the amount of reading was low. It does, however—by the incidence and size of family libraries, by the reading styles most typically employed, by the contents of collections, and by absence of participation in corporate shareholding lending libraries—reveal the limited va-riety of hardscrabble cultural participation. Moreover, informal borrowing rarely compensated for a basic lack of purchasing power.

The dominant characteristic of the hardscrabble living situation was its isola-tion from much of the vibrancy of commercial exchange and print culture's expansion in Windsor District. The occupational range among hardscrabble families confirms a severe limitation on material advancement. Few profes-sional, manufacturing, or commerce and trading families inhabited the farm-stead areas of the five isolated townships. Farm families (yeoman and tenant exclusively) accounted for fully 71 percent of all hardscrabble occupations, fol-lowed by artisan (15 percent), semiskilled laboring families (13 percent), and just three inland commerce and trading families (2 percent).

While very different in some aspects of their lives, the poor and the geo-graphically isolated, when they began a family library, purchased and retained almost identical books and pamphlets. Their almost wholly traditional uses of printed matter made their reading different from that of most every other segment of the district's population. Part of the group of artisan families rep-resented the only major exception. Relative solitude and pioneering conditions or, alternatively, access without regular purchasing power, kept 95 percent of all hardscrabble libraries to a bare minimum, selected from a limited range of printed matter. For every family with a private library in this human habitat there was another that may have purchased books and pamphlets but, if so, did not retain them through the death of the household head. Some of the poorest families did not participate in print culture at all; present evidence is thin, but it reveals that literacy rates were somewhat lower among the poor than in all other segments of Windsor District society.[14]

History of the Network of Human Habitats, 1760–1835

Human habitats change with time. The network of human habitats emerged in the founding generation, 1760–85, and continued to develop throughout the next half century. Material and cultural conditions of life were changing throughout the period of 1760–1835. We can identify three basic stages in the history of human habitats as a new form of rural community: emergence, elaboration and expansion in the hinterland of Windsor District, and eventual transformation of the network. Windsor District remains a valid indepth test case; with slight modification, its patterns held for the Upper Valley as a whole.

The initial formation of human habitats accompanied the settlement of Windsor District, 1760–85; economic locales became centered at Windsor and Chester. Sole reliance on the individual township for goods and services, if it ever was a reality in southern New England, quickly gave way on the northwestern frontier to clusters of two to four, and with further settlement four to eight, townships. By the mid 1780s the network of human habitats had emerged in full, and during the next decade several historical conjunctions capped the first stage in these habitats' historical evolution. Perhaps the most consequential development was the "transportation revolution" in rural New England. Road travel in the district was substantially improved through a series of turnpikes, improvements to other widely used roads, and construction of a critical bridge across the Connecticut River in 1796, which linked Windsor to Boston via Concord. The decade following the Peace at Paris also saw a sizable increase in the production, stock in bookstores, and distribution of print items throughout the district, led by initial diffusion of weekly newspapers. An early but short-lived attempt to sustain a second Windsor District newspaper, *The Morning Ray*, at Windsor in 1790, in competition with Spooner's *Vermont Journal*, was a signal event in the decentralization of communications within rural New England. More generally, the local market economy grew stronger between 1780 and 1795, and work patterns and the occupational structure began to shift concomitantly. These were also key years in the proliferation of the Vermont district school system, ensuring (perhaps with a small delay) the maintenance of extraordinarily high elementary literacy rates among the children and youth of new settlers. Together these changes in the basic structure of life created a stable preindustrial society, economy, communications network, and culture by 1795.

The second or expansion stage in the history of Windsor District human habitats encompassed the 1795–1825 period. It was marked by steady population growth through the early 1820s; thereafter population size stabilized, and the beginnings of rural decline set in except in the mountainous townships of Ludlow, Plymouth, and Weston. In the basic material and cultural structure of Windsor District as a whole, change accelerated between 1795 and 1825. Within another decade, the limits of commercialization were reached.[15]

By the late 1820s changes were under way in each of the eight factors undergirding the network of human habitats. In another decade further economic, social, and cultural integration had significantly altered the network and the fabric of daily life. The market economy continued to expand throughout Windsor District. The introduction of the railroad into the area in the late 1830s, initially bypassing Windsor District, likewise modified the transportation and communications systems. For the first time Windsor faced stiff local competition as a print center. In addition, newspaper reading was increasingly regular among a sizable majority of all families, strengthening the hold of an ideal of information diffusion based on the "latest intelligence." A third set of changes occurred as a result of the steady growth of the factory system of manufacturing in the district. Fourth, European immigrants arrived, as local residents moved away to New England's cities and mill communities. More generally, the cold years of 1816 and 1817, which were followed quickly by a general economic recession, had stimulated a steady outmigration westward. These four changes and others together transformed Windsor District's network of human habitats.[16]

Key Characteristics of the Network of Human Habitats

The network of human habitats helps us differentiate among five levels of engagement in a new rural civilization that enveloped much of Windsor District in the half century following the Revolution. If a Windsor District family of the time had actually moved eastward through the full set, from a hardscrabble grazing patch in Plymouth Kingdom to a fortunate village artisan shop in Windsor, it would have passed through a series of environments whose residents successively participated more actively in commercial exchange, were more aware of the distant contemporary world and its many influences on local life, and were better versed in contemporary theology, religious activities, public policy issues, fiction, and the Western intellectual tradition as understood at the time. Between 1780 and 1835 Windsor District residents lived in a world witnessing the erosion of geographical barriers to knowledge of distant events and places and thus of a central buttress of localism. The millennia-old divide between one's own face-to-face community and people in "distant climes" was being breached, and the final assault arrived with the telegraph in the 1840s.

Unusual complexity in the mix of conditions affecting daily life characterized each type of human habitat. On the one hand, families widely scattered
in living situations across Windsor District were affected by similar circumstances. On the other hand, interaction among the eight leading factors meant
that more than one combination of conditions accounted for the similar kinds
of participation in print culture found within each human habitat.[17]

One of the best illustrations of this complexity is the relationship between
physical placement within Windsor District and other combinations of factors: wealth and occupation frequently overrode geography. By 1815, for example, at least a quarter of all middle- and lower-middle-class families in Windsor District's four villages participated in print culture through subscription to
a weekly newspaper; maintenance of a sizable, fairly current family library of
at least twenty volumes; and ownership of a share in a local social library. The
local library supplemented private library reading with new publications and
expensive multivolume works. Among these two groups the proportions of
newspaper subscribers and of families retaining a library of more than twenty
volumes had risen to more than two-fifths by 1830. Subscriptions to periodicals,
mainly literary and religious, were also more prevalent. Lower-class families living in these same villages rarely enjoyed any of these cultural advantages. In
our group of thirty-two lower- and lower-middle-class village families, all of
whom owned less than $700 in total wealth, only two (6 percent) maintained
a library of twenty volumes or more; no more than three to five of these
households (9 to 16 percent) subscribed to a newspaper; only one (3 percent)
held a share in a local lending library; and no evidence survives that any family
in this group subscribed to a periodical. At best a few poor Windsor village
families borrowed fiction, travelogues, and light histories and biographies from
the Windsor Circulating Library, which opened in 1822.

The network of human habitats enables us to predict the contents of libraries as well as specific reading interests and styles. Though by no means
foolproof, it offers striking quantitative (see table 4–1) and qualitative (chapters
5 through 9) confirmation that material and cultural conditons combined in
varying ways to yield different kinds of participation in cultural life, public
and private.[18]

On the main body of evidence—nearly 650 family inventories documenting
400 private libraries (62 percent)—the network of human habitats clearly demonstrates that there were five distinct patterns of family library retention. Increases in the incidence and size of family libraries are summarized in table 4–3[19].

The incidence of family libraries rose steadily across all human habitats,
from a low of 50 percent for hardscrabble families to a high of 85 percent for
fortunate village families. A total of about 2,220 family libraries existed in
Windsor District's eleven townships in 1830. If we break them down by human
habitats,[20] we have the information a Windsor bookstore owner in 1830 could

Table 4–3: Patterns of Family Library Retention and Estimates for 1830 by Human Habitats[1]

	Fortunate Village	Fortunate Farmstead	Self-Sufficient Hamlet	Self-Sufficient Farmstead	Hard-Scrabble
1. Population	3,190	2,795	1,120	3,372	7,235
2. Percent of Total Population	18	16	6	19	41
3. Percent of Families with Libraries	85	72	65	60	50
4. Estimated Number of Libraries	544	402	146	405	723
5. Percent of All Libraries	24	18	7	18	33
6. Estimated Volumes of Printed Matter[2]	19,700	11,250	2,100	3,800	2,600
7. Percent of All Volumes	50	29	5	10	6

[1] Libraries have been located in 62% of all families with an inventory.

[2] Ratios of the percentage of families with libraries (from among all families with inventories) were used to estimate the total number of family libraries in 1830 for each habitat. This figure is reported in line 4 and multiplied by average number of print items per library (from table 4–1). This yields the "Estimated Volumes of Printed Matter" (line 6).

have wished for in deciding which books, pamphlets, and periodicals to stock. A third of all family libraries were minimal in size and character (hardscrabble). Almost another fifth (self-sufficient farmstead), also small, were dominated by intensive reading matter, both sacred and secular. Together these two most traditional human habitats accounted for about half of all private libraries. While reading matter and styles had begun to diversify even here by 1830, traditional intensive-reading works and steady sellers—works representing the wisdom of the ages in religion and practical earthly affairs—continued to command a substantial audience. If we pursue our analysis one step further, however, and multiply total estimated number of family libraries by average library size for each human habitat, we see that hardscrabble and self-sufficient farmstead families owned only a small share (16 percent) of all printed items, although they had half of all libraries.

As we move up the scale of human habitats toward steadier, more active participation in economic and cultural change, the proportions of print items and of libraries are reversed. Hardscrabble families, with 33 percent of all libraries, retained just 6 percent of all printed matter; and self-sufficient farmstead families, with 18 percent of all libraries, retained just 10 percent of all printed matter. Self-sufficient hamlet families held a share of printed objects almost equal to their share of libraries. The hamlet living situation, witnessing the initial encroachment of new commercial and cultural trends into the heartland of Windsor District, represented an important transition in reading tastes and kinds of participation in print communications. Hamlets marked the effective limit of direct bookstore sales. Only a tiny group of families in the professional, gentleman farm, commerce and trade, and artisan categories in self-sufficient farmstead and hardscrabble habitats made relatively frequent trips to the district's village bookstores. In the fortunate farmstead and village habitats in or near a village, whose residents were most informed and involved, families held just over two-fifths of all libraries but four-fifths of all volumes.

Wide variations in participation are even more clearly demonstrated in several other related criteria. The average size of family libraries shows a steady rise from 3.6 volumes per library among hardscrabble families to 36.2 volumes among fortunate village families (see table 4–1). A similar rise is evident for the range in library size and the median size of family libraries.[21] On all counts, enhanced material and cultural conditions led to greater incidence, range, and average and median size of family libraries through 1830. Similarly, shares in lending libraries increased in frequency across the network of human habitats. The retention rate for lending library shares rose from 1 percent (of families with a private library) among hardscrabble families to 4 percent for self-sufficient farmstead families, and then to 13, 12, and 16 percent for the three living situations more actively engaged in print communications and commercial exchange. In addition, the only shares in a Windsor District Encyclopedia Library (a small lending library specializing in encyclopedias) were found in the fortunate village living situation (two shares, or 3 percent of the families). In short, a family residing in a village or hamlet, or on a farmstead in a community with a major central village (Windsor and Chester) was four times as likely to participate in a lending library as one living elsewhere in Windsor District.[22]

Participation in print communications within Windsor District through 1835, then, was very widespread—considerably higher than the 62 percent of all families in 1787–1835 who retained a library at the death of the head of household. The character of that participation varied with the human habitat, however. A specific configuration of knowledge characterized each human habitat, but all habitats, at least within the one region during these decades, shared a common core of traditional information and opinion. Some types of publications managed to penetrate into all five human habitats. Bibles, hymnals, psalm books, devotional tracts, primers, and schoolbooks—what Rolf Engelsing has termed "intensive reading matter"—were retained by families in all living situations. Beyond these common books and pamphlets, some other publications were widely read in four of the five; others were widely read in three; and still others circulated through just one or two reading communities. Periodicals, the other major vehicle of print communications regularly saved, were mainly limited to the most active three of the five human habitats.[23]

Each type of human habitat constituted a separate reading community. While there was no rigid hierarchy, these five levels of involvement with print culture revealed successively broader concern with commercial exchange, market relations, and "modern intelligence." They showed greated involvement with banks, industrial growth, voluntary societies, and reform organizations, as well as more rapid information diffusion and enhanced participation in institutions of public culture. However, while a fresh fabric of sacred and secular thought and feeling was emerging in the American Northeast after 1800, participation in print culture did not necessitate any alteration in traditional attitudes. In fact, in most families reading initally reinforced the traditional wisdom of the ages instilled by Webster and others. Growing awareness of change did not automatically entail acceptance.

Other factors—political interest and religious affiliation and activity, including participation in the benevolent empire of moral reform—also helped shape Windsor District residents' relationship to print and written expression. Religion especially affected the proportion of sacred as opposed to secular works, the specific character of religious works retained, and their uses.[24]

Most societies regularly engage in interrelated and overlapping cultural debates and conflicts. Rhys Isaac, Anthony Wallace, and Paul Johnson, among others, have delineated several broad cultural rifts in America between 1750 and 1840. Randolph Roth is superb in translating these issues into Upper Valley terms. In the future we must develop ways of learning about the underlying web of knowledge and meaning possessed by the whole population—Schutz's general stock of knowledge at hand—and also about those forms of understanding prevalent in a particular community because of its living situation. These different funds of knowledge continuously shape understanding and action. The concept of a human habitat helps us comprehend the integuments of rural New England society, its material and cultural infrastructure, and the process of change.[25]

The next series of problems to be addressed involve the institutional structures underlying the spread of a new rural communications environment. How did the whole body of knowledge, including information and opinion, beliefs, and values, circulate through that society? How was the universe of available reading matter distributed? Which items circulated most widely? Within which groups were varying shares of the whole assimilated and used in daily life? Understanding how knowledge circulated, we can better understand the significance of major public policy issues and movements in the history of knowledge.

Part II
Print Communications
and Cultural Exchange

Chapter 5

The Communication System and the Book Trade in Rural New England: The Upper Valley, 1778–1835

'Tis to ye Press and Pen we Mortals owe,
All we believe & almost all we know.
All hail ye great Preservers of these Arts,
That raise our thoughts & Cultivate our Parts.

—George Fisher, *The Instructor; or,*
Young Man's Best Companion

Contact Points and the Life Cycle of Printed Objects

That a growing majority of residents of a rural area participated actively in transatlantic culture at the turn of the nineteenth century was a phenomenon so new that it startled European travelers. How could it have happened? What dynamic operated during the Early Republic to transform prerevolutionary rural New England communities such as Chebacco Parish in Ipswich, Concord, Dedham, Lynn? On the eve of the American Revolution these were all largely self-contained, inward-looking communities dominated by face-to-face oral culture. Vast changes indeed were required before an empire of public opinion based on print culture could rise to prominence in rural daily life.[1]

In 1760 a few traditional professional and mercantile members of each township kept attuned to "knowledge from distant climes" and shared some of what they learned with their neighbors.[2] By 1815 the "latest intelligence," delivered at an ever-increasing pace, was all the rage in rural as well as urban New England. The story underlying this shift is complex.

By 1810 major changes in information and opinion were under way in the Upper Valley. The new communications environment linked the five human habitats while diffusing print culture differentially within them. Print culture's institutional structure, itself a key participant in valley commercial exchange, reshaped all reading and writing. It made available an ever-widening variety of printed matter—works locally published and imports published throughout Anglo-American society but mainly in the American Northeast. Within this universe of available reading matter, the list of popular sellers lengthened, and the amount and quality of information and opinion steadily expanded, bridging the gap between urban and rural cultural worlds.

Within the Upper Connecticut River Valley by 1800, more than a hundred incorporated townships formed a political, economic, and cultural subregion whose inhabitants shared many habits and tastes based on their common southern New England heritage. This subregion's transportation and communication system consisted of two circulation networks, the book trade, and the different levels of access to print. The nature of the printed matter that was carried along Upper Valley roads and waterways during the half century following the Revolution accounts for both the stability of the "Standing Order" view of the world and the turmoil that eventually created one of the country's first burned-over districts.[3]

Two special emphases marked the Upper Valley communication system and the book trade. One was the overall unity of the communication system: the total circulation network for print culture and the institutional structure and internal workings of the book trade linking production, sales, and distribution with varying audiences for printed matter. The term "book trade" refers not only to books but to the entire range of printed vehicles for circulating ideas within the Upper Valley, whatever their point of origin. As used by contemporaries, vehicles were "instruments of conveyance." Thus Noah Webster noted, "Letters are vehicles of communications." The second special emphasis was the diversity of the effects of the transportation and communication system. Access to different types of vehicles—almanacs and novels, for instance—varied enormously within the Upper Valley. Knowledge was diffused differentially, resulting in the evolution of three distinct levels of access to printed matter and thus three zones of communications, reception, and cultural participation in public life. During the decades 1780–1830, printed matter formed part of daily life for a large majority of all residents, but the part differed radically from zone to zone.[4]

"Culture" must always be thought of as active. Every culture lives and breathes. The central purpose of a history of communications is to study not the making and trading of commodities but the differential access to, and uses of, knowledge in daily life. But reading and writing in the Early Republic were maintained and replenished by the circulation system, which carried a bewildering array of older and newer vehicles of printed and written communications. By conceiving of printed objects first as commodities, each variety of which passes through a series of points from creation through eventual destruction, it is possible to chart and analyze Upper Valley cultural participation.

Detailed evidence is available from a wide variety of historical sources.

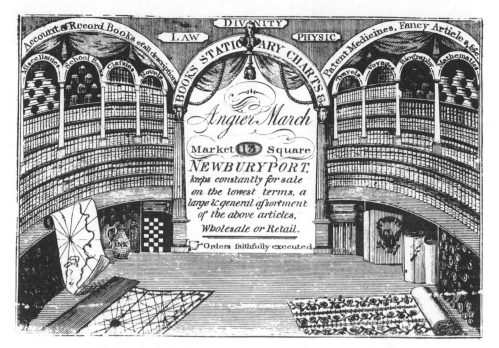

Angier March Bookstore, 13 Market Square, Newburyport. Trade Card Collection. Courtesy, American Antiquarian Society.

The typical range of products sold by New England bookstores is seen in this Trade Card: printed matter, stationery, account and blank record books, ink, paper, wallpaper, patent medicines, and maps.

The problem is one typical in history, however; each fund of evidence about printed matter disseminated in the Upper Valley in 1780–1830 offers only a partial view. It traces only some of the items circulating within the area in only a limited portion of their life cycle from pen and press to mulch. Each situation in which a book (or other printed object) was in the hands of Upper Valley residents represents evidence of contact between some books and some readers. We might, therefore, begin to think of the life cycle of a printed object as the external history of authorship, from the moment a manuscript was carried by a writer to a printing office or publisher until the work was listed as part of the estate inventory of a deceased household head, sometimes a half century later.[5]

Each print vehicle had its own life cycle, a series of situations when it was being used or was in contact with a group of potential readers. In the case of books, at each Upper Valley contact point a discernible share of all books in existence (within the total circulation system) were in contact with a specific portion of all residents. However, no single contact point could include transactions involving all books or all Upper Valley readers. Even the rich detail of the Walpole, New Hampshire, bookstore's annual stock list, for example, is limited by the fact that for some of the years it covers, there were two bookstores operating in the village. In fact, the total number of books circulating within an area at any given point in time cannot yet be determined. Partial evidence is the rule at every contact point, and the total set of contact points itself varies with the time frame, society, etc.

The Upper Valley was settled slowly after the French and Indian War and began to expand rapidly only after the American Revolution. The communication system connecting northwestern to southern New England remained quite primitive until the firm establishment of the Bennington *Gazette* and the Windsor *Vermont Journal*, accomplished by 1785. During the next forty years, before widespread use of stereotyped printing plates and steam presses, the life cycle of books in the Upper Valley was reasonably stable. The regional communication system determined the particular set of nine major contact points through which all books passed, once they had been printed in, or imported into, the Upper Valley. The nine contact points were: (1) an area writer's discussions about her or his manuscript with a printer or publisher; (2) printing and publishing situations; (3) shipping, distribution, and wholesaling of books; (4) retail sales, including the sales and stock of bookstores, general stores, peddlers, and even individual private sellers; (5) individual and family purchases; (6) borrowing situations; (7) private family libraries; (8) commentary about specific works or categories of works circulating in an area; and (9) evidence about print culture generally, including the new vocabulary of print communications.

Pamphlets, almanacs, newspapers, periodicals, and broadsides moved in parallel circuits, each with its own peculiarities. As each vehicle moved through the series of contact points, it moved through three increasingly specific fields of social influence: from the intentionality of authors expressing traditional or newer ideas; through the targeted influence achieved by its delivery to specific audiences, some intended and others not; to a field of direct influence based on reception, assimilation, and use by Upper Valley individuals and families.[6]

Authorship, printing, and publishing constituted the initial field of influence, a field of intentionality radiating outward from an author and her or his text and including the author's work and the printer-publisher's intentions, embodied in the concept of "ideal copy."[7] A locally authored book circulating within the Upper Valley first came in contact with residents when an area writer brought a manuscript to a printer or publisher. Subsequent negotiations, determining whether it would be published, involved a printer alone or a printer and another individual or group with funds, who served as the publisher. At this point, the scope of the contact was narrow, involving only two or a few individuals.[8]

Once agreement had been reached, the book was printed. Printing and publishing represented a second contact point and created an especially rich fund of documentary evidence. The text itself, supplemented by business records of printers and publishers, indicates how it was produced and suggests printing office practices,[9] including decisions about advertising, and initial edition and "batch" binding. During the period 1787–1830, three steps were involved in procuring copyright, as part of the legal process leading to publication. The title page, set in print, had to be deposited with the clerk of the federal district court. Next, at least one newspaper had to publish the text of the title page. Finally, a copy of the work had to be deposited with the secretary of state within six months after publication.[10] Procurement of copyright completed the second contact point.[11]

The area of circulation, or the field of delivery, constitutes the second field of influence for printed objects. After a book was published and bound, or when it was in sheets, before or after folding and gathering, it was distributed to a wide variety of sellers. The shipping, distribution, and wholesaling of books constitutes a third contact point.[12] Books were sold in a variety of settings within the Upper Valley; retail outlets constituted a fourth contact point and determined the universe of commodities available for purchase, whether new or second-hand, and whether published in the Upper Valley or beyond.[13]

The shipping and advertising records of books available for sale and lists of works actually sold enable us to begin determining the actual circulation patterns of published editions of books. Reading—actual consumption—represents the third and final field of influence, a field of reception, assimilation, and use by specific readers located throughout the Upper Valley. The consumption of printed matter began with individual and family purchases, a fifth contact point. These included purchases by private individuals; families; social, moral, and circulating libraries; and Sunday school, college, and encyclopedia libraries.[14]

Purchasing was not the only major avenue to reading in rural New England through 1830. Formal borrowing of books in the Upper Valley proliferated in village and hamlet areas after 1795. At least six social libraries, two moral libraries, one encyclopedia library, and a pair of circulating libraries existed within Windsor District's ten townships before 1830. There were also several academies in the district, and each typically maintained a small school library; even some Sunday schools maintained libraries. Families also borrowed informally from a member of another family. Borrowing situations thus formed a sixth contact point. Also included at this contact point was a third way an individual might obtain books (and a second avenue to reading without making a purchase), receiving them as gifts.[15]

Exceptionally rich and detailed evidence documents the accumulation of private family libraries, an important seventh contact point. Estate inventories list all print items in a household at the death of the household head and forming part of the legal estate. The chief weaknesses of estate inventories are that almanacs, newspapers, broadsides, and several types of books were rarely saved; that pamphlets and other items were sometimes not specified; and that only printed items retained till the death of the household head were included. Book carters roamed the Upper Valley collecting all manner of printed matter to be pulped and recycled. Nevertheless, the strengths of inventories are substantial. Works purchased and retained in the frugal family economy of the Early Republic offer the largest, most representative evidence of printed matter actually read. The evidence is very specific (title and author in New England) and exists for a large share of all families.[16]

Upper Valley residents also had indirect contact with printed matter. Books were discussed and excerpted both in private interchanges and in public vehicles of communication. Commentary on specific works or categories of works circulating in an area—discussions and mentions of a book in letters, diaries, journals, and daybooks, or in the work's own margins; excerpts in newspapers; and separately published letters, essays, and poems about books written by local residents and distant contributors—constitutes an eighth contact point. Such notices reveal much about the dissemination of books and the reception of the ideas they advocated. The ninth and final contact point broadens the evaluative framework by examining evidence about print culture generally, including the new vocabulary of print communications. Materials include comments, letters, essays, and other broad analyses of print culture. Such commentary often took the form of semantic comments—for example, about the meaning of "knowledge," "information," "communications," "modern intelligence," and "learning," or about the different types of reading matter and reading situations, the uses and misuses of each, and general attitudes toward print culture and its impact. These discussions buttressed a growing ideology of mass print culture.[17]

Among all vehicles of print communications we chose to concentrate in this book on those items retained in family libraries (books, pamphlets, and periodicals) or borrowed from lending libraries. Consequently, six of the nine contact points are emphasized: production and advertising; distribution; public borrowing records, in those cases where they exist for families with estate inventories; retention (family library) records in the form of household inventories and wills; reviewing and other private and public discussions of books and pamphlets; and contemporary understanding of print culture. Broad patterns in residents' understanding of the contemporary world derived from analysis of a myriad of specific instances, accurately weighed. It is hardly useful to learn that the Walpole bookstores stocked over 30,000 books in 1808 when the township held less than 2,000 people, unless somehow we can learn how the transfer of knowledge from author to bookstore to reader and back out to the world occurred. The circulation system and its resulting pattern of differential access constitute the first major clues to trends in the actual state of knowledge and to the interactive processes that led people in the Upper Valley to be preoccupied with printed and written matter.[18]

The Circulation System for Print Culture in the Upper Valley, 1778–1835

Transportation and communication systems remain mysterious elements in the ecology of civilizations. By themselves they do not do anything. No imposing steeples, columns, or facades adorn them, so their significance is far from obvious. When no one is out traveling they are quiet, serene, and just there, waiting to be used. Perhaps roads should have been made with built-in grand arches, or at least volume and weight meters so that we students of history would immediately comprehend their immense value to nearly all facets of everyday life. In a very real sense we have inverted the order of history. It was not that the long settled, large village residents of Windsor, Vermont, decided to create a transportation and communication system once more essential matters of survival and livelihood had been resolved. No, in the beginning God created the heavens, the mountains, and the Connecticut River.

Until now intellectual history has chosen to account for the dissemination of ideas and values by the easy trickle-down hypothesis. Its foundation assumption is that the dissemination of ideas, and hence of reading, and of specific types of reflection, proceeded in a hierarchical two-step fashion, from elites to the masses and from "high" to "popular" culture. This approach ignores the question of process: how a historical infrastructure, and particularly the transportation and communications networks that render knowledge available or unavailable, function. This chapter charts the ways in which knowledge as a commodity actually circulated throughout a rural society. Our focus is a series of fundamental questions more familiar to scholars of the European than of the American book trade. What were the basic transportation and communication systems undergirding the distribution of goods, services, and printed information and opinion in the Upper Valley? What were the institutional structures and the internal workings of the book trade (the latter linking production, sales, and distribution with varying audiences for printed matter)? What were the specific characteristics of each vehicle carrying information and opinion? And what geographical and cultural zones of access to printed and written matter, shaping various levels of cultural participation, existed between 1780 and 1835?

Elementary literacy was not equally distributed in the Upper Valley in 1760–1835. Nor did everyone acquiring basic literacy skills enjoy the same possibilities to learn about the distant world and apply that knowledge in daily

Township	Commencement and Duration of Printing Through 1830	Newspapers: Dates Published	Bookstores (n=40)	Periodicals: Dates Published
Barnard	1812–14		1	
Bellows Falls	1817–30	1817–30	1	
Bradford[2]	1809–13		1	
Brattleboro (P)	1797–1830	1797–30	5	
Chelsea	1826–30	1826–30	2	
Chester	1807–9;	1807–9;	1	
	1828–30	1828–30	1	
Dresden*	1778–79		–	
Hartford*[3]	1819		1	
Manchester*	1803–4		1	
Newbury*	1796–97	1796–97	1	
Norwich*	1830	1830	1	
Putney	1797–99	1797–99	1	
Randolph	1800–10	1800–10	1	
East Randolph*	1829	1829	1	
Royalton	1826–30	1826–30	1	
Thetford[4]	1827–29		1	
Weathersfield[5]	1813–16		2	
Westminster	1780–83;		–	
	1794; 1796		1	
Whitingham[6]	1796–c. 1806		1	
Windsor (P)	1783–1830	1783–1830	11	1803–04
Woodstock (P)	1804–6;	1804–6;	–	
	1818–30	1818–30	4	1820–30

P=Permanent print centers
* Fleeting print shops collapsing within two years
Source: Unless noted, a search of all extant issues of Chester and Windsor newspapers through 1830.

[1] McCorison, *Vermont Imprints*
[2] Engraving maps and making globes: McCorison, *Vermont Imprints*
[3] Printing and engraving maps: McCorison, *Amos Taylor; A sketch and bibliography*
[4] Bookselling only
[5] Also engraving, 1813: McCorison, *Vermont Imprints*
[6] Bookselling only: McCorison, *Taylor;* and McCorison, *Vermont Imprints*

Table 5–2: Upper Valley New Hampshire Counties – Print Center Record Through 1830[1]

Township	Commencement and Duration of Printing Through 1830	Newspapers: Dates Published	Bookstores (n = 20)	Periodicals: Dates Published
Charlestown*	1829–30	1829–30	1	
Enfield	1819–25		1	1819–25
Hanover (P)	1779:	1779:	–	
	1793–1830	1793–1830	5	1803–7
Haverhill (P)	1796–97;	1796–97;	–	
	1808–10;	1808–10;	1	
	1819–30	1819–30	1	1797
Jaffrey*	1812		1	
Keene (P)	1787–1830	1787–1830	4	
Lebanon[2]	1813–14		1	
Newport	1825–30	1825–30	1	
Plymouth*	1825–26	1825–26	1	
Walpole (P)	1793–1817;	1793–1813;	2	
	1825–26	1825–26	1	

P = Permanent print centers
* Fleeting print shops collapsing within two years
  Source: Unless noted, a search of all extant issues of Chester and Windsor newspapers through 1830.

[1] AAS Imprints Files; files of R. Murray, III.
[2] Bookselling only, apparently only during parts of two years

life. In conjunction with the other factors we have discussed, differences in access gave families living in the same county vastly different selections of British and American reading matter.

During the half century after initial settlement, an ever more elaborate road and water system brought new information and opinion (see tables 5–1 and 5–2 throughout). Wherever a book, pamphlet, periodical, almanac, newspaper, or broadside originated, it could reach readers only through the circulation system connecting printers and publishers, distributors, advertisers, and retailers. The circulation system in the Upper Valley in 1780–1835 was quite complex. There were two distinct circuits of print distribution, one formal and fairly stable (regularly available) and the other informal and irregular but also important because it supplied some works, including clandestine writings, otherwise generally unavailable.[19]

The formal circulation system became quite elaborate and highly integrated in the half century following the Revolution. Four essential components comprised the formal circulation system. First, rivers, bridges, and roads (post roads

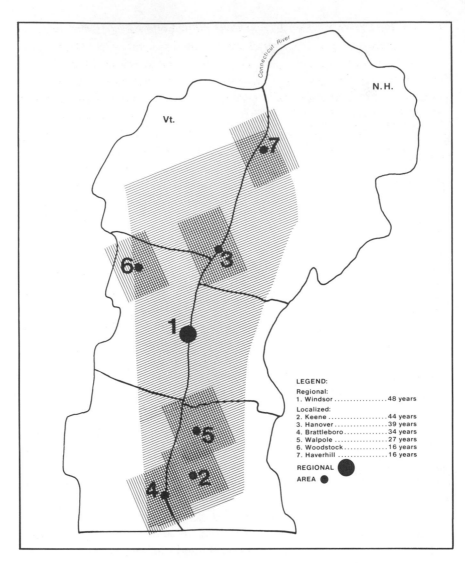

LEGEND:

Regional:
1. Windsor . . . . .48 years

Localized:
2. Keene . . . . .44 years
3. Hanover . . . . .39 years
4. Brattleboro . . . . .34 years
5. Walpole . . . . .27 years
6. Woodstock . . . . .16 years
7. Haverhill . . . . .16 years

REGIONAL

AREA

Figure 5–1: Upper Valley Permanent Print Centers, 1787–1830

and more local roads) served as conduits. Second, printing offices were established within what we have termed permanent and auxiliary print centers. Third, bookstores, mainly located in print centers, served as centers for the collection, storage, and distribution of printed and related items destined for sale directly (or indirectly, through general stores and peddlers) to the surrounding townships. Fourth, newspapers—all of which were published at full-fledged print centers—transmitted information about the holdings of each bookstore and served as an outlet for local opinion as well as the owners' ideas and values.

Windsor, Vermont, was the most elaborate Upper Valley communications center in 1783–1830, dominating the area's formal system for circulating print and written culture (see figure 5–1). The *Vermont Journal* initiated Upper Valley newspaper circulation in 1783. This weekly was the centerpiece of rural print communications. After 1790, two weekly newspapers were usually printed in Windsor. Between 1810 and 1816 there were three, and two again thereafter. No other Upper Valley community regularly sustained more than one weekly. Furthermore, bookstores independent of those attached to printing offices operated continuously from 1793. No other Upper Valley community was able to support more than two bookstores for more than a few years at a time through 1830. Another sign of substantial, steady publishing activity—increasing specialization within the book trade—also began in Windsor village. Bookbinders, both independent and affiliated with printing offices, resided there. Moreover, a Windsor *Village Magazine*, most of its contents written by local authors, lasted twenty-six weeks during 1803–1804. Certainly other townships, especially Hanover, laid more claim to being intellectual centers. And Walpole's *Farmer's Museum* was far superior to any newspaper published in Windsor. But with its size, stability, and commercial leadership; its location at the geographical center of the subregion; and its sometime role as governmental and legal center, Windsor dominated virtually every aspect of the production and dissemination of print culture in the Upper Valley.[20]

A permanent print center remained in active business for more than fifteen years, while an auxiliary print center operated between three and fifteen years (see figure 5–2). Auxiliary print centers also existed in fairly large secondary villages on main roads and waterways, generating print material from within the region and serving as wholesaling points for books, pamphlets, almanacs, and some periodicals published elsewhere. Windsor, the hub, was intricately linked by major roads and the Connecticut River to six other permanent print centers: Brattleboro to the south, Keene, and Walpole, Woodstock to the west, and Hanover and eventually Haverhill to the north. Each permanent print center was also connected to auxiliary print centers by the roads, the river, and the newspapers that traveled over them. Together the system had between fifteen and twenty-three township links (depending on the time period). Thus each print center had direct access to a broad range of printed materials. These two dozen or so townships disseminated awareness of burgeoning print culture throughout the remaining 100 to 120 settled places within the Upper Valley.

Windsor was the oldest permanent print center in the Upper Valley, having operated continuously since 1783. It was also, as we have seen, the center of the book trade for this subregion. Pamphlets, books, newspapers, almanacs, periodicals, and broadsides flowed outward from presses there, at the six other permanent print centers (see figure 5–1), and at eleven additional shorter-term

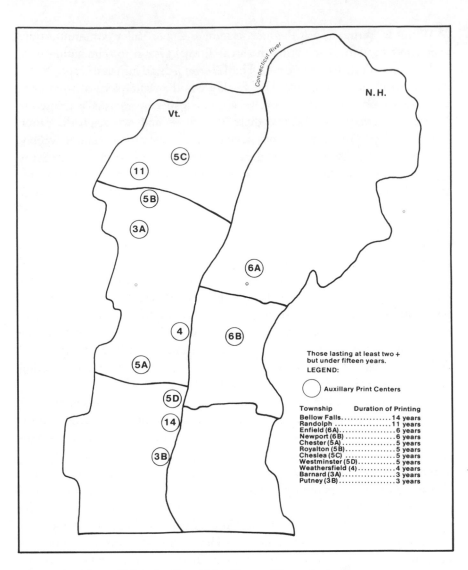

Those lasting at least two +
but under fifteen years.
LEGEND:

◯ Auxiliary Print Centers

Township	Duration of Printing
Bellow Falls	14 years
Randolph	11 years
Enfield (6A)	6 years
Newport (6B)	6 years
Chester (5A)	5 years
Royalton (5B)	5 years
Cheslea (5C)	5 years
Westminster (5D)	5 years
Weathersfield (4)	4 years
Barnard (3A)	3 years
Putney (3B)	3 years

Figure 5–2: Upper Valley Auxiliary Print Centers Through 1830

auxiliary print centers, each of which survived for three to fourteen years (see figure 5–2). These auxiliary centers filled the gaps between permanent print centers along the central artery, the Connecticut River, and also extended print culture into parts of the later-settled hinterland. Nine other more fleeting printing offices, lasting fewer than three years each, were excluded from most of the analysis of print centers to follow; they died shortly after birth because their economic locales did not grow enough to generate the business and advertising required for a newspaper's survival.

With 137 settled townships in the region by 1820, there were, theoretically at least, 137 possible print communication centers. However, the Upper Valley communication system was fairly centralized as early as 1790. This characteristic is crucial in accounting for the wide variation in availability of reading material among different segments of the population. In 1820 Windsor lay at the geographical center of eighteen permanent and auxiliary print centers. Windsor and the other six permanent print centers blanketed the most densely populated central corridor on either side of the Connecticut River. Eleven more auxiliary print centers, mostly founded during the 1810–30 period, operated on the perimeters of the central system as countryside population density increased. These eighteen print centers formed a new communications environment.

With their generators (presses) and disseminators (bookstores and newspapers) of print culture, print centers had an impact far beyond that indicated by lists of local imprints. A village with a printing office and newspaper served as a multipurpose communications center, completely dominating the communication of nonlocal and some local information in an area covering five to eleven townships. This broader role created a true nexus of print culture in the countryside.

Print centers served a series of specific functions. Their newspaper offices were the primary collectors—through the regular receipt of up to a hundred newspapers—of every conceivable kind of information about the non-local world. A digest of this news was widely disseminated through the four-page weekly. As we have seen, by its sustained attention to the whole array of businesses and economic opportunities seeking patronage within its subscription area, the weekly also functioned as the most important supporter of the emerging regional commercial economy. Advertisements and notices often amounted to nearly half the weekly's contents and were never less than a fifth in a modestly healthy newspaper. Print centers occasionally published periodicals, often published almanacs, and nearly always published broadsides. These documents usually contained information about the local scene as well as reports on distant places and events. Print centers also published most of the books and pamphlets that were written in the Upper Valley, and reprinted works written elsewhere. Furthermore, print centers were stationers selling pens, ink, paper, forms, blank books, letter seals, and usually a range of patent medicines. Finally, every print center served the additional functions of wholesale and retail bookstore for nearly all books, pamphlets, and other printed items sold in the area, wherever they had been published. By the late 1820s peddlers increasingly purchased their stock at Windsor and other Upper Valley permanent print centers.

The book trade, like everything else in the Upper Valley, was integrated into the seasonal agricultural cycle (see table 5–3). A Windsor advertisement in December 1806, for instance, noted that "a considerable addition to the

Table 5-3: Seasonal Pattern for Upper Valley
Advertisements: Month Advertisement of
Books First Appeared, 1802-30

Month	Number of Ads
December	31
January	26
November	19
October	18
June	14
March	13
July	13
February	10
April	9
August	8
September	8
May	6
Total	175 advertisements

Top Third   = 54 percent of all advertisements
Middle Third = 28 percent of all advertisements
Bottom Third = 18 percent of all advertisements

Source: VJ, sample of 175 advertisements, 1802-30.

above [advertised] assortment will be received by the first sleighing." The late fall and winter months were the most critical times for restocking printed and written items, which, like other heavy things, were most easily transported on frozen roadbeds, on the rivers in the fall, or on river ice. People and animals slogged along in the mud during much of the spring and early fall. Rough and slow in the summer, New England roads and rivers came alive in the late fall; after harvest, travel was brisk. By early winter, the frozen Connecticut and its tributaries provided relatively safe passage for books and people alike, so that 54 percent of all book advertisements appeared in the less than four months between mid-October and late January, while only 18 percent appeared in the quagmire seasons of spring (April and May), late summer, and early fall (August and September).[21]

The second leading component was the printing office. Most of the 137 townships and large unincorporated settlements existing in the Upper Valley by the 1820s never housed a printing office or even a satellite bookstore. In fact, printing facilities were established in only twenty-seven townships, or a fifth of the total, and only in eighteen townships (13 percent) survived long enough to qualify as print centers. The locus of supply for print culture was thus neither regional nor exactly local. Rather, like the emerging market economy of which it was an important component, the book trade was organized around distinct economic locales comprising (in whole or in part) four to ten townships. Moreover, a hierarchy existed among print centers.

The printing office, as noted above, was the physical core of each print center, thanks to that marvelously fecund early-modern machine, the printing press. In the Upper Valley in 1787–1830, most printing offices in permanent print centers had two active presses; auxiliary print centers often had but one. Normally a two-press shop had one master printer who was also a publisher, an apprentice, and perhaps two journeymen. Extra help was hired when necessary. Most printing offices were established to print not books or pamphlets but newspapers, and often a year or two passed before any additional item other than an almanac was attempted. Three-quarters of the twenty-seven Upper Valley printing offices through 1830 started in this way (see tables 5-1 and 5-2). None of the other seven offices lasted more than four years; a newspaper was essential to survival. Once stable, most printing offices also issued a yearly almanac in October or November and, throughout the year, produced books, pamphlets, and broadsides; ball, theater, and lottery tickets; blank forms, invitations, and legal notices. Occasionally (in four of the twenty townships with newspapers) periodicals were also printed.[22]

The bookstore, the third essential component of the formal circulation system, was the center for sales of wholesale and retail books, pamphlets, and almanacs, and some retail periodicals (see figure 5–3). Along with the meetinghouse service, the town meeting, the school session, and the multi-purpose general store, the bookstore was one of the most consequential social institutions in rural New England. As the most important secular connection with the nonlocal world, and also as a major connection to sacred knowledge, bookstores were uniquely complex businesses navigating between local and nonlocal, secular and sacred concerns. Through 1830, a fairly elaborate system totaling fifty-nine bookstores in thirty townships served as collection, storage, and distribution locations supplying their own and the remaining 107 townships. In location Upper Valley bookstores showed steady expansion: outward from the river townships between Brattleboro and Hanover by the mid-1790s, and then into the hinterlands during the next two decades, in accordance with settlement patterns. In the 1820s, printing offices proliferated in several new villages. By 1830 there were twenty townships with stable bookstores scattered throughout the area, and several other bookstores were showing signs of stability.

Only four bookstores independent of villages with printing offices existed in the Upper Valley through 1830. These unusual ventures reveal the emergence of another, more localized sort of bookselling. While no records of any of the four have been located, those of another business of exactly this type— Robert Thomas's independent bookstore in the truly rural township of Ster-

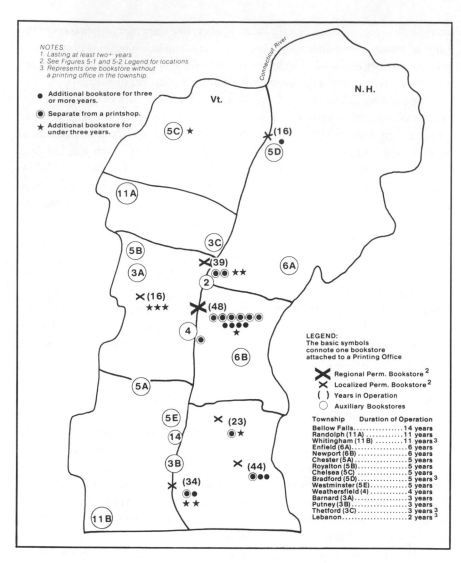

NOTES:
1. Lasting at least two+ years
2. See Figures 5-1 and 5-2 Legend for locations
3. Represents one bookstore without a printing office in the township.

● Additional bookstore for three or more years.
◉ Separate from a printshop.
★ Additional bookstore for under three years.

Vt.

N.H.

(5C) ★

✕(16)
(5D) ●

(11A)

(5B)   (3C)
(3A)   ✕(39)
        ●● ★★
        (2)   (6A)

✕(16)
★★★   ✕(48)
        ●●●●●●●
(4)   ●●●●●
●   ★

(6B)

LEGEND:
The basic symbols connote one bookstore attached to a Printing Office

(5A)

✕ Regional Perm. Bookstore [2]
✕ Localized Perm. Bookstore [2]
( ) Years in Operation
○ Auxiliary Bookstores

(5E)   ✕ (23)
(14)   ◉ ★

Township	Duration of Operation
Bellow Falls	14 years
Randolph (11A)	11 years
Whitingham (11B)	11 years [3]
Enfield (6A)	6 years
Newport (6B)	6 years
Chester (5A)	5 years
Royalton (5B)	5 years
Chelsea (5C)	5 years
Bradford (5D)	5 years [3]
Westminster (5E)	5 years
Weathersfield (4)	4 years
Barnard (3A)	3 years
Putney (3B)	3 years
Thetford (3C)	3 years [3]
Lebanon	2 years [3]

(3B)   ✕ (44)
          ◉●●
✕ (34)
●●
★★

(11B)

Figure 5–3: Upper Valley Bookstore Locations Through 1830

ling, Massachusetts, in 1790–1846, where there was no sizable village, no printing office, and no newspaper—reveal the tastes of agricultural and hamlet families. The best-selling items were a wider variety of almanacs, schoolbooks, dictionaries, hymnals, psalm books, and devotional works than that carried by general stores. Furthermore, as early as the mid-1790s, this bookstore also stocked a few copies of each of nearly two hundred newer books and pamphlets, especially novels, poetry, other kinds of modern literature, travels, works about the life cycle and individual stages of life, and theology. Like Thomas's Sterling

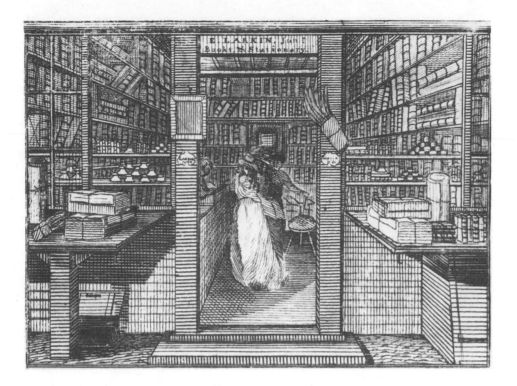

Ebenezer Larkin Bookstore, 147 Cornhill, Boston. Trade Card Collection. Courtesy, American Antiquarian Society.

Several New Hampshire and Vermont Upper Valley bookstores were well stocked with locally printed books and others imported from eastern cities. In this Boston bookstore trade card, bound books and others in sheets have been bundled for shipment.

bookstore, the four Upper Valley independent booksellers undoubtedly extended the habit of reading deep into the local countryside.[23]

All stable bookstores were affiliated with parent firms and distant print centers. In addition to selling locally printed books, pamphlets, and almanacs, the bookstore served as the prime distributor for the largest group of titles sold within the region: the imports, which the store obtained by exchanging part of each edition of a locally printed book or pamphlet with several other print centers within the Upper Valley and with some shops beyond its bounds. Only one title in seven available for sale in the Upper Valley in the period 1790–1830 was published there. Especially large numbers of titles came from Boston, Philadelphia, and New York. The preponderance of titles from distant presses, however, did not mean that they accounted for the greatest volume of sales. In total number of copies stocked and sold, popular sellers printed locally, including traditional "steady sellers" and many newer popular sellers, dominated purchases by 1800.

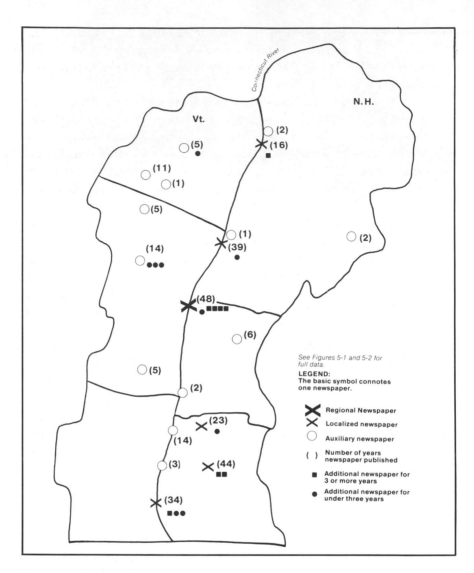

Figure 5-4: Upper Valley Newspaper Locations Through 1830

The distribution functions of a bookstore were central to its mission. Its connections with broader communications networks were firmly rooted in a shared North Atlantic Republic of Letters. All was not sweet reasonableness, however. Firms within the same village rarely traded stock, because competition within the local market was too intense. Beyond that market, the territory was often tacitly divided. When it was not, editors attacked each other in print and very occasionally also in court or in person.[24]

General stores formed the final sales outlets in the formal circuit of print communications. Most general stores sold printed items, but only a very limited line of almanacs, schoolbooks, dictionaries, hymnals, psalm books, and devotional treatises. By 1815 general stores existed in about half of the 123 townships that had been settled in the Upper Valley.[25]

Newspapers, which anchored the advertising system, were the fourth vital component in the communication system (see figure 5-4). They regularly carried elaborate series of advertisements on all respects of print culture: invitations to "subscribe to" (underwrite) books a publisher hoped to print locally or to help print somewhere else; announcements of forthcoming works; advertisements of at most three new works just printed in that printing office (or just received); and a basic advertisement that ran every six months to a year and listed many books printed there plus those recently received from other printing offices and most of the new arrivals from print centers elsewhere in America, Great Britain, and France. Each advertisement ran for between two and six weeks, usually consecutively for three weeks or biweekly. Because most general stores had a limited selection and retail mail ordering was infrequent before 1830, rural weekly newspapers functioned as book catalogues for area residents. There were relatively few formal book catalogues appearing in Windsor District through 1830. By 1810 the weekly came directly to the household or to a neighbor via the post rider in more than half of all Upper Valley townships. Within villages and hamlets, there were few serious delays in circulation, whether newspapers were delivered or were picked up. Currency was not usually required as payment until at least 1815; many advertisements concluded, "Most kinds of country produce will be received in payment." After 1815, this more personal system of bartering gave way to "strictly cash" and currency.[26]

In all respects the formal circulation system for printed items functioned within the basic rhythms of the agricultural year dominant in the Upper Valley into the 1820s. Reinforcing this pattern were annual almanacs, the trusty allies of newspapers. They advised their readers each November and December to prepare for winter, now that harvesting was complete, by equipping—and the equipment included schoolbooks—their children for school. Youth and adult readers were also advised to prepare themselves for the solitary weeks of winter by considering their own intellectual and spiritual improvement.[27]

A second circulation system through which printed matter was disseminated through the Upper Valley entailed more informal—irregularly available—circulation and sales. Several types of itinerant and local purveyors of printed matter included (1) paper mill owners selling stock received in trade from printing offices; (2) local authors selling their own works from their homes; (3) itinerant authors selling their own works and sometimes those of other people; (4) an occasional bookseller, or even more rarely a general store owner, who dealt in clandestine literature as well as advertised book trade titles; and (5) peddlers and other "flying stationers" and ballad sellers. The importance of these outlets was that each was in contact with a particular or unusual audience. Only some of the items they circulated and sold were typical reading fare, overlapping with works sold in bookstores and general stores. Peddlers especially, and others occasionally, distributed underground literature throughout rural New England.[28]

Peddling, the most important component of the informal circulation network, had a definite ecology. These itinerant hawkers and walkers in the Upper Valley usually circulated the widest variety of printed matter available in America, a selection broader than all but the most daring bookstores sold. Peddlers with books almost always avoided the few villages with printing centers. Beyond these, all Upper Valley townships were potential markets, but not all were visited regularly. All non–print center villages and their immediate farmstead surroundings had the highest priority, becasue they had relatively high numbers of potential customers. Peddlers and itinerant authors frequently visited Springfield, for instance. While it held several general stores with limited selections of printed matter, Springfield apparently lacked a bookstore although it was the second largest town in Vermont in 1810. Hamlets along main turnpikes and roads, plus farmsteads along the way and on decent local roads in nearby townships, had next priority. Peddlers and other traveling salespeople tended to avoid newly settled townships in settled counties, counties in the pioneer stage of social development, and isolated farmstead and shepherding communities.[29]

In all three active market areas—emerging fortunate village habitats, and hamlet and self-sufficient farmstead living situations—peddlers directly supplemented the fairly limited reading tastes of most residents. In these instances chapbooks served as the key bridge between traditional intensive reading fare and novels, travel accounts, and other newer forms of reading matter. Bookstore accounts of stock reveal that in several fields of knowledge many popular works—*Moll Flanders*, *A Pilgrim's Progress*, and *Robinson Crusoe*, for instance—were issued in chapbook form in abbreviated and often recast versions of between 12 and 64 pages. These texts proved more manageable to many readers than newer novels and other texts of hundreds of pages. Peddlers thus played a crucial role in providing forms of reading fare to bridge the gap between childhood and youthful family reading and schoolbooks, and the far lengthier and often more difficult texts typical of adult reading interests.

The special position of peddlers in the book trade rested on the fact that they traveled to customers rather than awaiting visits from customers. Further, they not only catered to families who were often already part of the market economy but also extended emerging capitalism farther into the countryside than general stores could. Families with access to general stores and other hamlet businesses, many of whom had an account with one or more by 1800–1810, were, however, the special targets of peddlers, as is evident from the pattern

Peddler James Fisk, Jr., of Burlington, Vermont. Courtesy, Vermont Historical Society.

As primary agents in the informal circulation system for printed matter, peddlers carried print culture into the countryside far from villages and their bookstores.

of resistance to peddlers and the attacks upon them. The limits of peddler activity in the countryside indicate where capitalism had yet to emerge in the Upper Valley in 1780–1830. Some families did have their first experiences with market products, and with money as a commodity, in dealing with peddlers. These experiences gave farm and hamlet families the taste for a wider range of printed matter than was available at local general stores, leading some to visit a village bookstore, subscribe to a weekly newspaper, or contemplate forming or joining a library. Most families, however, were merely adding to their variety of market transactions. In both cases the informal circulation system, especially through chapbooks, extended the habit of reading, and the diversity of reading matter available, to people living away from the fifteen to twenty-five print center villages and their surrounding farmsteads.[30]

One of the most interesting and unusual kinds of printed matter circulating through the informal distribution system was clandestine literature: obscene, pornographic, scurrilous, malicious, and radical political or religious works. A substantial part of an edition of John Cleland's *Memoirs of a Woman of Pleasure* (293 copies) remained in a special final stock accounting of Anson Whipple, the resident partner in Isaiah Thomas and Company's bookstore at Walpole, New Hampshire, in August 1817. That part of an edition of *Fanny*

Hill resided in an Upper Valley bookstore raises new questions. No Upper Valley bookstore ever advertised *Fanny Hill* through 1830. Presently it is safest to conclude that *Fanny Hill* was always sold under the counter and in only a few bookstores. In addition, it was disseminated in the Upper Valley through the informal circulation network of peddlers and other itinerants. Nor was this the only edition of *Fanny Hill*. Marcus McCorison has presented evidence attesting to at least one and perhaps two other editions in 1815–17, both "circulating in all parts of this [N.H.] and other adjoining States," according to a Concord bookseller's letter to the governor of New Hampshire. According to a second letter, the same writer supposed that four different booksellers and another, perhaps a general storekeeper, all named, were vendors of "the Book . . . entitled 'Memoirs of a Woman of Pleasure,' with 7 or 10 obscene plates." If the statement is accurate, then three of the five permanent print centers operating within the Upper Valley in 1810–17, were disseminating one of the most infamous of all clandestine works. Much more research is needed on other underground literature, which naturally left fewer traces than other texts. The print center's role in rural New England life was richly ambiguous.[31]

The print communication system did not end with local roads and waterways. Each township was connected with other townships, so that the Upper Valley was ultimately linked with Boston, New York, and Philadelphia, and through them with Edinburgh, London, and Paris. Moreover, information traveled in both directions in every part of the system. The local nodes of print communications generating cultural interchange throughout the Upper Valley were situated within a vast web of influence and power.

Dissemination: Zones of Access
to Print Culture in the Upper Valley

Before electronic communications, place and geography were central aspects of all human experience. Nowhere was this basic fact more clearly exemplified than in the vast differences in access to print culture that existed in the Upper Valley between 1780 and 1830 (see figure 5–5). Central in shaping cultural participation, access to print culture was a function not of an historical absolute distance, but of concrete circumstances combining geographical distance and historical habits of travel. When people calculated distance, they took into account the actual course of roads around physical barriers; the general quality of the road or waterway between homestead and bookstore; and the season of the year as it affected travel conditions.

As reading became a necessity of life in the Early Republic, the absence of ready access to printed matter became an ever more serious disability. So when we study the rise of print culture, groups with very limited access are

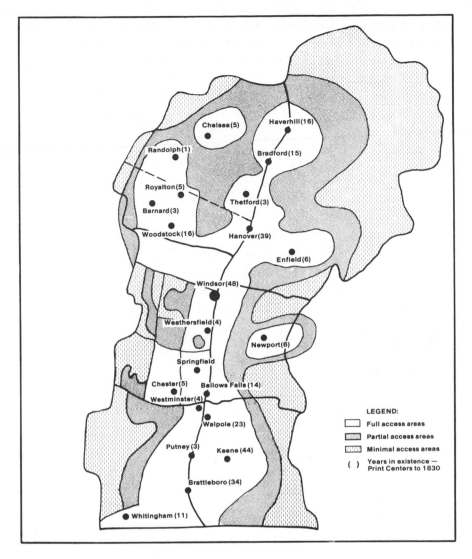

Figure 5-5: Upper Valley Differential Access Zones, 1820–30

as important as those with ready access. We can distinguish three levels of access to and participation in print culture within the Upper Valley in 1778–1830. Each defined a specific living environment with respect to print culture. First was the full-access zone (see figure 5-6). Encompassing approximately thirty-five communities by 1800, fifty by 1810, and at least parts of sixty communities in the 1820s, the full-access area was the central zone of print culture activity in the Upper Valley. It included all villages with bookstores and most of the surrounding farmsteads in these and contiguous townships. These areas were

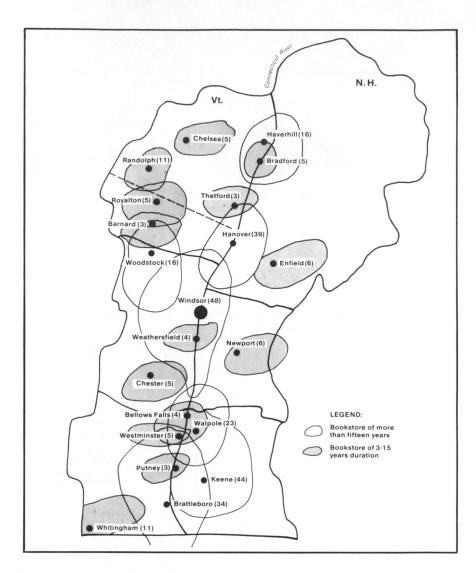

Figure 5–6: Upper Valley Full Access Zone, 1820–30

all within reach by a one-day round trip—about ten to fifteen actual miles for someone in a farm family who had completed her or his own essential daily chores. All homesteads were situated on post rider routes and hence were within subscription range of a newspaper (compare figures 2–5 and 5–6). Easy access to bookstores, newspapers, and other reading and writing resources was the main characteristic of the full-access area; residents of this zone could become informed of events and opinion as fully as the Upper Valley's stock of printed matter allowed. By 1825 the full-access zone embraced a little less than half the geographical region, just under half of the townships, and about 55 percent of the population, largely in the river valley.[32]

The second kind of communications environment was the partial-access zone (see figure 5–5), including portions of communities with some access to a regular newspaper but without easy single-day access to a bookstore. Residents were at best within ten to fifteen traveling miles of an auxiliary print center. Parts of forty-three communities, a third of the total, and a quarter of the land in the region lay within the partial-access zone, chiefly in a band around the full-access area. This zone held 25 to 35 percent of the population by 1825.

The minimal-access zone (see figure 5–5) constituted the third type of communications environment in the Upper Valley. Not only were these townships and parts of townships more than ten to fifteen traveling miles from even an auxiliary print center; they were also beyond the post riding circuit and hence lacked regular access to newspapers and to most peddlers. Geographically, minimal-access living environments constituted a full quarter of the region. Substantial parts of a fifth of all Upper Valley townships (twenty-seven, or 21 percent) remained in this access zone as late as 1825. Families in this zone comprised a third of the area's population through 1800; 20 percent by 1815; and 10 to 15 percent after the establishment of hamlets. By 1810 most were either extremely isolated homesteads or sparsely populated farmsteads in newly settled areas—in both cases mainly subsistence farming areas with little village life and rarely even a bustling hamlet. Roads were bad or nonexistent.[33]

The key factor determining access was the availability of a bookstore and of newspaper delivery, but this itself was a function of a township's population size; settlement patterns; stage of community development, social order, and commercial development; and geographical location. The stage of community development and the extent of interaction with neighboring townships were the most significant factors.[34]

Differential access to the basic vehicles of print and written communications was one of the most important distinctions among people in early America. Wide inequality of opportunity in this respect existed throughout the early national period; information reached people in widely varying amounts and kinds. In a time of considerable stability in material and cultural life this might have been a small matter, but as the pace of change accelerated, access to print offered people a means of ensuring that they would not be left behind in the economic, social, and cultural transformation. Certainly not everyone even at Windsor village bought or borrowed printed matter or read a newspaper regularly. Still, if people were inclined to do so and could afford it, they had the opportunity to keep abreast of much current information and opinion about the transatlantic civilization they were part of. This was decidedly not the case in distant Plymouth Kingdom or Stockbridge, however, where at best one could obtain some fragmentary information about the distant world from a well-stocked peddler or a rare traveler.[35]

In other words, in the life of the mind and heart, residents of Windsor and the other full-access communities were much closer to families in Boston than to residents of nearby minimum-access townships such as Plymouth and Weston. Most residents of Windsor District's central village townships had access to newspapers from the late 1780s onward. In contrast, many of the people in the five remote hardscrabble Green Mountain townships could not buy a current book or subscribe to a newspaper even if they had wished to. Only an occasional peddler and the stock of a general store alleviated the virtual embargo on the "latest intelligence." Isolation from newspapers and bookstores also meant that people did not know which books, pamphlets, and periodicals were available for sale, and so they remained unaware of reformulations of the Western heritage or of new contributions to it. For these residents the distant world remained mysterious and fascinating, abstract and mythical.

Within Windsor District, the communication system that divided fifty square miles of rugged hills and lush valleys into the three major access zones (follow figure 5–7 throughout) mainly proceeded up and down the Connecticut River and the turnpike that paralleled it. All print items, like all other commodities, passed up and down the Connecticut River, the spinal cord of the Upper Valley. Windsor District's two key east-west transit points along the river were the Cornish Bridge at Windsor (1796) and the Cheshire Bridge at Springfield (1808).[36]

Running south to north, four major roads progressed inland from the river valley. First and most important was the Green Mountain Turnpike, running diagonally from Rockingham township through the second largest village (Chester), on to Cavendish and Ludlow village (late blooming), and thence west to Rutland, a major village across the mountains. The second inland road, the Black River Turnpike, built just after 1810, started in Springfield at Cheshire Bridge and progressed west through the village, north to Perkinsville, along the Black River until it turned northwest around Hawk's Mountain, and on into Duttonsville, joining the Green Mountain Turnpike just beyond Proctorsville. The third major road moved west from the Four Corners through Weathersfield just south of Ascutney Mountain, joining the Black River road just beyond Amsden. The fourth road headed west out of Windsor village and went through West Windsor and Hammondsville on its way to Woodstock. These were the main arteries of land communication. Completing the primary transportation system of Windsor District were the Williams River from Rockingham through Chester, and the Black River from Springfield and Weathersfield through Cavendish and Ludlow to Plymouth far to the northwest (about thirty-five to forty traveling miles from Springfield).[37]

Along these road and water routes, the best that were available, actual travel

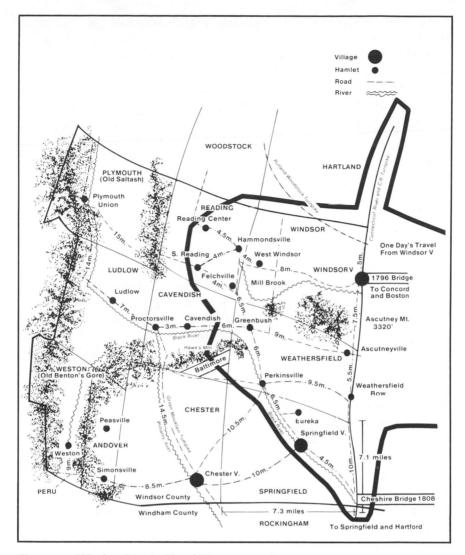

Figure 5–7: Windsor District Travel Distances, c. 1810

distances were frequently two or three times the theoretical distance between them on a map. There was almost no such thing as a straight road. Early roads were more irregular in their course than rivers because they had to avoid natural barriers, while rivers gradually carved their own pathways. Variable weather added problems. Take, for example, a trek from Plymouth Union hamlet to Windsor Village and back in 1810. The fifty-four to sixty-eight mile round trip in good weather took three days. Since there was no direct route, it was necessary to travel over the Green Mountain Turnpike down through Ludlow, eastward to Proctorsville, and then on to Amsden hamlet. From there, to avoid Ascutney Mountain and its nearby hills, one traveled either the southern route to Ascutneyville and then up the Connecticut Turnpike to Windsor village, or the northern route past Felchville to the West Windsor road into Windsor. An alternative route by more local roads proceeded over a bad road around Colby Pond to South Reading and then east over a major road through West Windsor hamlet. No village or even significant hamlet existed except on major roads and waterways. Off the beaten track, travel was horrendous in good weather and out of the question otherwise. The restrictions on travel and the life-threatening conditions with which early Americans coped in northwestern New England, unimaginable to us, defined the natural and human boundaries of Windsor District communications.[38]

Figures 5–8 and 5–9 sketch the three access zones in 1800 and 1825. The full-access zone encompassed the four villages and the farmstead areas surrounding each. Windsor and Chester villages, each controlling commerce and culture in several surrounding townships, were the main centers of print communications in Windsor District. Windsor village, called the "jewel of the Upper Valley" by contemporaries, was the largest settled place in the district with a population of 1,200–1,500 in the early 1830s. Here were printing facilities, several bookstores, and usually two newspapers continuously from the 1790s. Next most prominent was Chester village, the feeder center for the communication system's backbone. Windsor's newspapers were too much competition even for Chester, however; a single newspaper survived only for brief periods in 1807–1808 and in 1828–30. Chester village maintained a bookstore for a considerably longer period, however. Third in prominence was late-settled Springfield village, followed at some distance by Weathersfield's fragmented village.[39]

In 1800, the partial-access zone included the more remote portions of Windsor, Weathersfield, and Chester townships; much of Springfield; and the parts of Cavendish, Ludlow, and Andover that were near major roads. By the mid-1820s the situation had changed dramatically: among the four village communities, only small portions of Weathersfield and Springfield were limited to partial access. The central portion of Windsor District, radiating out from Cavendish along the main roads toward the Green Mountains, constituted the partial-access zone. Each of the seven nonvillage townships contained large partial-access areas. As road and water transportation routes improved, regular newspaper delivery and partial access cut a swath through minimal-access townships and gradually increased awareness of distant events and lifestyles. By 1810 Windsor weeklies were fairly widely disseminated in partial-access areas. It remained difficult, however, to buy a book that was not stocked in a general store; there were no bookstores in any of these townships. Consequently, the major obstacle to browsing and purchasing current works was a trip of twelve to twenty-five miles to Windsor or Chester. Traditional reading matter and almanacs could be purchased throughout the partial-access zone.

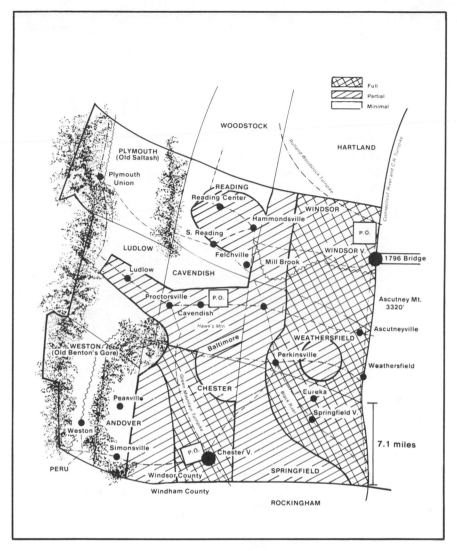

Figure 5–8: Windsor District Zones of Access and Communication System, 1800

Visits by peddlers and itinerant authors increased the variety of reading matter available to families in partial-access areas.[40]

In minimal-access areas there were many social and cultural limitations on obtaining knowledge, especially current information and opinion, from printed matter. Through the War of 1812, parts of at least seven of the eleven townships included at least some minimal-access areas. All or nearly all of Plymouth, Andover, and Weston townships; most of Baltimore, Reading, and Ludlow; a portion of Cavendish; mountain areas in the north of Weathersfield; and southern Windsor township remained minimal-access areas. Decent traveling

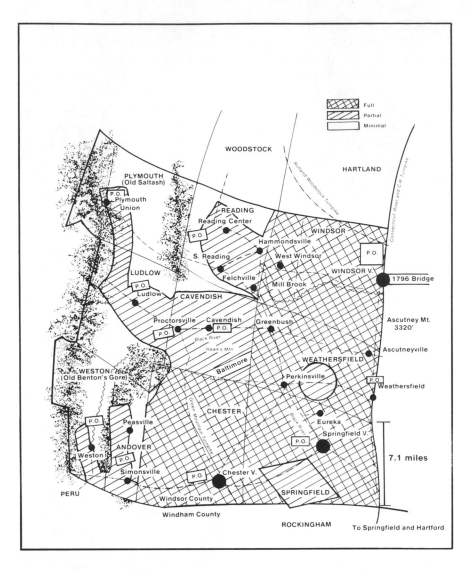

Figure 5–9: Windsor District Zones of Access and Communication System, 1825

roads were nonexistent, and local paths and trails were very poor. By 1815 road and river travel had improved substantially, so that even some of the western portions of the Green Mountain belt of townships had entered the partial-access communications zone.

Figures 5–8 and 5–9 highlight the changes in Windsor District's three communications environments over time. The decades of 1780–1802 saw slow growth. All print culture activity in Windsor District emanated from Windsor village. This period was followed by a half-decade of expansion, both in Windsor itself and in two other townships. Chester sustained a newspaper for a minimum of two years, 1807–1808, and Woodstock, just to the north of Reading, maintained a paper for three years (1804–1806). Outside of Windsor, contraction soon followed (1809–12). By 1811 Windsor once again had the sole village bookstores and sole wholesaling businesses within the district and the area surrounding it. By 1813, a second wave of expansion was under way in and beyond Windsor. Windsor village had expanded to three newspapers and five bookstores. Modest specialized printing facilities were also established at nearby Weathersfield. Soon, however, a second contraction set in; by 1817 efforts at Weathersfield had failed, and Windsor again had cut back to only two steady newspapers. Because population growth throughout the region had been sizable, a third period of expansion, in the dozen years of 1819–1830, saw additions to both permanent and auxiliary print centers; increasing newspaper, book, pamphlet, almanac, and periodical production; and more bookstores and binderies.[41] In 1830, Windsor District was in the middle of this third wave in the expansion of print culture, with two permanent print centers inside Windsor District and three more in communities contiguous to the district.

This pattern of ebb and flow highlights the complicated relationships between township and village life and the communication system through which printed matter flowed. When false optimism triumphed, as in the years 1803–1808 and 1813–17, failure was inevitable. The 1830s witnessed yet another period of contraction.

Substantial differences in Windsor District access zones are directly reflected in nearly all measures of the amount of cultural participation (see tables app. 2–1, 2–3, and 2–4). Family libraries in the full-access zone were almost ten times larger on average than those in the minimum-access zone, and their contents differed. The kinds of books retained in the libraries of ordinary families also varied from one access zone to another. Windsor township (village and farmstead) households with printed matter averaged thirty volumes per family library. Families in Reading, seven miles to the west, averaged four volumes per library. The same situation obtained in the southern tier of Windsor District, where Chester averaged twenty volumes per family library while its western neighbor, Andover, averaged five volumes per library. Variations in the depth and variety of reading matter, and in related reading styles and habits were even greater.

This pattern of print interchange cannot be explained by two-tier trickle-down hypotheses of dissemination. Our model, in contrast, comes to terms with such puzzles as the widely differing levels of print ownership and reading habits in two contiguous townships (e.g., Windsor and Reading) and in two groups of professionals, those living in print center village communities and those living in hinterland locations. By regarding culture as a several-tiered awareness of and knowledge about the world, we can describe the cultural geography of print communications and identify key influences on cultural participation and rates of change. To do so we will need to understand contemporary clusterings of cultural beliefs and values.[42]

Chapter 6

Upper Valley Vehicles of Print Communications and the World of Popular Sellers, 1778–1830

> As I have room, I would just hint . . . that the evenings are now
> long—that you have a number of good books (or ought to have)
> and have a Newspaper weekly without borrowing of your neigh-
> bours—and that you and your family have minds which need im-
> provement. 'A word to the wise is sufficient.'
>
> *Walton's Vermont Register and*
> *Farmer's Almanac for* 1828, "January."

For the past century most scholars studying intellectual life in early America have focused on an interesting but limited range of American-authored
printed works. More recent scholarship on economic thought, republicanism,
and Jefferson has expanded the canon considerably. In the process we have
learned that transatlantic intellectual traditions profoundly influenced reading
habits and public policy formulation for an expanding list of American "elites."
American intellectuals, we are learning, read mainly European authors in
many fields. Was the same true of the other 95 to 98 percent of the population? What did the vast majority of Americans generally read, assimilate, and
act upon? Which works shaped their understanding of the world? How were
they affected by transatlantic intellectual traditions? [1]

This chapter adds a broad history of American readership to an already rich
history of American authorship in the half century following the Revolution.
The origins of the present contribution lie in the work of Richard Beale Davis,
who demonstrated that American writings formed only a small portion of the
South's reading matter through 1840.[2] Our aim here is to expand our understanding of the beliefs and values that guided American families in daily life.
We shall consider the total reading population of the Upper Valley, determining some of the core reading matter assimilated by a wide range of Windsor
District residents, from children to local intellectuals, during the Early Republic.

Print Vehicles

During the early national era six distinct vehicles of print communication carried information to segments of the population: almanacs, broadsides, books, pamphlets, newspapers, and periodicals. The contents of each vehicle were a distinctive share of knowledge from Europe and America in 1780–1830; each vehicle had its own pattern and pace of presentation. Rural New England society had a mix of communications opportunities different from that available in the English countryside, in northern Germany, or in southern France, for example.

Differences among vehicles of print communication reflected the characteristics of the publication, circulation patterns, and—a subject hitherto neglected—the interrelationships among separate print vehicles. Operating within the same environment, Upper Valley print vehicles took on specific new characteristics and reshaped traditional ones partly in response to the presence of other vehicles. Generally, traditional knowledge was reconfirmed and newer knowledge freshly transmitted by every vehicle, though the proportions varied substantially. Almanacs, broadsides, books, and pamphlets were the dominant vehicles of print communications just after the Revolution. Over the next three decades the newspaper developed into a steady provider of much local economic information and other kinds of local knowledge as well as a steady flow of nonlocal news. Rural weeklies reached a sizable share of Upper Valley households by 1820. These five vehicles were joined in the 1820s by the periodical, which was just beginning to shed its elite image. A short sketch of each of the six primary vehicles of print communication, and its dissemination in the Upper Valley in 1780–1830, will help us appreciate the rapid spread of the habit of reading in the half century after the Revolution. Four of the six vehicles— almanacs, broadsides, books, and pamphlets—all reached a majority of households in the region by the mid-1790s, and newspapers approached this popularity about two decades later.[3]

After the Bible, the annual *almanac* constituted the most widely diffused vehicle of print culture in the Upper Valley until the 1820s. In 1810, for instance, at least twelve different almanacs circulated within the area. One Windsor almanac went through three editions; several others sold at least two full editions. Consequently, almanacs directly reached between three-fifths and three-quarters of all families in 1810.[4] Almanacs were amazingly cheap throughout the years 1780–1830. As late as 1817, the Burlington-based *Beers' Almanac* sold for five cents a copy; the price rose to six cents in 1818.[5] Produced on the cheapest paper and frequently used for a year and then laid aside, many almanacs disintegrated. Others were collected by teams of "book carters" who by 1810 moved regularly through "most of the towns of Vermont and in those of New Hampshire bordering upon the Connecticut River gathering up al-

The Heavenly Nine. David Claypoole Johnston, 1828, w.c. Courtesy, American Antiquarian Society.

Six of the nine Muses hold popular forms of printed matter. From left to right: Euterpe (no. 1 – music) inspects copies of *Theater Stars*, a broadside announcement; Calliope (no. 4 – epic poetry) an almanac, a book, *Jack Horner or other Poems*, and a *Directory* for 1823; Polyhymnia (no. 5 – sacred song) holds "Billy Taylor," broadside sheet music; sleeping Clio (no. 6 – history) rests on a stack of small fat chapbooks, including *Jack the Giant Killer, Tom Thumb, Goody Two Shoes, Wife of Colonel Pluck,* and *Cock Robin*; Erato (no. 8 – lyric and love poetry) rests on a broadside; and Thalia (no. 9 – comedy) holds a broadside, *Whims and Oddities* by T. Hood.

manacs, newspapers, old books, and rags for conversion into paper." As Simeon Ide, a leading Windsor publisher, recalled: "People ransacked their houses." Most almanacs, however, met the fate described by Andrew Ellicott in 1783: "One year passeth away and another commeth – so likewise 'tis with almanacs – they are annual productions whose destination and usefulness is temporary, and afterwards are thrown by, and consigned to oblivion." Although ephemeral, almanacs had a substantial impact in framing the secular year, reinforcing traditional wisdom about agricultural life, morality, and astrology.[6]

Rural families purchased a yearly almanac for several important reasons: for advice in planting and harvesting; for assistance in keeping track of the time of day, and of the heavens, by means of a detailed astrological calendar; for information about meeting schedules; and for lists of personnel at various institutions. Beyond these specific uses, Upper Valley residents saw the almanac's general purpose as "to rule and govern the year by." As another writer put it in 1808, "by this easy and familiar kind of instruction, every family may be led into some general acquaintance with the affairs and government of the universe."[7]

Whereas almanacs appeared annually in December, *broadsides* appeared whenever an event, tale, song, political opinion, or dream seemed relevant to the moment. Approximately ten percent of all imprints through 1830 were broadsides, meaning any item printed on one side of a single sheet of paper. Prior to 1800 and the spread of newspapers, they comprised about a fifth of all imprints. Broadsides served a wide variety of functions. Before 1830 the largest groups printed in Vermont and New Hampshire concerned government and politics; music, especially secular ballads; stories of unusual happenings in the natural or supernatural worlds; and popular literary efforts.[8]

Printed in villages, they circulated there and, especially in the case of broadside ballads, in the countryside. Press runs generally ranged between 500 and 1,500 copies. Normally there were not more than two editions. Broadsides were compact and often localized sources of both traditional and newer forms of knowledge. Broadsides mixed European and American subject matter. In addition to those printed in the Upper Valley, it is very likely that broadsides from communities near the borders of the Upper Valley made their way into the area, carried by itinerant authors and peddlers. Not many broadsides printed beyond rural Western New England appear to have circulated in the Upper Valley. Between 1780 and 1820 general-purpose broadsides were gradually replaced in most Upper Valley communities by fugitive pieces printed in newspapers. Except for sheet music, they were rarely saved by private individuals as part of family libraries.[9]

Books and pamphlets, taken together, were the most broadly circulating vehicles of print communication; they reached the largest total share of Upper Valley families. Yet with a few notable exceptions, books and pamphlets were targeted to particular groups within the population. The Bible was by far the most prominent exception. In fact, of 329 estates with all volumes identifiable, the Bible was retained in 293, or 89 percent. No other book approached this range of readership.[10]

Next to the Bible in importance were several types of works. Each distinct work within a specific area of knowledge was published in several editions, reaching a modest segment of the total audience. Five categories may be distinguished: (1) general works with strong appeal, a category including modern literature, popular theology and sermons, hymnals, devotional works, geographies, and, after 1815, histories; (2) schoolbooks and dictionaries, together constituting a quarter of all editions for sale in the region; (3) general works with medium appeal, encompassing travels and voyages, military affairs, philosophy, politics and government, and secular music; (4) works with limited appeal, including books about youth and adulthood as stages of life, children's books and primers, technology, classical writers, astronomy, science, agriculture, and economics; and (5) works appealing to professionals in the ministry, law, medicine, art, and architecture. Two characteristics are striking. One is the marked imbalance between secular works, accounting for a large majority of all editions for sale and 70 percent of known volumes retained, and sacred and religious works, with a quarter of all editions for sale and 30 percent of known volumes retained. The other is the large proportion of European-authored works, amounting to nearly three-quarters of all titles until the mid-1820s.

After the Bible and the almanac, the print vehicle with the widest circulation by 1820 was the rural weekly *newspaper*. Average circulation for stable weeklies rose (see table 6–1) from 850 copies per edition during the 1780s to 1,000 by 1800; 1,200 by the end of the War of 1812; and 1,400 by the 1820s. In 1810 between 33 percent and 45 percent of all households subscribed to a newspaper, and approximately a third of all families were steady subscribers. By 1830, more than half of all households were steady subscribers, an extraordinary sign of the depth and breadth of the rural New England mind in the era of its greatest formative influence.[11]

The deep penetration of newspapers in northwestern New England took place with astonishing rapidity, in just thirty years, 1785–1815. Upper Valley residents attached great significance to the rural weekly. The most concise statement of its main goals was Alden Spooner's masthead: "From realms far distant and from Climes unknown, we make the Knowledge of Mankind your own." The rural weekly's space was split between current nonlocal knowledge of all varieties and local economic and governmental information. The bulk of local and nonlocal newspaper knowledge could be interpreted equally well within "classical" late-eighteenth-century liberal republican theory, or within the alternative tradition of Christian piety described earlier. Editors took their central goal to be "the promotion of the general good of society, via the dissemination of useful knowledge, and correct information" to a very broad audience.[12]

Public opinion in the region, even apart from self-interested cultural figures such as newspaper editors, strongly asserted the special merits of regular newspaper reading. Further support for newspapers came from the only vehicle of communication larger in overall circulation, the yearly almanac. Inevitably, for one of the late fall or early winter months, the almanac would advise readers to stock up on books and a newspaper, as noted in the epigraph to this chapter.[13]

The rural weekly was unique among vehicles of print communications also with respect to distribution. Only the rural weekly came directly to its readers. Editors paid post riders to disperse newspapers along given routes encompass-

Table 6-1: Proportion of U.S. Households Subscribing to a Newspaper, 1780–1830[1]

	1780–89	1790–99	1800–9	1810–19	1820–29
1. Average Weekly Circulation	850	999	1,078	1,221	1,400
2. Number of Newspapers Surviving More Than Two Years	95	204	329	457	638
3. Percent of Households Subscribing to a Newspaper Surviving More Than Two Years	14%	22%	28%	33%	40%
4. Total Percent of Households Subscribing to a Newspaper[2]	18%–19%	30%–32%	36%–39%	42%–45%	51%–54%

[1] Several factors are masked by these figures, and each qualifies them up or down slightly. Overall, the higher and lower pressures balance each other out. First, these rates are for the country as a whole; New England estimates would be considerably higher. Second, the average per decade is calculated from evidence near the beginning of the decade. Thus it is possible that our averages understate circulation by as much as 10 to 15%. Third, about 8 to 10% of each newspaper's circulation was devoted to copies sent throughout the country to other editors, to provide a fund of non-local news. Fourth, the subscription period for households also varied. Line Number 3 offers, by decade, the most accurate available estimate of households subscribing upwards of two years. Halving these figures probably estimates subscribers receiving a newspaper for the entire decade.

[2] The percentage on the left is the total proportion of households subscribing, if we assume that one newspaper in four represents all the newspapers that survived two years and under. The percentage on the right is the total proportion using one newspaper in three, of those surviving two years and under. To calculate this larger proportion, we have divided papers not surviving more than two years per decade by 4 and then by 3, to include the low minimum subscription rates necessary to start a newspaper. The fragmentary surviving evidence suggests that 250–500 copies were necessary to commence a weekly newspaper (over 95% of those not lasting into their third year were weeklies); the higher figure was more appropriate for the 1810–30 decades. Hamilton, *Country Printer,* 213ff., and Webster's evidence in Read, "Noah Webster's Project," have figures on starting rates, and rates for newspapers within their first two years.

ing four to eight townships. As the transportation system improved, the distribution system became more complex. Stagecoaches carried bundles of papers to all post offices and also to many individuals living near post roads. Post riders dispersed papers into the hinterland from these main roads, remaining responsible for collecting fees throughout the distribution area. Together with the almanac, the newspaper was a leading agent in the regular dissemination of print culture within the 130 townships on both sides of the river basin.[14]

Periodicals, in this era serials appearing biweekly or less frequently, captured a relatively small share of the total audience for printed matter until the 1820s. Altogether nine periodicals were published within the Upper Valley through 1830. Only two lasted five years each, both in the 1820s, while four lasted three years each. Circulation statistics are unavailable, but editors' comments indicate that press runs ranged between 300 and 1,000 copies. Typically, a hefty portion of each issue was dispersed beyond the Upper Valley. Newspaper advertisements reveal that at least forty-five other periodicals printed throughout the United States and in Great Britain were at one time or another offered for subscription and/or sale in Windsor District, 1802–30. Nine of those were religious in character and thirty-six secular. Greater precision about periodical circulation is available from statistics on family library holdings. Approximately 155 volumes and groups of loose issues of periodicals were found among all extant Windsor District inventories, 1787–1830, accounting for 3 percent of all volumes retained. Periodicals reached 10 percent of all families with private libraries, and perhaps another 5 percent through lending library borrowing. These families represented mainly the wealthiest two-thirds of all estates. Both European and American writings, and traditional and more current perspectives, shared periodical pages; the direction of change was toward more American contributions, especially after 1815.[15]

Printed Matter Published in the Upper Valley, 1778–1830

Upper Valley print culture was extraordinarily rich in the first two generations of the new nation. The closest approximation of the total supply of printed items available for sale within the Upper Valley is a measure we term "the universe of available reading matter." Two broad classes of printed items constituted this universe through 1830: works produced in the area, and those imported from beyond the valley's boundaries. Both varieties were stocked by area bookstores, which sold them at retail, and also at wholesale to peddlers and general store owners. Thousands of works were published throughout the English-speaking world each year. The immediate reason to study the universe of available reading matter is to learn which works were printed in the Upper Valley, which found their way into the area, and which remained relatively unknown. The ultimate reason is to uncover those distinctive reading patterns that constituted the collective consciousness of rural New England. Detailed description of this kind of evidence allows us to draw a broad picture of rural cultural life in an era of rapid transformation, and eventually will allow comparative conclusions about shared cultural trends and leading differences among transatlantic societies.[16]

By the 1780s it was widely accepted in the Upper Valley that any information or opinion in need of quick and widespread dissemination beyond a single township should be printed. Powerful institutions took the lead, particularly in governmental and legal realms. The Vermont state government lured Judah and Alden Spooner to the Upper Valley as its first printers. On both sides of the valley, state printers were regularly retained to distribute the proclamations of governors and the acts, laws, proceedings, and addresses of state legislatures. The magnitude of state and federal government printing in 1790–1830 was extraordinary: almost a fourth of all known American imprints each year consisted of governmental decisions and deliberations. In 1830, 30 percent of all known American imprints issued from the presses of federal and state governments. Fulfilling republican theory about an educated citizenry, governments were among the chief promoters of reading and contributors to the supply of printed matter. To get a full view of the expansion of reading matter available in the Upper Valley generally, and in Windsor District specifically, we shall begin with the changing output and content of Upper Valley presses through 1830.[17]

The term "imprint" will be used here to include books, pamphlets, almanacs, and broadsides, as well as newspapers and periodicals which will be discussed later. During 1778, the first year in which full-scale printing was carried on in the Upper Valley, eight imprints were published, all at Dresden. One of the eight was a religious work, a sermon preached before the governor and legislature; six were secular works; and one title is lost. The six secular imprints all involved state politics and government. The volume and range of printed items was narrow as printing began. Strictly Vermont information and opinion predominated. A primary function of printed matter in the late 1770s was to reinforce traditional values; a second function was to provide new knowledge, but only in one dimension of life, political culture. Two of the most important realms of local life, religion on the one hand and government and politics on the other, were the first to enjoy widespread dissemination by printed books and pamphlets. It was not surprising that knowledge about America was the first to be captured locally in print.[18]

The most notable change in the relationship of printing and society between 1778 and 1784 lay in the gradual expansion of subjects treated in printed form. By the mid-1780s the annual volume of locally printed items had nearly tripled (see graph 6–1 throughout). Twenty-two imprints are known to have been published in the Upper Valley, all in Vermont, during 1784. Six (27 percent) were religious in nature, including two sermons, an autobiography, a general theological treatise, and a premillennialist forecast of doom bound together with a poem on the implications of the frequency of death among youth. The remaining sixteen imprints were secular works. Twelve of these were issued by the state government, but there were also two different almanacs, a primer used in both homes and district schools, and an antireligious Enlightenment philosophical treatise, Ethan Allen's *Reason the Only Oracle of Man*. The proportion of sacred works stabilized at about a quarter of the total. Among sacred texts, discussions of theological issues and personal religious experiences told for their didactic value were now added to reprints of sermons, traditionally the mainstay of oral culture. Among secular works, government and politics continued to dominate, but other interests included the de-

Graph 6–1: Vermont Imprints, 1778–1820

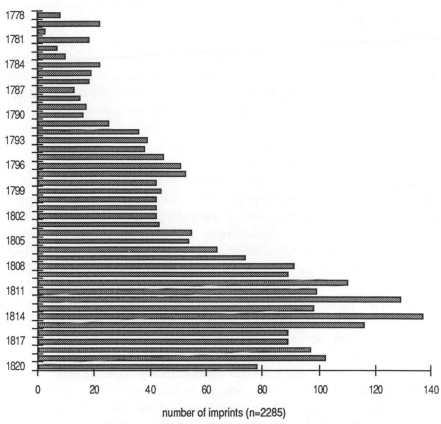

number of imprints (n=2285)

Source: Adapted from Marcus McCorson, *Vermont Imprints, 1778-1820*.

tails of the agricultural cycle, early childhood education, and opposition to traditional established religion. While the range of printed items broadened steadily throughout the 1780s, growth was uneven until the early 1790s, when a major explosion in the volume of print matter occurred.[19]

A large and somewhat more diverse locally generated print culture had emerged by the mid-1790s. Residents of Windsor District who read a rural weekly or visited a bookstore gained access to much that was printed in Vermont and New Hampshire valley counties. The reason was that most permanent and several auxiliary Upper Valley print centers regularly exchanged stock. Of works printed in the Upper Valley, a total of fifty-nine imprints were published in 1796, evenly split between Vermont (twenty-eight) and New Hampshire (thirty-one) publications.[20] The ratio of sacred to secular reading was about the same as in 1784: fifteen sacred and forty-four secular works. Religious publications were becoming more varied: seven sermons were published, half about death; three Baptist denominational reports; the writings of someone who had pretended to be a prophet and then recanted; another miscellaneous work; two dissenting hymnals (Baptist and Universalist); and a devotional tract. The subject matter of the forty-four secular works was no longer dominated by government and politics (eleven state and federal government pronouncements and local addresses), but the decline is deceptive since newspapers were becoming the preferred means of disseminating official documents. Treatment of other aspects of life had doubled during the preceding decade: in a total of thirty-three works, there were five editions of two almanacs; four schoolbooks; two works each in law and medicine; two Masonic orations; four secular songbooks; a geography and a map; and no fewer than twelve different publications in modern literature, including three captivity narratives and four volumes of poetry.[21]

As a group, these fifty-nine Upper Valley imprints reflected many traditional intellectual interests plus several new emphases. Locally printed almanacs were still expanding their readership. Among books and pamphlets, religion remained the broadest subject of concern. The most striking expansion, from 4 percent to 20 percent, came in modern literature. Of themes crossing more than one field of knowledge, death and violence, including crime and torture, were by far the most popular, being represented in nearly a fifth of all works (eleven of fifty-nine). Although they were only part of the normal reading stock of titles available to area residents, Upper Valley publications are a sound guide to many of the residents' most prominent reading interests because such works typically had larger average sales per title.

The total supply of available Upper Valley reading matter in 1796 also included weekly newspapers, with their voluminous reports of distant occurrences and local commercial and political life. Seven locally published weekly newspapers circulated through the area in 1796: two at Keene, and one each at Hanover, Haverhill, and Walpole in New Hampshire, and at Windsor and Newbury in Vermont. Four were stable weeklies, lasting over a decade each. In addition, one periodical with wide circulation in the valley was printed just across the western Windsor county line at Rutland village.

A wide variety of books, pamphlets, and periodicals (and to a lesser extent almanacs and newspapers) published outside the Upper Valley were also available within its boundaries. Large numbers of copies of a few types of works— particularly primers, schoolbooks, dictionaries, children's books, almanacs, and novels—were widely imported by area bookstores. In addition, a few copies of many other titles were stocked. The key point to remember about locally printed works is that many represent Upper Valley publishers' best guesses about what the local reading public was likely to purchase most frequently. Successful, stable print centers were those whose printer-publishers could anticipate the needs of various audiences and who made sound publishing choices on the basis of local reading tastes.

Locally printed information and opinion continued to increase throughout the Early Republic. The average yearly number of publications published in Vermont doubled between the early and the later 1790s, then more than doubled again, to one hundred per year, by early in the second decade of the nineteenth century. Valley publications regularly accounted for approximately 45–60 percent of these. Overall, the rate of increase in numbers of imprints within the Vermont Valley counties was nearly 600 percent between the late 1780s and the later 1810s, compared with a 274 percent increase in the population.[22]

Increases in both the quantity and diversity of reading matter produced in the area may be traced by comparing the Upper Valley print production figures in 1796, 1812, and 1826. Eighty-three Upper Valley imprints known to have been issued in 1812 accounted for more copies than the number of area residents. More than a third (37 percent) addressed religious concerns, an increase from the proportion earlier.[23] Expansion was most pronounced in sacred music, theology, and, in the wake of recent religious revivalism and conversions throughout the area, local editions of practical religious texts—prayer books, meditational and devotional treatises, and the Bible. Sermons remained the single largest genre of local religious publications. In the highly diverse denominational literature the Baptists remained most active. Among the fifty-two secular works (63 percent) printed in 1812, the largest category included twenty-four works of government and politics (29 percent of the total). The greatest increase came in the area of political thought and controversy. The War of 1812 and the revival of Federalist politics dominated, as an official party-supported Federalist print center at Windsor published the *Washingtonian*, a strident Federalist weekly; and half a dozen political tracts. The remaining twenty-eight local imprints emphasized schoolbooks and school-related works (nine), didactic works on various life stages (three), and secular music (three). A thin but diverse group of works included travels and modern literature (two each); single publications in astronomy, philosophy, and history; the autobiography of a local woman; and a monster story about a thirty-six-foot snake. There were also single editions of four different locally printed almanacs.[24]

Several broad shifts in the content of locally printed works were evident by 1812. Some reflect only random variation, such as a temporary decline in modern literature and in works about law and medicine.[25] Others represent longer-term changes in publishing. Most important of these latter was a decline in almanac readership and a concomitant rise in newspaper subscriptions. By 1810 newspapers had begun actively to compete with almanacs by reprinting most of the latter's contents in the appropriate season. Besides eighty-three books, pamphlets, almanacs, and broadsides, eight weekly newspapers were published in the Upper Valley during 1812, two at Keene and one each at Walpole and Hanover on the New Hampshire side, and three at Windsor and one at Brattleboro on the Vermont side. Five of these weeklies were stable. A periodical was also published nearby at Rutland, the *Vermont Baptist Missionary Magazine*. A second leading trend was continued growth in the number of locally published schoolbooks, reflecting widening district school opportunities. A third trend saw the first locally printed works on popular science and travel, and increases in the number of works about the life cycle and its stages.[26]

By 1812 print communications had an important place in the well-established market economy. Over the preceding three decades the volume and diversity of imprints published in the Upper Valley had increased markedly. Not until the 1800–1810 decade, however, was the communication system adequate to meet the Upper Valley population's demand for reading matter. By that decade Upper Valley print centers were themselves publishing a substantial share of all works selling well in their own bookstores. Shortly before 1810 a critical threshold was reached; now the audience of each Upper Valley print center was sufficient to encourage far greater diversity in both locally printed items and stock imported from outside the Upper Valley. The Walpole bookstore, for example, held well over 30,000 volumes in 1810. The original stock of most bookstores was provided by a parent firm. At one time or another, for example, Isaiah Thomas supplied Walpole, Brattleboro, and Windsor within the Upper Valley, and Rutland nearby. Gradually local publishing ventures and exchanges with other regional and extraregional firms supplied a new bookstore with a better balanced supply of imprints.[27]

Further expansion of reading interests occurred in the 1820s; we will take 1826 for a sample year. To date fifty-eight Upper Valley publications have been located; among these, forty-one or 71 percent were issued by Vermont presses. The proportion of religious works was only slightly down from 1812 (from 37 to 33 percent). Sermons, devotional works, and theological treatises continued to be in high demand. By the mid-1820s a greater effort was being made to publish Bibles locally (21 percent, up from 3 percent). Denominational pronouncements had also increased. Congregationalist and Episcopalian deliberations now supplemented those of Baptists and Methodists. Finally, benevolent reform, an occasional category previously, was now a subject about which people read regularly. All three areas of increase in religious reading reflected the same theme: increased application of religion to daily life and to social problems. As Rev. Asa Burton, a renowned area resident, put it in 1815, this was an "age of benevolence" in which "the whole Protestant world was newly alive to the great and blessed objects of relieving human suffering" and "redeeming the human character." Denominationalism, efforts to expand the ranks of Christians, and benevolent social reform merged into a militant evangelical

Christian activism, and Upper Valley reading reflected the heightened enthusiasm in the period 1800–1830.[28]

Allied to the rise of evangelical Christian activism was an even greater expansion in secular printed matter. Among thirty-nine secular items the largest area of interest was education, with nineteen imprints. Fourteen were targeted at the district school and the academy and four at colleges. The catalogue of a local social library was also published. The next most popular areas of interest were science and technology. One work each dealt with botany (in three-volumes), scientific agriculture, sheep raising and wool manufacture, navigation of the Connecticut River, and the department of medicine at Dartmouth College. Just four works were published in government and politics, including three addresses on the fiftieth anniversary of the Republic and a Vermont legislature directory. Another growing area, publications relating to the life cycle, accounted for four other books: a fictional story of youth by Barbara Hofland; two editions of Louisa Hoare's *Hints for the Improvement of Early Education and Nursery Discipline*; and an edition of Benjamin Franklin's *Way to Wealth*, bound with advice to young tradesmen. The remaining three items dealt with American history, modern literature, and law (a local rape trial). There were also single editions of three almanacs.[29]

By comparison with 1812, reading interests in 1826 were dominated by theology, religion and society, science and technology, education, and political discourse. By the 1820s the topic of education, which had accounted for under a fifth of all secular imprints in 1812, had claimed nearly half in 1826. A decline in works on politics and government was more apparent than real, since newspapers increasingly dominated political discourse. Even taking into account newspaper content, however, attention to Europe was declining in the 1820s; interest in Vermont and New Hampshire politics and government remained constant, and concern with federal policies and politics was much more prominent. Apart from education, the number of works devoted to science and technology, the rural Industrial Revolution, and the behavior of children and youth, showed sizable increases. Production of other books and pamphlets remained steady, while almanacs declined slightly in importance. Local publication of modern literature (both American and European works) had given way to large-edition regional publishing. The number of newspapers was increasing steadily, more than doubling from eight weeklies in five townships in 1812 to twenty-three in fourteen townships by 1830. Periodical publication fluctuated widely from year to year, but on the average, four periodicals were printed within the region during the 1820s.

Upper Valley production statistics have allowed us to begin reconstructing changing trends in reading tastes generally. The reason is that the twelve subject categories with the highest local publication levels were also the topical areas that local bookstores stocked most extensively with imported works. Especially when evaluated in the context of the area's total communication system, local imprints indicate the main emphases in both formal and informal sales circuits and offer an excellent guide to wider reading tastes in the area. While books and pamphlets reached the broadest total audience, the greatest change in reading habits came with the spread of the rural weekly newspaper with its steady diet of local and nonlocal, older and newer forms of knowledge. The keys to the newspaper's success were its broad format, cultural diversity, regularity, and steadily increasing number of copies printed. In 1810 ten weeklies were disseminating a total of between 8,000 and 12,000 copies per issue, reaching well over a quarter of all Upper Valley households. By 1830, there were twenty-three weeklies distributing between 20,000 and 30,000 copies per issue and reaching well over half and perhaps as high as two-thirds of all households. The next most important vehicle in the evolution of Upper Valley reading habits through 1830 was the yearly almanac, like the newspaper a general-purpose vehicle of communication. Almanacs were purchased by well over half of all families in the area through the mid-1820s.[30]

Upper Valley publishing and sales patterns meshed with the rhythms of everyday life in the forest society of northwestern New England. Farming permitted adults little time for prolonged reading during the planting and tending, harvesting and storage portions of the annual cycle, between late March and late October. During these busy periods the weekly newspaper, usually published between Thursday and Saturday, was ideal reading fare in both variety and length. By early to middle November there was time for winter school, for perusing books and pamphlets, and, among wealthier families perhaps, for reading a periodical.

By the late 1790s, a stable pattern had been established among publications other than the almanac and the newspaper. The leading subjects among books and pamphlets published within the area were politics and governmental affairs, general literature, and sermons and theology; then education, sacred music, and secular music. As late as 1812, the pattern remained basically the same, though sermons and theological studies had moved from third to second and education from fourth to third in numbers of editions disseminated. Some six years later a major shift in relative interest among subjects was under way, and several changes were noticeable by the mid-1820s. Religion, including church history, practical sermons and theology, and denominational affairs, had enlarged its share. Universalism and several newer evangelical denominations— Baptists and Methodists—were especially strong in the Upper Valley. Equaling print activity in religion was a branch of education devoted to children and youth. Next most popular in local production in 1820–30 were science and technology, the stages of life, government and politics, and geography.[31]

In attempting to define the universe of printed matter available to the Upper

Valley population, we find that the most significant development within Upper Valley printing in 1778–1830 was the diffusion of sacred works. This finding supports Randolph Roth's estimate of the importance of religion at this time. Although religious works rose from 22 percent of the total in the mid-1780s to a solid third by 1810, the content of religious beliefs, as expressed in these works, changed little. A severe Calvinism and a more moderate evangelicalism vied for supremacy throughout these years, with Universalism—stemming from Enlightenment rationalism—establishing a significant voice in opposition to both.

Among secular works, the proportions of conservative childrearing prescriptions and typically traditional schoolbooks rose, especially after 1800. Otherwise politics and government offered the largest reading matter—more than a quarter of all printed works through 1815. Thereafter, as foreign entanglements and interest in Europe waned, domestic politics and governmental affairs were increasingly relegated to the weekly newspaper.[32] Crime, death, violence, and torture loomed large as specific subjects of interest, seen in a fifth of all locally printed secular works through 1815. Afterwards the rural weeklies increasingly turned to these topics as well. Widely popular reading matter slowly but steadily diversified through 1830. Leading the way were science and technology and works on various life stages, expressing an increasingly rationalistic view of the world, the self, and the human life cycle. Locally printed editions of modern literature and history gradually increased until about 1820, then began to diminish in favor of imported editions, published primarily in Boston, New York, and Philadelphia (see figure 6–1).

In summary, Upper Valley publications suggest that values shifted slowly away from the leading themes and interests of the eighteenth century. Only a few strands in the fresh fabric of ninteenth-century thought were prominent among works issued by Upper Valley presses, apart from newspapers, through 1830; such works constituted a modest share of Upper Valley publications. These trends suggest an important generalization about locally printed reading matter: the newer the subject, the less likely a rural publisher was to reprint a current work about it or to publish the first edition of a fresh contribution to that subject. Older steady sellers in that area of knowledge were reprinted, however. Publishing and printing were international in scope and hierarchical in organization throughout the 1778–1830 period. Large urban publishers in every country of the North Atlantic set trends and, in the newest areas of knowledge, dominated vast rural hinterlands. Only gradually did rural publishers chance an edition in a new field or reissue a work with continuing, strong sales from urban printings.[33]

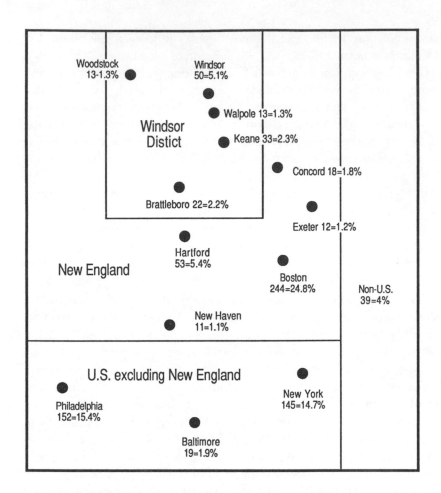

Figure 6–1: Places of Publication with Ten or More Editions for Sale in Windsor District, 1805–30

The World of Popular Sellers in the Upper Valley: Collective Cultural Trends, 1805–30

As Robert Darnton has noted with regard to eighteenth-century France, "what Frenchmen read was determined in part by the way in which their books were produced and distributed." Books are "economic commodities as well as cultural artifacts," after all, "and as vehicles of ideas, they have to be peddled on a market." The broad outlines of Upper Valley publishing, the major trends in reading interests that they reveal, and the system for circulating imprints tell us much about the life course of printed objects. But local production gives us only a partial picture of what was available. Apart from material printed in the Upper Valley, what else was available for people to read? Local distribution and sale of imprints published beyond the Upper Valley provide a way to answer this question.[34]

The usual sticking point in the study of print dissemination below the national level has been the lack of specific evidence beyond production data. In this predicament the *Annalistes* and scholars of Germany and England have turned to three other categories of evidence: "catalogues of private libraries, book reviews, and applications to the state for authorization to publish." All three types of sources exist for early America, and we have used them, but none offers detailed systematic evidence about the universe of available reading material.[35] Fortunately another enormous, largely untapped body of systematic data offers what Darnton terms "an over-all view of reading in general and by genre" throughout America. For at least one period—and often for two or more periods—of several weeks annually after 1800, Upper Valley booksellers, like their counterparts elsewhere, placed advertisements in local newspapers and in some that circulated in other areas. Each advertisement listed from one to as many as two hundred books and pamphlets just received and currently in stock, giving the author and a short form of the title (usually the binding's spine title). Newspaper advertisements are a treasure trove of vital information about the universe of available reading matter and the popular sellers in each region of the United States.[36]

Editors chose the wording of newspaper advertisements carefully and followed a set of conventions. When studied comprehensively (that is, if we examine every advertisement that reached Windsor District for twenty-six years), these notices enable us to distinguish among the universe of available works those books, pamphlets, almanacs, and even some periodicals that sold well among rural residents there from 1805 to 1830. The net result is a short list of works, wherever published, with sizable sales within Windsor District, organized in accord with contemporary understanding of the structure of knowledge (summarized in tables 6–2 and 6–3, and figure 6–1). With a minimum sales threshold and in the absence of comprehensive purchasing records from a Windsor District bookstore, our short list of popular sellers in all fields of knowledge offers a detailed guide to society-wide reading patterns. Popular sellers allow us to move beyond the helpful but partial picture obtained from social and circulating library records, book reviews, and production data alone. This massive fund of evidence (1,333 editions of 850 different popular books, pamphlets, almanacs, and periodicals), providing an overview of current and older vintage popular sellers, illuminates the intellectual traditions that shaped cultural participation in Windsor District in 1805–30.[37]

Far more than we have realized, landlocked rural residents in areas such as the Upper Valley kept up with many recent intellectual trends in the North Atlantic Republic of Letters. In many areas of knowledge—though not in all, to be sure—newly published works were shipped from London and Edinburgh

Table 6–2: The Structure of Knowledge Employed in Analysis of Sales and Retention Records, 1787–1830

Sacred Works
  Bibles and Concordances (total)
    Bibles (whole)
    New Testaments
    Concordances (including compendiums and dictionaries)
  Hymnals and Psalm Books (and combined)
  Prayer and Devotional Works (including catechisms and Sunday School works)
  Theology and Church History (including sermons, and personal religious accounts, e.g., of death)

Secular Works
  Schoolbooks (total)
    General Schoolbooks (including teachers' works, books on teaching, and letter-writing treatises)
    Readers (including combination readers-spellers)
    Spellers
    Grammars (total)
    English Grammars
    Latin Grammars
    Greek Grammars
    Mathematics (arithmetic, algebra, trigonometry and surveying)
    Geographies and Atlases[1] (including maps and gazetteers)
    Oratory[2] (including rhetoric and elocution)
    History Schoolbooks[3]
  Childrens' Books and Preschool Primers[4]
  Dictionaries[5]
  Almanacs
  Secular Music (including songbooks and orations about music)
  Military Affairs (and militia)
  History (including memoirs of historical personages)
  Travels and Voyages
  Philosophy (including aesthetics and works on Freemasonry)
  Classical Greek and Roman Writers
  Literature—Modern
  Medicine (including anatomy and psychology)
  Law
  Science and Technology (total)
    General Science (including chemistry, natural philosophy, and ornithology)
    Astronomy and the Occult
    Technology (including works on manufactures)
    Agriculture
  Stages-of-Life Reading[6] (including manners, cooking, stages of life training for youth and adulthood)

Continued

Table 6-2: Continued

Politics and Government
Economics
Art and Architecture
Miscellaneous

Other Unspecified Works
"Old Books," etc.

---

[1] It is impossible to distinguish usage in this area. Many state "for use in schools," and for convenience they have been combined here.

[2] Most of these were used in academies and colleges.

[3] There were far fewer history schoolbooks than expected until the early 1820s. Most of the substantial interest in history is reflected in category "History (including memoirs)."

[4] Children's books and primers were definitely a separate category distinguishing pre-school learning from schoolbooks in booksellers and residents' perceptions. See "Schoolbooks, Children's Books," VJ, 26 Dec. 1808, 8 Nov. 1813, 2 Nov. 1818, 29 Dec. 1823, 30 Aug. 1828, 14 Feb. 1829, 1 Aug. 1829 (all p. 3 or p. 4 advertisements).

[5] In contrast to the Geography category, it is difficult to decide which few were used in schools thus all have been combined here.

[6] This is a new category, the independence and importance of which I hope to establish in a future study.

to New York, Philadelphia, and Boston, and these works plus American reprints and other indigenous publications traveled along roadways and waterways into the hinterlands of the United States. By 1815 the amount of reading matter in Windsor District had increased dramatically, and among popular sellers, current works were gaining ground relative to traditional steady sellers. In the quarter centry after 1805, 850 different popular sellers constituted a new dimension of daily life in the allegedly backwater rural environment of Windsor District. In breadth and depth of interest, as measured by the number of editions in each subject area with popular sellers, Windsor District residents were suprisingly active readers. To a surprising extent, too, they were serious, mature readers.

The cultural geography of the rural American Northeast presents an interesting picture. As we have seen, the most consequential distinction in cultural participation was between major inland centers such as Windsor, in a full-access area, and geographically close but actually very isolated mountain and foothill communities in minimum-access zones where most residents had no easy access to a newspaper until the mid-1820s. The cultural gap between Stockbridge or Plymouth Kingdom, say, and Windsor was wider than that between Windsor and southern New England coastal cities such as Salem, or New Haven during the early national period. Nor was the gap between Windsor and Boston nearly as large—though it was considerable—as that between Stockbridge and Windsor.

Several surprising cultural trends are suggested by a study of Upper Valley popular sellers. First, the rise to dominance in public culture of secular interests was accomplished far earlier than has previously been suspected (see table 6–3). The transformation has generally been placed in the 1830s or 1840s. The argument has been that, following religion's temporary demise just after the American Revolution, with the second Great Awakening it regained lost ground and maintained great strength until the mid-1830s or later. Our present knowledge of Upper Valley reading suggests that the share of religious works rose in the 1790s as religion caught up with settlement. Between 1795 and 1830 that share fluctuated only narrowly, accounting for between a third and two-fifths of all reading matter. Although religion's influence on reading remained very widespread throughout the Early Republic, secular themes and more worldly concerns nevertheless were primary by the late 1790s and continued to be dominant thereafter.[38]

The proliferation of print communications after 1795 both helped to maintain continuity and exacerbated change in Windsor District daily life. Stability and change were both important, but not equally so in each major area of reading interest. Stability was the watchword in the realm of the sacred. There was the permanence of the Bible itself, a century-old steadiness in devotional literature and prayer books, and considerable continuity in popular hymnals and psalmodies. In the important area of theology, where Calvinism finally gave way to a more freewheeling evangelical theology and moral outlook, change proceeded very slowly indeed. Several categories of schoolbooks likewise stressed traditional information and opinion, and until the 1820s, schoolbook content changed little except to add currency and commerce to arithmetics. Change was also very slow in a few other areas, including political thought, classical literature, the professions of law and medicine, and dictionaries (until the late 1820s). Thus, in subject areas representing approximately two-fifths of all editions, stability in ideas and values far outweighed change.

The situation was quite the reverse in the remainder of popular-selling subject areas. Some fields, such as chemistry, novels, and the rationalist persuasion within the stages-of-life tradition, were relatively new in the scope of their interest. The novel, tale, and story engulfed the district after their rather sudden appearance among lists of popular sellers during the 1790s. Other popular fields reflecting significant new additions to intellectual traditions included modern literature generally, history, travel accounts, science and technology, children's books, general schoolbooks written for teachers, the schoolbook subjects of history and mathematics (especially general arithmetic, trigonometry, and sur-

Table 6-3: Largest Twenty-Five Categories of Popular Sellers in Windsor District, 1802–30 *

Subject Area	Number of Second Editions (or Shipments)
Modern Literature	193
Theology and Sermons	133+
Bibles with Concordances	83+
Hymnals and Psalm Books	76+
Children's Books, Toy Books, and Primers	72+
Mathematics (s)**	68+
Geographies and Atlases***	68+
History	62+
Schoolbooks: General (s)	51+
Spellers (s)	47
Travels and Voyages	46
Readers (s)	36
Grammars (s)	36+
Almanacs	35+
Science and Technology (combined)	33
Devotional and Prayer	31+
Law	30+
Medicine	29+
Military Affairs	25
Classical Writers	24
Dictionaries	24+
Oratory (s)	24
Stages-of-Life Advice	24+
Philosophy	21
Politics	16

*   All editions of books, pamphlets, and almanacs advertised and sold in
    Windsor District and contiguous communities, 1802–30.
** (s) denotes schoolbooks
*** Partly schoolbooks, partly general reading
+   Categories with additional unspecified works in one or more years

veying), and readers. The rural weekly's advertisements dramatically accented both change and continuity in reading interests and cultural participation.

If we turn now to the general content of Windsor District popular sellers in 1805–1830, we can sketch the intellectual foundations of the transformation that created a new, early modern order of rural life there and elsewhere in the American Northeast. Despite the strength of the eighteenth-century Anglo-American wisdom of the ages, a novel nineteenth-century framework of intellectual discourse was emerging in northwestern New England in the years 1805–1830. Perhaps it will be helpful to single out a few key elements in this framework—those which crossed several contemporary subject boundaries.

Five leading intellectual traditions dominated rural ways of thinking and all northwestern New England *mentalités*. The five must be understood in their broadest society-wide formulations before we can determine which parts of the whole were shared by various groups of readers within the Upper Valley. Three interrelated intellectual traditions had been evolving for some time: a shift from Calvinist to evangelical religion and morality; several neoclassical versions of republicanism; and the British connection, a result of the cultural parenthood of Great Britain. Two other conceptions were newly formulated: the spirit of fact and the life cycle as a chart of personal identity.

As the first step in a full-scale analysis of changing *mentalités* in the American Northeast during the first half century of the new nation, we attempt to distinguish these five conceptions from many narrower ideas. Let us begin with the rise of evangelical religion, with its ethical and moral imperative. Evangelical religion was a pervasive force in the Early Republic. Many historians have written about the gradual shift between the 1740s and the 1820s from Calvinist theology and morality to an evangelical outlook. Distinctions among the dozen leading Protestant denominations concerned important but nonetheless fine points of theology and church governance. By contrast, evangelical morality stormed through the Upper Valley between 1795 and 1815, winning broad agreement on some issues, such as the centrality of family morality, domesticity, the power of conscience, and, later, temperance. Several other moral and ethical issues, perceived by the evangelicals as pressing, such as commerce, war, slavery, and Masonry, provoked fundamental disagreement. A transdenominational evangelical or "Christian" morality rose to dominance in the 1810s, creating a ripple effect outward from theology and sermons to religious works of all sorts and into literature, history, the entire spectrum of schoolbooks, military biographies, secular music, children's books, the rationalist stage-of-life tradition, philosophy, politics and government, and even some almanacs.

Area newspapers were one of the very last print arenas to feel the force of the tidal wave of Christian morality, but after 1815 many rural weeklies gave increasing space to various aspects of Christian moral philosophy and benevolent reform. The key reason for the newspaper's delay in giving sizable coverage to religious and moral activities was an earlier eighteenth-century assumption that the newspaper's main function was primarily secular. Most editors could ill afford to side with or favor any denomination even if they wished to do so. By 1815, evangelical morality, if not actually triumphant, was so aggressive that it was perceived as a set of unquestionably true received principles separate from and above religion and hence appropriate for inclusion in rural

The Angel with the Book. Rev. 10, Daniel 7:7, *The Holy Bible: Containing the Old and New Testaments . . .* , 9th ed. (Brattleborough, 1817): opposite page 890. Courtesy, American Antiquarian Society.

The likely character of the final act in human history was a leading theme in the transition from Calvinist to Evangelical morality. Through Bible reading, rural New Englanders learned, from childhood, to view history through the sacred lenses of Protestant Christianity.

weeklies. By the mid-1820s, religion and benevolent moral reform had weathered the storms of a rapidly changing rural cultural scene and were well positioned to struggle mightily to regain their earlier dominance in public discourse. Their main competition came from a nonevangelical, Enlightenment-spawned rationalism, embodied in some forms of Universalist, New England Methodist, Freewill Baptist, Unitarian, and Episcopalian hymnals, sermons, and theological works. By 1815 periodicals represented this alternative theological tradition.[39]

While there were several varieties of neoclassical republican ideology, the overall conceptual framework of republican political economy and social theory was pervasive in this period and was nearly as apt to be evident in discussions of morality as of politics or economics. In fact, Windsor District popular sellers on government, politics, and economics, excepting the very few works in political theory, took the form of direct responses to perceived crises. By 1805, a serious search had begun for the meaning of America's republican experiment and for historical traditions of continued validity and vitality. Authors drew eleborate analogies between America at the time and past civilizations at various moments in their life cycles. Republican theory identified three major epochs and sets of institutions as being of special relevance: the ancient governments of Greece and Rome, a medieval order heralded by Sir Walter Scott and his numerous followers among British novelists and tale tellers, and "modern" transatlantic civilization. The ruling assumption was, however, the broader notion that virtually all known civilizations held lessons apt for America. Small wonder that travel accounts and historical novels were as popular as classical writings and histories.[40]

Third, through the British connection Americans understood themselves to be participants in a North Atlantic intellectual world dominated by British cultural perspectives. British influence was marked after 1800: two-thirds of all law books, four-fifths of all medical works, and seven-tenths of all works in modern literature had British authors. Suprisingly, even in rural New England, attention to British intellectual currents remained steady and dominant throughout the first half century of American nationhood, 1776–1825. Through 1815 a third of all nonlocal news in Windsor District's major weekly, the *Vermont Journal*, was about life in England, especially London. As reading increased in each successive decade of the Early Republic, lag time in the diffusion of British works diminished. In other words, a powerful and exceedingly widespread Anglo-American intellectual dialogue dominated the life of the mind into the mid-1820s. Its scope far exceeded that which has until now been attributed to it.[41]

The specific pattern of popular sellers indicates very strong interest in British culture until about 1810, a hiatus till Ghent, then high levels of British influence in a number of fields through 1825, and a gradual lessening thereafter. In the fields of greater popular interest, British works represented currents new in England, Scotland, and Ireland, as well as older intellectual trends. Many of the latest popular British works, especially novels, appeared in a major urban American edition within a few months after publication and were shipped to the Upper Valley later that same year or early the next. Rural New England functioned very much as a British intellectual province into the 1820s, particularly in fields such as the arts, law, medicine, and science, where America lacked a well-established indigenous tradition. British influence was not nearly so overpowering in theology, because there was a long American history of theological training.

Pro Patria: George Washington. Frontispiece engraved by Abner Reed. From [John Corry], *Biographical Memoirs of the Illustrious Gen. George Washington* (Barnard, 1813). Courtesy, Vermont Historical Society.

Washington most fully embodied the virtues of American neoclassical republicanism, and his experience was recommended to youth and adults alike as exemplary. "Dedicated to the Youth of America," Corry's *Memoirs* depicted the father of America in this frontispiece with a crest, including an angel with a trumpet, and a wreath. Through the mid-1820s sacred and secular were inseparable in basic cultural ideals.

Squire Thornhill Carrying off Olivia. Oliver Goldsmith, *The Vicar of Wakefield* (New York, 1803): opposite page III. Courtesy, American Antiquarian Society.

British novels were especially prominent among families living in river valley communities. The most widely read novel before the 1820s in Windsor District was Goldsmith's tale of the bumbling emigrant family of Dr. Primrose. Their travail of resettlement revolved about the Primrose's daughter, Olivia, Squire Thornhill, and a collection of rogues and sharpers.

Freemason's Heart, supported by Justice and Liberty. Broadside, published in Hartford, Vermont, c. 1814–20. Courtesy, American Antiquarian Society.

The Upper Valley rural ideal through the mid-1820s was capped by a highly moral philosophical ideal of rationalism and science, as seen in this broadside emblem of the virtues instilled by Freemasonry. The Enlightenment ideal of secular moral values survived in Freemasonry, a major institution in Upper Valley society.

Two other broad intellectual conceptions also gained widespread acceptance in the half century following the Revolution. Perry Miller's "hardheaded, utilitarian age" with its "spirit of fact" emerged slowly yet steadily within the Upper Valley in 1787–1830. One aspect entailed an almost religious devotion to concrete physical reality, as evidenced by attention to science, including geology, meteorology, zoology, mineralogy, astronomy, and chemistry. The thirst for knowledge about places and civilizations beyond the United States manifested itself in the proliferation of geography, both in schoolbooks and in works for the general population; of history, and of travel accounts. A third aspect of the spirit of fact related to the spreading fascination with intricate details and with design, planning, and blueprints. This characteristic led to the widespread popularity of surveying, trigonomety, tactical military science, and general technology. Inductive reasoning and empiricism, redefined as an "American scientific spirit," were on the rise by 1815.[42]

At what seemed to be the opposite end of the cultural universe was a newfound fascination with the human personality. A fundamental reevaluation of the relationship of the individual to the larger structures of society, polity, and economy was under way in Great Britain and was finding its way into the Upper Valley. This shift assigned greater importance than previously to parts of the life span other than adulthood and old age, traditionally favored in the eighteenth century. In particular, childhood and youth began to be considered as the most critical stages of life, each with its appropriate goals and objectives. Goals initially suggested during childhood education blossomed as virtues in the later stages of life. The stages of life were understood within a full-scale and increasingly rationalistic developmental framework purporting to account for all personality changes.

This "Voyage-of-Life" framework was later codified by Thomas Cole in four panels of this title. Early nineteenth-century Americans came to accept a four or five-stage conception (infancy was eventually distinguished from childhood) of the course of human existence from birth until death. Each stage had its own goals, problems, special emphases, and growth potential. This organic, Romantic approach to human personality took hold of the popular imagination in three phases: a threshold phase, 1795–1810; an early growth phase, 1810–1825, in which a well-defined series of stages of life was delineated; and a third phase, 1825–1850, marked by the widespread acceptance of this unified conceptualization of the cycle of life and death. The rational development of the self had become a leading concern among all classes of European-Americans, affecting more and more intellectual realms as the century progressed. Upper Valley readers shared in these developments. In addition to books and pamphlets, the periodicals, newspapers, and almanacs published after 1795 were full of essays, editorials, book excerpts, and letters from area residents offering helpful hints on each stage of life. The Voyage-of-Life tradition brought into focus many new concerns about the self in an increasingly commercialized agricultural society.[43]

The five key clusters of ideas and beliefs did not form part of any unified world view, but instead becamse interrelated through usage. In rural northern New England as elsewhere, the dawn of the nineteenth-century saw the slow decline of one array of world views and the beginnings of another, distinctively nineteenth-century, array. Calvinist and evangelical theology and morality, neoclassical republicanism, and the British connection meshed well with the reigning perception of the new nation's destiny. A rural, premodern Christian republic within the North Atlantic community was the resulting ideal.

This ideal was countered by the emerging concern with "objectivity" and "fact," with a new and different set of values and principles, and with a radically different concomitant view of nature, progress, and power. For American writers who were comfortable with the deepseated empiricism of a pioneer society and nurtured on British works, independence included ideas about technology and building, about exploring and exploiting, and about the workings of a heavily commercialized economy, society, and culture. As a cluster of values, the spirit of fact encapsulated all the altered circumstances of the new nation, from technological advances and inventions to geographical exploration and westward migration.[44]

The Voyage-of-Life tradition mediated between these two very different intellectual orientations, one avowedly sacred and the other implicitly secular. Most Americans, in their expression of ideas, values, and feelings, had become routinely conscious of life stages and of the requirements for self-development. The tasks and problems at any given stage of life were regarded as intervening to guide intellectual interests and to adjust inner feelings and external knowledge of the world. In this central strategic position, one's stage of life became the filter through which all other values passed. Gender ideology, with its divided consciousness, had become an important element in middle-class culture by the late eighteenth century. But it was only part of a broader approach to personality development which rendered life more manageable in an era of rapid fundamental change.

Popular Sellers and the Life Cycle

As Upper Valley residents came to view their life from birth to death in terms of a four- or five-stage life cycle, this set of perceptions directed actual personality development, intertwining culture and psyche. Much reading matter circulating in the Upper Valley after 1800 was intended for people in a specific stage—almost never more than two stages—of life. Countless prefaces, forewords, and introductions specified the intended audience of a work: chil-

Print Communications and Cultural Exchange

dren, young men or women (or both), parents, the elderly. By 1815, the rural New England reading public was increasingly divided into at least eight specific audiences.

How did the uses of printed matter vary by stage of life and by gender? Interestingly, a large number of the 1,333 editions read in Windsor District were intended not for adult men and women but for children between four and twelve years old. Works for children included most of the seventy-two publications in the category of primers, toy books, and children's books (see tables 6–2 and 6–3 throughout). Obviously some of these works would also be read by older children and others. Nearly all of the child works that were popular in Windsor District addressed both genders and assumed that boys and girls were far less different than similar until the onset of puberty. In view of the wide age range of the district school's population – from five through seventeen or eighteen years of age in many communities – it is best to break down the approximately 300 editions of schoolbooks (a fifth of all editions) by the functional level at which they were used rather than attempting to assign them to different ages artificially. All were intended to be read in connection with formal educational instruction, and distinctions were principally between elementary and advanced subjects, those taught mostly to district schoolchildren and those intended for scholars pursuing their education at the academy or college level or learning about more intricate subjects, perhaps to further a career.

Elementary schoolbooks included most of the fifty-four editions in the general schoolbooks category, excluding a few works for teachers and a few other treatises on educational theory; many of the thirty-six editions of readers and forty-seven editions of spellers; basic English grammars; arithmetics; and some of the school geographies and atlases. The more advanced schoolbooks included works on trigonometry, geometry, and surveying; a few of the advanced arithmetics; several of the more advanced texts and atlases in ancient

---

(Opposite): Frontispiece to George Fisher's *[American] Instructor; or, Young Man's Best Companion* (Walpole, 1794). Courtesy, Vermont Historical Society.

A scene of instruction in astronomy is depicted in the most popular self-education manual of the day, directed mainly at youth. Other books in the background offer materials for lessons in farriery, navigation, measuring, architecture, and arithmetic. The verse below the picture expressed the motto of an age of reading:

'Tis to ye Press and Pen we Mortals owe,
All we believe & almost all we know.
All hail ye great Preservers of these Arts,
That raise our thoughts & Cultivate our Parts.

John Taylor of Plymouth dated this copy on the reverse side of the frontispiece: "his book, March 2nd 1801."

and modern geography; some of the English grammars; the eleven Latin and Greek grammars; most of the twenty-four works in rhetoric and oratory; nearly all of the fifteen schoolbook history editions; and a few editions of basic dictionaries.[45] Youth was also the intended audience for many other books and pamphlets, and still other works found their audience among youth, whatever their authors' intentions. The leading reading interest of youth was modern literature, with novels and poetry at the forefront. Other categories of consequence included chapbooks of all sorts; devotional tracts, particularly works addressed to people hoping to undergo conversion; many stage-of-life publications discussing manners and mores or presenting letters from parents to their daughters or sons; and a smattering of history and travel books and even a few theological treatises and sermons. While it is difficult to be precise, we may reasonably estimate that about 175 editions (one-eighth of the total), exclusive of schoolbooks, were read by youth. A majority was intended by their authors for one gender only. The reading interests of males and females were assumed to differ beginning in late childhood.

Childhood and youth, the first two stages in the life cycle, accounted for two-fifths (about 550 of 1,333) of all editions of popular sellers available in Windsor District. Certainly this level of preadult reading should cause us to think differently about the knowledge that accompanied the acquisition of literacy and the first decade of reading experience in rural New England. In many cases reading began early in childhood and continued thereafter through the remaining stages of the life cycle. The stage for which it is most difficult to isolate specific categories or even portions of subject areas is old age. Not more than a half-dozen works addressed this stage of life, and even if we add some of the sermons and a few books concerning death, the total is only about twenty-five publications that may be assumed to correlate reasonably directly with the reading of the elderly. Obviously the elderly read far more widely, but through 1830 old age for the most part figured little in the intentions of writers. This pattern persisted despite steadily increasing targeting of other life stages.

Between 765 and 800 editions, or nearly three-fifths, cutting across most areas of knowledge, addressed adults. Another 100 or so works that overlap with material directed to youth should also be included—some novels, devotional works, and chapbooks for instance. Consequently almost two-thirds of all popular works were possible purchases for adult readers. We may identify three separate reading groups within this stage of life. First, most of the thirty editions of law books, twenty-five of the twenty-nine medical works, and nearly half of the most esoteric works in theology and church history were read by a small group of male professionals in these fields. They and a few curious general readers of professional works constitute a distinct segment of the Upper Valley adult reading population. Obviously this tiny reading public also read beyond professional areas.

A second audience, much larger in number, was married adult women, almost always presumed to be mothers. This group formed the intended audience of works, perhaps thirty popular editions, dealing with domesticity, child-rearing, and management of the home. To these publications we may add another 150 or so editions of other works. Modern literature (mainly novels, poetry, and plays) no doubt accounts for the largest single cluster, but devotional works and some theological texts were also very popular among adult married women. The tastes of some women—how large a group we do not yet know—extended to all areas of knowledge. To decide in advance of detailed research that women's reading was narrowly restricted is too eagerly to believe the rhetoric of the cult of domesticity. Newspapers, for instance, regularly sought adult women readers after 1815—through advertisements for commodities directed at women, through excerpts from books (available at the print center's bookstore and often published locally) on women's traditional role as wife and on the expanded role of the republican mother, through stories of female heroism and independence, through pieces about women rebelling against their traditional roles, through the poetry column, through announcements of educational and cultural opportunities for women only or equally available to men and women, and through general remarks which assumed women were regular newspaper readers.[46]

Beyond these two groups, one other reading public may be identified: adult male farmers and craftsmen in hamlets and villages. These readers paid particular attention to technical and practical works, including general science, technology, agriculture, architecture and building, history, politics and government. Almanacs and newspapers catered to this group of readers. This group also read in the areas of theology and modern literature, but the extent to which it did so is not yet known.

Apart from these three groups of adult readers—male professionals, adult women, and adult male farmers and craftsmen—it is not yet possible to identify specific audiences. It is useful, however, to make one other distinction, between utilitarian and leisure reading habits (I say "habits" rather than "works," since a leisure reading experience for one person might well have utilitarian value for another). In the former class were most frequently found devotional works; hymnals and psalmodies; prayer books and Bibles; some stage-of-life works; almanacs; publications on general science, technology, astronomy, and military affairs; and perhaps most important of all, newspapers. Most frequently specified as leisure reading were modern literature; history; accounts of voyages; writings about popular philosophy, politics, and government; the classics; and, again, newspapers. Bibles were also considered leisure reading material. While no absolute distinction was made between these two kinds of reading, works were usually written and published for one purpose or the other, the intention often being reflected in prefaces and advertisements.

The market distribution system for printed matter began to expand rapidly in the early 1790s and never ebbed through 1830. Extensive local production and growth in imports accounted for an explosion in the volume and diversity of matter stocked, sold, and read. From an annual stock of perhaps 50,000 copies of 1,500 works by 1805, Windsor District residents picked carefully, creating by their choices a small group of popular sellers each year. Readers could also pick from a reasonably broad selection of almanacs tailored to agricultural life in the area, a varied group of periodicals, and a regular and changing supply of broadside music, poetry, tales, and prose arguments. Reading patterns by stage of life, gender, and level of schooling allow us to identify according to their intellectual interests, eight specific reading publics among Windsor District residents.

The 1,333 editions of popular sacred and secular works and schoolbooks in 1805–30 catered to scores of particular reading interests. Five major intellectual traditions, spanning a broad range of beliefs and values, flowed through these works. Three of the five represented somewhat older intellectual traditions: evangelical Christianity, neoclassical republicanism, and the British connection. The other two traditions expressed newer trends of thought: interest in the facts of this world, numeracy as an ideal, and mensuration; and greatly expanded attention to human personality through a rationalistic developmental conception of the life cycle. Continuity vied with change in intellectual interests as lifelong reading characterized an ever greater proportion of families in Windsor District.

Part III
Family Foundations

Chapter 7

Varieties of Family Life:
The Material Anchors of Knowledge
in Windsor District, 1780–1830

The eye that mock-eth at his father, and scorn-eth to obey his
mother, the ra-vens of the val-ley shall pick it out, and the young
ea-gles shall eat it.

—Noah Webster, *The American Spelling Book*

The Family as the Foundation
of Collective Existence

In the Upper Valley, family circumstances, the availability of printed matter,
and an element of choice conspired to determine what was read and how
it was incorporated and acted upon. This chapter analyzes some of the most
important material determinants of knowledge among all strata of Upper Valley society between 1780 and 1830. These determinants include work; household organization; wealth; public position and prestige; and retention and size
of family holdings of printed matter, treated for now as collections of commodities. But at least a quarter and sometimes a third of Windsor District families appear to have shaped their participation in print culture in response to
factors not related to their occupations, wealth, or class interests, however
broadly conceived.

For the generations who founded the American nation, everyday life in the
Upper Valley was a mixture of toil, anxiety about the afterlife, stark and often
bluntly expressed appetites, and earthly pain and happiness. In these relentless
existences, occasionally an exciting interlude or moment of ecstasy occurred.
Many people burned with piety; others lived a lifetime in unnerving quiet.
The families of freehold and tenant farmers, artisans, semiskilled laborers, and
small traders predominated in the crowds at Fourth of July celebrations in
Windsor village during the Early Republic. Far more than any other influences, their families and clans and the circumstances of their collective exis-

tence formed and continued to shape the characters of these plain people. Southern New Englanders gathered in Vermont townships in clans; they moved on in the same way.[1]

The family was the center of both material and cultural life in the Early Republic. It was strained by the transformation of rural life in 1780–1835, but, against many forces that diluted its authority and competed for its traditional functions, the family remained the organizing force in collective existence through 1830. For most individuals, the family and its homestead remained the key unit of production in earning a living; the focus of work and love, twin cornerstones of collective experience; and the most powerful agent in cultural participation.

A great irony characterized the turn of the nineteenth century. With the spread of market capitalism, class relations for the first time were becoming important in rural New England. At the same time, however, print, one of the leading arenas of commodity exchange, was undermining all notions of one's "interests" based on material circumstances. As Susan Geib has noted, "the ability to think and choose is not given uniquely to people with full stomachs."[2] The first era of widespread literacy and mass culture based on the printed word was an era in which all the intellectual dynamite of a half millennium came within reach of literate people, largely untrained in the Western tradition. The habit of reading could reinforce the wisdom of the ages; become an agent of radical change, as in the exemplary cases of Joseph Smith and Orestes Brownson; or, more moderately, foster a mix of continuity and change.[3] Print commodities could serve conservative ends by offering routes of escape to better worlds and other lives, as a way of staving off revolt against existing authority and power. Printed matter conferred on the reader new capacities, however; people could now "visit" China and Africa who could not afford a stagecoach ride to Worcester or Boston. And on return from their reading, some of these men and women became leaders and bold adventurers, acting on their new knowledge in ways profoundly at odds with their allegedly "real" position within a system of class relations.

Great inequalities of condition marked rural family life: the richest family leaving an estate in Windsor District through 1830 owned worldly possessions worth 5,005 times the value of those of the poorest family. Reading became a necessity of life more slowly or more quickly in the half century following Independence based not on choice alone but also on life circumstances and the unequal availability of what we think of as enriching objects of curiosity. Our understanding has profited much from recent comparative work by Natalie Zemon Davis, Emmanuel LeRoy Ladurie, Darrett B. Rutman, and others. Davis speaks of the need for "more carefully defined milieus," and Rutman has written of the need to distinguish the country gentry, peasants, and townspeople (urban "middle class") among "the hearers of the preachers."[4] The point of analyzing the economic, social, and cultural milieus in which the life of the mind functioned is to understand the mix of factors affecting public value formation, persistence, and change over time. We will make this analysis in a comparative framework.[5]

The richest surviving evidence about the conditions of family life in the new republic consists of records relating to seasonal meetings of the probate court that members of a family attended following the death of the household head. The families in question are a large and quite representative portion of the entire population and are especially representative of all families participating in print communications. Furthermore, the evidence of inventories, supplemented by wills and other estate documents, is very specific, household by household. For larger dwellings, the inventory was often made room by room. For almost every household within this group of 643 families residing in Windsor District, 1780–1830, we have a fairly complete inventory. In includes amount and kind of land, house size when the dwelling was owned, livestock, agricultural implements and tools, the full range of material possessions in each room, and mills and other business structures. Records of church pew ownerships and rentals; shares in banks, turnpike companies, and lending libraries; and so forth were also maintained. The credit and debit status of the household rounded out the picture of material possessions. Supplemented with evidence of household composition for the period 1790–1840, with limited occupational data drawn form the 1810 and 1820 federal censuses, and with the 1820 federal census of manufactures, these inventories provide reasonably precise data regarding wealth, occupations, and work experience.

Evidence about the actual location of households and their relation to the area's transportation and communication systems enables us to sharpen the picture of family life. Our goal is to locate each major segment of Upper Valley society in terms of the material and cultural circumstances of family and clan life and to anchor differing family private and public activities in the circumstances of daily life. Windsor District's overall range of occupations, and the share of each, is well represented by estate inventories. Because those least well accounted for had the narrowest range of reading matter in nearly all known cases, the reading tastes in the cases most often lost to time can at least be sensibly approximated.

Household, Wealth, Work, and Public Position, 1780–1830

In this book I use the word "occupation" to mean the work of an entire household. "Work" in the Early Republic meant "the matter at which one is at work" or "a state of labor." Work included traditional male and female labor, "exertions of strength," "manual labor," and also "that which is produced by mental labor."

The narrower term, "occupation," was a quasi-legal category that was usually applied to male responsibility and public position: an "employment, business, trade, calling, or vocation." Employment meant "public office or business." Webster's 1828 codification defined it as "the principal business of one's life . . . the business which a man follows to procure a living or obtain wealth." Our usage distinguishes between the legal situation – the dominant power of males and the subordinate power of females in the ownership and management (occupation) of material resources in a patriarchal legal system – and the actual world of work as it was carried out. When using "occupation" we also mean to imply that nearly all males and females engaged in a wide range of work.[6]

Most Upper Valley families through 1830 – those above the lowest fifth of the wealth structure – farmed, did considerable artisan work, actively engaged in some commerce in products and services, regularly engaged in home manufacturing activities, and served in the public sphere in township, religious, and educational committees and positions. Many also served as doctors for their own families, kin, and neighbors. The variety and diversity of work in agricultural society illuminates a way of life which after 1810 increasingly came to be challenged. Greater specialization in work experience was the result of enhanced economic interdependence within each locale, an efficient but far less nurturing form of economic community, and a rising interest in private accumulation. In a rural household through 1830 work was an inherently collective experience, with particular contributions made by each male and female above eight or nine years of age. In early American society work reflected the labors of a group of workers more than the separable achievement of any individual. Gender was important in the division of work; no lone male ever ran a farm in the Upper Valley. These concerns are dealt with more extensively in appendix 3. The general discussion below takes into account all 643 Windsor District households with surviving inventories made just after the death of the household head in 1787–1830, and focuses specifically on the 396 families (62 percent) that maintained private libraries.[7]

Eight principal occupational designations accord best with all relevant evidence from the Upper Valley through 1830. These types of families are designated as: gentleman farm, yeoman farm, tenant farm, semiskilled laborer, artisan, commercial and trading, manufacturing, and professional (lawyers, doctors, clergy, and one editor/publisher/printer).

Gentleman Farm Families. Farming and grazing constituted the dominant work experience for the majority of Windsor District families. These are divided into three occupational groups, by rental or ownership of a farm and, among owners, by total wealth (real and personal), by type and amount of production for market, and by other economic activities (see table 7–1 throughout). Moving down the economic scale, a small group of wealthy farming and

Plymouth Ponds from the South, Plymouth, Vermont. From Edward Hitchcock et al., *Report on the Geology of Vermont* (Claremont, N.H., 1861), vol. 2: plate 38. Courtesy of Special Collections, University of Vermont Library, Burlington, Vermont.

Embodying the picturesque landscape tradition, this contemporary engraving presents a pastoral idyll of an unfettered life, in sharp contrast with the actual world of work analyzed here. Compare the photograph "Threshing Grain."

grazing families; a large group of "middling sort" families, some moderately well-to-do and some quite strained; and a sizable group of poor families inhabited Windsor District through 1830.

First among farmers were gentleman farm families. All of the twenty-five families in the study group—the same proportion of heavily commercial farmers Roth found in Upper Valley township tax records—owned property (real and personal) worth more than $3,000 at the death of the household head. Of gentleman farm families, 85 percent possessed property worth less than $5,000, placing the group at the upper range of the middle class if we use a three-tiered wealth scale. An eighth of gentleman farm families were headed by females—widows with a substantial legacy and children and perhaps with relatives living with them and working on the farmstead.[8] Compared with all

Table 7-1: Windsor District Occupational Data, 1787–1830[1]

Occupations of Households*	Number and Percent of Households in Group		Average Wealth (in $)	Median Wealth (in $)	Wealth Range (in $)
Commercial and Trading	45	(12%)	8,817	4,389	49–85,041
Manufacturing	7	(2%)	6,993	5,120	2,367–14,526
Professional	33	(9%)	5,459	3,326	100–38,242
Gentleman Farm	25	(6%)	4,077	3,607	3,080–8,742
Artisan	49	(13%)	1,496	864	49–5,740
Yeoman Farm	152	(40%)	1,340	1,166	129–2,998
Tenant Farm	47	(12%)	314	243	45–991
Semiskilled	25	(6%)	206	150	17–646
Total: n=383	$1,024,680		Av. $2,675	——	$17–$85,041

Occupations of Households*	Average Acreage	Overall Household Size[2]	Full and ¾ Contributors (16 and over)	All Active Contributors (10 and over)
Commercial and Trading	514.9[3]	7.9	4.9	6.3
Manufacturing	102.5[4]	8.6	4.1	6.4
Professional	274.5[5]	7.3	5.3	5.5
Gentleman Farm	160.4	9.2	5.9	7.9
Artisan	76.5[6]	7.1	4.1	5.1
Yeoman Farm	74.8	6.9	3.4	3.8
Tenant Farm	——	6.4	4	5
Semiskilled	——[7]	4.4	3.4	3.8
Total	147	7.1	4.1	4.9

* From Table 7-2

[1] Includes all inventories with private libraries and occupational data (n=383) and also a check of all families with an inventory but without printed matter for each of the eight occupations. Differences within occupations between print holding and non-print holding families are minimal.

[2] Data not available in some cases from the U.S. Census, thus 60 to 90% of occupations are represented.

[3] There were 5 renters; figure here is the average for the other 40 cases.

[4] Same situation as for note 3 (1 renter).

[5] Same situation as for note 3 (8 renters; 2 undetermined).

[6] Same situation as for note 3 (19 renters; figure here is the average for the other 30 cases).

[7] Data for 14 households; only 4 of 14 owned land.

other families whose major occupation was farming, gentleman farm families were distinguished by their wealth, power, and social status. The Leveretts' "old-fashioned coach, opening at the rear," moved swiftly down Windsor District roads on Sundays. Gentleman farm families were, on average, three times as wealthy as yeoman farm families, and tilled twice the acreage. They lived on full farmsteads ranging from 62 to 382 acres (167 acres on average) and usually owned other land, often including a separate woodlot. Most of their homesteads were worth at least $1,500, or nearly a third of their wealth. On all other measures, gentleman farm families lived very comfortably amid a considerable amount of household furniture, often of high quality. They had a family library, cooking equipment, dishes and utensils, bedding, and food supplies inside the house, plus orchards, beehives, gardens, livestock, farm implements, and saddles. Usually they had other buildings "and appurtenances" beyond the main house.[9]

Every gentleman farm family engaged in farming fulltime, growing for the market as well as for home use; in some grazing, especially sheepherding after 1815; and in either modest artisan activity or in home manufactures on a commercial basis. Excess production was sold or bartered within the economic locale. Major agricultural production efforts included raising stock for produce (for example, cheese, pork, and sides of beef); growing hay; cultivating corn, flax, wheat, oats, and barley; and tending bees for honey and apple orchards; and tapping maple trees for sugar in March and April. Specific commercial activity beyond farming included raising sheep to provide wool for trade and home manufacturing, home manufacture of cotton cloth for sale, carpentry, shoemaking, blacksmithing, and operation of a gristmill.[10] All through the farming population the number of active contributors to the labor force increased along with total wealth; gentleman farm families averaged eight contributors. Rural gentleman farm families were quite large, ranging from six to fifteen members. Households averaged 9.2 members, clustered at 6 to 7 and 9 to 11 residents. In a totally male political and legal structure, the combination of wealth and market participation with diversity of economic interests ensured gentleman farm families considerable local influence and social prestige. For male heads of household this power translated into political officeholding, religious influence (for example, as deacons) and other forms of public service at the community, district, and county level.[11]

Yeoman Farm Families. The largest group of Windsor District families (152 families in our study group, or 40 percent), were yeoman households. The term "husbandman" was used less frequently but interchangeably. In fully 86 percent of the cases, Yeoman families possessed less than $2,000 in real and personal property. Yeoman, as distinguished from tenant farm, households owned land. They typically became involved in local commodities markets by selling small but fairly regular quantities of one crop or sporadic surpluses of varying agricultural products. Whereas nearly all gentleman farm families sold at least one and usually several products annually, definite sales can be established for only a quarter of yeoman farm families before 1810; the percentage gradually rose to half of all families by 1830. Self-sufficiency aside, existence was far more rugged in the northern New England forest than in most rural areas to the south and west. Wealth varied considerably among yeoman farm families. They ranged in wealth: $251–$750, $1,001–$1,500, and $1,751–$2,251. Evidence of surprisingly few yeoman farm households headed by women survives.[12]

Yeoman farmsteads averaged a healthy 75 acres on the main homestead lot. About 30 percent also owned land or a share in land, usually a woodlot, away from the homestead. Of all farms, 77 percent had 1 to 100 acres, and just 11 percent had more than 150 acres. Most (87 percent) were located fairly far from villages. Yeoman families typically produced only one or two crops for market, plus occasional artisan and other services. Beyond the same farm products that gentleman farm families sold, the yeomanry engaged in commercial exchange in blacksmithing, shoemaking, carpentry, coopering, other artisan services, building and painting houses, trading small goods, sheepraising and wool production, spinning, and small-scale manufacturing. Notes and book accounts suggest that even households without signs of crop production or artisan services maintained between four and six ongoing commercial relationships. Households that manifestly engaged in commercial exchange maintained between eight and fourteen ongoing commercial relationships.[13]

Yeoman farm households averaged seven members. The most typical sizes were five to six (50 percent) and eight to nine members. In most households, between three and five people contributed regularly to the work cycle. There were an average of two more children under ten in yeoman households than in gentleman farm households, suggesting a larger concentration of younger families in this group. Yeoman farmers had a reasonable amount of social status, regularly occupying political and religious positions in their townships. In several cases, early settlers of some minor prominence spent little time accumulating material possessions. Their families were firmly of the "middling sort," and they invested large amounts of time and energy in local government and community progress. Beginning in central villages by the 1820s, specialization of local governmental affairs and the emergence of a semiprofessional class of township managers and officials curtailed the political influence of the yeomanry and raised tensions.[14]

Tenant Farm Families. Far less is known about tenant farm households, mainly because they were often much younger and were frequently less firmly rooted in their communities. They generally had few material possessions, and a majority lived in "hardscrabble" living situations. As Charles Danhoff has noted, tenancy "was common in the Northeast." Our study group of forty-seven tenant families were farmers without their own farms. Nor did they typically own any other lands, such as wild acreage or woodlots, or other real property such as pews in meetinghouses or lending library shares. In material condition, tenant farm households ranged from struggling to desperately poor. Average wealth was just $314, and median wealth was even lower, $243. Just over half of all tenant farm families owned less than $250 in property, and 70 percent owned less than $500. Most tenant farm families lived in isolated locations; Cavendish and four of the most mountainous townships accounted for 80 percent.[15]

Other studies tell us that some tenant farm families were new migrants to the Upper Valley who were just starting out in farming. Many remained tenants until they had accumulated enough money for a down payment on land of their own. Another group of tenant farm families, however, consisted of older, longer-term tenants who were unable to obtain or maintain ownership of a going farmstead of who chose not to own land, content to obtain their living by their labor. Most tenant farm families leased a parcel of land and worked it with their own farm implements, paying their rent in crops. That life was bearable, if difficult, is confirmed by the fact that personal property among tenanting households, which averaged $293, was two-thirds that of the yeomanry ($377). Tenant farm families generally owned less in the way of household furniture, beds and bedding, tableware, and expensive items such as saddles than yeoman farm families but had about the same amount of cooking utensils, farm implements, livestock, and food supplies. Tenant farm households were among the most migratory of Windsor District residents; consequently evidence of family size and structure is elusive. As it exists it reveals that tenant farm families were about the same in size as yeoman farm families: they averaged 6.4 members per household and were split into two groups. The first consisted of younger, small families, with 1 to 3 members, while the second group encompassed considerably older, large families, with 6 to 8 members each. Just three of forty-seven households are known to have engaged in production for the market and only about a fourth show any evidence of commercial exchange. Because property was the currency of participation and power, tenant farm heads held very few public positions and then only minor ones. Orestes Brownson's father, Sylvester, for example, served as a fence-sitter at Stockbridge in northern Windsor County in 1801 and 1802.[16]

Semiskilled Laborer Families. Semiskilled laborer families also left few traces beyond their inventories; there are twenty-five such families in our study group. These households generally lacked any "real property," which Webster and others, following Blackstone, defined as "things fixed, permanent, or immovable." Semiskilled laborer families survived by working for independent artisans, traders, farmers, or manufacturers. Nearly all semiskilled laborer families (90 percent) lived in Windsor District's villages and largest hamlets. Villages were fairly compact and intimate places through 1830. Like the tenant farm families, these people were generally powerless in the public sphere, although they were neither invisible nor socially anonymous. Females headed fully a quarter of these families, in all cases widows managing households that included several working individuals. Only a sixth of all semiskilled laborer households owned any real property and just a quarter farmed at all (the available evidence suggests that none did so fulltime) or owned any livestock or other animals. Average wealth for semiskilled laborer families was the lowest among all occupations, $206. No household owned more than $650 worth of property, and two-thirds held less than $250. Bare essentials dominated inventories. These families had no need for farm implements and lived without livestock or large amounts of food. Beyond food, shelter, clothing, and, in a narrow majority of all semiskilled laboring families, a small clutch of reading matter, small sets of artisan tools were often their only possessions. A third of gentleman farm families each retained more of this world's goods at inventory than all twenty-five semiskilled laborer families together.[17]

Semiskilled laborer families for whom evidence exists maintained the smallest households among Windsor District families, ranging from 3 to 7 members and averaging just 4.4. The correlation between the number of active contributors and lack of wealth was not accidental: in a labor-intensive rural economy, every contributor made a difference. All laborer households worked for other businesses and families. General and "common" village labor led the list of notes and payment methods in account books. The largest employers of labor were village and hamlet artisan shops, manufactories, stores, and, in season, farms. Manufacturing labor, at home and — increasingly after 1815 — in factories, was provided by at least a quarter of all semiskilled laborer families. Blacksmithing, masonry, cabinetmaking, and general carpentry and housebuilding were carried on by other families. The only signs of commercial exchange beyond notes for labor services were occasional notes of indebtedness and book accounts outstanding, usually one to two and never more than four. During the lengthy harvest season, July through November, many semiskilled laborer families went to work, and sometimes to live, as common wage laborers on farms. Otherwise, almost all families boarded or rented houses or space on the property of others. Semiskilled laborer families were usually far along in their family cycles at the death of the household head. Three types of households dominated: recent losers in life's fortunes, including those recently bankrupted; long-term laborer families now headed by widows; and mature, stable families who were poor and had been so for many years.[18]

Artisan Families. Artisan households played a complex and pivotal role in Upper Valley society. They were not just diverse in their work experience; their lifestyles differed widely as well. All artisan heads of household were economically independent skilled mechanics, most of whom, unlike more specialized urban artisans, worked for themselves, combining the roles of "worker, foreman, and merchant." Moreover, many rural artisans employed members of semiskilled laborer families. These aspects of work were all that united the artisans occupationally. Their wealth ranged from $49 to $5,740. Three-fifths owned land, while the rest rented. The artisan occupation was the most diverse in the Upper Valley, fragmenting in the face of massive changes in production, distribution, and consumption. Artisans were so close to the most rapid economic changes that we are tempted to assume that they were similar in outlook and in life experience. But at least in rural New England, for every two artisan families who welcomed cultural, social, and economic change, a third family resisted it fiercely. Moreover, the division was not a clean one between village and countryside families nor between rich and poor households.[19]

Moreover, although Windsor District artisans as a group were far better off financially than semiskilled laborer, tenant, or even yeoman farm families, artisan households tended to move quite frequently from one place to another. The connections between solvency and financial health on the one hand and permanence and roots on the other, traditional within rural society, had been severed here. Artisan ties to agricultural society were far less firm in 1815 than in 1790. In response to competition within their own and from other economic locales, many migrated, sometimes by choice and often by necessity. Artisan families moved sometimes to stave off the growing specialization of labor and at other times to take advantage of it. To do either, artisan households had to remain sharply attuned to varying economic and social conditions throughout their area. About two-thirds of artisan households nurtured diversity and change, and these families exhibited an essential feature of the early nineteenth century's new rural world. The majority of artisan families also exemplified a new social characteristic: three-fifths lived in the largest three villages, Windsor, Chester, and Springfield, and all but 10 percent resided in the six most populous townships.[20]

In material possessions artisan families varied greatly. A seventh of the households had property worth $3,000 or more and enjoyed lifestyles resembling those of gentleman farm families. An eighth were desperately poor, with property worth less than $500 and living circumstances like those of the majority of semiskilled laborer families. Nearly $5,700 in property value separated the poorest families from the wealthiest. Average value of property holdings at inventory was $1,496, higher than that for yeoman farm families, but median wealth was several hundred dollars lower. Just over half of all artisan families possessed less than $1,000 in real and personal possessions; three-quarters had below $2,000.[21] Long ago Percy Bidwell sketched the economic situation of rural New England artisan households, concluding that they exhibited "imperfect specialization of occupations" and "partial dependence on agriculture."

To the contrary, for a growing population of families, artisan labor was the primary and often the sole occupation. A substantial majority of artisan households engaged in some farming, including production for the market in many cases. A solid quarter of all artisan families (mainly village dwellers), however, lacking any livestock and having at best a garden and a few fruit trees, appear to have depended on barter and purchase for survival. Among property owners, a third maintained less than 11 acres each; a fifth owned enough land—between 26 and 50 acres each—to permit farming; and half owned full farmsteads of between 51 and 150 acres each. Other lands, including woodlots, meadowlands, and second farms that were rented out, were frequently owned and were sizable in several cases.[22]

The wealthiest Windsor District artisan families were carpenters specializing in house construction during an era of town building. They belonged to a larger group, a quarter of all artisan families, who were general carpenters and joiners. Other artisan households included several furniture and cabinet makers, coopers, shoemakers, and blacksmiths who made almost anything imaginable from iron; plus a few wheel, casket, and wagon makers, masons, glassmakers, specialized iron workers, and a person who made plow handles. Many artisan families also engaged in allied crafts on a minor scale. Artisan households varied enormously in size, from 3 to 15; 5 and 6 members were most typical (60 percent), and average size was 7.1, about the same as among yeoman farm families. Artisan families contained an average of 5 contributors aged ten and over, and size of household and wealth were strongly related. Artisan work (unlike several other occupations) was not usually assumed by a widow at her husband's death; the business was usually sold. Accordingly no record of female-head artisan households survives. Tools were often passed down to one or more sons (none to daughters in existing wills), who began or continued working for another shop.[23]

Artisan residence patterns involved them considerably in Windsor District public life; in three-quarters of all artisan families, workplaces were in or near a village. As a result most artisan families, with access to virtually all of the reading matter circulating through the district, shared with professional families a special relationship to print culture and to village life. Artisans, villages, and print culture thrived or declined together. In their diversity artisan families formed the crucial links between the wealthiest class—commerce and trading, manufacturing, gentleman farm, and professional families—and most of the farming and semiskilled laboring population.

Commerce and Trading Families. While the lower and middling orders of society formed the bulk of the population, most of these families enjoyed relatively little power or prestige. The final three occupational groups, together with gentleman farm families, wielded enormous wealth and power in nearly all aspects of Windsor District life.

First in commanding wealth, power, political and community influence, and prestige and respect were families in commerce and trading. Along with lawyers, they came closest to ruling Windsor District through 1830. These were mainly families of storekeepers engaging in retail business and wholesaling to Lilliputian general stores in hamlets; keepers of taverns and inns; and proprietors of traditional farm-related mills and industries, especially gristmills, sawmills, tanneries, cider mills, and pearlash works. Households engaged in commerce and trade (forty-five in our study group) represented the top level of entrepreneurship in the economic class structure of Windsor District. Land, buildings, and store stock accounted for a very large share (about 70 percent) of commercial households' total wealth, the highest among all occupations at an average of $8,817. A third of all families in this category possessed less than $2,000 in real and personal property; slightly more than a third retained between $2,000 and $10,000; and 30 percent were worth between $10,000 and $85,041. The generous variety of material circumstances among these families is striking testimony to the risks of business activity.[24]

Great diversity in wealth was also reflected in land holdings. Just six families (12 percent) owned no land at all. The other five-sixths each owned between 1 and 5,000 acres, averaging 515 acres per household. Typical estates (60 percent) ranged between 51 acres and 500 acres: a quarter owned relatively small plots (less than 50 acres); while 15 percent of trading families possessed more than 500 acres each. The forms of economic activity among these families were the most extensive in Windsor District. Most households engaged in full-scale farming, usually including production for the market; ran at least one shop, mill, tavern, or inn; and leased and/or transferred to kin or others the use of additional land holdings. Apart from land, real property often included shares in banks, cotton and woolen factories, turnpike companies (only the wealthiest owned shares in these), pews in local meetinghouses, and social libraries. Several families also lent money at interest. While the mix of financial resource allocation varied, trading in goods and services dominated, and farming remained secondary.[25]

Lowest in wealth, and nearly all below the median, were tavern and inn keepers, who usually also engaged in farming or artisan work. Stores were far more lucrative. Nearly two-thirds of storekeeping families were above the median wealth level; a large majority farmed as well. Storekeeping families in our study group ran a representative collection of businesses: a jewelry store; a hardware store; a combined cloth, clothing, and dyeing shop; and twelve general and dry goods stores. Failures were plentiful, however: the families of Watts Hubbard and Micah Lincoln did especially poorly, and five other families settled their considerable estates with less than $1,800. A third group of families engaged in traditional industries related to agriculture, and most succeeded; only two settled their estates in debt. Families in commerce and trading operated tanneries, distilleries, lime kilns, and gristmills and sawmills (which were often combined). The richest household, that of the Fullertons, operated a sawmill, a cooper's shop, a cotton factory, and a distillery (it shut down in 1820 but in earlier years annually produced gin valued at $6,500). Economic diversification proved a successful strategy in the harsh climate of the Upper Valley.[26]

Commerce and trading families were large, averaging 8 members and including 6.3 active contributors aged ten or over per household. Nearly three-quarters of all households clustered at 7 to 10 members each, combining economic stability and material accumulation. Several apprentices lived with trading families: six known apprentices worked for a general storekeeper, the owner of the distillery, and a tavern keeper. Almost all commerce and trading families located their stores, mills, taverns, and inns either in a village or around a major crossroads hamlet. They worked in the center of the communication network that enveloped their township and their economic locale. Since knowledge traveled the same paths as their wagons, horses, and sleighs, many trading families were active participants in print culture. Social prestige, community regard, and especially political clout and public office almost always accompanied wealth in Windsor District. At least two-fifths of the heads of trading families in our study group served in key leadership posts before 1830, including Windsor District's sole representative to the state legislature, its lone member of the Constitutional Convention of 1777, Chester's two original land assessors, and the first justices of the peace in Cavendish and Andover. This is about twice the rate of involvement of gentleman farm heads. In cultural leadership and general status, commerce and trading heads of household led the way, along with lawyers and manufacturers.[27]

Manufacturing Families. Ownership of facilities dedicated to the production of local factory goods distinguished a small but highly influential group of manufacturing families emerging shortly after 1800. The seven families in our study group were exceptionally wealthy, averaging just under $7,000 per family; median worth was highest among all occupations. In fact, only one family owned less than $3,000 in property. Average landholding was also substantial at 103 acres, but diversity was considerable: one family owned 360 acres, three retained between 41 and 125 acres, and three owned less than 25 acres. All seven manufacturing households were headed by men. Economic activity was rooted in factory production for the market. The Levi Nichols family owned the first manufactory erected in Springfield, a nail factory and saddlery. The Captain Henry Carleton and Nathan Mills families owned iron factories. The Mills family added needles, stirrups, rakes, and buckles to an expanding line of iron items. The Asa Gilmore, Benjamin Spaulding, and Abel Amsden families owned woolen factories. Amsden was also involved in commercial housebuilding. William Leverett managed a large cotton mill at Windsor.

These seven manufacturing families were scattered across five of the most populous townships. As in other occupational groups, household size grew in proportion to wealth and economic security. Average household size was nearly nine members, ranging from seven through twelve members. Only gentleman farm families were larger. The heads of four of the seven manufacturing families held local public office, and all enjoyed high prestige and social notoriety.[28]

Professional Families. The final group of Windsor District families included doctors, lawyers, ministers, deacons, and Alden Spooner, a newspaper editor-publisher. Similarities and also critical differences marked the three traditional professions. Professional families were high in average wealth ($5,459) but otherwise showed great internal differences. Real and personal property ranged in value from $100 to $38,242. Three levels of wealth may be distinguished: 43 percent under $2,000, almost all below $1,150; 24 percent between $2,001 and $5,000; and 33 percent above $5,000, most between $5,001 and $10,000. The families of lawyers were the richest, averaging $9,727 in wealth, with a median of $6,554. The families of doctors were either very wealthy or just modestly comfortable. Their average property was worth just a third that of lawyers, and doctors' median wealth was only $1,248, slightly above that of yeoman farm families. Ministerial families averaged just a sixth that of lawyers' families ($1,699); three were quite poor, having less than $400 in real and personal property, while three clustered around $3,300. Alden Spooner was worth $4,371. Professional families were also split with respect to landholding. A quarter of all families owned no land at all; physician households formed the bulk of renters. Just under a fifth of professional families owned less than 10 acres each, nearly a fifth retained 11 to 50 acres, and two-fifths owned between 225 and 1,200 acres each.[29]

In other economic activities the professional families were also split rather than united. The two ministers mainly tended to their denominational patrons, although Rev. Roswell Smith's family engaged in small-scale farming. The five deacons were farmers, and two grew hay, corn, wheat, and flax for market. Another sold honey. Physician families were as varied in their market interests as they were in wealth. A third of them produced crops for the market, and one spun wool and cotton for sale. Three of the most active physician farming families also ventured into other business: one regularly worked as an independent artisan; another owned a one-third interest in a forge; and the last held many shares: in area bridges and banks, and in a fire insurance company, an organ, and an "easy chair." Lawyers engaged in the broadest array of economic pursuits. Most carried on full-scale commercial farming. All but one lawyer family owned other lands (between one and fourteen tracts each), and more than half owned shares: in a woolen factory, two bridges, a bank, a mail route, a cider mill, an iron manufactory, a turnpike company, a granary, and a lime quarry.[30]

Nearly all professional families (80 percent) lived in the five most populous townships, and more than half inhabited Windsor and Chester. Professionals often resided in the countryside and kept an office in a village or hamlet. The families of lawyers, to take one group, usually maintained a full-scale farmstead (nine of thirteen cases). Consequently, three-quarters of all professionals provided services in a village or hamlet office, and nearly all of them owned their office buildings. Household size was uniform across the professions. Average size was 7.3 members, placing professionals at a midpoint among the eight occupations. The range of household size was quite broad, from 4 to 13 members, with 6 to 8, most typical, accounting for a small majority. Professional families were either newer families with several small children, or middle-aged with several adolescent children.[31]

Professional families held a curious position in rural New England. All three professions were deeply embedded in agricultural society, and lawyers and ministers exercised many public leadership roles; nevertheless, "the professions" were regularly attacked in weekly newspapers and periodicals. A special resentment was reserved for lawyers. Among the doctors, only Samuel Cobb ever held an important political office. Two of the deacons took leadership roles in educational and cultural organizations. Naturally, both ministers were very active in religious, educational, cultural, and social organizations. Among professional families, lawyers dominated participation in local and area politics. Eight of the thirteen in the study group held leadership positions at the community, district, or county level. These positions included: two registrars of the district probate court, a clerk of the county court, a county sheriff, two chief justices of the county supreme court, a township tax collector, two selectmen, a local treasurer, and a justice of the peace. Only commerce and trading families approached this level of public involvement. It should also be noted that all professional households were headed by men.[32]

Windsor District Society and the American Northeast, 1760–1830

Because, as Fernand Braudel has described, "fundamental inequality" had been the rule throughout the Western world for centuries preceding 1800, Windsor District's great disparity in average and median wealth across the set of occupations in 1780–1830 should come as no surprise (see table 7–1). Commerce and trading families possessed, on average, forty-three times the material goods of semiskilled laborer families and twenty-eight times those of tenant farm families. Comparative research demonstrating that many others were far worse off elsewhere—one of the oldest ruses of apologists for the wealthy—should not divert us from the palpable absence of material possessions among several groups of residents. The effects of such vast inequality on the basic texture of life, especially in a stern northern climate like that of Windsor District, form an essential subject for further study. It is noteworthy that most nineteenth-century burned-over districts were located in relatively harsh economic circumstances. The rural weekly, rising in a communications setting of rapidly spreading literacy, ensured that vast disparities in wealth, now divorced from any local conditions and personal knowledge of traits justifying them, would become ever more visible. Information about economic status was presented starkly by rural weeklies.[33]

Staggering inequality in real and personal property led to vast differences in basic standards of living, opportunities for material prosperity, and nearly all aspects of daily experience. This, and not the inequality itself, is the most striking finding about the occupational structure and work experience of the 643 Windsor District families who constitute our study group. Within the organizing framework of family survival and livelihood, differences in everyday life are evident in the indices of wealth and property, involvement in commercial production and market exchange, household size, labor force activity, homestead location, many gender-related issues, self-selection of titles, political activity, and prestige as seen in public positions. The Upper Valley, and more particularly Windsor District, did not embody the rural felicity and general prosperity that the populace had dreamed about during earlier Connecticut and Massachusetts winters. There, Christian and republican ideologies and such widely favored novels and tales as *Robinson Crusoe* and the *Vicar of Wakefield* had presented as a sensible ideal a moderately successful middle-class world.[34]

Reality was quite different. A significant share of the total population, at least a tenth, consisted of migrants unable to survive more than a year or two in any one township. Of those who stayed, a full fifth were extremely poor hardscrabble families, constantly struggling for merest survival. Averaging 5.6 members, hardscrabble families averaged less than $350 in total property. Earning a living sufficient to develop a plot of land and to avoid starvation during the long Upper Valley winter meant straining one's wits to capacity. A wide gap of $1,000 in property value separated semiskilled laborer and tenant farm families from the lower middle class and from "middling sort" artisan and yeoman farm families. The typical yeoman farm household held 4 times the property of a tenant farm family and 6.5 times the property of a semiskilled laborer family. Even for them, however, the regular tasks of farm life were extremely arduous in a forest society less suited to commercial agriculture than the homesteads most settlers had left behind in southern New England. For a third of artisan and yeoman farm families, the burden of life was much easier, as com-fortable as possible in generally rough terrain. Most professional, manufac-turing, commerce and trading, and gentleman farm families were, in the con-text of Upper Valley material life, exceedingly rich, and power accompanied wealth.

The "great diversity" Jackson Turner Main has noted in the economic class structure of the North before the Revolution continued in the Upper Connec-ticut River Valley through 1830. Variations in the size of households and the labor force meant that conditions that caused inequality were self-reinforcing and self-reproducing. Almost every viable farmstead, owned or leased, required at least three full- or three-fourths-time laborers, and four to five laborers were typical. Time spent away from the family farm working for others lessened chances that the farm would succeed or yield a tenant family sufficient profit to save a down payment. The impact of time away was all the greater because families forced to work for others were generally among the smallest and least able to steal hours from their own homesteads. Furthermore, because the Up-per Valley was essentially an agricultural economy geared to family produc-tion, farm land was crucial to a household's survival. Until Windsor District farmland had filled, as it first did in river valley townships in the mid-1820s, and in more mountainous precincts later, landholding was broad and exten-sive. Nearly three-quarters of all families in our study group (278 of 383 house-holds with private libraries) and two-thirds in the larger group of all families with inventories, owned land. Tenant farm families, moreover, at least had land to work and so might save enough to purchase their own homestead. The landless included the transients, almost all tenant farm and semiskilled laborer families, and a large minority of artisan families. A far higher than average share of young families were among the landless.[35]

No single set of historical evidence can ever be perfectly reliable. In general, the study group of families with private libraries (nearly two-thirds of 643 Windsor District inventoried families) accurately represents the larger group's occupation and work experience distribution (see table 7–2 throughout),[36] and also the total array of families inhabiting these eleven townships through 1830.[37]

For our primary purpose—gaining an understanding of survival, livelihood, material well-being, and participation in print culture—overrepresentation is far less serious a problem than underrepresentation. Professional, gentleman farmer, and commerce and trading families are all overrepresented among fami-lies with libraries, but because of the size and complexity of their holdings, this bias is useful. Accordingly, we may conclude that conditions of material life, reading habits, and cultural participation among all three groups of fami-lies well represent the Windsor District population as a whole. Artisan families were represented at their actual strength throughout Windsor District, ensur-ing a reasonably accurate picture of their material and cultural life. In two

Table 7–2: The Occupational Structure of the Upper Connecticut River Valley, 1787–1830[1]

Occupation: GILMORE (inventories)	Percent of Study Group[2]	Percent of All Inventories[3]	Occupation: ROTH (1828) (tax lists)	Percent
Professional Families	9%	4%	Professional and Business Families (excluding clergy)	5.7%
			P/B	2%/3.7%
Commerce and Trading Families	12%	9%	Commerce & Trading Families	9.2%
			Small Proprietors	2.6%
			Millers and Taverners	1.6%
			Clerks (in government, teaching, and salaried white collar)	1.3%
Manufacturing and Artisan Families	21%	25%	Manufacturing and Artisan Families	20.2%
Manufacturing Families (rural Industrial Revolution)	2%	3%	Master Craftsmen	8.8%
Artisan Families	13%	13%	Journeymen/Laborers	11.4%
Semiskilled Laboring Families	6%	9%		
Farming Families	58%	62%	Stable Farming Population	50.1%
Gentleman Farm Families	6%	5%	Commercial Farmers	6 %
Yeoman Farm Families	40%	42%	Family Farmers	22%
Tenant Farm Families	12%	15%	Subsistence Farmers	21 %
			Farm Laborers	17.9%
Total	100%	100%		100 %

[1] Roth, "Whence This Strange Fire," Table 1.3:97 and Appendix A:576–79. Actual numbers calculated for each percentage in Table 1.3, then Roth's occupations added and proportions calculated. Roth used tax lists for his occupational data and here calculated occupations for all church members in tax lists of 1828 for a diverse group of six Upper Valley townships [Windsor, West Windsor, Weathersfield, Barnet, Peacham, St. Johnsbury].

[2] I used Windsor District Inventories, 1787–1830 – and included here 396 families with printed matter in their inventories (covering about 2,800 individuals). Both Roth and Gilmore used all other known sources on the basic group of households to enrich the results.

[3] I used all Windsor District Inventories (without, as well as with, printed matter) here for the sample years 1803, 1808, 1813, 1818, 1823, and 1828 (n=133).

other occupational groups—yeoman and tenant farm families—the proportion of cases in our study group is slightly below that in the district as a whole and needs to be adjusted upward. Because of their sizable share of all families and also the limited range of their reading habits, however, our 199 families form a group sufficiently large to permit us to generalize about the scope of material life and print culture activity in each occupation. In six of eight occupations, then, our group of families with libraries is large enough to suggest the contours of experience among all such families. Our study group underrepresents the share of semiskilled laborer and manufacturing families in the entire population. The number of the former is, however, sufficient to enable us to generalize with confidence, since laborer families possessed such a tiny range of material possessions, including books. Because of the small number in our study group, we should be less confident about our picture of the material and cultural life experience of manufacturing families. In short, the total occupational picture changes markedly only for professioanl families, a group significantly overrepresented.

We must also consider how well the group defined by all surviving Windsor District inventories represents the total population of Windsor District and the Upper Valley. For comparative purposes, the best fund of detailed evidence comes from township tax records. The relatively small number that have survived for Windsor District cover only a few townships, but we are most fortunate to have Roth's research on religion and reform in the Vermont valley counties through the late 1840s.[38] Table 7–2 reveals that the two perspectives on the occupational structure validate each other. The single population group absent from both inventories and tax lists consisted of transient individuals and families who spent only a brief period in any single township. A comparison of Roth's occupational distribution with that presented here shows that professional families are represented far beyond their numbers in inventories, because all but one professional family retained a private library. According to Roth's data, professional families actually represented no more than 2 percent of Windsor District's total population through 1830. Differences in commerce and trading families are relatively small; again, Roth's percentages are more accurate. The wealth of trading families, and consequently their higher-than-average rate of family library retention, accounts for their greater share of inventories. Roth's master craftsman and journeyman/laborer categories are the equivalent of our artisan, semiskilled laborer (90 percent employed in villages), and manufacturing families. If some of the semiskilled laborer families without private libraries included in my listing of all inventories lived out in the countryside, the two general totals are almost identical.[39]

The largest occupational category in both estimates included most of the farming and grazing population. Despite slightly different criteria for placement, the two tallies generally agree regarding the basic material conditions of the life being described. Just as farmers are underrepresented among families with private libraries, among all families with inventories their proportion (62 percent) is slightly lower than in the total population. That is because tenant and semiskilled laborer families living on farms were quite poor and often inhabited isolated areas not reached by the probate court until the 1820s. The only divergence relates to tenant farm families, where inventory evidence appears sounder.[40]

The tight fit between tax lists and inventories confirms the strong representativeness of our study group for occupations and so establishes the general occupational structure of Windsor District, where three of Roth's six major townships are located. In addition, Windsor District's general representativeness for Upper Valley occupations is also confirmed.

Wealth levels require a similar comparative test of representativeness. Inventories measure total wealth at one moment in the family cycle—the death of the household head—permitting extrapolation backward. Because many kinds of real and personal property were accumulated and were used over long periods of time, this moment is most revealing of the total family life cycle. Furthermore, exclusions of wealth were systematic. Inventories did not include all the wealth that a family owned. The wife's dower and some of her personal property—the bulk of her clothing and some personal items—were exempted. Anything given away before death, hence outside the will division process, was also exempted. Such gifts were normally confined to small items of special personal meaning rather than consisting of valuable property, but we do not know the share of total property these gifts, female possessions, and nonwill bequests constituted.[41]

In this area Roth's analysis does not overlap sufficiently for comparative analysis, and I have therefore chosen the closest existing studies of rural New England wealth. The general material conditions of Windsor District families improved as settlement spread during the early national era. This led to generally higher wealth levels than prevailed among families in the Revolutionary era, which has been studied intensively by Jackson T. Main and others. In the Early Republic as in the previous generation, semiskilled laborer and tenant farm families were poorest except for transients, but in Windsor District, 1787–1830, $300 rather than $165 is a sounder minimum wealth level of severe poverty. While families in these circumstances were better off statistically, the circumstances of their material life remained unchanged, as did their relative position in the wealth scale of Windsor District. Similar findings obtain for other occupations. The key point is that, while people at all levels of the Windsor District economic class structure were somewhat wealthier than their predecessors, the significance of the increase is more ambiguous, since many items retained at inventory were more highly valued.[42]

To compare the wealth of Windsor District families, we have determined

Table 7–3: Comparative Economic Class Structure, Windsor District, 1760–1830

Economic class structure	Will makers with inventories 1787–1830 * (N=170)			Inventories with books 1787–1830 (N=314)		Inventories from 6 sample years * (N=129)		Population of entire Country in Revolutionary era **	Population of Windham, Conn. *** 1761–80	1781–1800
	N	Average wealth	%	N	%	N	%			
Wealthy: $6,601 +	16	$6,935	9.4	33	10.5	7	5.4	10%	4%	3%
Middle: $1,651–6,600	51	$3,678	30	109	34.7	31	24	30%	34%	34%
Lower Middle: $166–1,650	99	$ 997	58.2	146	46.5	81	62.8	40%	48%	50%
Poor: $1–165	4	$ 51	2.4	26	8.3	10	7.8	20%	14%	13%

* Ch. 7.
** Jackson T. Main, *Social Structure*, 42–43.
*** William Willingham, "Windham, Connecticut: Profile of a Revolutionary Community, 1776–1818" (Ph.D. diss., Northwestern University, 1972), 72 and 241ff.

the district's economic class structure using the study group, all inventories for selected years, all Windsor District will makers with wealth data available,[43] Jackson T. Main's findings and wealth designations, and also the results of a study of Windham, Connecticut, in 1760–1800.[44] This data is summarized in table 7–3.

Used with caution, these findings can assist us in assessing over- and under-representation by wealth, one of the most complicated problems associated with the use of inventories as historical documents. Gloria Main reports that inventory rates varied between 25 percent and 90 percent of all deaths for the seventeenth century. She and other scholars have found that the rate drops, though not uniformly, to between 40 percent and 50 percent by the late eighteenth century. We have no way of estimating the share of all deaths represented in Windsor District inventories through 1830. We can infer from decennial census data, however, that the 643 families represented in Windsor District inventories amounted to 8 to 10 percent of all resident households through 1830. This is the most pertinent measure. All comparisons between Windsor District and other rural settings depend on the accuracy of inventory wealth levels compared with those for the total population. Scholarly opinion is divided, but it seems plausible that inventories tended to overrepresent older families, and to underrepresent transients and the very poorest families, precisely because the valuation of real and personal family property was being assessed. In addition, they often underrepresented the very wealthiest families.[45]

Since for our purposes absolute precision is unnecessary, we will use the ranges established by Jackson T. Main and especially Willingham's data for 1781–1800 (see table 7–3, columns 4 and 5) as representing comparative wealth reasonably accurately for rural New England. Differences in the proportion represented by the very poorest class, between families with libraries and all families, are insignificant. Wills, by contrast, vastly underrepresented the poorest class. According to Main and Willingham, the proportion of the poorest was somewhat higher (between 13 percent and 20 percent); hence our figures should be adjusted upward. The share of wealth that Willingham found among the lower middle class is exactly that found for our study group, though considerably below that for our sample of all inventories. Main's estimate is very much lower. Both Willingham's and Main's share of wealth for the middle class is about the same as in our study group, but these estimates exceed that indicated by our sample of all inventories. For the richest group of families, the share of wealth in our sample of all inventories is close to Willingham's share. Main found a much larger upper class in the Revolutionary era generally.

Because its four valley and village center townships were most active in economic life and entrepreneurial thinking, represented the geographical center of the area, and stood at the crossroads of all aspects of the Great Transformation (in Polanyi's phrase), Windsor District might appear not to have been very representative of wealth levels in the rest of the Upper Valley. Nevertheless, the district was representative because it encompassed far more than these four central village townships. It encompassed sharp contrasts in its landscape and its people. The other two-thirds of Windsor District's townships were perfect specimens of the majority of Upper Valley hill country and crossroads townships, and the terrain was among the most rugged in the Upper Valley. In short, other Upper Valley districts contained somewhat larger proportions of farming households, and considerably fewer professional or wealthy commerce and trading families than did Windsor District.[46]

Wealth and Holdings of Printed Matter

Printed matter, constituting one important kind of family possession retained at inventory, is the visible sign of perhaps the most misunderstood aspect of Upper Valley life. Themselves owners of large professional libraries, scholars often naively believe that all other humans behave as they do and buy many books, even many that they may never read. There were few large collections of publications among ordinary families in rural New England.

The evidence from the Early Republic suggests, on the contrary, that printed matter was purchased sparingly, with care and purpose in most cases other than broadsides, and was sampled frequently. Single-volume holdings are the most deceptive. Eighty-seven families (22 percent) in our study group kept just one book. In three-quarters of these families this work was a Bible of 700 to 1,200 pages and two to sixteen parts, depending on the edition owned (see chapter 9). The Bible was treated as a sacred encyclopedia. Single volumes were found in an extremely wide variety of families—not just in very poor families for whom they represented all print communications past and present for which evidence of reading activity survives. Single volumes existed in families with wealth as low as $19 (second lowest in Windsor District; the family lowest in wealth, with $17, owned seven volumes) and as high as $8,743, in the richest 8 percent of all families. Families worth more than $1,000 accounted for nearly two-fifths of all single-volume holdings. Once we move beyond the very poorest families (those with less than $200) we see no substantial decline in families with a single volume until property has exceeded $2,000. Here we see the complexity of rural life and the impact of other factors on cultural participation.[47]

Wealth influenced participation in print culture, but it by no means determined it. Diversity in cultural participation within each wealth level characterized Windsor District through 1830 and offers a crude but important clue to the complex relationship between material and cultural life. A valuable distinction for our purposes is between inventories with printed matter and those without. Because the poorest families were underrepresented in all inventories, the 63 percent of inventories with libraries probably correspond to just under 60 percent of the total population. Another 5 to 10 percent of families with inventories (but no publications) may be inferred from other evidence—bookcases, writing implements and furniture, blank pocket books and/or account books, and journals for accounts—to have participated in print culture. Still other households would have participated by purchasing an annual almanac or in some cases a weekly newspaper; others would have given away their holdings, especially lone Bibles. In only a small share of families (about 5 to 7 percent) were skills associated with elementary literacy not present at all. Another, more sizable group of families (about 10 to 15 percent) had one literate parent. Some of these latter families read print matter apart from the almanac and quickly disposed of it; still others informally borrowed their reading matter. The actual share of families whose members engaged in some form of fairly regular reading activity was probably not less than 70 percent in 1800 and was probably as high as 85 percent by 1825.

The incidence of printed matter in families varied with wealth levels. Two findings are of particular importance.[48] First, wealth established a minimum threshold of cultural participation. Second, while retention of printed matter generally correlated with wealth, the correlation was not uniform.[49] Of families with property valued at less than $700, only a slight majority (52 percent) owned any printed works; above that divide (not a material but a cultural poverty level), ownership averaged 70 percent and quickly rose to 80 percent when property exceeded $1,500 in value (Main's economic middle class).

Among occupations, the lowest retention rates for printed matter were found among tenant farm and semiskilled laborer families; yeoman farm families held the next lowest rates. Artisan households once again were the crucial transitional group; 72 percent retained printed matter. Families in the other four occupations retained holdings in well over 80 percent of all cases. We should recall that the records tell us little about transient individuals and families. There was a causal relationship between wealth and occupation, on the one hand, and the minimal incidence of printed works among families on the other.[50]

Since the likelihood that families would possess printed matter increased sharply when family wealth rose above $700, perhaps wealth explains all or most variations, quantitative and qualitative. Books and pamphlets were material commodities, after all, bought and sold along with thread and crockery. Table 7–4 summarizes several aspects of the relationship of printed works to wealth levels, including the number of families with holdings, the number of printed items (volumes) retained, and shares in lending libraries. Surprisingly, once families had risen above $100 in total wealth, they showed no noticeable differences in numbers of imprints or lending library shares, until the family owned between $2,000 and $3,000 in real and personal property (that is, until it entered the upper 30 percent of all families). Consequently, unlike the incidence of family libraries, wealth remained of little consequence in determining the size of holdings until the family was well into the upper middle class. The average family retained about five volumes until estate wealth rose above $2,000, when the size of holdings tripled to fifteen volumes per family. Above $5,000, a typical family's holdings of printed matter averaged seventy-two volumes. The range of holdings also remained narrow until the $2,000 threshold had been reached and then expanded dramatically. Shares in lending libraries remained inconsequential until the $1,500 point. Median size of collection, perhaps the most conservative indicator, remained below six volumes until the $3,000 mark, then tripled in the next wealth group. Wealth directly affected the poorest and the wealthy. In between, however, where nearly two-thirds of all families fell, wealth was not a useful predictor of the quantity or variety of family holdings of printed matter.

A more precise way to understand the influence of wealth on holdings of printed matter is to distinguish four economic and cultural groups of families by wealth levels. We might regard these as cultural poverty (for convenience defined as $0–$700); the lower middle class ($701–$2,000); the middling sort ($2,001–$5,000); and the wealthy. The group least diversified in economic and

Table 7-4: Family Libraries and Wealth Levels, Windsor District, 1787–1830

Wealth Strata of Families with Libraries (in $)	Number of Libraries (n=386*)	Percent of All Libraries with Print Items	Number of Print Items (Total = 5,497)*	Percent of All Print Items	Average Size of Library (number of books)	Median Size (number of books)	Range of Libraries (number of books)	Shares in Lending Libraries (Total = 22)
1–100	19	5	56	1	2.9	1.5	1– 13	1
101–200	25	7	118	2.2	4.7	2	1– 40	0
201–500	71	18	291	5.3	4.1	3	1– 43	1
501–750	41	11	185	3.4	4.5	3	1– 38	0
751–1,000	22	6	240	4.4	10.9	5.5	1– 57	0
1,001–1,500	50	13	226	4.1	4.5	3	1– 34	1
1,501–2,000	35	9	191	3.5	5.5	3	1– 28	3
2,001–3,000	41	11	661	12	16.1	4	1–403	6
3,001–5,000	40	10	518	9.4	13	9	1– 85	5
5,001–10,000	24	6	1,864	33.9	77.7	16	1–909	3
10,001–20,000	12	3	660	12	55	33.5	3– 266	2
20,001+	6	1	487	8.8	81.2	86.5	38– 111	0

*No wealth figures available on the other 10 cases, for a total of 396 inventories with family libraries.

cultural participation embraced two-fifths (157) of all families with printed works in our study group. The average size of holdings in this first group of families was four volumes (see table 7–4 throughout), one of which was nearly always the Bible. Just 30 percent of these families retained a single volume. In addition, several kinds of works beyond traditionally steady sellers—Bibles, New Testaments, hymnals, psalm books, prayer and devotional works, dictionaries, and schoolbooks—were retained in households with little property. As holdings expanded, sermons, church history, and theology as well as works about history, geography, moral philosophy, politics and government, science and technology, travel accounts, and modern literature, particularly novels, were added. The connection between poverty and paucity of reading was strong but not uniform. Some poor families, like the vast majority of people at higher wealth levels, were treating printed matter as a necessity of life. Fifteen percent of the poorest families retained six or more volumes each, which we will term "expanding holdings"; and 7 percent retained collections of ten or more volumes each, which we will term "noteworthy holdings." In general, six volumes marked a threshold at which newer kinds of works and styles of reading began to appear, and ten volumes typically indicated real intellectual variety in reading. Two of the poorest families (1.3 percent) also retained shares in lending libraries.[51]

The second economic and cultural group, the lower middle class, with a quarter of the population but an eighth of all volumes, consisted of 108 families with holdings averaging 6.5 volumes. Nonetheless, sizable numbers of Windsor District families of very modest wealth were expanding their private libraries in the Early Republic. Single volumes were held by a solid quarter of the total in this group, but holdings of six or more volumes were becoming more numerous; expanding holdings accounted for a third of the total. Nearly a fifth of these families retained noteworthy holdings (ten to fifty-seven volumes). Double the share of poorer families (4 percent) also participated in lending libraries. The broadening range of family holdings among the lower middle class, and even in the poorest families, reveals the deep penetration of some of the newest kinds of reading matter.

Eighty-one solidly middle-class families, encompassing just over a fifth of our study group, comprised the third broad economic and cultural group. These families retained a greater share of volumes than their share of households. Their range of holdings was very broad, averaging 15 volumes per family. Single volumes dropped to just an eighth, and the proportion of expanding (55 percent) and noteworthy (36 percent, with 10 to 403 volumes) holdings increased dramatically. The first family retaining more than 100 volumes was worth between $2,000 and $3,000, solidly in the middle class.

Estates above $5,000 constituted the wealthy economic and cultural class in Windsor District (forty-two families in our study group). Their holdings, averaging 72 volumes each, accounted for 55 percent of all volumes among a ninth of all families. The John Leverett family had 909 volumes, by far the largest number in Windsor District (see appendix 5). In fact, most of the very largest private accumulations of printed matter in the district, thirteen of seventeen including more than 50 volumes each, were owned by the wealthy. Just one family with a single volume persisted. Fully 88 percent of all wealthy families kept expanding clusters of printed works, and four-fifths had noteworthy holdings (10 to 909 volumes). Almost all of the latter included intellectually rich and varied volumes, found primarily in professional, commerce and trading, gentleman farm, and manufacturing families, and in a few artisan families.

In conclusion, of 396 Windsor District families, just over a third (142) retained expanding holdings of printed works, and a quarter (95) retained noteworthy holdings. More varied types of collections usually reflected broader and more secular reading tastes in families at every wealth level, though in greater proportions at the higher end of the affluence scale. The general trend is clear enough: higher wealth levels meant larger and more varied family holdings and greater likelihood of other forms of participation in print culture. Still, this relationship holds mainly between one broad wealth level and another, and even here considerable variation existed. Each level of increasing wealth expanded variety in reading interests, involvement with social organizations, and cultural participation generally. The overall range of family holdings was very extensive. About 5 percent of all families retained more than fifty volumes each. Even among the poorest families, about a sixth does not fit the general picture of limited participation in print culture. Moreover, Windsor District's poor and lower middle class families demonstrated a phenomenon entirely new in transatlantic rural civilization—expanding types of imprints seen in one family in five. Overall, between a quarter and a third of all families show very loose connections between wealth and participation in print culture. Finally, it is not at all the case that the larger the inventory value, the greater the share of wealth spent on printed matter. As we advance along the scale of wealth, almost no appreciable increase occurred in the proportionate value of printed matter to estate wealth. Indeed, when property was worth more than $5,000, the share of wealth represented by printed matter sharply declined.

Increases in the average and median size of holdings, and in shares in lending libraries, accompanied greater wealth, as did broadening of reading interests and cultural participation. At every economic class level except the lowest, however, fully a third of all families manifested no invariable relationship between wealth and holdings of printed works. Many very small holdings were found in upper middle class families. Likewise, several large holdings existed at every wealth level down through $201–$500 among the poor group. Where people were poorest, minimum holdings were most frequent; a far looser relationship existed between increasing wealth and larger holdings. The looseness of the fit is striking. Variations within wealth levels in substantive types of family holdings are even more striking, as we shall see. One of the most prominent factors in expanding the range of reading matter held in family libraries was the relatively low cost of many print items by the mid-1790s and the resulting plenitude of printed works available. The profound result of this process was that, over the next forty years, print culture centered in family holdings, the almanac, and the newspaper, became an ever more necessary means of learning about oneself and the world, especially the distant world. For a substantial majority of all families whose estates were inventoried in the years 1787–1830, a permanent family library of printed matter, however small it might seem to us, had become a necessity.

Chapter 8

Deep Structure
and Rural New England *Mentalités*:
Reading and the Family Circle, 1780–1835

In some towns in Vermont there is a habit in family devotions
which ought to be discouraged . . . *sitting*. . . . When I go into a
family where all, penitent and impenitent, arrange themselves in
order during the reading and singing in the family, and then kneel
during prayer . . . I can be more collected in prayer, more fervent.
> —Missionary, "Family Prayer"
> VtC 24 June 1843.

Let them find it short, savory, simple, plain, tender, heavenly.
Worship, thus conducted, may be used as an engine of vast power
in a family. It diffuses a sympathy through the members. It calls
off the mind from the deadening effects of worldly affairs. It ar-
rests every member with a morning and evening sermon, in the
midst of all the hurricanes and cares of life. It says, "There is a
God! There is a spiritual world! There is a life to come!" It fixes
the idea of responsibility in the mind. It furnishes a tender and
judicious father . . . with an opportunity . . . to relieve the weight
with which subordination or service often sits on the minds of
inferiors.
> —*Cecil's Remains*, "On Family Worship,"
> VJ 4 Oct. 1824.

Family and Bible:
The Center of Reading Activity in Windsor District, 1780–1835

Contemporary American culture compounds the difficulties we face in understanding the uses of literacy skills and the beginnings of a mass culture of reading and writing in the Early Republic. Studying libraries and printed matter
distances readers of this book from the major direction of American culture
today, the delivery of a larger share of knowledge by an expanding array of

electronic media. Radio and several video formats, including television, are the core of electronic culture. Television has already replaced the newspaper as our primary way of learning about the distant world and the "latest intelligence." We are part of a culture in a transition as dramatic as that studied in this book: today reading abilities and the habit of regular reading are declining among a growing share of Americans. Living in a media-rich, competitive culture, how can we possibly understand the rhythms of daily life in families whose idea of a library was a Bible and whose notion of diversity was reading a different passage from it at each family service? How could knowledge possibly have been viewed as an important form of power in such a society?[1]

Low literacy levels and a scarcity of reading matter had traditionally marked rural culture in the West. Consequently, at first encounter daily life in the 1780s seems stable and slow to change when compared with our own ordinary experience. But between 1783 and 1830 this stability was shattered by changes in one major historical process after another. Print culture became as staunch an ally of change as of continuity, just as the computer and electronic culture generally would be in our day.

This book stresses the dual role of printed matter: as material commodity and as embodiment of immaterial ideas. Moreover, while each printed work had its own physical integrity as a "text," the ideas it contained were intelligible only within a complex web of intellectual traditions and other texts. This chapter studies the physical proximity of all printed items in a given home, and establishes pathways to link texts and embed them within the many intellectual traditions shaping American culture in the Early Republic. After discussing the ways families obtained materials to read, and their motives for doing so, we analyze the place of family libraries within the spectrum of print communications, focusing on different kinds of reading situations and acts engaged in within the family. Then, a comparative look at reading elsewhere in rural America helps to situate an analysis of 400 Windsor District family libraries surviving from the period 1787–1830. This latter analysis classifies six major types of collections. Appendix 4 specifies the benefits and drawbacks of inventories as evidence, traces the changing meeting places of the probate court within Windsor District in 1787–1830, and discusses the complex spine title system employed in bookbinding.

Public and private reading within the family unit was widespread and regular, even daily in some homes. Families obtained reading matter in several ways; we will proceed from the narrowest to the broadest. Village circulating libraries were the most geographically concentrated in their dissemination. Starting at Windsor village in 1822 and at Chester village in 1829, circulating libraries charged a small fee per item borrowed and mainly engaged in localized lending for reading at home. Because of higher literacy rates, circulating libraries probably reached a broader spectrum of families in America than in France, Great

Britain, and even Germany through 1830. In Europe, however, general-purpose lending libraries, usually located in cities, regularly served as reading locations and meeting places for reading societies. In rural Windsor District, lending libraries mainly fostered private and family reading; other institutions held discussions, starting with the Windsor Mechanics Association (1807), which held meetings below Alden Spooner's printing office for several years at least. Topics were usually chosen on the assumption that participants read at least the newspaper regularly. In 1828 Windsor families established the Windsor Debating Society, a literary reading and debating society that was also formally independent of all lending libraries.[2]

Social libraries formed a second way in which groups of fifteen to sixty families in a township could obtain materials to read. Such families established an incorporated lending library, sometimes accepting a few families living near in contiguous townships. The patriarchal nature of the rural American family was reinforced by rules frequently specifying that only a head of household could own a share and take books home for reading. Only one woman held a surviving Windsor District share among fifty-seven known families. Social libraries existed in seven of Windsor District's eleven townships between 1800 and 1830, all in full- or partial-access zones at their founding. These libraries made a greater variety of current imprints readily available, mainly for the wealthiest two-fifths of the population. As in all aspects of cultural participation, intensified connections with the commercialization process sweeping through Windsor District enhanced reading opportunities.[3]

In sharp contrast to these relatively limited avenues of family reading was a third route, the collecting of printed matter within the household. Families purchased printed matter, and sometimes expanded their holdings by inheritance and gifts. Into the 1820s, most Upper Valley residents did most of their regular reading from family holdings and those of neighbors and close kin. Most knowledge derived from printed matter was acquired in the home, because works purchased, subscribed to, and borrowed all ended up in the home and were read mainly there. The extent of a fourth avenue to reading, informal borrowing, frequently mentioned in the autobiographies of intellectuals and other public figures, is unknown. The account that follows draws on all known Windsor District evidence about private libraries, about every facet of reading, and about the total communications environment within which reading occurred.[4]

Families exercised authority over what knowledge available in printed form reached their members directly, or through closely controlled neighborhood district schools and through shares in social libraries, which were organized to supplement family collections. All household members beyond earliest childhood were at least potentially capable of reading works borrowed by the head of the family. Families exerted considerable influence, though not total control, over the reading experiences of members. Notwithstanding shared reading, discussion, and sometimes censorship, individuals did manage to read privately, at home and elsewhere, with an increasing degree of freedom after the Revolution.[5]

The books, pamphlets, and periodicals included in estate inventories were rarely scattered around a rural household. Comments in newspaper and periodical essays and in diaries reveal that they usually stood side by side in the main living room. With their spines facing outward, they awaited family members and perhaps other household members and visitors as well. Printed matter placed elsewhere was more specialized: a devotional manual or prayer book near a bed, or a professional library in an office. Almanacs were nearby, often tacked up beside the hearth. The generic terms regularly used by rural New Englanders (1750–1850) to describe printed matter kept among the family possessions were "library," "family library," and "private library," expressions that adapted the common meaning of "a collection of books" to the novel circumstances of ordinary rural households. I have included under this designation single works, typically one to six volumes in Windsor District households, so as to encompass all types of families in which the ongoing presence of reading matter can be established.[6]

Private diaries and letters, public comments on reading, and available quantitative data (see table 2–1) agree. Bible reading was the most common reading experience in rural New England through 1835. Many families ritually set aside a portion of the morning or evening for family prayer and Bible reading. But what kind of text was actually read? The two most widely owned texts, retained by half of all families holding any printed matter, were both very large Bibles. The most popular Bible was a full one-volume edition whose 1,000 to 1,100 pages included Old and New Testaments and much else besides. Imported into the valley and available from the early 1790s, thirteen editions of this behemoth were published in Vermont valley counties in 1812–20. Next most frequently owned was an imported four-to-six-volume family Bible. A "small" abridged work of 45 to 286 pages, containing just the two testaments, was typically a second Bible, often kept in the meetinghouse pew. Four editions were published in Vermont valley counties in 1811–19. There were also three single-volume editions of the New Testament (and one of selections) published there in 1811–19.

For nearly a fifth of all families with libraries through 1815 — and for more than three-quarters of those whose library consisted of a single work — a one-volume Bible was a sufficient family library. The reasons lie less in the supposed scarcity of printed matter than in the value system of rural New Englanders, and in the specific text owned. This was not a Gideon's Bible — simply Old and New Testaments. The rural New England Bible was usually so elaborate as to be best understood as, in the words of contemporaries, a "sacred en-

Search the Scriptures. Albert Alden, "Scriptures." Barre, Mass., Lithography Collection. Courtesy, American Antiquarian Society.

Virtually all Upper Valley residents shared a rich sacred core of knowledge, based on the Bible. The most typical experience of reading is a family scene such as this father and daughter. At least three-quarters of all families with holdings of printed matter retained a Bible—often referred to as a sacred encyclopedia—as the centerpiece of their library.

cyclopedia." Physically, it was a large work—eleven inches high, nine inches wide, and four inches thick.

Single-volume Windsor and Brattleboro Bibles (the latter the most popular in the Upper Valley, with twelve editions between 1816 and 1820) contained fourteen or fifteen parts among more than 1,000 pages. The brief opening section, "To the Reader," explained the process of translation. The heart of the text remained the Old and New Testaments. Also included was the Apocrypha—the fourteen books of the Septuagint, almost always included in these Protestant editions. And while the plain text of the Holy Word formed the core of Protestant Christianity, the rural one-volume Bible added all of the apparatus necessary to follow a sacred path to salvation: guidance in family continuity of several sorts; Christian principles, admonitions, and guidelines; devotional materials; church history; and aids to eschatology.

Family continuity was insured by the "Family Record," which included ample space for children's births and deaths, marriages, etc. While the overall share of those parents who chose children's names in accord with Biblical models of personality slowly declined during this era, the many who continued to do so had a ready reference to draw upon and a record book to personalize the process. Further assistance was provided by two other parts: "A Table of Kindred and Affinity," arranged to reveal who may not marry whom; and an "Alphabetical Table of Proper Names," from which to name one's children. While meanings were provided for most names, the list was not divided by gender.

Biblical admonitions, Christian principles guiding human behavior, and general wisdom readily could be extracted from the Bible and organized in rich lists of examples, using John Brown's fifty-six-page "Brief Concordance." Any principal word appearing in the Bible—in fact, the first three letters of it—would yield the appropriate sentence(s), proclaimed Brown. In many editions yet another part appeared, "Practical observations on the Old and New Testaments," arranged as an outline with excerpts from some chapters and summaries of others, and with key arguments highlighted for ready use in discussion. Illustrations further highlighted key themes and principles. Of the eleven known editions of Windsor and Brattleboro Bibles, nine could be purchased with various plates adapting Biblical themes to the local agricultural world (see visuals in this book for examples).

Christian principles and values were reinforced through frequent devotional practice. The staples of Windsor District meditation—Baxter, Doddridge, etc.—were easily supplemented by Bible passages offering solace to the troubled Christian, and by the model lives of Christian saints found in an "Account of the Lives, Sufferings, and Martyrdom of the Saints." The lives of the saints were viewed as a continuation of the "sacred pageant" on earth, and church history was critical knowledge for the Christian.

One of the central features of the rural Bible was to provide a complete explanation for human history. For a declining but nonetheless substantial number of Windsor District families, God's providence ruled human actions, whether close by in Windsor District or in London and Europe. In this regard, an unusual "Index" comprised an "account of the Most Remarkable Passages . . . Pointing to the Time wherein They Happened, and the Place of Scripture where They were Recorded." For a smaller group of families, secular history was unnecessary and irrelevant. The Bible provided these families with the story of Creation and all human occurrences through the final judgment. In this light we may understand why another section of the Bible lavished attention on a series of tables of weights, measures, coinage, and maps used in the text, and why a "Table of the Offices and Conditions of Men" described the hierarchical power structure of all peoples in Bible times, centering on the Jews from Patriarchs to Deacons—the lowest status noted. Another section offered a geographical description and historical discussion of the "Holy Land." The final section of extra assistance contained a "Chronological Index of Years and Times," a fascinating aid to future sacred history. This calendar of key Biblical years, for use in eschatological calculations, was the capstone of this system of sacred history, facilitating the many Upper Valley forecasts of the end of "things earthly." Anyone could calculate the timing of the last stage(s) without an exhaustive rereading of the text.

Especially after its local publication beginning in 1811, this was the Bible most frequently retained in Windsor District family libraries during the Early Republic. It was not just a book of faith or a repository of sacred principles, but a complex work designed to serve all the needs of a dedicated Christian household. With this sacred encyclopedia and guidebook for life on earth, a Christian family's basic religious needs were met. For the history of reading, the pattern of Bible reading makes plain that no correlation can be made between the number of volumes retained and the nature or amount of reading activity.[7]

Family libraries were neither random nor unified collections, but rather embodied several distinct purposes in their selection. They were as complex as rural life in an age of major transformation, and they offer evidence bearing directly on reading habits, knowledge of the world, and the texture of daily life. Family libraries were sometimes inherited, were frequently assembled over a period of time, and were usually preserved throughout the full life cycle of the family. Such libraries in our study included all printed matter belonging to a deceased person and to her or his "family"; newspaper reports of estate sales occasionally mention that wives purchased portions of the family library. Inventories excluded personal (as opposed to family) possessions of the wife of a male decedent. The existing evidence does not permit us to determine how regularly printed matter owned personally by wives may have been among the items that were excluded. (We must remember that inventories underestimate one portion of specifically adult female reading matter). The chief value of inventory data is that they document most common reading matter in the central institution of Upper Valley collective life. Reaching deeply into every major portion of the population, estate inventories allow us to trace the everyday reading habits and patterns among families.

The family was the center of Upper Valley reading activity, as of so much else in rural life, in the new nation. In Upper Valley society between 1787 and 1835, reading became a disruptive, mind-expanding experience as often as it was one that reinforced known values. Tension focused not on whether to read but on the selection of reading and manifested itself within the family, reflecting the rapid economic, social, and cultural changes occurring within rural life. Many of the family's traditional functions were being challenged, and in response a powerful ideology of the family emerged. It acknowledged rapid change but attempted to focus on the potential catastrophes that awaited the son or daughter, husband or wife who failed to honor traditional conceptions of hearth and home. Presented in countless works in two dozen subject areas, many new questions faced rural agricultural families in the early national era: Why follow in your father's footsteps if his artisan trade was crumbling? But then what career to follow? Why prepare for a life of farming in Weathersfield when factory work at Lowell or even Windsor seemed much more exciting? But then what about the evils of money, cities, strangers? On balance, Upper Valley families exercised fairly tight control over reading habits and subject matter, especially through the mid-1820s. By that time, people were increasingly reading beyond the family circle, developing greater independence from family norms. Complaints about novel reading often listed this as a pressing danger. Accounts of travels and voyages, biographies, histories, geographies, and weekly newspapers, like novels, all challenged the ideology of the family as a stable, secure, united sanctuary protected from tumultuous changes in the public sphere.

Several important functions of the Upper Valley family encouraged reading. First, families educated their offspring, relatives, and apprentices in the home during childhood and youth. To meet this need, increasing numbers of primers and other educational books and works addressed to the "family circle" were in local circulation by 1790. Parents also influenced the choice of schoolbooks used in neighborhood schools, through district school committees. In addition to instruction and religious and moral training, parents were admonished to train the "rising generation" to be good republican citizens. For women this second duty was embodied in the concept of republican motherhood. Men were encouraged mainly to keep up with public affairs—government, politics, and law—through newspapers and many types of books and pamphlets and to educate their sons in citizenship.[8]

Information about the increased array of goods circulating in an expanding market economy constituted a third incentive for a family to read. The spread of mass-produced goods and newspaper reading were inextricably linked: by 1810 every sizable store in Windsor District regularly advertised necessities and luxury goods. A fourth spur to reading was family involvement in the proliferation of religious, benevolent, and other social reform organizations. Every denomination disseminated periodicals by 1815, and within another decade almost every national and regional social reform group would be spreading word of its concerns. Locally printed sermons, tracts, denominational reports, and moral tales complemented periodicals. Religious and reform societies appealed directly to families for funding, support, and participation and were increasingly successful as the Second Great Awakening spread throughout the Upper Valley.[9]

Sometimes encouraged and sometimes just allowed, individual private reading at home expanded greatly during the Early Republic. Special reading situations allowed various household members to peruse works borrowed, purchased, and subscribed to. They constituted a fifth way in which family life encouraged reading within the home, now affording greater latitude and allowing individual preference to play a greater role. Private reading was not as often mentioned in general cultural commentary, but it was frequently discussed in letters and autobiographies and is evident in commonplace book entries. Orestes Brownson's childhood and youth in mountainous Stockbridge and Royalton during the years 1808–18 offers detailed evidence of this reading pattern.[10] Almost no reading rooms existed in Windsor District's villages and hamlets until after 1800 and relatively few until the 1820s; no free "public" libraries existed through 1830. Most private reading by all household members occurred either within the house or elsewhere on the homestead. Increased emphasis after the Revolution, on discreet stages of life, each with its own tasks and problems, directly encouraged private reading of advice in books, pamphlets, newspapers, and periodicals, and indirectly encouraged reading of novels, travel accounts, and other new genres.

Individual and private reading were sanctioned by guides to reading found in a wide range of works. These works often presented "complete" lifelong reading programs. Several copies each of a number of these works appear in Windsor District family libraries before 1830. Among the most popular were Isaac Watts's *The Improvement of the Mind*; William Pitt's *Letters Written by the Late Earl of Chatham to His Newphew, Thomas Pitt, Esq.*; and John Bennett's *Letters to a Young Lady*. The latter two works, both fairly popular among Windsor District families, offered full-scale reading programs for young men and women. The tendency to encourage further reading by lists and discussions of "valuable works" was widespread among stage-of-life books and also appeared in schoolbooks, memoirs, autobiographies, and devotional works.[11] By 1815, newspapers excerpted and printed commentary by editors, correspondents, and essayists for nearly every important book and pamphlet advertised for sale within Windsor District. Newspapers thus extended the readership of some key passages of books to a far broader audience while inviting eager readers to gain fuller knowledge by purchasing or borrowing the work excerpted. Periodicals read in the Upper Valley in 1787–1830 were mostly imported rather than locally published and carried regular reviews of major works and many briefer notices, further encouraging private and public reading.[12]

Each of these five major dimensions of family involvement with print culture – fundamental education, citizenship, economic exchange, religion and social reform, and private reading – promoted a different configuration of reading matter. Items purchased were not necessarily retained, however. Newspapers and almanacs were almost never saved for long. Many novels, primers, children's books, and schoolbooks were retained for between one and three years and were then discarded, destroyed by accident, loaned and never retrieved, given away, or sold to book carters who by 1810 were traveling throughout Windsor District. That together such printed items represented 20 percent of surviving holdings strongly suggests that considerably more reading was taking place than is indicated by family library holdings. The other 80 percent of the 5,630 volumes retained by 396 Windsor District families were books, pamphlets, and periodicals deemed worthy of long-term retention, for decades in many cases.

Although family libraries represent only a part of family reading, they hold one superordinate advantage over all other known sources: they allow us to analyze the core reading matter of a large representative group of nearly 400 ordinary Upper Valley families during a half century of change in cultural participation and in material life. During the early national era, about three-quarters of all Windsor District households established a family library, and nearly two-thirds sustained one throughout much of the full family life cycle. These people comprised the core of the first two generations of ordinary rural families in the Western world to do so. Between the Revolution and 1830, local communities of readers expanded in numbers and in the extent of their reading. What they read, how they read, and with what effects were matters of considerable importance in shaping the beginnings of the modern world.

In 1760 many rural reading communities mostly included the families of professionals; gentleman farmers; some individuals engaged in commerce, trade, and manufacturing; and a few artisans; as well as college students. Almost no bookstores were located in countryside villages. Peddlers and general stores extended the network of readers only gradually. Shortly after the Revolution, essays regularly were being written on the transition to an age of reading in New England. Apparently only in the American Northeast did yeoman, tenant farmer, semiskilled laborer, and artisan families join traditional participants in print culture. As early as 1792 the patronizing Connecticut author of "The

Metabasist" contended that "on the whole, I think, we may fairly conclude that reading is coming more into fashion than formerly." It was still "a new thing to many," but it was being widely encouraged in speeches, conversations, and essays; through the founding of social libraries; and by the purchase of small private libraries. The essayist ended with a few sarcastic "directions" to the unwashed "for the treatment of books."[13]

Family Libraries: Kinds of Works Retained and Reading Habits

Considerable evidence exists about the texture of reading experiences—acts of reading, situations of public and private reading, and the effects of reading—in different eras. Little of this evidence confirms two prevailing assumptions drawn from twentieth-century experience, namely that many rural New England families below the very wealthiest class maintained family libraries for ostentatious display and that many who accumulated private libraries retained a substantial number of unread works.[14]

In Windsor District, 396 family libraries averaged just fourteen volumes per collection, with a median library size of three volumes through 1815 and five volumes in 1816–30. The purchasing and discarding of printed matter, as of all other commodities in an economy of relative scarcity and limited access, was usually planned. The evidence presented here suggests that at least parts of most printed items in family libraries with fewer than ten volumes (76 percent of all collections) had been read or otherwise assimilated. Reading became a necessity of life in the Upper Valley during the Early Republic precisely because print culture was considered to provide valuable traditional and more current guides to specific situations and problems of daily life. How these works were understood is another question entirely; they were often enough understood differently by varying groups of readers.[15]

Rural New England family libraries consisted almost entirely of three of the six major vehicles of print culture: books, pamphlets, and periodicals. Eighty-five percent of family libraries either contained no expensive works or if they did have one, it was a fancy Bible. The libraries of ordinary rural families illustrate the pervasiveness of print culture in the early national era. The "middling sort" and the truly wealthy created lending libraries as an additional way (beyond purchase) to read expensive books and periodicals and newer works. The truly wealthy were the only people who, before the mid-1820s, could afford more than a few expensive volumes.

Reading styles were influenced by tradition, by the growth of knowledge in a field, by the variety of works available, and by the numbers of works purchased and read. New knowledge about many aspects of the world increased dramatically in the early national era and in popular form was widely disseminated. This development altered the overall character of reading. The way people read was usually but not always dictated by the type of work being read. Between 1780 and 1830 the typical Upper Valley family engaged in two very broad kinds of reading activities which traditionally had been pursued by fundamentally different audiences. Both styles of reading were purposeful, and both were extremely widespread. Each style had preferred texts which were usually read according to its dictates. Many families retained only intensive reading matter (works concerning traditional wisdom that were usually read in and reread); a somewhat larger share retained both intensive and extensive reading matter (works which extended a person's knowledge or beliefs beyond standard wisdom or offered a far more detailed presentation, and which were often read through); and a small proportion of families retained only extensive reading matter.

Intensive reading matter found in Windsor District libraries dealt with some aspect of the wisdom of the ages—specifically Protestant sacred and secular dimensions of the Western heritage. Noah Webster defined this wisdom as a "common body" of "essential truths" acquired together with literacy skills during childhood and youth. Wisdom was "the rule of known religious, moral, and political truths throughout the nation"; and this heritage was available in the "Bible and in the writings of eminent authors." For Webster these truths were most fully embodied in the literature of an earlier Augustan age. Other educators seriously disagreed as to which works most embodied true wisdom, but all agreed that the Bible was the central text and that religious ideas formed the core of the structure of knowledge. Works of this first type included both traditional steady sellers and newer popular sellers. In addition to the Bible and commentaries, they included psalm books and hymnals, prayer books and devotional works, primers, schoolbooks, dictionaries, almanacs, secular music, some stage-of-life works, and a small group of special works drawn from all histories, classical literature, works of modern literature, sermons, and light works in theology. Professionals and people engaged in commerce and trade also used reference works—basic compilations of the best wisdom and sometimes newest knowledge in a specific secular or sacred subject area—in a similar manner, reading in them for an interpretation of a theological issue, for the proper form of a legal agreement, or to calculate a sale or cast a purchase agreement in the proper form.

All of these varieties of printed matter were usually read intensively, over many years. Such reading might involve a particular passage or one or more segments of the work studied closely at any one sitting or occasion. The traditional task of reading, in Dennis Rusche's words, was to "recreate" and thereby to "reexperience the wise sentiments" of "accepted ideas." Learned during childhood and youth as an "oral activity," a performance "to induct students into a fixed realm" of established truths and to be continued thereafter, both private and group reading in the intensive style claimed to have a high moral purpose. *Robinson Crusoe*, for example, was viewed as a source of wisdom and pleasure and was often read intensively, perhaps once every couple of years for decades, by a family group or by one of its members. Novelty was only a minor consideration in this first style of reading, which savored familiar "memorable" passages. Schoolbooks varied this pattern only slightly: they were used very frequently over a short period of time.[16]

Intensive reading frequently drew comment in New England, especially after the Revolution, when the cultural ground was beginning to shift away from under it. In the 1780s, Joseph Buckingham recalled, "The houses of farmers, even those of the most affluent class, were not overstocked with books. . . . The Bible was the book for everyday reading, and, with a very few others, chiefly of a religious character, supplied the rural population with the greater part of its intellectual entertainment." A youth elaborated in his journal: "In the evening [January 2, 1814] I began the New Testament in hopes to read it more understandingly than I have ever before done." Thinking beyond the Bible and New Testament, Oliver Wendell Holmes, Sr., noted, "Some books never grow old. There are some authors, whose laurels will ever be as green as if they were garlands of immortal amaranth. But these are public property; they belong to every schoolboy that can read, and every scribbler that can quote."

Harriet Beecher Stowe, commenting on the joy of discovering a secular classic as a child, described this form of reading:

> But oh, joy and triumph! one rainy day she found at the bottom of an old barrel a volume of the "Arabian Nights," and henceforth her fortune was made. Dolly had no idea of reading like that of our modern days—to read and to dismiss a book. No; to read was with her a passion, and a book once read was read daily; always becoming dearer and dearer, as an old friend. The "Arabian Nights" transported her to foreign lands, gave her a new life of her own; and when things went astray with her, when the boys went to play higher than she dared to climb in the barn, or started on fishing excursions, where they considered her an encumbrance, then she found a snug corner, where, curled up in a little, quiet lair, she could at once sail forth on her bit of enchanted carpet into fairy land. One of these resorts was furnished by the third garret of the house, which had been finished off into an arched room and occupied by her father as a study. . . . Here Dolly loved to retreat and niche herself down in a quiet corner, with her favorite books around her.[17]

Availability, frequency of use, and the embedding of this type of reading experience in a ritual during childhood and early youth defined the intensive reading style of print consumption. While it is helpful to call specific kinds of works intensive reading matter on the basis of their most typical uses, the half century following the Revolution was not primarily an era of intensive reading. It was an era of transition in reading styles and subject matter, in which the acts, reading situations, and audiences of printed matter, at least in America, were expanding rapidly.

Another kind of text, very different in content and reading style, also deeply interested Windsor District families during the same era. In fact, a series of extensive reading alternatives to the intensive style existed. Extensive reading matter embodied new variations on older themes and subjects, newer knowledge—"the latest intelligence"—drawn chiefly from newspapers and periodicals, and it usually advocated change as positive and desirable.

Newspapers and periodicals, two examples of such texts, were ready sources of fresh advice, new information, and changing values and beliefs. Much else in their pages, however, represented continuity or set forth only minor variations on long-established themes and topics. A second group of extensive reading-works centered on brand new knowledge—many pamphlets; some varieties of schoolbooks; accounts of travels and voyages; modern literature, especially novels, tales, and poetry; political tracts and government manuals; works about personality development and the stages of life; sermons; essays in several fields; biographies; a new variety of nationalistic political history; works in science, technology, and economics; a large group of professional treatises; and a wide range of up-to-date compilations and summations, including many dictionaries, encyclopedias, gazetteers, and geographies. Many of these texts purported to make additions and modifications to older bodies of knowledge in time-honored fields of thought. Some of these works were purchased for repeated reading throughout life, but most were not. Rather, these works were purchased either because of the presumed currency of their ideas, opinions, and overviews, or for the aptness of their imaginative spirit. They were read entire or in part, either all at once or in several readings over a relatively short period of time. The common period of between one and three months for which books in most social libraries could be checked out is a useful standard. The greater the variety of works in a field, the more likely that new knowledge and unusual forms of presentation would stimulate additional purchases. Once a taste for Scott had developed, a reader would find it difficult to resist his latest work. For this reason title pages often noted that a work had been written "by the author of . . ." Items purchased for other than intensive reading might offer variety or currency, encourage curiosity, arouse excitement, or prompt an interest in new information about oneself, the world, or the realm of imagination. Sewall Cutting, patriarch of Windsor, reflecting on the years 1780–1830, expressed the basic distinction concerning the purposes of reading: between "universal truths and laws, and . . . under new forms, the subjugation of nature to the wants of man." The vast increase in knowledge of every conceivable aspect of this world, an increase ushered in by the Enlightenment, provided a context for "extensive" styles of reading. The progress of knowledge itself created what Bernhard Fabian, emphasizing periodical essays, novels, and travel books in his analysis of German reading habits, has termed "a craving for novelty." In Windsor District at least twenty different kinds of reading matter typically involved novelty, both in substance and in style of reading.[18]

Contemporaries frequently discussed the different moods of extensive readers and their reading fare. Many other reading situations and styles existed, in addition to serious and casual reading. George Keate, in his popular *Sketches From Nature*, commented that the "greatest obstructions to the successful journey of an author, arise from the different complexion and temper of his readers." The author "should defend himself against" some types of readers: "The Superficial Reader; The Idle Reader; The Sleepy Reader; and The Peevish Reader." Others he or she should "aim to please": "The Candid Reader; The Conjectural Reader; and The Learned Reader." A phenomenology of reading situations followed.[19]

A large share of the four-hundred Windsor District families in our study group, migrants from Massachusetts and Connecticut, were first- or second-generation regular readers and owners of a family library. When they first established the habit of reading, families most often engaged in intensive reading. The surviving private libraries in Windsor District strongly emphasized sacred works through about 1800. We would be mistaken to conclude that the small size of these earliest collections indicated infrequent reading. The size of a family library and the amount of reading engaged in by family members were rarely related. After 1800, the volume of local publishing and print importation in the Upper Valley expanded greatly, especially at Windsor, and gradually this increase was reflected in a proliferation of works that went beyond mirroring the wisdom of the ages. They provided many alternatives to intensive reading. As rural newspapers flooded the full- and partial-access zones of Windsor District by 1810 (see figures 5–8 and 5–9), they encouraged more casual and more short-term reading activity. They were also, as previously noted, the chief advertising medium for reading matter whose formats changed to meet new reading tastes.

Properly understood, family libraries offer the best insight available into precisely that deepest structure of the minds of their rural New England owners: the wisdom of the ages. Libraries identified, title by title in most cases, works read, reread, and retained for long periods of time. Libraries open to our view the most stable dimensions of information and opinion. These works were retained precisely because they provided a continuing, cumulative utility, a stable repository of the basic information, values, and beliefs embodied in print culture. Other works purchased near the time of the household head's death yield vital additional insight into more current intellectual interests of Upper Valley families through 1830. Both longer-term retention and more recent purchases illuminate key aspects of such families' basic *mentalités*. While the life of the rural mind and heart included much more, its deepest structures and most stable dimensions reveal the essential intellectual foundations for cultural participation. Rural cultural activity proceeded in a medium shaped by the vocabulary, grammar, and structures found in their residents' family libraries. All descriptions and evaluations of contemporary reality proceeded from constantly modified Windsor District *mentalités*. Many other kinds of cultural analysis are essential to a history of knowledge in the Early Republic, but none is more vital than a study of the form and content of its intellectual reservoirs.

In considering the meaning of the book, Lucien Febvre made the helpful point that it "is at least tangible evidence of convictions held because it embodies and symbolizes them; it furnishes arguments to those who are already converts, lets them develop and refine their faith, offers them points which will help them to triumph in debate, and encourages the hesitant." Windsor District families read works never purchased, and they read many works purchased but not retained for long. Virtually all available evidence leads us to conclude that, in Windsor District's spare rural economy, families—apart from those with the few largest private libraries—also read directly, listened to, or otherwise assimilated the contents of most works they purchased and retained. The general substance of these works became part of the active mentalities of their owners. Furthermore, material scarcity and exceptionally active neighborhood, family, and kinship networks insured the spread of some of the knowledge residing in family libraries to some of those without libraries, and even to some where elementary literacy had penetrated only partially or not at all.[20]

George Smart has stated the general point well: "With reservations as to completeness, it is fair to say, especially in regard to limited private libraries, that they provide us with an excellent picture of the reading habits of their owners." We now know that family libraries offer us not all but a substantial part of their owners' reading habits and reading fare. They do offer a view into the core of knowledge, the bases of owners' mental worlds. It is ironic that many historians readily assume that hoes and ploughs were used routinely to till fields, that cooking utensils were nearly always used to prepare food, and that clothing was recurrently worn, but then question whether printed texts were habitually read. The present study breaks with this tradition by assuming that most books and other print items retained were habitually read and that they were understood in many differing ways.[21]

Windsor District Family Libraries: Incidence and Size

Analysis of the overall study group of 396 families with private libraries, who retained 5,630 volumes of mainly books, pamphlets, and periodicals, moves us far beyond elite levels of intellectual interaction into the unknown daily lives of most ordinary rural families. As we have seen, the group is fairly representative of wealth, work, living situation, position, and status in Windsor District and closely reflects the geographical distribution of the population by township. Weakest in their representation were the four minimum-access zone townships in the foothills of the Green Mountains (see figure 5–9). Of crucial importance, Windsor District evidence survives for many of the area's very poorest families.[22]

The pace of material and cultural change in Windsor District penetrated the deepest mental structures of every human habitat between 1780 and 1830, setting off a tumultuous and often confusing struggle between traditional wisdom and newer varieties of "intelligence." To follow this struggle we begin with trends in a basic measure of Windsor District cultural participation in 1780–1830: the varying incidence and size of family libraries as described in probated inventories. These reveal a high and somewhat overstated initial incidence of family libraries among migrants from Connecticut and Massachusetts (see graph 8–1 throughout). Fairly small numbers of inventories, combined with a stationary probate court in 1787–1806, produce considerably greater fluctuation in the incidence of reported libraries (55 to 80 percent) than in the total population. But as the Windsor District probate court began to circulate more widely after about 1805, the number of estates inventoried increased steadily and substantially, considerably outdistancing earlier population increases. Over the next three decades, 1807–36, the share of families with libraries was slightly lower and fluctuated far less (57–65 percent) than in the early decades. Doubling from an average of ten to eleven per year in 1797–1811 to 22 per year in 1812–36, the number of inventories reflected fuller coverage of the District, and more accurately represented the entire population (see appendix 4). The result was that, during the first third of the nineteenth century, the probate court closely matched the entire social geography of Windsor District.[23]

Family library size increased sharply between 1787 and 1830, especially after 1810: from 5.3 volumes per library, 1787–1800 (67 libraries with 355 volumes); to 7.2 volumes per library, 1801–15 (143 libraries with 1,023 volumes); to 22.9 volumes per library, 1816–30 (186 libraries with 4,252 volumes). In the years 1787–1800, there were no social, moral or circulating libraries in Windsor District, nor were there any family libraries with more than thirty-five volumes. But by 1801–15 just under a tenth of all families retained a share in a lending library, and one family in twenty kept more than thirty-five volumes. At this time, too, we find the first collection with more than one hundred volumes. Library size increased further in 1816–30. A tenth of all families again retained lending library shares, and others borrowed from circulating libraries in Windsor (and, by 1829, Chester). Another tenth of all families with libraries (double the earlier proportion) maintained more than thirty-five volumes each. At

Graph 8–1: Windsor District Inventories: Proportions With a Family Library at Death of the Head of Household, 1787–1836

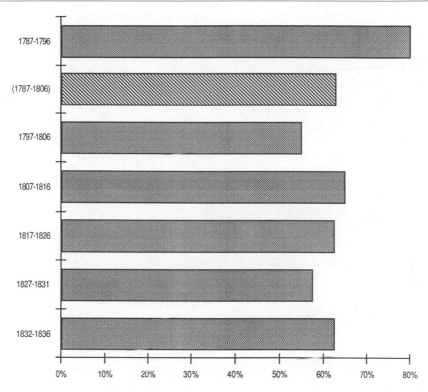

this time seven families (4 percent) had collections with more than one hundred volumes each. The average size of family libraries doubled between the late 1780s and the early 1820s (see graph 8–2). If we take into account the median library size we see that, coinciding with increasing numbers of inventories probated after 1796, a slight decline in median library size occurred, lasting through 1816. Therefore each half decade saw an increase, and by the late 1820s mean family library size in Windsor District had reached six volumes.

The key trend in Windsor District family library development was the addition of "extensive" reading matter to a large share of almost exclusively "intensive" reading libraries. The steady increase in the median size of libraries after 1812 highlights a significant decline in traditionally one-to-five-volume collections, from three-quarters to just half of all libraries. By the 1780s broader elementary literacy had translated into expansion in the share of families who continued the habit of reading throughout the life cycle, and for whom regular reading became a normal part of life.

Windsor District family libraries expanded steadily during the half century 1780–1830 (see table 8–1). At no time did one-volume libraries constitute more

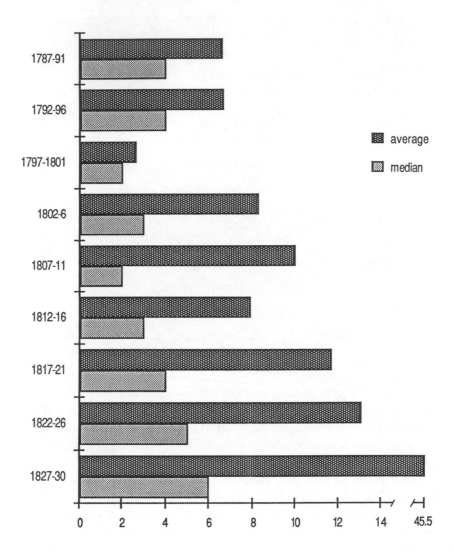

Graph 8–2: Windsor District Inventories: Average and Median Number of Volumes Per Family Library, 1787–1830

than a quarter of all libraries, but after the War of 1812, single-volume libraries amounted to less than a fifth of all libraries, even after we take into account the far better coverage of inventories. The proportion of families who retained more than ten volumes each grew after 1815 to 35 percent of all collections. These families, plus another 11 percent who retained six to nine volumes each,

Table 8-1: Size of Windsor District Family Libraries, 1787–1830

Number of Volumes in Library	I		2–3		4–5		6–9		10–14		15 +	
	No.	%	No.	%	No.	%	No.	%	No.	%	No.	%
1787–1800 (n=67)	17	(25%)	21	(31%)	15	(22%)	7	(11%)	2	(3%)	5	(8%)
1801–15 (n=143)	37	(25%)	48	(34%)	18	(13%)	17	(12%)	8	(6%)	15	(10%)
1816–30 (n=186)	36	(19%)	41	(22%)	23	(13%)	21	(11%)	20	(11%)	45	(24%)

Cumulative Percentages	Over 0 Volumes	Over 1 Volume	Over 3 Volumes	Over 5 Volumes	Over 9 Volumes	Over 14 Volumes
1787–1800	100%	75%	43%	21%	10%	8%
1801–15	100%	74%	40%	28%	16%	11%
1816–30	100%	81%	59%	46%	35%	24%

Source: All Windsor District inventories with family libraries, 1787–1830 (n=396)

constituted a major cultural phenomenon in the Early Republic. Most of them greatly diversified their intellectual interests and dramatically expanded Noah Webster's timeless core of knowledge.[24]

Family Libraries: Windsor District and Rural America, 1700–1850

Conspicuous expansion among every type of Windsor District family library began around 1810, closely following an earlier wave of expansion in newspaper circulation and printing facilities within Windsor District. By 1810, the dissemination of print culture had intensified in the hinterland, resulting in increasing accumulations. Even before 1800, slightly more than a fifth of all libraries (22 percent) held six or more volumes. By the years 1816–30, families with libraries of more than five volumes had more than doubled, to just under half of all households (46 percent). Within just a half century of the area's founding in the early 1760s, Windsor District family library holdings rose to a position among the highest in rural America. The incidence of family libraries in Windsor District in an earlier time period, before the widespread use of stereotyping, steam presses, and major improvements in transportation, had been much higher than that reported by Michael Harris for southern Indiana from 1800 through 1850. In southern Indiana the proportion was very low—20 percent (469 among 2,338 inventories drawn from sixteen counties) between 1800 and 1850. In Windsor District the proportion was 62 percent in 1787–1830. Perhaps most important in accounting for this difference is the far broader access to print culture in Windsor District, a result of higher levels of elementary literacy, especially among females. Furthermore, many of Harris's southern Indiana counties were not settled until after 1820, and schooling lagged behind settlement by a decade or more. The share of family libraries was probably greater in Windsor District than in less settled areas of the Upper Valley, but not by much. Rural Windsor District's slightly larger libraries in general, and much sharper curve of expansion after 1815, reflect all of the factors we have been discussing.[25]

In perspective, Windsor's 62 percent incidence of family libraries accords with recent scholarly attention to the critical role of social development, economic exchange networks, sizes and types of communities, and access to local and regional transportation and print communication networks. The major factors inhibiting the spread of regular reading were the lack of local schooling, and of access to economic exchange generally and to local bookstores specifically. In the absence of bookstores, general stores often assumed a somewhat greater burden, carrying a broader range of print items than in areas where bookstores were securely established. The supply side of print culture throughout early America accounts for a high or low incidence of family libraries and for varying sizes and kinds of collections retained.

It is no accident that retention rates were lowest in frontier areas and in other locales less advanced in settlement, social development, and market participation. Southern Indiana, 1800–1850, is a classic illustration. Because bookstores were scarce, general stores provided the major outlets for book sales; under these conditions only 20 percent of families had libraries. A similar situation in frontier Kentucky, 1780–92, yielded a 35 percent retention level. Frontier Missouri in 1800–1850 ranged between 30 and 60 percent, but the latter rate pertained mainly to settled urban centers with extensive economic exchange (for example, St. Louis). Elsewhere, 44 percent of families in the long-settled but rural Shenandoah Valley of Virginia in the Revolutionary era retained books, and 44–46 percent in rural Athens County, Ohio, did so somewhat later in 1813–59. In 1800, in frontier Washington County, Ohio, which was generally late developing but which had a small city at Marietta, 43 to 50 percent of all families retained a private library.[26]

Retention rates rose markedly and varied considerably beyond frontier, very recently populated, and fairly isolated settlement areas. Early on in the history of Massachusetts, retention was already quite high – 49 percent in two counties in 1635–91. And by the Revolutionary era, a remarkable 75 percent of all families with inventories in rural Worcester County retained a private library. Just after the Revolution, families in Suffolk County, including Boston, were retaining private libraries in 64 percent of all inventories probated. In eighteenth-century Maryland, with commercial ports, 60 percent of all inventoried families possessed private libraries, and on the eve of the Revolution that proportion reached 63 percent. Further south, in Virginia, retention rates in 1763–89 ranged between 59 and 68 percent, the latter in Richmond and its environs. A more detailed study by Kett and McClung reports a range of 32 to 62 percent incidence of family libraries in inventories encompassing urban and rural

Virginia in 1790–1830. In eighteenth-century South Carolina, including Charleston, retention rates were just under 45 percent but increased to 50 to 55 percent after the Revolution.[27]

Rural Windsor District's 62 percent incidence of family libraries in 1787–1830 is very high for a wholly rural setting, especially considering the relative recency of settlement and the geographical isolation. The continuing prevalence of the intensive reading style was to be expected, as was the fairly slim proportion of very large libraries. As some families increased their holdings and expanded their reading tastes, others joined the ranks of those retaining private libraries of any sort. It is very surprising, in view of the extensive coverage of all Windsor District wealth levels (see table 8-2), that more than a tenth (11 percent) of all libraries contained more than twenty-five volumes and that 25 percent contained ten or more volumes. Even more surprising, however, is the far larger share—46 percent—of families with six or more volumes, 1816–1830. Beyond this threshold newer kinds of works and alternatives to the intensive reading style proliferated. The commercialization of Windsor District and the spread of a new communications environment caused this major shift in rural reading habits and size of private libraries.[28]

As reading became a regular part of life for a larger share of all families, variety increased. Three-fifths of all families (twenty-seven of forty-four) who retained more than twenty-five volumes each had never engaged in a profession. Their libraries were either dominated by secular reading and newer vintage works (fourteen of twenty-seven), or were large general libraries (thirteen of twenty-seven) combining sizable holdings of both secular and sacred books of a serious intellectual nature. Four of these twenty-seven libraries were owned by gentleman farmer families living on a large homestead; the other twenty-three were owned by middle- and lower-middle-class artisan, yeoman farmer, and village families engaged in commerce, trade, and manufacturing.

At least through 1805, Windsor District was largely a frontier area. Only in 1810 did the first two of eleven townships (Windsor and Springfield) reach 2,500 inhabitants. At their population peak, in the mid-1820s, Windsor District's eleven communities averaged just 1,620 residents per township. Moreover, no city was mushrooming in their midst. Unlike similar communities elsewhere beyond New England, however, Windsor District pulsed with the steady rhythm of the printing press and the hum of the broader market economy. Family libraries were retained at double the rates typical for frontier and early subsistence farming areas. Only in sizable urban areas, in their immediate hinterlands throughout America, and in long-settled parts of rural southern New England did families retain family libraries at higher rates, from 63 to 75 percent.

The early national era encompassed the first two generations in the Western world in which almanacs, pamphlets, books, and newspapers were purchased

Table 8–2: Composite Size of Family Libraries,
         Windsor District, 1787–1830

Size of Library (in volumes)	Number of Libraries	Percent of All Libraries
I	90	22.7
2–3	110	27.8
4–5	56	14.0
6–9	45	11.4
10–14	30	7.6
15–24	21	5.3
25–99	36	9.1
100–199	4	1.0
200–499	3	.8
500–999	1	.3
Total	396	100.0

and read by most sectors of the rural population. In the Upper Valley private libraries were exceptionally prevalent and were increasingly supplemented by newspaper subscriptions. A desire to follow the War of 1812 throughout the North Atlantic, for instance, spurred families like the poor self-sufficient farmstead household of young Orestes Brownson to regular newspaper reading. The rural American Northeast shared with Sweden the highest literary rate in the West in 1780, followed closely by Scotland. In no other known rural area in transatlantic civilization through 1830 did the extent of cultural participation, especially for women and for ordinary men, compare with that in these three countries. All three inhabited peripheries of North Atlantic civilization. Apparently very different kinds of print matter were disseminated widely in each, as reading joined talking, singing, music, and dance as major forms of rural communication. If there was a key difference between Sweden on the one hand and the United States and Scotland on the other, it was in the greater variety of purposes to which elementary literacy was harnessed in the latter two countries. An expanding system of neighborhood schools joined with the family, apparently first in New England, to instill the rudiments of the Western tradition and to stimulate lifelong learning, secular as well as sacred, among the "rising generation." Among adults, America's status as a recently created New World Christian republic was regularly emphasized.[29]

Types of Family Libraries in Windsor District Through 1830

Most Windsor District family libraries were not random collections of works purchased in isolation from one another. Rather, the interrelationship among works, the way they were clustered to shape private libraries, is of central importance in the study of rural mentalities. Among the four hundred family libraries, six distinct types may be discerned, based on their contents and physical arrangement (see table 8–3 throughout). Two broad criteria distinguished types of libraries. One was the relative mix of sacred versus secular works. Sacred and secular works addressed different perceptions of reality and different life goals, using different means and sometimes even different languages. Several kinds of schoolbooks, especially spellers, grammars, and readers, and some stage-of-life works combined both religious and secular ideas and values. Otherwise, the two kinds of works demarcated increasingly different funds of knowledge.[30]

The second criterion, mentioned earlier, was the mix of works of traditional wisdom, which mainly were read intensively, and all other works, which were associated with newer knowledge and alternative "extensive" reading styles. These distinctions in reading matter and styles assume that most, but not all, readers used a work in accord with its stated function and basic intention.[31]

The six types of libraries were: sacred intensive-reading libraries, mixed secular-religious intensive-reading ("mixed intensive") libraries, sacred combined intensive-extensive-reading ("sacred combined") libraries, mixed secular-religious extensive-reading ("mixed extensive") libraries, secular extensive-reading libraries, and professional libraries. Just under a quarter of all families in our study retained the *sacred intensive-reading libraries* to be expected in a newly settled rural area of early national America. Most of these ninety-three libraries contained either one book (sixty-five cases) or two books (twenty-two cases); the range was one to ten volumes. Sacred intensive libraries averaged a Bible and one other religious volume—elementary religious works that encouraged Bible reading, family devotion, prayer, meditation, and sacred singing. The Bible dominated reading in these families, appearing in ninety of ninety-three libraries (97 percent). Next in frequency came psalm books (fifteen of ninety-three families, or 16 percent) followed closely by hymnals (nine of ninety-three, or 10 percent). Another defining characteristic of sacred intensive libraries was the absence of all secular works, including schoolbooks and typical farm and village utilitarian works. The reading interests of families with sacred intensive libraries were dominated by elementary sacred subjects characteristic of older, more traditional, and still marginally literate premodern societies.[32]

The largest group of families with a library, a third of the 400 families, retained a *mixed secular-religious intensive-reading library*. These families maintained a core of sacred works, most frequently a Bible, which was occasionally

Type of Library by Kinds of Books Retained*	Number of Family Libraries	Percent of All Libraries	Number of Volumes	Percent of All Volumes	Average Number of Books Per Library
Sacred (or Religious): Intensive Reading	93	23.5	144	2.5	1.6
Secular/Religious: Intensive Reading	131	33.1	524	9.3	4.0
Sacred: Mixed (or Intensive-Extensive) Reading	17	4.3	73	1.3	4.3
Secular/Religious: Extensive Reading	112	28.3	1,357	24.1	12.1
Major Secular: Extensive Reading	10	2.5	1,366	24.3	136.6
Professional:	33	8.3	2,166	38.5	65.6
a. Theological	7	——	109	2	15.6
b. Medical	12	——	542	9.6	45.2
c. Legal	13	——	1,514	26.9	116.5
d. Printer-Publisher	1	——	1	.02	1.0
Total	396	100	5,630	100	14.2

N=5,630 print items
   396 inventories with print items
*The two criteria employed are: mix of secular and religious (including theological) volumes; and primary use of reading material (intensive or maintenance of traditional wisdom versus extensive or expansion of knowledge base). For the latter distinction see ch. 8.

supplemented by a hymnal, psalm book, prayer book, or devotional work and rarely by a lone collection of sermons. In numbers of volumes, secular works dominated, accounting for a decisive 75 percent. This was the key feature of mixed intensive libraries. They contained basic information useful in rural life, primarily that gathered in small gazetteers, geographies, dictionaries, secular songbooks, and, most of all, schoolbooks. Almost all of the families with such libraries purchased a yearly almanac; few subscribed to a weekly newspaper or a periodical. Accounting for just a tenth of all volumes retained, these 131 libraries averaged just four volumes per library and ranged in size from one to twenty-one volumes. A typical mixed intensive library contained a Bible, perhaps a psalm book or hymnal, a schoolbook, and a dictionary, geography, or secular songbook.[33]

The collections of all other families (44 percent) were dominated by extensive reading matter, though most also contained intensive reading matter. A rare third type of library (only 4 percent of all collections) contained several volumes of sacred extensive reading matter yet none of a secular nature. Families with *sacred combined intensive-extensive-reading libraries* devoted intellectual attention almost exclusively to sacred concerns. The distinguishing feature of their reading was substantial interest in theological tracts and treatises, sermons, church history, and religious periodicals (sixteen of seventeen libraries), the Bible (fifteen of seventeen), and, to a lesser extent, psalm books and hymnals (twelve of seventeen). Usually there was a Bible, perhaps a psalm book or hymnal, and two or three theological treatises, sermons, works of church history, or periodical volumes. These families were part of a larger, very active reading group not satisfied with mere essentials of sacred life in an agricultural society. More determined and inquiring readers, they displayed interest in current as well as traditional religious disputes, in the history of Christianity, and in practical applications of theology. Sacred combined libraries averaged 4.3 volumes per library, and ranged between 2 and 9 volumes.[34]

The next-to-largest cluster of families (28 percent) retained *mixed secular-religious extensive-reading libraries*, the fourth type of family collection. Averaging a substantial twelve volumes each, and ranging between two and fifty-six volumes, the libraries of these families were actually almost all noteworthy in size. They typically featured four or more secular extensive works, especially modern literature, travelogues, history, philosophy, and works on classical culture. Frequently (in nearly half the cases) a volume of a periodical was included, and an eighth of all families also held a share in a local lending library. Sacred reading matter included one or more extensive-reading works in theology and usually a volume of church history or a collection of sermons. In addition, since these were Christian rural agricultural families, they retained one or more intensive-reading religious works, including Bibles (82 of 112 libraries, or 73 percent), psalm books, hymnals, devotional works, and an occasional concordance. They also usually held one or more schoolbooks (56 or 112 libraries) and two or more other works, including dictionaries, a geography or gazetteer, an elementary medical or law book, or a manual (60 of 112 libraries, or 54 percent). Overall, secular works dominated, accounting for 70 percent of all reading matter.

The 112 families retaining mixed extensive library collections constituted a substantial, actively reading group serious about ideas and their ramifications and alert to new information and opinions. Their library holdings in the "intellectual" and professional reading areas and in periodicals suggest that readers other than professionals and scholars were both far more cosmopolitan and more interested in modern intelligence than has previously been supposed. There can be little doubt—though detailed evidence is yet to be located—that most families retaining an expanding library of this type also subscribed to a newspaper regularly after 1800 and continued to purchase an annual almanac and perhaps occasional broadsides and chapbooks.

At the leading edge of new thought in Windsor District were the families of lawyers (3.3 percent of the study group; see below) and a small group of uniquely secular families (2.5 percent). The ten collections held by the latter group, each collection at least 75 percent composed of secular extensive reading matter, averaged 137 volumes per library. Together these ten libraries held 1,366 volumes, nearly a quarter of all the printed matter retained in our study group. These *secular extensive-reading libraries* ranged from a small collection in a family with a lending library share, to seven large libraries holding 38–91 volumes each, and one special library of 909 volumes, the collection of scholar John Leverett, whose family belonged to the gentleman farmer occupational category. Eight out of ten of these families engaged in commerce and trade (but did not sell books) and did some farming. Most of these households undoubtedly also subscribed to a local rural newspaper. Six of the ten families kept periodicals. Several probably also purchased an almanac annually. Inexplicably, just one family retained a share in a local lending library. All major secular extensive libraries reveal very broad secular intellectual interests. Two families owned no religious works, three did not keep a Bible, and six had no sacred texts beyond minimal intensive-reading prayer and devotional works. Still, though swamped by contemporary secular intellectual interests, a sacred perspective on the world did remain present in the majority of these families.[35]

Professional families—thirty-two doctors, lawyers, ministers, and deacons, plus newspaper publisher Alden Spooner—retained the most varied libraries, and their *professional libraries* represented the final library type. The most obvious distinguishing characteristic of these collections—the large number of print items devoted to the professional concerns of the head of household—was also their only unifying feature. Only in this group did the occupation of the household head (all of them men) make a library mandatory and dictate its size and structure. In eleven of thirteen lawyer households, for instance, law volumes accounted for more than one-quarter of all printed items. But works beyond the professional field and allied areas appeared clustered in professional libraries just as they did in other extensive-reading libraries. Following the practice of inventory assessors, we distinguish between the "professional library" as a specialized collection and the remaining "family library," using the latter term for convenience when designating the totality.[36]

The libraries of seven families of ministers and deacons survived in Windsor District inventories in 1787–1830. Rev. Samuel Sargeant's collection may be representative. Apart from a grammar, there were seven volumes on domesticity, six aimed at the family and one at young people. There were twelve volumes of sermons and sixteen volumes of strictly theological works, including several of a sophisticated and/or technical nature. Although Sargeant had a concordance, the absence of a Bible or any other basic religious works suggests that he may have given one or more volumes away before his death. The

Sargeant family retained no secular extensive works. The seven family libraries of ministers and deacons averaged just sixteen volumes.

All twelve family libraries of doctors contained a core (14 to 100 percent) of medical works, with just under half averaging between 42 and 56 percent medical and related professional volumes. The overall proportion of medical volumes was nearly half the total library holdings, which averaged forty-five volumes. Two-thirds of the libraries contained between nineteen and fifty-six volumes each. Secular works accounted for 80 percent of all volumes. Most family libraries of physicians contained works in several new areas of knowledge. (In all other families, shares in lending libraries made such works readily available.) Most popular among new reading categories were science, classical works, philosophy, and theology. The typical collection contained, on the sacred side, a Bible, a theological treatise, a collection of sermons, a psalm book or hymnal, and perhaps a devotional work; together with twenty-five medical volumes, a basic law book, a periodical outside the field of medicine, several other extensive-reading works, a farm-related work, and a couple of schoolbooks. Thus the family libraries of doctors revealed the same interest in newer forms of knowledge that was shown by families with mixed extensive libraries.

Thirteen family libraries of lawyers and one of a printer-publisher complete the tally of professional libraries. The 1,514 volumes found in these thirteen collections accounted for 27 percent of all print items in our study group. Averaging 117 volumes each, most holdings were sizable; six numbered more than 100 volumes each and two more than 400 volumes each. Only one was under 10 volumes, and ten of the thirteen (77 percent) held 24 or more volumes each. Three families maintained shares in lending libraries. Lawyers' families were exceptionally wealthy, averaging $9,645 per estate. Engaged in many public affairs, the families of lawyers had heavily secular libraries as varied as those among families with major secular extensive collections. Four of eleven lawyers' collections did not contain a Bible, and only six included any sermons, theology, or church history. While law books, periodicals, and texts in politics, government, and geography were prominent, in seven of the eleven enumerated libraries they were outnumbered by other secular extensive-reading works. Reading interests among the families of lawyers were extremely wide and up to date.[37]

The 396 family libraries in our study group have been classified into six basic types of collections, according to their contents. Collections of strictly sacred reading matter represented just over a quarter of all libraries, and libraries in which sacred works were dominant amounted to slightly under a third. Both types were considerably more prevalent before 1810. Families retaining these libraries showed relatively little awareness of the contemporary nonlocal secular world or of the three great revolutions (American, French, and commercial) that were affecting the North Atlantic. Probably only a tiny percentage of these families subscribed to a weekly newspaper through 1830. Another key indicator of the strongly traditional and conservative streak in Windsor District family libraries through 1830 is that among all libraries, a small majority (56 percent) was dominated by intensive-reading works that affirmed traditional beliefs and values. It is noteworthy that these two categories accounted for only a third of all libraries after 1820. Beyond Upper Valley villages, their immediate farmstead environs, and stable hamlets, newer varieties of knowledge and their associated reading styles emerged very gradually. Consequently, for a small majority of all known families with private libraries, old ways of thinking and living dominated their reading matter. Nearly half of this 56 percent chose to collect strictly religious works; the other half began to mix secular with sacred reading.

Windsor District family libraries reflected the relatively slow development of interest in secular extensive reading until about 1805. Just under two-fifths of all family libraries (149, or 38 percent) through 1830 retained one or more secular extensive works. But people who began to inquire actively about the contemporary secular world quickly found secular extensive reading exciting and tended to accumulate libraries far larger than those found in families who adhered to the wisdom of the ages. Where sacred works accounted for all or the overwhelming proportion of reading matter, intensive reading styles dominated, and collections remained very small — 3 volumes per library, as opposed to 14 for all family libraries. Nearly three-quarters of the 5,630 volumes retained in all family libraries were about life on earth and its many dimensions. Leaving aside primers, schoolbook spellers, readers, grammars, and a few stage-of-life and other works, texts presenting wholly secular concerns outnumbered those offering sacred knowledge two to one. By any standard, Windsor District family reading was increasingly dominated by secular thought and modern intelligence, especially after about 1805.

Part IV
Mentalités: Intellectual Reservoirs
and Their Replenishment

Chapter 9

Mending and Rebirth:
Human Habitats, Reading Communities,
and *Mentalités*, 1780–1830

Man in daily life . . . finds at any given moment a stock of knowledge at hand that serves him as a scheme of intepretation. . . . [It]
is by no means homogeneous, but shows a particular structure.
There is a relatively small kernel of knowledge that is clear, distinct, and consistent in itself. This kernel is surrounded by zones
of various gradations of vagueness, obscurity and ambiguity. Then
follow zones of things just taken for granted, blind beliefs, bare
suppositions, mere guesswork, zones in which it will do merely to
"put one's trust." And finally, there are regions of our complete
ignorance.

—Alfred Schutz, "Tiresias,
or Our Knowledge of Future Events" and
"The Stranger: An Essay in Social Psychology"

Art's cauldron is only on rare occasion gold and silver.

—John Gardner, *The Art of Fiction*

Continuity and Change in the Upper Valley Network of Human Habitats

Thomas Cochran recently expressed an important principle guiding inquiries
into cultural values. "What is perceived depends on what is already known:
one sees what is behind the eyes rather than in front of them." For rural New
Englanders it is necessry to rephrase the last part: Upper Valley residents saw
what was behind their eyes *more readily* than what was in front of them. In
a cultural area as flooded with Enlightenment religious and secular attitudes
(including theories of perception) as was Windsor District—Universalism was
the largest single denomination there until the late 1820s—residents increasingly began to identify more precisely exactly what was before their eyes. The
triumph of a spirit of fact, and an ideal of modern intelligence, entailing accuracy and precision in knowledge and speed in its diffusion, is one of the

signal developments of early nineteenth century culture. Family libraries enable us to delineate both dimensions of the mind's eye: traditional beliefs and values, and some newer aspects of knowledge deriving from a rapidly changing reality.[1]

This chapter studies the cultural geography of rural New England *mentalités* during the Early Republic, including intellectual reservoirs holding the stable core of knowledge and some current funds of information and opinion among each of five groups of ordinary rural families. Traditional family relations were alternately challenged and reinforced when family members read. To be sure, they learned new ways of maintaining and reinvigorating cultural traditions that had enriched New England family life for generations. But print culture also enticed families with enough novel secular knowledge, schemes, promises, elixirs, and current perspectives about God's ways to shake the foundations of the wisdom of the ages. As reading matter regularly reported on new developments occurring in transatlantic civilization, changes began to penetrate the most stable layer of family beliefs and values. Doubt, tension, and conflict multiplied as regular reading spread.

Upper Valley residents regarded the relationship between continuity and change as a choice between mending their lives and overturning older ways, most typically in a religious conversion or "rebirth." Continuity usually ruled the intellectual world of the Early Republic. People recognized change and participated in it, but since it was believed to lead inevitably to decay, in nature as in human societies, change was much feared. Transatlantic theories of social decay were applied in the popular New England conception of "mending" as a controlling metaphor for the course of daily life. Capturing a distinctly rural approach to change, the ideal of mending encouraged people to reuse land, material objects, and ideas as long as possible. The objective in mending was to perpetuate something while altering it as little as possible, whether the thing in question was a dam, a fence, clothes, shoes, farm implements, or conceptions of heaven and hell, natural history, or government. In the powerful opinions of the *New England Primer*, regular reading of the Bible could even mend a life. The spirit of mending so dominated traditional rural ways of thinking that, when mending proved insufficient, any amount of change became possible, even radical change that could remake a life. When sufficient change accumulated to overwhelm normal powers of assimilation, radical ideals of religious rebirth or secular transformation emerged.

Upper Valley residents had little experience with what later came to be an accepted feature of modern life, moderate change. They tinkered endlessly, but when small adjustments failed, they contemplated starting over. Radical change was not alien to Upper Valley residents; changes in the seasons were typically dramatic. The experience of "rebirth" in religious conversion aptly expressed a rural religious alternative to mending, appropriate to the sacred center of their beliefs. Continuity and change were deeply embedded in Windsor District cultural participation in the period 1780–1830. Residents strove both to preserve "universal truths" and to "subject nature to the wants of man." The two goals often proved incompatible, however. Most Windsor District residents between 1780 and 1830 tried to maintain stability in their values and beliefs amid increasing change in the world around them.[2]

What undergirded the self-confident, enterprising, tireless New England initiative seen in the spirit of mending? What accounted for the diversity of its manifestations? And, on the other hand, why did so many unusual sacred and secular leaders who had remade their own lives emerge from rural New England? Reformers, prophets, inventors, traders, and conservers all sprang from the same rural society during the same two generations. This is the great cultural puzzle. An extensive district school system—the factor most frequently cited—did spur people to acquire literacy skills. But until the 1820s pedagogy and schoolbook content aimed above all to form a sound conscience on the basis of longstanding intellectual traditions. By encouraging lifelong reading and writing, and by teaching the workings of a commercial economy, however, district schools unwittingly blazed pathways to far broader knowledge than most educators had anticipated. As intensely employed in preserving traditional ways of life as in actively seeking to alter them, rural New Englanders felt a driving passion grounded in the experience of reading and powered by the knowledge that it gave them.[3]

In light of the extensive commercialization of many dimensions of Windsor District life, answers to several crucial questions must be sought. What kinds of basic rural mentalities existed, and how did each incorporate the far-reaching economic, social, and cultural transformation enveloping Windsor District? Did responses and adaptations vary significantly from one group to another and, if so, how did diverse human habitats affect these responses? How did the mass culture of the printed word broaden intellectual interests, adapting reading habits and cultural participation to the changing circumstances of life within Windsor District?

Print culture presented a kaleidoscope of possibilities in the first age of widespread lifelong learning. The rural commercial exchange system and its communications environment spawned a fresh order of community based on the human habitat, a total environment of daily life. Human habitats are not a universal historical phenomenon; rather they emerged in rural societies along with diversity of commercial development and related social relations, of access to communications media, and of cultural participation. Just as the transportation system carried the material products of the market, the communication system directed specific cultural currents to particular arrays of families.

Drawing upon available reading, families in each living situation believed that the power of the printed word was a force as real as a snowstorm in January. An educated citizenry could preserve a republic.

Human habitats shaped distinctive vantage points, sets of material and cultural coordinates that created special interests and shared perspectives on life. Residents of separate habitats did not evolve wholly different visions of the world, however; the traditional Anglo-American wisdom of the ages was pervasive. To this core, each human habitat added its own interests, based on local material and cultural infrastructure. These interests were embodied in an expanding range of cultural, religious, political, and economic activities and organizations. The knowledge shared within each type of human habitat was coherent and continuous enough to differentiate it quite clearly from that of the other four into the mid-1830s. Thereafter, rural life was integrated throughout all but the most isolated areas of a small number of townships in the network.

The picture of rural life presented here differs sharply with the pre-social history, trickle-down model of cultural diffusion. We describe a situation in which some forms of knowledge were shared by all communities of readers. Other kinds were shared by smaller groups, drawn from just one or two types of human habitats. The spectrum was extensive; knowledge spread at its own rate in each major subject area. Consequently, the pace of print culture diffusion was regulated by varying circulation rates, not by a uniformly strong or weak flow, and rarely by a steady trickle. Each November almanacs flooded the whole network, reaching a large share of all families within two months. Until the mid-1820s, newspapers, and especially novels and poetry among books, passed quickly through the fortunate village and farmstead and the self-sufficient hamlet living situations, but then circulation came virtually to a halt except in a small group of mostly artisan families. Still other sorts of books, pamphlets, and periodicals were read widely in the four village townships but rarely beyond their bounds. Finally, some books and pamphlets, such as hymnals, psalmodies, prayer books, and schoolbooks, were widely retained and were nearly always available for purchase throughout the district, from the river valley to the foothills of the Green Mountains.[4]

Complexity in the Reading Experience:
Libraries, Texts, Interests, and Meanings

In each human habitat family diversity yielded to shared cultural perspectives. By this process a community of readers coalesced, sharing ideals, goals, and various forms of action. The intellectual foundations of cultural dialogue are evident to us in several sorts of records: in Windsor District family libraries, in social library chargeout records (those for Cavendish, 1815–37, were used here) and in other family-centered reading, including almanacs and newspapers. Family library retention rates varied widely, from 50 percent among hardscrabble dwellers to 85 percent among fortunate village families. Precisely because they included works purchased and retained often for decades, family libraries reveal deep reservoirs of knowledge from which residents drew principles appropriate in fashioning responses to the contemporary issues posed weekly in newspapers.[5]

As we have seen, the home was the center of reading activity in all human habitats through 1835. Common reading at family gatherings as formal as funerals or baptism and as informal as daily meals and discussions, greatly extended the influence of many texts. The presence of a work in the house meant that there were many opportunities for its contents to be read, listened to, and assimilated. In many instances, assumed and actual audiences differed in important respects, and works often had more than one audience, usually including the audiences that had been designated by the author or publisher.

Texts and material interests coincided frequently, yet material and cultural interaction was exceptionally complex. Students of intellectual history quickly discover that intellectuals did not all think according to the same principles of logic. In elaborating an idea, writers took many surprising routes, often drawing connections that we might find bizarre among specific phenomena. Our study of reading faces all of these problems, compounded by the fact that rural Windsor District participated in a brand new mass culture. Its eleven townships had fewer than 30 college graduates among nearly 17,000 residents in 1815, and no more than 4 percent of the adult population had ever attended an academy. As rural New England families first explored the rich repositories of the Western tradition, they sometimes developed unique perspectives on age-old problems.

What are the relationships among families, the texts their libraries contained, their other interests, and the meanings they assimilated from their reading? In general, we may not assume that meaning taken from a work fits with the general social class of its owner, nor that there is an unchanging readership for a work. Statements about the audience in one period cannot be extrapolated to earlier or later periods without attention to context as well as text.[6]

The research for this book has suggested the following general framework of relationships. The texts in a family library were chosen individually and retained as a group by that family. Each specific work had one or more intended audiences, hence a work's intended audiences are to be compared with the actual audience retaining each work. Where the family is part of an intended audience, the general perspective likely shaping that family's initial reading for that work is known. Where the family is not part of an intended audience, we learn about new meaning making exchanges. Moreover, each specific work, in the text read within Windsor District, was intended to present a particular fund of knowledge, including information and opinions, beliefs and values. Each text conveyed a basic perspective and set of messages, and much secondary knowledge. Sometimes secondary knowledge contradicted the basic perspective. The amount of knowledge assimilated varied with the behavior of readers, and also depended to a considerable extent on the type of work involved. For many types of the most common reading matter, the basic perspective and set of messages was usually assimilated. Because the accuracy with which the basic perspective and set of messages were understood varied, caution and further research in the history of reading are much needed here. Given the purposefulness of the reading experience, and where the family is part of an intended audience, the interests a family represented can generally be assumed to have coincided with the meanings its members assimilated from their reading.

History's lessons lie in the details. An example of the complexity of reading interests will clarify some of the issues. One of the most popular religious writers in Windsor District was Richard Baxter (1615–91). Both the eighteenth century prefaces and the mid–seventeenth century text of Baxter's *The Saints' Everlasting Rest* read by Windsor District families stressed the value of this work in persuading the unconverted "to maintain a heavenly conversation." A strong Manichaean cast streaked the work: "carnal minds," "earthly pleasures and vanity," and "the flesh" were sharply contrasted with the purity of the spirit realm and the afterlife. Next to living in sin, the most "dangerous hindrance" to "a heavenly life" was "an earthly mind." Baxter defines his intended audience as the rural poverty-stricken, those "under personal afflictions, tiring duties, disappointments, or sufferings," and those greatly discontented with their lot in life. Heaven, not this life, delivered "perfect endless enjoyment of both body and soul." The afterlife contained no earthly woes: neither grief nor sorrow, "nor is there such a thing as a pale face, a languid body, feeble joints, helpless infancy, decrepit age, peccant humours, painful or pining sickness, gripping fears, [or] consuming cares." The popularity of *The Saints' Everlasting Rest* owed much to the fact that many rural New Englanders could readily identify with its portrait.[7]

Baxter frequently distinguished among economic and social groups. The text favored the agricultural populace and the poor over the rich. Those in "ease and prosperity" knew little of "personal sufferings" and could scarcely appreciate heaven's reward, but to the "daily afflicted soul," thoughts of heaven were "delightful." Elsewhere the rich were taunted: "see if your credit, riches, or pleasures can help you." No, they would only invite everlasting wrath. Those "worldly minded" were castigated for "scrambling" "a step higher in the world than their brethren." Gold and "worldly glory" were no help toward salvation, because the world was "vile and deceitful." Indeed, "few of the 'mighty noble' are called," Baxter concluded.[8]

The *Saints' Rest* and other of Baxter's works appealed chiefly (eight of ten) to nonvillage families almost evenly split between the two predominantly agricultural human habitats: fortunate farmstead and self-sufficient farmstead. These were exactly the audiences Baxter sought to reach. Five of the ten families were primarily farmers (there were four yeoman families and a gentleman farmer family). Another family engaged in artisan labor, while the final four were all involved in localized, farmstead-related commerce and trade. Within the nonvillage population, and despite the book's sympathies with the poor, wealth posed no barrier to its reading. In fact, despite the work's perspective and structure of meaning, Baxter's keenest audience was not among the poorest Windsor District farmstead readers, as one might expect if economic motives and interests were uppermost in peoples' minds as they chose reading matter. The four yeoman farmer families, the artisan family, and one of the trading families were from the lower middle class, while three of the trading families and the gentleman farmer family were among Windsor District's richest 10 percent.

The reception given *Saint's Rest* teaches us the complexity of cultural appeals in the Early Republic. This book appealed mainly to traditional agricultural elements of the population rather than to villagers. Human habitat, not wealth or occupation, was the key to readership. Further, the text's primary structure of messages about salvation overrode all else. How its other messages were interpreted varied with living circumstances. Baxter's appeal to the majority group of lower-middle-class families in the countryside, away from the heaviest commercialization, is understandable in view of his abhorrence of urban life and the way to wealth, and his readers' anxieties about the dangers of luxury. Living among the rocks of rural Vermont, they could empathize with Baxter's picture of earthly woe and constant struggle. But what was the basis for his appeal to wealthy families? Baxter offers no justification for earthly riches and little comfort for the affluent. We must remember, however, that his central perspective was religious. This was first and foremost a devotional treatise addressed to an agricultural population. We do not yet know how rich agricultural families justified their material circumstances relative to Baxter's religious economy, but somehow they did so, in most cases choosing this alone among a wide range of devotional treatises. Baxter's steady attack on wealth and his thoroughgoing Manichaeanism may have played upon guilt feelings about wealth or fear of spiritual failure, or perhaps affluent nonvillage families simply ignored his criticism, regarding themselves as exceptions to Baxter's social portrait.

Cultural Life in the Hardscrabble Human Habitat

In hardscrabble families, not surprisingly, everyday chores consumed an enormous share of available time and energy. Hardscrabble households were comprised of a mixed lot of late youth, transients, new settlers, struggling families who were often at an early stage of their family life cycle, the physically and mentally disabled, failures, people with an assortment of legal and other problems, and families who preferred to have nothing to do with changing times. Characterized by geographic isolation and/or poverty that precluded more than minimal participation in print culture, the hardscrabble human habitat was the largest in population (41 percent) and in geographical extent (see figure 4–1 throughout). Farmstead areas in the five mountainous townships from Reading south to Weston and Andover were sparsely settled through 1830, none numbering more than 200 dispersed families. To this core we must add a group of families averaging just $361 in wealth who were scattered throughout other parts of the district. Hardscrabble families were united in cultural participation by a potent common denominator: they had access to only a narrow range of printed matter and most were cut off from newer trends in Windsor District life. The isolation of those geographically removed from the newer dimensions of the communications network was relieved only by local general stores and a rare peddler or traveling author. In however conservative a manner, over half of all hardscrabble families nevertheless did participate in the growing mass culture of the printed word.[9]

While some hardscrabble families participated in public life and half, notwithstanding their cultural isolation, retained family libraries, sharp financial restrictions limited the extent of their involvement. Hardscrabble families relied heavily on more traditional forms of cultural participation other than the printed word: religious meetings, political gatherings, and festive and ritual occasions such as the Fourth of July. Family, kin, and neighbors were the social center, but much of life was taken up with work, chiefly farming, grazing, and artisan activity. Hardscrabble families were not completely isolated from the commercialization of Windsor District, but their participation was thin and irregular, as described by Michael Merrill, James Henretta, Christopher Clark, and especially Susan Geib. Until the 1820s economic interaction mainly involved small inland general stores and the shops of country artisans; only after 1815 did a few small factories settle in (and sometimes establish) upland hamlets. Most hardscrabble land was in mountainous precincts. There parcels of land tended to be good for grazing but only fair for farming, with just a few choice strips between the hills. Some land was beautiful but proved barren.[10]

Even a majority of hardscrabble Vermonters were readers. These families took sacred matters very seriously, engaging in a much greater share of sacred reading than other groups of families did. Religious meetings were one of the

Farmhouse in winter in Randolph, Orange County, Vermont. Courtesy, Vermont Historical Society.

In mountainous Hardscrabble areas, poverty and isolation combined to limit access to printed matter and new trends in material and cultural life.

central foci of collective life among the poor throughout the district, especially upland hardscrabble people. Religion—both private devotion and public services—was one realm in which the individual's emotions were allowed free rein. No staid Episcopalian or Unitarian meetinghouses or societies were established beyond an informal cultural barrier running from Reading westward through Plymouth and then south through Ludlow to Weston and Andover through 1830. Congregationalists, remnants of an earlier southern New England Standing Order tradition, thrived among upland townships as they did nearly everywhere in New England, but these regions were above all preserves of the Universalists, Methodists, Freewill Baptists, and the Christian group. In addition, a new sect frequently would split off from one or more of these denominations, having decided, chiefly from its perusal of the Bible, that the world needed its special form of purification. It has been irrefutably demonstrated that hill country residents and the poor in all locations did not just passively assimilate an older sacred outlook on life; their strange fire grew and changed as it fed on opposition to many of the new forms of material and cultural life in the Early Republic. Most hardscrabble families grounded their more literalist strain of belief firmly in the Bible, in prayer and psalm books, and in hymnals and devotional treatises, the staples of their predominantly (81 percent) intensive libraries and reading styles.[11]

Township government and politics constituted a second realm of fairly active interest among hardscrabble families. While other human habitats were much more evenly split politically, the backcountry area inhabited by more than two-thirds of all hardscrabble families remained generally Jeffersonian in 1800–1824. In the 1808 election for governor, for example, Reading, Plymouth, and Ludlow all voted Republican in a losing cause by margins of 79–83 percent, whereas three of the four village townships went Federalist. In the closer gubernatorial election of 1813, Ludlow, Plymouth, and Andover maintained margins of more than 70 percent; Reading slipped somewhat (57 percent); and only Weston went firmly Federalist. Even the course of the war, which people throughout New England opposed on economic and other grounds, saw the backcountry remain quite staunchly Jeffersonian. By 1815 all but Weston were overwhelmingly Republican once again. Later the backcountry split off from the National Republicans and joined the Antimasons. In the gubernatorial election of 1834, Plymouth, Ludlow, and Weston all voted more than 60 percent Antimasonic in a three-party field; Antimasonry also carried Reading, though by a lesser margin. Very few other areas in Windsor District institutional life through 1830 — social, intellectual, or economic — elicited significant hardscrabble participation.[12]

Three families illustrate the nature of hardscrabble participation in print culture. Whether the household in question was the 130-acre farmstead of Levi Bixby's yeoman farm family in mountainous Ludlow or the poor five-member artisan family of Amos Tinkham in Windsor village, the stock of printed materials was slim. With a total estate valued at $529, the Bixbys retained a Bible and a psalm book at Levi's passing in 1798. Only an inexpensive Bible remained among the Tinkhams' $192 worth of possessions at Amos's death in 1829. Neither family seems ever to have owned a share in a lending library or a subscription to a periodical. Both families probably purchased a yearly almanac, however, eventually selling or discarding it. Both families may have borrowed books informally. The Bixbys almost certainly did not subscribe to a newspaper, and there is only about one chance in five that the Tinkhams began subscribing to one of Windsor's weeklies late in life (after 1810). Both families may have given away printed matter before the death of the household head; neither left a will. The kinds of printed works with which the Tinkhams and Bixbys most regularly came into contact reinforced traditional values and beliefs. The two were typical Windsor District hardscrabble families during the early national period, one on an isolated farm and the other poor and living in a village. They are representative of the vast majority of families in the hardscrabble human habitat.[13]

A fifth of all hardscrabble families constituted a divergent group that kept printed matter in newer areas of knowledge in addition to the typical intensive-reading matter. The Aaron Burdow tenant farm family of Reading, worth just $195 at his death in 1830, retained nine books, including a small Bible, a six-volume edition of Scott's *Family Bible* valued at $6, an unspecified *History of New England*, and an edition of *Travels through the Interior Parts of North America, 1766–1768*, by the eighteenth-century American John Carver. The Burdow family almost certainly never owned a share in a lending library or a subscription to a periodical. They most probably did purchase a yearly almanac, however, and may have borrowed printed matter. Their chances of subscribing to a weekly newspaper were at least one in two after 1810. Aaron may have given away books before his death. The Burdow family participated in print culture more extensively than, and its reading matter differed in content from, that of the Tinkhams and Bixbys. Aaron, a free black tenant farmer, read not just to reinforce existing values but for newer forms of intellectual stimulation, as we see from the history and travel books, from the broadranging commentary of Scott's *Family Bible*, and from the family's probable reading of a newspaper. Even among this variant group of hardscrabble families, only a third retained libraries of more than six volumes each, and just two (6 percent) held shares in social libraries.[14]

The history of reading derived from family libraries has much to contribute to the study of intellectual history. The location of printed matter in the home and the physical placement of works on shelves often offer clues to intellectual affinities within and among traditions, which would not be apparent from single works or separate categories of knowledge. Even fairly small libraries were frequently divided into sacred works, schoolbooks, and secular works. The following analysis will distinguish clusters of families within each broad reading community, as well as link specific reading tastes that are seen in all five reading communities.

Hardscrabble households retained the smallest private libraries in Windsor District, with an average of under 4 volumes each and a median size of just 2 volumes. Rarely did shares in social libraries supplement these collections, and few village families could afford even to borrow from the district's two circulating libraries. In addition, very few families subscribed to a weekly newspaper prior to the late 1820s, and fewer still to a periodical (3 volumes among 655, all held by one family). Most hardscrabble families never browsed in a Windsor or Chester bookstore in their lives. While they involved themselves in the new communications environment very narrowly, at least half of all hardscrabble families did retain a library, and a somewhat larger share engaged in some regular reading. They also read chapbooks and almanacs, especially two bestsellers that sustained traditional agricultural society, Robert Thomas's *Farmer's Almanac* and Truman Abell's *New England Farmer's Diary and Almanac*.[15]

Table 9–1: Hardscrabble Family Libraries

Type of Library	Number of Libraries	Percent of Hardscrabble Libraries	Percent of All Libraries of this Type	Number of Vols.*	Percent of Hardscrabble Volumes
Sacred Intensive	59	32	63	78	12
Mixed Intensive	90	49	69	289	44
Sacred Combined (Intensive/ Extensive)	8	5	50	31	5
Mixed Extensive	26	14	23	257 + 2s	39
Total	183	100%	41%	655 + 2s	100%

*s = shares in lending libraries

Nearly two-fifths[16] of hardscrabble families (table 9–1, types 1 and 3) retained only sacred reading matter, for the most part Calvinist but tinged with moderate Arminianism. Most of these families retained only religious reading matter of the most traditional kind: Bibles (fifty-eight volumes) and hymnals and psalm books (seventeen). Repeatedly used, these books reinforced traditional values and beliefs about vital piety and morality. All three types of printed matter served as supplements to preaching and singing, lending a "warming and purifying" spirit to public and private devotional practice. Excepting a rural almanac and perhaps an occasional chapbook, neither secular works nor contemporary theological works of any sort cluttered the vision of salvation in families with religious intensive libraries, and among whom writing implements were very scarce (two families, or 3 percent had them).

A second small group of eight families (none that of a deacon or minister) also retained only religious reading matter, but each kept at least one or two works in theology and devotional texts in addition to hymnals, psalm books, and Bibles. Approximating the backcountry denominational balance, old-line Calvinist, Universalist, and Methodist theological positions informed most of these treatises and collections of sermons. Solid Calvinism was the most active tradition of theological opinion, and even Universalist works were of the most conservative variety, hewing most closely to Calvinist tenets (favored by the Restorationist wing within the denomination). The centrality of vital piety was the dominant theme. Both post- and especially premillennialism marked many of these works. Other Enlightenment theological issues were not at all in evidence.

Fully half of all hardscrabble families retained about the same numbers and range of Bibles, hymnals, and psalm books as the first group of sacred readers but, not unlike our second group, added elementary biblical commentary, sermons, theology, and devotional manuals. Further expansion of intellectual interests first revealed itself in a modest cluster of mainly practical secular works. The largest group were district-level schoolbooks (twenty-seven); few texts known to have been used at local academies or colleges were retained. Several district schoolbooks, especially arithmetics, were purchased for farmstead use, as was common practice in the area. Other works included dictionaries (twelve); geographies and gazetteers (six); and a few miscellaneous secular songbooks and manuals. Six of the twelve authors most popular among all district libraries accounted for a large share of basic farmstead works: Webster's *Speller*, arithmetics by Nicholas Pike and Daniel Adams, Lindley Murray's readers, William Perry's *Royal Standard English Dictionary*, and Jedidiah Morse's various geographies and *American Gazetteer*. Each appeared in no fewer than fourteen (3.5 percent) and as many as forty-five collections (11 percent) throughout Windsor District (see table 2–1 throughout).[17]

Despite their poverty and isolation, modest inquisitiveness began to spread even among Windsor District's least advantaged families. Half of all hardscrabble families mixed a small group of elementary but nonetheless secular texts and also almanacs with more typical sacred reading matter. Their reading experience offers immensely important clues to the initial stage of expanding intellectual curiosity once ordinary families sustained the habit of reading. What kinds of intellectual interests were germinating in farming and grazing homesteads from Weston to Plymouth Kingdom and Reading? Just two types. A tiny share of families purchased no secular works but moved beyond intensive-reading matter by delving straight and solely into theology and sermon literature, while expanding their intensive-reading fare through devotional works. Most families in this group first expanded their reading interests by tasting secular fruit, however. In doing so they favored practical knowledge, including mathematics, market exchange, store accounts, and finance, as well as geography, elementary political economy, societal development, and world political structures (for example, Pike, Adams, and Morse). In addition, these families also began to take interest in an abbreviated version of the main themes in Western tradition: Anglo-American perspectives on the wisdom of the ages (Murray). Schoolbooks and other utilitarian works for home learning held great importance in shaping *mentalités*; they helped prepare a seedbed in which further interests germinated as reading occurred more regularly.

The three clusters of hardscrabble families described above displayed severely restricted intellectual interests overall. Nevertheless, an intellectual awakening was beginning to manifest itself in the lives of many families in limited-access areas of the new communications environment, and in other poor families. Moreover, a final cluster of hardscrabble families, a seventh of the total, had taken a critical second step in broadening their intellectual horizons. Mixed extensive libraries were found in a minority of the homes least touched by new developments in Windsor District commerce and culture through 1830, indicating that even in this group some were paying attention to the emerging new order of rural life. These few hardscrabble families maintained considerably larger collections, averaging ten volumes each, than all others living in similar straitened circumstances. They chose both religious and secular texts, though the latter dominated. They were able, moreover, to break free of the severe limitations placed on hardscrabble families by economic, geographical, and cultural circumstances, and to peruse more recent and varied reading matter in newer reading styles.

The hardscrabble families who moved beyond these intellectual constraints were not the wealthier families; rather they were concentrated by occupation and community setting. Artisan families living in hinterland hamlets (five of six artisan families) dominated those with the greatest amount and variety of serious reading matter about the local and distant contemporary world. They were joined by a few other families in a scattering of occupations, nearly all of whom lived in villages and hamlets. Accordingly, hamlet and village residence, hence optimal location in the communications network, and especially artisan work experience, encouraged richer, more diverse intellectual interests.

Calvinist, Universalist, and Methodist theological opinion dominated among this cluster of hardscrabble families as it did in the earlier group. Moreover, the share of families with devotional treatises was now much higher, approaching 40 percent. Each work was a classic devotional manual. Baxter, Willison, Flavel, Law, Doddridge, and Hervey, all British, were the most popular authors in this most diversified area of intensive reading. Among schoolbooks the authors favored by the majority dominated, but there was stiffer competition in readers. Several families replaced traditionally all-British introductions to the Western intellectual tradition with a newer type of reader including American selections. Starting with schoolbook readers, American nationalism spread through many fields of knowledge, supplementing the British view of the world.

Four large subject areas dominated secular reading: modern literature (seventeen volumes); history, travels, and military affairs (seventeen); "practical" affairs of political economy, including politics and government, law, and geography (ten); and works about the youth and adulthood stages of life (seven). Poetry and novels were the favorites in modern literature. Just two of the seventeen volumes were American authored, plus a volume of the *Rural Magazine*, which was edited by Vermonter Samuel Williams and printed at nearby Rutland. While the poetry books were almost all fairly mild eighteenth century and early Romantic British works, the novels were wild Gothic and Romantic tales, including Vulpius's *Rinald Rinaldini* and Trenck's racy adventures of a Prussian soldier. In their special role as forerunners of "modern" attitudes to knowledge, artisan families retained all hardscrabble habitat texts in literature. History, travels, and military affairs were evenly split in subject matter between America and Britain or Europe, and included several works about Vermont.

A constant theme in books and pamphlets about America was an aggressive patriotism which combined strident nationalism with praise for military life and heroism as exemplified by George Washington and Richard Henry Lee. Native American life also drew considerable attention in histories and travel accounts. Works in political economy included the usual commercially oriented works of Jedidiah Morse plus several volumes about Vermont law and political issues. Treatises on personality development amounted to practical guides to specified life stages.

In their emerging secular awakening, this minority of hardscrabble families exhibited concern with several traditions and themes to do with human and natural existence. These rested comfortably alongside Protestant visions of salvation; science and religion were still perceived as staunch allies by all but a few Windsor District families. Cosmopolitanism was a fundamental cultural stance of the era; hence the large majority of works retained were written by British authors from English and Scottish perspectives. Most works written by Americans expressed fervent patriotism, warm nationalism, and a tradition of fierce heroism in battle. Several of the British works also supported the martial spirit. The American-British cultural alliance was as uneasy yet persistent as the political one.

Increasingly, families read both works of the imagination and works in the new "spirit of fact." These parallel trends were among the most consequential of the age throughout the North Atlantic and crossed several subject areas. One category expressed fascination with the secular supernatural world of spirits, forces, and oddities of many kinds. In an agricultural society marked by so many regular and familiar rhythms, anything truly unusual commanded rapt attention. Rural newspaper editors filled their weeklies with fantastic beings and occurrences, all distractions from a life with too few thrashing monsters and too many utterly silent trees.

The rural imagination also craved support for a version of Jeffersonian republicanism that opposed many of the social effects of commercial life. Among this group of hardscrabble families, luxury and vice of a sort they associated with the city of London were perceived as leading villains. As Robert Mudie put it in *Babylon the Great*, London had become "the metropolis of the world . . . foremost and without a rival in every means of aggrandizement and enjoyment, and also of neglect and misery."[18]

It is especially noteworthy that the reading habits of most hardscrabble families inhabiting villages and hamlets differed little from those of people living on fairly isolated farmsteads. A particular social or geographical setting did not necessarily dictate lifestyle. Families were not shaped passively by one set of outward life circumstances. They were formed by a complex array of cultural as well as material influences, including inquisitiveness and intellectual passion. In their purchases of printed matter, most hardscrabble families, poor and/or isolated, remained oblivious to many of the intellectual as well as the material changes enveloping them. They adhered to a centuries-old intellectual heritage and so focused on continuity in the vortex of change. The overwhelming majority of hardscrabble families doggedly remained interested primarily in the afterlife, their collective mental reservoir remained deep and rich in sacred information and values. Three-quarters owned a Bible, and they retained secular works only very selectively. Sacred reading amounted to just a quarter of all works culturewide; it formed two-thirds of hardscrabble families' reading matter.

By adding the small group of families who developed an exclusive interest in current religious and theological trends we raise to about a fifth the share of hardscrabble families who were expanding beyond intensive reading matter. The other four-fifths held to one course, many of them purchasing books which confirmed their traditional sacred values. Only a few families (just one artisan family) living in Windsor and Chester villages, who owned less than $700 at inventory, took advantage of the wealth of printed matter surrounding them. We must, therefore, be more precise about the argument that even people who could not read assimilated print culture's values because they shared its environment. It would be false to assume that print inevitably dominated an environment once it entered it. Hardscrabble village households demonstrate that even many families engaging in reading were only minimally, if at all, shaped by their immediate environment.[19]

One of the central organizing themes of intellectual life in northwestern New England in 1780–1835 was the relationship between permanence and accelerating change. Hardscrabble families chiefly read works that stressed permanence and eternity. They responded to an array of intellectual traditions that seems narrow compared with the general, culturewide configuration. Oral culture, of great significance throughout Windsor District, particularly buttressed the dominant hardscrabble perspective. Life in the hardscrabble human habitat revolved about family and kin, neighborhood-changing works, religious meetings, and township public affairs. Neighboring and visiting were doubly important to people who lived outside villages, because of the isolation of farming and grazing areas nestled in the foothills of the Green Mountains, because cooperation among neighbors was critical to survival, and because conditions for travel were poor during parts of the year. In the rhythms of daily existence, village-dwelling hardscrabble families may well have been indirectly shaped by the broad religious, economic, political, and cultural factors altering their institutional infrastructure. Still, although literally they lived amid printing offices, newspapers, bookstores, lending libraries, post offices, general stores, and, by the 1820s, public lectures and discussion groups, most hardscrabble families remained too poor to participate very actively. We do not yet know which influences in this new communications environment may have begun to reshape their perceptions.

Some readers may well wonder whether economic, occupational, transportation, communication, and geographical factors could truly limit assimilation of newer cultural trends. The hardscrabble human habitat demonstrates irrefutably that they could do so. As Robert Darnton reminds us, print culture traveled the same roads and waterways as shoes, clocks, and iron plows. In hardscrabble mountain communities, people remained isolated long after the "pioneer" stage had passed. Recalling an incident from the mid-1820s, Horace Hubbard of Springfield, Vermont, noted that "without canals or railroads, with imperfect roads across our mountains, transportation was anything but satisfactory." One day "a man came from one of the mountain towns for rye. He said his children had been without bread for days." Material and cultural conditions severely limited cultural participation in the more rigorous environs of Windsor District.

The Tinkham artisan family living in Windsor village, the Bixby yeoman farm family of Ludlow, and the Burdow tenant farm family of Reading were all typical hardscrabble families. These were not illiterate families; they were families of readers. Yet because they were struggling, they were severely constricted in their ability to participate in the expansion of print culture. When survival and livelihood demanded intensive daily labor, the progress of knowledge slowed to a plodding walk. The limitations under which hardscrabble families lived and worked usually stifled the desire for newer forms of knowledge and the ideal of intellectual currency. But for them and for self-sufficient farmstead families, mending sometimes failed. When it did, rebirth and radical change came to be perceived as the true path to holiness. The cultural and material conditions of the hardscrabble and self-sufficient farmstead human habitats encouraged many to follow Mormonism, the Millerites, and many other radical religious movements of the day [20]

Cultural Life in the Self-Sufficient Farmstead Human Habitat

Self-sufficient farmstead families inhabited the second largest and second most populous living situation in Windsor District. It encompassed agricultural areas in four townships beyond Windsor and Chester but east of the mountains: Weathersfield and Springfield, river valley communities mixing farming and manufacturing; Cavendish, an important crossroads community connecting the river valley with the hill townships to the north and west; and tiny Baltimore. Farm families in these townships were neither particularly isolated geographically, as were families in the foothills of the Green Mountains, nor advantaged, as were their cousins living just outside Windsor and Chester villages. Self-sufficient farmstead families shared the middling sort of agricultural life they often read about.[21]

Rodney Loehr has aptly characterized economic life among self-sufficient farmstead families in this living situation:

> It appears quite likely that the general run of farmers constantly sought and produced for a market which they found in the towns, the local storekeepers, or various kinds of ambulating merchants. In turn the storekeepers found a market among the farmers for goods from the outside world. . . . There was specialization of endeavor. The storekeepers made [it] possible. . . . If we think of self-sufficiency as a relative matter and cease dealing in absolutes, we shall be on much safer ground.

Self-sufficient farmstead families ranged from the lower middle class up to the wealthiest farmers. Outright ownership was frequent, but so too were mortgages. A fifth of all families were tenants. Farmers accounted for three-quarters of all families, supplemented by professional families and families in commerce and trade (10 percent each), and a small share of manufacturing, artisan, and semiskilled laborer households (9 percent), almost all of whom also farmed on a regular basis. Weathersfield, Springfield, and Cavendish together contained much of the best soil in Windsor District. By 1810 most of the homesteaders in these areas were selling part of their farm production in the local markets. In return, they purchased an ever broader range of goods, including printed items and stationery.[22]

Agricultural life for self-sufficient farmstead families was not the simple independent existence of the agrarian myth. Interdependence, symbolized in "changing works," shaped agricultural existence, creating a life-sustaining web of localized social relationships. Farm life was regulated, but its clock kept agricultural time, tracking the cycle of the seasons. Winter and early spring were spent chopping wood and logging, storing up the next winter's supply of fuel and building materials. March and April were devoted to boiling sap for maple sugar and tool repairs. May and June saw harrowing, plowing, sowing, manuring, and hoeing, while July and August were devoted to tending and haying. Harvesting, then trading and selling other field and garden crops, and canning filled the fall, followed by care for special livestock and more repair of buildings, roads, machinery, and tools. Such was the annual routine of Alvah Carp's Chelsea family, in northern Windsor County, for example.[23]

Distance from a major central village meant that all purchase of recently printed and extensive-reading books, pamphlets, and periodicals was quite limited among self-sufficient farmstead families. Borrowing from a social, moral, encyclopedia, or circulating library also proved difficult. Seventy percent of families known to have subscribed to a lending library resided in Windsor and Chester townships, and fortunate farmstead families were three times as likely

Lovejoy Broad Brook Farm in winter in South Royalton, Vermont. Courtesy, Vermont Historical Society.

Families in Self-sufficient Farmstead areas shared a middling station: neither particularly isolated geographically nor advantaged by easy access to villages with bookstores.

to participate as self-sufficient farmstead families. Residents of these two farming habitats varied greatly in their cultural participation. Lifelong learning was growing, yet involvement remained constricted and, through 1815, heavily weighted toward traditional varieties of knowledge and reading styles. Until about 1815, relatively few self-sufficient farmstead families participated in the broader transatlantic processes of change in commerce and culture.[24]

Two families indicate the variety of cultural life in the self-sufficient farmstead reading community. Nicholas Williams's gentleman farmer family, worth $3,302 at inventory in 1813, owned four plots of land, including a 162-acre homestead. Family members engaged in considerable cloth spinning and weaving, and owned several looms and wheels and seventeen spools. Various tools and implements, including awls, a spike, a gimlet (used to bore holes), bellows and irons suggested some artisan activity. Williams was chiefly known in the public sphere for his active role in forming a local Springfield Baptist society. The family's six-volume sacred intensive collection included the typical Bible; a psalm book; two hymn books; and two "old books." The Williamses almost surely purchased an almanac regularly and probably subscribed to a newspaper as well.[25]

In contrast, the 126-acre artisan homestead of James Martin, Jr., worth a substantial $6,457 at James's death in 1789, included a house, a barn, and several outhouses and other buildings. Extensive notes in the Martins' inventory attested to a lively casket-making business. Many tools and implements of the trade remained, including fourteen-and-a-half dozen casket buttons, other paraphernalia, thread and thimbles for sewing, nine handkerchiefs, and 118 darning needles. Martin himself was a leading local political figure, serving as Springfield selectman in 1778 and from 1781 until his death.

The Martins' rich and varied mixed extensive family library numbered fifteen volumes, a very substantial collection for the 1780s. No Bible was present, though one may have been owned by James's wife or given away before James's death. There were, however, three devotional treatises, including Boston's *Human Nature*, Giles Firman's *The Real Christian*, and Eden Burroughs's *The Profession and Practice of Christians*; and a single volume of theology. Education was represented by George Fisher's *The Instructor: or The Young Man's Best Companion*, a favorite for self-instruction in artisan families. The other ten volumes were all popular extensive reading works. Geography was comprehensively treated in William Guthrie's two-volume *New Geographical, Historical, and Commercial Grammar*. History and politics maintained a decidedly sober Enlightenment perspective in Abbe Raynal's *Opinions on the Revolution in America*, and a Christian Enlightenment tinge in Robertson's *History of Scotland*. The Websters' basic manual, *The Clerk's Magazine*, and an unspecified work served the family's needs in law. More imaginative reading was offered by John Hawkesworth's two-volume *A New Voyage Round the World . . . Performed by Captain John Cook* and by single works in literature (Allen Ramsay's *Poems*) and philosophy (a copy of the Free Mason *Constitutions*). Writing paraphernalia included two desks, a blank book, and a pocket book usually used to record business transactions. Diversity and intellectual curiosity were the overall themes of the Martin family library, whose thirteen works represented six fields. Enlightenment tastes in secular reading balanced a strong emphasis on vital piety in religious works.[26]

Self-sufficient farmstead reading patterns were quite varied. About a fourth of the libraries were small, elementary, and limited to intensive sacred reading matter; another fifth, larger but still dominated by intensive works, maintained a balance of sacred and secular works. A small majority of these families participated more broadly in the North Atlantic Republic of Letters. Overall, self-sufficient farmstead family libraries were the second smallest in size (averaging 9.4 volumes, with a median size of 5 volumes). On all measures, reading in self-sufficient farmstead families was sharply lower than in all three fuller-access living situations. Although they held 22 percent of the wealth, these

Table 9–2: Self-Sufficient Farmstead Family Libraries

Type of Library	Number of Libraries	Percent of Self-Sufficient Farmstead Libraries	Number of Volumes[*]	Percent of Self-Sufficient Farmstead Volumes	Average Volumes Per Library
Sacred Intensive	18	26	25	4	1
Mixed Intensive	14	20	89	14	6
Sacred Combined Intensive/ Extensive)	1	2	2	——	2
Mixed Extensive	29	42	381+3s	59	13
Professional	7	10	153	23	22
a. Theological	3	——	56	——	19
b. Medical	2	——	56	——	28
c. Legal	2	——	41	——	21
Total	69	100%	650+3s	100%	9.4

[*]s=shares in lending libraries

families retained just 12 percent of all volumes, in 17 percent of the libraries. Wealth was overpowered by partial access in the new communications environment. Consequently, a third of the libraries were tiny (one to three volumes); and another third were small to medium size (three to nine volumes). Yet whereas just 6 percent of hardscrabble libraries were substantial (ten or more volumes), 29 percent of self-sufficient farmstead libraries were. Differences among townships were minimal.[27]

Among self-sufficient farmstead families as elsewhere in Windsor District, oral communication dominated daily life. It helped shape, and was in turn shaped by, printed matter. Music and dance were very strong cultural interests among hinterland farm families.[28] The growing habit of reading was founded on extremely high literacy rates for both males and females. Letter writing also increased after the turn of the century, and newspaper subscriptions rose significantly between 1810 and 1815. The parallel between increasing newspaper reading and rising female literacy rates is striking and warrants further research; male rates had remained constant for the previous two decades. Participation in cultural institutions and organizations that directly benefited from an expanding habit of reading grew, but at a modest clip. Self-sufficient farmstead families rarely traveled to Chester or Windsor village for a discussion, club meeting, lyceum lecture, play, musical performance, or lecture.[29]

As table 9–2 shows, three-fifths of all self-sufficient farmstead families maintained a private library, meaning that approximately 70 percent of them engaged in some regular reading. The most striking characteristic of their collections is the small average size and the compactness of the intellectual interests represented. Among sixty-nine families with libraries, none retained a major secular library; moreoever, professional family collections were only a third as large as the district average for these occupations. Compared with the hardscrabble living situation, however, cultural participation was increasing among self-sufficient farmstead families: half retained mixed extensive libraries containing both sacred and secular extensive reading matter. This marks the first critical shift in collective intellectual interests within Windsor District. Intellectual horizons were widening beyond the traditional sacred world view so dominant among hardscrabble families. Utilitarian work-related reading, moral improvement, and more fanciful reading were all on the rise.

Library size and content varied with work experience. Reading horizons expanded only modestly among yeoman and tenant farm families, who tended to retain small collections of one to nine volumes, with almost no works of contemporary interest, practical or imaginative. None owned a lending library share. Gentleman farm families frequently owned larger, more varied collections. Commerce and trading families owned both larger and smaller libraries. The strongest link between work and reading habits, however, was that which connected artisan and manufacturing families to broad-based intellectual interests.

Nearly half of self-sufficient farmstead families, continuing patterns found in hardscrabble family reading, maintained minimal interest in intellectual traditions beyond Calvinist and conservative evangelical Christianity and traditional secular knowledge. A quarter of all self-sufficient farmstead families with libraries held exclusively sacred works. These families each retained a Bible (often a large, elaborate one), but almost no other reading matter. These families, whether lower middle class or very wealthy, remained most comfortable with a wholly sacred version of the world. Another fifth of the families reflected the same trend but owned a few more hymnals, psalm and prayer books, plus district school texts and dictionaries. The major purpose of reading in these two clusters of families was to reinforce longstanding sacred and secular values rather than to learn about distant lands or new dimensions of life. Not all self-sufficient farmstead families with the most tradition-bound libraries were uninvolved with changes in Windsor District, but where they were involved, such interests had not yet affected deep-seated family reading habits.

A small majority of all self-sufficient farmstead families had libraries averaging fifteen volumes each (twenty-two volumes among professional families and thirteen otherwise), and engaged in both secular and religious extensive reading. Expansion of intellectual interests into more current topics centered on theology and devotional works among sacred reading, and law, geography, and history among secular works. The tastes of professional families, too, were

Mentalités: Intellectual Reservoirs

shaped by their material and cultural circumstances; their family reading had far more in common with that of their neighbors than with that of professional families living in Windsor or Chester townships. Professional family reading encompassed the interests just discussed and added three newer areas: American politics, secular music, and stage-of-life works.

Farming families who lived at some distance from a village with a bookstore continued to manifest only limited intellectual curiosity in book, pamphlet, and periodical reading. Learning about novels and works in many other fields, and then obtaining them to read, remained difficult, though considerably less so than for hardscrabble families. The small majority of the most intellectually active self-sufficient farmstead families supplemented their private library holdings with an annual almanac, and by 1810 about half subscribed to a newspaper. Just over a tenth retained a share in a local lending library after 1800. Some of these families may have read in areas of knowledge about which books could not be purchased readily. Size of libraries was directly related to connections to village life, increasing with greater participation in commercial exchange. The smallest libraries were among tenant farm families (three volumes per library), followed by yeoman (nine) and gentleman farmer (twelve). Considerably larger collections were owned by manufacturing, professional, and commerce and trading families (twenty-one to twenty-two volumes on average). The largest libraries—also those that most consistently reflected newer strands of thought—again belonged to artisan families (thirty-six volumes per collection), among whom intellectual currency was frequently an ideal.

Among the small majority of self-sufficient farmstead families with secular extensive reading interests, the Bible remained by far the most frequently retained work (86 percent). More than half of these families also owned a psalm book or hymnal. Devotional manuals—all but one written by a British author—were also a regular item of family reading. There were two general types: (1) warmer evangelical treatises centering on the need for conversion and advocating the "Evangelical scheme of justification," and (2) cooler Arminian-inspired works drawn from the sacramental tradition. Vital piety was the goal of both sets of works.[30] Church history, formal theological treatises, and sermons stood alongside biblical commentaries and concordances. Church history and biography reflected up-to-date (post-1760) versions of conservative theological views. The first major expansion of theological reading was represented by careful syntheses of previous knowledge. The most favored synopses stressed Calvinist and conservative evangelical theological portions. More concrete signs of a widespread Windsor District theological revolt, in full swing by 1810, were a strong minority of treatises advocating Baptist, Methodist, and Universalist theological positions and denominational affairs. In general, however, self-sufficient farmstead families favored old wine in new bottles.

Nearly three-fifths of more actively reading self-sufficient farmstead families maintained at least one schoolbook. American readers, works on public speaking, and academy-level texts also appreared frequently in these collections. Secular reading was anchored in law, geography, and history. A quarter of all families (including just two families of lawyers) kept basic law manuals. The Websters' *Clerk's Magazine* and Francis Clerke's similar *The Young Clerk's Companion* were the most popular "plain and practical" guides to procedures and forms.[31] Manuals and compilations also dominated geography reading: popular were those of Morse and Jacob Cummings' comprehensive *Introduction to Ancient and Modern Geography*. Half of all families retained at least one geography book. In an area closely related in contemporary thought, history reading matter, retained in just over a third of these families, was broad and philosophical. Conservative Enlightenment works emphasizing Christian rationalism predominated, including Robertson's various histories, Samuel Williams's *Natural and Civil History of Vermont*, Isaac Eddy's *Chronology*, and Daniel Sanders's *History of the Indian Wars*. Works setting forth alternatives to mainstream American self-images were also popular, e.g., Abbe Raynal's sobering assessment of the new nation's prospects in *The Revolution in America*. Works in eleven other areas of knowledge were scattered through these thirty-six libraries. The largest single group of self-sufficient farmstead families, those retaining extensive secular reading matter, collectively focused on issues of contemporary life and on more purely imaginative interests.

When a family participated in a lending library, its reading interests usually expanded substantially. Worth nearly $3,400 at inventory, Daniel Mason's successful gentleman farmer family worked a two-hundred-acre plot of land and engaged in commercial agriculture and home manufacturing. This ten-person family retained nine volumes at inventory. Only two were specified: a Bible and a New Testament. During the years 1816–22 and 1828–30, first Mason and then his widow borrowed works thirty-seven times (one work at a time, each being kept from two to eight weeks). A book from the Cavendish Social Library could be found in their farmhouse one of every two weeks during the six-year period of 1816–22. History accounted for two-thirds of all works that the Masons charged out. They especially enjoyed Enlightenment Christian history; they borrowed two works by Robertson and one each by Bigland, Rollin, and Samuel Williams. Several other borrowings revealed strong interest in military figures who were also powerful statesmen: Weems's *Washington*, O'Meara's *Napoleon*, and Voltaire's *Charles the Twelfth*. Other reading interests encompassed travel (Clarke), modern literature (Irving's *Sketch Book*), and theology (Buchanan's *Christian Researches in Asia*, and Ethan Smith's *View of the Hebrews*). Altogether eight secular and three religious works were read during the two periods of the most regular borrowing. Social libraries in inland townships without villages usually contained a more limited and less current selection of chapbooks, pamphlets, and periodicals than did those in village communities. Still, the lending library substantially complemented the family library.

Families retaining mixed extensive and modest professional libraries formed a solid middle rank. They differed from hardscrabble families in the larger size of their collections and in the variety of their holdings, both sacred and secular. Theology, devotional treatises, law, geography, history, and upper-level schoolbooks were far more frequent. Modern literature was not, partly because of the smaller number of artisan families, who were especially likely to choose novels, poetry, and plays. Reading in the self-sufficient farmstead family was not distinguished by works expressing current, challenging ideas. Several of the daily life interests prevalent in the hardscrabble living situation predominated here: family and kin relations, neighborhood and township affairs, and the health of the economic locale. For many self-sufficient farmstead families everyday life remained dominated by oral discourse, singing, dance, and the visual arts. Only gradually did more regular reading expand intellectual interests. Basic manuals, general synthetic overviews, histories, and biographies of renowned figures dominated both secular and sacred reading. Most self-sufficient farmstead family libraries continued to embody the more traditional Anglo-American versions of the wisdom of the ages. As family reading expanded, earlier Augustan perspectives for the most part continued to prevail. Religion and farming were the centers of daily life; Christianity determined the vision of the good life. For most self-sufficient farmstead families, an eternity in heaven was the primary life goal—the exclusive goal for some.[32]

The pace of the agrarian cycle was directly reflected in these families' reading habits. They favored many books which had been read for 150 years throughout the rural English-speaking world. Especially after 1800, however, as roads, stores, and post offices brought the commercial world of the villages and growing hamlets closer to these homesteads, half of all self-sufficient farmstead families displayed at least some interest in newer intellectual currents. Reading helped these families adapt to change by instilling a greater sense of the possibilities and dangers posed by an ever more connected world. While their ability to participate in the new communications environment remained limited through 1830, some families in the self-sufficient farmstead reading community did manage to explore new ideas abroad in the early nineteenth century.

Sacred reading among self-sufficient farmstead families was similar in most respects to that in the hardscrabble living situation. Only interest in premillennialism was noticeably less. However, the most important text, the Bible, was now frequently supplemented by commentaries. As the foundation of Windsor District cultural life, the Bible was earnestly studied in the Upper Valley. It is no wonder that Elias and Joseph Smith, William Miller, Orestes Brownson, Isaac Bullard, and so many other wanderers of the middle third of the century were products of hardscrabble and self-sufficient farmstead human habitats. One response to the Enlightenment's challenge to the Bible's authority and validity was the decision that all previous interpretations had been flawed. Several other kinds of religious works, including prayer books, devotional texts, histories of Protestantism and of religion generally, outlines of Christian morality, various denominational perspectives on theology, and sacred music, served to check more radical reinterpretations. Nearly all uses of printed matter in the religious area reinforced traditional Christian views of heaven and earth.

Apart from schoolbooks and dictionaries, sacred works continued to outnumber secular offerings in this reading community. Secular knowledge was taking hold, however, in breadth and depth of interest. Seven intellectual traditions, each involving more than one field of knowledge, rose to prominence in secular reading. Six had first arisen among a small minority of hardscrabble families. First was the whole area of competing loyalties and allegiances beyond the local world of Windsor District. Library holdings attested to moderate concern with Vermont affairs, as seen in Williams's *Natural and Civil History*, Russell's history of the Vermont state prison, various maps of Vermont, and several collections of *Laws and Statutes*. Loyalty to the American nation was widespread, as evidenced by broad concern with republicanism, nationalism, patriotism, and military valor. A broader allegiance to the North Atlantic world, especially Britain, was affirmed in nearly all readers, geographies, dictionaries, biographies, travel accounts, and works on politics and history.

A second key theme in reading matter was the Enlightenment. Scottish Common Sense philosophy was widely assimilated through Robertson, Raynal (rather than Buffon), and Sanders; Blair and Walker in their rhetoric texts; and Bigland, Williams, Rollin, and Isaac Eddy among more conservative historians. These works stressed Christian nationalism, environmentalism, and the triumph of reason and civilization over savagism.[33]

Practicality and usefulness, a third theme, leaned toward quantitative assessments. The spirit of fact was gaining prominence, along with a passion for calculation and "mensuration." Signs abounded in Fisher's *Instructor* and other educational works, and in geographies, gazetteers, maps, and atlases, for example.[34] A fourth, related theme was interest in science, medicine, technology, and allied trades.[35] Rationality and minute attention to detail were also associated with a fifth theme, conceptions of the life cycle and stages of life. Emotional life—the control of the passions—was the subject of parts of Blair's and Walker's popular rhetorics. Concern with the problems of character in adulthood also remained prominent.[36]

A sixth central theme was Romanticism, which often appeared as an extension of the Enlightenment's rationality into new areas of inquiry. Relevant works included Gessner's *Death of Abel* and Irving's *Sketch Book* in modern literature, several travel accounts, and biographies of Napoleon. A seventh and final major theme, new among self-sufficient farmstead families, was a growing attention to the bustling world of commerce, trade, city life, and entrepreneurial values.[37]

Expansion in reading tastes was a complicated phenomenon. Within each specific area of knowledge, reading interests did not grow steadily or uniformly as cultural participation increased. The learning associated with sacred reading remained strong among self-sufficient farmstead families, while gradual expansion of secular reading resulted in a complex mix of intellectual continuity and change. A development of the greatest importance occurred first among these families: the process of keeping up with newer versions of intellectual traditions through manuals and synopses. It is no accident that many works consolidating information and opinion in a broad subject area were written by Americans. This was the first, crucial step in the eventual spread of nineteenth-century thought deep into the countryside. On this basis the ideal of intellectual currency could be built later. Intellectual ferment was sustained in half of all self-sufficient farmstead families, whose overall religious and secular reading tastes were becoming recognizably modern.

Cultural Life in the Self-Sufficient Hamlet Human Habitat

The newest and most volatile Upper Valley settlement form was the unincorporated hamlet. Hamlet dwellers often hoped, in the long line of Vermont schemes, that they were part of a village that would burgeon in the wilderness. A step beyond the occasional random evolution of businesses and homes at countryside crossroads, hamlets, usually encompassing between fifteen and twenty-five households (75 and 150 residents), were more organized intersections of agriculture, commerce and communications. Thirteen surprisingly competitive such hamlets emerged in Windsor District through 1830. A choice location was essential for growth, hence, for every hamlet successful in 1830 there was another that had failed to thrive. While smallest in population, the self-sufficient hamlet human habitat spread farthest in Windsor District, emerging between 1800 and 1825 on main roads, often around a few mill sites, in nearly every township. Midway in social development between farmsteads and villages, hamlets were thriving by 1815 at West Windsor, Cavendish, Proctorsville, Ludlow Center, and Plymouth Union. Shortly thereafter Reading Center, South Reading, and Felchville sprouted, then Simonsville, Peasville, Weston Center, and Hammondsville. No Windsor District hamlet is known to have sustained a bookstore before 1830.[38]

Approximately two-thirds of all self-sufficient hamlet families retained family libraries. Because many hamlets were late in forming, the inventories span a shorter time period, 1800–1830. Sixteen family collections survived in our study group, averaging 14 volumes each and with a median size of 7.5 volumes. Family reading was greatly supplemented by borrowing from five hamlet lending libraries that were founded before 1830. The proportion of hamlet families with shares was double that among self-sufficient farmstead families, one in every five households and at least one in four in Reading, West Windsor, Cavendish, Andover, and Weston townships by 1820.

Who were these people? Families engaged in commerce and trade formed the largest group (about 40 percent), followed by artisan, manufacturing, and professional families (about a fifth each). This composition accords with the occupational picture of hamlets throughout the Northeast that Lemon, Prude, and Wallace have delineated. Half of all self-sufficient hamlet families engaged in some regular farming. In wealth, self-sufficient hamlet families were split almost evenly between lower-middle- and middle-class families on the one hand, and upper-middle-class ones on the other.[39]

Improved roads led to the establishment of several hamlets. Opening of a post office, which occurred regularly in hamlets between 1808 and 1830, was the most visible sign of a hamlet's economic stability. Hamlet settlers were moving away from poverty, with its material and cultural isolation. Average wealth was five times higher than for hardscrabble households.

Hamlet economic stability was paralleled by spreading cultural participation. Nearly three-fifths of all families engaged in extensive reading, and 75 percent kept five or more volumes, as opposed to 20 percent and 50 percent in the hardscrabble and self-sufficient farm reading communities, respectively. After about 1805, subscriptions to weekly newspapers and (among the fairly wealthy) to periodicals became more numerous, as did shares in lending libraries. Academies were established at Cavendish and later at Ludlow. Peddlers and itinerant authors began to visit more often, competing with and supplementing the reading stock of local general stores. These institutions collectively increased the range of available reading matter and extended cultural participation, often deep into the hinterland of Windsor District.[40]

Self-sufficient hamlets were moving toward the order of life characteristic of fully developed villages and their nearby farmsteads. The range of hamlet dwellers' wealth and the specialization of its occupational structure carried over from work into new realms of life, including the buying and borrowing of reading matter. Traditional oral expression was still primary, but print culture commanded an increasing share of attention. Literacy rates were extraordinarily high compared with those elsewhere in the West. Many self-sufficient hamlet families were active participants in local and area public life, and much of their interest flowed from more active reading about contemporary life in other parts of the transatlantic world.[41]

The most marked change in cultural participation was a dramatic increase

View of Cavendish, Vermont, w.c., c.1825. Anonymous. Courtesy, Public Library, Richfield Springs, N.Y.

Hamlets such as Cavendish were small but bustling settlements in transition between farmstead and village life. Many hamlet dwellers, imbued with entrepreneurial spirit, made full use of their heightened access to printed matter. Cavendish residents maintained a lending library and supported regular circulation of area newspapers.

in the attention paid to extensive-reading works (68 percent versus 21 percent and 45 percent in hardscrabble and self-sufficient farm human habitats). For the first time, modern literature—especially novels and poetry—was prominent among families that read actively; and interest intensified in personality development and the stages of life; geography, history, and politics; newer trends in theology and devotion; and newer professional works in law and medicine. Hamlets were the social, economic, and cultural focal points for the surrounding farming and grazing areas, bustling environments with a post office, general store, district school, and perhaps even a meetinghouse. In Glenn T. Trewartha's words, hamlets were "the first hint of thickening in the settlement plasm."[42]

Two families illustrate the split personality of the self-sufficient hamlet reading community. Oliver Farwell headed a very wealthy dry goods and general store family in Reading; at his death the family had property valued at $9,038. The Farwells also owned a half-share in a potash factory, a 70-acre farm, and 450 additional acres of fine farm land. The Farwells probably purchased a yearly almanac and, since they advertised in Spooner's *Vermont Journal* regularly after 1805, undoubtedly subscribed to it. Their private library included only intensive reading (six volumes), including a Bible, a psalm book, two dictionaries, and two schoolbooks (a grammar and an arithmetic). That the Farwells kept no extensive-reading works is not unusual, despite their occupation; more than two-fifths of all families in this living situation had similar collections.[43]

In sharp contrast to the Farwell family was the Plymouth Union hamlet household of Dr. James Willis, worth $476 at inventory. That the Willis family was struggling is confirmed by the husband's small practice (he had only fifteen book accounts). The family library was substantial in size (forty-three volumes worth $15.45, 10 percent of the Willises' total personal wealth) and rich in content. Under half the titles were medical works, including some standard works and seven volumes of the leading American journal, the *Medical Repository*. John Wesley's *Primitive Physic* and Nicholas Culpeper's *English Physician*, emphasizing "natural astrology" to predict disease patterns, were more unusual items. Religion was represented by typical small and large Bibles and a prayer book. There was also a concordance to the Bible and an autobiography of the peripatetic Elias Smith. Clues to a different intellectual orientation, found in Wesley, Culpeper, and Smith, were confirmed in five decidedly occult works. These texts embodied important aspects of an earlier Elizabethan view of nature which survived despite two centuries of attacks from natural philosophy. The Willises' library was noteworthy for its strength in popular science, astrology, and "ancient wisdom," in addition to medicine. Of the thirty identifiable volumes, twenty-seven were extensive-reading works, a proportion typical of a small majority of self-sufficient hamlet families.[44]

The Farwell and Willis family libraries suggest the complexity of the interaction between wealth and participation in print culture. While the Farwells were far wealthier, they kept a narrow selection of works. And whereas the Willis family was poor, it was typical in its general level of intellectual curiosity and unusual in some of its interests.

Self-sufficient hamlet families comprise the smallest reading community in our study group.

The range of self-sufficient hamlet library types was very broad, embracing two very different kinds of families: those whose family libraries focused exclusively on older intellectual traditions and interests and those engaged with the contemporary world, particularly secular affairs. The first group retained mainly intensive reading matter, chiefly in the religious and secular traditions previously discussed; and they did not expand their interests by joining lending libraries. Their private collections were built around the Bible, supplemented by sacred and secular works—hymnals, psalm books, prayer books, and sometimes devotional works, plus schoolbooks, dictionaries, and basic farmstead manuals. Surprisingly, all but one of these families were engaged in commerce and trading. Thus cultural participation lagged far behind changes in basic

Table 9–3: Self-Sufficient Hamlet Family Libraries

Type of Library	Number of Libraries	Percent of Self-Sufficient Hamlet Libraries	Number of Volumes*	Percent of Self-Sufficient Hamlet Volumes	Average Volumes Per Library
Sacred Intensive	1	6	2	1	2
Mixed Intensive	6	37	35	15	6
Mixed Extensive	3	19	44+2s	19	15
Major Secular:					
Extensive	3	19	94+1s	41	31
Professional	3	19	54	24	18
Total	16	100%	229+3s	100%	14.3

*s = shares in lending libraries

material and cultural conditions of life among these families. Moreover, families retaining only intensive-reading works averaged $900 higher at inventory than families with more extensive library holdings. Work experience helps us distinguish between the two types of hamlet dwellers. Among families with minimal reading interests, professional, manufacturing, and artisan families were underrepresented, while families engaged in commerce and trade were overrepresented. Throughout the Upper Valley, participation in print culture by families heavily engaged in commercial exchange was either surprisingly minimal or exceedingly active.[45]

While the material circumstances of this first cluster of families were quite comfortable, and despite the fact that market exchange was prominent in their daily lives, their family reading continued in traditional sacred ways. Able to survive changes in outward conditions, this tradition's twin pillars of strength were salvation and vital piety. Customary action continued to guide daily life. When people became aware of significant change, they tried to ignore it or just stored the information away. Sometimes they resisted change.

A small majority of self-sufficient hamlet families became more intimately involved in the changing world around them. They engaged in extensive reading and proceeded a step beyond reading for intellectual consolidation and cultivated ongoing concern for one or more newer forms of knowledge directly related to contemporary life. As they did so, their private libraries grew rapidly in size and variety and became dominated by secular works. The best measure of intellectual engagement is the two-thirds share of extensive-reading works. Furthermore, three of every four volumes in these collections concerned the secular world. Most of these families in fact subscribed to a rural weekly and participated actively in one or more local or state religious, reform, political, or cultural institutions. A third of this group maintained a share in a lending library.

The intensive reading matter retained by families who were intrigued with intellectual currency remained anchored in the traditional reading fare found in the first group of families but was supplemented by larger numbers of school-books, prayer books, and devotional treatises. One sign of shifting intellectual interests was that self-sufficient hamlet families held the lowest percentage of Bibles among all Windsor District human habitats (69 percent). Great diversity and sharp differences characterized theological works, nearly all of which were current in perspective and published after 1810. Especially attractive were Universalist, Baptist, and Methodist treatises, accounting for 70 percent of theological and denominational reading; emphases on premillennialism, Calvinism, and conservative evangelicalism were in the minority. Reading interest in social reform was also on the rise. True to form, an artisan family headed by John Dodge of Andover had in its library the most unusual work, a copy of *The Koran, Commonly called the Alcoran of Mahomet*. Actually, the *Koran* was a most interesting devotional manual. The Dodges did not retain a Bible at inventory but did own a copy of a mainstream Protestant hymnal, the *Village Harmony*.[46]

Secular holdings represented both older and newer intellectual traditions. There were four sizable areas of contemporary intellectual interest: geography, history, and politics; classical writings; law and medicine (works owned by professional families and by others); and modern literature. In addition, a smaller miscellaneous group of works introduced science, secular music, philosophy, and the stages of life. Enlightenment environmentalism dictated holdings in geography and history. State and regional works (Whitelaw, Spafford, and Samuel Williams) shared attention with universal geographies and histories. Vermont Federalism dominated reading in politics. Classical writings included three basic works of the classical heroic tradition: the *Iliad* and the *Odyssey* by Homer (Pope's translations), and *Plutarch's Lives* (the Langhornes' translation). Plutarch wrote of the rise, and especially the fall, of empires "grown too fat with riches," in Gordon Wood's phrase. Professional collections in law and medicine were fairly basic, excepting Dr. James Willis's. Works in nonprofessional households emphasized prevention in medicine—Buchan's *Domestic Medicine* was the favorite compendium—and basic manuals in law.[47]

Self-sufficient hamlet families with extensive reading matter either owned a single work in modern literature (five families) or held several works each (four of the nine families). Several intellectual traditions are conspicuous among the nearly forty volumes. One centered on rural felicity and included both older and newer works: Thomson, Cowper, Beattie, Samuel Rogers, and especially Scott and Byron. Further strong interest in the British literary heritage was exemplified by Milton, Addison and Steele, John Gay, and a dozen contemporary novels. Several late-eighteenth-century American texts—those of Trumbull, Tyler, Judith Sargent Murray, John B. Hunter, and runs of two periodicals of the day—rested alongside Augustan and more recent neoclassical British works.[48] The most prevalent tradition, in terms of numbers and variety of works retained, was Romanticism.[49] Many works exhibited what we might call a republican aesthetic. Connections between commerce, luxury, vice, and virtue drew regular critical comment from Gay, Murphy, and Addison and Steele and a mixed or more positive assessment from a large number of works that spanned several fields.[50]

Secular reading interests were expanding rapidly across a widening front in 57 percent of self-sufficient hamlet families. We may identify seven leading themes. One was concern with the distant world of cities, trade, and commercial values. Many works illustrated and advocated entrepreneurial values (arithmetics, geographies, law books, and works on Masonry); several other texts openly criticized this perspective (for example, Pope, Gay, Murphy, and Aikin's *Life of Howard*). A third cluster of works discussing struggles attendant on economic and cultural expansion had as a central theme victory achieved through severe competition and strife. A related intellectual trend was interest in rational organization, planning, and bureaucracy, leading to a greater degree of order and regularity, a major goal in the new rural world. This trend was evident in law books and manuals of several kinds, in an emphasis on prevention in basic medical texts, and in works on Masonry. It was confirmed in the greater visibility of professionals within compact hamlets.[51]

Two further intellectual concerns highlighted broad traditions of thought: the Enlightenment (conservative, moderate, and especially Christian phases, in Henry May's terms) and Romanticism. Both were very widespread among families with extensive reading matter. Enlightenment thought is apparent in the prevalence of environmentalism; nationalism and patriotism—the "rising glory of America"; Christian rationalism and progress; and a search for worthy eternal principles of secular behavior, especially public virtue. Romanticism encompassed an equally varied set of intellectual preoccupations: localism and historicism; a fascination with cataclysmic change, great events, and heroism; and increasing attention to exoticism, the East, and non-Western customs generally. Interest in nature was pronounced, and detailed descriptions of natural scenery were characteristic of both Enlightenment and Romantic texts.[52]

Intensified concern with the stages of life and with problems of personality development formed a fifth theme. Greater rationalization of life stages and their distinct problems and solutions paralleled deepening concern with the role of the passions in life as opposed to acceptable emotional expression. Competing political allegiances formed a sixth major intellectual theme, here as in our previous reading communities. A seventh entailed evangelical religion's social theory, centering on the family, domesticity, and the home as both a refuge and a moral training ground for the rising generation. The presence in one library of an alternative tradition of medicine and science that recalled medieval Elizabethan cosmology—*In the Shadows of the Enlightenment*, as Herbert Leventhal described it—and in another of *The Koran*, are intriguing indications of growing cultural diversity.[53]

Another social and cultural development that had considerable impact in Windsor District as a whole first becomes prominent in relation to self-sufficient hamlet families: greater visibility and diversity of female participation in the new communications environment. Female literacy in Windsor District had been expanding steadily since the late 1770s, and by 1800 the proportion of women engaged in lifelong reading and writing had risen to about 80 percent. This phenomenon was recognized in appeals to women readers in rural newspapers, in bookstore advertisements occasionally targeted to "female" reading tastes, in accounts of schooling experiences, in the share of women to whom letters remaining at post offices throughout the district were addressed, and in many family library books, pamphlets, and periodicals whose intended audience consisted of adolescent and adult women (see chapter 6).[54]

One other aspect of cultural participation increasingly prominent among self-sufficient hamlet families was that family members greatly expanded their reading interests by borrowing from a lending library. The Salmon Dutton family offers a good example. The Duttons showed the mental independence and the increasing relish for reading that more and more characterized the intellectually engaged hamlet families. Salmon Dutton, a fairly wealthy businessman, tavern owner, and local politician, pursued a religious quest that took him from the Standing Order to the Baptists and then to the Universalists. There he had a modest career as a publicist for universal salvation, producing three pamphlets. Readers of chapter 5 will recognize the sequence in places at which Dutton published: from Weathersfield to Windsor to Boston. To judge from the family library, religion, theology, normal homestead affairs, and local and state politics were the Dutton family's main intellectual interests. Secular reading was extremely limited in scope and entirely practical in nature. However, borrowing from the Cavendish Social Library in 1815–26 supplemented the family's private library.[55]

The Dutton household in the decade after the peace at Ghent consisted of Salmon; one of his younger daughters; his son, Salmon, Jr.; and the son's wife. Altogether, father and son borrowed and reborrowed twenty-two different volumes in the course of eleven years. All borrowed works were read between October 5 and April 14, after harvest and before planting, just as the almanacs recommended. As often as the father borrowed a work later borrowed and read by the son, the reverse occurred. Remarkably, the only work that overlapped family library interests was a collection of recent addresses by Vermont governors. As with Daniel Mason's self-sufficient farmstead family, a large share (three-quarters) of all reading was historical, with a division between Enlightenment Christian rationalism—newer as well as older works—and contemporary Romantic accounts of Napoleon, Washington, and New England. The remaining works were an exotic volume of travels (Clarke on Russia and Turkey); a work of political theory, Ferguson's *Essay on Civil Society;* and, soon after publication, Irving's *Sketch Book*, pamphlet by pamphlet. Worlds apart from Salmon's Universalist tracts, but building on the Dutton family library, which contained the foundations of the family's intellectual world, these more current borrowings reveal the growing complexity of hamlet reading interests. None of the borrowings contradicted the main orientation of family library reading, but they did substantially extend the family's mental horizons. Almost everywhere it flourished, broader secular reading expanded and modified rather than obliterated a core of religious knowledge.[56]

Transformation in the cultural participation of self-sufficient hamlet families is best seen by contrasting the presence of works in various areas of knowledge, with their roles in the libraries of habitats previously discussed. Hymnals, psalm books, other devotional books, and even Bibles were all retained by a lower share of families than previously. Among a small majority of families, reading in several categories of secular thought—including history, geography, law, the stages of life, and philosophy—expanded considerably. Works in several newer fields were retained in sizable numbers for the first time in this living situation. Growth was most dramatic in modern literature, which had been nonexistent in the previous reading communities aside from artisan families. At least a quarter of all self-sufficient hamlet families retained three or more novels, plays, peotry books, or essays. Another 20 percent of all self-sufficient hamlet families borrowed from lending libraries. Regular newspaper reading was also on the rise. Cultural participation by self-sufficient hamlet families was radically split. Family libraries were either stocked with works solely for intensive reading, or, if they reflected extensive reading, for the first time they included prominent current works reflecting purchases made right up to the year of the household head's death.

The texture of the family reading experience anywhere in the network of human habitats is difficult to capture. A rare glimpse of a reading activity mostly lost to history is afforded by Samuel Lane's journal, kept throughout 1739–1803 in a hamlet east of the valley, at Stratham, New Hampshire. Lane gave many books from the family library to his children, noting that he had done so and also noting other books he wished them to borrow and read. Separate copies of *Doddridge on the Religious Education of Children* were purchased for four of his children, prayer books for six, and a Bible and several other books for each daughter. Son Joshua also received an English-language dictionary, and son Jabez was given a Latin dictionary. The father's compulsiveness is evident in his instructions inside the front cover of the Protestant *Confes-*

sion of Faith. The work was intended for his three sons, "to go round amongst them one a year": "Each may Demand it in the following Months, viz—Samuel . . . Jan.-April, Joshua . . . May-August, Jabez . . . Sept.-Dec., or otherwise as they may agree." Nor were Lane's daughters forgotten, as he added, "with Liberty to my Daughters to Read, as often as they Request it of their Brethren in reason." Extensive reading matter was also specified, each book being carefully chosen by the male head of household for its intended audience.[57]

The self-sufficient hamlet reading community occupied a distinct intermediate geographical, social, economic, and communications status in the Early Republic. The rich intellectual ferment among a small majority of these families reflected the conditions of hamlet life. Midway between farmstead and village life, self-sufficient hamlet families were split intellectually. Some families adhered to an eighteenth-century mentality, though only one family in sixteen kept exclusively sacred reading matter. A majority participated in the gradual transformation of belief and values that characterized nineteenth-century thought. Increased reading encouraged mental and material growth and a newfound freedom of expression. Some families used this freedom to reinforce traditionally held values, mainly reading works which further confirmed them in their outlook. Others saw growth as bringing the distant world closer to their daily concerns. These families read to learn about new issues, problems, and solutions or simply to exercise their curiosity along more daring and imaginative paths. In one area of knowledge after another, people were breaking with longstanding traditional beliefs and values. Here for the first time among Windsor District reading communities, the fault line distinguishing the emerging cultural universe of the nineteenth-century from that of the eighteenth was unmistakable.

Cultural Life in the Fortunate Farmstead Human Habitat

"Cultivated farms lay beneath us, like a rich carpet of green, speckled with the cottage homes of industry," noted a traveler atop Ascutney Mountain, looking westward into Windsor township. "Vermont opens a rich field . . . her whole territory interspersed with hills and vales, inhabited by the bleating race, yielding comfort and wealth; and her winding streams where factory roars to factory, and the hum of bee-like industry is manufacturing, which disseminates the comforts and conveniences of life." The fortunate farmstead human habitat encompassing western Windsor township could be as beautiful as this 1842 report suggests. But Upper Valley forest society could also prove remarkably inhospitable to farmers, especially when summer collapsed in freezing evenings in mid-June or mid-August. Only a special breed of people lasted through a

Ascutney Mountain, Vermont, from Claremont, New Hampshire, 1862. By Albert Bierstadt. Courtesy, Fruitlands Museum, Harvard, Mass.

Residents of Fortunate Farmstead areas, such as this intervale along the Connecticut River at Claremont, New Hampshire, were split in their degree of involvement with contemporary currents of commerce and culture. Proximity to village bookstores, newspapers, and social and circulating libraries permitted wide diversity of participation in contemporary affairs.

year, 1816, with snow nearly every month; ravaging cholera epidemics in 1812–14; and normal snowfall averages ranging between 60 and 102 inches. Variety and extremes were watchwords in the weather as in manay aspects of material and cultural life.[58]

Pluralism thrived among fortunate farmstead families. As we have seen, participation in print culture did not automatically lead to intellectual change. Fairly ready access to print culture, in broadening the range of choice in reading matter, markedly increased the freedom often associated with life in the Upper Valley. Among families living close to, but not directly at the center of, rural change, reading interests varied enormously, from traditional wisdom to secular anticapitalist freethought ideology. Some families read more regularly to reinforce older, more traditional attitudes. Other families exploited the situation to become knowledgeable observers fascinated with contemporary change. Still others ignored or remained unaware of the new mass culture that was reshaping the world they inhabited. The last cluster, amounting to just over a quarter of all fortunate farmstead families, did not retain collections at the death of the household head. Little evidence regarding their intellectual interests survives.

We can learn much about the nearly three quarters of families who did retain a private library. A fifth of these families participated in print culture in the most traditional way, limiting their interest to sacred subjects. Another fifth, minus a few, supplemented traditional religious perspectives with limited secular reading. These families chiefly looked to the wisdom of the ages to sustain them in their daily existence, although they also frequently kept works of intellectual synthesis. A larger third group, comprising just under two-thirds of all fortunate farmstead families with libraries, participated more actively in various aspects of intellectual change. Overall, among fortunate farmstead families, the balance between continuity and change in beliefs and values shifted further toward change.

Proximity to a large marketing center, in which most families traded by 1810, differentiated fortunate farmstead families most from other Windsor District agricultural families. By the 1780s, Chester and Windsor had divided southern Windsor District between them. Farming homesteaders in Windsor and Chester townships profited greatly from the panoply of resources that their villages provided. About 2,800 individuals, a sixth of the Windsor District population, represented the fortunate farmstead reading community in 1830. Our study group includes sixty-six families. While the fortunate farmstead occupational range was broad, it was concentrated around full-time farming. Three-fifths of fortunate farmstead families were yeoman farm households, and another fifth were gentleman farmer households. Other occupations included artisan activity, commerce, and the professions.[59]

Fortunate farmstead families shared with their village counterparts the highest female and male literacy levels in Windsor District. Rates were extraordinarily high by the 1770s. From the 1780s onward, Chester and Windsor township readers, whether they lived in a village or out in the township on a farmstead, could choose among the offerings of several general stores, at least one bookstore, one or more weekly newspapers (at Windsor one was started in 1783, and there was one at Chester or nearby Bellows Falls in 1807–10 and in 1817–30), a social library (by 1801), and a circulating library (by 1822 in Windsor and by 1829 in Chester). Perhaps half of all fortunate farmstead families subscribed to a newspaper by 1805, and an eighth of our study group retained a share in one of three social and moral libraries. While Windsor offered even more opportunities for cultural participation than Chester, family libraries in both townships were quite similar in size.[60] Overall median size remained modest, at 7.5 volumes, because a substantial minority of families had very tiny libraries: 40 percent were under 5 volumes. Libraries of 10 or more volumes, or with a social library share, increased from 30 percent among self-sufficient farmstead families to 42 percent here. Average collection size, moreover, was quite large

(28 volumes). With 17 percent of all Windsor District libraries and an equal share of wealth, fortunate farmstead families retained more than double their share of printed matter (38 percent). Families ranged from wholly traditional to extremely current in their reading habits and in their uses of the printed word. Borrowing from circulating libraries further distanced fortunate farmstead reading habits in the 1820s from those in other nonvillage living situations.[61]

What conditions encouraged fortunate farmstead families to participate more actively in the expansion of print culture and to strive for intellectual currency? Wealth was especially powerful here. Whereas average wealth was $2,720 for all sixty-six families, it was $3,383 for those holding either ten or more volumes or a lending library share. Greater wealth, especially in personal property, prompted more regular use of a village's services, more frequent attendance at its functions, and so forth. It also increased contact with printed matter, whatever the family occupation.

Variety of cultural participation within the fortunate farmstead reading community is illustrated by three families. Consisting of an adult male, a female aged forty to forty-nine, and six children, the Joseph Parker artisan family of Chester engaged in carpentry and housebuilding. The Parkers, who were worth $1,889 at inventory in late 1830, also farmed a 135-acre homestead. Their intellectual interests remained entrenched in traditional intensive reading, in the form of a "Great Bible," a small Bible, and an unspecified hymn book. The only clue to their denominational affiliation is a pew in the Chester Union meetinghouse, which was used by Methodists, Universalists, and Baptists. Secular reading was evident only in an unspecified "geography," probably an abridged schoolbook, to judge from its valuation at seventeen cents. The Parkers were unlikely to have subscribed to a weekly newspaper but probably purchased a yearly almanac. A pocket book, doubtless for accounts of jobs performed, indicates that one or more of the family members could write. The Parker family is representative of the fifth of all fortunate farmstead families who, retaining small collections (one to four volumes), participated in print culture in limited ways and mainly for traditional ends.[62]

The Parnell Dean yeoman farm family of Windsor represents a second large cluster of families encompassing about half of all households. The Deans held slightly above-average wealth at Parnell's death in 1820 ($2,783) and had a typical ten-volume mixed extensive collection of reading matter. Religious reading encompassed an "old large Bible"; a "Psalm Book," perhaps used in the Old South Congregational Church, where the Deans maintained a pew; a copy of Hervey's *Meditations* for private devotional use; and one of Joshua Spalding's interesting premillennialist lectures, *Sentiments Concerning the Coming and Kingdom of Christ*. Secular reading was also prevalent. Educational books included a fancy reader with classical and more recent British selections, and a popular, comprehensive manual. Two of the most popular historical works in Windsor

District, Porter's *Narrative of the Campaign in Russia* and John Bank's *Life of Peter the Great*, reflect the strong curiosity in the fortunate farmstead and fortunate village reading communities concerning Russia and strong military leaders. The last two works dealt with New England Native Americans: *History of the Indian Wars* by Sanders and *The Redeemed Captive Returning to Zion* by John Williams of Deerfield. The Deans probably subscribed to a weekly newspaper and almost certainly purchased a yearly almanac.[63]

There was far greater variety in the reading of a third cluster of families with large collections. The family of Ebenezer Fisk, Sr., of Chester is representative. The Fisks were in the top ten percent of Windsor District wealth at Ebenezer's death in 1816; their property was valued at $5,847, just over half of it represented by eight pieces of land and by loans to various business people. If we may judge from the furnishings, the lawyer's household of six (Mr. Fisk; Mrs. Fisk, aged twenty-six to fourty-four; three young men aged sixteen to twenty-five; and a young woman, aged ten to fifteen) led a very comfortable existence. A surprisingly small proportion of the thirty-one-volume Fisk collection was devoted to sacred reading. There were two Bibles (one "large") and a copy of Dickinson's *Compendium to the Bible*. No hymnals or psalm books were kept at home; there may have been one or more in the family's two pews in the Congregational meetinghouse in Chester. Private devotion was assisted by Young's *Night Thoughts*. Schoolbooks were absent, but there were a pair of dictionaries. Fisk's professional books included eight standard volumes in law, and a five-volume collection of *American State Papers*; other volumes in government and politics were mainly tracts. Works in history included a volume on Washington and an unidentified history of "Modern Europe." Medicine was represented by Seaman on *Mineral Waters*, and geography by Morse's two-volume *American Universal Geography*. Other texts included the most popular Masonic songbook of the day, [Dunham's] *The Masonic Register*, and Goldsmith's very widely read *Vicar of Wakefield*.[64]

The most striking characteristic of fortunate farmstead families is the great diversity of their intellectual interests. In addition to traditional sacred reading, schoolbooks, and farmstead works, nearly two-thirds of all families in this living situation indulged their curiosity about newer trends in knowledge. Greater availability of print increased the breadth and variety of reading tastes, but as in previous reading communities, a series of shared intellectual interests dominated.

Fortunate farmstead families retained all of the types of private libraries that prevailed in Windsor District. Nearly three-quarters read both religious and secular works. Furthermore, unlike self-sufficient farmstead families, families here who read extensive works quite frequently each took an interest in several newer intellectual traditions and attitudes. Fortunate farmstead family libraries were well balanced, and a good spread of libraries existed relative to population growth in 1787–1830. Because five of eight lending library shares came from

Table 9–4: Fortunate Farmstead Family Libraries

Type of Library	Number of Libraries	Percent of Fortunate Farmstead Libraries	Number of Volumes*	Percent of Fortunate Farmstead Volumes	Average Volumes Per Library
Sacred Intensive	13	20	34	2	3
Mixed Intensive	11	17	37	2	3
Sacred Combined Intensive/ Extensive	5	8	31	2	6
Mixed Extensive	32	48	321+8s	17	10
Major Secular: Extensive	1	1	909	49	909
Professional	4	6	516	28	129
Total	66	100%	1,848+8s	100%	28

*s=shares in lending libraries

estates probated in the first half of the period, the overall proportion of fortunate farmstead families who engaged in social library borrowing was probably higher than the 12 percent for which evidence survives. In the 1820s some families also borrowed books from village circulating libraries (see table 9–4).[65]

Fortunate farmstead families may be divided into two broad clusters by the substance of their reading interests. Just over a third of families with libraries, all but two of whom owned their farmsteads (though some were mortgaged), retained small, solidly traditional intensive-reading collections. These families hewed close to the reading tastes of the large majority in hardscrabble and self-sufficient farmstead reading communities. Beyond these books and pamphlets, they mainly favored the yearly rhythm of the almanac. The intellectual interests of these fortunate farmstead families were either wholly religious or mixed sacred and secular but with little inclination toward extensive reading. The Bible, from small, cheap editions through Scott's six-volume *Family Bible* to a New Testament "with cuts," dominated religious reading. It was supplemented by hymnals, psalm books, and prayer books. Secular reading of families retaining mixed intensive libraries was limited to works that consolidated information, mainly dictionaries and schoolbooks—readers, arithmetics, and an occasional geography or American history text. Small concentrated collections and the most traditional Christian republican wisdom satisfied their sustained intellectual interests. As in earlier living situations, American nationalism informed the readers they retained. Signs of writing were found among half of this first cluster of mostly yeoman farm families.[66]

The second major cluster, nearly two-thirds, of fortunate farmstead families, were not satisfied with reaffirming the wisdom of the ages. Their reading tastes either mirrored the boldness of self-sufficient hamlet reading in theology, history, philosophy, modern literature, and so on, or went well beyond it, replicating the riches of fortunate village reading. In the latter case, large and varied private libraries were filled with examples of the latest and often the most sophisticated contemporary thought. A very small group of these families (8 percent of all fortunate farmstead families) expanded their mental horizons beyond intensive reading matter solely through theology and sacred history. The usual complement of Bibles, hymnals, psalm books, prayer books, and devotional texts served as a backdrop for serious theological and denominational works. As in the case of self-sufficient hamlet families, the common thread in virtually all religious works for extensive reading that these families kept was vital piety, expressed in regular family and individual devotion, considered essential to religious solace. Universalist, Baptist, and Methodist theology, history, and biblical criticism overshadowed mainstream Calvinist texts. Proximity to bookstores encouraged these families to hone their thinking about theological issues and religious practice rather than to develop any secular reading interests. In the process, they dissented from Standing Order positions. American works in theology and church history, while still a minority, came to account for just under two-fifths of all volumes.[67]

Among the thirty-seven families (55 percent of the total) with collections dominated by secular extensive reading, about one in four supplemented their reading with social library borrowing, and after 1810, at least two in three rounded out their reading with a newspaper. Most of these families also purchased an almanac. Four were headed by females, all widows. Their family reading did not differ significantly from that of households headed by men. Altogether, the thirty-seven libraries contained 1,746 volumes. For the moment, we will omit from consideration the two enormous libraries of the John Williams and John Leverett families (see appendix 5); the other thirty-five families retained 372 volumes, an average of 16 volumes each. Extensive reading accounted for a small majority of all known volumes, and secular works accounted for three-quarters of these.

The tone of the fortunate farmstead reading community was set by its most engaged families of readers. Greater ease of access to rich funds of printed matter reinforced, updated, and modified a strong religious bent and expanded the appetite for knowledge into ten main areas of secular thought. As in previous human habitats, Bibles and New Testaments were most prevalent. If we include typical social library reading, we see that more than half the families sustained an interest in theology. Almost half were interested in modern literature and history: two-fifths in geography; a third in schoolbooks, stage-of-life works, and devotional and prayer books; a quarter in hymnals, psalm books, dictionaries, law, and travel accounts; and a fifth in philosophy. Works on other subjects were read and retained by less than a tenth of all families.

Four-fifths of these thirty-five families retained a Bible, now regularly accompanied by commentary; half retained a four- or six-volume set of either Scott's *Family Bible* or Doddridge's *Family Expositor*. Moreover, several households without Bibles retained a meetinghouse pew, perhaps holding a Bible. The share of families with a Bible, consequently, could well have been nine-tenths. Hymnals and psalm books remained firmly under the influence of Watts. The same kinds of devotional works that we have previously noted were dominant here as well. Young's *Night Thoughts*; Bunyan's *Pilgrim's Progress*; the Stalwarts Baxter, Flavel, and Hervey; and a spiritual companion for farmers, Phineas Davison's *Evangelical Poems*, were popular. Whereas the small cluster of families retaining exclusively religious extensive reading favored dissenting opinions, the larger cluster retaining both secular and sacred extensive reading leaned more toward Calvinist and conservative evangelical theological strains. In this area fortunate farmstead families exhibited the same preferences as hardscrabble and self-sufficient farmstead families. Methodism, Universalism, and, for the first time, Episcopalianism, formed a minority reading interest. Such preferences were outnumbered two to one in total volumes by Standing Order theological opinion. The central underlying theme of vital piety was translated among these none-too-wealthy fortunate farmstead families as "patience under affliction." Thomas Boston's *The Crook in the Lot* best represents this intellectual position. Neither the extent nor the character of religious reading is readily predictable. Ownership of a pew—half of the thirty-five families owned one or more—did not make a family more likely to own theological works, hymnals, psalm books, or devotional treatises.[68]

Schoolbook reading expanded the pattern noted earlier for the self-sufficient farmstead human habitat. Especially those readers that included at least some American selections were very popular, including readers by Webster, Bingham, and Heaton. As before, Perry's *Royal Standard English Dictionary* dominated this category. Secular extensive-reading interests clustered in five subject areas: geography and travels; history, law, politics, and government; literature; stage-of-life works; and philosophy. As usual, Morse's several geographies and James Whitelaw's Vermont maps dominated geography reading. Travels emphasized exciting sea voyages, especially that of George Anson (1748) and Chetwood's account of Robert Boyle (about 1766). History, law, politics, and government were far more varied. In law several works were popular among nonlawyer families as well as among lawyers, including Blackstone, Nathaniel Chipman's *Reports and Dissertations*, various editions of the *Laws of Vermont*, and law manuals for citizens. Politics and government presented a mixed group, from Matthew Carey's *Olive Branch* and Ethan Allen's *Narrative* of his captivity, to a series of works on the republican tradition in Ireland, England, and America. History reading also stressed American contributions to the republican tradition. Other popular works were Banks's *Peter the Great* and Porter's *Narrative* of Napoleon's Russian campaign. In short, American history, the transatlantic republican tradition, military affairs, and the lives of heroic figures dominated law, history, and political life.[69]

Compared with the self-sufficient hamlet reading community, fortunate farmstead families had quite conservative tastes in modern literature, emphasizing mostly older mainstream British popular works such as *Paradise Lost* and Goldsmith's *Vicar of Wakefield*, and American captivity narratives. Only a single work, a five-volume set of the *Philadelphia Repository and Weekly Register* (1800–1806), spoke for recent trends in Anglo-American literature, although current works may have been borrowed from local lending libraries. Reading in the stages of life was scattered, but in philosophy interest coalesced around two widely read texts, Pope's *Essay on Man*, emphasizing the possibilities of virtue through a compact system of ethics, and John Mason's *Treatise on Self Knowledge*, a popular manual of moral philosophy.[70]

Interest in these five broad reading areas was fairly strong but was quite narrowly focused on some of the major conservative intellectual themes of the day. The fortunate farmstead habitat was a center of well-informed conservative opinion, both sacred and secular. Many of the reading interests prominent in the self-sufficient hamlet reading community were missing or minimal here: British Enlightenment history, contemporary Romantic concerns in modern literature, and science and technology. It should also be noted that the 909–volume library of the John Leverett family, one of two enormous collections among this group, suggests the possibilities and limits of reading in the family of a country scholar.

Fortunate farmstead families lived in the shadow of Windsor District's twin economic and communications centers. The distinctiveness of this human habitat was due not to its range of wealth or occupations, but to its placement within the communication system and its largely farmstead ecology. This is the crux of the matter. If isolation was the central characteristic of hardscrabble families, steady tradition that of self-sufficient farmstead families, and boldness that of self-sufficient hamlet households, then variety, leading to considerable intellectual richness, marked fortunate farmsteaders, who frequently kept libraries that increased the scope of their interests but confirmed their solid traditional values. That they needed to reinforce the foundations of their beliefs is clear from the extensive news of commercialization and distant events of the contemporary world which came in weekly four-page doses, challenging the traditional base. Fully 71 percent of all works owned by fortunate farmstead families consisted of extensive-reading texts (sacred and secular); just under two-thirds of these families retained at least one work of this type. This pattern represents a shift from that seen in hardscrabble, self-sufficient farmstead, and self-sufficient hamlet families. There was also a shift from basic works such as Bibles, hymnals, and psalm books to deeper and more regular devotional and theological reading. Yet while secular extensive reading was less evident in fortunate farmstead libraries than in those of self-sufficient hamlet families (43 percent versus 55 percent), newspapers, largely secular through 1830, were more widely read by fortunate farmstead families.[71]

The fortunate farmstead reading community updated and reinforced older, deeply Christian, and republican visions of American life and North Atlantic civilization. A sizable minority of families added signficantly to this heritage, gravitating toward the most contemporary intellectual issues and problems, especially to new secular reading interests characteristic of village and, less, to hamlet life. In their heavy holdings of intensive reading matter (Bibles, devotional works, schoolbooks, farm books, and dictionaries) fortunate farmstead families were closest to self-sufficient farmstead families. In some categories of extensive reading matter—theology, geography, history, and philosophy—they were positioned between self-sufficient farmstead and hamlet reading communities. In several newer reading areas (stages of life, science and technology, medicine and law, philosophy, travels, and politics and government), they were anticipating more pronounced trends among the fortunate village reading community. The unusual Leverett family maintained a far larger share of works than other fortunate farmstead families in one (and only one) large area: science, technology, and contemporary compilations of knowledge, including encyclopedias, dictionaries and the like.

Fortunate farmstead families were intellectually diverse. Differences in the size and content of family libraries and in other kinds of cultural participation increased with proximity to centers of distribution. Reading patterns reflected real ambivalence with regard to the changing cultural atmosphere of early national America. In the Leverett family collection, and in a few other libraries, the split was fairly pronounced and was itself the topic of some imprints. To an important degree, this reading community was poised unsteadily between firm adherence to the traditional wisdom of the Protestant New England agricultural farmstead, and greater attention to the more intensely secular contemporary affairs and commercial relations characteristic of village life.

Cultural Life in the Fortunate Village Human Habitat

The texture of life in the fortunate villages of Windsor District was so distinctive that Timothy Dwight and Anne Royall, travelers from opposite ends of the social and theological spectrum, could agree in the 1820s about its central features:

In this valley the principle commerce of the country within twenty miles of the river is carried on, and a great part of their mechanical business is done. Here the newspapers circulated throughout this region are printed and the bookstores kept. . . . Here also, the great body of information concerning this and other countries is first received and disseminated, and here fashions of all kinds are first adopted from abroad and diffused throughout the vicinity.

Windsor is the largest town in Vermont, and well built. The houses are close and compact, and many of them are very handsome buildings of brick. Many of the streets are planted with trees, which with the large public buildings, their steeples and cupolas, and a great number of stores, gives the place an air of wealth and grandeur. . . . The site is uneven, ascending from the river, but the scenery is rich and beautiful, the distant hills and mountains give a variety to the prospect, very imposing.[72]

Residents of the fortunate village human habitat through 1835 lived in Windsor, Chester, Springfield, and Weathersfield villages.

Within Windsor District's network of human habitats in 1830, the fortunate village was at the middle rank in population with about 3,200 souls (18 percent). While villages grew in 1800–1830, their share of the district's population had held steady because of continuing settlement of the hinterland. Our sample group for detailed analysis includes sixty-two families, or about a twentieth of all families living in a village for more than three years in 1787–1830. Because Windsor District village life emerged fully only in the 1790s, surviving inventories accent the last half of the period, 1809–30. Families in this living situation engaged in the full range of occupations apart from full-time farming. Some village families farmed, but usually farming was not their primary occupation. The largest three fortunate village occupational groups were: commerce and trading families, broadly conceived (40 percent); professional families (31 percent); and artisan families (22 percent). There were also tiny groups of manufacturing (5 percent) and semi-skilled laborer families (2 percent). While professional families were vastly overrepresented, their "family library" reading habits, apart from the "professional library" of the household head, were little different from those of almost all other fortunate villagers.[73]

In material circumstances, fortunate villages included families above $700 in property—our threshold for more than minimal cultural participation—living in the Upper Valley settings furthest advanced in the new rural economic and social order. The average wealth of fortunate village families was high—nearly three times the district average—but this statement obscures a deep division between lower-middle-class families and the wealthiest ones. Culturally, the villages included the central links in Windsor District's communications network and were in fact the only communities producing, importing, and distributing large volumes of printed matter. While villages were more internally

Mentalités: Intellectual Reservoirs

Windsor Village from Cornish Hills. Anonymous. Courtesy, Vermont Historical Society.

Nestled in the distance is "the jewel of the Upper Valley," Windsor, Vermont, in this view from the 1840s. Windsor's extensive village of 1,200–1,500 people in 1830 extended like a spider web, bounded by the Connecticut on its eastern flank, and the foothills of Ascutney Mountain to the south. Ascutney's prominence, a few miles south of Windsor village, was a reminder that, despite Windsor's size and self-importance, nature's monuments dominated the Upper Valley.

diverse than all other rural living situations, three of the four villages— Weathersfield, Windsor, and Springfield, in order of intensity—were strongholds of Federalism in politics and of conservative Standing Order denominational beliefs and forms of worship. Religious dissent in these three villages often took an elite liberal form, represented by Episcopalian and Unitarian societies. Only Chester was frequently Republican and heavily weighted toward dissenters in theology, especially Universalists, Methodists, and Freewill Baptists.[74]

For the large majority of village inhabitants, centrality of geographic location, community size and complexity, wealth, and access to print and written communications stimulated rich interaction with the full range of printed matter. The circumstances of village life bred a willingness to engage new information, more daring intellectual traditions, and more innovative applications of knowledge. Because rural villages were compact, fortunate villagers could purchase or borrow virtually every item of printed matter available in Windsor

District any day but Sunday. By the mid-1780s Windsor, the largest village in Windsor District, had already become the Upper Valley's first center of print dissemination. With the growth of other permanent print centers, Windsor's audience gradually constricted and localized to Windsor County. The proximity of Windsor to the other three district villages by major road and water routes, and its concentration of printing and publishing facilities, assured that through the mid-1830s Windsor would remain the only permanent print center in the district. Auxiliary print centers existed in each of the other three villages before the mid-1830s, but none was sustained for more than four years at a time.[75]

Differences among Windsor District's four villages, while important, were overshadowed by their similarities. Fortunate village families were most directly affected by the commercialization of Windsor District's economy, society, and culture in 1780–1835. The lives of Windsor District villagers increasingly differed from those of inland farmstead and even hamlet families—in their work rhythms, ongoing interests, and material possessions, and especially in the impact of print culture on their lives. Regular postal service, which came to Windsor in 1784, Chester in 1800, Weathersfield in 1806, and Springfield in 1817, intensified letter writing. Post riders delivered a constant flow of newspapers in the latter three villages, and periodicals in all four villages. General stores regularly supplied fortunate village residents with almanacs and all sorts of material for intensive reading, and bookstores at Windsor and Chester carried a very broad stock of printed matter. Supplementary reading opportunities were offered by three social libraries in Windsor and Chester from 1800 on and in Springfield by 1805, and by two circulating libraries at Windsor (starting in 1822) and Chester (1829). As high a share of fortunate village families maintained libraries as raised children (85 percent).

Print and written communications helped to reshape oral discourse in village settings. The proliferating reading matter changed the content of oral conversations, just as oral tradition influenced the understanding of printed works. Law manuals, for example, disseminated guidelines for various types of administrative procedures. Widespread male and female literacy, district schools (supplementing home instruction), and the encouragement of lifelong learning resulted in the very widespread retention of family libraries and encouraged the broad and rapid diffusion of print culture. Not only was the share of all families with libraries extraordinarily high, but libraries were much larger than in all other reading communities, averaging 36.2 volumes. Moreover, the median size of fortunate village collections, at 15 print items per library, was also much larger. Further, the circulation of newspapers, broadsides, and almanacs reached very high levels, and a quarter of all libraries included at least one volume of a periodical. Finally, the fact that the book trade (and allied institutions, especially newspaper publishing) was one of the three largest commodity markets in Windsor District added to the aura of print culture in the fortunate village reading community.[76]

The village's combination of compact space and variable wealth meant that printed matter was widely available outside private collections. Still fragmentary evidence reveals that informal borrowing occurred more regularly in villages and on nearby farmsteads than elsewhere in Windsor District. Families borrowing formally from social libraries mainly came from the top 60 percent of the population by wealth; poorer families could not afford the fees. Circulating libraries greatly extended the borrowing public, making current works affordable for the lower middle class. Not to be overlooked in the environment of the fortunate village habitat were voluntary organizations, institutions that most often met in villages and relied at least in part on printed materials for advertising, promotion, and dissemination of knowledge.

Fully four-fifths of all fortunate village families with libraries kept at least one volume of extensive reading matter. Wealth, specific community setting, and occupation all influenced collection size and variety. Once families owned more than $700 in property, wealth ceased to correlate closely with library size; but frequency of membership in a social library and of periodical subscriptions varied directly with wealth. Among villagers, Windsor families had somewhat larger and more varied libraries: collection size and variety remained very similar among families in the other three villages. Occupation powerfully affected village reading interests. Next to professional families, artisan families, as we have seen, were most likely to retain large collections reflecting a broad range of current interests. Among families with only intensive-reading collections, 75 percent (nine of twelve) were engaged in commerce and trade (in contrast to 40 percent of all fortunate village families). Despite intimacy with broader market exchange, business families were sharply divided in the extent of their participation in print communications. One group maintained solely traditional reading matter, while a second group was deeply absorbed in current intellectual interests.[77]

Two families displayed the dominant patterns of book holding among fortunate village families. Seth Grout, Jr., his wife, a male and a female child, and two persons in their sixties, perhaps grandparents, were very modest storekeepers and farmers (worth $1,716 at inventory), residing at Greenbush in western Weathersfield. The Grouts owned a family library of nineteen volumes at Seth's death in 1830. Religious works were limited to traditional fare, and no formal theology intruded. Schoolbooks were mainly typical ones (a speller, readers, and arithmetics), plus William Scott's more advanced *Lessons in Elocution*. Secular extensive works centered on three main intellectual interests: world geography, ancient and modern history, and Enlightenment philosophy and science. The collection featured a half dozen of the era's leading geographical and historical works, two Masonic works, a copy of Zadock Steele's autobiographical *Narrative of the Captivity and Sufferings of* . . . , together with an account of the burning of nearby Royalton, and a very interesting work on scientific agriculture, Lathrop's *Farmer's Library*. By 1810 regular almanac reading and a newspaper subscription probably supplemented family reading. The Grout family library was typical of nearly 60 percent of all fortunate village libraries that were inventoried. Reading tastes were expanding across a wide front and were deepening in a few areas.[78]

The Stephen Jacob family's library holdings were substantially broader than those of the Grouts. The Jacobs came to Windsor in the early 1780s, after Stephen, a 1778 Yale graduate, apprenticed at law with Theodore Sedgwick. When Stephen Jacob died in 1817 he was widely regarded as "one of the fathers of the state of Vermont," having served in countless leading public positions while practicing law at Windsor for more than thirty-five years. He left a substantial family estate (worth $11,516 in 1810) and a household of five other members: his wife, a young man, two young women, and a woman between twenty-six and forty-five. The Jacob family library was typical of the majority of large fortunate village collections. Midway in size among a dozen libraries that contained more than 50 volumes, the 114-volume collection included a professional law library of 32 volumes.[79]

Sacred reading included the typical Bible (two), compendia, and prayer books, plus seven volumes of fairly light devotional and theological reading. Secular reading was very diverse. Seven volumes concerned youth and adulthood as stages of life. Eight more volumes centered on history and geography. Russian history (Banks's *Peter the Great* and Thiebault's *Frederick the Great*), the French Revolution, and America were the main subjects here. Morse and Guthrie ruled in geography. Four volumes of travels were mainly concerned with Sicily and France (Brydon, Baron von Riedesel, and John Moore). There were also minor interests in philosophy and classical writers. With forty volumes, modern literature encompassed the largest reading interest. American authors included Freneau, Barlow, and Thomas G. Fessenden. British writers dominated with thirty-six volumes. Poetry included Parnel, Thomson, and Dryden, while novels and plays included Goldsmith, Fielding, and Smollett. Other works included an eight-volume set of Addison and Steele's *The Spectator*, a seven-volume collection of *The Works of Laurence Sterne*, and several minor texts.[80]

A family of regular readers, using printed matter as a guide to life and also as a spur to the imagination, the Jacobs showed how easily books and periodicals now could be purchased. Their religious and theological works reveal their considerable attention to current issues without displaying great daring. The medium-sized law library was weighted evenly between basic and more technical works. Schoolbooks and classical works suggest that one or more children attended an academy or perhaps an area college. Works on the stages

Table 9–5: Fortunate Village Family Libraries

Type of Library	Number of Libraries	Percent of Fortunate Village Libraries	Number of Volumes*	Percent of Fortunate Village Volumes	Average Volumes Per Library
Sacred Intensive	2	3	3	.1	2
Sacred Combined Intensive/ Extensive	10	16	52	2	5
Mixed Extensive	24	39	385+4s	17	16
Major Secular: Extensive	7	11	368	16	53
Professional	19	31	1,440+7s	64	76
a. Theological	3	5	55	3	18
b. Medical	7	11	417+3s	18	60
c. Legal	9	15	967+4s	43	107
Total	62	100%	2,248+11s	100%	36

*s=shares in lending libraries

of life represented a broader strain of Enlightenment rationalism, seen also in travel accounts and the history of Europe, Russia, and the New World. Modern literature reveals exceptional curiosity. In all likelihood the family purchased a yearly almanac and subscribed to a Windsor newspaper.

The riches of fortunate village cultural participation are immediately evident from the distribution of library types. The most striking finding is that extensive reading had spread through four-fifths of all fortunate village families, penetrating deeply into the lower middle class. Secular reading engaged virtually all families. Just over a third read mainly secular works; over half (56 percent) split their reading between secular and sacred concerns; and a tenth engaged almost exclusively in sacred reading.

Families with mixed (secular-sacred) extensive-reading libraries (40 percent) and professional families (31 percent) formed the largest groups. The sizable number of professional family libraries offers us a full view of reading done by one of the most advantaged and influential opinion groups in the region; many of these families assumed leadership positions in Windsor District. Families with major secular libraries, usually containing only tiny caches of religious works, formed a prominent minority for the first time in our exploration of the network of human habitats, accounting for a ninth of all fortunate village households. In contrast to these three groups of families, those holding mixed intensive-reading libraries accounted for only a seventh of the total, a far smaller share than in previously described reading communities.

Table 9–6: Fortunate Village Reading Interests

Type of Reading Matter	Total Volumes*	By Area	Percent of All Fortunate Village Volumes
Sacred Works:	385		17
Bibles and Testaments		101	
Hymnals and Psalm Books		40	
Devotional Treatises		42	
Sacred Extensive Reading			
Theology (incl. Sermons			
and Church History.**		202	[9]***
Secular Works:	1,686		75
Schoolbooks:		110	[5]
Spellers		12	
Readers		22	
Arithmetics		22	
Grammars		11	
Geographies and Histories		5	
Upper Level		34	
Misc.		4	
Secular Extensive Reading:	[1,538]		[68]
Law**		485	
Modern Literature		246	
Medicine[1]		198	
General Knowledge, Arts,			
Science, and Technology		177	
History		126	
Geography and Gazetteers		77	
Politics and Government		57	
Classical Literature		44	
Philosophy		44	
Stages of Life		43	
Miscellaneous Periodicals		5	
Windsor Newspapers		2	
Almanacs		1	
Misc. Fields		33	[2]
Miscellaneous Books (unspecified):	153		7
Unidentified Volumes:	24		1

*   Grand Total: 2,248 volumes + 11 Lending Library Shares
** Includes a sizable proportion of works from "professional collections." Study group includes 62 family libraries.
***[ ] = subtotal

Fortunate villagers became the most avid readers in rural New England. The most useful strategy in analyzing their intellectual interests is to view this reading community as one coherent yet diverse group of families (see table 9–6 throughout). Early-nineteenth-century thought encompassed continuity and change across a wide spectrum of fields of knowledge, as longstanding intellectual traditions, in older and reformulated versions, vied with a need for the "latest intelligence" in a rapidly changing world. At the root of all reading was a growing fascination with change itself and with speed and accuracy in information diffusion, as central aspects of the emerging "modern" world. No better example exists than Carey's lament over the near impossiblity of keeping up with the great changes that had occurred in the world during the four years between editions of his atlas. By 1800, change was regularly discussed; its vocabulary and the rhetoric of speed, precision, and accuracy were treated as wholly positive virtues until the mid-1830s.[81]

Only 19 percent of families predominantly engaged in commerce and trade, retained exclusively traditional intensive-reading fare: Bibles, hymnals, psalm books, prayer books, devotional works, schoolbooks, dictionaries, and homestead manuals. However, since several of these families advertised in Windsor District newspapers, they undoubtedly received a local weekly. All of the other family libraries suggest how firmly established broad intellectual interests were among villagers as a group. Compared with intellectual interests in human habitats previously discussed, the fortunate village reading community revealed far broader and deeper intellectual curiosity, and its family libraries display far more coherence among individual works retained.

Fortunate village families engaged in more religious *and* more secular reading than families in all other human habitats. While secular works vastly outnumbered sacred ones, the latter were both rich and varied. The Bible remained the anchor of sacred intensive reading, though its retention rate fell to three-fifths, lowest among all human habitats. Secularization, evident among self-sufficient hamlet families and fortunate village families, was an important cultural trend during the Early Republic.

Most families with sacred reading matter extended their quest for salvation to several related types of works. They made greater use of commentaries in Bible study. Prayer books, mostly variants of the *Book of Common Prayer*, were also very popular. Psalm books and especially hymnals were owned by two of every five families. Watts continued to rule very firmly in general, though another kind of church music was gaining wide attention. As Jonathan Worst has noted, a shift from psalmody to newer types of hymnody texts was especially strong during the 1800–1830 decades. In devotional reading, though diverse, a few common purposes dominated. The white heat of vital piety burned in many works, the most popular of them by Thomas á Kempis, Baxter, Law, Mason, and Rowe. Venn, Boston, and Doddridge were no less committed to conversion and salvation as central life goals, but their approach and tone were milder. Hervey was a bit more abstract in a pair of popular works. Works by Bunyan and Young were also widely retained.[82]

Nearly half of all fortunate village families with libraries engaged in theological reading. Theology's importance in these collections—it was third after law and modern literature—owed little to professional interest. Calvinist topics and a broad array of evangelical themes dominated. A complex mix of Scottish philosophical thinking buttressed much, though not all, of Anglo-American theology during the early national era. Conservative Calvinists such as Samuel Williams, as well as most evangelicals, profited from the Christian Scottish Enlightenment. In perspective, theological change was slow in modifying Calvinism's fundamental points, which were regularly reinforced in hymn books, devotional tracts, theological treatises, sermons, and accounts of model Christian lives. With the emergence of a conversion-dominated religious practice, piety was once again seriously contending with intellect for the center of Protestant experience within the Calvinist legacy. Theological disputes took second place.

As in devotional reading, the key split in theology proper was between cooler liberal evangelical and rationalist on the one hand, and warmer Calvinist and conservative evangelical positions on the other. Two groups of texts received the most attention. One represented theological questions raised by Enlightenment thinkers. Small clusters of works favored Universalism (Ballou, Huntington, and several copies of Dan Foster's *Examination*) and Episcopalianism (Tillotson, Bowden, and the *Churchmen's Magazine*). Far outnumbering these works were mainstream Calvinist and evangelical writings, usually by Standing Order clergy, though interest in Methodism was growing. A few, such as the writings of Spalding, who argued against Universalism, were defensive in nature. Most were more straightforward expositions of some variety of the Calvinist-evangelical theological universe. Church history also drew considerable attention. There were several copies each of the *Works* of Josephus and of Hannah Adams's lengthy *View of Religions*. Works by Macgowan, Harwood, and Hunter discussed Jesus. Surprisingly, fortunate village families shared with hardscrabble families an interest in millennialism. Two-thirds of all works were by premillennialist authors, including Bishop Newton, Kinne, and Langdon. Significantly, interest in eschatology was high.[83]

Congregationalism reigned in the religious reading as well as in the practice of each of Windsor District's four villages. Universalism, Methodism, and Episcopalianism offered the main denominational alternatives. In all cases, more recent religious and theological works were the rule rather than the exception among these families. Among the four-fifths of all libraries that retained extensive-reading works, no purely sacred libraries existed. Sacred reading had not at all declined among fortunate village families; rather it had been swamped by secular interests.

Secular reading covered a remarkably broad range for an inland rural society. Apart from schoolbooks, there were 1,538 secular volumes, 4 for every religious volume retained. Among scores of subjects we may isolate nine major strands of secular thought. First is the very broad area of competing political and cultural allegiances. Beyond local life, interest in Vermont and New England was exceptionally widespread, especially after 1810.[84] Attachment to America as a nation grew even more rapidly, however, and showed itself in nearly every field of knowledge. For the first time, in the latter half of the 1820s, a slight majority of all works purchased and retained were written by Americans. Cultural nationalism particularly found expression in an ideal of American Christian republicanism. It encompassed both religious and more secular notions, with intense and aggressive Christian nationalism and more than passing interest in militarism at its core. Schoolbooks proclaimed this credo vigorously; American historical writing and most American contributions to modern literature were uniformly nationalistic.[85] Most works on politics and government proclaimed the virtues of the new nation. Militaristic concern with America's prowess, its military history, military technology, and values was widespread. This republican martial aesthetic was best summed up in Abel Bowen's sublime phrase, the "brilliant celerity of their electric execution," referring to the accuracy of American gunnery during the War of 1812.[86]

Cosmopolitanism, particularly attention to Great Britain, Western Europe, and Russia, was the third and broadest circle of intellectual commitment. Its interests pushed far beyond those of republicanism into liberalism. Concern with the commercial and religious aspects of other nations was especially strong, combining a longstanding focus on the North Atlantic Republic of Letters with a narrower view of the world as one large and varied market for America's goods and Christian values. Abundant evidence includes works on trade and business, business arithmetics, and intense interest in international trade and commerce in the regional press. Geographies reinforced cosmopolitanism, as did travel books, modern literature, and mercantile and business law. Interest in foreign affairs and political life in Europe first began to wane in the early 1820s, partly replaced by attention to foreign trade. Cosmopolitanism also took several other forms: histories of Great Britain, works on London life, and works on British politics and government; numerous schoolbooks that presented a predominantly British view of culture and learning; serious interest in Russia; world geographies and atlases; a series of works on the French Revolution and on the Napoleonic Wars; discussions of the transatlantic dimensions of republican and of liberal political thought; and more than 100 volumes of British literature that covered the preceding three centuries. All levels of allegiance expanded throughout the 1787–1835 decades. After 1825 nationalism overtook cosmopolitanism as the leading framework of extraregional thought.[87]

The second and third major strands of secular thought were the continuing appeal of both the Enlightenment and romanticism. In the former category, Scottish Common Sense Realism and moral sense theory dominated, especially after 1800, as Henry May has noted. The standard-bearers included Witherspoon and Samuel Stanhope Smith among Americans and Kames, Dugald Stewart, Adam Smith, and William Robertson among the British. Idealism had very little influence beyond Swedenborg, but a lighthanded liberal Christian utilitarianism was represented by several writers, notably William Paley, and skepticism survived in Palmer and Paine. Locke persisted as well, usually reinterpreted through Scottish lenses. Aspects of Enlightenment thought beyond strict philosophy included church and secular history. Freemasonry attracted considerable reading interest, as did classical traditions and travelogues in an Enlightenment spirit. Environmentalism, Christian rationalism, and progressive views of America's place in the historical cycle of nations highlighted the fortunate village Enlightenment tradition. Many works sustained a search for universal, eternal principles of human conduct and charted the triumph of reason and order over barbarism and chaotic "primitive" societies.[88]

By 1815 Romanticism was as pervasive as Enlightenment thought, providing the richest fund of new insights and styles of living among fortunate village families. Specific aspects of human experience were beginning to seem more consequential, and organicism was becoming a constant criterion for human appraisal, infusing historical accounts as extensively as it did stage-of-life works. There was a trend toward a cult of the representative historical leader, but introspection and literature of the private self also gained in prominence, and the picturesque approach to natural scenery attracted new attention. Science and literature joined hands in the quest for a clear view of the constitution of the natural world. Accounts of new and different places with exotic mores and values gained legions of dedicated readers.[89] Modern literature was rich enough among the libraries of fortunate village families to illustrate any scholarly account of the shift from Augustan thought to early Romanticism. During the transition and first stages of Romanticism, the pantheon included Sterne, Cowper, Scott, Byron, Southey, Henry Kirk White, and Wilson, plus popular romances by Jennings, Roche, Porter, West, and Genlis.[90]

The rise of romantic themes and treatments in several fields of knowledge helped to foster individualism as an underlying intellectual orientation toward life, especially after about 1805. Concern for the well-being of the individual, Band not just of the group (even the family), was gaining ground. Genius and the uniqueness of great leaders drew frequent comment in newer texts about Washington, Napoleon, Nelson, and Peter the Great. Introspective individualism figured in the Romantic literature of Sterne, Byron, Southey, and Scott. Works of a more mundane sort, on the human life cycle and on the Christian road to salvation, increasingly emphasized the special value of personal experience.[91]

A fourth strand in early-nineteenth-century fortunate village thought encompassed attention to the spirit of fact—defined as "practicality" and "utility," and encompassing planning, scheduling, and the rational details of organizational behavior—and, above all else, to quantity and a "calculating" mentality. At the root of this cluster of interconnected values was a fascination with the material world before residents' eyes and the particularities of its constitution. As we have already seen, Carey expressed anxiety about precision, accuracy, and speed in the collection and dissemination of new knowledge. Two-fifths of all fortunate village families owned a dictionary, most frequently Perry's or Walker's. Two-fifths owned a volume in science and technology, more than a third owned a work of geography, a third retained a private aid to personality development, and nearly a third owned at least one law book (there were twice as many libraries with law books as there were lawyers). To an important degree, the early national era in America, especially after 1800, was an age of "method" and practical rationality, as exemplified in many kinds of manuals. These interesting works, Americanizing every field of knowledge, provided basic assistance in the process of intellectual consolidation or synthesies, so essential as preparation for fresh thought. Encyclopedias, dictionaries, schoolbooks, and other compilations all illustrate a bent to summarize, arrange, and disseminate the "latest intelligence." To "modernize" knowledge, as contemporaries expressed it, also meant making it available to a far broader audience.[92]

Measuring and arranging knowledge, presenting it more "usefully," and then transmitting it as rapidly as possible were, by 1815, the goals of the day in information management. The result was a rapid Americanization of knowledge, by means of not only manuals but also works about economic and social organization and about personality development. Planned intellectual development was also on the rise, as is evident from the popularity of reading programs. Finally, there was a vast increase in the number of syntheses of all knowledge available in a single field, such as Adams's *Natural Philosophy*. Americans were learning to enjoy ordering the universe and reducing it to comprehensible proportions. Paley's utilitarianism or another more generalized form usually provided the philosophical underpinning.[93]

Closely allied to the "spirit of fact" was interest in topics more compatible with newer liberal than with older republican perspectives. Aspects of commercialization and its links with cities, trade, and the entrepreneurial ethos were subjects widely examined. Paul Faler, Alan Dawley, Anthony Wallace, and other writers have well described people's fascination with a protoindustrial set of values within a most conservative Christian work ethic. A set of cultural rules, promoted as mandatory for Christian survival, treated life on earth essentially as work for a commercial enterprise. The rules embraced orderliness, cleanliness, frugality, economy, industry (including an abhorrence of idleness as wastefulness), seriousness, efficient use of time, rational management of material resources, and the Christian duty of assisting the less fortunate. Few observers outside freethought circles noticed that these values fit well with the needs of factory work and were mainly advocated by wealthy spokesmen of an emergent commercial and factory management class.[94]

From the standpoint of Windsor District's fortunate villagers, cities were fascinating yet dangerous places. They perceived the transatlantic social world as split between alternative ideals: a felicitous rural lifestyle and an urbane urban one. In their strong commitment to a rural ideal, they emphasized the new commercial order and communications environment that were familiar from their daily lives. A thinner range of writers lauded urban ways, especially those of London but also of New York, Philadelphia, and less frequently, Boston. Cities were most conspicuously exciting and perilous but were also sophisticated, full of "natural occasions of wit," and rife with "evil" influences. Still other works, again in several different fields of knowledge, provided advice for the curious. This reading community was surprisingly uncritical of the whole commercial and urban world. Criticism was chiefly found in Aiken and Pope, in several sermons, and in devotional and a few stage-of-life works.[95]

Science and mathematics constituted yet a seventh strand in secular thought; it gained the widest possible range of supporters, from materialists to the conservative Princeton theological phalanx studied by Theodore Bozeman. Widespread fascination with science was often seen in purely secular, nondoxological terms: science seemed to be the "great deliverer of mankind," to use George H. Daniels' phrase. Fortunate village families showed scientific interest to a striking degree. Their libraries included eight recent vintage encyclopedias (plus two shares in encyclopedia libraries); several works each in scientific agriculture, astronomy, biology, and natural philosophy; several general works; and six periodicals.[96] Technology had a similarly important place. Works describing and advocating technology stressed the superiority of practical skill and, increasingly, of American practicality and technique. They included the half-dozen periodicals mentioned above, which regularly noted technological advances; newspapers; the eight encyclopedias, each of which had technological articles; and several individual works.[97].

Two strands of secular thought also had only recently emerged as popular reading interests. The Voyage-of-Life tradition of personality theory relied on a highly rationalistic and chiefly evangelical and Romantic approach to life and death, and a reformulated description of the life cycle and stages of personality development. Works on rhetoric, elocution, and oratory discoursed at length on the emotions and passions and their differences. Stage-of-life works specifically addressed childhood, parent-child relations, young men and young women, and death.[98] Evangelical social theory offered a group-centered alternative to egocentric Romanticism. Concern for private morality and benevolent reform activity proliferated in sermons, devotional treatises, works on the stages of life, and books and pamphlets advocating a particular reform or reformer. An important part of the explosion of voluntary benevolent reform activity focused on Christianizing the heathens, whether they were Native Americans shepherded by Rev. David Brainerd and Rev. Eleazer Wheelock or non-Western peoples discovered by Harriet Newell. The cult of domesticity and family, the largest area of interest, ranged from the coquettish advice in *The Wife* to Anthony Willich's eminently serious and practical *Domestic Encyclopedia*.[99]

A profound shift in knowledge occurred among Windsor District's fortunate village families between 1780 and 1830. It both triggered and simultaneously reflected a growing transformation in the circumstances of daily life. Intellectual innovation and daring intensified year after year in the first third of the nineteenth century, as new knowledge and an altered outlook led many rural Americans into what appeared to be an entirely new world.

The Dawn of a "Modern Age": Historical Conclusions and Public Policy Implications

As I was Walking through the spacious wilderness of the world . . .
  —John Bunyan, *The Christian Pilgrim*

Rural economy, society, and culture underwent a startling transformation between the Revolution and the mid-1830s. The outlines of an early modern rural commercial world and a mass culture were recognizable by 1835. Regional integration intensified in the middle third of the nineteenth century, as technological change accelerated. Windsor and Springfield became leaders in the machine tool industry. What Perry Miller termed "a machine civilization" emerged in the American Northeast. Commerce, industry, and technology were able to thrive in Windsor District precisely because residents, through reading, had come to believe that each of the three could provide them with important benefits in everyday life. Before the first machine shop opened, and well before the first telegraphic news reached Windsor District newspapers in the mid-1840s, cultural understanding had caught up with, had begun to direct, the pace of material change.

Windsor District had become a diverse early modern rural commercial area by 1835, but its development did not proceed in the manner usually described by social scientists relying on modernization theory. The wellsprings of commitment to change were embedded in the mix of rural institutions reshaping life on the narrow patches of good farmland between the forested hills of northwestern New England. Commercial relations, technological change, and a spirit of "modernness" gradually transformed traditional agricultural practices. The persistence of farming and grazing as central elements in an economy mixing subsistence and commercial agriculture, widespread commercialization of daily life, rural industrialization, and a new mass culture has obscured the character and scope of change by the mid-1830s.

Between 1780 and 1835, instead of an essentially stable, uniform pattern of agricultural existence, the district saw commercialization spread throughout the economy, society, and culture, in a cycle of settlement, stability, and peak rural commercial expansion, of surge and partial retreat. By 1835 the population balance had also shifted, and Windsor District, following all other parts of the Upper Valley except northern Orange County, began to lose residents faster than it gained new ones. Everywhere people perceived decline. The failure of premature railroad and steamboat schemes exaggerated forecasts of imminent "ruin," in no small measure because regional commercial exchange and a new mass culture had spawned intense awareness of the superior fortunes of actual and imagined competitors. Ironically, for Windsor District residents an unintended consequence of access to "the latest intelligence" was the knowledge that local development had been matched and surpassed by other American locales.

We have much to learn from our last major era of fundamental material and cultural transformation. The cycle of economic development, prosperity, and crisis that occurred in Windsor District during the first half century of the American republic has swept through most of the countryside regions of the world during the last two centuries. Two characteristics regularly associated with urban modernity, for instance, widespread involvement in commercial exchange and a mass culture founded on an integrated print communications environment, were dominant characteristics of rural New England well before the industrial era. As Upper Valley residents built the foundations of an early modern rural civilization, they participated to varying degrees in a whole series of major historical developments. Final thoughts about five such developments, each with material and cultural aspects, will be discussed here. Their combined impact on rural transformation is especially instructive today, as all societies on earth seek to understand the changing infrastructure of our contemporary world.

The constriction and gradual diminution of rural New England localism in the first third of nineteenth century has important implications for the increasingly international character of commerce, communications, and culture in our contemporary world, and for America's role in that world. As rural New England became integrated into regional transportation and communications networks in 1780–1835, localism gave way to new perspectives on the role of one's community in a nation-state and on the impact of distant events on local decision making. A parallel development is occurring today, also affecting commerce, communications, and culture as it constricts nationalism in favor of broad regional and international perspectives and activities.

The Dawn of a "Modern Age" in Rural New England, 1780–1835

As increasing numbers of Windsor District residents in 1810–30 accurately perceived that they were living through a fundamental transformation in rural life, they began to develop a vocabulary for understanding and expressing what was happening to them. Essentially, they came to believe that they were living in a modern age. The emergence of this vocabulary and social grammar to make sense of modernizing trends throughout the spectrum of contemporary knowledge constitutes the first major Upper Valley historical development in the Early Republic. The modernization of knowledge has five aspects.

While a few positions in the two-century-old intellectual debate between the ancients and the moderns garnered minor Upper Valley reading attention in 1780–1830, many writers of books, pamphlets, and especially newspapers were using the term "modern" and its variants in new contexts by 1815. Transatlantic civilization was perceived as "modern" in specific practical ways. The term "modern" assumed a definite temporal referent; all the most widely-used dictionaries after 1790 defined modern as "recent" and "pertaining to the present time." Newspaper editors and other contributors took as an important goal, to "modernize" knowledge. By this they meant to "render modern" by presenting the "latest intelligence." As they did so, editors and others also used the designation "moderns" to refer to "the people of late or present times," "those who have lived lately." Finally, writers regularly employed "modernness" to mean "newness," "novelty," "recentness of origin," and "the state of being unknown to former times." By 1815, in the minds of Upper Valley residents, they lived in a "modern age" or a "modern time." Whether contemporaries were accurate or not, if we are to understand and evaluate the era, it is valuable to approach this issue using their own mental framework.[1]

A slow but relentless "modernizing" of substantive knowledge was diffused through the network of human habitats in Windsor District after the Revolution. As the process progressed, it reshaped regional mentalities in several ways. First, it fostered secularization in reading matter of all kinds, especially in the fortunate village and fortunate farmstead reading communities, and also in a broad range of self-sufficient hamlet families, in a narrower group of self-sufficient farmstead families, and in artisan and a few other households within the hardscrabble living situation. Books borrowed from social libraries, chapbook reading, and newspaper and almanac reading, were heavily secular. Even in family libraries, the most stable core of reading, interest in secular affairs rose substantially.

Three fundamentally different intellectual orientations to life on earth and thereafter existed throughout Windsor District's five human habitats. Together these determinations formed the intellectual foundations of early modern thought in America. While each orientation drew on intellectual traditions going back

Table 10–1: Windsor District Basic Mentalités, *1780–1830*

Intellectual Orientation by Type of Library*	Hardscrabble (n=183)	Self-Sufficient Farmstead (n=69)	Self-Sufficient Hamlet (n=16)	Fortunate Farmstead (n=62)	Fortunate Village (n=66)
Sacred: 108 27%					
Religious Intensive	59	18	1	11	2
Religious Intensive/Extensive	8	1	0	5	0
Professional:					
–Theological	0	1	0	1	1
Sacred/Secular: 271 69%					
Sacred/Secular Intensive	90	14	6	13	10
Sacred/Secular Extensive	26	29	3	32	24
Professional:					
Theological	0	2	0	0	2
Legal	0	2	0	2	6
Medical	0	1	2	0	6
Printer/Pub.	0	0	0	0	1
Secular: 17 4%					
Major Secular Extensive	0	0	3	1	7
Professional:					
Legal	0	0	1	0	2
Medical	0	1	0	1	1

* Professional libraries have been distinguished by their contents.

centuries, all three nurtured contemporary beliefs and values as well. A heritage of Protestant Christianity, shared by residents of all five human habitats, wholly dominated families who centered their mental lives on religion, conversion, and salvation; these people perused only sacred reading matter. A second orientation blended a growing range of sacred and secular concerns. And a third, minor but gaining in influence, was almost completely secular in perspective. Table 10–1 organizes the 396 family libraries in our study group according to these three distinct intellectual orientations.

The uses of printed matter in Windsor District were as varied as a Vermont day. Lifelong learning nourished both rapid change and constancy. Between 1790 and 1830 two of three main groups of families held strong to moderate allegiance to a new order of life shaped by commercial exchange and print communications. Families exhibiting both religious and secular reading interests comprised the majority intellectual orientation (69 percent). Those exhibiting only sacred interests, mainly intensive reading matter, comprised a sizable but declining minority (27 percent), while families exhibiting almost exclusively secular reading interests formed a tiny minority (4 percent) living in the district primarily after 1810.[2] The relationship between sacred and secular reading was complicated. While an exclusively religious view of the world greatly diminished in the half century after the Revolution, some families strengthened their exclusive reliance on sacred perspectives, not despite but *because* they participated in print culture. By 1815 those relying largely on sacred perspectives were, generally speaking, firm resisters of most and sometimes all currents of economic and cultural change. But even isolated farming and grazing families, and their poor cousins throughout the district, were regularly poring over their Bibles for arguments against change and often for signs of a Second Coming. Through careful selection from available printed matter, many families in the hardscrabble, self-sufficient farmstead, and hamlet human habitats, and some in the fortunate farmstead and village living situations, chose to reconfirm an essentially sacred world view.

Most Windsor District families read not less but more about religious subjects in 1825 than in 1795; a noticeable decline in sacred reading occurred only among families with overwhelmingly secular reading interests. The point is that reading in secular affairs dramatically increased and swamped religious reading, as measured in numbers of volumes owned (70 percent to 30 percent). The persistence of intensive reading (an experience very different from that engaged in most of the time by most of the readers of this book) cautions us against assuming that few books meant little reading. Both sacred and secular reading were actively engaged in by a majority of the population of Windsor District by about 1805 and continued thereafter. Secularization rarely led to desacralization.

Concluding a discussion of Benjamin Silliman's mind, John C. Greene pinpointed the volatile interaction of sacred and secular in early-nineteenth-century American thought: "Piety, patriotism, science, practical invention, and business were welded together in a fervent vision of the noble destiny prepared by God."[3] We may now add other equally central clusters of ideas: cosmopolitanism, nationalism, regionalism, and localism, all competing for political allegiance; Enlightenment and Romantic perspectives on human and natural existence; an emerging spirit of fact and of "modernness," leading to fascination with the particularities of commerce and trade and with the technology and inventions of the early Industrial Revolution; and finally, a major new theory of personality development, the Voyage-of-Life tradition, premised on gender distinctions and efforts to rationalize all tasks and problems facing each stage of life.

A second aspect of the modernization of knowledge concerned a shift from mainly intensive reading matter and styles to a mix of intensive and several newer extensive reading styles and subject matter. Changing emphases in reading styles accompanied new additions to the reading repertoire. It is noteworthy that even two-fifths of the 1,403 specified volumes of sacred reading were extensive reading matter—formal theology, church history, and sermons. Among the 3,217 secular volumes, an astounding 85 percent were extensive reading matter, spread throughout some eighteen subjects. Altogether, 71 percent of all known works were usually read in a reading style other than the intensive. Between 1780 and 1830 and especially after 1800, the fortunate village, fortunate farmstead, and self-sufficient hamlet reading communities were dominated by extensive reading styles and subject matter. Intensive styles and subject matter retained a powerful hold on hardscrabble and most self-sufficient farmstead families.

Related to secularization and changing reading styles was a third aspect of the modernization of knowledge: greater acceptance of change as a normal part of daily life. Particularly after 1815, local commentary about intensifying economic, social, and cultural changes increased markedly. Some families wished nothing to do with earthly striving. Their life goal was salvation and a return to eternal life in heaven (see chapter 2). Change was welcomed by other families, but many—good republicans of all varieties—remained profoundly ambivalent about the moral implications of commercialization. Slowly, however, acceptance and even advocacy of change won a greater following, spurred on by its overall dominance in public dialogue, especially in weekly newspapers. Varying dramatically across the network of human habitats, a newfound ideal of intellectual currency imputed great value to "timeliness" and accuracy in information diffusion. Fascination with the technology of information dissemination and with speed in the circulation of knowledge via stagecoach, steamboat, and railroad comprised an important element in a vibrant style of thought: the "technological sublime."[4] The initial view of the telegraph in the mid-1840s was that it annihilated time and space; actually this assessment emerged out of a longstanding interest in the speed with which knowledge circulated. Although specific criticism was expressed in an organized way by the Workingmen's movement on behalf of those directly suffering the effects of change, much broader anxiety was vented in response to economic downturn. After the bubble of unlimited prosperity burst in the mid-1830s, assessments of the character of the age became more tempered, ambivalent, and realistic.

Among all Windsor District occupational groups, artisan families were most profoundly impressed by the new communications environment. A large majority took great advantage of print culture and sustained the most active intellectual interests of any occupational group except professional and manufacturing families. This was the case in all human habitats. The other third of all artisan families, no poorer by wealth but mostly living in the countryside away from villages, mainly held to traditional intensive reading styles and texts.

With an ideal of intellectual currency came a fourth aspect of the modernization of knowledge: the decline of localism as a vibrant intellectual stance and its replacement by integrative regional, national, and international perspectives. "Modern intelligence" in its contemporary trans-local frame of reference became a cultural ideal. As speed in the diffusion of news about area commerce and distant climes increased, localism turned defensive. When Lafayette visited Windsor on the Fourth of July, 1825, the traditional image of rural felicity was initially evoked by one of the village's leading citizens. General Forbes presented to his guest a rural people "plain and hardy, but intelligent and virtuous: industrious cultivators of the earth, but enjoying on their lofty hills, and in their lowly vallies, comfort and independence." Then the speaker made a surprising addition. He said he understood well that this was not Lafayette's first stop in America: "Our hearts are not the less full. They have, indeed, been constantly and tenderly alive to all your movements, and whatever concerned you, while traversing the union." The emotion underpinning this peculiar sentiment was empathy; but the statement also attested to the power of Windsor's weekly newspapers to report Lafayette's tour of America for months and to assess its impact. This is a striking example of a phenomenon wholly new in rural areas of the Western world. Ordinary countryside citizens were presumed regularly to have been following the distant course of travel by and celebration of a transatlantic military and political hero. Intelligence in rural New England of the 1820s no longer meant native ability; this was taken for granted. "Intelligence" meant awareness of the contemporary world and, in particular, accurate, timely knowledge of distant current occurrences.[5]

The local world and the distant world, then, were being drawn much closer together and newly seen by a large share of families as parts of an interrelated whole. This was a remarkable achievement for a forest society on the periphery of North Atlantic civilization. The chief effect of expanding print culture after 1783 was that an ever-increasing share of Windsor District families began to keep up with the course of public life beyond their own township, and with both newer and older vintage intellectual developments in the Western world generally. They also saw themselves as participants in a vast transformation. Any family reading a weekly newspaper learned about many of the political, social, economic, and cultural affairs in their economic locale, about other reading matter available at Windsor, and about current events of every imaginable sort occurring in Boston, New York, London, and Europe. By 1815 interest in the nonlocal world, viewed through British cultural lenses, was widespread in Windsor District, and it led to a more concrete understanding of interaction among cities, villages, and the countryside, among regions and nations, and across transatlantic civilization.

A fifth aspect of the modernization of knowledge was its gradual Americanization, especially after 1815. Americanization occurred in stages: initial awareness, intellectual consolidation, adaptation, construction, and criticism. In his 1821 *Travels*, Timothy Dwight noted that Americans generally supplied their wants in "every art, science, and path of literature" from British authors. The central reason was, as Dwight put it, that the book "of almost every kind on almost every subject are already written to our hands." Seven years later (1828), James Fenimore Cooper lamented in his *Notions of the Americans* that "compared to the books that are printed and read, those of native origin are few indeed." He believed this to be a phenomenon new in history: "the United States are the first nation that possessed institutions, and, of course, distinctive opinions of its own, that was ever dependent on a foreign people for its literature." Until the 1820s, the basic mold for all five principal rural New England *mentalités* was European. During the 1820s this situation changed rapidly and, for the first time, a majority of works available for sale came to be of American origin.[6]

The vast modernization of knowledge had an energizing effect on everyday life in Windsor District. The rural American Northeast was the first place in the Western world where much of society—all but the poorest families, and a few of those, and females as well as males—came to accept the integration of local and distant worlds. Geographically isolated near the western fringe of North Atlantic civilization, Upper Valley residents during the Revolutionary era and Early Republic learned the Western heritage, as translated through Augustan and late-eighteenth-century British and American cultural perspectives, in an environment less limited by the traditional forces of wealth, occupation, and social status than in other early modern Western nations.

Employing mainly intensive reading styles at first, readers pored over a narrow range of sacred and secular texts. Then, although they actually observed the world through these lenses, they assumed that their eyes were clear and their minds unobstructed. The results often proved unsettling. Countless private interpretations of the world were spun during the long, isolated Upper Valley reading period from late November through early April. Counterweights to private interpretations existed but were no match for a vivid imagination applied in intensive chant-like reading, thinking, speaking, and singing. Joseph Smith could found a religion, Orestes Brownson could prophesy a new world, and William Miller could "calculate" the end of life on earth. Most residents, of course, lived within more traditional bounds than this trio, but they and a few hundred like-minded souls together exerted an extraordinary influence on antebellum cultural affairs. Rural New Englanders took their versions of the Western intellectual heritage seriously and literally, and believed the world should follow their lead.

The Commercialization of Economic, Social, and Cultural Life, and the Creation of an Early Modern Rural Infrastructure

Among other important Upper Valley historical developments through the early 1830s, perhaps the broadest was commercialization. Along with the new mass culture, commercialization created a novel early modern rural infrastructure in a harsh forest environment. Sustaining life in the Upper Valley had never been easy. As Asa Smith noted in the early 1850s, "only enterprising and efficient men would settle in a region rough and forbidding as this once was."[7] Steady, purposeful development, hammered out amid adversity in northeastern forests, is one of the taproots of American inquisitiveness and adventurousness. The commercialization of the economy, the society, and the culture restructured rural life.[8] During this half century an agricultural economy came to be centered on commercial exchange. Traditional social relations, exemplified by the system of "changing works," were profoundly altered in the process.

Commercialization evolved in steps in 1780–1830, attracting ever more families to produce for and purchase from businesses in their economic locales. Each step furthered the integration of human habitats spreading from the river valley into the foothills of the Green Mountains. The difference in commercial activity between 1790 and 1830 was astonishing.[9] Participation in commercial exchange activity rose in the fortunate village and surrounding fortunate farmstead habitats from some households by 1800, to most by 1815, and to all but the poorest households by 1830. In later settled self-sufficient hamlet habitats (mainly after 1800), participation spread from some households by 1815 to all but the poorest by 1830. The self-sufficient farmstead habitat saw participation spread more slowly, from a few households by 1800, to some by 1815, and to most by 1830. Hardscrabble households rarely participated as late as 1800, by 1815 a few did so, and even by 1830 only about a third did so.

The career of Orestes A. Brownson, a native son of Windsor County, vividly illustrates a basic paradox in our understanding of rural New England infrastructure. One of the Americans most prophetic about the nature of early industrial society, Brownson apparently grew up among the poorest families in one of the last settled and least commercially developed parts of the American Northeast. Born in 1803 in the mountainous hardscrabble township of Stockbridge, Brownson was raised there and in a slightly larger self-sufficient upland grazing community far beyond South Royalton village. Notwithstanding his completely agrarian, sheepherding origins and the lack of any later work experience as a factory operative, by the late 1820s, well before the modern factory system had spread widely, Brownson somehow developed one of the most knowledgeable and detailed critiques of the coming of the modern world in America. How could this be? Our understanding either of Brownson's life and world view, or of the material and cultural conditions of the world he inhabited, must be very inadequate. That he developed his views of early commercial and industrial society from such an unlikely vantage point starkly suggests how little we yet understand about rural New England at the dawn of the modern era.[10]

Brownson may have had a prophetic spark, but he was also an astute observer of the changing texture of rural lifestyles. The overwhelming majority of Americans experienced the coming of industrial society not in the spread of large factories, cities, or elaborate bureaucracy, but indirectly, in new and ever more frequent contacts that led to increasing domination by distant centers of commerce and culture. Material and cultural change in the Upper Valley did not entail the urbanization of rural society. Rather, rural villages took on some functions traditionally provided solely by cities, and developed several new functions. The decentralization of printing and publishing into rural Upper Valley villages after the Revolution was a development new in transatlantic society. It created a vigorous communications environment that spurred a fundamental transformation in rural *mentalités*. Forever afterwards it was possible to remain rural and yet no longer be culturally isolated from the experience of other human beings. Works written by people in the next county or region, or halfway around the world, all circulated widely through rural areas. As rural literacy spread, print—not electronic—communications created the first rural dimension of an international community of commerce and culture. In 1783, when Alden Spooner chose his newspaper masthead—"knowledge from distant climes"—he reflected this new reality.[11]

In this book we have portrayed a rural society breaking out of what Braudel terms the "rules which [had] enclosed the world in stability for such a long period."[12] By sharing in a new order of rural existence, Windsor District's forest people became a commercialized forest people, informed about local affairs and the distant world through a new mass culture. Rural factory and shop production of many necessities and luxuries, including printed matter, and widespread commercial exchange supplemented farming, grazing, and artisan labor as basic elements in the economy. In the social sphere public voluntary organizations multiplied affiliative bonding, subtly changing the social fabric for youth, adults, and the elderly. Marked by narrowly segmented and specialized concerns, over a hundred extrafamilial "associations" proliferated in Windsor District by the late 1820s. Expanding access to knowledge led to vast differentiation in economic and social as well as cultural participation.[13]

During the first third of the nineteenth century, Windsor District thrived, experiencing great if uneven prosperity that reached all but hardscrabble families. By 1815, material and cultural isolation and insularity were being replaced by awareness and interaction, extensively in three of the human habitats of Windsor District and haltingly in the other two. By the late 1830s, the network of human habitats in Windsor District was again changing its basic form, creating a more uniform rural ecology.

The Emergence of an Age of Reading in America

A third historical development of great significance in rural New England between 1780 and 1835 was the emergence of an age of reading, marked by the prevalence of reading as "among the necessaries of life." Elsewhere in the North Atlantic in 1800—from Sweden and Germany to Scotland and the cities of the American Northeast—a reorganization of cultural life had been under way for decades, but it was limited to the upper- and solidly middle-class social groups living mostly in urban settings. After the Revolution, in the rural areas of the American Northeast, print culture became pervasive, even reaching some of the poorest families. The ideology of literacy gave tacit approval for all social classes to participate in public life, in order to sustain America as a Christian republican nation. This was the proper role of an American citizen. What a wonderfully rational ideological goal this was. The age of reading that commenced in the first third of the nineteenth century has continued into our own time.

Certainly by 1810 regular reading could ease the workload noticeably and improve the quality of individual and family life in Windsor District. Regular reading made available a far wider range of choices for participation in public life; rendered a tough, exhausting life more varied and interesting; and facilitated diverting inward voyages and experiences. These—and not primarily whether it improved the material conditions of life—are some of the standards appropriate for measuring the impact of literacy in rural New England.[14]

Except for an as-yet-undetermined share of the 20 percent of families who were poorest and most isolated, living in the hardscrabble habitat, by 1810 virtually all males and nearly all females were acquiring literacy during childhood and youth. By that date a substantial and growing majority of families maintained a relish for reading and engaged in a habit of lifelong learning. While absolute precision will always elude us, based on all known sources for the total Windsor District population, we estimate that the share of families engaging in some regular reading reached at least 70 percent by 1810 and perhaps 80 percent by the late 1820s. Even among the poor and isolated, elementary literacy had made monumental progress, especially relative to other rural societies in the Western world.

What general causes accounted for the rise of reading as a necessity of life, beyond the acquisition of elementary literacy skills? There were two long-term and three more immediate basic causes. Among long-term factors, the influence of the ideal of public political involvement, a heritage of the Revolution and Confederation periods now embodied in the conception of republican citizenship, was profound. The responsibilities of citizenship in the new republic demanded of both males and females new forms of knowledge. In the new republican experiment initial curiosity quickly turned to political commitment between the 1790s and 1815, supplemented by anxiety about the nation's perilous position within the European balance of power. In the generation following the Revolution, American political and cultural leaders assumed that it was necessary to ransack the fund of human experience in several fields of knowledge. They read about and endlessly debated what the wisdom of the ages revealed concerning the proper course of development for a republic. By following this dialogue, a republican citizenry was defining a central characteristic of America as a New World republic: America became a republic of knowledge. America's ambivalent position throughout the early national era, as both an independent nation-state and a cultural province of Great Britain, exacerbated the need for current information. Sweden and Scotland, the other countries with the highest literacy levels in the Western world, were also peripheral to many of the main currents of European civilization. This position greatly intensified local consumption of printed matter within Windsor District.

A second long-term cause of the rise of reading was Protestant Christianity's emphasis on the printed word, especially the Bible. By the time of the Great Awakening, printed matter had become a normal element of religious services and devotional practice throughout New England. Increased denominational competition thereafter further intensified reliance on printed matter to interpret the way to salvation.

At least three other factors were more immediate to the historical position of rural New England in the Early Republic. First was the expansion of a market-based economy throughout the Northeast, linking local and international commercial exchange. Growing markets encouraged more frequent consumption of a wide variety of commodities, including printed matter. The new communications environment and the emergence of new educational, political, religious, and general cultural institutions further encouraged reading. Another factor was the widespread establishment of a neighborhood district school system and a broad ideology stressing the multiple benefits of literacy and reading. Third was the decentralization of print centers throughout the rural New England countryside; as a result, printed matter circulated ever more widely, closely following the diffusion of commerce. After mid-1783 printed matter circulated south from Windsor through the river valley townships and west into the hinterlands.

As reading became an accepted part of everyday life two among the initial group of widely literate rural generations evolved. The proportions of the male, and especially the female, population actively engaged in continuing learning throughout life were among the highest in the Western world. Active lifelong learning by means of printed matter became a normal element of existence for both genders. Taking hold in various ways, a process of cultural evolution involved different amounts, kinds, frequencies, and styles of reading. In its initial stage, the acquisition of elementary literacy, this evolution progressed through the different access zones in the communications network of Windsor District in the manner described previously.[15]

Home instruction and district schools were the primary agents in the inculcation of literacy skills. The content of household and school instructional books aimed at providing a foundation in the wisdom of the ages. Most of the popular textbook readers, arithmetics, and geographies, and even some spellers, also encouraged the spread of commerce. That schoolbook reading material failed to introduce students to broader problems and current issues of the public world they were soon to enter should not be surprising. The main goal of primary education in rural New England through 1830 was the formation of a sound conscience and a well-grounded world view. Academies furthered this objective, and through their opportunities for academic specialization also provided a means of economic and social ascent. Interest in public life, it was widely assumed, would develop naturally during its proper season of life, late youth and early adulthood.

In and of itself, the widespread acquisition of literacy skills and basic knowledge did not necessitate a vast increase either in continued reading or in available printed matter. This is, at present, the inference to be drawn from the history of literacy in Sweden.[16] However, the era in which literacy became very widespread for both males and females in rural New England, 1780–1835, was also marked by rapid commercialization of social and cultural as well as economic relations. As a result, the maintenance of literacy skills throughout later life was facilitated by multiplication of reading occasions and exponential growth in the variety of printed matter suited to them.

By 1810 numerous institutions furthering lifelong learning had emerged in Windsor District. We may follow their evolutuion by assessing institutional encouragements to reading at three moments in time: 1790, 1810, and 1830. First, in 1790 there were businesses directly encouraging the spread of reading, including two printing offices, newspapers, and bookstores, and several general stores, itinerant authors, and peddlers. The comprehensive role of the rural

Mentalités: Intellectual Reservoirs

weeklies in fostering business of all sorts has already been discussed. In addition, about two dozen subsidiary institutions included district schools in the river valley and the central tier of townships, several religious denominations throughout these same townships, and a post office at Windsor. State and national governments also stimulated reading as their proceedings and laws were reprinted in local newspapers.

Twenty years later, in 1810, the situation had changed dramatically. Within Windsor District alone, three weekly newspapers and an equal number of printing offices supplied four bookstores, two other binders, and a far larger number of general stores and peddlers, plus an unknown number of itinerant authors. Windsor District authorship had increased substantially, and Windsor village had already spawned a short-lived literary periodical, the *Village Magazine*. The range of stores, shops, and manufactories seeking customers through notices and advertisements in the rural weeklies had expanded greatly (to 120); just after harvest some newspapers looked like business directories.

A second element of life supporting lifelong learning in 1810 encompassed over two hundred subsidiary social institutions, each relying partly on printed matter to foster its ends. Approximately one hundred district schools were located in ten of the eleven townships, and a mixed academy (and a dancing school) thrived at Windsor. Lending libraries were active in Windsor, Chester, and Springfield. Two colleges sought Windsor District male students through local advertisements. State and national governments, Federalist and Jeffersonian political parties (county and occasionally township organizations), more than a dozen branches of various religious denominations, and post offices in six of Windsor District's eleven townships all sought patronage and the attention of readers. Windsor newspapers published quarterly lists of all letters not yet claimed from each district post office. Moreover, local branches of a half dozen benevolent, moral reform, and other social organizations such as the Masons had been founded; each wished to obtain more members and to spread "intelligence" about its cause.

By 1830 the list of institutions fostering involvement through printed matter read like a greatly expanded directory of Windsor District public life. A panoply of printing offices, newspapers, bookstores, binderies, general stores, peddlers, and itinerant and local authors performed primary dissemination functions. District newspapers catered to 173 businesses in 1830. In addition, an astounding number and variety of groups and organizations sought adherents through the district's print communications network. About 110 district schools provided summer and winter instruction at the elementary level. There were also Sabbath schools in several townships and a county organization coordinating their activities. There were three academies at Windsor (two male and one female), another academy at Chester, a writing school at Windsor, and a Universalist ministerial training school at Reading. Dartmouth College, Middlebury College, and the University of Vermont also sought male students through the rural weeklies.

Informal educational opportunities included the Windsor Lyceum and a separate series of lectures on chemistry, also held at Windsor. New social libraries had been established at West Windsor, Cavendish, Andover, Weston, and Reading, in addition to the three libraries previously established at Windsor, Springfield, and Chester. Windsor and Chester villages also had initiated cheaper circulating libraries during the 1820s, and a mysterious encyclopedia library had opened. Rounding out educational institutions, Windsor and Chester villages sported a total of four reading rooms.[17]

In the political arena, organizations of both national political parties, the Jacksonians and the National Republicans, plus two other regional political groups, Antimasons and Workingmen, were active. The usual proceedings and laws of state and federal governments were published, plus commentary on specific issues affecting Windsor County residents, such as a bridge or canal, or a whole region, such as steamboat service on the Connecticut River. Each township except Baltimore had at least one post office in 1830; altogether there were fifteen in the district. Other cultural institutions included theaters at Windsor and Chester and a dancing school at Windsor. At least thirty-one religious groups were strewn across the district, led in numbers by Methodists, Congregationalists, Universalists, and Baptists but also including Unitarians, Episcopalians, Christians, and Freewill Baptists. More than a dozen local branches of reform and other social organizations also sought adherents.

In the half century following the Revolution, many different vehicles of print communication vied for attention. Insight into their relative popularity may be gained by arranging all evidence on the purchase, borrowing, and gifting of printed matter in layers of diffusion, each affecting different elements of the total population in 1825.[18] The first and broadest layer of diffusion included Bibles, Testaments, and Commentaries, etc., read by approximately 80 percent of all families with readers. A second layer included almanacs (c.65 percent), schoolbooks (c.60 percent), and weekly newspapers (c. 50–55 percent). A third layer of diffusion embraced hymnals and psalm books, dictionaries, primers, and children's books (all at c. 40 percent). A fourth layer of diffusion encompassed theology, sermons, church history, and modern literature (at c. 30 percent); and devotion and prayer books, travel and voyages, geography, history, and stages of life (at c. 20 percent). Least widely read were science/ technology, law, philosophy, and politics/government (at c. 10 percent) followed by medicine, and classical writings (at c. 5 percent).

Each type of imprint formed its own pattern of circulation through the five types of human habitats. Diffusion proceeded at widely differing rates through the network. Moreover, both the networks of habitats and the overall knowledge flow for each type of imprint changed with time. Overall, with vastly increased penetration, between 1780 and 1830 printed matter became a powerful agent of change among ordinary people, as it had been among elites for three centuries. By the 1820s the vast array of available ideas and opinions had accelerated rural cultural diversity to a degree unimaginable in the 1780s. Moreover, as Roth's study of Upper Valley political, economic, and religious life demonstrates, it had significantly intensified conflict.

Intellectual change bred instability. The search for life's meaning amplified diversity; by 1815 conflict was everywhere. The major terms of American culture, the nature of a Christian republican nation, and the proper role of its citizens provoked the greatest disagreement. The wisdom of the ages remained a touchstone, but as individuals and families began to read more regularly, they confronted their own intellectual assumptions, often for the first time. As Nathan Hatch puts it, "people on a number of fronts began to speak, write, and organize against the authority of mediating elites, of social distinctions, and of any human tie that did not spring from volitional allegiance." Cultural life in rural New England involved a struggle between "a hierarchic and ordered society" and "demands for root and branch reform." The dialogue sometimes yielded startling clarity, more frequently led to cacophony and confusion, and almost always charged the atmosphere with earnestness.[19]

By 1815, the material and cultural landscape within the Upper Valley had changed enough for the nature of American society to become the central cultural question. What kind of a society was this? What kind of a society could it be? Life in rural New England was dynamic, rent with contradiction, positively electric with arguments, solutions, prophecies, schemes, plans, conspiracies, paranoia, and plain delusion. Abel Tomkins reflected this when he threw up his hands in frustration and asked: "Why all these false prophets, these ringleaders, and founders of new orders?"[20] By the second quarter of the nineteenth century it was too late to return to an earlier way of life. The second generation of Windsor District readers held too many conflicting views about change and permanence to return to a mythical past of clarity, order, and acceptance. That so many longed to return to a golden age of simple material life and cultural authority indicates the difficulties they experienced in adjusting to a new rural infrastructure.

Rural Pluralism and Cultural Diversity

The fourth major development of rural life between 1780 and 1835 was the dramatic growth of rural pluralism and cultural diversity. To understand their forms and their differing intensities in rural New England, we have developed a broad conceptual framework encompassing rural life. First we elaborated a conception of a network of five distinct living situations. Employing this formulation we then sketched the varying but generally increasing penetration of hardscrabble through fortunate village living situations by a new rural commercial order. The analysis of human habitats is based on the interaction of eight factors exerting influence in varying combinations (see the introduction). Neither material nor cultural aspects of change were ever exclusively dominant for long; their interaction was too intimate. Combinations of factors represented the building blocks of rural life, as we have been able to reconstruct them from available evidence. Five sets of combinations gave shape to a rural infrastructure exhibiting an early modern order of rural life.

The concept of a series of rural living situations shaping distinctive reading communities has important implications for the study of cultural life and of the formation of public opinion in a nation more than five-sixths rural in 1830. Public opinion was a phenomenon of print culture much commented on in urban settings by the mid-eighteenth century, as middle-class readership increased substantially throughout Europe and America. In rural New England between 1780 and 1830, public opinion was discussed as if it were a physical substance permeating the atmosphere. Actually, the apparent uniformity of Upper Valley cultural life hid enormous diversity; the cultural atmosphere was quite localized. And its formation was a complicated process. Newspaper editors played a central role as gatekeepers, while authors, publishers, printers, bookstore owners, clergy, other professionals, merchants, manufacturers, and gentleman farmers, made important contributions. But the affiliative choices and involvements of Windsor District families also depended on other factors, including kinship history, private myths families lived by, religious preferences, and political interests. Public opinion incorporated many reading publics or intended audiences, "those to whom authors and publishers addressed their works."[21] Five broad rural audiences selected varying mixes of printed matter, from which they constructed differing collective *mentalités*. On some issues public opinion was uniform across all five human habitats; at other times it varied from one reading community to the next.[22] Thus, between 1780 and 1835, it is less accurate to speak of a democratization of knowledge than of a partial democratization of access to knowledge.

The conceptual framework outlined above is able to account for the enormous diversity in nineteenth-century American life. The entire array of major and minor Upper Valley figures contributing actively to cultural life rose to maturity within the network of rural human habitats. For instance, an understanding of human habitats provides important insights into the life of Joseph Smith, who purportedly "outgrew his culture" while living within the rural world of the Upper Valley.[23] The specific cultural and material roots of Mormonism lay in the sacred fundamentalism of the hardscrabble and self-sufficient farmstead reading communities. The Smith family lived a fairly typical farmstead existence from the time of its migration to Vermont in 1791 through its departure a quarter century later, in 1816. The Smiths owned their own farm for a time but struggled to eke out an existence, leaned to religious practices popular in these habitats — anti-Standing Order Universalism and Methodism — when they became active churchgoers, and remained opposed to many elements of commercial life, partly in response to family financial reversals. The Smiths exhibited enduring fascination with the sacred world and an ideal of salvation reinforced by a harsh standard of vital piety. But they also participated actively in a longstanding secular approach to the supernatural world of magic and spirits. Eventually Joseph Smith merged religion and magic in a manner that attracted a growing following. Whatever one's position on Smith as a religious prophet, his finding and translating a set of golden tablets containing a long-lost version of sacred history recalls the intensive reading style and longing for return to Christian fundamentals found in many hardscrabble and self-sufficient farmstead families. Smith incorporated almost as much of the wisdom of the ages as he rejected.[24]

A Shift in the Meanings of Human Happiness

Among the material and cultural changes of 1780–1830 another "subtler occurrence," as invisible yet powerful as the pull of gravity, emerged. A shift in the meaning of human happiness constituted a fifth major development of the Early Republic. By 1820 people were far more openly mounting a characteristically modern search for happiness on earth. While the subject had of course been discussed since ancient times, possible roads to earthly happiness now were studied with a new urgency. With growing material prosperity, for the first time in the history of a rural Western people human happiness on earth for the many seemed a realistic possibility. Heaven on earth had long been a marvelous postmillennialist fantasy, but this newer vision captured serious-minded farming, artisan, business, and manufacturing families as well as the usual array of true believers. Sacred and secular aims mixed, as this primary, controlling vision grew in importance after 1815. Both scientists and semi-skilled laborers went to New Harmony in a "quest for the new moral world."[25]

The main reasons why human happiness on earth now appeared possible to so many more families are embedded in the remarkable transformation of material and cultural conditions detailed in this book. Many of the newest members of reading communities were experiencing the most basic changes in their material and cultural conditions of life. These included changes in the production, distribution, and consumption of material goods. At the same time, rural families learned about a wide range of potential lifestyles through the pages of weekly newspapers and on trips to villages and hamlets. Additionally, for the first time in rural society, worldly goods used by the richest elements of society were on display, divorced from the homes of their intended purchasers. The commercialization of rural society offered worlds of dreams to families who otherwise would have learned far less about the lifestyles of wealthier groups. The possibilities of prosperity provoked endless fantasies in people who had always believed that invisible supernatural (secular and sacred) forces determined the course of daily existence.

By the late 1830s many of these hopes had been blasted. Some gave up longing for earthly happiness; chief among these were the Millerites. Many more continued to strive for human happiness on earth, adjusting and readjusting the means employed toward this end. The term "reform" has never quite encompassed this ferment. The possibilities for human happiness on earth constituted the central issue of the age after 1815, requiring several social philosophies to broaden their goals far beyond mere reform of the existing world.[26]

Why did the search for human happiness on earth become more persistent, relentless, and sometimes desperate after 1815? Perhaps the most important reason was the extreme variability in actual family prosperity. Increased awareness of differences in material worth, and in the comforts that wealth, social position, and religious and political power brought, were hammered home weekly by the newspapers and other printed matter. Awareness of possible gain quickened the search for happiness. Providing support for all readers, print culture also advanced compensations for those who failed or who chose not to pursue material success. Many were bought off with a literature offering escape, fantasy, and dreams as compensation for the lack of material goods and services.

The quest for human happiness on earth created unprecedented cultural turmoil between 1815 and the 1850s. A sense of declension was almost as prevalent as a sense of opportunity. Resignation and the hopes of future perfection struggled in nearly every realm of life. The spread of lifelong learning altered the traditional standards by which many families made decisions about acceptable levels of material prosperity. Many families and individuals sought to augment their material circumstances by organizing their lives in new ways.[27] Others migrated and began again, hoping to create new conditions more likely to enhance material and cultural prosperity. Both choices were very popular after about 1810, as Lewis Stilwell long ago demonstrated. For those who stayed, several decades of struggle over the direction and control of public life ensued, documented fully by Roth. In the intensification of their search for happiness on earth, rural New Englanders manifested distinctly modern behavior.[28]

One key question posed by the conception of a network of human habitats is this: Was it generally the case that enhanced participation in rural material and cultural life followed increasing exposure to variety in commerce and culture? The answer is decidedly yes. Five examples of cultural exchange will suggest the basic relationship. The large majority of Windsor District students attending the nearest college, Dartmouth, came from just two living situations, fortunate village and fortunate farmstead. Likewise, the subscription pattern for many extensive-reading works—for instance, a new Charlestown, Massachusetts, edition of Edward Young's *Works* (1811)—was almost wholly (95 percent in the example) limited to these same two human habitats. Similarly, a study of all Windsor District residents obtaining a patent through 1830 reveals that twelve of thirteen (92 percent) resided in the four village townships, and nine of thirteen (70 percent) lived in fortunate village and farmstead human habitats. Also, nearly all active participants in the several attempts to improve navigation of the Connecticut River (including steamboat schemes) were residents of the fortunate village, farmstead, and self-sufficient hamlet living situations. The same held true for early advocacy of a railroad route through Windsor District.[29] Consistently, residents of human habitats where knowledge of change was most accessible provided the core group of participants. Full discussion of the specific *mentalités* of Windsor District residents, and of the texture of their daily lives, will be presented in another study; here we have attended to the fundamental framework of rural daily life.

Drawing on the important findings of scores of recent scholars, this study highlights both the web of connectedness binding rural civilization together between 1780 and 1835, and the increasing diversity pulling it apart. Integrating a broad set of factors influencing everyday life, we have described and analyzed the material and cultural matrix out of which distinctive New England characteristics emerged. Key factors included combinations of moral fervor, Christian republicanism, entrepreneurship, acquisitiveness, mechanical ability, intellectual currency, and cosmopolitanism, personal dynamism, and eccentricity— all notions drawn from a wide variety of reading matter.

Beginning after the Revolution, what can only be described as an outwardly self-confident instructional and crusading mentality permeated rural New England cultural life. Other Americans reacted strongly and often: favorable and thankful when they were receptive, indignant and resentful when they were not. A mysterious brew of enervation, vibrancy, and eccentricity has long been recognized as central to rural New England religious and moral life in 1780–1830. The results included scores of benevolent and other reform organizations and two generations of more radical religious leaders, social experimenters, prophets, and quacks. Rural New England reformers were activist and single-mindedly interventionist. Daily life in a forest society required this personality style; John Brown and Lyman Beecher are its archetypal exemplars.[30] Two other characteristics of New England secular life also owed much to activism and intervention: a much-vaunted aptitude for mechanical invention and tinkering, and an entrepreneurial spirit amounting to a passion for commerce and trade.[31] The great surprise is that these special characteristics are rarely considered together in attempts to explain peculiarities of New England life in the Early Republic.

The longstanding dominant rural ideal in Windsor District throughout the Early Republic was that of the traditional "middle station." Defoe described it as well as any, in the preface to one of the best-loved books of these decades, *Robinson Crusoe.* The realities of life in a forest society and the transformation of rural life in the half century after the Revolution conspired to modify this ideal drastically. By 1815 peace and plenty were rapidly vanishing from Windsor District, and industry and intelligence had taken on new meaning. Rural life was now full of complexity and contention.[32]

Public Policy Implications: History and the Study of Context

The administrations of the last four elected U.S. presidents have become enmeshed in public policy blunders they should have known enough to avoid or at least not to compound. The failures of Democrats and Republicans alike have contributed to bewilderment, at home and around the world, about what America stands for. These failures have also led to growing concern about what is missing in the training of government leaders. A common thread in events surrounding Vietnam, Watergate, the Iranian hostage crisis, and the conduct and implementation of recent American foreign policy has been the absence of even elementary appreciation of the dangers involved in each fiasco. Hopes for short-term gain seem to have obliterated all sense of long-term national principles or even a rudimentary ability to anticipate serious complications. Missing in the education and preparation of government and business leaders is historical perspective. While there is much talk of "street smarts" these days, we need to teach "world smarts."

Historical perspective is essential to sound public policy formulation. History's role in public policy thinking decreased in the 1960s, replaced by an ideology of fervently nationalistic civics. This parochialism, which treats world complexity as paralyzing uncertainty and dismisses it, has left many American politicians and bureaucrats unsophisticated about the taproots of our distinctiveness as a people. At a time when greater resourcefulness in public policy thinking is sorely needed, a reassertion of historical perspective has much to recommend it.[33]

Unlike Isaac Asimov's Harry Seldon, historians cannot predict future events.[34] At its best, history is a discipline of reflection and evaluation. But the skills historians develop in analyzing past complexity are critical to identifying the array of factors manifest in contemporary problems. By creating a sense of the complex dynamics of the contemporary historical moment, historians can bring to discussions of public policy indispensable insights about broader patterns shaping current situations. One of the missions of historians is to remind other professionals engaged in planning that to ignore fundamental processes of historical change and specific stages of development is virtually to guarantee failure.

One way historical perspective can assist in public policy planning is by applying specific historical knowledge to current issues—a political crisis, a negotiation, or an issue such as gender equity in jobs. The lessons of history about Watergate, Yalta, and women in the workplace are all prominent recent cases in point. Such attempts are valuable and should continue, but the fact is that history usually lacks the level of finality required for the burdens some would like to place upon it. Part of a new frankness about the value of history is to avoid misuses of history.[35] Another approach, while not avoiding ideological clashes on public policy issues, uses historical insight to offer perspective in the area history is best equipped to discuss: the broad context within which contemporary affairs occur. That every issue or event is embedded in a rich historical context is precisely the working assumption most in need of emphasis in public policy planning.

When they are consulted at all, historians too often accept the narrow assumptions of public policy planners. They respond to the question: What specific information can you as a historian contribute to the particular problem we are dealing with?[36] This is the wrong question for the historian. Historians need to become active in public policy planning at an earlier stage of formulation. There they can at least make their case: that historians provide perspective on fundamental contexts and relationships that should constitute essential elements in the planning process. Such an approach gains in effectiveness if historians draw on one of their most practiced but least appreciated skills: their ability to analyze relationships between evidence and inference.[37]

Part of the difficulty in reinvigorating the role of history in American life lies within the profession itself. Two decades of experimentation with new research methods have left many historians beset by self-doubt. The enormity of the literature contributes further anxiety. At a time when so much information is gathered and so little is evaluated, historians can ill afford to ignore their first responsibility: to synthesize and offer broad interpretations within their own areas of expertise.

To profit from the experience of the first two generations of Americans inhabiting a rural mass culture of the printed word, we have looked anew at America in the Early Republic. This book has reconstructed the foundations of material and cultural life for the entire population of half a rural New England county during the early national era. The basic contours of commerce and culture began to change in older rural southern New England by the 1750s.

The timing of Upper Valley settlement in 1760–90 accelerated the pace of change there during the next half century.

The broader view taken here of interactions among commerce, communications, and culture in the beginnings of an early modern rural order of life holds insight for America's present historical moment. This broader view allows us to explore a novel historical parallel between the Early Republic and contemporary America. The basis of the parallel is comparison between two periods of fundamental material and cultural change. Precisely because transformation in rural life throughout America in 1780–1835 brought into being a distinctively early modern economy, society, system of communication, and culture, it is of critical relevance to contemporary civilization. Today we are living amid another series of basic changes in communications, culture, and economic life, which together are shaping an international electronic-based civilization.

Specifically, a fascinating historical parallel exists between America in 1780–1835 and America since the early 1960s. They and we inhabit remarkably similar historical moments—each at the beginning of a vast communications revolution creating a new mass culture; each inhabited by pioneer generations in a new mass culture, print and electronic; each witnessing rapid and often tumultuous transformation in private life and in the public sphere. Then as now, new systems of economics and communications were expanding. As a result, participants were forced to live amid changes both exciting and yet difficult to comprehend. Then as now, pluralism was at the center of American cultural dialogue. Then as now, pluralism's effects were perceived as unsettling, even threatening, to the essential fabric of a shared culture.[38] Then as now, knowledge, in league with commerce and communication systems, was perceived as a predominant form of power. Then as now, myriad new forms of knowledge were beginning to reshape the order of power on earth.

The transformation of life in the late eighteenth and nineteenth centuries may appear to have been a slow process, but it eventually led America from New World obscurity to world power. Basic realignments among and within the nations most actively participating in international electronic civilization have already begun. The potential impact of these shifts on America are so profound that it is time they were studied intensively rather than merely being casually alluded to. The results of such study should become part of the planning process throughout American institutions. The central question is: What is necessary, valuable, and timely for America as a nation and for the American people who are also participants in an international electronic-based civilization?

Our approach emphasizes both the similarities and the differences between two communications revolutions, and the powerful impact that communication systems made on life in the Early Republic and are making in contemporary America. This parallel suggests a different way of thinking about changes

America is presently undergoing. In public policy planning, sound fundamentals are critical to successful outcomes. Comprehension of basic processes of historical change and specific stages of development are essential to sound fundamentals.

The greater the rate of contemporary change, the greater the need for historical perspective to distinguish between the evanescent and more lasting dimensions of change, and to discern meaning in the latter through comparative historical analysis. In a time of fundamental transformation in the world's infrastructure, a fresh look at the last historical period of similarly profound transformation can provide insights invaluable in public policy understanding and planning. As part of that process, the findings of this book begin to reorient our understanding of the nature, timing, and pace of change creating an early modern rural order of life in 1760–1835.

Nearly all recent overviews of American history in the period 1780–1850 stress that "the spirit and direction of American life became so strikingly different after the War of 1812 that the period around 1815 must be regarded as a major turning point in American history." Problems arise in accounting for the Great Transformation, as it is often termed. While increasingly precise about the process of economic change, current explanations attribute only marginal relevance to cultural dimensions of life. At best, culture is seen as a structure of rational response: advocacy or opposition. "Economic changes were primary," conclude Sellers, May, and McMillen, authors of a leading American history overview. This stance determines the key question asked: "How, then, did this economy become a dynamic *industrial economy* by the Civil War era?" The answer is that "the critical shift in the pace, direction, and spirit of the economy had occurred decades before, as a result of the 'market revolution' which had brought most American economic activity into the orbit of an intricately intermeshed national market system." Transportation is usually singled out as underpinning the market revolution.[39]

In periods of major change, the "Hobbesian populism," in Fred Matthews' term, that "ideas and emotions are always determined by social circumstances" must be called into question.[40] Economic changes were significant but not primary in America's first Great Transformation. Rather, an integrated process encompassing economic, social, communication, and cultural factors propelled historical change. The present study has disentangled several of these major factors and reintegrated them. Its main finding is that an interactive transformation extending over two generations, 1780–1835, affected many of the fundamental building blocks of rural civilization. Randolph Roth's recent book on Upper Valley religion, politics, and reform in 1790–1850 confirms and deftly elaborates the pattern of change presented here. Supplemented by David Ludlum's now-classic analysis of "social ferment" and the important research of

Donal Ward on religion and theology, and of Hal Barron on life in Chelsea, Orange County, Vermont, 1840–90, a vastly different and far richer picture of early modern rural life in the American Northeast is emerging.[41]

The implications of the historical parallel between the Early Republic and contemporary America may be seen in five major areas: economic changes; cultural changes resulting from vast expansion of the communication system; a new set of communities of knowledge, reflecting changes in the infrastructure; a society's adaptation, in a series of stages, to new funds of knowledge; and a stable underlying core of beliefs and values important in cushioning the impact of development. In each area, issues arising in the Early Republic resonate with contemporary relevance.

As in the Early Republic, the arena of the greatest change today is the relationship between economies and communication systems. Most residents of developed nations, and many in developing ones, comprise the first generations living in an emerging world civilization based on international electronic communications and a world economy. These two central features of global transformation have already begun to reshape society, politics, and culture around the world. Based on transatlantic experience in the last Great Transformation, we should expect—and in fact have begun to experience—major economic changes in daily life. These include: repositioning in economic leadership among nations, considerable shifts in economic power among regions within nations, and the beginnings of major shifts in geographical centers of world commerce and culture. Economic and cultural forms of production, the transportation and communication routes of distribution, and patterns of material and cultural consumption are already changing in response to the rise of a worldwide industrial economy, international communication system, and global cultural perspective.

In addition to economic changes in daily life, during the past twenty years major cultural transformation has created the first generation of young adults nurtured by electronic visual and aural communications. As in the Early Republic, today a fundamental reconfiguration of cultural participation is occurring, as the direct result of vast expansion in the communication system. The onset of an age of reading in the Early Republic heralded the first modern rural mass culture of the printed word. As that culture matured, it integrated rural and urban civilization throughout the North Atlantic. By 1815, a substantial majority of all Windsor District families engaged in forms of regular reading that were in keeping with the rhythms of their agricultural existence. Moreover, for the first time in the nearly four-hundred-year history of print communications, extensive reading matter and styles were permanently spread through all of society, reaching deep into the low middle class and even into some of the poorest families.

Wide variation accompanied the diffusion of early modern cultural change.

Rather than triumphing quickly, change competed for expression with the reigning "wisdom of the ages," for at least two generations. A broad measure of general reading activity, the proportion of families retaining a family library, varied between 50 percent for hardscrabble families and 85 percent for fortunate village families. The substance of rural *mentalités* showed even greater variation. In a manner reminiscent of today's rampant religious fundamentalism and fringe-group advocacy of simplistic unitary solutions to all problems, simple solutions were enticing in the Early Republic. The desire to regress to an earlier, less complicated world powered many nineteenth-century American responses to change. The presidencies of Andrew Jackson and his successors symbolized one response to accelerating change, that of the venturesome conservative. A similar approach, especially strong at present, has dominated contemporary American culture for nearly two decades.[42]

Today, electronic communications media appear to be the dominant ways most Americans — of all wealth levels, racial and cultural groups, and genders — learn about the world they inhabit. Inspired by historical perspective, careful analysis of access to networks of distribution for each type of media, and to their interaction and overlap, promises valuable insight into electronic communication's impact at home.[43] Long-term analysis of the spread of electronic media and their dissemination of the values of Western industrial societies to the rising generations of all other civilizations is also much needed.

Each major medium of communication carries enormously varied sets of messages. Moreover, the leading vehicles of communication in an emerging mass culture open far broader opportunities to express new perspectives than their creators and early proponents ever imagined. As could be expected, considerable turmoil and confusion are in evidence. In the 1830s, new readers and writers, such as Orestes Brownson, Joseph Smith, and William Lloyd Garrison, came to be widely known throughout transatlantic print culture for their differing analyses of large problems of the times. Today, Bishop Desmond Tutu, Bob Geldof, and Moammar Khadafy are known throughout world electronic culture for their vastly different approaches to current world problems. In early nineteenth century America one important reaction to an expanding cultural dialogue was a wave of vigilante action: riots, government intervention, and attempts at repression through a series of trials for libel and blasphemy. Many contemporary societies are following a long tradition of ineffective responses to cultural change, based on military control, political repression, and stifling the free flow of information. At the same time, electronic communications media seem to have been captivated by peoples and traditions we hardly knew existed two decades ago. This situation offers a great challenge to develop regional and global perspective as a critical part of the education of all Americans.[44]

A third dimension of rural New England material and cultural change in

1780–1835 with contemporary relevance was the intricacy of the network of rural communities of knowledge, which reflected several modifications to the infrastructure. During the era when pioneer generations in a new mass culture thrived, an early modern network of human habitats emerged, thrived, and eventually was transformed. Intricate relationships among economic, social, communication, and cultural elements of civilization were central to rural New England life for three-quarters of a century, 1760–1835. Today, electronic communications, in interaction with many other aspects of American life, have begun to evolve their own series of widely varying habitats of learning and communities of knowledge. Studying this differentiation in all its complexity will enrich our understanding of the impact of change, and of shifts in contemporary American *mentalités*.

The place of beliefs and values in contemporary civilization is in need of extensive study, informed by comparative historical perspectives. Along with international commerce and finance, the rise of a worldwide communication system based on electronic media is the most potent source of a global cosmopolitan culture. As the array of material goods and services in urban and suburban areas throughout the contemporary world is consolidated, communications networks in these areas are also converging. A new field is needed to study the processes of cultural and material change and their interaction. It should include a sophisticated history of habitats and communities of knowledge and a history of cultural and material infrastructure.

The actual impact of different vehicles of communication on the process whereby values are formed must occupy a central place on the research agenda of a history of knowledge and its uses. Americans' continuing reliance on the primary agents that created a mass culture of the printed word – the family and the school – to shape current rising generations reveals the poverty of today's public policy in the absence of historical perspective. In value formation, electronic communications are parents, kin, and institutions for the young. Analyses of the impact of these media frequently rely on materialist perspectives and overly rationalist assumptions. Incorporating historical perspectives into research designs can enrich analyses of audience "demographics" and suggest ways to track Americans' changing stock of knowledge about the world and its uses in daily life. For instance, in the diffusion of knowledge, homogenization in a society's perspectives and beliefs is not the usual result of greater integration in the types of media. In the Early Republic an intricate structure of knowledge evolved: an international layer with some uniform elements, regional layers, and national and even more localized layers. Interaction among these layers on major public policy issues is a fascinating area of study.

The history of the last Great Transformation in America carries an important message about the workings of the infrastructure undergirding all life. We have often tended to think of infrastructure too narrowly, and mainly in material terms. The concept of the network of human habitats between 1760 and 1835 helps us clarify key elements of rural infrastructure and understand their complex interaction. This understanding has much to offer students of contemporary civilization. In distinguishing nine aspects of modern industrial societies, Clark Kerr finds "great discontinuities" between "patterns of belief" and "other aspects of society": politics, industrial production and distribution, and general economic trends. Confirming a consensus in the literature that these factors do not mesh with beliefs and values, Kerr closes his discussion with Milton's statement that "the mind is its own place." This book demonstrates that the mind is crucial to historical change, but that it is not its own place.[45]

Even apparently universal forms of knowledge are never received as pure information; they are always translated through local circumstances. Control of the production and distribution of knowledge does not always lead to corresponding control of its selective reception and uses. If the world is entering a "new stage of history," as Kerr believes, then communication systems will play a crucial role, not by themselves but embedded in a new worldwide network of human habitats. Understanding the historical role of human habitats in the spread of a mass culture of the printed word in 1760–1835 in America suggests several phenomena we should pay closer attention to in the contemporary world.[46]

The historical parallel between the Early Republic and contemporary America is valuable in a fourth area, the process of cultural change that a communications revolution engenders. The technology of communications did not transform America into a "modern society." Literacy rates soared long before technological innovation struck the book trade, and cultural values changed very slowly for over a generation (through 1810). America was a Republic of Knowledge at its birth in the 1770s; this is one of the signal constants throughout American history.

Shaped by a relatively new array of media, in the Early Republic American culture proceeded through a complex evolution. The overall pattern entailed a transformation from a culture which in 1760 was strongly localized although marked by pockets of interest in provincial and transatlantic affairs, toward a far richer cultural mix in 1835, based on a strongly regional culture with an expanding national focus, a narrower set of transatlantic interests, and less intense and more porous localism. All through these modifications in the geographical locus of cultural exchange, an underlying shift was occurring in the fundamental cultural perspective informing all dialogue, from British to American. American perspectives in schoolbook readers began to replace English ones, as Lyman Beecher began to crowd out George Burder in rural sermon reading.

The process of cultural adaptation in the Early Republic holds important lessons for the contemporary diffusion of values by electronic media. The key relationships are among networks of production, distribution, and consumption. The electronic communications revolution has already spawned an initial stage of cultural evolution, one which appears every bit as complicated as that seen in the Early Republic. In America and elsewhere, electronic communications have intensified national culture while taking two very different new directions: toward an expanding global culture, and toward ethnic or racial fragmentation into countless subcultures within and between nations.

The advertisements and products, the substantive ideas and beliefs, that Americans see and hear about conjure up a modern, fully developed, high-tech information society, and a strongly American version of the world. Moreover, during the past two decades radio, television, video, film, videotext, and telecommunications have been spreading this American perspective, expanded to encompass several varieties of Western consumer culture, across the globe. American values are supplemented in major regions of the world by English, Brazilian, Australian, Chinese, and Japanese variants, and within each country by national cultural products, entertainment programs, and newscasts. In many countries modern, Western, and American are synonyms.

World news, and the products and services of a global economy, are central elements of life in America. Nationalism remains the central focus of beliefs and values, but international information, opinion, and products have been gaining in importance within America. Global opposition to apartheid, world hunger relief, and international terrorism are but three issues on which a national perspective has proved inadequate. We should expect other much broader developments as the diffusion of international electronic civilization intensifies. This is not to suggest that an international culture is likely to replace national cultures. But the balance among local, regional, national, and international aspects of cultural and material life is shifting, leading toward a new equilibrium in which global perspectives are ever more critical.

Historical comparisons must assess differences and their meanings as thoroughly as similarities. Among many dramatic differences between America in the Early Republic and in the contemporary world, one is ominous. In the 1780s an almost universal framework of sacred and secular principles and mores — the wisdom of the ages — and an integrated series of embedded social institutions, beginning with the rural family and the printed word, existed to cushion the impact of economic development and vastly expanded print communications. These factors served to insure stability in lifelong expectations and continuity in beliefs and values. Such values, the common fund of knowledge buttressing them, and their institutional support system protected rural New Englanders from the worst ravages of change. They knit and reknit a web of daily customs, assimilating some elements of change and rejecting others. This was the initial and most essential function of print culture in the Upper Valley in 1780–1835.

No parallel world view or set of social institutions exists in America today. Our culture, by nearly all accounts, is marked by fragmentation in public thought and ambiguity and confusion over the proper relationship between public and private spheres. Within the private realm, isolation and loneliness is continuously reinforced. Nor is any comparably influential set of social institutions sufficiently widespread to reinforce cultural stability in America. In the absence of such institutions, international electronic communications appear to be exacerbating divergence in conditions of life and cultural perspectives, and, above all else, social atomization and radical privacy.

History raises many new questions about this grim picture of contemporary life. From its Native American and then colonial origins, America has been an enormously diverse culture. Reflected only modestly in rural New England's network of human habitats, in what by all contemporary accounts was the most homogeneous of all America's regions, the level of material and cultural pluralism within America as a whole was very great in 1780–1835. Perhaps the contemporary cultural fragmentation and retreat into privacy—*Habits of the Heart* by Robert Bellah and his colleagues, and the many commentaries on it, offer perhaps the clearest discussion—mask a set of underlying beliefs and values. In the absence of systematic study, all American commentators are in the worst possible situation: having to conclude that, at present, it is not possible to know.

In historical perspective, rather than the idea that a set of shared values and social institutions exists but cannot easily be pinpointed, it seems more likely that American civilization, buffeted by unruly changes of many sorts, is well along in a vast material and cultural transformation, one of whose most prevalent symptoms is agreement among conservatives and liberals that something is very wrong in the heartland. This was precisely the cultural situation in 1835 as well. While the parallel does not render the contemporary historical moment any less ominous, it does suggest a few reasons to rethink the nature of some current problems: (1) pluralism has always been more fundamental to the American character than we have understood; (2) basic changes in beliefs, values, and institutions such as those actively under way, especially in the rising generation, are unsettling; and (3) commentators, many of whom themselves represent a passing order, dismiss the necessity to probe the enormous vitality and promise that other elements of America's pluralistic society hold.

History also suggests a more pessimistic insight on shared culture. In broader comparative perspective, traditional belief systems seem likely to remain stronger in some nations less heavily commercialized and industrialized than America and Western Europe. This is especially the case in populous countries with enormously rich and longstanding cultural systems; Thailand and China are among the premier examples. Reconfirmation of ancient values, knitting and reknitting the web of custom, as these countries seem to be doing, might well provide for a smoother process of cultural adaptation. It may be that countries initially implementing major changes in communications technology are not the ones most likely to maintain a leadership role internationally, if their own cultural heritage is easily cast aside or reduced to the simplicity of a docu-drama. American historians must redouble their efforts to reestablish the central role of lifelong learning about American history as a necessary activity for every citizen of the Republic, and certainly for the half who attend college.

World news today seems to belie Marshall McLuhan's prediction that global consciousness would evolve in tandem with global systems of communications. Or does it? What values and models of social organization will be consolidated as international electronic communications spread? Should we expect another lengthy wild period of new visions of life on earth, like the one that emerged in rural New England and elsewhere and spread throughout transatlantic civilization in the nineteenth and early twentieth centuries? However exciting the prospect, the recent use of mass communication skills by Adolf Hitler and many lesser tyrants, and the apparent susceptibility of contemporary peoples across the world to electronic persuasion is unsettling. Only through the lens of a new historical realism can problems, which may seem monstrous at a given moment, be viewed more accurately in the clearer light of the ages.

Appendixes

Print Culture and Evidence
for Other Forms of Cultural Expression

While the cultural evidence for this study centers on printed matter, it is important to consider the other major ways Upper Valley residents expressed themselves in daily life: in oral discourse, music and singing, dance, visual expression, and writing. Far too little is known abaout the traditions of oral culture in early national America; their history is yet to be fully explored. Two positions have tended to dominate the fragmentary research completed to date, representing opposite views of oral discourse. One assumes a richly textured world of "popular culture," while the other, far more usual in literacy study and in social and intellectual history, assumes that much of the populace was passive and culturally impoverished and that, as long as reading remained the preserve of elites, life was mean, nasty, and brutish. What needs study is how those with the least developed skills of print literacy lived and communicated, earned a livelihood, and participated in cultural life beyond simple survival. Thinking about the various audiences of culture from this vantage point requires us to broaden our understanding of cultural participation. In fact, daily life in Windsor District's forest society frequently was quite brutish, even for regular readers.[1]

In the half century following the Revolution, a fundamental shift in the communicative economy occurred. An oral-based culture gave way to a much more complex cultural situation, with print culture playing an increasingly important, synergistic, and integrative role. All means of cultural expression, and their myriad forms of value transmission, overlapped during the early national era. In fact, as chapter 6 suggests, many of the first examples of printed material reflected local cultural trends in other realms of expression.[2]

Lately historians have been discovering in the period 1815–50 a deep contemporary fascination with oratory—in the pulpit, at camp meetings, and on the "stump," as well as on the lyceum circuit and in Congress. Indeed, this era became known throughout the country as the "Golden Age of Oratory." Interest followed the explosion in print and written forms of expression, and interacted with it in many ways. As Donald Scott has shown, the power of printed and written matter in diffusing information – advertisements, notices, and reports and evaluations of speaking occasions – was enormous.[3]

As was true of other cultural forms, by the early nineteenth century oral and print culture reinforced each other in maintaining cultural values. An example of their close relationship is seen in public newspaper reading. The newspaper was commonly read aloud in post offices, general stores, and taverns throughout the Upper Valley as elsewhere in America. Richard Caton Woodville and William Sidney Mount captured this experience in genre paintings, for instance in Woodville's *War News from Mexico* (1848) and Mount's *California News* (1850). This process of community newspaper reading, as well as reading aloud in the home and among neighbors, enabled even some remaining nonreaders to share in the fruits of print culture.[4]

Oral traditions were reconfirmed in the way reading was understood (as speaking to the mind's ear) and taught at home, in district schools, and, after 1815, in Sunday schools. As Dennis Rusche has noted, the 1770–1840 decades form an "age of oral reading" instruction. Throughout early America a widespread assumption of rural New Englanders was that memory was the first faculty developing in children. Aided by their first skill, oral expression, children were taught to employ their memories regularly in "engraving" the contents of the Bible, countless maxims and mottoes, and other brief secular pieces on their "tender" and "impressionable" minds. The early reports of Sunday schools in Windsor and elsewhere in the valley proudly detailed lists of the number of verses the best pupils were able to memorize. James Axtell has wisely commented, "As if Gutenberg and Caxton had never lived, colonial schools forced their pupils to use the diminishing power of a smaller, more personal, oral culture – verbal memory – to control and order the proliferating, impersonal products of a print culture."[5]

Until the early 1820s, challenges to the dominance of the oral mode of childhood education in the Upper Valley were minimal. Oral transmission retained its age-old position as the most powerful and pervasive form of cultural expression throughout rural society. The addition of regular silent reading to reading practices, involving greater parity between the mind's eye and the mind's ear, came only gradually. The pace at which private reading, and silent reading in public places, rose to dominance is an enormously important topic for the history of knowledge and reading, and holds considerable promise for studies of the rise of individualism, privacy, etc. Adult reading experience was gradually being transformed by increased contact with print and written culture in 1790–1820.[6]

Music and singing offered another major form of family and community-wide cultural participation. Several traditions of New England psalmody, hymn singing, and secular music emerged before the American Revolution and flourished in the early national period. In fact, Jonathan Worst has concluded that in 1760–1810 the first distinctively American musical idiom emerged and flowered. The pervasive influence of psalm, hymn, parlor, and ballad singing and of singing schools was intimately related to print culture, as is seen in the virtual explosion of printed (and manuscript) compilations of sacred and secular music. Works in music comprised nearly 6 percent of all Windsor District popular sellers through 1830, and were owned by 111 of the 396 families (28 percent) with family libraries surviving in 1787–1830. Two hundred music works accounted for a twentieth of all printed volumes retained.[7]

Singing was not the only form of expression in the Upper Valley emanating from widespread interest in music. Dance offered a third form of widespread cultural participation. Little has been written about informal rural dancing in the Upper Valley before the 1830s; however, several collections of "the Newest Cotillions and Country Dances" were published locally and advertised in Upper Valley newspapers alongside advertisements of dancing instructors. One of the best sources of information about country dance customs is genre painting, especially William Sidney Mount's three pictures, *Rustic Dance After a Sleigh Ride* (1830), *Dancing on the Barn Floor* (1831), and *Dance of the Haymakers* (1845). All three paintings attest to Mount's special interest in rural tavern and barnfloor dancing customs. Mount himself was an "expert fiddler," and his brother William was a dancing instructor.[8]

Visual culture, the expression of values and beliefs in visual objects, comprised another powerful tradition of cultural expression, and it too interacted with print culture. Scholars of American art have begun to suggest that the visual life and acuity of early Americans was far richer than was previously imagined. A rich cache of information on cultural values and beliefs awaits us here.[9]

So many different physical objects were made by local and itinerant artists that Upper Valley residents were virtually surrounded by crafted items. Between 1780 and 1835 these included: the whole range of building design, including diverse specialized forms such as meeting house steeple design; furniture, some of which carried additional artwork in the form of stenciling; sculptured items ranging from weathervanes to tombstones; ship figureheads, sternboards, and decoys; pottery; various other carved forms such as canes and scrimshaw; toys; samplers and other needlework pictures; quilting; designs and scenes on dishes and wallpaper; painted objects, including canvas portraits, land and seascapes, genre, still life, and religious, literary, and historical subjects; cutouts, paddlewheel art, fireboards, signs on vehicles and buildings, overmantels, murals, panoramas, calligraphic pictures, and cornices with stenciled renderings; costumes and clothing; and book illustrations, engravings, lithographs, etc.

Beyond academic traditions, American art was copious and extremely varied. This folk art tradition of limners and other local artists has been much studied but remains largely undeciphered. At least from the mid–eighteenth century on, the visual world both sustained and advanced early American cultural values and beliefs. Art objects were a constant facet of daily life for all Upper Valley residents; most of the art objects listed above appeared in the wills and inventories of area residents or were known to have been a part of their visual world, as in village meetinghouses, signs, etc. But the intensity of visual bombardment varied greatly among human habitats. Because of their concentrations of people, wealth, and structures, villages and hamlets offered especially rich surroundings in terms of visual art.[10]

The proportion of the population actually engaged in creating and making visual objects was substantial. Especially prolific were makers of samplers, clothing, other costume items, and quilting. In Windsor township, with a population of 2,800 in 1815, approximately 2–3 percent of the total engaged in one or another specialized visual art or craft; this is about the same share as contributed actively to print culture. Another 10.4 percent participated in more general art-producing craft skills, for a total of at least an eighth of the population (see table App. 1–1).[11]

Writing was the least widely practiced major mode of cultural expression in early America. Little is yet known about the cultural context of writing. Prior to the late eighteenth century, limitations on all forms of writing included the lack of an effective school system, inadequate postal and private carrier systems, and poor conditions of roads, where they existed at all. The circulation of information over any long distance appears to us very slow even in New England until at least the early nineteenth century. There were two main functions of writing in the 1780s, dissemination and preservation. Dissemination entailed communicating to others "at some distance" via letters, whereas preservation included jotting down information concerning one's own household or some aspect of the community at large (e.g., earmarks) or keeping a record of one's internal development, tribulations, or travels.[12]

The share of New Englanders writing letters before the late eighteenth century was quite small. Until the porportion of children and youth attending school grew, many people lacked the writing skills. In addition, the expense of paper and implements, and of sending a letter, was prohibitive for most families. General economic circumstances, the scarcity and expense of paper and ink, insufficient time, and lack of inclination also limited diary and journal keeping in the seventeenth and eighteenth centuries. The cultural and economic context of letter writing changed gradually in 1787–1812. Between 1799 and 1816, the rates for letters actually rose, from six to eight cents per sheet, though the minimum distance limits also rose, from 30 to 40 miles. In northwestern New England this meant that nearly all townships in each economic locale were within the minimum rate zone in 1799–1816. Letter writing in-

Table Appendix 1–1: Estimated Crafts and Arts Makers, Windsor, Vermont, 1815 [*]

Specialized Arts and Crafts	*Approximate Number of People Engaged*
Steeple design	2
Furniture making	3
Stencilling	2
Weathervanes	5
Tombstones	3
Ship figures	n.a.
Sternboards	n.a.
Scrimshaw	5
Canes	2
Decoys	4
Pottery	5
Toys	10
Dish design	3
Wallpaper	n.a.
Paintings:	
Portraits and silhouettes	2
Landscapes and seascapes	1
Genre and religious	1
Literature, history, still life	n.a.
Cutouts	3
Paddlewheel art	n.a.
Fireboards; murals; overmantels	1
Panoramas	n.a.
Signs	4
Calligraphic pictures	1
Cornices	2
Book illustration; lithography; engraving	3
Total:	62 = 2.2% [**]
More Generalized Crafts	
Costumes and clothing	75
Samplers (girls/young women aged 6–18)	50
Needlework pictures	50
Quilting	100
Building houses, etc.	15
Total:	290 = 10.4%
Total of Crafts and Art Makers	352 = 12.6%

Note: In addition, many visitors from outside the township were contributing to the fund of visual culture.

[*] Windsor's population in 1815 was about 2,800.

[**] Information unavailable for six other arts and crafts.

creased slowly through about 1805 and more steadily thereafter. Lower rates (back to six cents per single sheet within 30 miles in 1816), especially given more post offices and better roads covering shorter actual distances, cheaper prices for paper, plus generally rising prosperity, accelerated communication by letter. A letter writing system in which the receiver paid, however, remained an extremely risky and relatively expensive proposition through about 1810.[13]

Until the turn of the nineteenth century, among adult males preserving information was far more frequently the purpose of writing than disseminating it. Public record keeping was the chief secular function of early American written culture. The act of preserving countless elements in a community's collective experience had much in common with its sacred counterpart, the Sunday service. Both reinforced values of stability, regularity, steadiness, and collective responsibility for each member of one's community. Combining oral and written forms of expression, record keeping was an essential part of public culture. Each township appointed or elected a sizable proportion of its adult male property holders—sometimes as high as 45 percent—to governmental, judicial, social, and economic positions, all of which required some writing ability. Females were regularly excluded from these responsibilities. In the first decades of the Republic, however, voluntary organizations placed an increasing number of individuals in new situations where preserving information was deemed necessary. A direct result of changing attitudes toward female education was that women began to fill some of these positions. A new ideal of female improvement, nurtured in the Revolution's necessities, had revealed the inadequacy of traditional assumptions about female abilities.[14]

Beyond individual memory retention, through the late nineteenth century most information was preserved by making and storing written documents, an activity consuming much time and effort. Print culture expanded mainly in areas where dissemination, not preservation, of information, was the important consideration. Nearly all of the considerable quantity of record keeping at the township level in New England in 1600–1800 was by hand. Some individuals, in 1780–1830 as earlier, kept separate private records duplicating the official copies maintained elsewhere in the township or county, but we do not know the extent of this practice. Others kept their own daybooks. More elaborate records were also retained by some, especially on large farmsteads where multiple transactions with other families and businesses occurred, or where production or work period information was needed, as in a local factory, print shop, or bookstore. The extent of female participation in all these forms of cultural accumulation remains a mystery. Apprentice contracts and agreements also appeared mainly in written form before 1830.[15]

Professionals and other public officials also kept records. Ministers and elders kept parish and denominational records, a task which increased dramatically after the Revolution with the rise of regional consociations and national denominational organizations. "Tell us about any 'season of revival' in your congregation, and how many were converted this year," a new breed of publicists and bureaucrats requested. Doctors frequently kept registers of patients, with diagnoses of ailments, treatments, and fees. Lawyers kept parallel records of client transactions. Within the governmental-legal structure itself, most townships kept yearly tax listings of real property owned, often employing several assessors. Constables were given written warrants by the selectmen and sent in written returns after, for instance, removing individuals from a township. Court records of various sorts were also maintained. Guardianship records were kept, along with appropriate documents certifying the transfer. Earmarks on animals, deeds on property, township minutes, and records of births, deaths, and marriages, however irregularly kept, were all preserved. Personal wills and inventories of estates were kept by the clerks and judges of the county probate courts in the Upper Valley, along with reports of commissioners sent to evaluate net worth and depositions of witnesses and heirs. Militia and criminal records were also kept. Finally, voluntary organizations kept their minutes; the schoolkeeper often kept an account of books, pens, and board; and the storekeeper kept elaborate books, receipts, and notes on credit and debit. As with singing and music, much early Vermont and New Hampshire Valley printing consisted of constitutions, articles, acts, laws, minutes, proceedings, and catalogues. Several imported books of forms and procedures were also found among steady sellers.[16]

Writing remained the more functionally specific and male-dominated among cultural transmission skills through about 1810. Most New England families did not have the financial resources to engage either in letter writing, except perhaps in extreme emergencies, or in diary or journal keeping. Nor did they have to write in order to live in mainly agricultural communities. A sizable share of male household heads and a few females did keep public and business records, however. By 1810 changes were evident: letters, and indeed all forms of writing, were spreading. Printed matter played an important role in encouraging writing. Letter writing manuals were steady sellers in the Upper Valley; and several schoolbooks and stage-of-life works contained sections on letter writing.

Windsor District Human Habitats, 1780–1835: Interrelationships among Primary Factors

Our goal is to differentiate five distinct living situations encompassing five different audiences of print communications. Participation in the public market economy, wealth and its uses and dispersion, type of local community setting and ecology, placement within the transportation and communications network (access zone), and family situation in a rural economy, including work rhythms (occupation), constituted five key elements determining Windsor District's rural infrastructure. Each impacted Windsor District families differently; together they helped determine residents' approach to the world, including reading habits, in 1787–1835.[1] Interaction among the five factors defines the complicated interrelationship among material and cultural bases of Windsor District human habitats. We have constructed the network of human habitats from many kinds of data.

Expanding participation in the market economy has been described in chapter 2. Among other central factors shaping the network of human habitats, wealth was the least subtle in its impact. Distribution of wealth within the district was sharply uneven. Poverty erected an initial barrier to starting, building, and diversifying a family library, severely restricting purchasing power and the ability to receive credit. Families below $700 in total wealth were far less likely to start and to maintain a family library than all others. At every wealth level above this threshold, not of poverty but of cultural participation, wealth had little effect on the incidence of family libraries. The size of a collection was also very limited below $700: families rarely retained anything more than a Bible and perhaps a schoolbook, hymnal, and/or a psalm book. Wealth was the most significant factor in defining minimum participation in print culture.

The third factor was the type of community a family lived in: the geographical location of the household in village, hamlet, or farmstead. In contrast to wealth, community type held considerable influence at the top end of the scale of cultural participation, especially in Windsor and Chester. These villages contained newspaper publishing, bookstores, and social, encyclopedia, and circulating libraries. Ease of access to the broadest range of print matter encouraged high levels of participation.

The other two bases of rural infrastructure were far more precise in shaping participation in print culture among families above minimum wealth but outside of print center villages. One was access within Windsor District's communications network. Access zone shaped habits of buying and borrowing printed items. Placement within the configuration of access zones could mean either full or severely limited access to all items printed within, plus all those imported into, the Upper Valley. Limited access meant no bookstore within a day's travel, no newspaper circulation close by, and no regular mail service within easy travel distance. Figures 5–8 and 5–9 depict two configurations of access zones, in 1800 and 1825. The limitations on life in the minimum access zone were such that, except for the very wealthiest families in just a few occupational categories, existing private libraries were kept to a bare minimum, and families had few opportunities to expand their reading beyond intensive matter and styles. The fifth strong influence on daily life was the primary occupation of the household. The character of a family's primary work experience usually exerted a major influence on the extent and variety of its participation in print communications.

None of these five factors worked in isolation. Primary occupation combined with access zone to account for the largest number of individual households tending toward one or another human habitat. Social geography most often functioned as a liberating factor in terms of living situation, as did family participation in general commercial exchange. Wealth established a minimum threshold for active participation in print culture. Less powerful in differentiating households by their retention and reading habits were wealth at the top of the scale, and type of community setting at the bottom (farmsteads). The central point is that each of these five factors helped shape reading patterns in important ways; together they explain very precisely the participation in print culture of between two-thirds and three-quarters of all families.

Each human habitat in the network encompassed a limited number of mixes of these basic factors. Each mix of wealth, occupation, participation in the market economy, community setting, and access zone produced an identifiable pattern of participation in print communications. Each household in a human habitat was mainly affected by a portion of that habitat's set of leading causative agents. The fit between human habitats and cultural participation is reasonably snug but not airtight. To take one example, the leading causative agents defining the hardscrabble living situation were serious poverty and extreme isolation from the main arteries of the communications system. Occupation and type of community were far less significant factors for this human habitat.

One group of hardscrabble families lived in Andover on farms in the foot-hills of the Green Mountains during the 1820s. They owed their placement within the hardscrabble living situation primarily to their position on the outer fringes of the communications network in the limited access zone (see figure 5–9 and table 4–1). Community setting—farmstead rather than hamlet or village—was a secondary contributing factor; wealth and occupation were far less significant. A second group of hardscrabble families, artisans, with almost identical participation in print communication, libraries, and knowledge lived during this same decade in Windsor village. They owned their placement within the hardscrabble human habitat mainly to their real poverty (averaging below $250 in total wealth). Superb placement at the center of the communication system, occupation, and community type were outweighed by the absence of active purchase or borrowing of printed matter. These two types of families demonstrate clearly a basic phenomenon of the network: different mixes of conditions yielded similar patterns of participation in print culture. The network of human habitats enables us to predict that, in a newly discovered group of families with libraries, a mix of factors weighted in this manner would result in a configuration of participation and knowledge compatible with that of the hardscrabble human habitat and no other.

With the earlier discussion of commercialization in mind, let us look more closely at the other four major factors shaping the network of human habitats.

The Communication System and Community Type

The communications network carved Windsor District into three zones of access to all printed matter (see chapters 5 and 6), thereby greatly influencing the character of print culture. Our general conclusion is that, as with other commodities, access to print was widely unequal. This meant, to take the extremes, the difference between a five-minute walk along a village street and a two-day, forty-mile walk or horse ride around two sets of mountains and hills.[2] Certain circumstances, especially community type, wealth, and occupation, moderated the restrictions imposed by geography and communications. At the top end of the wealth scale this meant the likelihood of increased travel to Windsor, or the ability to pay someone to ride and purchase books, or (very rarely) purchase by mail. Occupation played its role, too, influencing homestead location, amount of travel likely to central villages, and amount of work-related and leisure time available for reading.

There were significant differences in participation in print culture by access zones across Windsor District. Table App. 2–1 combines all known data on living locations (village, hamlet, and township) and access zones within the communications network of Windsor District. Access zones begin to differenti-

Table Appendix 2–1: Participation in Print Culture, by Community Type and Communications Access Zone: Windsor District, 1787–1830 [*]

	Number of Print Items (n=5,630)	Number of Libraries	Average Number of Print Items per Library	Shares in Lending Libraries
Full Access Zone	4,259 76%	178 45%	23.9	20 77 %
Windsor Township	[2,470]	[80]	[30.9]	[11]
Village	1,359	40	34	9
Farmstead	1,111	40	27.8	2
Chester Township	[1,282]	[70]	[18.3]	[8]
Village	468	21	22.3	2
Farmstead	814	49	16.6	6
Springfield Village	309	14	22.1	0
Weathersfield Village	198	14	14.1	1
Partial Access Zone	850 15%	120 30%	7.1	3 11.5%
Weathersfield Farmstead	241	44	5.5	0
Springfield Farmstead	240	39	6.2	1
Ludlow Hamlet	86	2	43	0
Plymouth Hamlet	50	2	25	0
Cavendish Township	[233]	[33]	[7.1]	[2]
Hamlet	51	6	8.5	1
Farmstead	182	27	6.7	1
Minimal Access Zone	521 9%	98 25%	5.3	3 11.5%
Plymouth Farmstead	57	8	7.1	0
Weston Township (Hamlet & Farmstead)	50	12	4.2	0
Andover Township (Hamlet & Farmstead)	48	11	4.4	1
Ludlow Farmstead	182	25	7.3	1
Reading Township	[184]	[42]	[4.4]	[1]
Hamlet	38	11	3.5	1
Farmstead	146	31	4.7	0
Total	5,630 100%	396 100%		26 100 %

[*]Zones of access are for around 1825. See Figure 5–9.
Source: All Windsor District inventories with family libraries, 1787–1830 (n = 396).
[ ] = subtotal

ate families by incidence of family libraries, quantity of print items retained, and borrowing from lending libraries. Evidence is provideed for total library size, numbers of libraries, average library size, and family shares in lending libraries.

We began constructing the set of human habitats by combining type of community and access zone; through the mid-1820s, no township's land lay exclusively within a single access zone. Even Weston and Andover in the Green Mountains had a slice of partial-access land by 1815, while a portion of southern Windsor township leading into Mount Ascutney remained a minimal-access area through 1830. The main finding about the relationship of community type to access zone is that the full-access area was sharply differentiated from both partial- and minimum-access zones in every factor related to print communications (table App. 2–1). Full-access zone families, with just 45 percent of libraries, retained three-quarters of all printed items and also three-quarters of all shares in lending libraries. Nearly half of families with lending library shares retained very small libraries, under nine volumes each, and over two-thirds retained libraries of under twenty-five volumes. Consequently, adding lending library shares to family library holdings further clarifies the concentration of active readership by access zone (see figures 5–8 and 5–9 throughout). Enhanced access sharply intensified cultural participation.

Outside the full-access area, size of libraries and likelihood of a share in a lending library dropped dramatically. Full-access areas had regular newspaper delivery, hence advertisements of bookstore holdings, as well as easy access to a bookstore. Minimal-access areas had none of these. Partial-access zone libraries remained a third larger on average, and of a far greater range, than those among families in the minimum-access zone, even in 1830. Communities in the partial-access zone had fairly regular access to newspapers via postrider routes but were far from a bookstore. Purchase of a wide variety of print items beyond those carried by peddlers, especially most current works, unavailable at local general stores, remained difficult. The net result in partial-access areas was great diversity in book ownership from one library to the next. In the partial-access zone, enhanced possibilities for greater access to print attracted only some families.[3]

Wealth

Wealth by township (table App. 2–2), a helpful but fairly crude criterion of wealth differences among the many geographical locations, reveals the following pattern. Wealth and differential access were highly correlated: the four richest townships encompassed the full-access zone; the two poorest were two of the three full townships in the minimal-access zone; and the other three

Table Appendix 2–2: Windsor District Wealth, by Township, 1787–1830

Township	Number of Households**	Total Wealth	Average Wealth	Median Wealth
Chester	69	$ 233,701	$ 3,386	$ 1,450
Windsor	78	$ 248,303	$ 3,183	$ 1,350
Springfield	52	$ 165,466	$ 3,182	$ 1,400
Weathersfield	56	$ 142,260	$ 2,540	$ 1,111
Plymouth	10	$ 22,024	$ 2,202	$ 543
Andover	11	$ 21,706	$ 1,973	$ 1,890
Cavendish	31	$ 56,528	$ 1,823	$ 1,200
Ludlow	26	$ 36,239	$ 1,394	$ 983
Reading	41	$ 50,838	$ 1,240	$ 701
Weston	12	$ 11,546	$ 962	$ 686
Baltimore*				

*Insufficient Data

**All Windsor District inventories with print items, 1787–1830 (n=386).

townships, comprising the partial-access zone, were in the middle of the wealth scale.

Table 4–2 breaks wealth down more fully by access zones; the same geographical divisions are employed in table App. 2–1). When divided by access zone, it is clear that wealth is related to levels of print retention, but only in a general way. The maintenance of family estates above the subsistence level required access to the same transportation system as undergirded the communication system; however, other factors, especially high migration throughout the region and the hereditary transmission of wealth, modified the relationship. If we compare wealth averages with the average number of print items per library within each access zone (table App. 2–1), we see that the correlation between family wealth and print retention is not strong. Sizable increases in wealth greatly enhanced the possibilities for (but certainly not the necessity of) substantially larger print collections. Size increase most often took the form of either a broader distribution of books among various areas of knowledge or greater depth in a few areas. This complex relationship between access zone, wealth, and books was pronounced in distinguishing the full-access zone as a whole from the other two. Full-access zone families, comprising 45 percent of the population, owned 66 percent of the wealth and 76 percent of the print items retained. By contrast, minimal-access families, with a quarter of the families, retained just 13 percent of the wealth and 9 percent of the volumes. But within each access zone, about half of the time no close fit holds. Wealth was one of several key factors contributing to cultural participation.

Occupation

A fourth factor, operating somewhat independently of the other three, occupation substantially modifies the effect of both geography and wealth on print retention. In chapter 7 we discuss the relationship of wealth to occupation (see table 7–1), concluding that while a general relationship existed, each occupation had its own wealth range. In this respect, occupation functioned within each access zone both to enhance and to counteract wealth.

The relationship between the primary occupation of a household, and the size of its private library and likelihood of a share in a lending library, is presented in table App. 2–3. When arranged by occupation, a three-tiered division in the average and median sizes of family libraries is apparent. Highest were professional and gentleman farm family libraries. Professional libraries constitute an important instance where occupation, in conjunction with wealth, overrode the limitations of minimal- and partial-access zones. Gentleman farm libraries followed more closely the limitations set by access zones; smaller libraries were found in areas away from the river valley and closer to the mountains.[4] The second tier, ranging in average size from 10 to 20 volumes per family, included commerce and trading, manufacturing, and artisan families. These occupations were not uniform in their relationship to wealth. Families in the first two occupations were by far the richest families in the region, while artisan average wealth was quite low. Surprisingly, despite enormously high wealth averages, highest in the district by over $2,000, commerce and trading household libraries were not uniformly large. There were three sizes: small (1–7 books), substantial (11–16), and very large (21–71). These almost perfectly matched access zones. Windsor and Chester commercial families averaged 28 and 25 volumes, respectively, whereas Weston, Andover, Plymouth, and Reading combined to average only 4.5 volumes per library. Among all families, those engaged in commerce and trade varied least from their basic living conditions.

The third and lowest tier of occupations in numbers of print items, ranging between three and four volumes each, encompassed yeoman and tenant farm, and semiskilled laborer households. Averaging $1,340 per household, yeoman farm family libraries were more affected by variations in wealth, with significant differences in family library size depending on access zone. Tenant farm (averaging $314) and semiskilled laborer households ($206) were too poor for consequential variations in family library size by access zone. With nearly three-fifths of all libraries, families in these three occupations retained only 15 percent of all print items. In general, occupation inhibited family library establishment and expansion in one group of partial-access-zone families and encouraged them among another group of families residing in the minimal-access zone.

Table Appendix 2-3: Windsor District Family Library Size, by Primary Occupation, 1787–1830

Primary Occupation of Households	Number of Families (n=386)	Number of Print Items (n=5,630)	Percent of all Print Items	Range in Library Size	Average per Library	Median per Library	Number of Shares in Lending Libraries	
Tier One:								
Professional (Households)	33	2,153	38.5 %	1–465	65.2	29	7	21%
Lawyers	13	1,501	26.9 %	3–465	115.5	106	4	
Doctors	12	542	9.7 %	1–266	45.2	28.5	3	
Ministers/Deacons	7	109	2.0 %	1–48	15.6	6	0	
Printer/Publisher	1	1	.01%	1	1.0	1	0	
Gentlemen Farm	26	1,170	20.8 %	1–909	46.8	9	2	8%
Tier Two:								
Commercial and Trading	45	888	15.9 %	1–91	19.7	8	4	9%
Manufacturing	7	91	1.6 %	1–29	13.0	17	2	29%
Artisan	50	468	8.4 %	1–57	9.4	5	2	4%
Tier Three:								
Yeoman Farm	152	623	11.1 %	1–25	4.1	3	6	4%
Tenant Farm	48	169	3.0 %	1–21	3.5	2	0	
Semiskilled	25	68	1.2 %	1–10	2.7	1	0	

Source: All Windsor District inventories with print items and occupational data, 1787–1830 (n = 386).

Something in the nature of professional, manufacturing, and artisan families, shared by only a small portion of yeoman and tenant farm families (10 percent), led to much more frequent retention of print items and to larger and more varied family libraries, regardless of type of community and access zone. These three occupations were the avant garde following newer trends in material and cultural life. In addition, artisan families, a group especially important for our overall understanding of the spread of print communications, showed marked independence from the restrictions imposed by wealth. For instance, they frequently retained novels, and retained some even within the hardscrabble living situation. One final point is illuminating. If we take occupations by access zone (see table App. 2–4), we find major differences in patterns of residence. Commerce and trading, artisan, and professional families most often settled in full-access zones. Manufacturing was the only occupation in which families maintained a high average library size while living outside the full-access zone.

The Placement of Households in the Network of Human Habitats

To capture the richness of rural life in 1780–1830, we need to expand our two-term formulation of ecological and communications dimensions to a four-factor series of coordinates, by incorporating the social and economic bases of knowledge. The conception of a network of human habitats offers such a comprehensive perspective. Five clusters of conditions yield five different groups of families. These five living situations, each combining the four sets of material and cultural conditions of life, constitute a set of sets, an analytical model for differentiating within Windsor District, five separate audiences, each somewhat varied in its makeup. This is a typology of five varying sets of conditions under which all forms of print communications thrived or were inhibited. We are not suggesting that there were five different social groups, economic groups, etc. Nor are we contending that each human habitat represented an alien or even a separate structure of knowledge about the world. Rather, each human habitat manifested similarities to, as well as differences from, the other living situations. Different *mentalités*, encompassing significant variations in Windsor District reading patterns, 1780–1835, were shaped by the mix of these material and cultural conditions of life existing within each human habitat.

To consolidate the foregoing analysis, one further step is necessary: combining sets of material and cultural conditions to form a number of broader groupings of daily life circumstances. Our goal is a limited number of more comprehensive cultural and material coordinates. A careful look at evidence from tables App. 2–1, App. 2–3, and App. 2–4 suggests a five-category array of households by access zone:

1. Full-access village families—all village homes within the full-access zone.
2. Full-access farmstead families—all farmstead homes within the full-access zone.
3. Partial-access hamlet families—all hamlet homes within the partial-access zone.
4. Partial-access farmstead families—all farmstead homes within the partial-access zone.
5. Minimal-access families—all homes within the minimal-access zone, whether located on farmstead or in hamlet.

To move from this categorization to that of human habitats requires shifting 27 percent of the libraries. The shift recognizes the significance of occupation and especially of wealth—in addition to community type and zone of access—among the poorest and relatively poor families, in restricting participation. That, 98 percent of the time, a family under $700 in total wealth could not either establish credit to participate in the market economy, despite living in Windsor village, or subscribe to a newspaper or social library was due to the conditions we are delineating. A notion fashionable among historians who study the lower classes—that because their resilience was great, they could find routes of access to reading—shows naivete about how difficult it has been to escape the constrictions of disadvantage.

Rural New England's network of five human habitats combines in an interrelated system of coordinates the three zones of access to the communication system, the three Windsor District living locations, the four wealth levels discussed earlier, and the eight primary occupations. Table 4-1 embodies the results of this rearrangement.

First the procedure and then the rationale. The procedure leading to this set of cultural locations included the following adjustments to the data presented in tables 4-2, 7-1, App. 2-1, App. 2-3, and App. 2-4:

1. Arrangement of this data into one table, 4-1.
2. Adjustments to arrangement of data by community type and zone of access:
   a. Dividing the full-access zone into two categories: fortunate village and fortunate farmstead families.
   b. Dividing the partial-access zone into self-sufficient hamlet and self-sufficient farmstead categories. There were no partial-access zone villages in Windsor District.
   c. Combining all minimal-access zone living units into one category (those referred to above as the geographically isolated) and changing the designation of the human habitat to hardscrabble. This term was used often in early Vermont to designate particularly barebones subsistence grazing and hilly areas where farming seemed to consist of cultivating roots and hoping for rich harvests of wild fruits and berries.[5] Hardscrabble life, whether in a village or in the foothills of the Green Mountains, was exactly that: hard.
3. Adjustments to the present arrangement of data by wealth and occupation:
   a. Shifting into the hardscrabble human habitat all those households in table 7-1, occupations 5 through 8 (artisan, yeoman, tenant, and semiskilled families) falling below $700 in total wealth. Only a small proportion of all families with

Table Appendix 2–4: *Windsor District Occupations, by Access Zone, 1787–1830*

	Professional	Lawyer	Minister	Doctor	Printer/ Publisher	Commerce and Trade	Manufacture	Artisan	Gentleman Farmer	Yeoman Farmer	Tenant Farmer	Semi- skilled
Full Access Zone	23	10	4	8	1	29	3	30	14	52	9	14
Windsor Township												
Village		3	1	5	1	10	2	11				4
Farmstead			1			1		3	6	24	5	2
Chester Township												
Village		1	2	1		6		7				3
Farmstead		2		1		3		2	8	28	4	1
Springfield Village		2				2	1	4				3
Weathersfield												
Village		2				7		3				1
Partial Access Zone	6	2	1	3		11	1	9	9	53	25	3
Weathersfield												
Farmstead		1		2		2		2	4	21	9	1
Springfield												
Farmstead						3		4	3	19	8	1
Ludlow Hamlet						2						
Plymouth Hamlet				1		1						
Cavendish Township												
Hamlet						2		3				
Farmstead		1	1			1	1		2	13	8	1
Minimal Access Zone	4	1	2	1		5	3	6	3	47	14	8
Plymouth Farmstead						1		1	1	3	1	
Weston Township				1			1	1		4	3	2
Andover Township						1	1	1	1	6		
Ludlow Farmstead			1			2		1		14	3	5
Reading Township												
Hamlet		1										
Farmstead			1			1	2	2	1	20	7	1

Source: All Windsor District inventories with books, 1787–1830 (n = 386).

wealth below $700 clustered between $500 and $700. The average wealth of all households below $700 was $343 and the median wealth still lower. The $700 wealth total establishes a useful threshold below which participation in most dimensions of change affecting Upper Valley life, material or cultural, was minimal. As discussed in chapter 8, $700 is the best cutoff point in relation to the changing incidence of family libraries. Above the $700 threshold, library incidence rose markedly. This means shifting to the hardscrabble human habitat all households below $700 in total wealth in these four occupations, regardless of living location.

b. Shifting two other tiny groups of families (2 percent) up one step in the scale of human habitats. First, we shifted a tiny group of four gentleman farm and manufacturing families (the only ones among the thirty-two living in the minimum-access zone) away from the hardscrabble to either self-sufficient hamlet or self-sufficient farmstead human habitat (depending on whether they lived in a hamlet or elsewhere in one of the mountain townships). This shift was based on the extraordinary wealth of these four families. Clearly their occupation and wealth altered their ability to participate in print culture in a way completely at odds with their living location and community type. Second, we shifted the three minimum-access zone professional families in a similar manner. This tiny but important shift was made because of the peculiar nature of the professional occupation: each family was very actively involved in the region's transportation and communication system, and, in fact, all three families lived in farmstead areas where new roads had created hamlets at or nearby their homesteads by 1815.

The adjustments to living locations and zones of access relative to the full- and partial-access zones reflect finer distinctions based on evidence already presented. The reasoning behind merging minimum-access zone households with all those at the bottom end of the wealth scale into the hardscrabble human habitat rests on their common isolation from most of the fruits of print culture; one group was isolated by its geographical location, the other by its poverty. Even within Windsor village, when a family's wealth level was low, its occupational skills limited, and its work both rigorous and lengthy, little time or money remained to build beyond a small intensive-reading library. In these instances occupation and wealth simply overwhelmed geography, community size, and favorable placement within the communication system.[6] The rationale behind the other small adjustments by wealth and occupation is very similar. Even within minimum-access areas, the material and cultural conditions, and therefore opportunities, for gentleman farm, manufacturing, and professional families were almost always sufficient to free them from the restrictions imposed by access zone and geographical location. In five of the seven cases, these families lived in emerging hamlets; they were shifted up one notch in the scale of participation, to the self-sufficient hamlet human habitat. The other two families were shifted to the self-sufficient farmstead living situation.

The Upper Valley Occupational System, 1780–1835

Our broadest unit of analysis is the whole of Upper Valley society. In addition to the adult males on whom interest has traditionally focused, we include adult women, children, youth (about age 13 to marriage), and the elderly of both genders, all of whom have until recently been excluded in occupational analyses. These latter groups contributed substantially to the household as the locus of agricultural production and consumption. No occupational scheme we have encountered directly considers the participation of those beyond adult and late youth males; hence we must develop a full family/household occupational designation system.[1]

The quality of evidence about occupations presents problems. Federal census takers, where they identified the occupations of individuals before 1840 – in the 1810 and 1820 schedules – only included some males. No female occupational data appeared; this remained the policy in Upper Valley counties, even where females headed households. In addition, census takers exercised great discretion concerning males other than male heads of household. Especially in the group sixteen to twenty-five years of age, many were not included in occupational data. The same absence of all female occupations exists in annual tax assessment rolls at the township level. Since a list of those ratable for voting was the main object, women were systematically excluded.

The approach we have adopted is to take the full household, the locus of agricultural production and consumption, as the central unit for understanding the occupational systems. Agriculture represented the chief occupation for over 70 percent of all households in the Upper Valley through 1830, and into the 1820s many other occupations existed mainly to further the interests of the farming and grazing population. The system of household contributions will be assumed to include fulltime labor by both the offiicial "head" of the household and his wife, except where the head was a widow.[2] A contribution of roughly three-quarters will be assumed for all additional male and female adults and elderly, as well as all youth. Children nine to twelve are assumed to have contributed a half share.

Recognizing that nonfarm occupations provided primary income for a sizable and extremely influential minority of households, and that a patriarchal legal system governed property ownership and transmission, we will understand the occupational designations rural New Englanders employed as a set of cultural symbols which only partially encompassd the world of work. In discussing the occupations, we will always intend the household unit as a human totality. By this strategy we are able to overcome the wide difference between theory and practice in work experience. Without a "helpmate," few males would have had a household to "head." While 1 to 3 percent of all Upper Valley households in each census between 1790 and 1830 were headed by widows, usually with no male over age sixteen, almost no households existed without a full-time female contributor. A viable agricultural household demanded the full time labor of two adults, including at least one female, plus supplementary assistance.

A second difficulty pertains to the meaning of the designations employed by contemporaries, and too easily accepted by some historians. The conventional set of categories assumes that each individual—in this case, the "head"—followed one primary occupation. Except at the very lowest and highest ends of the wealth scale, this was not the case; specialization was limited to the extremes of wealth and work. Very poor farm laborer, tenant farm, and some yeoman farm families spent virtually all their time in agricultural pursuits. Otherwise, multiple occupations were the rule—in yeoman and gentleman farm households, in most of the artisan class, in a reasonable proportion of manufacturing and commerce and trading households, and in the case of some professionals, particularly ministers and some doctors. Only at the very top of the wealth scale, including the richest few families of doctors, some of the families of lawyers, and some merchant and manufacturer families, was there significantly more specialization. Many of these families lived in villages and, after 1800, no longer farmed. In short, diversity in work activities was high for most of the population into the 1820s.

In the occupational listings employed in the federal censuses for Windsor County before 1840, just three categories are distinguished: agriculture, commerce, and manufacturing. While this tripartite distinction is useful, further research reveals serious limitations in this data. The enumerations do not cover all households. Occupational information, available first in the 1810 census, is minimal: data on home manufacture of cloth and on different kinds of establishments beyond the home exist only for a minority of townships.[3]

The quality of evidence in the 1820 census is somewhat better. Ludlow, Vermont, schedules contained occupational notations for 95 percent of the households, the highest rate; whereas occupations exist for 83 percent of Windsor township households. This range is typical for Upper Valley townships in 1820. A more serious limitation in the 1820 census is that, where other data permitted crosschecking, the designations in the commerce and manufacturing listings were reliable in only 43 percent of the cases. The 1830 census contained no occupational listings. In short, the federal censuses—there were no state censuses through 1830—offer a helpful but limited starting point. Given these three difficulties—a unitary occupation system, the masculine bias, and vagueness and errors in the application of the three-category federal census system in use before 1840—additional information on occupations had to be found.[4]

The new set of occupational categories used here is based on full household work activities. They take into account the several valuable occupational systems suggested in previous scholarship. These latter fall into two types (see table App. 3–1 throughout this discussion). General systems have tended to speak more of social classes than occupations per se. Those offered by Emmanuel LeRoy Ladurie for Languedoc, and Darrett Rutman and Kenneth Lockridge for seventeenth- and eighteenth-century New England, fall in this group. A similar set of categories, discussed as occupations, was developed for early nineteenth-century New Hampshire by Donald Cole. Nearly all such arrays distinguish three general social classes or occupational groupings. Most identify peasant and farmer households, containing the bulk of the population. LeRoy Ladurie then distinguished a bourgeois class (landowners, merchants, and officeholders) and artisans. Rutman set apart country gentry and an urban middle class. Cole distinguished a business class and a professional class (lawyers, doctors, and ministers).[5] The problem with these systems of designation is precisely their generality. Even in the best example, that of Lockridge, which seeks to collapse occupations into a three-tiered class structure, the categories are too general to represent the actual range of Upper Valley occupations and their important features. As Howard Russell has demonstrated, the movement away from agricultural subsistence progressed considerably beyond these limited occupational sets well before 1800.

The second type of occupational system eschews broad social classes, preferring more limited, precisely structured occupations. The most elaborate breakdown for preindustrial America was developd by David Hackett Fischer for urban areas, from data supplied by membership directories of the Washington Benevolent Societies of New York and Boston. With his customary zealousness, Fischer catalogued 223 occupations, quite sensibly grouped into ten larger categories. Several categories are relevant only to the urban scene. The remaining categories provide the foundations for a workable system, when taken in conjunction with two other notable scholarly efforts, those of Jackson T. Main and Percy Bidwell.[6] Neither Fischer nor Main cites Bidwell's pioneering and, for our purposes, more directly applicable analysis. Yet the similarities among these three occupational systems are greater than the differences.

Table Appendix 3-1: Occupational Systems for Preindustrial America

A. Rutman
  Peasants
  Country Gentlemen
  Urban Middle Class

B. Lockridge
  Farmers
  Artisans
  Laborers
  Merchants
  Professionals
  Gentry

C. LeRoy Ladurie
  Rural Peasants (including farm laborers)
  Artisans (esp. clothworkers)
  Urban Bourgeoisie (including landowners, merchants, and officeholders)

D. Bidwell
  Farmers
  Professionals
  Businessmen (including taverner, inn-keeper, country trader, and proprietors of various directly farm-related mills and tanneries)
  Village Artisans or Country Mechanics
  Manufacturers (including hats, iron, shoes, woolen cloth, and cotton spinning)

E. Cole
  Farmers
  Businessmen
  Professionals (lawyers, clergy, and doctors)

F. Fischer
  Farmers
  Gentlemen
  Professionals (including lawyers, ministers, doctors)
  Merchants
  Shopkeepers
  Clerks
  Lesser Public Officials
  Artists
  Mechanics and Petty Tradesmen
  Semiskilled and Unskilled Laborers
  Manufacturers

G. Main
  Farmers
  Esquire; Gentlemen
  Lawyers
  Doctors
  Ministers
  Merchants
  Shopkeepers
  Innkeepers
  Artisans
  Miscellaneous Non-Farmers
  Unknown

Sources:

A. Rutman, *Puritanism.*
B. Lockridge, *Literacy,* 25ff.
C. LeRoy Ladurie, *Languedoc,* 155ff.
D. Bidwell, *Rural Economy,* 253–75.
E. Cole, *New Hampshire,* 166ff.
F. Fischer, "Federalists and Democracy," table 16, I: 257–64.
G. Main, *Social Structure,* esp. 257.

Bidwell, Main, and Fischer are in accord that farmers, merchants, and professionals (doctors, lawyers, and clergy) constitute three essential categories. All agree likewise on merchants, shopkeepers, and inn and tavern keepers as constituting one or two more major designations; we will consider them as one occupation – commerce and trade. The three also concur on another occupational slot, for artisans and mechanics.

Beyond these similarities across five basic occupations, divergences must be reconciled. Since all "Gentlemen" and "Esquires" found in the Upper Valley were part of the normal occupational structure, they will be treated as such. Gentleman farm families may be distinguished from other farm families but other "gentlemen" are covered by previously discussed occupations.[7]

Developing a fund of evidence sufficiently rich to describe each occupational designation proved difficult. The present research design combines: all available federal decennial census date for the period 1771–1830, including the various censuses of manufacturers; all wills; all deeds; and all (643) surviving inventories (396 of which contained family libraries and were analyzed fully). In addition to analysis of the full inventory of each household where the head died and left printed items among his or her possessions (396 cases), material from the other 247 households without a family library was included to flesh out the overall occupational and wealth structure. Whereas the census serves as a rough starting point, the inventories represent very valuable evidence useful in creating a thorough reconstruction of occupational designations. Further refinement and confirmation were necessary, however, and were provided by a third type of evidence, a combination of modern historical accounts and traditional local history and genealogy. The major Windsor District newspaper, the *Vermont Journal*, 1787–1830, and its lesser competitors also contributed key information about the occupational structure.

Building on the work of Bidwell, Main, and Fischer, modified to fit Upper Valley work experience, the present occupational designation system also makes use of all surviving evidence from each of the eleven townships of Windsor District.[8] Works studying single townships, such as Dedham or Hingham, Massachusetts, or Windham, Connecticut, offer a valuable comparative perspective. Together they provide detailed evidence for models of the kind advanced by Edward Cook and Robert Doherty. But the variety of townships in Windsor District confirms the parallel need for multiple township analyses. In this instance, Windsor District is a better unit than either Windsor or Chester economic locales separately, because Windsor District encompassed a broad enough geographical area (roughly one-eleventh of the Upper Valley) to contain most of the different economic characteristics and types of townships found within the entire region. Neither of the locales by itself did. Ten of the eleven townships (one an "incorporated place," Baltimore) fit Bidwell's basic "typical inland township" criteria, none topping his 3,000 population ceiling till Windsor did so just after 1820. It was nearly 1800 before any of the other ten saw its 2,000th resident.

Windsor District's diversity during the early national era was quite striking. At one extreme was Windsor, the largest township in the Upper Valley, with its communications center, located along the river, and a substantial inland hamlet. Next came Chester, with a sizable village, and Cavendish, with two bustling crossroads hamlets. Like Windsor, both were balanced between mill-sites and crop lands. Then there were Springfield and Ludlow, each shifting late in the period (after 1810) from a predominance of farming and grazing to a variety of mills. Springfield, with an important factory village, was far larger, growing rapidly by 1820. Further down the scale of diversity came communities devoted mainly to pasturing and farming. Purest of this type was Reading, emphasizing grains and fruits as well as pasturing. Finally, there were the mountainous townships, including Weathersfield on the river, with its fine grazing farms, lumber mills, and fractionated village; and Andover, Weston, and Plymouth on the eastern slope of the Green Mountains. These latter three townships included relatively hardscrabble areas, and there were no significant villages in any of the three through 1830. Andover and Weston were particularly mountainous; but still there were a few fertile farms in addition to several lumber mills. Plymouth held many limestone deposits, and there were several scattered mills. The soil of Plymouth was poor for most crops but decent for grains and grasses.[9]

As one might expect, the occupational balance varied rather dramatically as one moved from a regional commercial and communications center to a balanced, successful farming community; to a mill village; to poorer grazing and pastureland; and to truly hardscrabble and mountainous conditions. The chief benefit of including the full range of township types is to arrive at an accurate total representation of rural society. A precise proportionate analysis of occupations for the district is impossible because there is no present way to determine the complete occupational structure of Windsor District, household by household.

The crucial missing evidence is the precise number of households for each of our eight occupational categories. In the absence of such information, and any way to approximate it, we must fall back on the best evidence we have: the 396 inventories with printed items, supplemented where helpful by the 247 without family libraries, and by Roth's analysis (see table 7–2). Wherever possible (extreme caution was exercised here), comparative studies with fuller evidence were used.

Inventories, Spine Titles, and Family Libraries, 1787–1835

Evidence from inventories took the form of a list of the contents of a household estate, written down by the (usually just one) officially appointed assessor shortly after the death of the household head. Inventories comprise a very large and detailed fund of evidence, part of which documents those print items purchased and also retained for at least some portion of the family life cycle. Inventory records complement advertising and sales records, allowing us to compare what was actually purchased with the broad universe of works advertised and to distinguish more precisely what was actually read from among all works available for sale.

A most vexing characteristic of inventories is the way printed items were listed. An abbreviated author-title notation system was universally employed. The title frequently contained the last name of the author. One or more words representing the essence of the work were also included, but they were not always drawn from the exact title of the book as found on the title page. A word or words not on the title page appeared in 10 percent of all works listed in Windsor District inventories. Moreover, even when title words were all drawn from the full title, the words included often were not the first words of the full title. This occurred in a majority of all works listed, so that the brief title was often not a "short title" (an abbreviated version of the full title) at all. Titling did not follow modern bibliographical transcription procedures governing library card catalogues, sequentially ordering words appearing on the title page. American spine titling in the 1750–1830 era followed a premodern bibliographical word notation system. Even an easy example, such as John Banks, *A New History of the Life and Reign of the Czar Peter the Great, Emporer of all Russia . . .*, which was listed as "Peter the Great," suggests the potential confusion. William Pitt's *Letters Written by the Late Earl of Chatham to His Nephew Thomas Pitt, Esquire* appears as "Letters to Mr. Pitt" on the spine of the editions retained in Upper Valley inventories through 1830. Notations such as "Adams, Philosophy" pose another order of problem. Without the additional information "4 vols." there would be no way to identify the precise work read, let alone the particular edition and "text."[1]

The derivation of the inventory appraisers' shorthand description of books, pamphlets, and periodicals has never been adequately discussed. Books and bound periodicals were almost always described in the inventories by the words appearing on the spine of the volume. Spine titles usually closely followed variations in the size of print set on the title page by the publisher: the larger the print size, the more likely the word or phrase was to appear on the spine binding. For pamphlets, loose periodical issues, and books without spine titles, the title page (and sometimes the running title) was consulted and a brief descriptive title copied or concocted. Unfortunately, the spine title is almost never included in modern bibliographical description of printed items. Locating the precise work being described via the spine system has proved an enormously time-consuming task. Worse, each scholar identifying works from inventories has had to duplicate the procedures followed here because of the absence of any general bibliographical conversion table.[2]

One major benefit of spine or binder's title evidence is that it often helps us to differentiate, once the basic work has been identified, the specific edition (or editions) which could have been retained in a particular family library. For instance, Sir Robert Porter's *A Narrative of the Campaign in Russia* was printed in five editions during 1814 and 1815. Without the spine title, no way exists to identify which edition was retained. By comparing several copies of each edition, however, it is possible to identify the edition(s) in question. The spine title appearing in Windsor District inventories, "Campaign in Russia," appears only on the Philadelphia 1815 edition, which was advertised for sale in Windsor District. The Hartford 1814 and 1815 editions carried "Russian Campaign" on their spines; the Baltimore 1814 edition carried "Porter's Narrative"; and the Trenton 1814 edition carried "Porter, Campaign in Russia."[3] For all those works with more than one edition, and especially those with text variations in different editions, spine titles often prove enormously valuable, pinpointing the exact edition retained. In the process of checking some 1,250 different works, we have discovered that full edition and/or large batch binding was becoming common by the 1780s and was prevalent by 1800, especially for the large majority of those works most widely read through 1835. These usually were works with several editions each.

The basic procedure we followed was to compare all British and American editions prior to the date of the inventory for each work listed in a Windsor District inventory during the period 1787–1835. Knowledge of the universe of reading matter available within Windsor District assisted in locating the edition most probably read. Since the large majority of works retained were of recent origin, the task was easier than it might have been. In addition, perhaps 15 percent of all works were issued in only a single English-language edition through 1830. Altogether, 10 to 12 percent of all cases proved irresolvable as to the specific edition. By this we mean that, while it is possible to identify the work retained, it is impossible to discriminate further among several editions possibly purchased. The proportion of works we could not identify at all is surprisingly small, approximately 1.5 percent of all 1,250 titles.[4]

Estimating the proportion of books carried over more than one generation is impossible without the spine title system of bibliographical description. Even with this system, works purchased secondhand complicate the task, although little evidence exists of secondhand sales in any printed advertisements circulating in Windsor District until 1829.[5] Individual works and a few whole libraries were handed down within families between 1787 and 1830, but many of these works appear in surviving inventories. To take a rare but illustrative example: William Spaulding's household library of eight books (excepting one Bible) was given in 1805 to his brother, Benjamin, Sr. When the latter died in 1812, twelve of his expanded family library of twenty volumes passed to his son, Benjamin, Jr., and two more to Benjamin, Sr.'s brother Peter. They both died shortly: Benjamin, Jr., in 1813 and Peter in 1814. Some of Benjamin's and all of Peter's family library passed to the former's son, William. William's family accumulated several more volumes before his death in 1825.[6]

Over 90 percent of all volumes found in Windsor District inventories in 1787–1830 represent works with at least one American or British edition after 1787. All known evidence suggests that Upper Valley families treated works passed down over the generations as important and meaningful family possessions. The scarcity of such inherited works is mainly due to the lower literacy rates prevailing in Vermont and in southern New England before the 1780s. After the Revolution, the pool of families with private libraries at the household head's death grew. Furthermore, the amount of printed matter available to read began to expand dramatically in the early 1790s. This fact, combined with the small size of most household libraries before about 1805, suggests that intergenerational accumulation and transmission of libraries, apart from the few great libraries traditionally studied, were phenomena of the early national era. This line of reasoning argues against the notion that libraries were often long held, relatively inactive collections inherited over several generations and not reflective of actual contemporary reading.

Like all sources, estate inventories have specific strengths and weaknesses as evidence about family libraries. Perhaps their greatest strength is that the print items listed truly represented the central core of stable intellectual interests among family members. Not only may this core be discerned from actual holdings, but there were also many contemporary references to inventory holdings as "family libraries."[7] In the formal legal sense, inventories included all family property remaining in the household estate at the time of death of the household head. All family property was legally owned by the household head. Males accounted for 94 percent of all heads of household with inventories in Windsor District through 1830.[8]

A second strength of estate inventories is that they represented wide sections of the wealth and occupational structure of the population. Inventories were generally more representative of the total wealth structure of the Upper Valley than wills (the latter are regularly used in determining elementary literacy levels). Inventories offer a reasonably accurate profile of the entire population by wealth and occupation. Their weakest coverage is for the bottom fifth of society by wealth. Whereas only 2.4 percent of wills represented the lowest 20 percent of Windsor District families by wealth, using comparative studies to establish wealth levels, 8.3 percent of inventories with family libraries derive from the bottom fifth in wealth. Furthermore, no significant change in the proportion occurs when all inventories (with and without private libraries) are considered. Offsetting the under-representation of the bottom fifth of the population in the data, proportions reported for lower-middle and middle economic classes were slightly higher than their share of the entire society. In short, inventories depict extremely well the lifestyles of 80 percent of all families by wealth. Furthermore, within the lowest 20 percent, a sufficient proportion of inventories survive for us to learn about most important patterns in the limited library collections of this group.

A third strength of Windsor District family inventories is that the assessors were far more likely than in earlier periods (and some other places) to enumerate specific print items retained. Fully 85 percent of all Windsor District libraries in 1787–1830 specified at least some of their print items, compared with only 31 percent in colonial South Carolina, for instance.[9]

A final strength of Windsor District inventories is that they best reflect the state of affairs at the latest and, unlike wills, the best possible single moment in family ownership of material possessions: at the end of the full family cycle. Not all print items ever purchased were retained throughout the remainder of that family's existence. Consequently, the addition of records from other moments in the life cycle is desirable, in line with the general principle of multiple-moment research. Such evidence is extremely rare, however. Lists of printed items read by individuals are also very helpful, but these too are rare.[10]

The strengths of estate inventories as a source of information on family libraries are considerable. Family libraries are by far our richest single source of evidence about reading habits and patterns in early national America. But the limitations of estate inventories also need to be understood. First is under-representation of the bottom fifth of the population by wealth. For some kinds of studies, this might be a serious flaw. But because the range of family libraries at this wealth level was very narrow, little is lost in our case. Inventories offer us less than full, but nonetheless vital, insight and in fact constitute the only detailed picture of Windsor District's poorest households.[11]

Table Appendix 4–1: Share of Population and Share of Inventories for Windsor District Townships, 1787–1830

Township	Share of Inventories 1787–1830 (n=396)	1830 Census[1]	Difference
Chester	17.1%	13.1%	+4.0%[2]
Windsor	19.9%	17.6%	+2.3%
Reading	10.1%	7.9%	+2.2%
Cavendish	9.5%	8.5%	+1.0%
Weathersfield	13.5%	12.7%	+ .8%
Ludlow	6.1%	6.4%	− .3%
Springfield	14.1%	15.6%	−1.5%
Weston	3.0%	5.5%	−2.5%
Plymouth	4.3%	7.1%	−2.8%
Andover	2.4%	5.6%	−3.2%
Baltimore[3]	————	————	————

[1] Using either the 1810 or the 1820 census yields approximately the same results.
[2] The + figures show an overrepresentation in inventories; the − figures an underrepresentation, as compared with the population share of each township.
[3] Insufficient evidence of inventories.

A second limitation is potential bias in coverage among the eleven townships in Windsor District. Table App. 4–1 compares the share of inventories for each township with that township's share of the total population in 1830. While no township was greatly overrepresented or underrepresented, representation was weighted toward townships closest to the probate court's home base at Windsor (see figure 1–2 throughout).

The main explanation for variations in rates of inventories lies in a subject often neglected in state inventory research: the travel patterns of the probate court. During its first two decades, 1787–1806, Windsor Probate Court typically met at a single location (Windsor), frequently twice a month, and at each of two other locations (Chester village and Cavendish hamlet) once every four months. Notification of deaths had to reach one of these locations in order for legal proceedings to begin. The process then entailed the assignment of assessors, a visit, the filing of a completed inventory, division into shares, contested estate hearings, etc. Through 1806 the numbers of estates probated remained small. During the next decade, 1807–16, the probate court meeting pattern was extended. By 1819 the Windsor District Probate Court was meeting in Cavendish (fourth in positive correlation) on the first Wednesday of each month save September, and in Chester (first) "on the last Wednesday of February, and the fourth Wednesday of August," in addition to regular biweekly sessions in Windsor's main, east village (second) and three meetings that year in a West Windsor home adjoining Reading (third). By the late 1820s the probate court had extended its meetings out into mountainous Weston and therefore into half the townships of the district. With 53 percent of the population, communities in which probate court met accounted for only a slightly larger share (57 percent) of all district inventories through 1830. Least represented in 1787–1830 were more isolated farming and grazing townships in the foothills of the Green Mountains (16 percent of inventories and 20 percent of the population). As meetings of the probate court increased in frequency and spread into the hinterland, the numbers of estates probated rose, substantially faster than previous population increases. The net result was a marked increase in the representation of the Windsor District population in 1807–30.[12]

A third and more intriguing limitation of estate inventories is that they only included a portion of the total amount of printed matter read, and only a portion of print items purchased over the course of the family cycle. This deficit helps us to focus on the precise nature, general contents, and length of retention of works in family libraries. Presently known evidence does not permit an accurate estimate of the volume of print items read, but not purchased and retained, by families. As we have seen, both informal and formal borrowing existed throughout the Upper Valley. It is also impossible to estimate with accuracy the number of kinds of works owned by wives as part of their dower and other personal holdings, since these were part of the household but not legally part of the family holdings. Nor can we estimate the number or character of works involved in gifting; or inheritance, either from a member of another family or from an earlier generation in one's own family. Comparative work on the Indiana frontier in 1805–50, by Michael Harris, suggests extensive informal borrowing.[13]

The more frequently and regularly a print vehicle appeared, the more quickly and regularly it was discarded. This was particularly true of newspapers. Almanacs too were purchased widely and by even larger a proportion of the population than that of newspaper subscribers, at least into the 1820s. But less than 10 of 396 households with print items kept even a single almanac, and none retained more than two of these annuals through 1830. Like newspapers, almanacs were either discarded—they may have worn out or just outlived their usefulness—or resold, probably to be recycled. The quality of the paper in surviving almanacs and newspapers, and the type used, in almost all cases was of poorer quality than that used in books published by the same press the same year. Periodicals, on the other hand, were treated quite differently. Many were kept. Among our 396 libraries with print items, 55 (14 percent) contained at least one periodical (mainly bound volumes, though a few loose issues also survived). The whole or parts of over one hundred separate volumes were retained. The fairly small numbers of American periodicals printed in the Upper Valley, and of British and American periodicals advertised there in 1802–30 suggest that the total proportion of families subscribing to a periodical through 1830 was not significantly higher than the 14 percent retaining copies.[14]

Books and pamphlets varied in their retention patterns from one category of knowledge to another. Two kinds of works were retained for short periods, if at all. Primers, children's books, toy books, and pamphlets, whatever their subject matter, were often not retained. Children's books, toy books, and preschool primers were fifth among all popular sellers, accounting for at least 6 to 7 percent of all sales, whereas they represented only .4 percent of all works retained through the family cycle, twenty-fourth among twenty-nine categories. Pamphlets were too varied to measure precisely, but their share of bookstore stock at hand suggests the same rough disparity. Many were sold across almost all categories of knowledge, yet relatively few were retained. Moreover, most of these were not even specified further than "pamphlet" or "small group of pamphlets."

A second category of works widely purchased but with a relatively short half-life (about two to four years), included modern literature, especially novels, and district-level schoolbooks. Modern literature was by far the best selling of all types of books, commanding nearly a sixth of the entire market. But among works retained over four years, modern literature was only fourth, with no more than one-twelfth of the total number of volumes retained. The disparity was even greater because of the large numbers of works involved. More than half the copies of each of the 193 editions of modern literature selling well were not retained for more than two to four years each. As in Germany and elsewhere in Europe after 1750, novels were perceived as a new and different form of reading matter, books to be read and perhaps reread in part but then discarded, sold to a bookseller (to be resold secondhand to another reader), or sold to book carters by weight. In two-thirds of all cases novels retained had been purchased within four years of the death of the household head.[15]

Limited use was also the rule for some varieties of schoolbooks, especially spellers and grammars, and an enormous quantity of chapbook selections of tales and stories. The two stablest areas of schoolbooks in content through 1820, geographies and readers, sold very well. Recent geographies were regularly used as reference books, especially in families reading a rural weekly full of news from "distant climes." Book-length readers were retained as general introductions to the Western intellectual tradition. In other subject areas, where knowledge was changing more rapidly, families retained purchases for shorter periods of time. What was most often kept was the item most recently purchased. Works in the professions offer a special case; once purchased, works in law, medicine, and theology often remained serviceable for decades.[16]

Upper Valley families, then, did not keep nearly all the print items they purchased. Moreover, different print vehicles and works in different fields of knowledge were not saved for equal lengths of time. The length of an item's retention in a family library often varied inversely with the pace of change in knowledge within that field and the frequency and regularity with which new works were issued. One might have presumed that in a field with the most rapid change, the greatest number of works would be accumulated. Rather, the opposite was often the case. More up-to-date works replaced older, less useful ones. Competition for a market share in a popular, active field of knowledge further increased total sales in that subject area (see table 6–3 for the twenty-five most active sales fields). Long-term retention patterns in family libraries differed substantially from sales patterns. The length of time an item was retained depended upon the kind of work it was and upon contemporary perceptions of the work's utility. Upper Valley residents took a functional view of knowledge in print form and approached print commodities with a particularly traditional, spare view of consumption, part of a broader trend in market purchasing activity. Just as they did with farm implements and cooking utensils, Upper Valley residents retained part of their purchases of print a short time and part for longer periods. The retention of printed matter was partly a matter of rural capital formation.

Snuff and an "Electrikl Machine":
A Scholar in the Wilderness

While living in a forest society, the John Leverett family's involvement in the North Atlantic Republic of Letters was substantial, as exemplified in their 909-volume family library (see table App. 5–1). A wealthy ($6,140) upper-middle-class gentleman farm family could indeed keep up with many of the leading North Atlantic intellectual trends. The Leveretts led a quietly refined life in a true mansion on a 150-acre homestead just a horse sprint up the Connecticut River from Windsor village. Gentleman John Leverett and his family combined the slowly dying neo-classical America, of which Windsor village was an arresting symbol, and the new world of commerce, factories, and intellectual currency. No less than four snuff boxes were among Leverett's possessions. But the same room held "an Electrikl Machine." While only a handful of Windsor District families had such collections, the Leveretts' library offers us a rich glimpse of the dilemmas and opportunities of changing rural life in the Early Republic. Changing beliefs and values penetrated deeply into rural America, and the Leverett family library highlights trends circulating through many Windsor District families.[1]

Born in Boston in 1758, Mr. Leverett counted among his ancestors a seventeenth-century governor of Massachusetts and an early eighteenth-century president of Harvard. John Leverett himself received an A.B. from Harvard in 1776, and while trained for the law he did not practice. Married three times, Leverett fathered eleven children. Three of his five sons graduated from college, and the other two apprenticed to urban merchants and settled in Boston and New York City. Three of the six daughters married professionals (two lawyers and a minister). At its most bustling, in 1815–25, the household numbered fifteen. Simeon Ide recalled the sight of the Leveretts going to church on Sunday: "John Leverett, gentleman and scholar, [his] old-fashioned coach, opening at the rear, brought the family to church, leaving him and one of two daughters at the Baptist [Church]; and depositing Mrs. Leverett and the rest at the [Congregationalist] Old South."[2]

An 1829 eulogy by a president of Middlebury College noted that, "possessing an uncommon thirst for literary information, [Leverett] devoted much of his time to reading and studious research. Metaphysical inquiries were particularly his delight. He did not, however, neglect the study of other sciences." Accounting for a twelfth of the $6,140 estate, the family library was largely (at least 75 percent) purchased between 1795 and 1829. Secular reading dominated (636 to 265, or 71 percent) but works of theology, sermons, and church histories formed the largest single cluster; with devotional reading they accounted for 267 volumes (see table App. 5–1). In counterpoint to this trend was the second largest cluster, 203 volumes (22 percent), which encompassed science, technology, mathematics, trade, and general compilations of knowledge about these subjects. Schoolbooks, classical writers, and modern literature, each with 75 to 85 volumes, were the next largest groupings, combining for a tenth of all holdings. French, Latin, and Greek language works were all prominent, seasoned by Hebrew and German treatises. Philosophy, and history and geography, each had 50 to 60 volumes. Another 90 volumes embraced smaller clusters in medicine and law, politics and government, the stages of life, travels, and social reform. This was the kind of household whose walls included paintings, prints, and "French verbs conjugated and framed . . . $25."[3]

While a full discussion of the Leveretts' intellectual interests must await another publication, a few overarching themes may be noted. Calvinist theology reigned supreme among sacred reading. John Leverett was a staunch orthodox Baptist and strong supporter of infant baptism. But Congregationalism, the religion of Leverett's third wife, Elizabeth Salisbury, was also prominent. This was the collection of a serious polemicist; argumentative treatises abounded. The theology collection also included Universalist, Unitarian, and Methodist perspectives, often in works pointing out their weaknesses. On the limited issue of infant baptism, the Leverett collection contained all major transatlantic positions and serious criticism of each. Secular reading was also rich with older and newer strains of thought. The ultimate anchor of new thought was present: a full (87- to 92-volume) set of Abraham Rees's *New Cyclopaedia*, the most important contemporary compilation of knowledge in the English language. Beyond Rees, works in many fields were guided by a scientific, nationalist, Enlightenment-oriented, secular perspective: natural philosophy generally, chemistry, astronomy, zoology, botany, electricity, and scientific farming. Eight major treatises, including the important perspective of Thomas Chalmers, considered the relationship between science and religion.[4]

The Leverett family library was a curiously somber collection: no secular music, no fine arts, and very few novels—almost none by the leading contemporary writers. However, imaginative literature other than novels, well represented the full sweep of British and continental literary traditions from the sixteenth through the early nineteenth centuries. America and British history

Sacred Works: 265 volumes (29%)

  Bibles and Testaments 8

    a. Bible 1

    b. New Testament: Greek 4

    c. New Testament: Latin 2

    d. New Testament: English 1

  Psalm Books and Hymnals 6

    a. Psalm books 3

    b. Hymnals 3

  Devotional Works 32

  Theology (incl. Church History and Sermons) 218

Secular Works: 636 volumes. (70%)

  Schoolbooks 109

    a. Spellers 1

    b. Grammars 9

    c. Readers 6

    d. Geographies 2

    e. Mathematics 19

    f. History 5

    g. Misc. Upper Level (Logic, Rhetoric, Elocution, etc.) 18

    h. Latin Schoolbooks 16

    i. Greek Schoolbooks 6

    j. Combined Latin and Greek Schoolbooks 1

    k. Hebrew Schoolbooks 1

    l. German Schoolbooks 1

    m. French Schoolbooks 24

Continued

and contemporary life held great interest; Hamiltonian Federalism was Leverett's political philosophy. As in theology, modern literature, and public affairs, several hundred years' worth of major philosophical positions, culminating in the Scottish Enlightenment and the Skeptical Enlightenment encompassed 57 volumes. Scottish philosophy was represented by Alison, Hutcheson, Reid, Stewart, Smith, Kames, Blair, Robertson, Beattie, and Thomas Brown. In the Skeptical Enlightenment (to use Henry May's phrase), Mandeville, Hume, Helvetius, Hartley, Locke, Rousseau, and Berkeley were prominent. The material and cultural context of the Leverett family library is crucial. Families living in or near villages with bookstores were able to attain intellectual currency in rural New England before 1830. For these families, progress in knowledge was no longer limited to urban habitation.

Education (Teachers' Manuals and Theory of Education) 5

Dictionaries (English Language) 7

Classical Writings 59

    a. New Testament Greek and Latin Lexicons 2

    b. Roman Civilization: Writings of 39

    c. Greek Civilization: Writings of 13

    d. Combined Greece and Rome 4

    e. Hebrew Writings 1

Law 8

Medicine 23

Travel 6

Geography 11

History 39

Politics and Government 22

Philosophy 58

Modern Literature 78

Science, Technology, Trade, and General Compilations 184

Social Reform 3

Stages of Life 22

Newspapers 2

Miscellaneous (Unidentified) 8 volumes (1%)   Total Volumes: 909

Source: WDPR.

Notes

Preface

1. The phrase is Arthur Schlesinger, Jr.'s, in *Orestes A. Brownson: A Pilgrim's* Progress (Boston, 1939), 6.

2. See Ralph Samuel and Gareth Stedman Jones, "Editorial: Ten Years After," HW 20 (1985):1–4, quote on 3. In these notes, sources frequently cited are abbreviated. See list of abbreviations preceding the bibliography.

3. See William J. Gilmore, "Elementary Literacy on the Eve of the Industrial Revolution: Trends in Rural New England, 1760–1830," PAAS 92, pt. 1 (1982): 87–178.

4. The best recent discussion of the concept of *mentalités* is André Burguière, "The Fate of the History of *Mentalités* in the *Annales*," CSSH 24 (1982): 424–37. On its application, see Robert Darnton, *The Great Cat Massacre and Other Episodes in French Cultural History* (New York, 1984), esp. 3–7, 257–63, and 283, n. 2.

5. See *Moby Dick*, ch. 47, "The Mat-Maker." For all books, pamphlets, broadsides, almanacs, and periodicals read by Windor District residents and found in estate inventories and wills, or otherwise known to have been read, I have decoded the spine title system of bibliographic description to ascertain the precise work in question and then sought the specific edition most likely to have been used by each family (see app. 4). Between a 1795 edition and an 1818 edition, say, texts frequently were changed by authors and publishers who liberally substituted and added forewords, commentary, etc. To avoid confusion, and since the full list of all editions consulted approximates a complete bibliography of every edition of approximately 1,250 different works, 1780–1830, full bibliographical information for the most frequently consulted edition is supplied in a distinct section of the bibliography. The first use of each primary source work does not duplicate this information; rather, the note uses an author–short title format. The reader wishing full bibliographical information should refer to the bibliography. In all cases where a work is quoted, and in all uses of other primary source imprints, the normal first citation conventions appear. On historical realism see the brooding analysis of Arthur M. Schlesinger, Jr., *The Cycles of American History* (Boston, 1986).

Introduction

1. Perhaps the most interesting theory is David Riesman's, positing a transition in national character types from tradition-directed to inner-and then to outer-directed. See Riesman, Nathan Glazer, and Reuel Denney, *The Lonely Crowd: A Study of the Changing American Character* (New Haven, 1960); and Riesman, *Individualism Reconsidered* (Glencoe, Ill., 1954).

2. See, for example, Paul Seaver, *Wallington's World: A Puritan Artisan in 17th Century London* (Methuen, 1985); Alan Macfarlane, *The Family Life of Ralph Josselin, a Seventeenth Century*

Clergyman (Cambridge, England, 1970); and Carlo Ginzburg, *The Cheese and the Worms: The Cosmos of a Sixteenth Century Miller* (Baltimore, 1980).

3. Manuel, "The Use and Abuse of Psychology in History," DAED 100 (1971):187–212, quote on 196.

4. See Daniel Czitrom, *Media and the American Mind: From Morse to McLuhan* (Chapel Hill, N.C., 1982).

5. See the bibliography for citations of this work. For much of the literature on the extent of economic and social transformation through the late eighteenth century, see James A. Henretta, "Wealth and Social Structure," in *Colonial British America: Essays in the New History of the Early Modern Era*, ed. Jack P. Greene and J.R. Pole (Baltimore, 1984), 262–89, esp. 277–79.

6. VtR&J 18 Dec. 1831.

7. Ibid., 29 Mar. and 5 Apr. 1833: p. 3, editorials unless noted. On the three-way 1834 gubernatorial election, for instance, see ibid., 4 Sept.–20 Nov. 1834, for returns by townships.

8. See Drew McCoy, *The Elusive Republic: Political Economy in Jeffersonian America* (New York, 1980).

9. VtR&J 29 Mar., 5 and 12 Apr., 5 July, 2 Aug., 6 and 27 Dec. 1833; 13 and 27 Feb. and 6 Mar. 1834. Throughout this book all underlining, etc., is as in the original unless noted.

10. Ibid., 24 Feb.; 6, 13, 20, and 27 Mar.; and 3 Apr. 1834. The 3 April issue reported the proceedings of the Young Men's County Convention at Woodstock, at which mechanics and farmers attempted to evaluate their situation, by noting that "the position of the people of this county may be, in part, inferred from their geographical situation."

11. Abel Tompkins, *Miller Overthrown: or, the False Prophet Confounded. By a Cosmopolite* (Boston, 1840), 132. I was led to read this tract by Randolph Roth.

12. DHI IV:413, and "Sense of the Tragic," IV:411–17.

13. See Randolph Roth's excellent "Whence This Strange Fire? Religion and Reform in the Connecticut River Valley of Vermont, 1791–1843," 2 vols. (Ph.D. diss., Yale Univ., 1981); and his *The Democratic Dilemma: Religion, Reform, and the Social Order in the Connecticut River Valley of Vermont, 1791–1850* (Cambridge, Eng., 1987).

14. Lewis D. Stilwell, *Migration From Vermont* (Montpelier, Vt., 1937).

15. Whitney Cross, *The Burned-Over District: The Social and Intellectual History of Enthusiastic Religion in Western New York, 1800–1850* (Ithaca, N.Y., 1950), bks. IV–VI, pp. 171–357.

16. See Roth, "Whence This Strange Fire?" and *Democratic Dilemma*.

17. See Gilmore, "Elementary Literacy;" Gilmore, "Orestes Brownson and New England Religious Culture, 1803–27" (Ph.D. diss., Univ. of Virginia, 1971); and Thomas R. Ryan, *Orestes A. Brownson: A Definitive Biography* (Huntington, Ind., 1976), 15–83.

Chapter 1

1. See, for instance, Richard D. Brown, *Modernization: The Transformation of American Life, 1600–1865* (New York, 1976); his "Modernization and the Modern Personality in Early America, 1600–1865: A Sketch of a Synthesis," JIH 2 (1972):201–28; and Douglas T. Miller, *The Birth of Modern America, 1820–1850* New York, 1970). I checked over three dozen current textbooks (through 1987).

2. Fifteen years ago, in a draft overview for a multivolume social history, "America, A Social History: The Main Lines of the Subject, 1650–1975" (unpublished manuscript, 1974), David Hackett Fischer advanced a useful concept of "deep change" to characterize the 1790–1830 era.

3. Family libraries, maps, and writing implements (along with other sources of reading matter borrowed and subscribed to) attest to a cultural revolution; see chs. 8 and 9.

4. Daniel Webster, "The Bunker Hill Monument," in Edwin P. Whipple, ed., *The Great*

Speeches and Orations of Daniel Webster With an Essay on Daniel Webster as a Master of English Style (Boston, 1879), 123–35; quotes on 125–27 and 131.

5. Joseph Story, "*Discourse Pronounced at Cambridge Before the Phi Beta Kappa Society, on the Anniversary Celebration, August 31, 1826*," in Story, *The Miscellaneous Writings, Literary, Critical, Juridical and Political, of Joseph Story, LLD., Now First Collected* (Boston, 1835), 3–33; quotes on 3–8, mainly following points of argument.

6. For the apparently different situation in Virginia, see Joseph F. Kett and Patricia A. McClung, "Book Culture in Post-Revolutionary Virginia," PAAS 94, pt. 1 (1984):98–137. On the importance of Boston in the New England book trade, see Rollo Silver, *The Boston Book Trade, 1800–1825* (New York, 1949). On the importance of a broad international perspective, see Bernard Bailyn, "The Challenge of Modern Historiography," AHR 87 (1982):1–24.

7. For the literature on early communications revolutions, see Elizabeth Eisenstein, *The Printing Press as an Agent of Change: Communications and Cultural Transformation in Early Modern Europe*, 2 vols. (Cambridge, England, 1979), 1:3–159.

8. See Egil Johansson, *The History of Literacy in Sweden, in Comparison with Some Other Countries* (Umea, Sweden, 1977), reprinted in *Literacy and Social Development in the West: A Reader*, ed. Harvey J. Graff (Cambridge, England, 1981), 151–82.

9. See Albert Ward, *Book Production, Fiction, and the German Reading Public, 1740–1800* (Oxford, 1974); Rolf Engelsing, "Die Perioden der Lesergeschichte in der Neuzeit," in *Zur Sozialgeschichte deutscher Mittelund Unterschichten4* (Gottingen, 1973): 112–54; and Engelsing, *Der Burger als Leser: Lesergeschichte in Deutschland zwischen feudaler und industrieller Gesellschaft* (Stuttgart, 1974).

10. The sources for this and the next several paragraphs include six months' reading on literacy and print culture in the North Atlantic world. For an excellent guide to this literature, focused on literacy but much broader in coverage, see Graff, *Literacy in History: An Interdisciplinary Research Bibliography* (New York, 1981), Sec. 4: pts. 1–3, 6, 7. There is no adequate bibliography in English on the book trade. On print culture, see especially the bibliography in Eisenstein, *Printing Press*, II:709–67 and I:ix–159. See especially Lucien Febvre and Henri-Jean Martin, *The Coming of the Book: The Impact of Printing, 1450–1800*, trans. David Gerard (London, 1976); Terry Belanger, "From Bookseller to Publisher: Changes in the London Book Trade, 1750–1850," in *Book Selling and Book Buying: Aspects of the Nineteenth-Century British and North American Book Trade*, ed. Richard Landon (Chicago, 1978), 7–16; A.S. Collins, *Authorship in the Age of Johnson* (London, 1928), and *The Profession of Letters, . . . 1780–1832* (London, 1928); D.F. McKenzie, "The London Book Trade in the Later 17th Century," *The Library* 33 (1978): 242–46; Marjorie Plant, *The English Book Trade: An Economic History of the Making and Sale of Books* (London, 1974); Giles Barber, "Pendred Abroad: A View of the Late Eighteenth Century Book Trade in Europe," in *Essays to Graham Pollard*, ed. John Carter, (Oxford, 1975), 231–77; Sten G. Lindberg, "The Scandinavian Book Trade in the Eighteenth Century," in *Buch und Buchhande in Europe in Achtzehnten Jahrhundert*, ed. Giles Barber and Bernhard Fabian (Hamburg, 1981), 225–48; Wallace Kirsop, "Literary History and Book Trade History: The Lessons of L' Apparition du livre," *Australian Journal of French Studies* 16 (1979): 488–535; Roger Chartier and Daniel Roche, "Le livre: un changement de perspective," *Faire de l' histoire III: Nouveaux objets* (Paris, 1974), 115–36; Chartier, "Livre et espace: Circuits commerciaux et geographie culturelle de la librairie lyonnaise au XVIIIᵉ siecle," *Revue francaise d' histoire du livre*, nos. 1–2 (1971):77–108; Darnton, *The Literary Underground of the Ancien Regime* (Cambridge, Mass., 1979); and Darnton, *The Business of Enlightment: A Publishing History of the Encyclopedie, 1775–1800* (Cambridge, Mass., 1979); and Ward, *Book Production*. The finest study of literacy is Graff's *The Legacies of Literacy: Continuities and Contradictions in Western Society and Culture* (Bloomington, Ind., 1987).

11. Gilmore, "Elementary Literacy," 87–178. Research is needed on the contents of popular texts used as agents of literacy in homes and schools.

12. Ibid., Roy Wiles, "The Relish for Reading in Provincial England Two Centuries Ago," in *The Widening Circle: Essays on the Circulation of Literature in Eighteenth Century Europe*, ed. Paul J. Korshin (Philadelphia, 1976), 85–115.

13. For the population data here and in the next paragraph, see tables 1 and 4 in Blake McKelvey, *American Urbanization: A Comparative History* (Glencoe, Ill., 1973), 11, 52, and "Part One," 3–74; table 3 in Roy Porter, *English Society in the Eighteenth Century* (New York., 1983), 383; and table 5 in George Rogers Taylor, "Comment," in *The Growth of the Seaport Cities, 1790–1825*, ed. David T. Gilchrist (Charlottesville, Va., 1967), 39 and 26–53.

14. Seven English urban places were larger than Philadelphia, the second largest American urban center. By comparison with New York City, Paris, Constantinople, Cairo, Moscow, and Vienna, all held more then 230,000; Berlin and Mexico City ranged between 120,000 and 180,000; and Glasgow and Edinburgh ranged between 77,000 and 83,000.

15. New York was now the largest city in the New World, just ahead of Mexico City's 175,000 residents.

16. In Gilmore, "Elementary Literacy," I included evidence drawn from other parts of rural New England. I have since completed a full-scale study of another extremely rural area in the American Northeast. The findings were presented in "Elementary Literacy on the Eve of the Industrial Revolution: Trends in Southern New Jersey, 1760–1840" (unpublished paper delivered at the Princeton Univ. Seminar for Historians of New Jersey, Nov. 1982. Literacy trends for villages and their immediate environs paralleled those found in the Upper Valley, but rates were somewhat lower for both genders in satellite hamlets and considerably lower deeper in the countryside. Denominational schools assumed the burdern of primary education for residents of villages and some hamlets, in the absence of public schools in southern New Jersey until the 1840s. Where neither commerce nor schooling penetrated, literacy and reading activity progressed far more slowly.

17. See Richard D. Brown, "The Emergence of Urban Society in Rural Massachusetts, 1760–1820," JAH 61 (1974):29–51.

18. The literature is large. See, for instance, Louis Wright, *Cultural Life on the Moving Frontier* (Bloomington, Ind., 1955); and, for a broader context, Henry Steele Commager and Elmo Giordanetti, eds., *Was America a Mistake? An Eighteenth-Century Controversy* (New York, 1967).

19. The first Vermont printed book-length work of fiction, John Filson's *Adventures of Colonel Daniel Boone*, (1793) was preceded by fifteen years of printing and more than 300 other imprints. See Marcus McCorison, *Vermont Imprints, 1778–1820* (Worcester, Mass., 1963), p. 61, no. 264; [First] *Additions and Corrections* (Worcester, Mass., 1968), p. 5; [Second] *Additions and Corrections* (Worcester, 1973); and [Third] *Additions and Corrections to Vermont Imprints, 1778–1820* (Worcester, 1985).

20. In the Upper Valley, nearly two-thirds of all Windsor District families with inventories in 1787–1830 retained family libraries. Members of many other families, at least another 10–15 percent, engaged in reading without retaining a private library. They either did not save or gave away printed materials, including almanacs, pamphlets, broadsides, newspapers, and several categories of books (e.g., novels and children's books). Thus, approximately three-quarters of all families maintained the habit of reading; see chs. 5, 6, 8, and 9.

21. See n. 10 above.

22. Comparative study of transatlantic populations as they pursued mass literacy and active reading through a long time period offers a central challenge to history. Fundamental change in material and cultural life had differing effects in London and Paris; in the provincial capitols of Great Britain, Germany, France, Sweden, and America; and in the rural countryside areas

of each nation. Varying motives and patterns in commerce and culture need to be explored, in the spirit of Bailyn's "Challenge" (see n. 6 above).

23. Many studies (e.g., Genevieve Bollème, *Les almanachs populaires dux XVII* et *XVIII* *siècles* [Paris, 1969]; and David Lundberg and Henry May, "The Enlightened Reader in America," *AQ* 28 (1974):262–93) center on the nation-state as an appropriate geographical unit of analysis, taking an important aspect of the "social history of ideas" as their subject. National level research masks the enormous variety within American life in the Early Republic. Sometimes the whole is far less than the sum of its parts. A major alternative strategy, based on the single-township case study, offers clarity, compactness, and the ability to study many aspects of life in the same setting. But I judged the danger of the one-town pattern to be too great for cultural analysis: eight random township studies among two-hundred towns might produce four interesting pairs of exceptions to dominant cultural patterns. See Darrett Rutman, "People in Process: The New Hampshire Towns of the 18th Century," *Journal of Urban History* 1 (1975):268–91.

24. E. J. Hobsbawm argues well for the importance of the French and Industrial Revolutions as "the twin craters of a rather large regional volcano," in *The Age of Revolution, 1789–1848* (New York, 1962), quote on 18. Even beyond America, the American Revolution was more influential than in Hobsbawm's view. On this point, Gordon Wood's "Social Radicalism and Equality in the American Revolution," *B.K. Smith Lectures in History: Univ. of St. Thomas* (Houston, Tex., 1976), 5–14, is useful.

25. Raymond D. Gastil, *Cultural Regions of the United States* (Seattle, 1975), 45.

26. The other subregions are: the coastal area, encompassing parts of all states except Vermont; the upland mountains, comprising substantial portions of Vermont, New Hampshire, and Maine; and the Lower Connecticut River Valley, first settled in the 1630s. Connections between the Lower and Upper Valley areas were of great importance throughout the latter's settlement.

27. Insights from several disciplines—including cultural geography, economics, anthropology, sociology, and enviornmental-natural history—and studies in the new history related to each, influenced my perspective on the Upper Valley. The choice of New England, rather than the Middle Atlantic area, was arbitrary. On the Upper Valley, see Gastil, *Cultural Regions*, 128–38, esp. 138–56; John L. Rice, "Dartmouth College and the State of New Connecticut, 1776–1782," in *Connecticut Valley Historical Society, Papers and Proceedings, 1876–1881*, ed. Rice (Springfield, Mass., 1981), 152–206; Fischer, *The Revolution of American Conservatism: The Federalist Party in the Era of Jeffersonian Democracy* (New York, 1969), app. 1; Timothy Dwight, *Travels in New England and New York*, ed. Barbara Miller Solomon, 4 vols. (Cambridge, Mass., 1969), esp. I:219–33; Margery D. Howarth, *New Hampshire: A Study of Its Cities and Towns in Relation to Their Physical Background* (Concord, N.H., 1936); H. Nicholas Muller, III, "Shifting Boundaries, Elusive Settlers, and the Population of the 'Republic of Vermont': A Review Essay on *Vermont 1771 Census*," VtH 51 (1983):179–89; Donald Cole, *Jacksonian Democracy in New Hampshire, 1800–1851* (Cambridge, Mass., 1970), 136–159; and Roth, *Democratic Dilemma*. Referring to the valley towns of Vermont and New Hampshire, David Carlisle, editor of the Walpole, N. H., *Farmer's Museum, or Literary Gazette* (hereafter FM), noted that "the business intercourse between the two states was constant, and similarity of taste and habits existed among the inhabitants of both," quoted in Joseph Buckingham, *Specimens of Newspaper Literature*, 2 vols. (Boston, 1852), 2:174, and see 177.

28. See Roth, "Whence This Strange Fire?" chs. 1 and 2. This study relies heavily on a fascinating historical account of Vermont life in 1749–84: Donald Alan Smith, "Legacy of Dissent: Religion and Politics in Revolutionary Vermont, 1749 to 1784," 3 vols. (Ph.D. diss., Clark Univ., 1981).

29. Isolation was somewhat mitigated by talking with residents who did share in the fruits

of commerce and print communications. The extent of this exchange network is yet to be determined. See David Hall, "The World of Print and Collective Mentality in Seventeenth-Century New England," in *New Directions in American Intellectual History*, ed. John Higham and Paul K. Conkin (Baltimore, 1979), 166–80.

30. We will use the term "township" to mean the legal unit encompassing all Windsor land, including farmstead, hamlet, and village living situations. The contemporary terms most frequently used were "town" and "township." We prefer the originally English "township"— widely used in the Upper Valley—to avoid a narrower use of town (as opposed to countryside), where town means city or village. See John A. Graham, *A Descriptive Sketch of the Present State of Vermont* (London, 1797), 125; Jedidiah Morse, *The American Gazetteer* (Boston, 1797), vii; and Edward A. Hoyt, ed., *General Petitions, 1788–1792*, vol. 9, *The State Papers of Vermont* (Montpelier, Vt., 1955), 97ff, for examples.

31. Ten townships plus Baltimore, a small incorporated settlement. To ensure accurate basic information on the Upper Valley, I have collated all maps, atlases, gazetteers, and geographies published through 1840, as well as modern compilations of rudimentary data on the river valley counties of each state. The special card files of maps at the VHS and the AAS's subject catalogues were indispensable. A most helpful caution regarding how maps become outdated is J. Kevin Graffagnino's thoughtful "Representation of a Turbulent Land: Some Vermont Maps, 1755–98" (unpublished paper, 1980). See also his *The Shaping of Vermont: From the Wilderness to the Centennial, 1749–1877* (Rutland, Vt., 1983); David A. Cobb, "Vermont Maps Prior to 1900: An Annotated Cartobibliography," VtH 39 (1971):169–317.

32. The exact portion of rural New England being discussed will be specified throughout.

33. No single factor had dominant impact on the course of material or cultural change. In various combinations, however, the material and cultural infrastructure had a substantial impact on how much and what kinds of printed matter most residents read; on what kinds of letters, if any, they sent and received; and on what other forms of writing and recordkeeping they undertook.

34. Central to my understanding of these issues are Nancy Cott, *The Bonds of Womanhood: Woman's Sphere in New England, 1780–1835* (New Haven, 1977); Linda Kerber, *Women of the Republic: Intellect and Ideology in Revolutionary America* (Chapel Hill, N.C., 1980); Mary Beth Norton, *Liberty's Daughters: The Revolutionary Experience of Women, 1750–1800* (Ithaca, N.Y., 1980); and John Mack Faragher, *Men and Women on the Overland Trail* (New Haven, 1979).

35. Henretta, *The Evolution of American Society, 1700–1815: An Interdisciplinary Analysis* (Lexington, Ky., 1973), 187–223.

36. In addition to dedicated factory villages, many other Upper Valley villages and hamlets each contained from one to six factories. Most factories retained between three and twenty workers. Children and youth of both genders were employed as workers alongside a majority of adult males. For specifics on Upper Valley population and some of the rudiments of economic life and manufacturing, we have used the U.S. Censuses for 1790 through 1840, as well as the separate Censuses of Manufactures for 1820 and 1832. For another view, see Richard D. Brown, "Emergence of Urban Society," 29–51.

37. Herbert Gutman, Review of Alan Dawley, *Class and Community: The Industrial Revolution in Lynn*, in *New York Times Sunday Book Review*, 12 June 1977.

38. See Gilmore, "The 'Mystic Chords of Memory': Needs and Opportunities for a History of Reading to 1876" (Paper presented at AAS Conference on the History of the Book, 3 Nov. 1984).

39. Eisenstein, *Printing Press*, 3–159.

40. See the discussion of the push for literacy in Lee Soltow and Edward Stevens, *The*

Rise of Literacy and the Common School in the United States: A Socioeconomic Analysis to 1870 (Chicago, 1981), 58–66.

41. Rollo Silver is a leading contributor to several of these areas; see his *The Boston Book Trade* and Lawrence Wroth and Rollo Silver, "Book Production and Distribution from the American Revolution to the War Between the States," in *The Book in America: A History of the Making and Selling of Books in the United States*, ed. Hellmut Lehmann-Haupt, 2d. ed. (New York, 1952), 63–136.

42. See Walter Ong, *Ramus: Method and the Decay of Dialogue* (Cambridge, Mass., 1958); *The Presence of the Word: Some Prolegomena for Cultural and Religious History*, rev. ed. (Minneapolis, 1981); and *Orality and Literacy: The Technologizing of the Word* (Methuen, 1982). See also Marshall McLuhan, *The Gutenberg Galaxy: The Making of Typographic Man* (Toronto, 1972); and *Understanding Media: The Extensions of Man* (New York, 1964). Some critics of novel reading were pioneers in exploring an important aspect of the relationship between the medium of communication and the messages it contained.

43. Rusche is the most careful student of Webster's educational philosophy; see "An Empire of Reason: A Study of the Writings of Noah Webster" (Ph.D. diss., Univ. of Iowa, 1975), 270.

44. See E. Jennifer Monaghan, *A Common Heritage: Noah Webster's Blue Back Speller* (Hamden, Conn., 1983), 31–56 and 196–210; and Rusche, "Empire of Reason," 260–95. Webster's *The American Spelling Book* (Bennington, Vt., 1794) was the most popular book of reading instruction.

45. Webster, *American Spelling Book*, vii. In late Reformation Sweden (c. 1650–1725), the emphasis in reading instruction was on visual and not oral communication. As Egil Johansson puts it, "Learning should pass from what was concrete for the eye, via memory, to a complete understanding and application." Children were taught to "learn to read and see with their own eyes what God bids and commands in His Holy Word." See his *History of Literacy*, quotes on 156–57 and 164. On reading orally in France in the 1760s, see Darnton, "Readers Respond," in *Great Cat Massacre*, 225.

46. Rusche, "The Empire of Reason," 271.

47. See Monaghan, *A Common Heritage*, 1–90.

48. Rusche, "The Empire of Reason," quotes on 265–66 and 269; also see Monaghan, *A Common Heritage*.

49. Rusche, "The Empire of Reason," 295; Engelsing, "Die Perioden," 112–54; and David Hall, "The Uses of Literacy in New England, 1600–1850," in *Printing and Society in Early America*, ed. William Joyce et al.(Worcester, Mass., 1983), 1–47.

50. On novel reading see Robert Winans, "The Growth of a Novel-Reading Public in Late Eighteenth-Century America," *Early American Lit.*9 (1975): 267–75: G. Harrison Orians, "Censure of Fiction in American Romances and Magazines, 1789–1810," PMLA 52 (1937):195–214; and Soltow and Stevens, *Rise of Literacy*, 11–22 and 58–88, on types of reading matter advocated generally and in the common school movement after 1834. Davidson kindly allowed me to read several draft chapters of her *Revolution and the Word: The Rise of the Novel in America* (New York, 1986). The Miller quotes are from Orians, p. 200.Throughout this study, unless noted, all quotes have been checked in the original.

51. See Rusche, "Empire of Reason."

52. See n. 42 above.

53. Mason was later a storekeeper. Daniel Mason, Account Book, 1804–20, Cavendish, Vt. (Manuscripts Collection, VHS). The writing exercises are in the front of the book, and the sentence noted was copied seven times across two facing pages, an exercise book pattern common in district schools because the books were signed and handed in opened up for easy perusal by the teacher.

54. Leavitt, *Easy Lessons in Reading for the Use of Younger Classes in Common Schools* (Watertown, N.Y., 1827), quotes on 14 et passim.

55. Toward evening's end Mr. Metcalf (of Boston) fondly referred to Fessenden's fine poem, reiterating his view that printing was indeed "the art of speaking to the eye." Jefferson Clark, *Address Delivered at the Anniversary Celebration of the Franklin Typographical Society, Jan. 17, 1826* (Boston, 1826), quotes (including poem) on 19 and 22.

56. See Patricia Cline Cohen's intriguing study, *A Calculating People: The Spread of Numeracy in Early America* (Chicago, 1982), 134–41.

57. Throughout this discussion see Kerber, "Daughters of Columbia: Educating Women for the Republic, 1787–1805," in *The Hofstadter Aegis: A Memorial*, ed. Stanley Elkins and Eric McKitrick (New York, 1974), and reprinted in *Women's America: Refocusing the Past*, ed. Kerber and Jane DeHart Mathews (New York, 1982), 82–94, quote on 83; Kerber, *Women of the Republic*, 3–32, 137–155, and 185–288; Cott, *Bonds of Womanhood*, 63–125; Norton, *Liberty's Daughters*, 256–99; Ruth H. Bloch, "American Feminine Ideals in Transition: The Rise of the Moral Mother, 1785–1815," *Feminist Studies* 4 (1978):101–26; and Norma Basch, *In the Eyes of the Law: Women, Marriage and Property in Nineteenth Century New York* (Ithaca, N.Y., 1982), 15–112.

58. Kerber, "Daughters," 86.

59. Kerber, "Daughters," 83; *Women of the Republic*, 203ff.

60. See Laurel Thatcher Ulrich, *Good Wives: Image and Reality in the Lives of Women in Northern New England, 1650–1750* (New York, 1982), p. 7. I used the wording of Blackstone, in the Oxford, 1769, facsimile ed., Chicago, 1979, p.II:433. See also Kerber, *Women of the Republic*, esp. 115–37 and 185–288, quote on 190; and Marylynn Salmon's excellent comparative essay, "Equality of Submersion? Feme Covert Status in Early Pennsylvania," in *Women of America: A History*, ed. Carol Ruth Berkin and Mary Beth Norton (Boston, 1979), 92–113.

61. Kerber, "Daughters," 90–92; Norton, *Liberty's Daughters*, 293–94.

62. Kerber, *Women of the Republic*, quote on 200.

63. For the following paragraphs I have read all of the district school records known to have survived in Windsor Distrct through 1830 (mainly found interspersed through the vital records of each township) and culled all notices, essays, editorials, and letters from Windsor District newspapers, 1783–1835. For examples see: VJ for 19 May 1784, 27 Oct. 1794, 17 Nov. 1806, 1 Jan. 1810, 30 July 1821, 27 Nov. 1829, 6 Mar. 1830, 5, 22, and 29 May 1830, 10 July 1830, 28 Aug. 1830, 4 Sept. 1830, and 20 Nov. 1830; Wash for 17 Sept., 1 Oct., and 3 Dec., 1810; and VtC for 12 Feb. 1830. See also Thomas Tolman to James Whitelaw, 13 Nov. 1813, Mss 30 #17, June-Dec. 1813, VHS. See also Kathryn Kish Sklar, "The Founding of Mount Holyoke College," in *Women of America*, ed. Berkin and Norton, 177–201, esp. 177–81.

64. For examples of lists, see Kerber, Norton, and Cott. For instance, Rev. John Bennett wished no attention to "politics, philosophy, mathemetics, or metaphysics," lest "disengaged ease and softness" be destroyed; quoted from Norton, *Liberty's Daughters*, 264.

65. Kerber, "Daughters," 86–87, and *Women of the Republic*, 209ff.; Cott, *Bonds of Womanhood*, 101–25; Norton, *Liberty's Daughters*, 263ff., quote on 286.

66. Cott, *Bonds of Womanhood*, 101–25, quotes on 123 and 125; Norton, *Liberty's Daughters*, 294.

67. Norton, *Liberty's Daughters*, 271–72.

68. See VtC 12 Feb. 1830; VtR&J 25 Sept. 1830; and "Proctorsville Reading Club Journal," MSC 150, VHS.

69. Norton, *Liberty's Daughters*, 257 and 288ff.; Cott, *Bonds of Womanhood*, 125; and Celia Morris Eckhardt. *Fanny Wright: Rebel in America* (Cambridge, Mass., 1984).

Chapter 2

1. McCorison, *Vermont Imprints* and *Additions and Corrections.*

2. See Linda Kerber, *Federalists in Dissent: Imagery and Ideology in Jeffersonian America* (Ithaca, New York, 1970), esp. 1–22.

3. There is a large and growing literature on this topic. For a valuable contribution, see Jonathan Prude, *The Coming of Industrial Order: Town and Factory Life in Rural Massachusetts, 1810–1860* (Cambridge, England, 1983), and its bibliography.

4. See Noah Webster, *An American Dictionary of the English Language* (New York, 1828), Vol. 1: "Commerce."

5. Recent literature on the political economy of the Early Republic is discussed in Daniel Walker Howe, "European Sources of Political Ideas in Jeffersonian America," RAH 10 (1982):28–44. I derived the estimated share of families participating in market exchange from two sources: the percentage of inventories and estate settlements with debts, and a tally of all households with book accounts drawn from a canvass of all known Windsor District account books, 1780–1835. For a partial list, see Gilmore, "Elementary Literacy," table 4; pp. 118–19. I used the 643 families with inventories.

6. Hobsbawm, *Age of Revolution*, 17–73, quotes on 50; Mick Reed, "The Peasantry of Nineteenth-Century England: A Neglected Class," HW 18 (1984):53–76; and Edwin Burrows, "The Transition Question in Early American History: A Checklist of Recent Books, Articles, and Dissertations," *Radical History Review* 18 (Fall 1978):173–90, quote on 178. All varieties of Marxism assume, as Burrows puts it, "that every social system is characterized by a distinctive mode of production" which is the engine of historical change. Marx's thinking, and that of his followers, explicates a later stage of urban, industrial (wage labor) capitalism more adequately than it accounts for developments within a rural, agricultural society becoming increasingly commercial in its forms of consumption (the American Northeast c. 1740–1835).

7. Burrows, ibid., 173–90; quotes on 173 and 178(2). Burrows accurately predicted that "the next major subject of controversy in American history is almost certainly going to be the transition from precapitalist to capitalist society."

8. Susan Geib, "'Changing Works': Agriculture and Society in Brookfield, Mass., 1785–1820" (Ph.D. diss., Boston Univ., 1981).

9. When a printing office in a village closed, as occurred in Walpole by 1817, all local production of printed materials ceased. Local consumption continued, however, as customers sought out new sources of production. Keene and Windsor newspapers replaced the Walpole weekly when it folded in 1813; after 1817, their books and pamphlets replaced those previously printed and stocked in Walpole.

10. Adams, *The Scholar's Arithmetic* (Leominster, Mass., 1801), vii and 184. In the language of elementary numeracy, barter was "the exchanging of one commodity for another, and teaches merchants so to proportion their quantities" to avoid loss. See William Perry, *The Royal Standard English Dictionary* (Brookfield, Mass., 1806), 80, for the prevailing definition of cash as ready money. See also other popular Windsor District schoolbooks: Nicolas Pike, *A New and Complete System of Arithmetic*, (Boston, 1809), 275–79; Caleb Alexander, *A New and Complete System of Arithmetic* (Albany, New York, 1802), 142–44; Nathan Daboll, *The Schoolmaster's Assistant* (New London, Conn., 1800), 117–19; Thomas Dilworth, *The Schoolmaster's Assistant* (New York, 1802), 72; and Daniel Staniford, *Practical Arithmetic* (Boston, 1818), 104–07. In general see Cohen, *A Calculating People*, ch. 4: "Republican Arithmetic," 116–49.

11. Among several hundred account books virtually all were based on converting goods and services into money equivalents.

12. Fernand Braudel, *Civilization and Capitalism, 15th–18th Century: The Wheels of Commerce*

(New York, 1982); and Immanuel Wallerstein, *The Modern World-System*, 2 vols. (New York, 1974 and 1980).

13. All advertisements appearing in Windsor District newspapers, 1783–1830, were studied.

14. See Douglas North, *The Economic Growth of the United States, 1790–1860* (New York, 1961), and Percy Bidwell, *Rural Economy in New England at the Beginning of the Nineteenth Century* (New Haven, 1916). The latter's own data (p. 367) shows this, though he draws the opposite conclusion. Also see n. 6 above.

15. This proportion is derived from all Walpole Bookstore "Accounts of Stock," 1796–1817, in Isaiah Thomas Papers, Box 9, AAS. For the specific figures, see "Account of Stock," 28 June 1808.

16. In this overview we emphasize newspapers, almanacs, periodicals, and the most popular books and pamphlets retained by our study group of 396 families with private libraries.

17. As Crowley puts it in *This Sheba Self: The Conceptualization of Economic Life in Eighteenth Century America*, (Baltimore, 1975), p. 15: "Mandeville sought to demonstrate that . . . public virtue as self-denial and justice toward others was at odds with a definition of the public good as prosperity." The only American edition of Mandeville (Boston, 1811) was a reprint of the original edition (a short poem) of the fable. See also Thomas A. Horne, *The Social Thought of Bernard Mandeville: Virtue and Commerce in Early Eighteenth Century England* (London, 1978); and McCoy, *Elusive Republic*, esp. 25–27, throughout this discussion. One of the 396 libraries (the largest) retained a copy of a British edition of Mandeville.

18. As Crowley notes, its practical target was consumption, and its ideal was abstinence. Crowley, ibid., 16–18.

19. Ibid., 18–20.

20. As Crowley puts it, this position "provided Americans with an empirical understanding of their economy and its health." Its popularity was great, partly because it "supplied terms for the assessment of economic life": ibid., 34–49 and 147–57.

21. The British commercial and financial revolution of the early eighteenth century was "unscrutable and dangerous" to the Bolingbroke circle. Selfishness leading to vice ruled public life: "they associated . . . selfishness with luxury, and considered luxury to be the natural outcome of trade." William Cobbett, one of the leading British radicals, in the words of Craig Calhoun, "indeed thought it a pleasant and quite possible prospect that commerce and manufactures could be greatly diminished, the clock turned back and the factory system averted." See Crowley, ibid., 24–26; Calhoun, *The Question of Class Struggle: Social Foundations of Popular Radicalism During the Industrial Revolution* (Chicago, 1982), 103; and Isaac Kramnick, *Bolingbroke and His Circle: The Politics of Nostalgia in the Age of Walpole* (Cambridge, Mass., 1968).

22. Another complication is that an author's statements were often used to buttress positions different from those espoused by that author. To understand local cultural dialogue we must combine the traditional intellectual history of Crowley, McCoy, and others with the newer history of "the book." See Robert Darnton, "What Is the History of the Book?" DAED III (1982):65–83.

23. This discussion is based on reading matter found in 396 Windsor District family libraries (c. 5,630 volumes). See table 2-1 for the most popular titles in family libraries.

24. McCoy, *Elusive Republic*, 241, quoting an 1813 essay by Dr. E. Bollman.

25. See E. J. Ferguson, "Political Economy, Public Liberty, and the Formation of the Constitution." WMQ 3s 40 (1983):389–412; and McCoy, *Elusive Republic*, 13–104. Specific contemporary positions present in Windsor District reading included Hamiltonian Federalist, Adamsonian Federalist, Madisonian Republican, Jeffersonian Republican, old Republican (e.g. John Taylor), Country Radical, Court Radical, and Agrarian. Many Windsor District residents adopted the

substance, if not the name, of one of these eight positions; others held less coherent, more syncretistic views.

26. On American factories as distinct from British ones, see Charles L. Sanford, "The Intellectual Origins and New-Worldliness of American Industry," *Journal of Economic History* 18 (1958):1–16. Philip Lampe has kindly shared with me his data and his unmatched knowledge of Windsor District political behavior and elections into the 1840s.

27. This was true of the major home and school instructional work, George Fisher's *The Instructor, or The Young Man's Best Companion*, and of the two basic arithmetic texts used in district schools, Adams' *Scholar's Arithmetic*, and Pike's *System*. All three of the most popular school readers, Lindley Murray's *The English Reader*, *The Hive*, and Caleb Bingham's *American Preceptor* contained several excerpts each from authors stressing the benefits of commerce. Also see Cohen, *A calculating People*, 116–49.

28. In science and agriculture, Leonard Lathrop's *Farmer's Library* was favorably disposed to commercial agriculture. Thomas Chalmers' various sermon and works were evaluations of life set in a thoroughly commercial England. Ten general works about law included Blackstone, *Commentaries on the Laws of England*; Nathaniel Chipman's *Reports and Dissertations*, compilations of the laws of Vermont; Zephaniah Swift's *Laws of Connecticut*; Isaac Espinassi's *Nisi Prius* [civil actions]; and half a dozen introductory works for nonlawyers. In addition, there were several more specialized works on commercial subjects.

29. The three included George Washington's *Farewell Address*; Matthew Carey's *The Olive Branch*; and the *American State Papers*, which contained considerable information about, and advocacy of, many aspects of commercial life. Other popular procommercial works included, Abraham Rees', *The New Cyclopaedia*; several works of history (Charles A. Goodrich's *A History of the United States*, Hannah Adams's *A Summary History of New England*, John Banks's *Peter the Great*, and Sir Robert Porter's *A Narrative of the Campaign in Russia*); and three works of philosophy (William Paley's *Principles of Moral and Political Philosophy*, [Dunham's] *Masonic Register*, and Benjamin Franklin's autobiography and his *Works*.

30. McCoy, *Elusive Republic*, 13–47, 170, and 236–37.

31. Excerpts appeared in the readers by John Hubbard, Murray, and Bingham, in *The Hive*, and in Webster's *Speller* (in snippets). Full editions of these writers were prominent in Windsor District libraries.

32. Sacred works included collections of sermons by John Wesley, Elias Smith, Samuel Niles, and Abraham Booth, and devotional works by Richard Baxter and John Flavel, Philip Doddridge's *Rise and Progress of Religion in the Soul*, and a popular collection hymns, *The Village Harmony*.

33. William D. Liddle, "Virtue and Liberty: An Inquiry into the Role of the Agrarian Myth in the Rhetoric of the American Revolutionary Era," *South Atlantic Quarterly*, 77 (1978):15–38, quotes on 16–17, 19, 21, and 27.

34. Kerber, *Federalists*, 1–22, and McCoy, *Elusive Republic*, 13–75. Crucial to this fixed image was a profoundly anticity bias. London, the center of international trade, was perceived as an exciting but inherently dangerous, vice-ridden city.

35. See, amid a growing subfield, Henretta, "Farms and Families: *Mentalités* in Pre-Industrial America," *WMQ* 3s 35 (1978):3–32; Christopher Clark, "Household Economy, Market Exchange, and the Rise of Capitalism in the Connecticut River Valley, 1800–1860," *Journal of Social History*, 13 (1979):168–89; Michael Merrill, "Cash Is Good to Eat: Self-Sufficiency and Exchange in the Rural Economy of the United States," *Radical History Review* 4 (1977): 42–71; Winifred B. Rothenberg, "The Market and Massachusetts Farmers, 1750–1855," *Journal of Economic History* 61 (1981): 281–314; Robert E. Mutch, "Yeoman and Merchant in Pre-Industrial America: Eighteenth Cen-

tury Massachusetts as a Test Case," *Societas* 7 (1977):279–302 and Bettye Hobbs Pruitt, "Self-Sufficiency and the Agricultural Economy of Eighteenth-Century Massachusetts," WMQ 3S 41 (July, 1984): 334–64. Students and research assistants have helped me to refine a method of mining the rural weekly newspaper to analyze every conceivable piece of information about economic life, broadly conceived, printed in Windsor District newspapers in 1783–1830. I added to this file every additional business from all surrounding weeklies, to be sure no businesses were missed. These materials have been supplemented by extensive work in three other sources: (1) Windsor District Account Books, 1755–1851; see partial list in Gilmore, "Elementary Literacy," table 4, p. 118; (2) Windsor District inventories, 1787–1840 (1831–40 initially canvassed by Ray Morgenweck for a history research paper); and (3) local journals, diaries, letters, and family papers of Windsor District residents.

36. The best study of migration into or out of Vermont remains Stilwell, *Migration From Vermont*. Average household size ranged from 5.3 at Plymouth to 6.4 at Windsor. Throughout this discussion, Smith, "Legacy of Dissent," has been extremely useful for the years through 1784. One community, tiny Baltimore, remained a hilly agricultural settlement.

37. Rich farmland areas of Reading, Cavendish, and Weathersfield were first settled by full families and maintained the greatest proportion of females (96.8–98.4 females per 100 males). Windsor, Chester, and Springfield, combining farming with village commerce, had a lower share of females (93.6–95.4 per 100 males). Mountainous townships, last settled and least stable (Andover, Ludlow, and Plymouth Kingdom), averaged just 88.2 females per 100 males. Calculated from the First U.S. Census, *Heads of Household* (Washington, 1909), 10. See also Rutman, "People in Process," 276ff.

38. Once townships passed projects they petitioned the state legislature to approve local taxes used to make improvements.

39. This discussion is drawn principally from Bidwell, *Rural Economy*; Howard S. Russell, *A Long Deep Furrow: Three Centuries of New England Agriculture* (Hanover, N. H., 1976), 151ff., 276ff., and 325ff.; extensive farm diary reading in VHS, NHHS, and the historical research division of Old Sturbridge Village; and careful inspection of New England genre painting of the 1790–1840 years.

40. Russell, *A Long Deep Furrow*, 25ff., (quote) and 120ff.

41. These connections have been culled from an analysis of all 643 Windsor District household inventories, 1787–1830. In many cases, partners and others with shares in a business are listed, usually with any relationship to the deceased. Further crosschecking that could be accomplished (via wife's maiden name) was included. To take just one group, lawyers, see, for instance, the inventories of Luther Mills, Windsor, 1830, WDPR, vol. 12:132ff.; John Hunt, Windsor, 1796, 2:232ff.; Lucius Hubbard, Chester, 1809, 5:217ff. and 305ff.; Ebenezer Fiske, Chester, 1816, 7:36ff., 244ff., and 526ff.; and Stephen Jacob, Windsor, 1817, 7:345ff. and 512ff. Lawyers' economic base was consistently the most diverse, usually including 5–10 properties beyond the farmstead or village mansion house; shares in turnpike companies, manufactories, and banks; and tenant rentals of additional property. Less extensive nonfamily business involvements may be seen in the deeds and inventories of merchants, manufacturers, and an occasional doctor or gentleman farmer.

42. [Rutland] *Farmer's Library*, 2 Sept. 1793. As a result, "Vermont will rear," he or she thought, "beautiful, athletic, hardy, wise, and endearing young men, whose northern constitutions will beget enterprising plans. . . . "

43. All societies recognize, as Florence Kluckholm notes, "that individuals are biologically and culturally related to each other through time. There is . . . always a lineal principle in relationships." There are also two other fundamental dimensions, collateral and individualistic. Collaterality recognizes that "the individual is not a human being except as . . . part of a social order,

and one type of inevitable social grouping is that which results from laterally extended relationships." Every society, then, balances these three "relational orientations:" lineal, collateral, and individual. Henretta's perspective in "Farms and Families" (esp. 31–32) fails to weigh the kinship structure within the lineal orientation, and underestimates the import of broader social networks, especially the community, within the collateral orientation. Our data on economic life in the Upper Valley both reinforce and modify recent scholarship, including Henretta, Clark, Merrill, Mutch, Pruitt, and Rothenberg. See Kluckholm, "Variations in the Basic Values of Family Systems," in *A Modern Introduction to the Family*, ed. Norman W. Bell and Ezra Vogel (Glencoe, Ill., 1962), 304–15.

44. The Windsor economic locale consisted of the northernmost half of the district and the riverbed settlements south of Windsor village which bartered or exchanged goods and services there. The Chester economic locale consisted of the southernmost half of Windsor District, excepting the riverbed settlements.

45. The number and range of estate debts and notes has been calculated from the occupational breakdown discussed in ch. 7, specifically the yeoman and husbandman occupations. The inventories are in the WDPR, vols. 1–12 (1787–1830). For advertisements threatening suits (with interest charges), see VJ, Jan. 1790 (1st week), Benjamin Greene's store; VJ, July 1790 (3rd week), Greene and Leonard; and VJ, 3 July 1815.

46. See, for instance, Samuel Cobb, Springfield, 1806, WDPR 5:224ff., one-third share in a forge on the falls of the Black River; William Leverett, Windsor, 1817, 7:504ff., share in two turnpike companies; and Abel Amsden, Reading, 1828, 11:370, half of a carding machine, and half share in a 70-acre tract. In a sample of 50 households from all occupations and wealth levels, 1795–1805, at least one economic relationship of nonfamily shared ownership was identified in a third (16) of the cases. Sharing and its proportion of total estate value both increased with wealth.

47. Geib, "Changing Works."

48. A complete inventory of all businesses advertised in Windsor District, 1783–1830, was compiled. Local histories yielded a few additional dispensers of goods and services.

49. Compiled from all 1790 issures of VJ. The four stores and two artisan shops in a handful of villages considerably north of Windsor (Lebanon, N.H., etc.) were not advertising primarily to attract Windsor District customers, but because the *Journal*, as the northernmost newspaper in the Upper Valley in 1790, circulated throughout their townships.

50. The first advertisements appear in 1788. For the quotes, see VJ, 30 Nov. 1790; the advertisement takes up three-fourths of a column. In describing his Chester village location, Porter placed it firmly in its market context, "on the great road from Walpole to Rutland and Canada." Most business notices in the *Journal* were dated and often numbered, aiding the compositor and us. Porter placed just one advertisement in 1790, but it had a second run of six weeks.

51. VJ, 10 Feb. 1790. See McCorison, *Vermont Imprints*, 35–45. That more printed items were available is certain; Spooner's printing office published at least 3 other items in 1788, 6 in 1789, and 1 in 1790.

52. There were a few advertisements for the following: doctors (6), lawyers (1), hotels (1), taverns (1), gristmills (2), the brewery (1), and other factories (3). Notices for apprentices appeared regularly and four notices seeking the return of runaways. On manufactures, see VJ, 6 July, 28 Sept., and 28 Dec. 1790 issues. On workers, see VJ, 31 Mar. 1790.

53. See Merrill, "Cash is Good to Eat," 42–71, esp. 52–53; and Christopher Clark, "Household Economy," 168–89, esp. 175. Money or cash is crucial to commodity relations, in Merrill's view: "It follows that where money does not play the role Marx assigned to it in the circulation of commodities, the products we are dealing with are not commodities at all."

54. See Merrill and Michael Wallace, "Marxism and History," in *The Left Academy: Marxist Scholarship on American Campuses*, ed. Bertell Ollman and Edward Vernoff (N. Y., 1982), 202–41.

55. VJ, 7 Apr. 1790, and 16 and 30 Nov. 1790; after produce Chandler noted "and etc." In Windsor District, Porter's store was atypical in omitting cash as an acceptable form of payment. A third general store, Bissel & Mann of Orford, N. H., acknowledged that its commerce was not determined by the existence of cash: it had a "quantity of English and Westindia Goods, which they will exchange cheap for wheat, rye, corn, oats, foxskins, peas, beans, red and white cloverseed, flax, pot and pearlash, and CASH will not be refused."

56. Notices were scattered throughout VJ, 1790 issues.

57. See n. 55 above.

58. Perry, *Royal Standard*; John Walker, *A Critical Pronouncing Dictionary* (London, 1822 ed.); Noah Webster, *A Compendious Dictionary* (New Haven, 1806); and his *American Dictionary*, vol. I: "Currency." Webster's 1806 American dictionary defines cash as "any money, but properly ready money." Currency and money included all varieties of paper money; all notes, including U.S. Treasury notes, notes between businesses, and some notes between individuals; and metal coinage.

59. Perry, *Royal Standard*; Webster, *A Compendious Dictionary*.

60. Changing social and economic dynamics of class are more useful than static calculations of occupation and wealth. See, most recently, Sean Wilentz, "On Class and Politics in Jacksonian America," RAH 10 (1982):45–63, esp. 52.

61. E.P. Thompson, "Eighteenth Century English Society: Class Struggle Without Class?" *Social History* 3 (1978):133–50, esp. 149–50.

62. See Gilmore, "Elementary Literacy."

63. In this respect, Windsor District and the area surrounding Keene, N. H. (where the only other 1790 Upper Valley weekly was published) were somewhat atypical and more developed than other areas in northwestern New England.

64. Donald A. Smith, "Legacy of Dissent," is the most up-to-date account of Vermont history, 1749–84.

65. *Second Census of the United States: Heads of Household–Vermont* (Washington, 1979), 10 and 156–81. Gender ratios equalized to 99.6 females per 100 males in the mountain communities as forests were cleared, land was cultivated, and more young two-parent families took their chances in New Connecticut. In 1800, three-quarters of Plymouth families included a male and a female aged 26–44.

66. Within a year (3 March 1801), still another newspaper would be established at Windsor, the *Federal Gazette*. It survived for four years and then changed its name to the *Windsor Post-Boy*, lasting until 31 March 1807. See Clarence S. Brigham, *The History and Bibliography of American Newspapers, 1690-1820*,2 vols. (1947; rpt. ed., Hamden, Conn., 1962) 2:1097–1103.

67. VJ, 7, 14, and 21 Jan., 25 Feb., 22 Apr., and 2 Dec. 1800. Other townships in Windsor and Orange counties were probably covered by additional riders. The same pattern is found in letters remaining to be picked up at the Windsor post office. See, for instance, VJ, 14 Jan. 1800.

68. Windsor (14), Woodstock (6), Hartland (4), and Cornish (1) in 1800, versus Windsor (7), Chester (2), and Claremont (1) in 1790. No Chester stores or shops advertised in the VJ during 1800, but advertisements for 1799 and 1801 identify at least two general stores. Windsor township's stores and shops rose at a rate twice its 40% population increase. Within Windsor economic locale, too, the growth rate for comercial activity (100%) exceeded a dramatic population increase (80%). In Windsor District as a whole, 27 shops and stores actively vying for local business in 1800 (versus just10 in 1790) represented a 160% rise, greater than the population increase of 86%.

69. The source is VJ advertisements for 1800. Five-sixths of all firms were located in Windsor and eastern Orange County.

70. This is the case even if just half of those households first subscribing to a newspaper

in the 1790s began to participate in commerce. As earlier, this estimate derives from analysis-of estate inventories and a survey of Windsor District account books.

71. For instance, see VJ, 24 June (Fitch); 13 Oct. (Green and Choate); 17 Nov. (Blodget); and 15 Dec. (J. Leverett) 1800. Within the rural transaction system, the usual general store advertisement now announced a fresh shipment of goods, "all of which they will sell very low for Cash, Wheat, Butter or short and approved Credit."

72. See VJ, 7 Jan., 4 Feb., 24 June, 22 Sept., 8 and 22 Dec., 1800. Firms in other product areas manufactured joiner's tools, shingles, boots and shoes, cabinets, chairs, and stone lime. Production outside of the household was expanding rapidly and included nails, liquors, a wide variety of cloth, glass and crockery, shoes, hats, paper and stationery, blank books and forms, books, pamphlets, broadsides, newspapers, and almanacs.

73. While the spread of commerce lowered Windsor township's share of all business slightly, from 33% to 28%, the actual number of firms grew from 14 to 31. Among Upper Valley businesses seeking local customers in 1810, those residing outside Windsor county fell, from a quarter in 1800 to an eighth, the direct result of additional localized newspaper circulation elsewhere.

74. Compiled from all issues of Windsor and Chester newspapers for 1810. For the Chester economic locale, surviving Chester newspaper issues, 1807–1809, were analyzed.

75. See Roth, "Whence This Strange Fire?"; his *Democratic Dilemma*; and David Ludlum, *Social Ferment in Vermont, 1790–1850* (New York, 1939).

76. See n. 74 above. No local businesses beyond small general stores and artisan shops are known to have existed in Plymouth, Weston, or Baltimore. In general, I assume that a more local level of artisan services existed throughout Windsor District.

77. All 1810 general stores not in existence in 1800 were traced back to the first notice of their existence.

78. See table 4 in Gilmore, "Elementary Literacy," 118–19. Records mainly survive from stable enterprises. Many products later to become the basis for specialty stores first appeared in general store advertisements and purchases.

79. Wills, inventories, and local histories are the sources used. No Windsor District lawyers or doctors advertised in 1810. On the medical society, see Wash, 20 Aug. and 24 Sept. 1810.

80. See n. 74 above. All but two artisan shops were located in Windsor District or in contiguous townships.

81. Ibid. Four more clothiers beyond Windsor District advertised regularly in local newspapers.

82. For examples, see VJ, 18 June 1800 (Dana); and Wash, 10 Dec. 1810 (Hickok and Munson).

83. VJ, 1 Oct. (Allen, Williams, and Hall) and 23 Apr. (J. and S. Cutting) 1810; Wash., 26 Nov. (S. Edson and Co.) and 5 Nov. (Parker and M'Farland) 1810; and VJ, 3 and 17 July (3 ads) and 4 and 18 Dec. 1815.

84. See VJ, 18 June (Dana; and Allen, Williams, and Hall) and 16 July (Justin and Elias Lyman) 1810; and Wash, 5 Nov. (Parker and M'Farland), 19 Nov. (Lyman, Mower, and Co.), and 24 Dec. (William and Luther Dyer) 1810. Vermont paper money included "Vermont bills" or "Vermont Bankpaper," usually at par, meaning "sold at their nominal amount for coin or its equivalent": VJ, 23 Apr. 1810 (J. and J. Fessenden). By 1810 cash was also being used more broadly, to include all payment made on the spot versus by credit. See Webster, *American Dictionary*, I, "Cash: It is properly silver or gold; but since the institution of banks, it denotes also bank notes equivalent to money."

85. By 1810 the favorite term for payment not by credit but at purchase time was "cash," with its expanded meaning of paper or coinage; "ready money" and "ready pay" were also fairly popular. Both meant to pay on the spot, either in coinage or paper money. See Webster, *American Dictionary*, "Money"; and Perry, *Royal Standard*, "Cash". Also see Wash, 1 Oct. (J. and S.

Cutting) and 24 Dec. (William and Luther Dyer) 1810; and VJ, 1 Oct. 1810 (Allen, Williams, and Hall). A final payment twist involved delinquent accounts: if payment were not made by a certain date, then the account would be turned over to an attorney "for immediate collection, when current money will be expected."

86. As earlier, this estimate derives from analysis of estate inventories and a survey of Windsor District account books.

87. For examples, see Wash, 30 July, 6 and 27 Aug., 10 and 24 Sept., 1, 8, 15, 22, and 29 Oct., 12 and 26 Nov., and 3, 10, and 31 Dec. 1810. See also VJ, 29 Jan., 19 Feb., and 1 Oct. 1810; and VtR 26 Feb. and 5 and 19 Mar. 1810. Topics commented on extensively include: the Embargo and commercial policy; the Vermont State Bank (with a branch just south of Windsor District at Westminster in 1810, and soon a branch at Windsor); currency matters; selling buildings and farms; vendues; the apprenticeship system; manufacturing at the Vermont State Prison; inventions; road, bridge, and turnpike companies; prospects for local canals; newspaper circulation; postrider routes; and post office letters remaining.

88. See VJ, 18 June for the Gallatin Report; "The Debtor," 28 Jan. 1800; and 17 and 24 Sept., 1 Oct., and 12 Nov. 1800. See also Wash, 10 and 24 Sept., 1 and 8 Oct., 12 Nov., and 3 and 31 Dec. 1810. Also see VJ, "Communication," 21 Jan. 1800. A rich Mason and brigadier general of the militia, Chase was honored by a large, carefully organized procession. Among qualities "worthy" of emulation was "a spirit of toleration and forbearance to those indebted to him, which, if imitated by the traders of the present day, would greatly conduce to the happiness and prosperity of the country."

89. For examples, see Wash, 8 and 22 Oct., 26 Nov., and 3 and 10 Dec. 1810; and VJ, 15, 22, and 29 Jan., 26 Mar., 29 Apr., 11 June, 30 July, 13 Aug., and 12 Nov. 1810.

90. VJ, 11 Feb., 4 Mar., 15 and 22 July, 9 and 22 Sept., and 3 Nov. 1800. For instance, the 22 Sept. piece, "The Triple Pleas" by S.D., perhaps Salmon Dutton (see ch. 9), related a dispute among the three over which was the superior. When judgment was turned over to sober, honest, wise men," then "away must trudge" all three: "if men fools and knaves will be, they'll be ass-ridden by all three."

91. In an enormous literature, see Brian L. Foster, "Development, Modernization and Comparative Parochialism: A Review Article," CSSH 20 (1978): 319–28; George Modelski, "The Long Cycle of Global Politics and the Nation-State," ibid., 214–35; and Cyril E. Black, ed., *Comparative Modernization: A Reader* (New York, 1976).

92. For a generation before discussion of scientific agriculture emerged, newspaper readers received the false impression that farming was declining in importance in Windsor District.

93. Rates of growth were 4%, 2%, and −2%, respectively. See Roth, "Whence This Strange Fire?", ch. 6, 388–462.

94. E.g., VtC, 25 Dec. 1830; and William Wilgus, *The Role of Transportation in the Development of Vermont* (Montpelier, Vt., 1945).

95. VtR&J, 22 May 1830; and VtC, 12 Feb. 1830.

96. These were four of the largest twelve townships in Vermont by 1810.

97. The localization of newspapers accounts for the only anomaly in the data, an apparent decline in general stores. In Windsor District beyond Windsor and Chester townships, where the number of general stores declined to 9 (from 12 a decade earlier), general stores rose from 7 to 17 between 1810 and 1830.

98. Fully 70% of all Upper Valley firms selling actively in Windsor District now were located either in the district or contiguous to one of its townships.

99. We searched all extant 1828 and 1829 issues of Chester newspapers, all issues of both Windsor newspapers for 1830, and all local histories. In 1830 wholesaling firms in ten cities and large villages outside Vermont and the New Hampshire Valley counties—Baltimore, Philadel-

phia, New York, Albany, and several eastern Massachusetts cities—sought customers through regular advertising at Windsor and Chester, versus three in 1810.

100. The estimate derives from extant estate inventories and Windsor District account books. Windsor District's river valley villages, and also Chester, were now fully commercialized. With 29 firms, Springfield replaced Chester as second in commerce to Windsor. Weathersfield's fragmented village added another 19 businesses. All 15 Windsor District specialty stores, all 4 print centers, 17 of 20 taverns, 28 of 35 manufactories, and 34 of 40 artisan shops in 1830 were located in the four village townships.

101. Roth, "Whence This Strange Fire?" offers a superb analysis of what he terms "a new order of life" developing in townships with sizable villages. Windsor and Weathersfield are among the communities he studied in detail for 1790–1843. Chs. 2 through 6 provide foundations in economic life and in basic modes of communications, for Roth's detailed analysis of the workings of a rural commercial society and polity.

102. See Roth, "Whence This Strange Fire?", 107–544; and *Democratic Dilemma*, 80–310.

103. This typology was drawn from a complete inventory of all forms of printed matter available to read in Windsor District, 1780–1830, plus analysis of the contents of all issues of rural newspapers circulating in Windsor District, 1783–85, 1790, 1800, 1810, 1815, and 1 Jan. 1820 through 31 Dec. 1830.

104. See Wilentz, "On Class and Politics," 45–63, for a recent overview.

105. See VJ, 1817–29. Religious controversy, central to rural New England life, pitted a few rich, some middling sorts, and many poor Freewill Baptists, Christians, Universalists, and Methodists against rich, middling, and poor Congregationalists, Presbyterians, and others. Religion mitigated wealth distinctions while it intensified differences over benevolent reform and social action. Benevolent moral reform societies and the resurgent freethought movement warred openly—even violently—after 1815, just when the encroachment of rural industrialization might have led to strong class-based agitation. See, e.g., *The Christian Repository*, ed. Samuel C. Loveland (Woodstock, Vt., 1820–29). On violence, see Anne Royall, *The Black Book*, 2 vols. (Washington, 1828).

106. Chs. 6–9 discuss ways in which other forms of reading also cemented a shared culture.

107. See Robert Wiebe, *The Segmented Society* (New York, 1975), and *The Opening of American Society: From the Adoption of the Constitution to the Eve of Disunion* (New York, 1984). Ironically, organizational activity before c. 1810 was mostly limited to the wealthiest members of society; thereafter, activity encouraging class-based action included societies of workingmen in Windsor, Chester, Springfield, and Woodstock, just to the north of Reading.

108. For example, each newspaper frequently urged paying bills on time, reinforcing proper credit and payment behavior; see, e.g., VJ, 16 Aug. 1803. Other pieces discussed punctuality as essential to business, but until the 1820s it remained more an ideal than a general practice; see, e.g., VJ, 10 Mar. 1806.

109. VJ, 13 Feb. and 20 Mar. 1815.

110. Dwight, quoted in *Gospel Herald* 6 (21 May 1825), n.p. Children should be brought up to "useful industry" by "habituation." As an 1815 almanac pronounced, whoever's "mind is engaged by the acquisition or improvement of fortune . . . escapes the insipidity of indifference and the tediousness of inactivity"; quoted in an unidentified New England almanac bound in *Vt. Almanacs*, vol. 1 (1814–21), VHS.

111. Some lotteries justified themselves by a purpose beyond profit, e.g. a Groton, Conn., lottery to build a town monument and one to benefit the First Ecclesiastical Society of Canaan; VtR&J, 16 Jan., 17 and 24 Apr., and 1 May 1830.

112. Two sets of local and regional meetings were held in 1830; two organizations were formed to lobby for these proposals, each with a report: VtC, 8 Jan. 1830; VtR&J, 9, 16, and

23 Jan., 6, 13, 20, and 27 Feb., 6 and 13 Mar., 3 and 10 Apr., 1 and 15 May, 5 June, 3 and 31 July, 14 Aug., 18 Sept., 20 Nov., and 4 Dec. 1830.

113. See, e.g., VtC., 1 and 29 Jan., and 12 and 19 Feb. 1830; and VR&J, 23 and 30 Jan., 13 and 27 Feb., 24 April, 10 and 17 July, 25 Sept., 2 Oct., 27 Nov., and 25 Dec. 1830. The workings of nature were of wide interest: "The Barometer," "The Age of Improvement" (on inventions), the "Aurora Borealis," the "Aeronaut's Address," the "Velocity of Light," and "India Rubber Balloon."

114. On temperance see VtR&J, 9, 16, and 30 Jan., 13 Feb., 13 and 27 Mar., 19 June, and 18 Sept. 1830. On timeliness, see "Take Care of Your Time," VtC, 15 Jan. 1830. The "science of nature" was especially prized in this new earth-bound calculus.

115. By the mid-1820s the proper role of "mechanicks" and "the laboring classes" in society was being debated hotly in Windsor District. Initially vague, rural definitions of mechanics gradually identified them as wage-earning workers in factories and large artisan shops, as opposed to yeoman and tenant farmers. Sometimes self-employed artisans and other small-scale businesspeople were included in this group: see "Mechanicks," VtR&J, 4 Sept. 1830; 16 Sept. 1830 and "Politicks for Farmers," 9 Oct. 1830. In the late 1820s a Windsor District resident could denigrate the laboring classes, praise mechanics, and remain consistent, with contemporary usage. The "laboring classes" usually included farmers and semiskilled laborers, plus the groups mentioned above. See Webster, *American Dictionary*, II: "laboring," "mechanic," and "mechanical"; and the excellent discussions in Alan Dawley, *Class and Community: The Industrial Revolution in Lynn* (Cambridge, Mass., 1976); Paul Faler, *Mechanics and Manufacturers in the Early Industrial Revolution: Lynn, Massachusetts, 1780–1860* (Albany, N. Y., 1981); Prude, *Coming of Industrial Order*; and Bruce Laurie, *The Working People of Philadelphia, 1800–1850* (Philadelphia, 1980).

116. See VtR&J, 13 Feb., 6 Mar., 3 July, 7 Aug., 4 and 16 Sept., 9 Oct., and 27 Nov. 1830.

117. See VtR&J, 20 Feb. (two pieces), 24 July, 7 Aug., 4 Sept., and 11 Nov. 1830. Also see Carl Siracusa, *A Mechanical People: Perceptions of the Industrial Order in Massachusetts, 1815–1860* (Middletown, Conn., 1979), chs. 4 and 5.

118. Discussions of mechanics and the laboring classes originally took place in two contexts: in the columns of Windsor newspapers where local businessmen, manufacturers, and other public figures commented freely on these newly conspicuous groups; and in more informal settings where mechanics and members of the laboring classes themselves discussed conditions in their daily lives. In Sept. 1830, Nahum Haskell sought to rectify the absence in the mainstream press of essays or letters by mechanics with the Woodstock *Working-Man's Gazette*, a weekly journal "devoted to the interests of the laboring classes." It served as the first sustained public forum expressing the beliefs of these groups in Windsor County. See the "Prospectus" in the first issue, 23 Sept. 1830. The co-editor was William Prescott of Chester (whose newspaper there had just failed).

119. See *The Genesee Republican*: "The Necessity of Reform, No. 2," 18 Aug. 1830; "The Producing Classes," 6 Oct. 1830; "The Workingmen," 20 Oct. 1830; and "The Spirit of Reform, No. 5," 8 Dec. 1830; and *The Cayuga Patriot*, 14 July, and 11 and 25 Aug. 1830. These views were discussed in the Woodstock *Working-Man's Gazette*, Sept. 23, Oct. 14 and 28, and 8 Dec. 1830.

120. *Genesee Republican*, 18 Aug. 1830 and 8 Dec. 1830. Brownson's basic distinctions were between the "poor" and the "rich," the "unproductive" and "productive" classes. These groupings of social classes were widespread among Upper Valley advocates of the laboring classes by the late 1820s. Brownson proposed abolition of imprisonment for debts, and unspecified changes in laws governing financial obligations; abolition of monopolies generally; altering the militia to promote greater equality; avoiding "all despotisms of the law"; and guarding against any union between church and state.

121. *Genesee Republican*, 6 Oct. 1830 and 8 Dec. 1830. Brownson stressed equal education for

all children and youth, and the encouragement by families and schools of regular reading and inquiry about American politics and economics. In 1830 Brownson believed firmly in the power of public opinion to effect change. The structure of commercial society was the root cause of inequality; in Brownson's view, luxury created poverty, exactly the reverse of Mandeville's position. Brownson wondered whether humankind had really "gained much by establishing republics" in place of monarchies. This was a radical view. In his ideal community, only "superior knowledge and superior virtue" were distinctions conveying legitimate power.

122. See Gilmore, "Elementary Literacy," 78–187, for evidence that literacy was growing among these groups in 1780–1830. Sources do not tell us the extent to which they followed the emerging critique discussed above.

123. Through his editorials and coverage of rural New England economic woes, Simeon Ide's Windsor *Republican and Journal* provided the precise evidence critics of the new rural economic order needed to increase support for their perspective.

124. See Edward Pessen's overview in "Wealth in America Before 1865," in W.D. Rubinstein, ed., *Wealth and the Wealthy in the Modern World* (New York, 1980), 167–88, esp. 177 and 185.

125. A symbiotic relationship existed between the explosion of newspapers and periodicals, and the rapid expansion of voluntary organizations concerned with public life. The number of newspapers and periodicals surviving for more than two years each, and hence reasonably stable, increased dramatically between 1780 and 1830: for newspapers see table 6–1; periodicals lasting more than two years rose from 7 in the 1780s, to 40 in the years 1800–9, and to 118 in the 1820s.

By 1810, most villages settled for two decades or more and not surrounded by longstanding print centers maintained rural weeklies. The data is from tables 9 and 10 in Gilmore, "The Process of Thought and the Circulation of Print: Event and Awareness in American Consciousness: Rural New England as a Case Study, 1780–1840" (Paper delivered at the Annual Meeting of the Organization of American Historians, 1980).

126. Marx's own understanding of the capitalist mode of production was first formulated in the 1840s, at a mature stage of a divergent mode of production in a differently constituted social order. While extremely valuable, Marxist approaches are of limited use in understanding the mix of material and cultural conditions of life in rural New England during the early national decades.

127. See McCoy, *Elusive Republic.*

128. See Clark, "Household Economy"; Henretta, "Farms and Families"; and Merrill, "Cash is Good to Eat."

129. The closest estimate of the share of Windsor District families participating in market exchange, based on all Windsor District inventories and selected account books through 1830 may be seen in table N–1.

130. On fashion, see Nicholas Hayes Ward, "Pianos, Parasols, and Poppa: The Migration of Vermont Farm Girls to the Massachusetts Mill Towns" (M.A. Thesis, Brown Univ., 1974).

131. Howard Russell, *A Long Deep Furrow*, esp. ch. 30, "Tools and Tillage," 308ff. By 1800 many other products were advertised regularly in Windsor District (e.g., shoes and hats from Boston). See VJ, 1790–1829.

132. There is discussion of versatility with much confirmation from contemporary observers in Howard Russell, *A Long Deep Furrow*, esp. 25ff. and 200ff. Also see Henretta, "Families and Farms," esp. 19. The extent to which declining diversity in work performed on a rural farmstead accompanied the growth of specialization is in need of detailed research.

133. On this broad theme, see Marvin Meyers, *The Jacksonian Persuasion: Politics and Belief* (rev. ed., Stanford, Calif., 1960).

134. See Henretta, *Evolution*, 187–226.

135. See the full discussion in Anthony F.C. Wallace, *Rockdale: The growth of an American*

Table N-1: Share of Windsor District Families Participating in Market Exchange

	Four Village Townships	Seven Agricultural Townships	Entire District
1790			
Percent of Population Living Here	73	27	100
Percent of Residents Participating in Market Exchange	40	30	38
1800			
Percent of Population Living Here	66	34	100
Percent of Residents participating in Market Exchange	55	42	50
1810			
Percent of Population Living Here	61	39	100
Percent of Residents Participating in Market Exchange	75	55	67
1830			
Percent of Population Living Here	58	42	100
Percent of Residents Participating in Market Exchange	82	65	75

village in the early Industrial Revolution (New York, 1978); and Sean Wilentz, *Chants Democratic: New York City and the Rise of the American Working Class* (New York, 1983).

Chapter 3

1. By "print culture" I mean all of the knowledge Upper Valley residents learned about the world, distant and local, through printed and written matter. Print culture is a shorthand term for printed and written forms of cultural expression embodying the heritage of "written communications within the Commonwealth of Learning." See Eisenstein, *Printing Press*, xiv.

2. Considerably less then 3% of all Upper Valley residents ever published a piece. Active participation in cultural life through writing letters and keeping accounts and journals was much more widespread. Most residents were assimilators rather than direct creators of public opinion.

3. See Gilmore, "Elementary Literacy." The initial problem then is to see what forms of oral, visual, and written/printed cultural expression may be recovered, and to determine what elements of Upper Valley society are represented by each fund of evidence. In the following discussion we shall leave aside dance, and singing and music only because the evidence we have collected is fragmentary.

4. See Natalie Zemon Davis, "Anthropology and History in the 1980s: The Possibilities of the Past," JIH 12 (1981):267-75. As the eighteenth century waned, oral culture in New England began a slow decline, but only relative to other forms of expression, especially print and written communications. The dominant oral mode began to shift to one emphasizing printed matter. This process reflected the increasing need to disseminate information to a greater proportion of strangers over an ever larger area.

5. Cremin, *American Education: The National Experience* (New York, 1980), ix.

6. To understand the breadth of cultural life we must push well beyond print culture.

While it is immensely more difficult to investigate the several other dimensions of culture beyond print expression, only a comprehensive view will enable us, eventually, to weigh accurately the impact of printed matter.

7. See Gilmore, "Elementary Literacy," 87–178; and Johansson, *History of Literacy*, 151–82, esp. 161–64. Far more work on the Swedish book trade and the history of knowledge is needed to follow the incursion of secular dimensions of thought into print communications.

8. See Brown, "Emergence of Urban Society."

9. See Raymond Williams, ed., *Contact: Human Communications and Its History* (London, 1981), 127–50.

10. See especially Cott, *Bonds of Womanhood*; Norton, *Liberty's Daughters*; and Kerber, *Women of the Republic*.

11. *Analectic Magazine* 9 (Apr. 1817):285–300, quote on 286–87.

12. The following section presents an overview expanding on an earlier study of elementary literacy and schooling in the Upper Valley, 1760–1830, Gilmore, "Elementary Literacy."

13. Ibid., 95ff. In working up the concept there I did not recall that Linda Auwers had used this research strategy in the study of literacy in America in her report, *The Social Meaning of Female Literacy: Windsor, Connecticut, 1660–1775* (Newberry Papers in Family and Community History, no. 77-4A [Chicago, 1977]). Having since reread her work, I gladly acknowledge its influence.

14. Gilmore, "Elementary Literacy," esp. 114–55. Also see Auwers, "Reading the Marks of the Past: Exploring Female Literacy in Colonial Windsor Connecticut," *Historical Methods* 13 (1980):204–14, esp. 206, and 212 on "multiple data bases."

15. See Gilmore, "Elementary Literacy," graph 5B, 6B, and 7A (Plymouth Kingdom, 1812–16, and Weston, 1822–26). Skepticism regarding the self-reports in the 1840 federal census is warranted, given the intensity of the push for mass literacy by then. See Soltow and Stevens, *Rise of Literacy*, chs. 2–4.

16. See Soltow and Stevens, *Rise of Literacy*, and Johansson, *History of Literacy*. Far lower literacy rates for males (50%) and females (40%) in the bottom fifth of the population assumes that approximately 40 inventories below $165 represent only half the actual share of Windsor District's poorest families. This is probably a conservative assumption. It may well be that the ceiling for the bottom fifth of families by wealth should be raised. At about 3% inflation, 1790–1830, the ceiling would be raised to $289 by 1810 and $522 by 1830. A fifth of all inventories, 1787–1830, contained wealth of levels between $17 and $335. Account book customers excluded those too poor to be able to establish credit accounts with any shops and stores. Deed makers excluded those without land, and this share varied between 15% and 35%. Petitioners in a township may have included some of the poorest and the landless, but it is best not to make too much of this source. Will makers, finally, included only 2.4% of those owning less than $166 in total wealth. Thus, even multiple-moment research leaves gaps in our knowledge about acquisition levels for the lowest fifth of the population by wealth. Fragmentary results suggest that the lowest wealth levels were accompanied by lower rates of literacy (see the findings of Ross W. Beales, Jr., "Studying Literacy at the Community Level: A Research Note," JIH 9 (1978):93–102, and Auwers). It is possible that when literacy reached a threshold of approximately 70% for females as well as males, in an active reading environment with strong kinship ties, and a campaign for mass literacy, literacy rates rose rapidly among the lingering minority of "illiterates." Perhaps, therefore, lack of wealth did not inhibit the acquisition of literacy but rather restricted its maintenance and particularly the formation of family libraries.

17. Literacy's proper context is cultural participation generally. Literacy precedes the history of knowledge in printed and written forms. The social and cultural context of the history

of knowledge and of reading—in all its situations, experiences, and meanings—included how literacy skills were acquired, what was learned in the process, reasons for the achievement of literacy levels, and the ways reading and writing skills were used in daily life.

18. There were 15 verified American editions of Fisher in 1748–1800. The book's table of contents is an excellent outline of the forms of literacy and knowledge that were valued in the world of work.

19. The basic outlines of Cremin, *American Education*, vols. 1 and 2 are applicable. On the Upper Valley, see Clyde Fussell, "The Emergence of Public Education as a Function of the State of Vermont," VtH 28 (1960):179–96; Charles Kinney, *Church and State: The Struggle for Separation in New Hampshire, 1630–1900* (New York, 1955), esp. 152ff.; and the Walpole and other "Accounts of Stock," 1796–1823, Isaiah Thomas Papers, AAS. The numbers of primers and spellers circulating in America in 1783–1810 is almost beyond belief: 160 editions of the *New England Primer* in editions of 2,000–4,000 copies; 124 editions of Webster's and 45 similar editions of Dilworth's speller; and another 100 editions of other spellers and primers averaging perhaps 500 copies each. This amounts to 1,137,000 copies in circulation, or probably enough for every nonslave household in America during these 28 years.

20. On education at home and in schools, see Barbara Finkelstein's excellent essay, "Reading, Writing, and the Acquisition of Identity in the United States: 1790–1860," in *Regulated Children, Liberated Children: Education in Psychohistorical Perspective*, ed. B. Finkelstein (New York, 1979), 114–39.

21. This was nine to ten times higher than Carlo Cipolla's finding in *Literacy and Development in the West* (Baltimore, 1969) that "until 1800 the most favorable cases [for expanding literacy in the Western world] were those in which, apart from the parish priests and other kinds of informal teachers, there was one formal teacher per 1,000 inhabitants" (p. 115). The Vermont Constitution (1777) included a provision for schools in each township, using revenue from school lands. See Gilmore, "Truants and Scholars: Daily Attendance in the District School—A Rural New England Case," VtH 53 (1985):95–103; and Gilmore, "Elementary Literacy," 98–114. New data from West Windsor hamlet confirm these findings.

22. See the fine chapter on rural schools in Carl Kaestle, *Pillars of the Republic: Common Schools and American Society, 1780–1860* (New York, 1983), 13–29, esp. 16–18. If we can learn the range of schoolbooks used in district schools within the Upper Valley after 1787, we will be able to close a major gap in our comprehension of the knowledge and skills acquired in childhood and youth.

23. See David Hall's discussion of steady sellers in "The Uses of Literacy." As research in this area proceeds, it is important that "steady sellers" be specified. Those works most aligned with traditional, intensive-reading styles and subject matter form only one group among "steady sellers." Robinson Crusoe was a steady seller at least through 1830. But did the act of reading also change over time? Steady sale of a particular work does not necessarily imply continuity of reading style for that work. On writing as a regular part of district school instruction, see Finkelstein, "Reading, Writing, and Identity," and (for a slightly later period) Soltow and Stevens, *Rise of Literacy*, 102–114. It is possible to estimate the share of all families engaging in letter writing over time, during 1783–1830. Data from several Upper Valley post offices (often in general store and bookstore account books) enables us to calculate the rough share of households receiving letters. If we compare these results with newspaper notices of letters remaining at the end of each quarter in those same towns, we can construct a changing ratio: of households with a letter not yet picked up to the share of households picking up one or more letters. Since we can learn, in selected cases, the proportion of families receiving a letter, the full data on letters not picked up found in nearly all rural weeklies enables us to estimate the total share of families

receiving letters. I hope to illustrate this procedure in a future essay on increasing maintenance rates for skill in writing beyond one's name.

24. Johansson, *History of Literacy*, 182. For the concept of a push for literacy, see ibid., 154–55. Kenneth Lockridge was the first to point to the importance of population density and schools in his *Literacy in Colonial New England: An Enquiry into the Social Context of Literacy in the Early Modern West* (New York, 1974). See his later summary in "Literacy in Early America, 1650–1800," in Graff, *Literacy and Social Development*, 183–200, esp. 186. Lockridge minimizes, among other factors, economic exchange patterns and emphasizes rather an "intensive, widespread, and uniform Protestantism" which in turn "encouraged systematic schooling" (p. 192). For Edward Cook's typology, see *The Fathers of the Towns: Leadership and Community Structure in Eighteenth Century New England* (Baltimore, 1976). On my earlier formulation, see Gilmore, "Elementary Literacy," esp. pt. 4, "Factors Accounting for Different Levels of Elementary Literacy."

25. Compare graphs 2A–6B in Gilmore, "Elementary Literacy," and figures 5–8 and 5–9 here.

26. Smith, "Legacy of Dissent."

27. See figures 5–8 and 5–9 here; Gilmore, "Elementary Literacy," graphs 5A–6B; and Auwers, "Reading the Marks of the Past."

28. Reading's first post office was established in 1818, Cavendish's first in 1800 and its second in 1821.

29. See Auwers, "Reading the Marks of the Past." Weston attained post office status in 1815, eight years before much earlier settled Reading. On Weston, see Ernestine Pannes, *Waters of the Lonely Way: A Chronicle of Weston, Vermont, 1761–1978* (Canaan, N.H., 1982).

30. Soltow and Stevens, *Rise of Literacy*, 58–88.

31. See Cott, *The Bonds of Womanhood*; Norton, *Liberty's Daughters*; and Kerber, *Women of the Republic*.

32. See Soltow and Stevens, *Rise of Literacy*, 48; and Kerber, *Women of the Republic*, chs. 6–8.

33. The conception comes from the field of literacy. See the essays in Graff, *Literacy and Social Development*. Hall has recently adopted it in his "The Uses of Literacy." Cohen, *A Calculating People*, wishes to see it as a skill different from reading and writing (pp. 4–13). But the links between arithmetic, reading, and writing are too close, in my view, to sustain this interpretation. Numeracy was a subsidiary (but increasingly important) skill, learned only after a basic reading ability had been acquired. A rule was read, written down, and then problems worked at—this is the pattern found in rural New England schoolbooks and in scratch books analyzed in Gilmore, "Elementary Literacy," 98–114.

34. See n. 11 above; Soltow and Stevens, *Rise of Literacy*, 11–22.

35. For an excellent example of collective reading situations at home, see David Hall, "The Mental World of Samuel Sewall," in *Saints and Revolutionaries*, ed. Hall and John Murrin (New York, 1984); and Hall, "The World of Print."

36. See Francis Grubar, *Richard Caton Woodville: An Early American Genre Painter* (Washington, D.C., 1967), the catalogue of the Corcoran Museum exhibit. To take just one example, Woodville's *War News from Mexico* (1848), some 14,000 impressions of which were distributed to American Art Union subscribers in 1851, offers rich insight into this phenomenon. In historical perspective, the extraordinarily small share of the Windsor District population cut off from printed matter after 1810 suggests that nearly all residents assimilated at least some of the information and opinion circulating through the network of print and written communications. But exactly what? It should not be assumed that the core wisdom of the ages, transmitted as part of the acquisition of literacy at home and in district schools, was also the most prominent dimension of knowledge transmitted orally. After 1787, the cultural situation was far more complex

in Windsor District, with its high literacy levels; forms of knowledge, like material possessions, were distributed very unequally.

37. We use the term "knowledge" comprehensively. As formulated by Alfred Schutz and elaborated by Berger, Luckmann, and others, it includes information and opinion, beliefs and values. See Schutz and Thomas Luckmann, *The Structures of the Life-World*, tr. Richard M. Zaner and H. Tristram Engelhardt, Jr. (Evanston, Ill., 1973); Schutz, *Reflections on the Problem of Relevance*, ed. and tr. Richard M. Zaner (New Haven, 1970); Schutz, *The Phenomenology of the Social World*, tr. George Walsh and Frederick Lehnert (Evanston, Ill., 1967), and Peter Berger and Thomas Luckmann, *The Social Construction of Reality* (Garden City, N.Y., 1966). The fact that the mind, as an object of study, was banished from much of the new history until recently, has had a stultifying effect on scholarship.

38. For a somewhat different perspective, see Gordon Wood, "The Democratization of Mind in the American Revolution," in *The Moral Foundations of the American Republic*, ed. Robert H. Horwitz (Charlottesville, Va., 1977), 102–28.

Chapter 4

1. See Raymond Williams, "Communications Technologies and Social Institutions," in R. Williams, *Contact*, 225–38.

2. See Richard D. Brown, "Emergence of Urban Society."

3. See Laurence Veysey, "Intellectual History and the New Social History," in Higham and Conkin, *New Directions*, 3–26.

4. See Henretta, "Farms and Families"; Paul Johnson, *A Shopkeeper's Millennium,: Society and Revivals in Rochester, New York, 1815–1837* (New York, 1978); and Rhys Isaac, *The Transformation of Virginia, 1740–1790* (Chapel Hill, N.C., 1982). To date each has stopped short of a clean break with one or the other of these powerful historiographical traditions. On the general issues, see the assessments of Bailyn, "Challenge," and Geoffrey Barraclough, *Main Trends in History* (New York, 1978).

5. For the traditional intellectual history position, see George Fredrickson, *The Inner Civil War: Northern Intellectuals in the Crisis of the Union* (New York, 1965), vii–viii, and Lewis Perry, *Intellectual Life in America: A History* (New York, 1984). Among many calls to rethink the field, Gene Wise's was the most insightful: "The Decline of American Intellectual History: A Diagnosis and a Possible Reprieve" (unpublished Paper, Case Western Reserve Univ., 1975).

6. I have learned much from scholars who have directly confronted the problem of social milieu and cultural evidence, esp. Natalie Zemon Davis, "Printing and the People," in *Society and Culture in Early Modern France*, ed. Davis (Stanford, Calif., 1975), pp. 189–226, and 326–36. On socioeconomic and sociopsychological groupings, see Davis, "Interview," in *Visions of History: Interviews with [thirteen historians]*, ed. Henry Abelove et al. (New York, 1984), 97–122, esp. 109. Also see Emmanuel LeRoy Ladurie, *The Peasants of Languedoc*, tr. John Day (Urbana, Ill., 1974); Darrett Rutman, *American Puritanism: Faith and Practice* (Philadelphia, 1970); and Wallace, *Rockdale*. In the end we rejected using prevailing notions of "social milieu" and the "social basis of knowledge" because many such formulations assume that culture is a mirror and not a generator, and because these concepts are too narrow to encompass the mix of factors at work in rural New England.

7. For a marvelously thoughtful comparative work moving beyond this situation, see Braudel, *Civilization and Capitalism, 15th–18th Century*. Few historical studies blend social and economic with cultural history in an analysis of what Alfred Schutz termed the stock of knowledge at hand and its role in daily life. See Schutz, *Reflections*, 53–166; Schutz and Luckmann, *The Structures of the Life World*, 99–331. For a recent behaviorist attempt, see Christine Heyrman,

Commerce and Culture: The Maritime Communities of Colonial Massachusetts, 1690–1750 (New York, 1984).

8. The study of differential access and print communications networks generally is in its infancy. The classic study remains Febvre and Martin, *Coming of the Book*, chs. 4, 6, and 7.

9. The same access zone, and settlement site within that access zone, whether a grazing area in the Green Mountain foothills or a river valley village, held an array of cultural interests. The array was narrower or broader due in part to its location and community type, in part to its relationship to commercial exchange, and in part to the further factors of wealth and daily work experience.

10. We shall use the term "human habitat," as in "fortunate villge human habitat," to include all examples of this type. Variations among examples of each type were fairly minimal.

11. The few very poor professional and commerce and trading families below $700 remain in their respective human habitats because their unusual poverty at the time of the household head's death typically represented a brief phase in the family's life cycle. No extensive farms, hence no substantial numbers of the three farming occupations existed in the village and hamlet human habitats. See Joseph S. Wood, "The Origins of the New England Village" (Ph.D. diss., Pennsylvania State Univ., 1978), esp. ch. 6, pp. 203–85; Jack Larkin, "Interim Center Village Report," Old Sturbridge Village, (n.d.) p.3 and charts 3 and 4; and the Woodstock *Vermont Mercury*, 27 May 1842.

12. Until about 1810 there were no sizable hamlets in any of these townships, and it was 1809 before the first post offices (in Ludlow and Plymouth hamlets) were established in these townships. Not until the early 1820s did all five townships, expanding along with the major district road system, boast at least one active hamlet.

13. The 86 families in the five mountainous farmstead areas averaged just $754 in total wealth, a third of these were below $700 in total wealth.

14. Ross Beales, Kenneth Lockridge, and others have found this to be the case for earlier periods. We do not know whether the choices of printed matter made by hardscrabble families in their few purchases were dictated by a desire to maintain the traditional values they learned as they acquired literacy skills, or by an inability to obtain more, and more varied, printed matter. Our tentative conclusion is that financial stringency arrested curiosity and growth and so reinforced traditional beliefs and values.

15. Thompson, *History of Vermont*, 209–10, gives a summary of U.S. Census data, 1790–1840.

16. See Thomas Dublin, *Women at Work: The Transformation of Work and Community in Lowell, Massachusetts, 1828–1860* (New York, 1979); Dublin, ed., *Farm to Factory: Women's Letters, 1830–1860* (New York, 1981); and Roth's detailed explanation of the impact of these changes in "Whence This Strange Fire?", 463–544. The rise of factory villages, especially Springfield, Windsor, and Ludlow, created an ever more distinctive human habitat in these communities by the late 1830s.

17. In ch. 9 we discuss life in each type of human habitat. In a future work, each living situation and its *mentalité* will be discussed fully. We emphasize that, in particular families, individual will, interest, and whim often played a key role.

18. The basic mix of conditions constituting each human habitat was constructed independent of later research on the incidence, size, and content of our 396 family libraries. Formulation of the system was accomplished using the full set of 643 inventories (1787–1830), before extracting the data on family libraries. Once the system of human habitats was delineated, I then arranged the 643 inventories accordingly to evaluate the number, size, and range of family libraries found in each. Then I backtracked, adding several kinds of evidence about participation in printed

and written communications (See app. 2 for the specific procedures). The first test of the system of human habitats was on the purely quantitative aspect of elementary literacy, especially female patterns, in Gilmore, "Elementary Literacy," 125–38 and 156–67. This chapter tests several aspects of family library collections and also shares in lending libraries from the sole detailed body of Windsor District evidence: estate inventories. We have also identified each print item retained, making possible a far more critical test of the distribution and contents of family libraries by living situations (in chs. 8 and 9). An ideal next step would be to analyze bookstore sales records, almanac sales, newspaper and periodical subscriptions, general store sales, post office records of letters received, and peddlers' sales records for Windsor District businesses.

19. The incidence of family libraries in each human habitat has been estimated from the best available evidence: the proportion of families with libraries in their inventories (among all families with inventories), 1787–1830.

20. Based on the proportions of all inventoried families with private libraries, an accurate representation for this purpose. Some periodicals were subscribed to by mail, mainly after 1820; most were advertised per issue and sold that way in Upper Valley bookstores.

21. One exception: median size was identical for hamlet and fortunate farmstead families.

22. Estimated from the federal censuses of 1820 and 1830. By "elsewhere" we mean families in the two largest living situations, the self-sufficient farmstead and hardscrabble human habitats, constituting over half of all Windsor District residents in 1830. Only two families with a lending library share failed to retain a private library at inventory. Many self-sufficient hamlet, and all fortunate farmstead, families resided in townships establishing lending libraries between 1800 and 1820.

23. See Engelsing, "Die perioden" and *Der Burger als Leser*.

24. See Roth, "Whence This Strange Fire?" In a future work we will note religious membership and activities for our 643 families where these have turned up in wills, inventories, or other biographical and historical studies.

Chapter 5

1. See Christopher M. Jedrey, *The World of John Cleaveland: Family and Community in Eighteenth Century New England* (New York, 1979); Robert Gross, *The Minutemen and Their World* (New York, 1976); Stephen Roper Davis, "From Ploughshares to Spindles: Dedham, Massachusetts, 1790–1840" (Ph.D. diss., Univ. of Wisconsin, 1973); and Faler, *Mechanics and Manufacturers*.

2. Elizabeth Carroll Reilly, "The Wages of Piety: The Boston Book Trade of Jeremy Condy," in Joyce et. al., *Printing and Society*, 83–131; Richard D. Brown, "Spreading the Word: Rural Clergymen and the Communications Network of Eighteenth Century New England," *Proceedings of the Mass. Historical Society*, 94 (1982):1–14. Brown is at work on a major study of cultural communications in this period. See also Allan R. Pred, *Urban Growth and the Circulation of Information: The United States System of Cities, 1790–1840* (Cambridge, Mass., 1973), esp. 1–103.

3. See Roth, "Whence This Strange Fire?"; Ludlum, *Social Ferment*; and Donal Ward, "Religious Enthusiasm in Vermont, 1761–1847" (Ph.D. diss., Univ. of Notre Dame, 1980).

4. Webster, *American Dictionary*, 2: "vehicle." Social historians have demonstrated the necessity of thinking in terms of scale; cultural historians confronting evidence about a particular dimension of *mentalités* may profitably employ this perspective in studying the process of creating a book, printing and publishing, circulation patterns, and intended and actual readership attained through purchase, borrowing, or gifting.

5. Or became mulch in a paper mill. Here we shall not consider the subsequent history of a book through later owners, except where direct evidence survives of books gifted or willed

to another Windsor District family whose household head also died before 1831 and left a private library.

6. This approach is similar to Robert Darnton's analysis of the European book trade in "What is the History of the Book?" Some printed items were also brought to the area by travelers. Occasionally a private letter or journal entry illuminates this more elusive contact point. We have excluded from this discussion the interesting ephemera printed at each press (lottery tickets, forms, etc.).

7. See Fredson Bowers, *Principles of Bibliographical Description* (Princeton, 1949), 113–23; G. Thomas Tanselle, "The Concept of *Ideal* State," SB 33 (1980):18–53; and his "Title-Page Transcription and Signature Collation Reconsidered," SB 38 (1985):45–81, esp. 53–57. For the terms "fields of intentionality," "delivery," and "reception," I have adapted the terminology of Robert Jauss, "Literary History as a Challenge to Literary Theory," *New Literary History* 2 (1970):7–37, and "Levels of Identification of Hero and Audience," *New Literary History* 5 (1974):283–317.

8. Private correspondence is the norm here. See, for instance, Samuel Hall to E. P. Walton 1833, MSS 20 #74, VHS; and a superb source, the James Whitelaw Papers, VHS. For an instance of a publisher separate from a printer, see McCorison, *Vermont Imprints* 397, no. 1901. Throughout this section I have relied on Upper Valley sources wherever possible. The best general study of book production and distribution in early America remains Wroth and Silver, "Book Production." For American works originally published outside the area, copyright permission to reprint locally was secured by correspondence between publishers.

9. This evidence documents the acutal production circumstances of a book. See, for instance, McCorison, "A Daybook from the Office of the Rutland *Herald* Kept by Samuel Williams, 1798–1802," PAAS 76, pt. 2 (1967):293–395. A comprehensive listing of this data, keyed to extant imprint inventories, is much needed. Present reliance is often on number of editions, usually an unreliable guide to the number of copies printed. See G. Thomas Tanselle's excellent essay, "The Bibliographical Concepts of Issue and State," PBSA 69 (1975):17–66. Sometimes production data includes the number of copies per edition. The basic source is the comprehensive imprints inventory. I used McCorison's splendid *Vermont Imprints* for Vermont imprints (excepting newspapers) through 1820, and the parallel work of Robinson Murray, III, for New Hampshire through 1800. Murray kindly allowed me full access to all of his work and files, including his extraction of New Hampshire imprints, through 1830 from Shaw, Shoemaker, et al., *American Bibliography* (New York, 1958–). I have similarly extracted Vermont imprints, 1821–30, used the AAS town of publication card catalogue for both states through 1830, and consulted James K. Ready, "A Checklist of Imprints for Vermont, 1821–35" (Master's thesis, Catholic Univ., 1955), and Glenn B. Skillen, "Additional Vermont Imprints, 1821–1835" (Master's thesis, Catholic Univ., 1964).

10. See G. Thomas Tanselle's most helpful "Copyright Records and the Bibliographer," SB 22 (1969):77–124, esp. 79–80, and McCorison, *Vermont Imprints*, xi–xii. No Vermont or New Hampshire Upper Valley records are listed in Tanselle's inventory, 122–24. The register of copyrights received by the Vermont secretary of state's office contains notices of deposits, and the records of the U.S. District Court at Burlington, now housed at Waltham, Mass., contain Vermont copyright entries; both sources rarely reveal the size of editions. Where systematic lists of imprints do not exist, we can use title pages of books to be published, set by the printer and often advertised reprinting a reduced facsimilie; newspaper announcements of a work's future publication; subscription papers and notices of them; and separate announcements—once a work was published—in bookstore lists, catalogues, and advertisements for individual books. For an example of a title page facsimile, see the Concord N.H. *Mirror*, 6 May 1799 (William Hubbard's *A Narrative of the Indian Wars*). This announcement also opens subscription papers

(the project apparently failed). For a later-stage announcement collecting subscription papers, see the Hartford *Connecticut Courant*, 22 Sept. 1778 (*The Annals of the Netherlands*). For later announcements, see VJ 8 June 1812 (Banks, *Peter the Great*). On book catalogues, see Robert Winans's excellent *A Descriptive Checklist of Book Catalogues Separately Printed in America, 1693–1800* (Charlottesville, Va., 1981).

11. On binding practices, see Giles Barber, "Continental Paper Wrapper and Publishers' Bindings in the Eighteenth Century," *Book Collector* 24 (1975):37–49; William H. McCarthy, Jr., *An Outline of the History of the Printed Book: Being the 3rd Number of the Dolphin* (New York, 1938); and Helmut Lehmann-Haupt, *Bookbinding in America: Three Essays* (Portland, Me., 1941). The details of binding just down the valley at West Brookfield, Mass., may be followed in "William Merriam's Account Book, 1831–33," AAS.

12. Publishers' shipping records, including information about the means of shipment, stagecoach routes, teaming practices, roads and waterways taken, etc., detail wholesaling to other bookstores, exchanges of stock with other publishers, and auction and literary fair activities. See Wroth and Silver, "Book Production," 121–24 and esp. 131ff., and Charles L. Nichols, "The Literary Fair in the United States," in George P. Winship, ed. *Bibliographical Essays: A Tribute to Wilberforce Eames* (Cambridge, Mass., 1924), 85–92.

13. Together with wholesaling exchange records, records of the sales and stock of bookstores, general stores, peddlers, and even individual private sellers yield comparisons between the proportion of works published in the Upper Valley and all works for sale there. An example of a bookstore's stock is *A Catalogue of Books for Sale by Thomas and Thomas* (Walpole, 1803). An unpublished list for a later period is the complete stock, with numbers of copies per item, of the "Buffalo Bookstore, 180 Broadway, New York City for 1840" (Book Trades Collection, Box 2, Folder 3, AAS). Sales records of a print shop may be found in McCorison, "Daybook." Two general store records of the stock of print items, both for Windsor, Vermont, have been located: James Tarbox Account Book, XMSC-15, VHS; and Harris and Morrills' Stock on Hand, 1st of April 1833, XMSC-15, 1833, VHS. That private individuals sold books may be seen in Robert Foster, ed., *Hymns and Spiritual Songs* (Portsmouth, N.H., 1818), title page. For an Upper Valley peddler's stock see "Invoice of Peddler's Goods, 31 Dec. 1842," MSC–174, VHS. On used books as part of the normal advertising system, see [Concord] *Courier of New Hampshire*, 22 Feb. 1800.

14. An instance of social library purchases, including the stock of the library, is the "Dummerston, Vermont, Social Library Records, 1808–40," Alderman Library, Univ. of Virginia. A published listing is Anthony Haswell, *Constitution and Catalogue of the Pawlet Library* (Bennington, Vt., 1799). For a catalogue of Dartmouth College's general library see *Catalogue of the Library* (Hanover, N.H., 1813). College societies also kept library collections. On Dartmouth, see Lowell Simpson, "The Development and Scope of Undergraduate Literary Society Libraries at Columbia, Dartmouth, Princeton, and Yale, 1783–1830," JLH 12 (1977), 211–21.

15. The borrowing records of the Cavendish Social Library have been discovered: "Memorandum of Books delivered from and returned to Cavendish Library, 1815–1840," MS974.31 C315L, VHS. Informal borrowing may be picked up in the occasional letter or other written source, as in Henry Steele Wardner, *Historical Address Delivered at the Recent Dedication of the Old South Meeting House* (Windsor, Vt., 1923), 8; On Sunday School libraries, see F. Allen Briggs, "The Sunday School Library," *Readings in American Library History*, ed. Michael H. Harris (Washington, D.C., 1971), 64–71; and the remarkable family borrowing records of Samuel Lane, in *A Journal for the Years, 1739–1803*, ed. Charles Lane Hanson (Concord, 1937):8–15. Other data about borrowing is found written in books, e.g., the AAS copy of Jonathan Mayhew, *Sermons Upon the Following Subjects* (Boston, 1755), 1769 inscription, first blank leaf, verso.

16. The richest systematic source for the reading habits of large numbers of ordinary fami-

lies, estate inventories, exist for each probate district (interspersed with wills, which rarely itemized books assigned for this region) and have been preserved systematically for the Upper Valley. For recycling, see Louis W. Flanders, *Simeon Ide: Yeoman, Freeman, Pioneer Printer* (Rutland, Vt., 1931), 76ff.

17. Contemporary published commentary mainly came from writers offering independent estimates of specific works. By the early 1820s regularly, and more randomly earlier, the VJ and most other Upper Valley weeklies reprinted both extensive and brief excerpts from at least a third of all works available for sale that year. While comments in private sources are exceedingly scattered and too fragmentary for systematic assessments of reading tastes, they do offer rich insights into local reception and reading habits.

18. We underemphasized those contact points for publication, sales, and purchases. In this book we have utilized almanacs and especially newspapers for culturewide trends, but the breadth of newspaper and almanac information renders us incapable of determining, from known sources, what was read by specific population groups.

19. Much valuable insight has been gained from studies of the European book trade, especially those of Davis, Febvre and Martin, Roche, Darnton, and Chartier. Eisenstein guides her readers through much of the literature in *Printing Press*, 709–67.

20. A third bookstore opened in 1793 and a fourth in 1808; thereafter never less than four bookstores (whether related to printing offices or independent) competed in Windsor village through 1830. During 1813–14 and again in 1827–1831, there were six in operation (see graph 6–1 for the coincidence of peak print production and numbers of bookstores). The first independent bindery was established in 1808, funded by Isaiah Thomas, who was an absent partner of Preston Merrifield. Just after the War of 1812 it was replaced by another which flourished through 1830. In 1827 a second independent bindery opened.

21. See Gilmore, "Elementary Literacy," 87–178.

22. See Rollo Silver, *The American Printer, 1787–1825* (Charlottesville, Va., 1967), 28–62, on the workings of printing offices.

23. Most Upper Valley bookstores were located in sizable villages as part of permanent print centers. Four exceptions were located in communities without printing offices: Whitingham, Vt., known only from the title pages of itinerant peddler Amos Taylor's own imprints, c. 1796–1806; Bradford, Vermont's bookstore (1809–13), known from maps and globes produced there; and stores in a relatively populated township, Lebanon, N.H. (1,800 people), open for just over a year in 1813–14, and at Thetford, Vt., surviving for just over two years, 1827–29, both known from newspaper advertisements. On Thetford see Charles Latham, Jr., *A Short History of Thetford, Vermont, 1761–1870* (Thetford, Vt., 1972). For Whitingham, see McCorison, *Amos Taylor, a sketch and bibliography* (Worcester, Mass., 1959), 44–45. On Robert Thomas, see Gilmore, "Profile of an Independent Hamlet Bookstore: Robert B. Thomas and the Book Trade in Sterling, Mass., 1790–1815" (Paper presented at meeting of the Society for Massachusetts History, Mar. 1984).

24. In Windsor District, the following nonvalley bookstores advertised on a regular basis before 1831: Samuel Mills of Burlington, Vt.; Thomas and Thomas of Worcester, Mass.; E. & H. Clark, Middletown, Conn.; Monroe and Francis of Boston, Mass.; Greenbanks, and Godey's of Philadelphia, Pa.; and Peter Force of Washington, D.C. Wroth and Silver, "Book Production," 63–136, discusses the domination of Boston, New York, and Philadelphia in American book production. On steady sellers, see Hall, "Uses of Literacy," 16–20 and 29ff. See also the Walpole Bookstore's "Records of Sales," for 1809, Isaiah Thomas Papers, AAS. On territorial disagreements, see "A Postrider Wanted," FM 3 Aug. 1802, p. 3.

25. See D.H. Hilton General Store Day Book, 1827–29, UVt.

26. Each newspaper editor sold space for advertisements to booksellers from many communi-

ties. Other Upper Valley print centers and those in cities outside the area advertised regularly in Spooner's VJ between 1800 and 1830.

27. For advice, see "January," *Walton's Vermont Register and Farmer's Almanac* (Montpelier, Vt., 1828). A superb full study of the life cycle of printed objects is Darnton, *Business of Enlightenment*.

28. The informal circulation system is treated at greater length in Gilmore, "Peddlers and the Dissemination of Print Culture in Rural New England, 1780–1840," in *Dublin Seminar Series: Itinerancy*, ed. Peter Benes (Boston, 1986).

29. Ibid. In many cases village booksellers supplied peddlers. An unwritten code recognized that competition in the same place between two sellers supplied by the same regional wholesaler was ultimately unproductive to the wholesaler.

30. Petitions came not from the bookstore owners but from general store owners and other merchants who felt keenly the competition from peddlers. Even without trading in clandestine literature, peddlers offered a wider variety of printed items than general stores; and because they purchased from large booksellers, often at a "trade discount," they could offer their stock at cheaper prices. See the correspondence between Isaiah Thomas and Robert B. Thomas of Sterling, Mass., for 1793 and 1799, and that between Anson Whipple of Walpole, N.H., and Isaiah Thomas, 1812–13, in the Isaiah Thomas Papers, AAS.

31. The daybooks of the firm for these years have not survived, not has any other evidence of direct sales to customers. One edition was presumably published at Brattleboro, the other at Windsor. See McCorison, "Two Unrecorded American Printings of 'Fanny Hill'," VtH 40 (1972):64–66, quotes on 65, and Gilmore, "Peddlers." Evidence is sufficient to consider the circulation of clandestine literature one among several key functions of the informal distribution system for printed matter. The circulation of *A Woman of Pleasure* awakens us to the similarities in book trade patterns throughout the North Atlantic Republic of Letters. See Darnton, *Literary Underground*.

32. Seven villages with print centers lasting betwen 16 and 44 years between 1787 and 1830 formed the core of a full-access zone. Another 13 print center villages with at least one bookstore, each disseminated print matter for between 3 and 15 years in the full-access zone. Sizable portions of another 40 or so contiguous townships completed the full-access zone. By the 1820s, the proliferation of Upper Valley auxiliary bookstores markedly shortened the travel distance to the nearest bookstore (see fig. 5-3). The most interesting early American attempt to map levels of access is Ralph H. Brown, *Historical Geography of the United States* (New York, 1948), 109ff.

33. See fig. 2–5 for postrider routes in 1800. Nearly three-quarters of minimal-access zone townships were in the most rugged mountainous parts of the Upper Valley. The other quarter represent townships isolated from Upper Valley print culture but under the distant influence of nonvalley print centers. On the Vermont side, Stockbridge and Plymouth Kingdom in Windsor County were in slightly closer proximity to Rutland than to any valley print center. Townships such as Williamstown and Washington, in northwest Orange County, were in the Montpelier orbit, again for reasons of geography and travel conditions. On the New Hampshire side, communities such as Springfield, Goshen, and Washington, in what became Sullivan County, were influenced by Concord. These patterns of influence have been confirmed by a scan of local news and notices in Rutland, Montpelier, and Concord newspapers, 1800–1830.

34. Of the six most populous townships in Windsor County for 1810, all with between 2,100 and 2,800 residents, only the largest (Windsor at 2,752) maintained a newspaper (three weeklies). Woodstock, with only 85 fewer souls in 1810, had no newspaper until a decade later. Chester, fourth in population (2,370), established a newspaper which apparently folded after two years (1807–8). Location and size, a result of differing patterns and levels of societal development, distinguished Windsor. Four townships fell within Windsor's distribution network. Chester was far enough away to attempt early autonomy.

35. The range of printed matter available in northwestern New England was far broader than previous understanding of rural society suggests. Even in Windsor, some lag time existed in obtaining current information or the latest novel, versus Boston, Philadelphia, or even Concord. But this gap steadily diminished after 1787. See Pred, *Urban Growth*.

36. The following sketch is derived primarily from the rich maunscript and print collections of AAS, VHS, UVt, and the Vermont State Papers.

37. Important secondary routes included: a well-traveled local road from Weathersfield through northwest Springfield and Chester village to Andover and Weston hamlets and then into Peru; a road from Windsor along Mill Brook through West Windsor, Hammondsville hamlet (and Reading Center) into South Woodstock village; and a road connecting Springfield and Chester villages.

38. Travel off the main roads and rivers or streams was extremely difficult for humans and almost impossible for any regular sizable transport of store goods or farm products.

39. Timing is quite important in identifying zones of access; the proportion of Windsor District full- and partial-access areas grew substantially between the 1790s and 1810. Through 1810 a portion of each township remained far removed from full access. By 1825 nearly all of Windsor and Chester townships, most of Weathersfield, and an ever-expanding portion of Springfield were within the full-access zone. By 1840 the full-access zone embraced all but the most mountainous precincts of Windsor District.

40. The effect of enhanced steady newspaper delivery on book purchases was gradual; a sizable increase in bookstore starts awaited the late 1820s. Books purchased through local hamlet general stores, which could obtain specific volumes the customer saw advertised in Windsor newspapers, offered competition to itinerant booksellers. The store owner, or his or her agent, would post a notice in the store, after a time take the list along on a trip to Windsor, obtain the books, and sell them to customers. Analysis of family libraries by township, 1787–1830, reveals marked expansion in the acquisition of print items in partial-access areas after 1810. Springfield was a favorite Upper Valley township for peddlers before it established its own bookstore in the mid-1830s. Probably one or more of its general stores carried a larger-than-normal selection of books, as occurred throughout the Midwest. See Michael Harris, *The General Store as an Outlet for Books on the Southern Indiana Frontier, 1800–1850* (AAS misc. pamphlet, reprinted from JLH, 1973); and his "Bookstores on the Southern Indiana Frontier, 1833–1850," *American Book Collector* 23 (1973):30–32.

41. In 1818 a stable print center (a newspaper and a bookstore lasting into the 1830s) was established at Bellows Falls, Vt., just to the south. In 1820 Woodstock, Vt., to the north, gave a print center a second try, supporting a newspaper, eventually two bookstores, and even a periodical. Accordingly, Bellows Falls and Woodstock became the second and third permanent print centers catering to some Windsor District residents. Chester made its second attempt at establishing a print center in 1828 by beginning a newspaper, opening another bookstore, starting a circulating library, and printing books. Charlestown, N.H., just across the river from Weathersfield, followed suit within a year.

42. The initial geographical breakdown into different zones of access enables us, to specify within reasonable limits the cultural geography, structure, and timing of diffusion for any cultural value and belief prevalent in this subregion. To date, the movement of a cultural value cluster from initial entrance to widespread awareness in any large social unit has only been speculated upon without any clear grounding in the society's communication system. The effect has been rather like attempting to model a clay figure without an armature. Through 1830, nearly all noteworthy belief clusters embodied in print and written sources and not originated locally, arrived first in Windsor District through Windsor, Chester, or Springfield (see fig. 5–7). After moving rapidly through bookstore communities and those near enough to be serviced regularly

by a newspaper, clusters of belief next spread through partial-access zone communities (see fig. 5–5). Here, in townships within reasonable distance of an auxiliary bookstore, belief clusters were diffused quite rapidly. Dissemination proceeded haltingly (if at all) in the mountainous portions of the minimal-access zone. The concept of idea clusters is adapted from Clifford Geertz's *The Interpretation of Cultures* (New York, 1973).

Chapter 6

1. See Crowley, *This Sheba Self*; Howe, "Republicanism"; and Gary Wills, *Inventing America* (New York, 1976), which spawned a considerable controversy.

2. See esp. his *Intellectual Life in the Colonial South, 1585–1763*, 3 vols. (Knoxville, Tenn., 1978); *Intellectual Life in Jefferson's Virginia, 1790–1840* (Knoxville, Tenn., 1964); and *Literature and Society in Early Virginia, 1608–1840* (Baton Rouge, La., 1973). Davis's main interest was in establishing indigenous southern contributions to intellectual life.

3. For the rise of the weekly newspaper in one area, see John C. Nerone, "The Press and Popular Culture in the Early Republic: Cincinnati, 1793–1848" (Ph.D. diss., Univ. of Notre Dame, 1982).

4. Between 24,000 and 40,000 almanacs were sold annually in the Upper Valley, 1787–1820 — editions published within the region (standard press runs of 2,000–3,000 copies per edition), plus small lots and shares of editions published elsewhere but advertised in Upper Valley weeklies. An estimate of the size of lots and shares was drawn from G.&C. Merriam Co. Sales Records, 1818–36; e.g., sales records for 27 Oct. 1828–16 Mar. 1829 (when sales began and ended for that year's stock of almanacs) reveal 4,585 copies sold at the Brookfield, Mass., store. Eight varieties of almanacs were sold, including 3,020 copies of their own issue and 1,565 copies of seven others taken for resale (microfilm copy of records at AAS, originals at Beinecke Library, Yale Univ.).

5. Even the most expensive almanacs available for sale, the *New England Farmer's Diary and Almanac* and the *Ladies' and Gentlemens' Diary, and Almanack*, sold for 12.5 cents a copy in 1818, far less than a day's wage for all but a few semiskilled laborers. On the role of the almanac in the Early Republic, see Jon Wenrick, "For Education and Entertainment: Almanacs in the Early American Republic, 1783–1815" (Ph.D. diss., Claremont Graduate School, 1974), esp. ii.

6. Flanders, *Simeon Ide*, 76ff.; *Baltimore Almanac for 1784* (Baltimore, 1783). Also see Isaiah Thomas's wish that people would save almanacs, in *Massachusetts, Connecticut . . . Almanac for 1783*, quoted in Georgia Bumgardner, "American Almanac Illustration in the Eighteenth Century," in *Eighteenth Century Prints in Colonial America: To Educate and Decorate*, ed. Joan D. Dolmetsch, 51–70, (Charlottesville, Va., 1979), quote on p. 65. Only three almanacs remained among 5,630 volumes in 396 family libraries inventoried in Windsor District, 1787–1830. Often hanging on a peg near the fireplace (seen in contemporary prints and paintings of house interiors) the current year's almanac was too short-lived to be inventoried.

7. "A Pack of Cards Turned Into an Almanack," [Chester]*The Vermont Phenix*, 25 Nov. 1829, p. 1, col. 2; Amos Cole, "Preface," *The New Hampshire and Vermont Almanac for 1809* (Windsor, 1808). See Bumgardner, "Eighteenth Century Almanacs," 65, for almanacs as "encyclopedic magazines . . . on a much smaller and less expensive scale." The finest explanation of the actual functional uses of the almanac in early America is Richard Anders, "Introduction: The New England Almanac" (typescript prepared for ASS exhibit, 1979–80).

8. Georgia Bumgardner, "Vignettes of the Past: American Historical Broadsides Through the War of 1812" (unpublished paper, 1980). Bumgardner reports that William Miller found 19% broadsides among Franklin and Hall's imprints, 1728–66. McCorison, "Daybook," 293–395, suggests the difficulties in ascertaining total imprints. In *Vermont Imprints*, McCorison had iden-

tified 27 items from the shop of the *Herald*. The daybooks raised this figure to 98 items: 4 more books and pamphlets; 7 more broadsides or pamphlets; 34 more broadsides; 10 more dance invitations; and 16 legal forms, for a rate of one survival per 3.7 items printed (27.5%). Robinson Murray, III, in correspondence with author, estimates that broadsides comprised about a quarter of all New Hampshire imprints, 1756–1800.

9. Data compiled from McCorison, "Daybook"; Ready; Skillen; and Shaw, Shoemaker, et al., *American Bibliography*, on Vermont; and on New Hampshire, Murray's files and Shaw, Shoemaker, et al. Nineteenth-century genre paintings are a rich source for the existence and placement of various types of broadsides. See, for instance, Willaim Winner's *The Pie Man or a Civic Procession* [1856] (Historical Society of Pennsylvania; reproduced on the cover of *Antiques*, July 1980).

10. Analysis of all Windsor District newspaper advertisements of imprints for sale through 1830, and all imprints retained by Windsor District families at the death of the household head, 1787–1830, enable us to speak with precision about the circulation of books, pamphlets, and periodicals within the region (see chs. 8 and 9). Based on inventory share, I estimate that no less than three-fifths of all Windsor District homes, and probably three-quarters, retained a Bible. Many household heads passed on their Bible before death, and other families removed it prior to inventory assessment.

11. Because previous estimates of the size of newspaper editions varied widely, table 6–1 summarizes contemporary evidence from a broader study conducted of the proportions of households subscribing to a newspaper in 1780–1830. See Gilmore, "The Process of Thought," 43–59, and table 8 there. These are nationwide figures based on all known sources. The three Vermont weeklies averaged 1,070 copies for 1800, and the three New Hampshire weeklies 1,133, in keeping with the national average of 1,078. The 1810 calculation is as follows: 40% at 1,100 copies, plus taverns, stores, etc.; minus 50 copies exchanged with other editors; minus short-term weeklies; equals about 33%. The 1830 calculation is: 75% at 1,200 copies, plus taverns, stores, reading rooms, etc.; minus 100 copies exchanged with other editors; minus short-term weeklies; equals 55–65%. We have omitted any estimate of distant newspapers received in the Upper Valley through the mails; evidence is rare, but see the Ryegate, Vt., Post Office Records, 1825–26, VHS.

12. Between 1783 and 1824, excepting the War of 1812, most rural weeklies turned political at national election time; otherwise they carried relatively little political opinion (as distinct from government affairs) on a regular basis. See VJ, 7 Aug. 1783, 5 Aug. 1826, and 10 Feb. 1827. Upper Valley editors were convinced of the elementary educational value of the rural weekly: e.g., a weekly was "almost equal to a school," contended VJ, 26 Feb. 1821. See Joyce Appleby, "Republicanism in Old and New Contexts," WMQ 3s 43 (1986):20–34, quote on 31; and Lance Banning, "Jeffersonian Ideology Revisited: Liberal and Classical Ideas in the New American Republic," WMQ 3s 43 (1986):3–19.

13. *Walton's Vermont Register and Farmer's Almanac for 1828* (Montpelier, Vt., 1827), "January" for the quote; VJ 28 Dec. 1818; Dwight, *Travels*, 4:251 (Letter VII); Jacob Abbot, quoted in Cott, *The Bonds of Womanhood*, 10; Bidwell, *Rural Economy*, 347ff.

14. See McCorison, "Daybook," 306–7, for Eleazer Wheelock, a postrider in the Rutland area, 1798–1802. I have traced the postrider system through VJ advertisements, from summer 1783 through 1830; also see John Lambert, *Travels in Lower Canada and North America*, 2 vols. (London, 1810), 2:498–99. The postal acts of the early national era provided an incalculable stimulus to newspaper quality and rapid circulation. See Frank Luther Mott, *American Journalism: A History, 1690–1960*. 3d ed. (New York, 1962), 160–61.

15. A full list of periodicals offered for sale and/or subscription was compiled from VJ advertisements, 1802–30. Family library holdings of periodicals were calculated from WDPR inven-

tories, 1787–1830. Only 6% of periodicals holders fall in the lowest two-fifths of family wealth, whereas 47% fall in the top fifth. Five-sixths (32 of 38) of these families were from the top two-thirds of the wealth structure.

16. Comparisons of reading matter by similar groups within different nations are also possible.

17. For the relationship between printers and the state government, see documents and correspondence in the manuscript volumes of Vermont State Papers. For the period 1777–87, e.g., see 8:18, 37, and 41; and 9:10, 50, and 193. On Spooner, see Graffagnino, "'We Have Long Been Wishing for a Good Printer in This Vicinity': The State of Vermont, the First East Union and the Dresden Press, 1778–1779," VtH 47 (Winter 1979):21–36. McCorison, *Vermont Imprints*, permits accurate work on the Vermont valley counties, and Robinson Mrrray's research files are invaluable for the New Hampshire valley counties. Shaw, Shoemaker, et al., *American Bibliography*, reports 1,693 governmental imprints among 5,609 total imprints for 1830.

18. See McCorison, *Vermont Imprints*, 3–4 (changes from his *Additions* and *Corrections* have been incorporated in all citations to the work). Invitations, legal forms, and several other ephemeral items were also printed. Two imprints were addresses to the citizenry from politicians, one a proclamation by the governor and the other three, documents issued by the General Assembly.

19. Ibid., 20–24.

20. For exchanges, see Walpole Exchange Books, 1802–9, Isaiah Thomas Papers, AAS. For 1796, 154 Vermont and New Hampshire imprints have been discovered (several times the 1784 total): 50 in Vermont and at least 94 in New Hampshire. See McCorison, *Vermont Imprints*, 82–93, and Murray, New Hampshire imprint files.

21. McCorison, *Vermont Imprints*. Vermont state printing was now contracted at Rutland and Bennington, hence the absence of Vermont laws, etc. The 11 state and federal government imprints included 2 proceedings of the state government; 2 copies of Washington's *Farewell Address* and another political oration; 2 Fourth of July orations; 3 copies of the last words of local criminals about to be executed; and a document relating to the Canadian government.

22. We used data from McCorison, *Vermont Imprints*, on Vermont, employing a time series with five-year intervals. Less complete New Hampshire evidence suggests the same pattern.

23. At least 68 almanacs, books, pamphlets, and broadsides have been identified as published within the Upper Valley Vermont counties in 1812, up 242% from 28 volumes printed in 1796. For New Hampshire valley counties we must rely mainly on Shaw, Shoemaker, et al., *American Bibliography*, which lists only 15 imprints; this compares with 31 New Hampshire Valley imprints 16 years earlier. We proceed assuming that we are missing a sizable group of New Hampshire imprints. If we consider just Vermont-side imprints, where we have fuller evidence, 38% were devoted to sacred subjects.

24. Sacred works included an edition of the Bible, a catechism, 2 hymnals, 3 editions of Watts' *Psalms of David*, 4 devotional-meditation works, 10 sermons, 3 Baptist denominational works, and 7 other theological works and tracts. For the religious context, see Roth, "Whence This Strange fire?", chs. 1–3. Among secular works in politics and government were 6 position statements on the war, 3 New Hampshire valley county convention reports, a report on the state prison located at Windsor, and 14 political addresses (13 Federalist). Several orations were sponsored by Washington Benevolent societies; five political addresses commemorated the Fourth of July, and 4 memorialized Washington's birthday. Washington's *Farewell Address* was reprinted 4 times. See the *Washingtonian*, 1812–16; and Fischer, *Revolution in American Conservatism*.

25. At Walpole, the correspondence of resident partner Anson Whipple, 1812–15, notes shortages in paper and typeface in anticipation of and during the war; the longest works were the first to be delayed. Isaiah Thomas Papers, AAS.

26. McCorison, *Vermont Imprints*, 282–307; and Murray files, culled from Shaw, Shoe-maker, et al., *American Bibliography*, for 1812 (and rechecked).

27. See Walpole, N.H., Accounts of Stock, 1796–1818, Boxes 8–11. Isaiah Thomas Papers, AAS.

28. The absence of bibliographies of imprints of the quality of McCorison's is a serious limitation. The known 1826 total is just one above the 1796 level, and far below the 183 imprints for 1812. Supply by distant producers was far easier in the mid-1820s because of stereotyping and a superior regional transportation system. The 41 known 1826 Vermont-side imprints (from Shaw, Shoemaker, et al., Ready, and Skillen) represent a drop from the 1812 figure of 68 imprints. New Hampshire's 17 imprints are up 2 from 1812, though still well below the 31 for 1796. In 1826 there were 4 Bibles and a dictionary-encyclopedia explaining Biblical terms; a catechism and a sacred music text; 3 sermons, including 2 on death; 4 works of theology and religious experience; 3 denominational publications; and 2 works of benevolent social reform. The apparent decline in sermons (32% to 16%), and in works of devotion and meditation, reflect either the peculiarities of 1826 or our lack of evidence; analysis of all imprints, 1820–30, reveals no such trend. The Burton 1817 quote is in Ludlum, *Social Ferment*, 51–52.

29. Educational imprints included: 5 readers, 3 geographies, 2 arithmetics, 2 spellers, and one each in history and grammar. There were also 2 college-level catalogues, a text in astronomy, and a commencement program. The final item, a catalogue of the Charlestown, N.H., Social Library, included regulations and a list of works owned.

30. Ninety-two percent of all known Upper Valley imprints through 1830 were issued from permanent print centers. The dozen largest areas of stock at Walpole, where detailed records exist for 1796–1818, were exactly replicated in choices of subjects to print locally. See Walpole, N.H., Accounts of Stock, 1796–1818, Boxes 8–11, Isaiah Thomas Papers, AAS.

31. The strength of religion is confirmed in Upper Valley periodical publication through 1830; half were religious.

32. See Roth, "Whence This Strange Fire?"; his *Democratic Dilemma*; Ludlum, *Social Ferment*; and Ward, "Religious Enthusiasm."

33. The voluminous correspondence among printers and publishers in the Isaiah Thomas Papers, AAS, reveals constant checking with publishing conditions in Boston, other eastern cities, and Great Britain.

34. Darnton, "Reading, Writing, and Publishing in Eighteenth Century France," *Daedalus* 100 (1971):214–57, quotes on 226 and 238.

35. Ibid., 224. Rural booksellers' catalogues were rare in the Upper Valley; I have found twelve printed, 1787–1830 (none in the inventories). Catalogues of private libraries, both manuscript and printed, exist, and while they offer one of the closest measures of the reading of elites, they represent an inordinately limited sample of wealthy families. Book reviews are also both valuable and limited, providing an important segment of contemporary opinion – that of particular periodical editors and writers – about specific works. They are of limited utility in systematic study of general reading patterns. We have used periodical reviews extensively in estimating the interpretations of particular works by their readers. Widespread continuing readership of steady sellers presents more complex problems of changing interpretation. Applications to the state (a type of data used by scholars of France in their studies) are not helpful here, as they do not usually give statistics on the number of copies printed of Vermont and New Hampshire imprints. McCorison, *Vermont Imprints*, used existing copyright records.

36. Darnton, "Reading and Writing," 219. Two helpful studies represent fundamental research of the kind most needed. See John E. Molnar, "Publication and Retail Book Advertisements in the Virginia Gazette, 1736–1780," 2 vols. (Ph.D. diss., Univ. of Michigan, 1978). As Molnar puts it, "The present study was predicated upon the premise that materials offered in

the *Gazette* advertisements were indeed purchased by the newspaper's readers" (p. 296). Walter B. Edgar, "The Libraries of Colonial South Carolina" (Ph.D. diss., Univ. of South Carolina, 1969), makes the same assumption about advertisements (pp. 13 and 49–94) but rightly emphasizes the necessity for utilizing many different kinds of sources to understand reading patterns.

37. The process of preparing this evidence for analysis involved three steps: (1) newspaper advertisements were distinguished by type (copyright notice, announcement of local imprints just published, bookstore catalogue, and catalogue of partial "fresh supply"); (2) all imprints were identified (98% success rate); and (3) a procedure was devised to narrow the universe of all works available for sale in Windsor District to popular sellers—works which provide demonstrable evidence of sales.

38. Winthrop Hudson, *Religion in America*, 3rd ed. (New York, 1981), 131ff., 158, 159ff., 182ff., 199–205, 209ff.; Cross, *Burned-Over District*; and Wallace, *Rockdale*.

39. Nathan O. Hatch, "Elias Smith and the Rise of Religious Journalism in the Early Republic," in Joyce et al., *Printing and Society*, 250–77; and Stephen A. Marini, *Radical Sects of Revolutionary America* (Cambridge, Mass., 1982).

40. For an alternative intellectual tradition alongside republicanism, see Appleby, "Republicanism."

41. A few historians, esp. Frank Thistlethwaite, argued for a more intimate connection; see his *America and Atlantic Community: Anglo-American Aspects, 1790–1850* (New York, 1959); and also see John Clive and Bernard Bailyn, "England's Cultural Provinces: Scotland America," WMQ 3s 11 (1954):200–213.

42. See Perry Miller, *The Life of the Mind in America: From the Revolution to the Civil War. Books One Through Three* (New York, 1965), 269–327; George H. Daniels, *American Science in the Age of Jackson* (New York, 1968); John C. Greene, *American Science in the Age of Jefferson* (Ames, Iowa, 1983); and Daniel Calhoun, *The Intelligence of a People* (Princeton, 1975).

43. This discussion is drawn from work in progress on conceptions of the life cycle, 1787–1830.

44. Daniel Boorstin's perspective is relevant here; see esp. *The Americans; The Colonial Experience* (New York, 1958), *The Americans; The National Experience* (New York, 1965), and *The Lost World of Thomas Jefferson* (Boston, 1960); and Appleby, esp. "Republicanism," 20–34.

45. Subtracting the few editions intended for teachers, and adding about an equal number of editions of dictionaries.

46. I have completed extensive research on this subject, to be reported in a future work. In general, see Kerber, *Women of the Republic*, 185–288. Kerber relies on detaile manuscript research which serves as a model for a history of reading.

Chapter 7

1. See Richard Bushman, *Joseph Smith and the Beginnings of Mormonism* (Urbana, Ill., 1984), 9–42.

2. Geib, review of Robert Doherty, *Society and Power: Five New England Towns, 1800–1860*, in the *New England Quarterly* 51 (1978):442–44, quote on 443.

3. See the brilliant essay, Darnton, "Readers Respond to Rousseau," *Great Cat Massacre*, 215–56 and 279–82.

4. See Natalie Davis, "Printing and the People," 189–226; LeRoy Ladurie, *Peasants*; and Rutman, *American Puritanism*, 74–80, quote on 74. Rutman also adds a fourth category—those within each category "not particularly influenced by the preachers."

5. See esp. Doherty, *Society and Power; Five New England Towns, 1800–1860* (Amherst, Mass., 1977); Bernard Farber, *Guardians of Virtue: Salem Families in 1800* (New York, 1972);

Stephen Davis, "From Ploughshares," on Dedham; Daniel Scott Smith, "Population, Family, and Society in Hingham, Massachusetts, 1635–1880" (Ph.D. diss., Univ. of California at Berkeley, 1973); William Willingham, "Windham Connecticut: Profile of a Revolutionary Community, 1775–1818" (Ph.D. diss., Northwestern Univ., 1972); Charles Danhoff's helpful *Change in Agriculture: The Northern United States, 1820–1870* (Cambridge, Mass., 1969); Cook, *The Fathers of the Towns*; and Roth, "Whence This Strange Fire?"; and *Democratic Dilemma*.

6. See Walker, *Dictionary*; Perry, *Royal Standard*; and Webster, *A Compendious Dictionary* and *American Dictionary* "employment," "labor," "occupation," and "work."

7. See Jackson T. Main, *The Social Structure of Revolutionary America* (Princeton, 1965); Fischer, "America"; Prude, *Coming of Industrial Order*, 7–13; and Geib, "Changing Works," esp. 92–148. On female work patterns, see Norton, *Liberty's Daughters*, chs. 1 and 5; and Cott, *Bonds of Womanhood*, 19–62.

8. Wives owned some personal property not recorded in inventories; no regular evidence of the specifics has been found. On the rights of widows, and married women's property rights in Vermont, see the following Vt. Probate Laws: 1787, 1793, 1797, 1804, 1816, 1818, 1821, 1823, 1824, and 1829. Items "exempted from execution" in 1779–97 included "such household goods as are necessary for the support of life" (*Vt. Laws of 1779:* 59). Thereafter, a widow kept "her apparel, and such other personal estate, as the judge of probate shall think proper, according to her quality and degree" (*Vt. Laws of 1797*, p. 225, and repeated until the 1821 *Laws*. Except as part of a dower, the status of printed items used mainly by wives and young women is unclear in Vermont probate law through 1830. Gifted works were almost surely exempted. Single women — *femme sole* — who married during the term of a probate court proceeding were rendered legally dead. The chilling wording in the law was: "all the trust and authority of such administratrix, in and over such estate [a *femme sole* as an estate administrator] shall thereupon cease" (*Laws of 1816*, ch. 132).

9. Simeon Ide, "Reminiscences," *Centennial Memorial of Windsor, Vermont, July 4, 1876* (Windsor, 1876), quote on 39. Not all village lots were small (10 acres or under) or all townships lots large, so size is not an infallible guide to actual location. Local history and map sources confirm these findings. Gentleman farm households (25) were drawn from WDPR vols. 1–12; and see app. 3, n. 9.

10. For example, Lot Norton, Weathersfield, 1813, WDPR 6:250ff., 274–80, and 8:475ff.; Nathan Adams, Plymouth, 8:231–33; Abner Bisbee, Springfield, 1819, 8:unpaged, and 1810 Federal Census — 70 yds. wool, 60 yds. linen annually; and Elias Watkins, Chester, 1813, 6:300ff. and 613ff., and 1810 Federal Census — 160 yds. wool, 200 yds. linen annually. Other services gentleman farm families engaged in included justice of the peace, probate court clerk, and postrider delivery.

11. Gentleman farm households mostly consisted of family, kin, and fosterlings, plus an occasional single apprentice. Newspaper advertisements and notices culled from all Windsor District weeklies through 1830 reveal the persistence of apprenticeship. Fosterlings show up in guardianship records; see *Windsor District Guardian Records, 1805–55* 2 reels, microfilm copy, Vermont Public Records Division, Montpelier, Vt. Family size was calculated from U.S. Census schedules for Vermont, 1790–1830.

12. This discussion of yeoman-husbandman farm households is drawn from analysis of the 152 yeoman-husbandman inventories with books, briefer analysis of those without books (about 115), and the other sources listed in app. 3, n. 9. See also Main, *Social Structure*, 218; and Liddle, "Virtue and Liberty."

13. Evidence exists in 82 cases. See, e.g., Joseph Pierce, Chester, 1809 WDPR 5:343ff.; Samuel Page, Saltash [Plymouth] 1796, 2:294ff.; Richard Guild, Chester, 1820, 8:unpaged; and David Burton, Andover, 1822, 9:336ff.

14. For examples of families devoting significant time to public affairs, see James Whitney, Ludlow, 1813, WDPR 6:315ff.; and William Hosmer, Sr., Chester, 1813, 6:467ff. and 499ff. Stephen Davis examines specialization, in "From Plowshares," 160–89.

15. On tenancy, see Danhof, *Change in Agriculture*, 87–94; and Donald L. Winters, *Farmers Without Farms: Agricultural Tenancy in 19th Century Iowa* (Westport, Conn., 1978), 14 and 106–107. Overall Windsor District tenancy rates (about 15%) are in the same range as two-fifths of Iowa counties during their initial decades of settlement, 1845–75, versus 18%–22% in the remaining three-fifths of Iowa counties. The present discussion is drawn from analysis of the 47 tenant farm household inventories containing libraries, briefer analysis of inventories without printed matter (38), and the materials in app. 3, n. 9. See also VtR&J, 3 July 1830.

16. Two families engaged in artisan activity; another household, that of a single free black male over 45, Aaron Burdow, engaged in sheep raising and the home production of wool. For Brownson, see Stockbridge, Vt., Town Meeting Minutes, 1801–03: Vt. Public Records Division, Montpelier, Vt. For a very different pattern of experience in central Massachusetts, see Prude, *Coming of Industrial Order*, 3–33 and 67–132.

17. See Webster, *American Dictionary*, 2. Comparative data from elsewhere in New England (e.g., Bidwell, *Rural Economy*, 262–68) points to a slightly larger share of semiskilled laborer families. The present discussion is drawn from analysis of 25 family inventories with libraries, briefer analysis of 23 without libraries, and materials cited in app. 3, n. 9. See the discussion of Roth's evidence in Part C below, and table 7–2.

18. Household size and composition were calculated from U.S. Censuses, 1790–1840. On work activities see, e.g., Polly McRoberts, Springfield, 1829, WDPR 11:488ff.; Susannah Bagley, Windsor, 1814, 7:500ff. and 8:m.p.; and Captain James Martin, Springfield, 1801, 2:9ff. For typical families see Sally Lewis, Windsor, 1825, 10:150ff.; and Moses Blanchard, Reading, 1818, 7:140ff. For a slightly later period see Roth, "When This Strange Fire?", 576–79; he categorizes this group as farm laborers. By 1828 there were farm laborers who just happened to live in hamlets, villages, or farm households out in townships. For the earlier period, living situation within a township, combined with work experience flowing from household placement, yields the most accurate evidence of occupation (see table 7–2).

19. For a fascinating portrait of artisan experience in an urban setting, see Wilentz, *Chants Democratic*.

20. Hitherto this process had only begun among professional families in rural areas. See Daniel Calhoun, *Professional Lives in America, Structure and Aspiration, 1750–1850* (Cambridge, Mass., 1965). The discussion of artisan families is drawn from analysis of 49 artisan household inventories with family libraries, briefer analysis of 6 families without collections, and the materials in app. 3, n. 9. Research on artisan lifecenters on cities. In addition to Wilentz, see Laurie, *Working People*, 25ff., quote on 26; Howard Rock, *Artisans of the New Republic: The Tradesmen of New York City in the Age of Jefferson* (New York, 1979); and I.J. Prothero, *Artisans and Politics in Early Nineteenth Century London: John Gast and His Times* (Baton Rouge, La., 1979). On rural artisans, see Geib, "Changing Works," 137–40; and Prude, *Coming of Industrial Order*, xi, 71, 121, 133, 143, 219, 235, and 262.

21. See table N-2.

22. See Bidwell, *Rural Economy*, 262–68. Bidwell quoted Tench Coxe to the effect that even village artisans owned land, hence almost all farmed. Actually, 40% of Windsor District artisan families owned not a rod of land; they rented. Moreover, a quarter of artisan families did not farm at all. Geib, "Changing Works," 137–40 found "few full time" artisans (4 of 204 families) at Brookfield, 1785–1820. Crop produce in storage may mean production on that homestead or it may mean payment for services rendered.

Table N-2: Wealth of Artisan Households at Inventory

Wealth (in $)	Number of Families	Percent of Families	Cumulative Wealth of Artisan Households (percent)
251–500	12	25	——
501–1000	14	28	53
1001–2000	11	23	75
2001–3000	5	10	85
3001–5000	5	10	95
5001–6000	2	4	100

23. Throughout this book I have relied on Eric Sloane, *A Museum of Early American Tools* (New York, 1973), quote on 90.

24. Roth, *Democratic Dilemma* studies economic leadership in detail. Commerce and trading is a variant of Stephanie Wolf's usage in *Urban Village: Population, Community, and Family Structure in Germantown, Pennsylvania, 1683–1800* (Princeton, 1976), ch.3, esp. 107. Bidwell, *Rural Economy*, 256–62, includes artisans as well. This discussion of commerce and trading families is drawn from analysis of inventories of 45 households with private libraries, briefer analysis of those without collections (12 or so), and materials cited in app. 3, n. 9. Average wealth would be $7,100 without the semifeudal estate of Thomas Fullerton, Esq., worth $85,041 in 1825, WDPR 10:22ff., 13:632ff., and 14:510ff. Just one female-headed household (Mary Leverett) appears among the 45 families (39 with acreage).

25. For typical shares, see Elisha Phelps, Windsor, 1819, WDPR 8:194ff., shares in two banks; and Daniel Brooks, Springfield, 1817, 8:296ff., 4 shares in a cotton and woolen factory.

26. For illustrations of these trends, see Nathan Sprague, Plymouth, 1812, WDPR 6:108ff.; John White, Springfield, 1826, 10:442ff.; and Watts Hubbard, Windsor, 1802, WDPR 4:150ff.; Hill, Ludlow, 1809, 5:338ff. and 455ff. ($460); Captain Ebenezer Lakin, Plymouth, 1808, 5:278–93, and 324ff.; and for Fullerton, see n. 24 above. Also see Horace Hubbard and Justus Dartt, *History of the Town of Springfield, Vermont, with a Genealogical Record, 1752–1895* (Boston, 1895), 39 and 142–43; and Hamilton Child, *Gazetteer and business directory of Windsor County, Vt., for 1883–84* (Syracuse, N. Y., 1883).

27. For apprentices, see, e.g., Blake, Chester, 1813, WDPR 16:500. For politically active figures, see, e.g., Salmon Dutton, Cavendish, 1824, 10:30ff.

28. This discussion of manufacturing families is drawn from an analysis of the 7 families with private libraries, briefer analysis of those without collections (3), and the materials in app. 3, n. 9. See also Horwitz, *Anthropology*, 68–69; and Wallace, *Rockdale*.

29. This discussion of professional families is drawn from an analysis of 33 (all) inventories with private libraries, and the materials cited in app. 3, n. 9.

30. See Sargeant, Chester, 1818, WDPR 7:476ff.; Smith, Windsor, 1825, 10:200ff.; and Mann, Chester, 1824, 9:304ff.

31. Four of five deacons lived out on farmsteads. They have been grouped with professional families in keeping with usage in the Upper Valley. They designated themselves as deacon by occupation and also in all legal documents; in addition, they held a highly respected, semiprofessional status in the denominations they belonged to.

32. See, e.g., Lucius Hubbard, Chester, 1809, WDPR 5:271ff.

33. In median wealth, commerce and trading families were 29 and 18 times wealthier than

semiskilled laborer and tenant farm families, respectively. See Braudel, *Wheels of Commerce*, 2: 466–67.

34. For another perspective, one with which I largely disagree, see Prude, *Coming of Industrial Order*, 12–13; he stresses the "limited consequences" of material inequality and believes that "affluent citizens enjoyed only limited leverage over the less wealthy" and that there was "no way—no continuing, established institutional structure—through which wealth was translated into domineering economic power."

35. In general, see Jackson T. Main, *Social Structure*, 7–43. Families without land included all 47 tenant farm families: 21 semiskilled laborer families (84%); 20 artisan families (40%); 10 professional families (30%); 1 manufacturing family (14%); and 6 commerce and trading families (13%). Upper Valley land varied greatly in quality and provides only an indirect measure of economic wellbeing. Main, *Connecticut Society*, (Hartford, 1977), 12, finds that "fully one-third of the men owned little property"; see also 15 and 17–22. Robert Gross found that a quarter of the Concord, Mass., population was landless in 1771, rising to 42% in 1801 and to 56% in 1826. See Gross, "Culture and Cultivation: Agriculture and Society in Thoreau's Concord," JAH 69 (1982):42–61. Land shortage began in the 1820s in Windsor District.

36. In addition to 383 families with full data, another 13 families have print items enumerated but only partial supporting data. To compare differences in wealth levels between households with and without printed matter, I took each fifth year in 1803–1830, and included all estates. During these years 133 inventories were probated: 84 with printed matter (63%), exactly the share for all inventories probated through 1830.

37. As Gloria Main notes, the issue is the degree to which probate inventories harbor sources of bias which distort the picture of society contained in those records. See Main, "Probate Records as a Source for Early American History," WMQ 3s 32 (1975):88–99, esp. 96; her marvelous *Tobacco Colony: Life in Early Maryland, 1650–1720* (Princeton, 1983); Jackson T. Main, *Society and Economy in Colonial Connecticut* (Princeton, 1985); Daniel Scott Smith, "Underregistration and Bias in Probate Records: An Analysis of Data from Eighteenth Century Hingham, Massachusetts," WMQ 3s 32 (1975):100–112; Alice H. Jones, *American Colonial Wealth*, 3 vols. (New York, 1977), and her *The Wealth of a Nation To Be* (New York, 1980); Linda Auwers's review of *The Wealth of a Nation To Be* in *Historical Methods* 12 (1979):39–45; Gilmore, "Elementary Literacy," 145; and Kett and McClung, "Book Culture," 106.

38. Tax lists also have limitations. Roth first analyzed tax lists for six townships in 1828, at the end of the period we are concentrating on. A full analysis of the proportion of occupations for these townships is not presented; Roth's data is for household heads who were members of seven mainstream Protestant denominations. Unitarians, Freewill Baptists, the "Christian" sect, and all nonchurch members ("in the best of times the churches reached fewer than half of the valley's adult males") are absent. Thus, his sample includes about 45% of all "adult male tax payers and household heads." It is likely that semiskilled laborer and tenant farm families are underrepresented by tax data. See Roth, "Whence This Strange Fire?", 477 and 576. Important for comparative purposes is the array of townships studied. Four of the six were river valley townships, and the data is esp. biased toward manufacturing communities and major marketing towns like Windsor. The majority of all Upper Valley townships were in the hill country (foothill and upland townships such as Andover, Weston, Ludlow, Reading, Baltimore, and Plymouth); this group is absent. Likewise, the far smaller but nonetheless significant number of internal crossroads townships, with active hamlets (e.g., Cavendish) but no sizable villages, and internal market towns (e.g., Chester) are also absent. With these limitations in mind, Roth's analysis is enormously helpful. To facilitate accurate comparison, I have rearranged Roth's occupational designation system.

39. Roth, "Whence This Strange Fire?", 576–78, admits that he "left a good deal of white

collar wage earners as Journeyman/Laborers." I find virtually no clerks among deceased household heads through 1830. Roth defines clerks as heads whose full-time occupation was clerk, government employee, or teacher. It is also the case that some commerce and trading families appear as journeyman/laborer in Roth's occupational scale.

40. I picked Plymouth, Weston, and Reading because I had studied their deeds for an earlier study of male and female literacy trends (see ch. 3).

41. Roth included Windsor, West Windsor, and Weathersfield from Windsor District. Roth's and my emphases differ primarily because of our different research agendas. I have the highest admiration for his work.

42. The relative wealth of yeoman farm families also increased with time. Jackson T. Main, *Social Structure*, 7–43, reports that an eighth of Revolutionary era yeoman farm inventories had personal estates below £50 (about $165), whereas only 4% did so in the early national era. Even a greater difference obtained for artisan families. Main found that about 30% "left very small estates" (under $165), whereas only 8% of Windsor District artisan families were below $200, and 12% were below $250 a generation later.

43. This includes relatively minor (15%–20%) overlap with column 2. Some wills include summary wealth data but no inventory; most wills are of estates inventoried, with or without libraries.

44. Converted from pounds to dollars at the value used in Windsor District, 1787–1830: one pound =$3.33, with minor fluctuations of +/− 4%. For conversions, see Simmons, Andover, 1797, WDPR 2:418ff.; Philbrook, Reading, 1797, 2:264ff.; and, outside the valley at New Haven in 1802, in Francis James Gagliardi, "The Babcocks of New Haven, Connecticut: Printers, Publishers, and Booksellers, with a Bibliographical Checklist of their Publications, 1764–1800" (Master's thesis, Southern Connecticut State College, 1965), 66. In general, see Jackson T. Main, *Social Stucture*, 42–43; and Willingham, "Windham," 72 and 241ff.

45. See Gloria Main, "Probate Records," 98; and n. 37 above.

46. See Jackson T. Main, *Social Structure*, ch.9, 270ff.; and Alice Jones, *Wealth of a Nation*, 35, 44ff., 162–64, and 172–74.

47. Actually there were 91, but in 4 cases the family also retained a share in a lending library. Thus, their habit of reading was considerably more developed than at first glance appears to be the case.

48. See n.37 above.

49. See n. 44 for money conversions.

50. See Atwood, Windsor, 1797, WDPR 2:324ff., and Child, *Windsor Gazetteer*, 116. Also see Susannah Bagley, Windsor, 1814, 7:500ff. and 8:n.p., listed as a semiskilled laborer. Bagley had lived most of her adult life as the spouse of a comfortable artisan cabinetmaker, and the family owned a farm.

51. Dugger, "Book Trades in Missouri," 103, comments on the flexibility of the link between wealth and ownership of printed matter. See also Slotow and Stevens, *Rise of Literacy*, 79–80 and 200–01.

Chapter 8

1. See Jonathan Kozol, *Illiterate America* (New York, 1985).

2. See VJ, 5 Jan. 1807; and VtC, 28 Nov. 1828. On European patterns see Ward, *Fiction and the German Reading Public*; Wiles, "Relish for Reading;" Barney Milstein, *Eight Eighteenth Century Reading Societies: A Sociological Contribution to the History of German Literature* (Bern, 1972); and Darnton, *Business of Enlightenment*, 319ff. Information about Windsor District reading beyond the bounds of the homestead in 1780–1830 is limited: genre paintings depict widespread informal reading, especially of newspapers and broadsides, in village and hamlet public places.

Several libraries offered avenues to reading, sometimes including reading on the premises: occasional Sunday school libraries (after 1815) for children and early youth; academy libraries at Cavendish, Chester, Windsor, and Reading; college and literary society libraries at Dartmouth and Middlebury colleges, and at the Univ. of Vermont for a handful of Windsor District students; and eleven social, moral, and circulating libraries. For an interesting study of the Dartmouth Literary Society library, see Simpson, "Development and Scope."

3. Lending libraries were established at Windsor (and a moral library at West Windsor), Springfield, Chester, Cavendish, Reading, Andover, and Weston. We have included all known evidence in our analysis.

4. Among many studies of early American inventories see: Richard B. Davis, *Colonial South, Jefferson's Virginia*, and *A Colonial Southern Bookshelf: Reading in the Eighteenth Century* (Athens, Ga., 1979); Jackson T. Main, *Social Structure*, esp. ch. 8; Edgar, "Libraries"; H.H. Dugger, "Reading Interests and the Book Trade in Frontier Missouri" (Ph.D. diss., Univ. of Missouri, 1951); Michael Harris, "Books on the Frontier: The Extent and Nature of Book Ownership in Southern Indiana, 1800–1850," *Library Quarterly* 42 (1972):416–30; and Joseph T. Wheeler, "Literacy Culture and 18th Century Maryland," *Maryland Historical Magazine* 34 (1943):273–76. See also the many works of Edwin Wolf, 2nd, esp. "Great American Book Collectors to 1800," *Gazetteer of the Grolier Club* 16 (June 1971):3–25; the Introduction to Marie Korey, ed., *The Books of Isaac Norris (1701–1766) at Dickinson College* (Carlisle, Pa., 1976); *The Library of James Logan of Philadelphia, 1674–1791* (Philadelphia, 1974); and "The Library of Ralph Assheton: The Book Background of a Colonial Philadelphia Lawyer," PBSA 58 (1964):345–79.

5. See Cavendish Social Library Records, 1815–33, VHS; and ch. 9 below for a discussion of passing around books within a family. No family retained more than one share of any single lending library. For uses of the term "neighborhood" see, e.g., "An Act for the Settlement of Testate and Intestate Estates," *Acts and Laws of the State of Vermont. 1779* (Dresden, 1779).

6. Webster, *A Compendious Dictionary* and *American Dictionary*; John Walker, *Critical*; and William Perry, *Royal Standard*: "library," "collection." A "collection" was consistently defined as "things gathered together," and "the body formed by gathering an assemblage" or "an assembly." Webster added that a collection also referred to a single book, in the case of "a book compiled from other books by the putting together of parts," such as "a collection of essays or sermons." Webster's 1828 dictionary added that these collections belonged "to a private person or to a public institution or a company." Usage of library, family library, and private library abounds, e.g., in WDPR 9:135 and 12:160; and in the loose Isaac N. Curtineus inventory, 27 Apr. 1824, Misc. Coll. of Inventories, VHS. For a professional household distinguishing between family and professional libraries, see WDPR 12:160 and the Curtineus inventory.

7. On Bible reading, see Lorenzo Dow, *The Life and Travels of Lorenzo Dow* (Hartford, Conn., 1804), 8–9 and 43. For an example of contemporary commentary on Bible reading, see *The Hive*, 23–27. On the Bible as a sacred encyclopedia, see *American Penny Magazine and Family Newspaper*, Feb. 15, 1845, p. 30. For Vermont editions of the Bible, see McCorison, *Vermont Imprints*, and the three *Additions and Corrections*: for the massive one-volume edition of the *Bible*, see Windsor, 1812, and Brattleboro, 1817, editions, pp. 287 and 379. The two most popular multi-volume Bibles were Thomas Scott, *The Holy Bible*, 6th ed., 6 vols. (Boston, 1817–18); and Philip Doddridge's New Testament *Family Expositor*, 6 vol. (Charlestown, Mass., 1807–8). One version of the Family Bible (by Thomas Scott) included only the New Testament. See Margaret Hill, ed., *The English Bible in America: A Bibliography of Editions of the Bible & the New Testament Published in America, 1777–1957* (New York, 1961), 20 and 26. For placement of family libraries, see Chester, Vt., *Freedom's Banner:* 6 Jan. 1829.

8. On wives purchasing portions of the library, see Edgar, "Libraries of Colonial South Carolina," 12 and 67. Little evidence of specifically "female books" appears in the Windsor Dis-

trict inventories of female household heads. On women and family education, see Kerber, "Daughters," and *Women of the Republic*, chs. 7–9; and ch. 1 above.

9. See McCorison, *Vermont Imprints*, for imprints. In general, see William McLoughlin, *Revivals, Awakenings, and Reform* (Chicago, 1979).

10. See Henry Brownson, *Early Life*, I: 1–63; and Orestes Brownson, *The Convert; or, Leaves from My Experience* (New York, 1857), 1–35.

11. I used the New York, 1804, ed. of Pitt; the New York, 1824, ed. of Bennett; the Exeter, N.H., 1793, ed. of Watts; the Philadelphia, 1800, ed. of Mathias; and the New York, 1803 (2 vols.), ed. of Miller. For encouragement of adult reading, see fairly popular works such as Thomas James Mathias's *The Pursuits of Literature* and Samuel Miller's *A Brief Retrospect of the Eighteenth Century*; and autobiographies such as Dow, *Life and Travels*, 4–5, 8–9, 12–13, 43, and 304.

12. By 1815, for instance, the VJ carried over 100 excerpts, at least 50 comments encouraging reading, and several pieces recommending works to read each year.

13. Metabasist added that private libraries were started either because their owners "love books, or because they would wish to be thought to have a taste for reading." The Windsor *Morning Ray*, 29 May 1792, reprinted from the Danbury, Conn., *Farmer's Journal*, 30 Apr. 1792. The general attitude of the author may be seen in the other 16 numbers of the series published in 1792. In general, see Reilly, "The Wages of Piety," esp. 104–17, and Richard D. Brown, "Spreading the Word."

14. See Darnton, "Readers Respond," and Gilmore, "The Mystic Chords of Memory." The progress of literacy in the Upper Valley, the small size and limited range of most family libraries, and their limited wealth proves largely false these contentions as well as that many families in 1787–1830 retained coffee table books. Uncut pages, books inherited over several generations and disregarded, and casual buying habits are noted as evidence for the second assumption. My experience, working with rare books for twenty years, has been that uncut pages usually appear only in a handful of volumes of uncertain provenance. Some of these would have been copies unsold at the time. Only a small minority of the 5,630 volumes held by 396 ordinary rural New England households could have been inherited from before the Revolution. These works were just as likely more revered as less revered than contemporary purchases. No substantial evidence supports the hypothesis that inherited works were treated casually and regularly disregarded; few commodities were, and few other aspects of family heritage.

15. This is the argument of Ginzburg, *Cheese and the Worms*.

16. See Hall, "The Uses of Literacy," 1–47; and Bernhard Fabian, "English Books and Their Eighteenth-Century German Readers," in Korshin, *The Widening Circle*, esp. 169–75. The original research and interpretation reported by Fabian is that of Rolf Engelsing. On wisdom and reading, see Rusche, "Empire of Reason," esp. 253–302, quotes on 254–55, 294, and 317; and contemporary understanding of "wisdom" in the dictionaries cited in n. 31 below, esp. Webster's 1828 dictionary and Johnson's dictionary. For further confirmation, I sampled the books and pamphlets conveniently grouped under "wisdom" and "knowledge" in the ASS *Dictionary Catalogue*, 20:377–81.

17. Buckingham, *Boston Courier*, 9 Apr. 1849 (semiweekly version); *New England Magazine* 2:7 (1 Jan. 1832), 46; Catherine Beecher, *The Poganuc People*, (New York, 1878), where she describes her own upbringing in the study of her father, Lyman Beecher. See Barbara Cross, "Stowe, Harriet Beecher," in *Notable American Women, 1607–1950: A Biographical Dictionary*, ed. Edward T. James, Janet Wilson James, and Paul S. Boyer, 3 vols. (Cambridge, Mass., 1971), 3:394.

18. See Fabian, "English Books." Engelsing coined this term; see his "Die Perioden" and *Der Burger als Leser*. For the Cutting quote, see the epigraph to ch. 1.

19. Keate (Boston, 1793), 59–66; see also "Light Reading," VtC 23 Feb. 1827.

20. Febvre and Martin, *Coming of the Book*, quote on 288. Also see Hall, "The World of Printing" and "The Uses of Literacy."

21. George K. Smart, "Private Libraries in Colonial Virginia," *American Literature* 10 (1938): 24–52, quote on 25. See also Michael Harris, "Books on the Indiana Frontier," 428; Louis Wright, "The Purposeful Reading of Our Colonial Ancestors," *E.L.H. A Journal of English Literary History* 4 (1937):85–111, esp. 86 and 88; H. Trevor Colbourn, *The Lamp of Experience: Whig History and the Intellectual Origins of the American Revolution* (New York, 1974), v; Edgar, "Libraries of Colonial South Carolina," ch. 16, 171ff.; and Richard B. Davis, *A Colonial Southern Bookshelf*, 8.

22. Death rates vary greatly among communities: compared with Middleborough, Mass., 1779–1801 (Willingham, "Windham," p. 69), Windsor District's 643 probated inventories, 1787–1830, represent 10% –20% of household heads dying through 1830; but compared with evidence for Windham, Conn., 1780–1817 (Isaac Thompson, "Bill of Mortality of the town of Middleborough, from the year 1779 to 1801," *Collections of the Mass. Historical Society for the Year 1801*, 8:180), Windsor District evidence represents about 40%–45% of those deceased. No evidence of actual death rates has yet been located for the district or the area immediately surrounding it. Seven other inventories have either a title which cannot be made out due to a mark on the original manuscript page (which cannot be deciphered), or an ambiguous reference to what may be a blank-page, lined notebook. These seven cases have been excluded throughout; they would only raise the total by 1%. All WDPR 1787–1830 records were checked three times. Because of the mass of data (12 record books of 450–550 pp. each plus loose records), it is highly recommended that at least three separate sweeps be made.

23. Inventories fairly represent all three zones of access and participation in print communications. To discuss the full range of family library holdings, we have classified all works retained in the 396 libraries. Decoding the spine or binder's title identification system allowed us to locate and read nearly all approximately 1,250 titles (5,630 volumes). In doing so I constructed a classification system based on both the actual contents of the works and the contemporary classification system within which they were understood. This study expands on John Demos's pathbreaking efforts in the material culture of colonial Plymouth, described in *A Little Commonwealth: Family Life in Plymouth Colony* (New York, 1970). Inventories probated in 1831–36 were added to follow the trend slightly beyond the period under analysis. Inventories increased quite suddenly, doubling in 1812, and sustaining the higher rate over the next quarter century. The population increase in 1790–1810 was 143%, dropping off sharply to just 10%, 1810–40.

24. The share of the very largest libraries, of 15 or more volumes, rose from 8% in 1787–1800, to 11% in 1801–15, and then exploded in the 1816–30 years to 25% of all libraries retained. Large libraries were growing in size as well as in prevalence. The average size of libraries of 15 or more volumes rose from 27 in 1787–1800, to 38 in 1801–15, and to 81 in 1816–30 (60 without the John Leverett library of 909 volumes). Also see Edgar, "Libraries of Colonial South Carolina," 216; and Joseph T. Wheeler, "Literary Culture."

25. Both areas profited from reasonable proximity to a major regional printing center (Boston and Cincinnati). See Michael Harris, "Books of the Frontier," esp. 418 and the table on 419, which shows 469 of 2,338 or 20%. Harris's totals for 469 southern Indiana libraries, 1800–50, drawn from all inventories, are listed in titles rather than total volumes, therefore his percentages will slightly understate the size of Indiana libraries. That Harris's findings include two later decades counterbalances this difference.

26. Ibid.. See Michael Harris, *The General Store*; "Books Stocked by Six Indiana General Stores," JLH 9 (1974):66–72; and "Books for Sale on The Illinois Frontier," *American Book Collector* 21 (1971):15–17. Also see Dugger, "Reading Interests in Missouri," 47 and 100–104; Freeman

H. Hart, *The Valley of Virginia in the American Revolution, 1763–1789* (Chapel Hill, N.C., 1942), 167; and Soltow and Stevens, *Rise of Literacy*, 68–70, and n. 36 and 37, pp. 212–13.

27. Samual E. Morison, *The Puritan Pronoas: Studies in the Intellectual Life of New England in the 17th Century* (New York, 1936), 138; Jackson T. Main, *Social Structure*, 254–55; Joseph Wheeler, "Literary Culture," 273–76; Edgar, "The Libraries of Colonial South Carolina," 15ff., who reports rates of 43.6% for 4,700 inventories, 1737–76; and Kett and McClung, "Book Culture," 109ff. and tables at end of essay.

28. Even in frontier Missouri during these same decades, where the share of family libraries with 10 or more titles reached a third, it must be remembered that the proportion of families retaining libraries outside St. Louis was exceptionally low (30%–40%). With 77,860 residents in 1850, St. Louis had become the eighth largest city in the country. Dugger, "Reading Interests in Missouri," 106ff.; and on St. Louis see McKelvey, *American Urbanization*, table on p. 37. Wheeler found that about a quarter of Maryland family libraries, 1700–76, contained more than 10 titles: Jackson T. Main, *Social Structure*, 256, citing Wheeler's evidence. The proportion of libraries with more than 20 titles in Windsor District parallels the findings for Missouri, including St. Louis, 1800–1840.

29. See Gilmore, "Elementary Literacy"; Johansson, *History of Literacy*; and Gregory A. Stiverson,"Books Both Useful and Entertaining; Reading Habits in Mid-Eighteenth Century Virginia." *Southern Librarian* 24 (1975):52–58. A subscription list containing a few Vermont residents survives for Orestes Brownson's *The Philanthropist*, Ithaca, N. Y., 1831–32, Brownson Papers, Univ. of Notre Dame Archives, South Bend, Ind.

30. Each of the 396 libraries was examined as a unit, and then libraries were organized into groups by similarities in holdings.

31. This was the most basic distinction in forms of knowledge shared throughout rural New England. It was drawn from my reading of the contents of 98% of all titles (the other 2% could not be identified). Clear statements of the distinction are found in the dictionaries of N. Bailey, J. Walker, W. Perry, C. Alexander, T. Sheridan (and T. Sheridan, *Improved*), W. Woodbridge, S. Johnson, and N. Webster (1806, 1817, 1828, and 1837). These comprise all dictionaries widely available for sale and retained in Windsor District libraries through 1840 (see table 2–1).

32. See Lockridge, *Literacy in Colonial New England.*

33. No scholarly or professional works – either in theology, on the sacred side; or in law, medicine, or a dozen related areas, on the secular side – nor any periodicals were retained by this group of families.

34. A rather puzzling absence from this type of library was any significant trace of devotional reading or works concerned with moral uplift.

35. An exception was made for the Leverett library (69%) because of its collection of secular works (620 volumes); the share of extensive reading works in all other cases but one well exceeded 80%. Even excluding the Leveretts' holdings, major secular extensive libraries averaged 51 volumes per library. The most typical sacred reading included a Bible or New Testament, often with a compendium, plus a hymnal or psalm book, one or more devotional works or prayer books, and more rarely, a religious periodical or theological treatise. The library of the Elisha Phelps family is illustrative. This was a rich ($38,222) Windsor commerce and trading family. Phelps's wife Susannah, four small children (two sons and two daughters), and two youths (male and female) between 16 and 25 survived him at his death in 1819. The library contained 59 volumes. Modern literature dominated, with 20 volumes. One lot was clustered together in the Phelps' cherry bookcase above a desk in the living room in this sequence: Dryden's *Virgil*, Wirt's *Letters of the British Spy*, Johnson's *Lives of the Poets*, a couple of recent minor collections of tales, Cowper's *Collected Poems*, and Thomson's *Seasons*. Separated from this group were

Pope's *Homer, Don Quixote*, 2 other minor works, and 6 volumes of a major American literary periodical, the *Analectic Magazine*, featuring Irving, Paulding, and Verplanck. History was also prominent, with 14 volumes. Bigland's very popular Christian perspective, *A View of the World*, and his *Letters on History* were present, alongside Marshall's *Washington*. Prentiss's *Life of Eaton* and a work on the French Revolution were also paired. Next was Samuel William's *Natural and Civil History of Vermont*, paired with another work in natural history, Preston's *Wonders of Creation*. Stage-of-life works represented the third largest cluster of volumes (11). One work, *The Wife*, offered a plan of domestic life and a list of duties, while another was a collection of Elizabeth Hamilton's *Letters on Education*. Both were probably read by Mrs. Phelps and her oldest daughter. A six-volume edition of Willich's *Domestic Encyclopedia* contained much of interest to several family members. Two other works, the *Young Gentleman's and Ladies Magazine* and Blair's *Lectures on Rhetoric*, probably served the youth and perhaps their parents. No works in philosophy or political thought were retained. Bigland and Williams offered the only detailed forays into geography. Theology and religious affairs were represented by 4 volumes of the leading organ of the Protestant Episcopal Church, the *Churchman's Magazine*. See WDPR 8:194ff.; and U.S. Census for 1810, Vermont: Windsor.

36. See, for instance, WDPR, 12:158, where the "Family Library" and the "Law Library" are distinguished in the estate of the John P. Williams family of Chester. We will use the generic term "family library" to include all print items retained, distinguishing further in discussion of the particular occupations of household heads.

37. Only one volume appeared in Alden Spooner's inventory, despite his long publishing career, editorship of the VJ, and a four-term career in the Vermont legislature. Perhaps he gave to his wife, or otherwise gave away or disposed of printed matter before his death. See WDPR 11:160–69.

Chapter 9

1. Thomas C. Cochran, *Frontiers of Change: Early Industrialization in the United States* (New York, 1981), 11.

2. See McCoy, *Elusive Republic*, 13–47. On mending, see, for instance, Lydia Baldwin's Diary, MS-B-B1930, 4, for 20 Jan. 1796, VHS; the John Campbell Diary, 1, for 4 and 7 Mar. 1807, NHHS; Comfort Chafee's Account Book, MSC 150, 30 Mar. 1821, VHS; and the Diary of Nathan K. Abbott, 1:131 (May, 1845) and 2:63 (May, 1849), NHHS. See also Bushman, *Joseph Smith*.

3. Rusche, "An Empire of Reason," ch. 6; see Kaestle, *Pillars of the Republic*, ch. 2.

4. For a work with a very limited subscription, see the list for a three-volume edition of Edward Young, *The Works of Rev. E. Young* (Charlestown, Mass., 1811). The list included 17 Windsor District families; 16 of these were residents of the fortunate village or farmstead human habitats.

5. A full analysis of material and cultual life in each of the five types of human habitats has been completed and will be presented in a future work. Here we can give only a brief summary of a very detailed study (1,100 pp. in manuscript). Families without a private library or borrowing records in a lending library remain silent in this analysis; within the limited confines of each human habitat, their lives were partly shaped, and therefore may be partly represented, by the values and beliefs of families with private libraries. But further research is necessary.

6. Beyond data for a few intellectuals, relatively little has been published about the reading experience and the interpretation and influence of texts. Elizabeth Eisenstein wisely alerts us to the danger of simply assuming the influence of a work on a particular "class" of readers. An assumed audience or public expresses the intentionality of the writer, and may or may not have constituted actual readership. Eisenstein notes, for instance, that "booklets pertaining to

the behavior of young ladies did not necessarily attract feminine readers and were probably also of interest to male tutors, or confessors or guardians." But surely Eisenstein means "*exclusively* female readers"; in rural New England, diaries make plain that while others may have also read them, booklets on the behavior of young ladies were regularly read by this group. Her useful distinction, between a real and an assumed audience, is a modification of Natalie Z. Davis's usage of T.J. Clark's distinction between an audience and a public. Eisenstein, *Printing Press*,I:64; Davis, "Printing and the People," 192–93; T. J. Clark, *Image of the People: Gustave Courbet and the Second French Republic, 1848–1851* (New York, 1973), 11–15.

7. I used the Philadelphia, 1830, and the London, 1962, editions of Baxter's *Saint's Rest.* The latter has an excellent introduction by John T. Wilkinson. The quotes are from the 1830 edition, pp. 17, 18, and 17; see also 31, 36, 89, 102, 180–82, 282, 363–70, 386, and 502–3. Several scholars place *Saint's Rest* in the way-to-wealth tradition of works which "exhorted the Protestant middle class to get wealth, yet remain ascetic, grow rich but not relax their spiritual energy"; see, e.g., Howard Mumford Jones, *O Strange New World—American Culture: The Formative Years* (New York, 1964), 199. On Baxter's *Saint's Rest*, also see Hugh Martin, *Puritanism and Richard Baxter* (London, 1954); Richard Schlatter, *Richard Baxter and Puritan Politics* (New Brunswick, N.J., 1957); and Geoffrey Nuttall, *Richard Baxter and Phillip Doddridge: A Study in a Tradition* (London, 1951). For contemporary commentary, see Benjamin Fawcett's introduction to the Philadelphia, 1830, edition of *Saints' Rest*, 5–13.

8. Baxter, *Saint's Rest*, (1830 ed.) quotes from 24, 89, 102, 180–82; also see 291–327.

9. The two groups of hardscrabble families overlapped; just under a third of all relatively poor families with private libraries lived in the five hinterland townships. The economically isolated usually could not afford to browse in newspapers or bookstores regularly enough to follow most changes occurring in the distant world, intellectual developments, or currents of public life–all actively pursued by other Windsor District families. On peddlers, see Gilmore, "Peddlers and Dissemination."

10. Merrill, "Cash is Good to Eat"; Clark, "Household Manufactures"; Henretta, "Farms and Families"; Geib, "Changing Works."

11. For a similar situation in rural England, see James Obelkevich, *Religion and Rural Society: South Lindsey, 1825–1875* (Oxford, 1976). See also Marini, *Radical Sects*; and Hatch, "Elias Smith."

12. VJ, 19 Sept. 1808 and 4 Oct. 1813. Roth, "Whence this Strange Fire?", 106. On 1815 and 1816, see Roth, 302; the Sept. and Oct. issues of VJ and VR; and data obtained from Philip Lampe.

13. Tinkham, Windsor, 1829; WDPR 11:470 (p. 490 is marked 470 by mistake); Bixby, Ludlow, 1798; WDPR 33:37ff. Only if families such as the Tinkhams of Windsor came into fairly frequent contact with a weekly newspaper would the judgement about traditional beliefs require modification, but, due to their economic circumstances, this is highly unlikely.

14. Burdow, Reading, 1830, WDPR 12:277.

15. In the analysis to follow, undue emphasis on any single work or family has been avoided; rather the discussion centers on groups of families constituting reading communities, and their collective holdings. The intellectual foundations of hardscrabble public and private life were very concentrated. There were no professional family libraries and, more importantly, no major secular-extensive family libraries either. For the Abell almanac, I used 1814–20 Weathersfield and Windsor eds. For the Thomas almanacs, I used the Boston eds., 1793–1842

16. The remainder of this section, and the discussions of family libraries in succeeding sections of this chapter, rely on an analysis of each of the 396 family libraries, derived from inventories of estates, WDPR, 1787–1830, and involved identification of the accurate text for, plus analysis (including full reading) of, all works–5,630 volumes in some 1,250 titles. An important part of the process entailed compilation and analyses of all available Upper Valley written and

Table N-3: *Hardscrabble Libraries, 1787–1830*

	Libraries		Volumes		
Years	Number	Percent	Number	Percent	Shares
1787–1808	64	35	166	25	1
1809–30	119	65	489	75	1
Total	183	100	655	100	2

printed contemporary opinion about each work. Discussion of the full set of procedures must await a future publication, but see app. 4 here.

17. Titles and prefaces often state this, and these works often show up in families without children or any other minors living with them.

18. *Babylon the Great: A Dissection of Men and Things in the British Capital.* 2 vols. (Philadelphia, 1825); quotes on I:2, 3, and 12–13. See also Samuel Austin Allibone, *A Critical Dictionary of English Literature, and British and American Authors.* 5 vols. (Philadelphia, 1870–91), II:1384.

19. Another aspect of hardscrabble family libraries important in evaluating reading patterns is their representativeness over time. The basic findings are summarized in table N-3.

A comparison of these proportions with population trends in Windsor District reveals that our 183 families fairly represent reading patterns throughout the Early Republic. The average size of family libraries rose from 2.6 vols. per library in 1787–1808, to 4.1 vols. in 1809–1830. Even in the late 1820s, hardscrabble family libraries had risen only to 4.5 vols. each, as they reinforced older views of the role and uses of printed matter in daily life.

20. Hubbard and Dartt, *Springfield,* 57.

21. The overwhelming majority of families lived in Springfield (23), Weathersfield (23), and Cavendish (16). Just 3 Baltimore families with libraries reached inventory.

22. Rodney C. Loehr, "Self-Sufficiency in the Farm," AgH 26 (1952):37–41, quote on 41. Tenancy here approximates the share for midwestern farms toward the mid–nineteenth century, reported in Paul Gates, "Problems of Agricultural History, 1790–1840," AgH 46 (1972):42–44. In general, see Clark, "Household Manufactures," esp. 173; Roth, "Whence this Strange Fire?", 16 (map); and Pruitt, "Self-Sufficiency."

23. See Liddle, "Virtue and Liberty"; and Geib, "Changing Works," chs. 1–4. For Carp's diary, 1861–63, see Hal Seth Barron, "The Impact of Rural Depopulation on the Local Economy of Chelsea, Vermont, 1840–1900," AgH 54 (1980):318–35. Carp's view is confirmed by Gates, "Problems," 345, and two rich series in the Bellows Falls *Gazette:* 5, 12, 19, and 26 Jan.; 2 Feb.; and 2, 16, and 23 Mar. 1839. One series consisted of essays on regular monthly and seasonal farming activities; the other was a farmer's diary for the same month during each of the past six to eight years. Both were by the same local writer.

24. Nearly all self-sufficient farmstead families lived within a long day's ride of Chester or Windsor village in decent traveling weather, but many families did not take advantage of this circumstance. Residents in the more southerly towns were also within a day's ride of Bellows Falls, which maintained a printing office and bookstore in 1817–30.

25. The inventory is in WDPR 6:304ff. and 527ff. See also Hubbard and Dartt, *Springfield,* 51 and 83.

26. Other print and writing activity probably included almanac purchases and occasional letter writing and account keeping. Given Martin's early death date (1789), a newspaper subscription was extremely unlikely; see WDPR 1:7ff, and Hubbard and Dartt, *Springfield,* 385 and 519.

27. See table N-4.

Table N-4: Self-Sufficient Farmstead Libraries: Comparative Size

Size of Library in Volumes	Springfield		Weathersfield		Cavendish	
	Number	*Percent*	*Number*	*Percent*	*Number*	*Percent*
1–9	18	78	17	74	11	69
10–19	2	9	3	13	2	12
20 +	3	13	3	13	3	19
Total	23	100	23	100	16	100

28. This is confirmed by the sizable number of secular and religious singing books—48, or a ninth of all known volumes.

29. Male literacy rates in Cavendish, where they have been studied in detail, were 90% or above throughout the era. Female levels varied more widely: from 60% by the early 1780s, to 70% by the early 1790s, and up to 90% for 1812–31. Gilmore, "Elementary Literacy," graph 3B, p. [174].

30. Works on one or another stage of life sparked little intellectual interest among these families.

31. Thomas Peake's *A Compendium of the Law in Evidence* was the reigning manual of the rules of evidence in cases with judge and jury. There were also a series of basic explanatory treatises, and collections of the laws of Vermont and Connecticut.

32. On Augustan-age influences, see Kerber, *Federalists in Dissent*, ch. 1. When matched with population growth, the share of self-sufficient farmstead libraries in our study group is stable across the decades: see table N–5.

33. Strands of American nationalism infused readers; texts in mathematics and rhetoric; Webster's *A Compendious Dictionary*; geographies; a series of *Patriotic Addresses*; Weems's *Washington*; and in politics, Carey's *Olive Branch*. Other strains of Enlightenment thought were found in Franklin's *Autobiography*, Voltaire, and the moral quietude of a pair of works on Freemasonry.

34. See Cohen, *A Calculating People*. Other examples of calculation include law manuals and books of forms; Williams's "rational organization of society" in his history of Vermont; the proliferation of Biblical compendia, etc.; and Watts's *Improvement of the Mind*.

35. Fisher's *Instructor* devoted space to farming methods and trade. Love's *Geodaesia*, Buchan's *Domestic Medicine*, Lathrop's *Farmer's Library*, and a hefty portion of Williams's history of Vermont shared these subject interests.

36. On character, see Weems's *Washington*, the several biographies of Napoleon, Virgil, and Voltaire's *History of Charles the XII*. Relatively few formal stage-of-life treatises were retained.

37. Pike's and Adams's schoolbooks in mathematics paid special attention to the world of business, as did lawbooks and manuals—including those retained beyond professional families—such as Blackstone's *Commentaries on the Laws of England*, with its powerful articulation of patriarchal property rights, and Powell's *Law of Contracts*.

38. Data on Windsor District hamlets was extremely difficult to come by. We searched local histories, manuscripts at the VHS, Univ. of Vermont, AAS, and Old Sturbridge Village, petitions to the state legislature, wills, deeds, and township records. See James T. Lemon, *The Best Poor Man's Country: A Geographical Study of Early Southeastern Pennsylvania* (New York, 1976), 114–15, 119–21, 145, 148. Also see Wallace, *Rockdale*, 39 and 41ff.: a variety of occupations "allowed each [mill] hamlet to a considerable extent . . . to be a self-reliant community insofar as specialized personalized services were concerned. People grew up and lived in intimate awareness of the nature of the lives and work of others; they performed services for the benefit of

	Libraries		Volumes		
Years	Number	Percent	Number	Percent	Shares
1787–1808	21	30	167	26	0
1809–30	48	70	483	74	3
Total	69	100	650	100	3

persons whom they knew; each was aware of his dependence upon and his responsibility for other people. . . . Each [mill] hamlet was unique and the sense of place was strong." See also Glenn T. Trewartha, "The Unincorporated Hamlet: One Element of the American Settlement Fabric," *Association of American Geographers Annals* 33 (1943), 32–81, quote on 32. The establishment of a local post office branch offers perhaps the clearest indication of active hamlet status. See George Clarke Slawson, *The Postal History of Vermont* (New York, 1969), 183–222: Cavendish (1800), Plymouth and Ludlow (1809), Reading (1818), Proctorsville (1821), Peasville (1823), Simonsville and West Windsor (1828), and Hammondsville, also called Felchville (1830).

39. The 16 households were spread throughout 8 hamlets in 6 townships: 4 families each in Reading and Cavendish, and 2 each in Ludlow, Plymouth, Andover, and Weston townships. Just one library survives from the 1790s (1797). On hamlets, see Lemon, *The Best Poor Man's Country*; Wallace, *Rockdale*; and Prude, *Coming of Industrial Order*, chs. 1–4.

40. However, many related cultural institutions, such as lecture series, lyceums, discussion clubs, and theater, so important in transmitting and ramifying the knowledge learned through reading, did not reach this far into the countryside.

41. See table N–6.

42. Trewartha, "The Unincorporated Hamlet," quote on 32. See also Wood, "Origin of the New England Village," esp. 203–85; and Thomas R. Lewis, Jr., "From Suffield to Saybrook: An Historical Geography of the Connecticut River Valley in Connecticut Before 1800" (Ph.D. diss., Rutgers Univ., 1978), an excellent topical treatment.

43. The Farwells sold a small selection of very basic, intensive-reading works in their store: various children's books, primers, blank writing books and writing implements, and schoolbooks (readers and grammars in quantity are mentioned). Oliver Farwell, Reading, 1817, WDPR 7:370ff. and 399ff.

44. The occult works are: Heinrich Agrippa von Nettesheim's *Three Books of Occult Philosophy or Magic*; the pseudonymous Erra Pater's *Book of Knowledge, Treating of the Wisdom of the Ancients*; John Heydon's *Theomagia, or the Temple of Wisdom, in Three Parts, Spiritual, Celestial and Elemental: Containing the Occult Powers of the Angels of Astromancy in the Telesmatical Sculpture of the Persians and Egyptians*; and Thomas Burnet's *The Theory of the Earth*. On Culpeper and the general phenomenon, see Herbert Leventhal, *In the Shadow of the Enlightenment: Occultism and Renaissance Science in Eighteenth-Century America* (New York, 1976), esp. 27–29. On Burnet and his place between Renaissance and later science, see Charles Coulton Gillispie, *Genesis and Geology: The Impact of Scientific Discoveries Upon Religious Beliefs in the Decades Before Darwin* (New York, 1959) chs. 2–5; and Basil Willey, *The Eighteenth Century Background: Studies on the Idea of Nature in the Thought of the Period* (Boston, 1961), ch. 2.

45. WDPR, passim. While just two of the 7 business families held extensive reading matter, these were both among the largest three libraries in this human habitat. Major economic pursuits of these 7 families included: a clothing store, a dry goods store, a general store (the

Table N–6: Self-Sufficient Hamlet Family Libraries and
Participation in Lending Libraries

Size of Library (in volumes)	Number of Libraries and Lending Library Shares	Percent of Libraries
1–4	4 + 1s*	25
5–9	7	44
10 +	5 + 1s	31
Total	16 + 2s	100

* s = shares in lending libraries

Farwells), a tavern with a farm attached, a tannery, a sawmill and a gristmill plus a substantial farm, and a small farm.

46. I used the Springfield, 1806, ed. of the *Koran*. See Wiener, DHI,I:258a; II:29b, 344b–45a, 474b, 640–50b; III:90b; and esp. IV:230–31. See also Seyyed Hossein Nasr's fascinating essay, "Islamic Conception of Intellectual Life," in DHI, II:639–52. R.B. Davis notes a copy in a Virginia lawyer's family in *Intellectual Life in Jefferson's Virginia*, 81; see also *Museum of Foreign Literature* 3 (1823):13–26.

47. All three of the classical works were in English in these estates. I used the two-volume Baltimore, 1812, ed. of *The Iliad*; the two-volume Philadelphia, 1813, ed. of *The Odyssey*; and the eight-volume New York, 1816, ed. of Plutarch's *Lives*. See Gordon Wood's comments on Plutarch's *Lives* in *The Creation of the American Republic, 1776–1787* (Chapel Hill, N.C., 1969), 51, quote on 35.

48. On rural felicity, see Thomson's *The Seasons*, Cowper's *Collected Poems*, Beattie's *The Minstrel*, Samuel Rogers's *The Pleasures of Memory*, and the works by Scott and Byron in table 2–1. In other British literature, see Milton's *Paradise Lost*, Addison and Steeles' *Spectator* series, John Gay's *Fables*. For American literary contributions, see Trumbull's *M'Fingal*; Royall Tyler's *The Algerine Captive*; Judith Sargent Murray's *The Gleaner* series, and John B. Hunter's *Manners and Customs*.

49. In poetry, Romantic writers included Thomson as a precursor, Cowper, Rogers, Scott, and Byron. There were no dominant figures among novelists; wild, exotic tales such as Thomas Moore's *Lalla Rookh* contrasted with tales of moral improvement such as *Lucinda; or The Mountain Mourner* and Barbara Hofland's *Says She to Her Neighbor, What*.

50. Varied intellectual traditions were represented by the fifth, miscellaneous category. Philosophical writings included several treatises on Masonry, all of which centered on virtue as the "foundation of honor and esteem, and the source of all the beauty, order, and happiness in nature." For the quote, see *Beauties*, Haverhill, Mass., 1822, p. 18; the Huntington Library, San Marino, Calif., generously provided a microfilm of the only known copy. On virtue, see Wood, *Creation*, 65–70; and McCoy, *Elusive Republic*. Stage-of-life works were split between concerns of social status and middleclass manners and mores, and those of social reform. Other works included teatises on surveying and domestic architecture.

51. Backus's *History*, Elias Smith's *Life*, Milton's *Paradise Lost*, and McCrie's *Life of John Knox*.

52. See Henry May, *The Englightenment in America: A History* (New York, 1976), xvi. On environmentalism, see Williams and Bigland; on nationalism and patriotism, see Trumbull, Tyler, and Murray; on Christian progress, see Robertson, Bigland, and Williams. On localism and historicism, see Weems, and Parish and Morse's *Compendious History of New England*; on

cataclysmic change and heroism, see Byron, Bourne, and O'Meara; on exoticism and the East, see Moore's *Lalla Rookh*, Buchanan's *Christian Researches*, the *Koran*, and Clarke's *Travels*; on alternative customs and mores, see Scott's *Vision of Don Roderick*, Hunter's *Manners and Customs*, and Aikin, *Life of Howard*, which highlighted his travels among leper colonies.

53. On stages of life, see Young, Murray, Beresford, Opie, Edgeworth, and several novels; on personality development, see Cowper, Byron, and Rogers; on Evangelicalism's social theory, see More, Hofland, Opie, Edgeworth, Murray, and the fashionable *Boston Magazine*.

54. For the general context of female lives, see Cott, *Bonds of Womanhood*; Kerber, *Women of the Republic*; and Norton, *Liberty's Daughters*.

55. See Dutton, "A Short History," 53–64 in his *An Examination*; Dutton's inventory (Cavendish, 1824) is in WDPR 10:30ff. Most of the biographical data is taken from Dutton, "A Short History," and Child, *Gazetteer*, 104–8. The three tracts were published in 1814, 1815, and 1819.

56. Dutton, WDPR 10:30ff.; and Cavendish Social Library borrowing records, 1816–30, VHS. I used the New York, 1819–20, ed. of *The Sketch Book* here because the Duttons did; it did not contain all of the stories in later editions.

57. Daughter Mary was given Bunyan's *Sighs from Hell*; Susie received Moril's *Preparation for Eternity*; and Martha and Bathsheba each received a different volume of Mall's *History of the Martyrs*. Even grandson James Lane was given Bunyon's *Grace Abounding*. Lane's vigorous campaign is in Samuel Lane, *Journal*, consisting of excerpts from his daybooks in the NHHS; quotes on 8–9.

58. N. Sizer, "The Beauties and Grandeur of Vermont," in [Woodstock] *Vermont Mercury*, 11 Nov. 1842; Stilwell, *Migration from Vermont*, 64–74, and 97–103. On cholera, see VJ, 1812–14. Undue concentration on one staple crop was apt to lead to failure. Thus, fortunate farmsteaders raised "wheat, corn, rye, beans, oats, barley, flax, peas, and turnips." In addition, they grazed animals on meadows and pasture lands and grew fruits and vegetables in orchards and gardens, often including a "sugar-orchard" of maple trees. Surpluses could come in any of the above areas: wheat and beef, and later sheep, were most frequent, together with potash used for soaps and pearlash used for baking powder.

59. West Windsor was populated sufficient to petition for separate township status after 1810. See Mary Fenn, *Parish and Town: The History of West Windsor, Vermont* (Montpelier, Vt., 1977). Families living in its village after 1810 were placed with the fortunate village habitat. One tenant farm family and one semiskilled laboring family, both above the $700 threshold, round out fortunate farmstead occupations.

60. See table N–7.

61. See table N–8. Two enormous libraries, of 465 and 909 volumes, inflate the average. The figures for collections of 1–9 volumes include only libraries without a lending library share. Seven libraries of 1–9 volumes held a share. According to Cavendish Social Library Records, 1816–30, VHS, average borrowing amounted to 16 volumes per family during the period for which records exist (1816–30).

62. The household, perhaps including boarders, consisted of males aged 10–14 and 15–19, and females 0–4, 10–14, and 15–19 (2). See the U.S. Census schedules for 1820 and 1830, Windsor Country; and the 1820 Census of Manufactures, Windsor County (the listing is 2 in agriculture). For Parker's inventory, see WDPR 12:230ff.

63. The educational works included Nathaniel Heaton's *The Pleasing Library*, and George Fisher's *The Young Man's Best Companion*. For Dean's inventory, see WDPR 8:341ff.

64. The dictionaries were Perry's and Johnson's, abridged. The law books included Blackstone's *Commentaries*; Chipman's *Reports and Dissertations*; the Simmons' manual, *The Gentleman's Law Magazine*; and *Laws of Vermont* (2 vols.). Modern literature also included the minor

Size of Library (in volumes)	Chester		Windsor	
	Number of Libraries and Library Shares	Percent	Number of Libraries and Library Shares	Percent
1–9	27 + 4s*	71	18 + 3s	64
[1–4]	[19 + 3s]	[50]	[15 + 3s]	[54]
10 +	11 + 1s	29	10	36
Total	38 5s	100	28 3s	100

* s = shares in lending libraries

work, *The Lucky Mistake*. Fiske's inventory is in WDPR 7:205ff. and 262ff.; also see the U.S. Census schedules for 1810, Windsor County.

65. See table N–9.

66. Webster's *An American Selection of Lessons in Reading and Speaking* (Boston, 1797), e.g., contained half American selections, as part of a planned attempt to "diffuse the principles of virtue and patriotism" while teaching the history and politics of the country.

67. These works included popular ones such as Winchester's *Universal Restoration*, the periodical *American Baptist Magazine*, and Methodist commentaries on the Bible; several other Methodist treatises, all radiating fervent piety (e.g., John Ffirth's biography of Rev. Benjamin Abbott, and John William Fléchière's *Appeal to Common Sense*). Mainstream Calvinist works were dominated by two popular writers, Doddridge and Robert Russel (*Seven Sermons*). Located close to these works were devotional treatises, also strongly Calvinist (e.g., Richard Allestree's *Whole Duty of Man*).

68. The next most popular hymnal was Worcester's conservative collection, *Christian Psalmody*. The most popular Methodist works were sermons by Wesley and church histories. Universalists favored Winchester's *Universal Restoration* and Lucy Barnes's *The Female Christian*. The most popular Episcopalian text was the *Works* of William Smith, a liberal Philadelphia minister.

69. The subject areas refer to clusters of texts in libraries, as well as to contemporary structures of knowledge. The most popular works on the republican tradition in Britain were Henry Care's *English Liberties*, a collection of documents beginning with the Magna Carta: and John Dale Burk's *History of the Late War*. On America, James Lyon's *Scourge of Aristocracy* was the most popular work. In history were works on George Washington (several copies) and the War of 1812, Sanders's *Indian Wars*, and William's *History of Vermont*.

70. The most popular captivity narratives were Williams, *Redeemed Captive*, and Susanna Hastings, *Narrative of the Captivity of Mrs. Johnson* (1796).

71. Actually, far more secular volumes were retained per family than previously: 12 versus 1, 3, and 8 for earlier reading communities. Religious volumes per library was twice the rate for self-sufficient farmstead and hamlet human habitats (7 versus 3.2 and 3.4 volumes, respectively).

72. Dwight, *Travels*, II:232; Royall, *The Black Book*, II:359–60.

73. Families moved to the hardscrabble human habitat, including most semiskilled laborer families and a few artisan households, averaged $312 in total wealth per household (see table N–10). The second group of families was evenly split; half the household heads died in 1810–19.

74. See Roth, "Whence this Strange Fire?", maps on 100ff. Weathersfield and Windsor had

Table N-8: *Fortunate Farmstead Libraries and Participation in Lending Libraries by Size of Library*

Size of Library (in volumes)	Number of Libraries	Percent	Number of Libraries with No Lending Library Shares
1–9	45 + 7s*	68	38
[1–4]	[34 + 6s]	[52]	[28]
10 +	21 + 1s	32	20
[10 + (and 1–9 with a lending library share)]	[28 + 8s]	[42]	——
Total	66	100	58

* s = shares in lending libraries

Episcopalian societies before 1829; Springfield established one thereafter. Windsor established a Unitarian society after 1829.

75. On the four villages generally, see Slawson, *The Postal History*; Child, *Windsor County*; and Lewis C. Aldrich and Frank R. Holmes, *History of Windsor County, Vermont* (Syracuse, N. Y., 1891). On Windsor, see Henry Steele Wardner, *The Birthplace of Vermont: The History of Windsor to 1781* (New York, 1927), 349ff. and 477ff.; Ide, "Reminiscences," 61; and *Vermont's Susquicentennial: The Celebration at Windsor, July 8, 1927* (Windsor, Vt., 1927), 11ff. On Chester, the district's second major village, see esp. Alice M. Lawton, "History of Chester," Paper read at the Review Club, 28 Oct. 1930, Ms 974.31 C426L, VHS; B.H. Albee, *A Short History of Chester, Vermont* (Springfield, Vt., 1890); *Proceedings at Chester, Vermont, June 29, 1909, on Old Home Day* (Montpelier, Vt., 1909); "Chester Past and Present," in *Ludlow and Her Neighbors* (Ludlow, 1899), 45ff.; and the surviving issues of the *Chester Phenix, Freedom's Banner*, and *Green Mountain Palladium*. In 1789–91 and 1805–6, a series of petitions to the legislature attempted to establish a new county—termed Alba—with Chester, sixth largest township in the state in 1805–25, as its seat. The attempt failed. See Hoyt, *State Papers of Vermont*, 9:96–99, 204–5, and 250–52; and Vermont Secretary of State Petitions, 45:195–200; 46:71 and 78–79. Cultural life remained very active into the early 1830s: local post office service and a social library began at the end of 1800; an academy opened in 1814; in the late 1820s began regular productions of a theater company, a newspaper, a lyceum, a course of lectures on chemistry, an evening writing school, a circulating library, and a special female branch of the academy. Weathersfield Bow, after very promising early growth, bogged down in competition among several sites in the township. Weathersfield supported an auxiliary print center (1813–1816) and otherwise was supplied by Windsor. On Weathersfield, see esp. John S. Hurd, *Weathersfield: Century One* (Canaan, N.H., 1975). A shift in Springfield's town center from Eureka to Springfield village on the Black River, effected before 1810, encouraged a large factory village. In 1817, Springfield village received its post office, and by the 1820s, Springfield was overtaking Chester as the district village next largest to Windsor. See George, *Pocket Gazetteer*; Zadock Thompson, *Gazetteer of Vermont* and *History of Vermont*; Mary E. Baker, *Folklore of Springfield* (Springfield, Vt., 1922); Albee, *Chester*; Whitelaw's maps of Vermont, 1796–1822; Hubbard and Dartt, *Springfield*; and Rev. L.H. Cobb, *The Old Paths: Delivered at Springfield, Vermont . . . May 30, 1959* (Claremont. N.H., 1869).

Table N–9: Fortunate Farmstead Libraries and Participation in Lending Libraries,
1787–1830

Dates of Inventories	Libraries	Volumes and Library Shares	Average Volumes Per Library
1787–96	3	15	5
1797–1816	32	200+7s[*]	6.3
1817–26	20	172+1s	8.6
1827–30	11	1,461	132.8

[*] s=shares in lending libraries

76. No less than 2,248 volumes were distributed reasonably well across the 62 collections (see table N–11).

77. Daniel Roche found that in provincial cities of late-eighteenth-century France, business families were often amid, but not directly engaged in, newer forms of thought: *Le Siècle des Lumières en province. Académies et académiciens provinciaux, 1680–1789* (Paris, 1978).

78. Geography included Zadock Thompson's *Gazetteer of Vermont* and Morse's *American Universal Geography*; history included Frederick Butler's *A Complete History of the United States of America*, another unspecified American history, David Humphreys's *Life of the Honorable Major-General Israel Putnam*, and an unspecified (probably Rollin's) *History of the Ancients*. Information on Grout is drawn from his inventory, WDPR 12:218ff. Also see Child, *Windsor County*, 244.

79. Jacob was of "an aristocratic bearing," a "high strung Federalist" in the words of a contemporary. His home was pronounced "among the most elegant in the village" by a traveler as early as 1797. See Jacob G. Ullery, *Men of Vermont: An Illustrated Biographical History of Vermonters and Sons of Vermont* (Brattleboro, Vt., 1894), I:178; Henry S. Wardner, "Judge Jacob and Dinah, *Vermonter* 19 (1914), nos. 5–6, pp. 1–87, and *Birthplace of Vermont*, esp. 523–24; Tanselle, *Royall Tyler* (Cambridge, Mass., 1967), 41–43 and 239–40; Marius Peladeau, ed., *The Prose of Royall Tyler* (Rutland, Vt., 1972), esp. 388–94; Ide, "Reminiscences," 63; Graham, *Description of Vermont*; Russell S. Taft, "Windsor," *Windsor Journal*, 16 Jan. 1892; Child, *Windsor County*, 34; and WDPR 7:345ff. and 512ff. The law library included laws of the United States, Vermont, and New York State, the latter probably related to Jacob's mediator role as a commissioner in the land disputes between Vermont and New York, settled in 1789. Blackstone was supplemented by 22 volumes of reports and specialized treatises.

80. Works in philosophy and the classics included Franklin's *Autobiography*, Pope's translation of *The Odyssey*, and Horace's *Serenissim Delphini*. American works included a volume of Phillip Freneau's *Poems*; Joel Barlow's *Vision of Columbus* and *The Columbiad*; and Thomas G. Fessenden's *Terrible Tractoration: A Poetical Petition*. Poetry included Thomas Parnell's *Collection of Poems . . . from the Most Celebrated Authors*, James Thomson's *The Seasons*, and John Dryden's *Poetical Works*. Novels and plays included Goldsmith's *The Vicar of Wakefield* and *The Citizen of the World*, Fielding's *Tom Jones*, and Tobias Smollett's *The Adventures of Roderick Random*.

81. See Gilmore, "The 'Annihilation of Time and Space': The Transformation of Event and Awareness in American Consciousness, 1780–1850," Paper delivered at Conference on Printing and Society, AAS, 1980.

82. See Jonathan Worst, "New England Psalmody, 1760–1810: Analysis of an American Idiom" (Ph.D. diss., Univ. of Michigan, 1974), 1–41. Commentaries on the Bible included several copies each of Dickinson's *Compendium* and Doddridge's massive *Family Expositor*.

Table N–10: Fortunate Village Libraries, 1787–1830

Years	Number	Percent of Total	Windsor District Population Share (%)
1787–1808	13	21	30
1809–30	49	79	70
Total	62	100	100

83. Enlightenment theology included John Tillotson, Charles Chauncy, Jonathan Mayhew, Adam Clarke, Charles Crawford, William Paley, and Samuel Stanhope Smith. Emmanuel Swedenborg, *Works*, and Lorenzo Dow, *Life and Travels*, represented a related tradition of truly independent thinkers. The most popular writers of mainstream theology included Jonathan Edwards, Philip Doddridge, John Wesley, a Methodist denominational *Discipline*, Hugh Blair, Edward Griffin, and Vicesimus Knox. Among the more conservative writers were Samuel Niles, Humphrey Prideaux, Alexander Proudfit, Thomas Ridgely, Herman Witsius, Joshua Spalding, John Tillard, and John Witherspoon. Other defensive works included Charles Leslie's arguments against Deists, and Timothy Merritt's against Hosea Ballou. Among periodicals, the *New York Theological Magazine* and *The Panoplist* were the most widely read. In church history, other popular writers included John L. Mosheim and John Martin.

84. Interest in Vermont and New England is seen in several copies of Whitelaw's maps and Samuel Williams's *History*; over a dozen volumes of Vermont *Laws and Statues*, several in libraries of families not headed by lawyers; and several other works (e.g., Zadock Steele's *Captivity and the burning of Royalton*, Zadock Thompson's *Gazetteer of Vermont*, and Nathaniel Chipman's *Reports and Dissertations*). Several histories of New England were also retained, including those by John Winthrop, William Hubbard, George Minot, Hannah Adams, and Daniel Sanders.

85. The most popular of these writers included Royall Tyler, William Wirt, Joel Barlow, John Trumbull, Phillip Freneau, Judith S. Murray, and Mercy Warren.

86. Abel Bowen, *The Naval Monument Containing Official and Other Accounts* . . . (Boston, 1816), x. Most popular works on politics and government were Federalist-inspired, including works by Matthew Carey, Robert Walsh, Nathaniel Chipman, Fisher Ames, and George Washington, and the *Federalist* essays. Military affairs included Daniel Sanders and William Hubbard on the "Indian Wars"; Horace Kimball and Samuel Williams on the War of 1812; and homage to LaFayette, Putman, Eaton, the American Navy, and the Puritan Founders. There was a cult of Washington as well. Fascination with militarism overflowed into interest in foreign military heroes: Napoleon, Frederick the Great, Nelson, and Victor Moreau. Interest in other aspects of American nationalism abounded.

87. See Thistlethwaite, *America and the Atlantic Community*, and Michael Kraus, *The Atlantic Civilization: Eighteenth-Century Origins* (Ithaca, N. Y., 1966).

88. In general, see May, *Enlightenment*, pt. 4. For Enlightenment church history, see Hannah Adams, John L. Mosheim, Henry Hunter, and Edward Harwood. In general, see Robert R. Clemmer, "Enlightenment Church History in the United States, 1800–1850" (Ph.D. diss., Univ. of Pennsylvania, 1961), esp. 8–10 and 90–93. For Enlightenment secular history, see William Robertson's histories: Frederick Butler's *View*, *History of the United States*, and *Letters on History*; Daniel Sanders, *Indian Wars*; John Banks, *Peter the Great*; William Russell, *Modern Europe*; Charles Rollin, *Alexander the Great*; Isaac Eddy, *Chronology*; and Samuel Williams, *History of Vermont* and *Sketches of the War*.

89. Fortunate village families followed the travels of Patrick Brydon through Sicily, James

Table N–II: *Fortunate Village Libraries and Participation in Lending Libraries By Size of Library*

Size of Library (in volumes)	Number of Libraries and Library Shares	Percent of All Fortunate Village Libraries
1–5	17+1s[*]	27.4
6–10	10	16.2
11–50	23+6s	37
51–403	12+4s	19.4
Total	62+11s	100

[*] s=shares in lending libraries

Bruce through Abyssinia, John Campbell into South Africa, Constantin Volney through Egypt and Syria, James Riley and Judah Paddock among the Arabs, Aeneas Anderson and George L. Staunton among the Chinese, François Depon through South America, Louis Grandpré across the Indian Ocean, Claudius Buchanan in Asia, and Alexander Mackenzie throughout the American Northwest.

90. British literary traditions preceding the Neoclassical and Romantic were also well represented. Readers were enthralled with Shakespeare, Milton, Pope, James Beattie, James Thomson, and Samuel Johnson. Popular American authors included Tyler, Wirt, Trumbull, Warren, and Barlow.

91. The literature is growing rapidly. Two pioneer studies are Lawrence Stone, *The Family, Sex and Marriage in England, 1500–1800* (London, 1977), and Alan Macfarlane, *The Origins of English Individualism: The Family, Property, and Social Transition* (New York, 1979).

92. See Webster, *American Dictionary*, 2: "modern" and variants.

93. On reading programs, see John Bennett, *Letters to a Young Lady; the Parent's Friend*; Thomas James Mathias's *The Pursuits of Literature*; and William Pitt's *Letters to His Nephew*.

94. See Paul Faler, "Workingmen, Mechanics, and Social Change: Lynn, Mass., 1800–1860" (Ph.D. diss., Univ. of Wisconsin, 1971), esp. chs. 6 and 7, and the briefer published version, *Mechanics and Manufacturers*.

95. Among the many other rural advocates from several branches of knowledge were James Thomson, Robert R. Livingston, Elias Smith, Phillip Freneau, Miss Grierson, George Zollikofer, and Johann Georg Zimmerman. On urban life see, e.g., John Britton's *Pleasures of Human Life*, Charles Macklin's *Man of the World*, Edward Moore's *Gamester*, Goldsmith's *Citizen of the World*, Montesquieu's *Persian Letters*, Thomas James Mathias's *Pursuits of Literature*, James Beattie's *Minstrel*, Robert Southey's *Letters from England*, Richard Cumberland's *Memoirs*, Charles Pigott's *Jockey Club*; and Chesterfield's, Pitt's, and Junius's separate *Letters*. All spoke rather well of London life, as did the leading British periodicals, *The Spectator, The Rambler, The Looker-on*, and *The Mirror*. For advice on urban ways, see Edward Clarke, John Simmons, and *The Civil Officer*, among manuals; and Daniel Fenning's *Ready Reckoner*, the *Dictionary of Trade*, William Jackson's *Book-keeping*, Richard Hayes's *Negociator's Magazine*, Daniel Johnson's *American Shipmaster's Daily Assistant*, *Valuable Secrets in the Arts, Trades, etc.*, William Guthrie's *New Grammar*, Blackstone's *Commentaries*, and most of the arithmetics which were increasingly aimed at future commercial dealings.

96. See Theodore Dwight Bozeman, *Protestants in an Age of Science: The Baconian Ideal and Antebellum American Religious Thought* (Chapel Hill, N. C., 1977), 11–22 and 167ff. While the centers of eastern Presbyterian power embraced the Baconian ideal in its most conservative

doxological fit with Biblical literalism, many scientists and others used the label to praise a scientific attitude free from the arcane theological freight of old-school Presbyterianism. See Daniels, *American Science*, chs. 3 and 6, esp. 198–200; and William Duncan, William Jackson, Richard Hayes, and Daniel Fenning, who embraced "the spirit of fact" in a limited practical pursuit of knowledge and were careless and often naive about the implications of their findings and their reports of the work of others. For interest in science, see Robert Livingston's *Essay on Sheep*, Leonard Lathrop's *Farmer's Library*, John Dick's *New Gardener's Dictionary*, *The Complete Farmer*, and Samuel Deane's *New England Farmer*. Scientific knowledge, like politics and government, changed rapidly and therefore usually was reported in newspapers, periodicals, pamphlets, and broadsides. Key works include Benjamin West's account of the transit of Venus, Locke's *Outline of Botany*, several works in medical libraries, George Adams's comprehensive *Lectures on Natural and Experimental Philosophy*, William Nicholson's *Introduction to Natural Philosophy*, Goldsmith's hodgepodge *History of the Earth*, Daniel Preston's *Wonders of Creation*, *Valuable Secrets*, Jefferson's *Notes*, Samuel Miller's *Brief Retrospect*, Samuel Williams's *Natural and Civil History of Vermont*, Anthony Willich's *Domestic Encyclopedia*, and half a dozen periodicals, including the *American Review*, *The Polyanthos*, *The Atheneum*, the *Museum of Foreign Literature*, *The Massachusetts Magazine*, and *Analectic Magazine*.

97. See Daniel Johnson's *American Shipmaster's Daily Assistant*, Fenning's *Ready Reckoner*, Fessenden's *Terrible Tractoration*, Maria Edgeworth's *Practical Education*, John Marshall's *Washington*, Abel Bowen's *Naval Monument*, Horace Kimball's *Naval Temple*, John Banks's *Peter the Great*, Robert Porter's book on Napoleon, and several works on Nelson. A thoughtful work on these last four strands of thought is John A. Kouwenhoven *Made in America: The Arts in Modern Civilization* (New York, 1962).

98. See esp. Hugh Blair's *Lectures*, William Scott's *Lessons in Elocution*, James Burgh's *Art of Speaking*, and William Enfield's *Speaker*. A pioneer study in this area is Michael Kammen, "Changing Perceptions of the Life Cycle in American Thought and Culture," *Proceedings of the Mass. Historical Society* 91 (1979):35–66. Works retained include: on childhood and parent-child relations, [Anon.], *Manners and Customs*, James Janeway's *Token*, and Samuel Stennett's *Monitor to Parents*; on death, John Willison's *Afflicted Man's Companion*; on youth, Pitt's *Letters to his Nephew*, John Bennett's *Letters to a Young Lady*, and Chesterfield's *Letters to His Son*. Many other works were directed to both youths and adults, including Defoe's *Religious Courtship*; *The Young Gentleman's and Ladies Magazine*; Johann Zimmerman's *Solitude Considered*; John Aikin's *Life of Howard*; John Mason's text on moral philosophy, *Self-Knowledge*; John Britton's *Pleasures of Human Life*; Eden Burroughs's *Narrative of Polly Davis*; and George Lyttleton's *Dialogues*.

99. Modern literature and many periodicals elaborated further on the stages of life. These include Maria Edgeworth's treatises and tales about true womanhood and morality; William Kenrick's *Whole Duty*; Regina Roche's *Children of the Abbey*; and general works such as Elizabeth Hamilton's *Letters on Education*, Edgeworth's *Practical Education*, Hester Chapone's *Letters on the Improvement of the Mind*, Maria Rundell's *New System of Domestic Cookery*, Hannah More's *Strictures on the Modern System of Female Education*, and John Bennett, *Letters to a Young Lady*. For Newell, see Leonard Woods, *Memoirs of Harriet Newell*. For Wheelock, see McClure and Parish, *Memoirs of Wheelock*. For Brainerd, see Jonathan Edwards, *The Life of Brainerd*.

Chapter 10

1. See Walker, *Dictionary*; Perry, *Dictionary*; Noah Webster, *Compendious Dictionary* and *American Dictionary*: "modern," "modernize," "moderns," "modernness," and "novelty."

2. Fourteen of the seventeen estates were probated after 1818, and the earliest in 1806.

3. John C. Greene, "Protestantism, Science, and American Enterprise: Benjamin Silliman's Moral Universe," in Leonard G. Wilson, ed. *Benjamin Silliman and His Circle. Studies*

on the Influence of Benjamin Silliman on Science in America: Proceedings in Honor of Elizabeth H. Thomson (New York, 1979):11–27, quote on 22.

4. See Perry Miller, *Life of the Mind*, 269–329.

5. VJ, 8 *July* 1825.

6. Dwight, *Travels, IV*:226–27. The Revolution, in Cooper's mind, "effected no immediate change in the nature of their studies, or mental amusements. The works were reprinted, it is true, for the purposes of economy, but they still continued English." Cooper, (2 vols.), New York, 1963 quotes on II:99–101.

7. Asa Smith, *An Address . . .* (Boston, 1853), 8.

8. By the early 1830s the population balance had shifted: Windsor District lost 2% in 1830–40, and the rest of the Upper Valley also declined (except Orange County, which gained 2%). The same decline showed west of the mountains; Rutland, Bennington, and Addison counties all lost population in 1830–40. See U.S. Censuses, 1790–1840, and table 1–1 in this book.

9. See ch. 2.

10. Since Arthur Schlesinger, Jr.'s work in the late 1930s, Brownson's early life and world view have been accurately understood. See Schlesinger, *Orestes A. Brownson*, and Schlesinger's 1939 Harvard University Bowdoin Prize essay, which also treated Brownson: "Orestes Brownson, An American Marxist Before Marx," *Sewanee Review* (1939):317–23.

11. See, by contrast, McLuhan's notion of a global village in *Gutenberg Galaxy*, 5–79, esp. 31 and 26, and *War and Peace in the Global Village* (New York, 1968). That the vehicles of communication were few and extremely slow in circulating knowledge, compared with electronic culture, does not negate the fact that Windsor residents who subscribed to a newspaper in 1815 were able to learn, on a weekly basis, about events occurring in scores of other countries as well as in many other parts of the U.S.

12. Braudel, *Capitalism and Material Life, 1400–1800* (New York, 1973), x.

13. Alan Macfarlane, *Reconstructing Historical Communities* (Cambridge, England, 1977), 12–13, on kinds of communities and the problem of multiple "communities."

14. This is the argument of Harvey J. Graff, *The Literacy Myth: Literacy and Social Structure in the Nineteenth-Century City* (New York, 1979).

15. Gilmore, "Elementary Literacy."

16. Johansson, *The History of Literacy*.

17. See chs. 3 and 8.

18. To give a full overview, the data incorporates all types of printed matter read, both works comprising family libraries and works selling briskly but not retained for long. The percentage is drawn from all sources discussed earlier (see ch. 6). The preliminary figure in each category was multiplied by .62, the proportion of families with a library, among all families inventoried. The only major source of printed information not specified here is broadsides, for which information is too fragmentary. The field most underrepresented in the absence of broadside production and distribution data is secular music, because of the large number of broadside ballads.

19. Hatch, "Elias Smith," 250–77, quotes on 257 and 258; Joseph J. Ellis, *After the Revolution: Profiles of Early American Culture* (New York, 1979), esp. 81–82.

20. Abel Tompkins, *Miller Overthrown*, 132.

21. See Natalie Davis, "Printing and the People," esp. 192–93; and T.J. Clark, *Image of the People*, 11–15.

22. See C.B.A Behrens, "Porn, Propaganda, and the Enlightenment," *New York Review of Books*, 29 Sept. 1977:32–33.

23. Bushman, *Joseph Smith*, 3–8, quote on 7.

24. Thereafter, the Smiths inhabited a western New York fortunate farmstead human habi-

tat, two miles south of a major villge with a permanent print center (Palmyra), but lived as a struggling tenant farm family: ibid., 3–78.

25. J.F.C.Harrison, *The Quest For the New Moral World: Robert Owen and the Owenites in Britain and America* (New York, 1969); see also Jan Lewis, *The Pursuit of Happiness: Family Values in Jefferson's Virginia* (New York, 1983).

26. Roth, "Whence This Strange Fire?", chs. 4–6; and *Democratic Dilemma*, chs. 3–8.

27. On mending and planting as creating see, e.g., William Dow, Account Books, 1839–65, vol. 3: entries for Nov. 1842, 3 Feb. 1843, 30 Apr. 1845, and Dec. 1846, VHS; and Lydia P. Baldwin, Diary, 20 Jan. 1796, p. 4, VHS.

28. See Stilwell, *Migration*; Donald A. Smith, "Legacy of Dissent"; and Roth, "Whence This Strange Fire?" Sufficiently detailed voting records do not exist to permit comparison of Windsor District political divisions and the network of human habitats. But there were tendencies. Thus, among fortunate village and fortunate farmstead townships, Weathersfield was the seat of Federalism and Windsor and Springfield were mostly Federalist, while Chester often went Republican. That Chester decidedly dissented in religion, while the other three village townships were either Standing Order or moderate Liberal, may help explain its difference. All of the backcountry except Weston was usually Republican territory. By 1840 all townships were Whig, but Chester least so.

29. Marcus McCorison, "Patents Granted to Vermonters Before the Year 1831," MS 608.743 M136, VHS.

30. See Roth, "Whence This Strange fire?" and *Democratic Dilemma*; Ludlum, *Social Ferment*; Ward, "Religious Enthusiasm."

31. See ch. 3, n. 11.

32. *The Wonderful Life and Surprizing Adventures Of that Renowned Hero, Robinson Crusoe* (Boston, 1779), 1–4.

33. See Bailyn, "Modern Historiography"; Geoffrey Barraclough, *Main Trends in History* (New York, 1978); Lawrence Stone, *The Past and the Present* (Boston, 1981); Frances FitzGerald, *America Revised*, (New York, 1980); Morgan Kousser, "The Revivalism of Narrative," *Social Science History* 8 (1984):133–50; and Richard E. Neustadt and Ernest R. May, *Thinking in Time: The Uses of History for Decision-Makers* (Glencoe, Ill., 1986).

34. Isaac Asimov's mysterious psychohistorian in the science-fiction series *The Foundation Trilogy*, 3 vols. (New York, 1964–66). Occasionally the jargon of the behavioral sciences blinds the profession, but then it recovers, as it is doing presently. See Robert L. Jacobson, "Humanists Cheer a Call to Arms over Specialization," *Chronicle of Higher Education*, 1 May 1985.

35. Controversies over the treatment of Watergate in Paul Johnson's popular history of the last sixty years, Theodore Draper's essay on "neo-conservative" history, and the testimony of Rosalind Rosenberg and Alice Kessler-Harris in the case of EEOC v. Sears Roebuck and Co. all point to the difficulties of applying one form of historical insight to contemporary life. See Paul Johnson, *Modern Times: The World from the Twenties to the Eighties* (New York, 1983), 613–96; Andrew Hacker, "Women at Work," *New York Review of Books* 33 (14 Aug. 1986):26–32; Theodore Draper, "Neoconservative History," *New York Review of Books* 32 (16 Jan. 1986):5–15; and a series of replies, esp. *New York Review of Books* 33 (24 Apr. 1986):49–51, involving Robert Nisbet and others.

36. During my year as a Fulbright Fellow at Thammasat University in Bangkok, Thailand, accidentally but most fortunately, I became regularly involved in public policy research. I served as a consultant to Dr. Chira Hongladarom, Executive Director, Human Resources Institute, and Vice-Rector for Research and Academic Services at Thammasat. The three major Thai projects I worked on entailed consulting and research in: Agriculture and Scientific Manpower

[sic] Training, Information Technology and Its Impact, and Economic Forecasting for Human Resource Management and linkages between Education and Human Resource Development.

37. Applied to public policy decision-making processes, this means entering the planning process at the earliest possible stage. This can be accomplished by reading and contributing to all drafts. Immersion in the sources is as essential for successful contribution to public policy planning as it is for historical research. An informed feeling for the problem is the trigger to historical understanding. On the lack of perspective in problem solving, see James Bamford, *The Puzzle Palace: A History of America's Most Secret Agency* (New York, 1983). Barbara Tuchman presents a notable and inspiring exception to the silence of historians. See most recently *The March of Folly: From Troy to Vietnam* (New York, 1984). This treatment has profited from discussions over several years with my colleague and friend, John W. Sinton, and from Jonathan Berger and Sinton, *Water, Earth, and Fire: Land Use and Environmental Planning in the New Jersey Pine Barrens* (Baltimore, 1985).

38. See the fascinating analysis in Robert N. Bellah et al., *Habits of the Heart: Individualism and Commitment in Americna Life* (New York, 1986 ed.), esp. vi–xi, 3–51, and 250–96.

39. Charles Sellers, Henry May, and Neil R. McMillen, *A Synopsis of American History*, 6th ed. (Boston, 1985), 110–11. Even when communications are mentioned, they are treated in strictly material terms, as technologies and quantities. See Mary Beth Norton et al., *A People and a Nation: A History of the United States*, 2d. ed., vol. 1, (Boston, 1986), 224. For an excellent recent treatment, see Wilentz, *Chants Democratic*, 3–19.

40. Fred Matthews, "'Hobbesian Populism': Interpretive Paradigms and Moral Vision in American Historiography," JAH 72 (1985):92–115, quotes on 104 and 113.

41. See Roth, "Whence This Strange Fire?" and his book, *Democratic Dilemma*. See also Ward, "Religious Enthusiasm;" Ludlum, *Social Ferment*; and Hal Seth Barron, *Those Who Stayed Behind: Rural Society in Nineteenth Century New England* (Cambridge, England, 1984).

42. See Clark Kerr, *The Future of Industrial Societies: Convergence or Continuing Diversity?* (Cambridge, Mass., 1983); and J.F.C. Harrison, *Quest for the New Moral World*.

43. See Czitrom, *Media and the American Mind*; and W. David Bolter, *Turing's Man: Western Culture in the Computer Age* (Chapel Hill, N.C., 1984).

44. Russell B. Nye, *Fettered Freedom: Civil Liberties and the Slavery Controversy, 1830–1860* (Urbana, Ill., 1972); Leonard Levy, *The Emergence of a Free Press* (New York, 1985); and Constance Rourke, "P. T. Barnum," in her *Trumpets of Jubilee*, (New York, 1963), 276–319.

45. Kerr subsumes all cultural expression under two of the nine factors: "the content of knowledge" ("professionals" and "high culture" or "knowledge within their specialties," which is becoming internationalized at a late stage of industrial society) and "patterns of belief" ("vital ideas by which peoples and societies live"). Kerr's general conclusion is that, at present, the tendency across the industrial world, capitalist and socialist, is toward a common material order of daily life, based on similar means and methods of production, but with enormous diversity persisting in all major cultural patterns. See Kerr, *Industrial Societies*, 64–65 and 72–75.

46. Ibid., 72–75 and 110–26.

Appendix 1

1. See Gilmore, "Elementary Literacy," 87–95. See the interesting study by Richard Hoggart, *The Uses of Literacy* (New York, 1970).

2. See Natalie Zemon Davis's use of this term and discussion in "Interview," *Visions*, 97–122, 111 for the quote.

3. On oratory, see Robert T. Oliver, *History of Public Speaking in America* (Boston, 1965), chs. 3–7; Donald Scott, "The Popular Lecture and the Creation of a Public in Mid-Nineteenth

Century America," JAH 66 (1980):791–809; idem, "Print and the Public Lecture System, 1840–1860," in Joyce et al., *Printing and Society*, 278–99.

4. See Hall, "World of Print." On Mount, see Alfred Frankenstein, *Painter of Rural America: William Sidney Mount, 1807–1868* (Stony Brook, N. Y., 1968), esp. 45. On Woodville, see Theodore E. Stebbins, Jr., et al., *A New World: Masterpieces of American Painting, 1760–1910* (Boston, 1983), 259–60.

5. James Axtell, *School Upon a Hill: Education and Society in Colonial New England* (New York, 1974), quote on 184–85.

6. Recovering oral culture obviously presents severe problems, though contemporary short stories, novels, and newspaper reports describing oral traditions are rich sources. Gesture, costume, visual representation, posters and handbills, singing and music, dance, and oratory all combined to commemorate and reinforce the mixed sacred and secular liturgy of American nationalism. For a model analysis of ritual, see Edward Muir's pioneering study, *Civic Ritual in Renaissance Venice* (Princeton, 1981). On reading strategies, see Rusche, "The Empire of Reason," ch. 8.

7. Worst, "New England Psalmody."

8. See Frankenstein, *Mount*, 14–16 and 36; and McCorison, *Vermont Imprints*, nos. 439, 738, 1029, 1065, and 1285. About two dozen imprints in music to accompany dancing appeared in VJ advertisements, 1783–1830.

9. But see the rich series of *Annual Proceedings of the Dublin Seminar for New England Folklife*, ed. Peter Benes, 11 vols. (Boston, 1976–86).

10. A collation was made of all objects noted in Windsor District wills and inventories probated through 1830.

11. Approximately 30 to 40% contributed indirectly to written expression through letters, accounts, journals, and the like.

12. See Ray Nash, *American Penmanship, 1800–50: A History of Writing and a Bibliography of Copybooks from Jenkins to Spencer* (Worcester, Mass., 1969); Allan Pred, *Urban Growth and the Circulation of Information*.

13. In the U.S. Congress's first law on the matter (1792), a single-sheet letter cost 6 cents if sent under 30 miles, rising to 25 cents per sheet over 450 miles: two-sheet letters cost twice the single-sheet rate. Only for five sheets and above—a minuscule proportion of extant Upper Valley letters—was there a savings. By comparison, a farm family could buy their yearly almanac or a primer for only 5 cents through 1818 and 6 cents in 1819. On letter writing, see Pred, *Urban Growth and the Circulation of Information*, 81. On its relatively high cost, see François Furet and Jacques Ozouf, *Reading and Writing: Literacy in France from Calvin to Jules Ferry* (Cambridge, England, 1982), I:131. That youth away at school expected their parents to write, and became almost frantic when they failed to, is evident in the 1824 "Vermont Journal of Riley M. Adams," *Vineland Historical Magazine* 5 (1920):86, 108–09, 127, 129, and 130.

14. See Norton, *Liberty's Daughters*, 256–94, e.g., 268 and 272ff.; Kerber, *Women of the Republic*, 185–231, e.g., 215ff., 221ff., and 227ff.; and esp., Cott, *Bonds of Womanhood*, 101–25 and 132ff. For the ratio of elected officials to polls, compare election results and tax records, e.g., for Stockbridge, Vt., WDPR.

15. Cott, *Bonds of Womanhood*, 125, notes "unpredicted" consequences of women's schools and, 126–96, discusses women's associational activities.

16. The preservation of information—for, e.g., deeds, some wills, inventories, and guardian records—frequently took the form of single-copy recordkeeping, with the store, agency, institution, or functionary with whom one dealt retaining the official copy, which the customer signed or marked. After about 1815, paralleling increases in the paper supply, decreases in its cost, and accelerating in- and outmigration, a gradual shift toward keeping duplicate documents and records occurred. On printing, McCorison *Vermont Imprints*, 3ff., is the best source for Ver-

mont, while the Murray files are for New Hampshire. The spread of female participation in the written preservation of culture during the nineteenth century needs to be traced in each of these realms.

Appendix 2

1. Helpful are Raymond Williams, "Base and Superstructure in Marxist Cultural Theory," 31–49, and other essays in *Problems in Materialism and Culture: Selected Essays,* ed. Raymond Williams (London, 1980); idem, *Marxism and Literature* (Oxford, 1977), 75–141.

2. Virtually no tenant farmer or semiskilled laborer household ever owned a horse, and over half the yeomanry were also without a horse, or a share in a horse, at inventory.

3. Ludlow and Plymouth hamlets were supplied by the Green Mountain Turnpike through Chester rather than directly from the river valley.

4. Gentleman farm households were limited to farmstead community settings, and thus were more susceptible to the influence of their communication access zone. Noteworthy internal variations among types of professional family libraries are discussed in chs. 8 and 9.

5. Webster's *American Dictionary* notes that "to scrabble" meant "to scrape, paw or scratch with the hands; to move along on the hands and knees by clawing with the hands. . . . A word in common popular use in New England, but not elegant."

6. A few families rose above these material and cultural constraints, e.g., the family of Joseph Holmes. Amid $17 in total wealth were 7 books. This is all the more remarkable in that Joseph, a resident of Weathersfield, died not in 1830, after the full explosion of the world of print, but in 1795.

Appendix 3

1. That groups other than white males over 16 did not participate equally in power or responsibility is obvious: Norton, *Liberty's Daughters*; Geib, "Changing Works." For major discussions of occupations, see Lockridge, *Literacy in Colonial New England*; Rutman, *Puritanism*; Jackson T. Main, *Social Structure*; LeRoy Ladurie, *The Peasants of Languedoc*; Fischer, *Revolution of American Conservatism*; and Horwitz, *Anthropology Toward History*.

2. Women worked in the fields planting and harvesting regularly in some areas and only when necessary in others. See Geib, "Changing Works"; Russell, *A Long Deep Furrow*; W. Elliot and Mary M. Brownlee, eds., *Women in the American Economy: A Documentary History, 1675 to 1929* (New Haven, 1976), pt. 2, 91–143; and local histories, where evidence of women working the fields is widespread. See, e.g., Warren R. Cochrane and George K. Wood, *History of Francestown, N.H., 1758–1891* (Nashua, N.H., 1895), 360; and Edward Miller and Frederic P. Wells, *History of Ryegate, Vermont* (St. Johnsbury, Vt., 1913), 207.

3. Census schedules, Third Census of the United States, 1810, for Vermont and New Hampshire Valley counties.

4. Fourteen individuals known to have been heavily engaged in commerce as the primary occupation of their household were checked in the 1820 census schedules. Six were fully accurate; six of the other eight were listed as in agriculture, with no household members listed in commerce. See WDPR 9:84ff., 90ff., and 492ff.; 10:30ff. and 70ff.; 11:56ff.; and 12:76ff. and 218ff. No occupational designations were listed for the other two households, both including proprietors of large general stores: 8:n.p. and 12:242ff. In the oddest case of all, the family of Abel Amsden, Sr., one of the area's most prominent manufacturers, owner and operator of the only carding factory among families with inventories, was listed as limited to agriculture. Abel Amsden, Sr., Reading, 1828, 11:370ff.

5. LeRoy Ladurie, *Peasants*, 155ff. He terms these groups "different milieus of sociocultural classes." Rutman, *Puritanism*; Lockridge, *Literacy*, 25ff; and Cole, *New Hampshire*, 166.

6. See David Hackett Fischer, "Federalists and Democracy" (Ph.D. diss., Johns Hopkins Univ., 1963), 2 vols., I:257–64 category no. 8, clerks; 9, lesser public officials; and 10 artists); and idem, *Revolution of American Conservatism*, where the "manufacturer" category was added, p. 120. In rural areas, individuals in a wide variety of occupations served as public officials; these were customary and expected roles, secondary to their primary occupations. See Jackson T. Main, *Social Structure*, esp. 257; and Bidwell, *Rural Economy*, 253–75.

7. See Webster, *American Dictionary*, I: "esquire" and "gentleman"; and Perry's and Walker's dictionaries. Fischer and Bidwell include a manufacturer category. Fischer and Main include a category covering semiskilled and unskilled laborers and another for "gentlemen" and "esquires," but their designations, esp. in the latter case, confuse social standing and role with occupation.

8. I used T.D. Seymour Bassett's superb *Vermont: A Bibliography* (Boston, 1981); McCorison, *Vermont Imprints*: the AAS Imprints Catalogue; the collections of VHS, Old Sturbridge Village, and Dartmouth College; and the Vermont State Papers.

9. This information has been drawn from (1) local and county histories; (2) VJ, 1795–1829; VtR, 1809–29; and VtR&J, 1829–30; (3) the Federal Censuses, 1790–1830; (4) 396 inventories with printed matter and 247 without, arranged by locales and then by townships (esp. helpful here was comparative evaluation of land under cultivation); and (5) the 1820 Federal Census of Manufactures schedules.

Appendix 4

1. In this case I used the New York, 1804, edition and consulted all English-language editions. For each edition used in this study I have attempted to locate at least 3 copies in original bindings. See G. Thomas Tanselle, *The History of Books as a Field of Study*, [Chapel Hill, N.C.], 1981, on the importance of establishing the text to be analyzed.

2. Jacob Blanck, comp., *A Bibliography of American Literature*, 6 vols. (New Haven, 1955–75), is one of the few major bibliographies including notations of spine titles, which Blanck referred to as "binder's" titles. He included those only for works where "the title on the binding varies from that on the title page." An example is T.B. Aldrich's *Pampinea and Other Poems* (1861). The spine title, *Poems of a Year*, is listed (I:xxxiii). Had the spine title been "Aldrich Poems," under Blanck's procedure it would not have been added to the entry. Some notations each have taken me up to 40 hours.

3. All extant editions (to 1830) were consulted; AAS, VHS, Library of Congress, Harvard Univ., and Princeton Univ. were the repositories most regularly checked.

4. In almost every case just one copy of these works was retained in a Windsor District library.

5. Secondhand sales were an important part of the book trade in the English countryside by the late eighteenth century. See Plant, *English Book Trade*.

6. This sequence has been compiled from WDPR, 1789–1830, and, for household data, the federal censuses.

7. Wives often had to purchase parts of household collections they wished to retain (and were not willed). See Edgar, "Libraries of Colonial South Carolina," 12 and 67, for examples elsewhere. Within the Upper Valley, see the inventory of John P. Williams of Chester (a lawyer who died in 1830), WDPR 12:60ff. Several similar profesional libraries distinguish the "family library" from the "law," etc., library.

8. See William Slade, comp., *The Laws of Vermont of a Public and Permanent Nature: Coming Down to, and Including the Year 1824* (Windsor, Vt., 1825), index of laws on probate court; and specific cases, WDPR 2:366ff. and 5:27ff.

9. E.g., Edgar, "Libraries of Colonial South Carolina," 12ff. and 21ff.

10. See, e.g., the 370-volume "Catalogue of Allen Wardner's Library" (1832), Doc Box 169, Stone and Green Coll., VHS. For evidence from other moments in the family cycle, see, e.g., Robert H. Irrmann, "The Library of an Ohio Farmer [1824–25]," *Ohio Archaeological and Historical Quarterly* 42 (1948):185–93. The farmer, also a justice of the peace, was still living in 1837. A second list is reprinted in N. Tiffany, *The Tiffany's of America* (n.p., n.d.), 145–46. This is a list of Consider Tiffany's library in 1788; he died in 1796 (pp. 140–47). For an extraordinary reading list, see Edwin R. Lancaster, "Books Read in Virginia in [the] Early Nineteenth Century, 1806–1823," *Virginia Historical Magazine* 42 (1938):56–59.

11. Our study group of 396 families with libraries includes 38 estates valued at $165 or less, whereas a fully representative sample would have 50–70.

12. See VJ, 29 Dec. 1806, 27 Jan. 1807, 20 Dec. 1819, and 9 Jan. 1830 for the 1830 meeting places; and also n. 8 above. The share of the four foothills communities was calculated from the five federal censuses, 1790–1830.

13. Edward Cook to Gilmore, 16 Nov. 1978, notes that with inventories, "you can't always distinguish between books someone went out and got, and books that were gifts or inheritance, and really didn't interest the owners." There is no known evidence that gifted and inherited print items typically "didn't interest the owners." On the rights of widows, and married women's property rights in Vermont, see ch. 7, n. 8. By comparison, see Harris, "Books on the Indiana Frontier," 428; Irrmann, "Library of an Early Ohio Farmer," 186; and Edgar, "Libraries of Colonial South Carolina," 69. Within Windsor County, see Gilmore, "Orestes Brownson," ch. 5. On gifting, see, e.g., Amasa Allen's 1820 will, WDPR 9:135ff. Phillip Bruce, *An Institutional History of Virginia in the Seventeenth Century*, 2 vols. (New York, 1910), 402–459, esp. 405; and Wolf, "Library of Ralph Assheton: The Book Background of a Colonial Philadelphia Lawyer," PBSA 58 (1964):345–79, p. 349.

14. I compared the imprints of Upper Valley presses every four years, 1787–1830. Differences in paper quality are confirmed in the printing office practices of the Walpole print center. See the extensive correspondence between it and the Isaiah Thomas parent firm at Worcester, Mass., 1797–1817, Isaiah Thomas Papers, AAS.

15. See Ward, *Fiction and the German Reading Public.*

16. On schoolbooks, see Cohen, *A Calculating People*, 116–49. On grammars and spellers see Monaghan, *A Common Heritage.*

Appendix 5

1. The John Williams family library of about 465 volumes was not specified in the inventory. All details of the Leverett estate come from the inventory filed 7 Oct. 1829, WDPR 11:508–16. See Harvard Univ., *Quinquennial Catalogue of the Officers and Graduates, 1636–1925* (Cambridge, Mass., 1925): *New England Historical and Genealogical Register* 2 (1848):326, on John Leverett's third wife's death; [Charles Edward Leverett], *A Memoir Biographical and Genealogical of Sir John Leverett, KNT., Governor of Massachusetts . . . and of the Family Generally* (Boston, 1956), 154–58, for most family details; Lawrence Brainerd, *Epitaphs, Old South Burying Ground* (Windsor, Vt., 1914), 78:79ff.; and Rev. Joshua Wyman Wellman, *Descendants of Thomas Wellman of Lynn, Mass.* (Boston, 1918), 269.

2. The data on size of household is from manuscript census schedules for Windsor, Windsor Co., Vt., 4th U.S. Census, 1820.

3. Leverett inventory, WDPR 11:508–12. The sketch and quote are in [Leverett], *A Memoir*, 157–58.

4. N.B. Harte, "Rees's *Cyclopaedia* as a Source for the History of the Textile Industries in the Early Nineteenth Century," *Textile History* 5 (1974):119–27; and Wallace, *Rockdale*, 115–16.

Abbreviations

AAS	American Antiquarian Society
AgH	*Agricultural History*
AHR	*American Historical Review*
AQ	*American Quarterly*
CSSH	*Comparative Studies in Society and History*
DAED	*Daedalus: Journal of the American Academy of Arts and Sciences*
DHI	Philip P. Wiener, *Dictionary of the History of Ideas*
FM	[Walpole] *Farmer's Museum, or Literary Gazette*
HW	*History Workshop: A Journal of Socialist and Feminist Historians*
JAH	*Journal of American History*
JIH	*Journal of Interdisciplinary History*
JLH	*Journal of Library History*
NHHS	New Hampshire Historical Society
PAAS	*Proceedings of the American Antiquarian Society*
PBSA	*Papers of the Bibliographical Society of America*
RAH	*Reviews in American History*
SB	*Studies in Bibliography*
UVt	Rare Books and Manuscript Division, University of Vermont
VHS	Vermont Historical Society
VtC	[Windsor] *Vermont Chronicle*
VtH	*Vermont History*
VtJ	[Windsor] *Vermont Journal*
VtR	[Windsor] *Vermont Republican*
VtR&J	[Windsor] *Vermont Republican and Journal*
Wash	[Windsor] *Washingtonian*
WDPR	Windsor District Probate Records
WMQ	*William and Mary Quarterly*

Bibliography

I. Primary Sources

A. Manuscripts.

Burlington, Vt. University of Vermont Library. Rare Books and Manuscript Division. D.H. Hilton General Store, Day Book, 1827–29.

Charlottesville, Va. University of Virginia. Alderman Library. Dummerston, Vermont, Social Library Records, 1808–40.

Concord, N.H. New Hampshire Historical Society. John Campbell Diary, vol. 1, 1807.

————. Nathan K. Abbott Diary, vols. 1 and 2, 1845–46.

Montpelier, Vt. Vermont Historical Society. Account Books, Windsor District, 1755–1851.

————. Daniel Mason Account Book [Cavendish, Vermont], 1804–20.

————. James Whitelaw Papers. Author-Publisher Correspondence.

————. Misc. Collection of Inventories. Isaac N. Curtineus Inventory, 27 Apr. 1824.

————. Post Office Records, Ryegate, Vt., 1825–26.

————. Stone and Green Collection. Doc Box 169. A Catalogue of Allen Wardner's Library, 1832.

————. William Dow Account Books, 1839–65.

————. MS-B-B1930. Lydia P. Baldwin Diary.

————. MS 608.743 M136 "Patents Granted to Vermonters Before the Year 1831," Prepared by Marcus McCorison.

————. MS 974.31C315L. Cavendish Social Library. "Memorandum of Books Delivered from and Returned to Cavendish Library, 1815–1840" and other Cavendish Social Library Records, 1815–33.

————. MSC-150. Proctorsville Reading Club Journal.

————. MSC-150. Comfort Chafee Account Book.

————. MSC-174. Invoice of Peddler's Goods, 31 Dec. 1842.

————. MSS-20 #74. ALS. Samuel Hall to E.P. Walton [?], 1833.

————. MSS-30 #17 Je.–Dec. 1813. ALS. Thomas Tolman to James Whitelaw, 13 Nov. 1813.

————. XMSC-15, 1833. Windsor, Vt., General Store Records of Harris and Morrills' Stock on Hand, 1 Apr. 1833.

————. XMSC-15. James Tarbox Account Book, Including General Store Stock Records [Windsor, Vt.]

Montpelier, Vt. Vermont Public Records Division. Stockbridge, Vt., Town Meeting Minutes, 1801–3.

————. Windsor District Guardian Records, vols. 1–4: 1805–55. Microfilm copy.

———. Windsor District Probate Records. Wills, Inventories, and Estate Settlements, vols. 1–20: 1787–1840. Microfilm copy.

———. U.S. Census Schedules for Vermont for 1790–1840. Microfilm copy.

———. U.S. Census Schedules of Manufactures for 1820 and 1832. Microfilm copy.

Montpelier, Vt. Vermont Secretary of State Papers. Petitions, vols. 45–46.

New Haven, Conn. Yale University. Beinecke Library. G. & C. Merriam Co. Sales Records, 1818–36.

South Bend, Ind. University of Notre Dame Archives. Orestes A. Brownson Papers. Subscription List for *The Philanthropist*, Ithaca, 1831–32.

Worcester, Mass. American Antiquarian Society. Account Books, Windsor District, Vt., 1755–1851.

———. Book Trades Collection. Box 2, Folder 3. Complete Account of Stock, "Buffalo Bookstore, 180 Broadway, New York City for 1840."

———. Isaiah Thomas Papers. Correspondence between Isaiah Thomas and Robert B. Thomas, 1793–1799.

———. Isaiah Thomas Papers. Boxes 8–11. Isaiah Thomas Print Center Network, Bookstore Accounts of Stock, 1796–1823.

———. Isaiah Thomas Papers. Boxes 8–11. Walpole, N.H. Bookstore Accounts of Stock, 1796–1818.

———. Isaiah Thomas Papers. Walpole, N.H. Bookstore Record of Sales for 1809.

———. Isaiah Thomas Papers. Walpole, N.H. Print Center Exchange Books, 2 vols.: 1802–9.

———. Isaiah Thomas Papers. Walpole, N.H. Correspondence between Walpole [N.H.] Print Center and the Isaiah Thomas Parent Firm at Worcester, 1797–1811.

———. Isaiah Thomas Papers. Walpole, N.H. Correspondence between Anson Whipple, Walpole, N.H., and Isaiah Thomas, 1812–17.

———. West Brookfield, Mass. William Merriam's Account Book, 1831–33. Microfilm copy.

B. Newspapers and Periodicals.

A few newspapers were not specifically listed in notes but are listed here because they were used extensively to compile the directory of businesses in chapter 2, the fund of evidence for perceptions of print communications in chapter 6, and the universe of available reading in chapter 8.

American Baptist Magazine and Missionary Intelligencer. Boston. 1817–19. 2 vols.

American Penny Magazine and Family Newspaper. New York. 1845.

American Review of History and Politics, and General Repository of Literature and State Papers. 4 vols. Philadelphia. 1811–12.

Analectic Magazine. 14 vols. Philadelphia. 1813–20.

Analectic Magazine. "Systems of Elementary Education." 1817: 285–300.

The Atheneum: Or, Spirit of the English Magazines. Boston. 1817–23.

Bellows Falls Gazette. Bellows Falls, Vt. 1839.

Boston Courier (semi-weekly version). Boston. 1849–50.

Boston Magazine. Boston. 1803–6.

Brownson's Quarterly Review. Brownson, Orestes. "Liberalism and Progress," 21 (1864):454.

Cayuga Patriot. Auburn, N.Y. 1830.

Cheshire Advertiser. Keene, N.H. 1792.

The Christian Repository. Woodstock, Vt. 1820–29.

The Churchman's Magazine [of the Protestant Episcopal Church]. New Haven. 1804–15; 1821–27.

Concord [N.H.] Mirror. Concord, N.H. 1799.

Courier of New Hampshire. Concord, N.H. 1800.

Democratic Republican. Walpole, N.H. 1812.

Farmer's Journal. Danbury, Conn. 1792.

Farmer's Library. Rutland, Vt. 1793–94.

Farmer's Museum, or Literary Gazette. Walpole, N.H. 1793–1809.

Freedom's Banner. Chester, Vt. 1828–29.

Genesee Republican and Herald of Reform. LeRoy, N.Y. 1830.

The Gospel Herald. New York. 1820–27.

Green Mountain Palladium. Chester, Vt. 1807–8.

Hartford Connecticut Courant. Hartford, Conn. 1778.

Henry Clay and Advocate of the American System. Woodstock, Vt. 1830.

The Looker-On. London. 1792–93.

The Massachusetts Magazine: or Monthly Museum. 8 vols. Boston. 1789–96.

The Medical Repository. 23 vols. New York. 1797–1824.

The Mirror. 2 vols. Edinburgh. 1779–80.

The Morning Ray. Windsor, Vt. 1791–92.

Museum of Foreign Literature, Science, and Art. 17 vols. Philadelphia. 1822–30.

New England Magazine. 1832.

New Hampshire Sentinel. Keene, N.H. 1799.

Northern Memento. Woodstock, Vt. 1805.

The Panoplist [various titles]. 5 vols. Boston. 1805–9.

Philadelphia Repository and Weekly Register. 5 vols. Philadelphia. 1800–1806.

Political Observatory. Walpole, N.H. 1803.

The Polyanthos. 11 vols. Boston. 1805–14.

The Rambler. 4 vols. London. 1750–52.

Rising Sun. Keene, N.H. 1795.

Rural Magazine: or Vermont Repository. Rutland, Vt. 1795–96.

The Spectator. 8 vols. London. 1711–14. Reprint. 2 vols. New York. 1826.

Theological Magazine, or Synopsis of Modern Religious Sentiment On a New Plan. 3 vols. New York. 1795–99.

Vermont Baptist Missionary Magazine. Rutland, Vt. 1812.

Vermont Chronicle. Windsor, Vt. 1827–43.

Vermont Courier. Rutland, Vt. 1810.

Vermont Intelligencer [various titles]. Bellows Falls, Vt. 1820, 1830.

Vermont Journal [various titles]. Windsor, Vt. 1783–1829.

Vermont Mercury. Woodstock, Vt. 1842.

Vermont Phenix. Chester, Vt. 1829.

Vermont Republican. Windsor, Vt. 1809–29.

Vermont Republican and Journal [various titles]. Windsor, Vt. 1830–40.

Village Magazine. Windsor, Vt., 1803–4.

Washingtonian. Windsor, Vt. 1810–16.

Weekly Wanderer. Randolph, Vt. 1810.

Windsor Federal Gazette. Windsor, Vt. 1801–4.

Windsor Post-Boy. Windsor, Vt. 1805–7.

Woodstock Observer. Woodstock, Vt. 1820.

Working-Man's Gazette. Woodstock, Vt. 1830–31.

The Young Gentleman's and Ladies Magazine. 2 vols. London. 1799–1800.

C. Other Printed Primary Sources, and Paintings.

For all books, pamphlets, broadsides, almanacs (and also periodicals, included above) read by Windsor District residents and found in estate inventories and wills, or elsewise known to have been read, I have decoded the spine title system of bibliographic description to ascertain the precise work in question and then sought the specific edition most likely to have been used by each family. Between a 1795 edition and an 1818 edition, texts were changed by authors and publishers, who liberally substituted and added forewords, commentary, etc. To avoid confusion, and since the full list of all editions consulted approximates a complete bibliography of every edition of some 1,230 different works, 1780–1830, here full bibliographical information is given only for the edition most frequently consulted.

Abell, Truman, comp. *New England Farmer's Diary and Almanac.* Weathersfield and Windsor, Vt., 1814–20.

Adams, Daniel. *The Scholar's Arithmetic: or Federal Accountant.* Leominster, Mass., 1801.

Adams, George. *Lectures on Natural and Experimental Philosophy. Considered in its Present State of Improvement.* 4 vols. Philadelphia, 1806–7.

Adams, Hannah. *A Summary History of New England.* Boston, 1799.

————. *A View of Religions in Two Parts.* 2d ed. Boston, 1791.

Agrippa von Nettesheim, Heinrich Cornelius. *Three Books of Occult Philosophy or Magic*(1533). Translated. London, 1651. Reprint. New York, 1971.

Aikin, John. *A View of the Life, Travels and Philanthropic Labours of the Late John Howard.* New York, 1814.

Alexander, Caleb. *The Columbian Dictionary of the English Language.* Boston, 1800.

————. *A New and Complete System of Arithmetic.* Albany, N.Y., 1802.

Allen, Ethan. *A Narrative of Col. Ethan Allen's Captivity.* Walpole, N.H., 1807.

————. *Reason the Only Oracle of Man; or, A Compendious System of Natural Religion.* Bennington, Vt., 1784.

Allestree, Richard. *The Whole Duty of Man.* Williamsburg, Va., 1746.

American Antiquarian Society. *Dictionary Catalogue,* vol. 20, pp. 377–81. Books on "knowledge" and "wisdom."

American State Papers. State Papers and Public Documents of the United States from the Accession of Thomas Jefferson to the Presidency [through 1815]. 5 vols. Boston, 1814–15.

Ames, Fisher. *The Works of Fisher Ames, Compiled by a Number of His Friends, To Which are Prefixed Notices of His Life and Character.* Boston, 1809.

Anderson, Aeneas. *A Narrative of the British Embassy to China, In the Years 1792, 1793, and 1794.* Philadelphia, 1795.

Anson, Commodore George. *A Voyage to the South Seas, and to Many Other Parts of the World.* Edited by John Bulkeley. London, 1748; facsimile ed., London, 1974.

Backus, Isaac. *A History of the Baptists in New England from 1622 to 1804.* 3 vols. Boston, 1777; Providence, 1784; and Boston, 1796.

Bailey, Nathan. *A Key to the English Language.* Middletown, Conn., 1807.

Ballou, Hosea. *A Treatise on Atonement.* Randolph, Vt., 1805.

————. *Universalist Hymn Book.* Boston, 1821.

Baltimore Almanac for 1784. Baltimore, 1783.

Banks, John. *A New History of the Life and Reign of the Czar Peter the Great, Emperor of all Russia.* New York, 1804.

Barlow, Joel. *The Columbiad.* 2 vols. Philadelphia, 1809.

————. *The Vision of Columbus.* 1st Hartford, Conn., 1787 ed.

Barnes, Lucy. *The Female Christian, Containing a Selection from the Writings of Miss Lucy Barnes.* Portland, Me., 1809.

Baxter, Richard. *The Saints' Everlasting Rest.* Introduction by Benjamin Fawcett. Philadelphia, 1830. Also reprinted ed. Introduction by John T. Wilkinson. London, 1962.

Beattie, James. *The Minstrel; or the Progress of Genius.* New York, 1812.

Bennett, John. *Letters to a Young Lady.* New York, 1824.

[Beresford, James]. *Miseries of Human Life, or Groans of Samuel Sensitive and Timothy Testy, with a Few Supplemental Signs from Mrs. Testy.* Boston, 1807.

Bible. *The Holy Bible: Containing the Old and New Testaments: Together With the Apocrypha.* Windsor, Vt., 1812.

Bible. *The Holy Bible: Containing the Old & New Testaments: Together With the Apocrypha.* Brattleboro, Vt., 1816.

Bigland, John. *A Geographical and Historical View of the World.* 5 vols. Boston, 1811.

———. *Letters on the Study and Use of Ancient and Modern History.* Philadelphia, 1814.

Bingham, Caleb. *American Preceptor.* Boston, 1811.

Blackstone, William. *Commentaries on the Laws of England.* 4 vols. Oxford, 1769; facsimile ed., 1979.

Blair, Hugh. *Lectures on Rhetoric and Belles Lettres.* 2 vols. Philadelphia, 1793.

Book of Common Prayer [of the] Church of England. New York, 1810.

Booth, Abraham. *An Apology for the Baptists.* Philadelphia, 1788.

Boston, Thomas. *The Crook in the Lot: or, the Sovereignty and Wisdom of God in the Afflictions of Men, Displayed.* Philadelphia, 1792.

———. *Human Nature in its Fourfold State.* New York, 1811.

Bourne, George. *History of Napoleon Bonaparte: Emperor of the French and King of the Italians.* Boston, 1806.

Bowen, Abel. *The Naval Monument Containing Official and Other Accounts.* Boston, 1816.

Bradley, Joshua. *Some of the Beauties of Freemasonry.* Haverhill, Mass., 1822.

[Britton, John]. *The Pleasures of Human Life.* Boston, 1807.

Brownson, Orestes. *The Convert; or, Leaves from My Experience.* New York, 1857.

Bruce, James. *An Interesting Narrative of the Travels of James Bruce, Esquire, into Abyssinia, to Discover the Source of the Nile.* Abridged ed. Boston, 1798.

Brydon, Patrick. *A Tour through Sicily and Malta. In a Series of Letters.* Boston, 1792.

Buchan, William. *Domestic Medicine: or a Treatise on the Prevention and Cure of Diseases, by Regimen and Simple Medicines, with an Appendix for the Use of Private Practitioners.* Fairhaven, Vt., 1798.

Buchanan, Claudius. *The Works of . . . Comprising His Christian Researches in Asia.* Montpelier, Vt., 1813.

Buckingham, Joseph. *Specimens of Newspaper Literature.* 2 vols. Boston, 1852.

Bunyan, John. *Grace Abounding.* Exeter, N.H., 1793.

———. *The Pilgrim's Progress.* Brattleborough, Vt., 1815.

———. *Sighs from Hell.* Boston, 1708.

Burgh, James. *The Art of Speaking.* Baltimore, 1804.

Burk, John Dale. *History of the Late War in Ireland.* Philadelphia, 1799.

Burnet, Thomas. *The Theory of the Earth, Containing an Account of the Origins of the Earth.* 2 vols. London, 1684–90.

Burroughs, Eden. *A Faithful Narrative of the Wonderful Dealings of God Towards Polly Davis.* Windsor, Vt., 1792.

———. *The Profession and Practice of Christians Held Up to View by Way of Contrast to Each Other.* New London, Conn., 1793.

Butler, Frederick. *A Complete History of the United States of America Down to the Year 1820.* 3 vols. Hartford, Conn., 1821.

———. *Sketches of universal history, sacred and profane, from the creation of the World, to the year 1818 [Letters on History].* Hartford, Conn., 1818.

Byron, George Gordon. *English Bards and Scottish Reviewers.* Boston, 1814.

———. *Works of the Right Honorable Lord Byron.* 4 vols. New York, 1821.

Campbell, John. *Travels in South Africa Undertaken at the Request of the Missionary Society.* Andover, Mass., 1816.

Care, Henry. *English Liberties, or the Free Born Subject's Inheritance Containing the Magna Charts.* Updated by William Nelson. Providence, R.I., 1774.

Carey, Mathew. *The Olive Branch: or Faults on Both Sides, Federal and Democratic.* 7th ed. Philadelphia, 1815.

Carp, Alvah. Chelsea Vermont Diary, 1861–63. In "The Impact of Rural Depopulation on the Local Economy of Chelsea, Vermont, 1840–1900." Edited by Hal Seth Barron. AgH 54 (1980):324ff.

Carver, John. *Travels through the Interior Parts of North America. [1766–68].* London, 1768.

Cervantes Saavedra, Miguel de. *Don Quixote of La Mancha.* 4 vols. New York, 1815.

Chalmers, Thomas. *The Application of Christianity to the Commercial and Ordinary Affairs of Life, in a Series of Discourses.* Hartford, Conn., 1821.

———. *Discourses on the Christian Revelation.* Andover, Mass., 1818.

———. *Sermons Preached in St. John's Church, Glasgow.* Philadelphia, 1824.

Chapone, Hester. *Letters on the Improvement of the Mind, Addressed to a Lady.* New York, 1826.

Chauncy, Charles. *The Benevolence of the Deity, Fairly and Impartially Considered.* Boston, 1784.

———. *Seasonable Thoughts on the State of Religion in New England.* Boston, 1743.

Chesterfield, Phillip Dormer Stanhope. *Letters Written by the Late Right Honorable . . . To His Son.* 2 vols. Baltimore, 1813.

[Chetwood, William Rufus]. *The Voyages and Adventures of Captain Robert Boyle in several parts of the world.* Montpelier, Vt., 1812.

Chipman, Nathaniel. *Reports and Dissertations.* Rutland, Vt., 1793.

The Christian Economy. Tr. from the original Greek of an old manuscript, found in the Island of Patmos. Windsor, Vt., 1788.

The Civil Officer, or the Whole Duty of Sheriffs, Coroners, Constables, and Collectors of Taxes. Boston, 1809.

Clark, Jefferson. *Address Delivered at the Anniversary Celebration of the Franklin Typographical Society, Jan. 17, 1826.* Boston, 1826.

Clarke, Adam. *A Discourse on the Nature, Design, and Institution of the Holy Eucharist.* New York, 1812.

———. *The Holy Bible With Commentary and Critical Notes.* New York, 1811.

Clarke, Edward D. *Travels in Various Countries in Europe, Asia, and Africa, Commencing January 1, 1801.* 14 vols. New York and Hartford, Conn., 1811–17.

[Cleland, John]. *Memoirs of A Woman of Pleasure.* In Accounts of Stock, Walpole, N.H., 1817. Isaiah Thomas Papers. AAS.

Cole, Amos. *The New Hampshire and Vermont Almanac for 1809.* Windsor, Vt., 1808.

The Complete Farmer: or, General Dictionary of Agriculture and Husbandry. 5th ed. London, 1807.

Cooper, James Fenimore. *Notions of the Americans.* (1828). 2 vols. New York, 1963 ed.

Cowper, William. *Collected Poems.* 3 vols. New York, 1821.

Crawford, Charles. *The Christian: A Poem in Four Books.* Philadelphia, 1783.

Culpeper, Nicholas. *The English Physician Enlarged, containing 369 Receipts for Medicines Made From Herbs.* Taunton, Mass., 1826.

Cumberland, Richard. *Memoirs*. Boston, 1806.

Cummings, Jacob. *An Introduction to Ancient and Modern Geography on the Plan of Goldsmith and Guy*. Boston, 1814.

Cutting, Sewall. "Historical Address." In *Centennial Memorial of Windsor, Vermont, July 4, 1876*. Windsor, Vt., 1876.

Daboll, Nathan. *The Schoolmaster's Assistant*. New London, Conn., 1800.

Dartmouth College. *Catalogue of the Library*. Hanover, N.H., 1813.

Davison, Phineas. *Evangelical Poems*. [Palmer, Mass., 1810].

Deane, Samuel. *New England Farmer; or Georgical Dictionary*. Worcester, Mass., 1790.

Defoe, Daniel. *The Religious Courtship. Being Historical Discourses on the Necessity of Marrying Religious Husbands and Wives Only*. Montpelier, Vt., 1810.

————. *The Wonderful Life and Surprizing Adventures Of that Renowned Hero, Robinson Crusoe*. Boston, 1779.

Depon, François R.J. *A Voyage to the Eastern part of Terra Firma, or the Spanish Main in South America*. 3 vols. New York, 1806.

Dick, John. *The New Gardener's Dictionary; or the Whole Art of Gardening Fully and Accurately Displayed*. London, 1771.

Dickinson, Rodolphus. *A Compendium to the Bible*. Greenfield, Mass., 1815.

Dictionary of Trade [No copy located].

Dilworth, Thomas. *The Schoolmaster's Assistant*. New York, 1802.

Doddridge, Philip. *Four Sermons on the Religious Education of Children*. London, 1796.

————. *New Testament Family Expositor*. 6 vols. Charlestown, Mass., 1807–8.

————. *Rise and Progress of Religion in the Soul*. New York, 1809.

Dow, Lorenzo. *The Life and Travels of Lorenzo Dow*. Hartford, Conn., 1804.

Dryden, John. *The Poetical Works of John Dryden With the Life of the Author*. 2 vols. London, 1798.

Duncan, William. *The Elements of Logick in Four Books. Designed Particularly for Young Men at the University*. Albany, N.Y., 1814.

[Dunham, John M.]. *The Vocal Companion and Masonic Register*. Boston, 1802.

Dutton, Salmon. *An Examination of the Modern Doctrine of Future Punishment*. Boston, 1819.

Dwight, Timothy. *Sermons*. 2 vols. New Haven, Conn., 1828.

————. *Travels in New England and New York*. Edited by Barbara Miller Solomon. 4 vols. Cambridge, Mass., 1969.

Eddy, Isaac. *Chronology Delineated to Illustrate the History of Monarchical Revolutions*. Weathersfield, Vt., 1813.

Edgeworth, Maria. *Practical Education*. 2 vols. Boston, 1815.

————. *Tales of Fashionable Life*. 2 vols. Boston, 1810.

Edwards, Jonathan. *An Account of the Life of the Rev. David Brainerd, Minister of the Gospel*. Worcester, Mass., 1793.

————. *History of the Work of Redemption; Containing the Outlines of a Body of Divinity in a Method Entirely New*. Worcester, Mass., 1792.

————. *A Treatise Concerning Religious Affections*. Worcester, Mass., 1808. Edited by John E. Smith. New Haven, Conn., 1959.

————. *The Works of President Edwards*. 8 vols. Worcester, Mass., 1808.

Enfield, William. *The Speaker: or, Miscellaneous Pieces Selected from the Best English Writers. With an Essay on Elocution*. Boston, 1795.

Erra Pater [pseud.]. *The Book of Knowledge: Treating of the Wisdom of the Ancients. In Three Parts*. Albany, N.Y., 1809.

Espinassi, Isaac. *A Digest of the Law and Actions and Trials at Nisi Prius*. 2 vols. Walpole, N.H., 1801.

The Federalist, on the New Constitution, Written in the Year 1788, *by Mr. Hamilton, Mr. Madison, and Mr. Jay; With an Appendix.* Hallowell, Me., 1826.

Fenning, Daniel. *The Ready Reckoner, or Traders' Useful Assistant in Buying and Selling All Sorts of Commodities.* New York, 1803.

Ferguson, Adam. *An Essay on the History of Civil Society.* Philadelphia, 1819.

[Fessenden, Thomas G.]. Caustic, Christopher. *Terrible Tractoration!! A Poetical Petition.* New York, 1804.

Ffirth, John. *The Experience of Gospel Labours of the Reverend Benjamin Abbott.* Philadelphia, 1802.

Fielding, Henry. *The History of Tom Jones. A Foundling.* 3 vols. New York, 1816.

Firman, Giles. *The Real Christian: or a Treatise of Effectual Calling.* Boston, 1742.

First U.S. Census, Heads of Household. Washington, D.C., 1909.

Fisher, George. *The Instructor, or The American Young Man's Best Companion.* Walpole, N.H., 1794; Philadelphia, 1801.

Flavel, John. *A Token for Mourners.* Andover, Mass., 1820.

———. *Two Select Works.* Boston, 1815.

Fléchière, John William. *An Appeal to Matters of Fact and Common Sense, or a Rational Demonstration of Man's Corrupt and Lost Estate.* New York, 1813.

Foster, Dan. *A Critical and Candid Examination of the Doctrine of Eternal Misery.* Walpole, N.H., 1803.

Foster, Robert, ed. *Hymns and Spiritual Songs.* Portsmouth, N.H., 1818.

Franklin, Benjamin. *The Life of Dr. Benjamin Franklin.* New York, 1825.

———. *The Way to Wealth.* Worcester, Mass., 1790.

———. *Works.* 2 vols. New York, 1807.

Free and Accepted Masons. *Masonick Constitutions.* New York, 1789.

Freneau, Phillip. *The Miscellaneous Works of Phillip Freneau.* Philadelphia, 1788.

———. *Poems.* 2 vols. in 1. New York, 1815.

———. *Poems Written Between the Years 1768 and 1794.* Monmouth, N.J., 1795.

Gay, John. *Fables.* 1727 and 1735 series. Philadelphia, 1808.

Genlis, Stéphanie Félicité Ducrest de St. Aubin de. *Alphonso and Dalinda: or, The Magic of Art and Nature. A Moral Tale.* Fairhaven, Vt., 1799.

George, Henry. *A Pocket Geographical and Statistical Gazetteer of the State of Vermont.* Haverhill, N.H., 1823.

Gessner, Salomon. *The Death of Abel.* Concord, N.H., 1793.

Goldsmith, Oliver. *The Citizen of the World.* 2 vols. Philadelphia, 1802.

———. *An History of the Earth, and Animated Nature.* 4 vols. Philadelphia, 1795.

———. *The Vicar of Wakefield. A Tale.* Brattleborough, Vt., 1814.

Goodrich, Charles A. *A History of the United States of America, on a Plan Adapted to the Capacity of Youths.* Bellows Falls, Vt., 1827.

[Goodrich, Samuel Griswold]. *The Child's arithmetic, being an easy and cheap introduction to Daboll's, Pike's, White's and other arithmetics.* Hartford, Conn., 1818.

Graham, John A. *A Descriptive Sketch of the Present State of Vermont.* London, 1797.

Grandpré, Louis M.J. O'Hier de. *A Voyage in the Indian Ocean and to Bengal, Undertaken in the Year* 1790. Brattleborough, Vt., 1814.

Grierson, Miss. *Pierre and His Family: or, A Story of the Waldenses.* New York, 1827.

Griffin, Edward. *A Series of Lectures, Delivered in Park Street Church, Boston, on Sabbath Evening.* Boston, 1813.

Guthrie, William. *A New Geographical, Historical, and Commercial Grammar; and Present State of the World.* 2 vols. Philadelphia, 1809.

Hamilton, Elizabeth. *Letters on the Elementary Principles of Education.* 2 vols. Philadelphia, 1813.

Harwood, Edward. *The Life and Character of Jesus Christ Delineated.* Philadelphia, 1819.

Hastings, Susanna. *A Narrative of the Captivity of Mrs. Johnson.* Windsor, Vt., 1807.

Haswell, Anthony. *Constitution and Catalogue of the Pawlet Library.* Bennington, Vt., 1799.

Hawkesworth, John. *A New Voyage Round the World. Performed by Captain James Cook.* London, 1780.

Hayes, Richard. *The Negociator's Magazine, or the Most Authentic Account Yet Published of Monies.* London, 1777.

Heaton, Nathaniel. *The Pleasing Library. Containing a Selection of Humorous, Entertaining, Eleant and Instructive Pieces in Prose and Poetry.* Wrentham, Mass., 1801.

Hervey, James. *Meditations and Contemplations.* 2 vols. Brattleborough, Vt., 1814.

Heydon, John. *Theomagia or the Temple of Wisdom in Three Parts, Spiritual, Celestial and Elemental: Containing the Occult Powers of the Angels of Astromancy in the Telesmatical Sculpture of the Persians and Egyptians.* 3 vols. London, 1663–64.

The Hive: or a Collection of Thoughts on Civil, Moral, Sentimental & Religious Subjects. Worcester, Mass., 1796.

Hoare, Louisa. *Hints for the Improvement of Early Education and Nursery Discipline.* Salem, Mass., 1826.

Hofland, Barbara Wreaks. *Says She to Her Neighbor, What.* 4 vols. in 2. New York, 1815.

Homerus. *The Iliad of Homer.* Translated by Alexander Pope. 2 vols. Baltimore, 1812.

———. *The Odyssey of Homer.* Translated by Alexander Pope. 2 vols. Philadelphia, 1813.

Horace. *Opera, Interpretation et notis illustravit Ludovicus Desperez in usum Serenissim Delphini.* Philadelphia, 1814.

Houghton, Asa, comp. *The Ladies' and Gentlemen's Diary, and Almanack.* Bellows Falls, Vt., [1818].

Hoyt, Edward A., ed. *General Petitions, 1778–1787,* vol. 8, and *General Petitions, 1788– 1792,* vol. 9. *The State Papers of Vermont,* Montpelier, Vt., 1952.

Hubbard, John. *The American Reader.* Bellows Falls, Vt., 1817.

Hubbard, William. *A Narrative of the Indian Wars in New England.* Brattleborough, Vt., 1814.

Humphreys, David. *An Essay on the Life of the Honorable Major-General Israel Putnam.* Brattleborough, Vt., 1812.

Hunter, Henry. *Sacred Biography; or the History of Jesus Christ.* 4 vols. Walpole, N.H., 1803.

Hunter, John D. *Manners and Customs of Several Indian Tribes Located West of the Mississippi.* London, 1824; facsimile ed., Milwaukee, Wis., 1964.

Huntington, Joseph. *Calvinism Improved.* New London, Conn., 1796.

Irving, Washington. *The Sketch Book of Geoffrey Crayon, Gent.* 7 pts. New York, 1819–20.

Jackson, William. *Book-keeping in the True Italian Form of Debtor and Creditor By Way of Double Entry.* Philadelphia, 1801.

Janeway, James. *A Token for Children.* Bennington, Vt., 1815.

Jefferson, Thomas. *Notes on the State of Virginia.* Newark, N.J., 1801.

Jennings, W. *The Foundlings of Belgrade, a Translation from the French.* New York, 1808.

Johnson, Daniel. *The American Shipmaster's Daily Assistant.* Portland, Me., 1807.

Johnson, Samuel. *Dictionary of the English Language.* London, 1790.

———. *The History of Rasselas, Prince of Abissinia.* Brattleborough, Vt., 1813.

———. *The Lives of the Most Eminent English Poets.* 3 vols. Philadelphia, 1819.

Josephus, Flavius. *The Genuine Works of Flavius Josephus.* 6 vols. New York, 1825.

Junius [pseud.]. *The Letters of Junius. With Notes and Illustrations, Historical, Political, Biographical, and Critical.* Boston, 1826.

Kames, Henry Home, Lord. *Elements of Criticism.* 2 vols. Boston, 1796.

Keate, George. *Sketches From Nature.* Boston, 1793.

Kenrick, William. *The Whole Duty of Woman*. Exeter, N.H., 1794.

Kimball, Horace. *The Naval Temple, Containing a Complete History of the Battles Fought by the Navy of the United States, From Its Establishment in 1794, to the Present Time*. Boston, 1816.

Kinne, Aaron. *An Explanation of the Principal Types, the Prophecies of Daniel and Hosea, the Revelation, and Other Symbolical Passages of the Holy Scriptures*. Boston, 1814.

Knox, Vicesimus. *Christian Philosophy*. Philadelphia, 1804.

Lambert, John. *Travels in Lower Canada and North America*. 2 vols. London, 1810.

Lane, Samuel. *A Journal for the Years, 1739–1803*. Edited by Charles Lane Hanson. Concord, N.H., 1937.

Langdon, Samuel. *Observations on the Revelation of Jesus Christ to Saint John*. Worcester, Mass., 1791.

Lathrop, Leonard. *Farmer's Library; or, Essays Designed to Encourage the Pursuit and Promote the Science of Agriculture*. Rutland, Vt., 1825.

Law, William. *A Serious Call to a Devout and Holy Life*. London, 1728; reprint, London, 1955.

Leavitt, Joshua. *Easy Lessons in Reading for the Use of Younger Classes in Common Schools*. Watertown, N.Y., 1827.

[Leslie, Charles]. *A Short and Easy Method With the Deists*. Windsor, Vt., 1812.

Livingston, Robert R. *Essay on Sheep; Their Varieties*. New York, 1809.

Locke, John. *An Essay on Human Understanding*. London, 1690; facsimile ed., 2 vols. New York, 1959.

Locke, John. *Outlines of Botany, Taken Chiefly from Smith's Introduction: Containing an Explanation of Botanical Terms and an Illustration of the System of Linnaeus*. Boston, 1819.

Love, John. *Geodaesia: or, the Art of Surveying, and Measuring Land Made Easy*. New York, 1793.

The Lucky Mistake: A New Novel, or The pleasing story of Rinaldo & Atlante. Brattleborough, Vt. [n.d., c. 1803–8].

Lyon, James. *The Scourge of Aristocracy and Repository of Important Political Truths*. 4 nos. Fairhaven, Vt., 1798.

Lyttleton, George. *Dialogues of the Dead*. Worcester, Mass., 1797.

McClure, David, and Elijah Parish. *Memoirs of the Rev. Eleazer Wheelock, DD., Founder and President of Dartmouth College and Moor's Charity School*. Newburyport, Mass., 1811.

McCorison, Marcus, ed. "A Daybook From the Office of the *Rutland Herald* Kept by Samuel Williams, 1798–1802." PAAS 76 Pt. 2 (1967): 293–395.

McCrie, Thomas. *The Life of John Knox*. New York, 1813.

Macgowan, John. *The Life of Joseph the Son of Israel, Chiefly Designed to Allure Young Minds to a Love of the Sacred Scriptures*. London, 1771.

Mackenzie, Sir Alexander. *Voyages from Montreal on the River St. Laurence, Through the Continent of North America to the Frozen Pacific Ocean in the Years 1789 and 1793*. New York, 1813.

Macklin, Charles. *The Man of the World*. Boston, 1795.

Mall, Thomas. *A History of the Martyrs Epitomised. A Cloud of Witnesses; or the Sufferers Mirrour*. 2 vols. Boston, 1747.

Mandeville, Bernard. *The Fable of the Bees; or, Private Vices, Public Benefits*. 2 vols. London, 1795.

———. *The Fable of the Bees; or, Private Vices, Public Benefits*. Original poem. Boston, 1811.

Manners and Customs. Windsor, Vt., n.d.

Manvill, Mrs. P.D. *Lucinda, or the mountain mourner*. Ballston Spa, N.Y., 1807.

Marshall, John. *The Life of George Washington, Commander in Chief of the American Forces and First President of the United States*. 5 vols. Philadelphia, 1804–7.

Martin, John. *The Conquest of Canaan*. Frankford, Pa., 1811.

Mason, John. *A Treatise on Self-Knowledge; Showing the Nature and Benefit of that Important Science, and the Way to Attain It*. Montpelier, Vt., 1813.

Mathias, Thomas James. *The Pursuits of Literature.* Philadelphia, 1800.

Mayhew, Jonathan. *Sermons Upon the Following Subjects.* Boston, 1755.

Melville, Herman. *Moby Dick.* 1851. Indianapolis, Ind., 1964.

Merritt, Timothy. *Strictures on Mr. Ballou's Sermon.* Boston, 1818.

Methodist Episcopal Church. *The Doctrines and Discipline of the Methodist Episcopal Church.* New York, 1805.

Miller, Samuel. *A Brief Retrospect of the Eighteenth Century.* 2 vols. New York, 1803.

Milton, John. *The Poetical Works.* 2 vols. Springfield, Mass., 1794.

Minot, George R. *Continuation of the History of the Province of Massachusetts Bay, from the Year 1748 to 1765, With an Introductory Sketch of Events from its Original Settlement,* vol. 1, Boston, 1798.

Montesquieu, Baron. *Persian Letters.* 2 vols. in 1. Edinburgh, 1773.

Moore, Edward. *The Gamester: A Tragedy in Five Acts.* New York, 1806.

Moore, John. *Voyage to Georgia in the Year 1735.* London, 1744.

Moore, Thomas. *Lalla Rookh. An Oriental Romance.* New York, 1824.

More, Hannah. *Strictures on the Modern System of Female Education.* 2 vols. in 1. Charlestown, Mass., 1800.

Moreau, Victor-Marie. *The Life and Campaigns of Victor Moreau. By an Officer of His Staff.* New York, 1806.

[Moril]. *Preparation for Eternity* [No copy located].

Morse, Jedidiah. *The American Gazetteer.* Boston, 1797.

———. *American Universal Geography.* 2 vols. Boston, 1793.

———. *Elements of Geography.* Boston, 1795. Schoolbook version.

Mosheim, John Lawrence. *An Ecclesiastical History, Ancient and Modern, From the Birth of Christ to the Beginning of the Present Century.* 6 vols. Charlestown, Mass., 1810.

Mount, William Sidney. *California News* (1850). Suffolk Museum and Carriage House, Stony Brook, N.Y. Painting.

———. *Dance of the Haymakers* (1845). Suffolk Museum and Carriage House, Stony Brook, N.Y. Painting.

———. *Dancing on the Barn Floor* (1831). Suffolk Museum and Carriage House, Stony Brook, N.Y. Painting.

———. *Rustic Dance After a Sleigh Ride* (1830). Suffolk Museum and Carriage House, Stony Brook, N.Y. Painting.

Mudie, Robert. *Babylon the Great: A Dissection of Men and Things in the British Capital.* 2 vols. Philadelphia, 1825.

Muhammad, the Prophet. *The Koran, Commonly called the Alcoran of Mahomet.* Springfield, Mass., 1806.

Murphy, Arthur. *The Citizen. A Farce.* New York, 1823.

Murray, Judith Sargent. *The Gleaner. A Miscellaneous Production in Three Volumes.* 3 vols. Boston, 1798.

Murray, Lindley. *The English Reader.* Rutland, Vt., 1819.

New England almanac [unidentified]. Bound in *Vermont Almanacs, Vol. 1: 1814–21.* VHS.

The New England Primer, or An easy and pleasant guide to the art of reading. All Upper Valley editions, 1809–30. Burlington, Vt., 1815.

The New Testament of our Lord and Saviour Jesus Christ, translated out of the original Greek; and with the former translations diligently compared and revised. Windsor, Vt., 1816.

Newton, Bishop Thomas. *Dissertations on the Prophecies which have been fulfilled, and at this time are fulfilling in the world.* Northampton, Mass., 1796.

Nicholson, William. *An Introduction to Natural Philosophy.* 2 vols. Philadelphia, 1807.

Niles, Samuel. *The True Scripture Doctrine of Original Sin.* Boston, 1757.

———. *A Vindication of Divers Important Gospel Doctrines.* Boston, 1752.

O'Meara, Barry. *Napoleon in Exile, or a Voice from St. Helena.* Philadelphia, 1822.

Opie, Amelia. *Tales of Real Life.* 2 vols. Boston, 1813.

Paddock, Judah. *Narrative of the Wreck of the Ship Oswego on the Coast of Southern Barbary and of the Sufferings Among the Arabs.* New York, 1818. Bound with Riley.

Paine, Thomas. *The Age of Reason, Being an Investigation of True and Fabulous Theology.* New York, 1827.

Paley, William. *The Principles of Moral and Political Philosophy.* Boston, 1818.

Palmer, Elihu. *Principles of Nature.* New York, 1802.

The Parent's Friend: or Excerpts from the Principle Works on Education. Philadelphia, 1803.

Parish, Elijah, and Jedidiah Morse. *A Compendious History of New England.* 3d ed. Charlestown, Mass., 1820.

Parnell, Thomas. *A Collection of Poems from the Most Celebrated Authors.* Elizabeth Town, N.J., 1797.

Patriotic Addresses. Boston, 1798.

Peake, Thomas. *A Compendium of the Law of Evidence.* Walpole, N.H., 1804.

Perry, William. *The Royal Standard English Dictionary.* Brookfield, Mass., 1806.

[Pigott, Charles]. *The Jockey Club: or, A Sketch of the Manners of the Age.* New York, 1793.

Pike, Nicolas. *A New and Complete System of Arithmetic.* Boston, 1809.

Pitt, William. *Letters Written by the Late Earl of Chatham to His Nephew, Thomas Pitt, Esq.* New York, 1804.

Plutarch. *Plutarch's Lives, Translated from the Original Greek, with Notes Critical and Historical, and a Life of Plutarch.* Translated by John and William Langhorne. 8 vols. New York, 1816.

Pope, Alexander. *Essay on Man.* Concord, N.H., 1817.

Porter, Sir Robert. *A Narrative of the Campaign in Russia.* Philadelphia, 1815.

Powell, John J. *Essay Upon the Law of Contracts and Agreements.* 2 vols. London, 1796.

[Prentiss, Charles]. *The Life of the Late General William Eaton; Several Years an Officer in the United States Army.* Brookfield, Mass., 1813.

Presbyterian Church in the U.S.A. *The confession of faith; the larger and shorter catechisms.* Philadelphia, 1813.

Preston, Daniel. *The Wonders of Creation, Natural and Artificial.* 2 vols. Boston, 1808.

Prideaux, Humphrey. *The True Nature of Imposture Fully Displayed in the Life of Mahomet.* Fairhaven, Vt., 1798.

Proudfit, Alexander Moncrief. *Lectures on the Parables, to Which are Added Some Occasional Discourses.* Salem, N.Y., 1820.

Ramsay, Allan. *The Poems of Allan Ramsay; With the Life of the Author, and His Collection of Scots Proverbs.* 2 vols. Philadelphia, 1813.

Raynal, Abbé. *Opinions on the Revolution of America.* Norwich, Conn., 1782.

Rees, Abraham. *The New Cyclopaedia; or Universal Dictionary of Arts, Sciences, and Literature.* 41 vols. plus 6 vols. of plates. Philadelphia, 1805–25.

Ridgely, Thomas. *A Body of Divinity.* Glasgow, 1770.

Riedesel, Johann Hermann, Baron von. *Travels Through Sicily and That Part of Italy, called Magna Graecia.* 2 vols. London, 1773.

Riley, James. *An Authentic Narrative of the Loss of the American Brig Commerce.* New York, 1818. Bound with Paddock.

Robertson, William. *The History of America.* 2 vols. Philadelphia, 1821.

———. *History of Scotland During the Reigns of Queen Mary and of King James VI.* 2 vols. Philadelphia, 1811.

Roche, Regina. *Children of the Abbey.* 2 vols. Hartford, Conn., 1822.

Rogers, Samuel. *The Pleasures of Memory and Other Poems.* New York, 1820.

Rollin, Charles. *Ancient History of the Egyptians, Carthaginians, Assyrians, Babylonians, Medes and Persians, Macedonians, and Grecians.* 8 vols. Philadelphia, 1825.

———. *The Life of Alexander the Great, King of Macedon.* Providence, R.I., 1796.

Rowe, Elizabeth. *Devout Exercises of the Heart in Meditation, Soliloquy, Prayer, and Praise.* Windsor, Vt., 1792.

Royall, Anne. *The Black Book.* 2 vols. Washington, D.C., 1828.

Rundell, Maria Eliza. *A New System of Domestic Cookery Formed upon the Principles of Economy: and Adapted to the Use of Private Families, Throughout the United States.* New York, 1817.

Russel, Robert. *Seven Sermons.* Wilmington, Del., 1801.

Russell, John. *An Authentic History of the Vermont State Prison; from the Passing of the Law for its Erection in 1807, to July, 1812.* Windsor, Vt., 1812.

Russell, William. *A History of Modern Europe.* 5 vols. Philadelphia, 1802.

[Sanders, Daniel]. *History of the Indian Wars With the First Settlements of the United States, Particularly in New England.* Montpelier, Vt., 1812.

Scott, Thomas. *The Holy Bible.* 6th ed. 6 vols. Boston, 1817–18.

Scott, Walter, Sir. *The Bridal of Triermain, or The Vale of St. John. A Lover's Tale.* Philadelphia, 1813.

———. *Chronicles of the Canongate.* 2 vols. New York, 1827.

———. *The Lady of the Lake: A Poem in Six Cantos.* Montpelier, Vt., 1813.

———. *Rokeby: A Poem.* New York, 1818.

———. *The Vision of Don Roderick.* New York, 1818.

———. *Waverley.* 2 vols. New York, 1815.

Scott, William. *Lessons in Elocution, or a Selection of Pieces in Prose and Verse, for the Improvement of Youth in Reading and Speaking.* Montpelier, Vt., 1820.

Seaman, Valentine. *A Dissertation on the Mineral Waters of Saratoga.* New York, 1793.

Second Census of the United States: Heads of Household–Vermont. Washington, D.C., 1979.

Shakespeare, William. *The Plays and Poems of William Shakespeare.* 8 vols. Philadelphia, 1795–96.

Sheridan, Thomas. *A Complete Dictionary.* 5th ed. Philadelphia, 1788.

———. *Sheridan Improved. A General Pronouncing and Explanatory Dictionary of the English Language.* Edited by Stephen Jones. Wilmington, Del., 1801.

Simmons, John. *The Gentleman's Law Magazine: Containing a Variety of the Most Useful Practical Forms of Writing, Which Occur in the Course of Business.* Middlebury, Vt., 1804.

Slade, William. comp. *The Laws of Vermont of a Public and Permanent Nature: Coming Down to, and Including the Year 1824.* Windsor, Vt., 1825.

Smith, Adam. *An Inquiry into the Nature and Causes of the Wealth of Nations.* 3 vols. Philadelphia, 1789.

———. *The Theory of Moral Sentiments.* 2 vols. Boston, 1817.

Smith, Asa. *An Address.* Boston, 1853.

Smith, Elias. *The Life, Conversion, Preaching, Travels, and Sufferings of Elias Smith.* Portsmouth, N.H., 1816.

———. *Sermons Containing an Illustration of the Prophecies.* Exeter, N.H., 1808.

Smith, Ethan. *A View of the Hebrews; or the Tribes of Israel in America.* Poultney, Vt., 1825.

Smith, Samuel Stanhope. *An Essay on the Causes of the Variety of Complexion and Figure in the Human Species.* 2d ed. New Brunswick, N.J., 1810.

Smith, Reverend William. *The Works of William Smith, Late Provost of the College and Academy of Philadelphia.* 2 vols. Philadelphia, 1803.

Smollett, Tobias. *The Adventures of Roderick Random.* 2 vols. Philadelphia, 1794.

Southey, Robert. *Letters from England*. Boston, 1808.

Spafford, Horatio Gates. *A Gazetteer of the State of New York*. Albany, N.Y., 1813.

Spalding, Joshua. *Sentiments Concerning the Coming and Kingdom of Christ*. Salem, Mass., 1796.

———. *Universalism Confounds and Destroys Itself*. Northampton, Mass., 1805.

Staniford, Daniel. *Practical Arithmetic*. Boston, 1818.

Staunton, Sir George Leonard. *An Authentic Account of an Embassy from the King of Great Britain to the Emperor of China*. 2 vols. Philadelphia, 1799.

Steele, Zadock. *A Narrative of the Captivity and Sufferings of With an Account of the Burning of Royalton*. Montpelier, Vt., 1818.

Stennett, Samuel. *Monitor to Parents. Selected from Stennett's Christian Duties*. Hartford, Conn., 1816.

Sterne, Laurence. *The Works of Laurence Sterne*. 7 vols. Dublin, 1794.

Stewart, Dugald. *Elements of the Philosophy of the Human Mind*. Philadelphia, 1793.

———. *Philosophical Essays*. New York, 1811.

Story, Joseph. "Discourse Pronounced at Cambridge Before the Phi Beta Kappa Society, on the Anniversary Celebration, August 31, 1826." In Story, *The Miscellaneous Writings, Literary, Critical, Juridical and Political, of Joseph Story, LLD., Now First Collected*, p. 3–33. Boston, 1835.

Stowe, Harriet Beecher. *The Poganuc People*. New York, 1878.

Swedenborg, Emmanuel. *Miscellaneous Theological Works*. Philadelphia, 1797.

Swift, Zephaniah. *A System of the Laws of the State of Connecticut*. 2 vols. Windham, Conn., 1795.

Thiebault, Dieudonne. *Original Anecdotes of Frederick the Great, King of Prussia, and His Family, His Court, His Ministers, His Academies, and His Literary Friends*. 2 vols. Philadelphia, 1806.

Thomas, Robert. *The Farmer's Almanac*. Boston editions, 1793–1842.

Thomas à Kempis. *The Imitation of Christ*. Manlius, N.Y., 1816.

Thomas and Thomas. *A Catalogue of Books for Sale by Thomas and Thomas*. Walpole, N.H., 1803.

Thompson, Isaac. "Bill of Mortality of the town of Middleborough, from the year 1779 to 1801." *Collections of the Massachusetts Historical Society for the Year 1801*. 8:180.

Thompson, Zadock. *A Gazetteer of the State of Vermont*. Montpelier, Vt., 1824.

———. *History of the state of Vermont, from its early settlement to the close of the year 1832*. Burlington, Vt., 1833.

Thomson, James. *The Seasons*. Middlebury, Vt., 1815.

Tillard, John. *Future Rewards and Punishments Believed By the Ancients* [no copy located].

Tillotson, John. *The Works of the Most Reverend Doctor John Tillotson*. 3 vols. London, 1752.

Tompkins, Abel. *Miller Overthrown: or, the False Prophet Confounded. By a Cosmopolite*. Boston, 1840.

Trenck, Fredrich von der. *The Life of Baron Fredrich Trenck*. New York, 1815.

Trumbull, John. *M'Fingal, or the Tory's Day of Judgment. A Modern Epic Poem in Four Cantos*. Middlebury, Vt., 1815.

Tyler, Royall. *The Algerine Captive, or the Life and Adventures of Dr. Updike Underhill Six Years a Prisoner Among the Algerines*. 2 vols. Walpole, N.H., 1797. Reprint, New Haven, Conn., 1970.

Valuable Secrets in the Arts, Trades, etc. New York, 1808.

Venn, Henry. *The Complete Duty of Man*. Middlebury, Vt., 1811.

Vergilius Maro, Publius. *The Works of Virgil Translated by Dryden*. 2 vols. New York, 1825.

Vermont. *Acts and Laws of the State of Vermont* and *Laws and Statutes of Vermont*. Dresden, Burlington, Montpelier, and Windsor, Vt. Volumes for 1779, 1787, 1793, 1797, 1804, 1816, 1818, 1821, 1823, 1824, and 1829.

"Vermont Journal of Riley M. Adams." *Vineland Historical Magazine* 5 (1920), pp. 86, 108–9, 127, 129, 130.

The Village Harmony: or, New England Repository of Sacred Music. Boston, 1817.

Reading Becomes a Necessity of Life

Volney, Constantin. *Travels through Egypt and Syria.* 2 vols. New York, 1798.

Voltaire, Jean François-Marie Arouet de. *The History of Charles the XII.* Frederick-Town, Md., 1810.

Vulpius, Christian. *History of Rinald Rinaldini.* 2 vols. Boston, 1824.

Walker, John. *A Critical Pronouncing Dictionary and Expositor of the English Language.* Philadelphia, 1803.

Walsh, Robert. *An Appeal from the Judgments of Great Britain Respecting the United States of America.* Philadelphia, 1819.

Walton's Vermont Register and Farmer's Almanac for 1828. Montpelier, Vt., 1827.

Walton's Vermont Register and Farmer's Almanac for 1829. Montpelier, Vt., 1828.

Warren, Mercy Otis. *Poems, Dramatic and Miscellaneous.* Boston, 1790.

Washington, George. *Washington's Farewell Address to the People of the United States.* New York, 1809.

Watts, Isaac. *Hymns and Spiritual Songs.* Montpelier, Vt., 1814.

——. *The Improvement of the Mind: Containing a Variety of Remarks and Rules for the Attainment and Communication of Useful Knowledge in Religion, the Sciences, and in Common Life.* Exeter, N.H., 1793.

——. *The Psalms of David, Imitated in the Language of the New Testament.* Montpelier, Vt., 1814.

Webster, Charles, and George Webster. *The Clerk's Magazine: Containing the Most Useful and Necessary Forms of Writings Which Commonly Occur Between Man and Man.* Albany, N.Y., 1803.

Webster, Daniel. "The Bunker Hill Monument." In *The Great Speeches and Orations of Daniel Webster With an Essay on Daniel Webster as a Master of English Style,* pp. 123–35. Edited by Edwin P. Whipple. Boston, 1879.

Webster, Noah. *An American Dictionary of the English Language.* 2 vols. New York, 1828. 7th ed., 2 vols. in 1. New York, [1831].

——. *An American Selection of Lessons in Reading and Speaking.* Boston, 1797.

——. *The American Spelling Book.* Bennington, Vt., 1794.

——. *A Compendious Dictionary of the English Language.* New Haven, Conn., 1806.

——. *A Dictionary of the English Language Compiled for the Use of Common Schools in the United States.* Hartford, Conn., 1817.

Weems, Mason Locke. *The Life of George Washington.* Philadelphia, 1819. Reprint, Cambridge, Mass., 1962.

Wesley, John. *Primitive Physic; or an Easy and Natural Method of Curing Most Diseases.* New York, 1818.

——. *Sermons on Several Occasions.* 4 vols. Philadelphia, 1794–1801.

West, Benjamin. *An Account of The Transit of Venus upon the Sun June, 1769.* Providence, R.I., 1813.

White, Henry Kirk. *The Remains of Henry Kirk White.* 2 vols. Philadelphia, 1811.

Whitelaw, James. *Maps of the State of Vermont.* Burlington and Ryegate, Vt., 1796–1822.

The Wife, Interspersed with a Variety of Anecdotes and Observations. Boston, 1806.

Williams, John. *The Redeemed Captive Returning to Zion.* 1707. Facsimile ed., Amherst, Mass., 1976.

Williams, Samuel. *The Natural and Civil History of Vermont.* Walpole, N.H., 1794. 2d ed., 2 vols., Burlington, Vt., 1809.

[Williams, Samuel]. *Sketches of the War.* Rutland, Vt., 1815.

Willich, Anthony. *Domestic Encyclopedia: or, A Dictionary of Facts, and Useful Knowledge Comprehending a Concise View of the Latest Discoveries.* 6 vols. Philadelphia, 1803.

Willison, John. *The Afflicted Man's Companion.* Boston, 1795.

——. *Sacramental Meditations and Advices Grounded Upon Scripture Texts.* Philadelphia, 1794.

Wilson, John. *Light and Shadows of Scottish Life. A Selection from the Papers of the Late Arthur Austin.* Philadelphia, 1822.

Winchester, Elhanan. *The Universal Restoration Exhibited.* Boston, 1792.

Winner, William. *The Pie Man, or a Civic Procession* (1856). Historical Society of Pennsylvania. Reproduced on the cover of *Antiques Magazine*, July 1980. Painting.

Winthrop, John. *History of New England From 1630 to 1649.* 2 vols. Boston, 1825–26.

Wirt, William. *The Letters of the British Spy.* Baltimore, 1813.

Witherspoon, John. *The Works of the Rev. John Witherspoon.* 3 vols. Philadelphia, 1800.

Witsius, Herman. *The Oeconomy of the Covenants Between God and Man, Comprehending a Complete Body of Divinity.* 3 vols. New York, 1798.

Woodbridge, W. *A Key to the English Language, or a Spelling, Parsing, Derivative, and Defining Dictionary.* Middletown, Conn., 1801.

Woods, Leonard. *Memoirs of the Life of Mrs. Harriet Newell, Wife of the Rev. Samuel Newell, Missionary to India.* Lexington, Ky., 1815.

Woodville, Richard Caton. *War News from Mexico* (1848). Painting.

Worcester, Samuel. *Christian Psalmody.* Boston, 1815.

Young, Edward. *Night Thoughts; or Life, Death, and Immortality.* Haverhill, Mass., 1820.

―――. *The Works of Rev. E. Young.* 3 vols. Charlestown, Mass., 1811.

The Young Clerk's Magazine: or, English Law Repository. 8th ed. Philadelphia, 1795.

Zimmerman, Johann Georg ritter von. *Solitude Considered.* Boston, 1804.

Zollikofer, George J. *Exercises of Piety; or, Meditations on the Principle Doctrines and Duties of Religion.* Worcester, Mass., 1803.

II. Secondary Sources

Abelove, Henry, et al., eds. *Visions of History: Interviews With [thirteen historians].* New York, 1984.

Albee, B.H. *A Short History of Chester, Vermont.* Springfield, Vt., 1890.

Aldrich, Lewis C., and Frank R. Holmes. *History of Windsor County, Vermont.* Syracuse, N.Y., 1891.

Allibone, Samuel Austin. *A Critical Dictionary of English Literature, and British and American Authors.* 5 vols. Philadelphia, 1870–91.

Anders, Richard. "Introduction: The New England Almanac." AAS exhibit, 1979–80.

Appleby, Joyce. "Republicanism in Old and New Contexts." WMQ 3s 43 (1986):20–34.

Asimov, Isaac. *The Foundation Trilogy.* 3 vols. New York, 1964–66.

Auwers, Linda. "Reading the Marks of the Past: Exploring Female Literacy in Colonial Windsor Connecticut." *Historical Methods* 13 (1980):204–14.

―――. Review of *The Wealth of a Nation To Be*, by Alice H. Jones. *Historical Methods* 12 (1979):39–45.

―――. *The Social Meaning of Female Literacy: Windsor, Connecticut, 1660–1775.* Newberry Papers in Family and Community History, No. 77–4A. Chicago, 1977.

Axtell, James. *School Upon a Hill: Education and Society in Colonial New England.* New York, 1974.

Bailyn, Bernard. "The Challenge of Modern Historiography." AHR 87 (1982):1–24.

Baker, Mary E. *Folklore of Springfield.* Springfield, Vt., 1922.

Bamford, James. *The Puzzle Palace: A History of America's Most Secret Agency.* New York, 1983.

Banning, Lance. "Jeffersonian Ideology Revisited: Liberal and Classical Ideas in the New American Republic." WMQ 3s 43 (1986):3–19.

Barber, Giles. "Continental Paper Wrapper and Publishers' Bindings in the Eighteenth Century." *Book Collector* 24 (1975):37–49.

————. "Pendred Abroad: A View of the Late Eighteenth Century Book Trade in Europe." In *Essays to Graham Pollard*, pp. 231–77. Edited by John Carter. Oxford, 1975.

Barraclough, Geoffrey. *Main Trends in History*. New York, 1978.

Barron, Hal Seth. "The Impact of Rural Depopulation on the Local Economy of Chelsea, Vermont, 1840–1900." AgH 54 (1980):318–35.

————. *Those Who Stayed Behind: Rural Society in Nineteenth Century New England*. Cambridge, England, 1984.

Basch, Norma. *In the Eyes of the Law: Women, Marriage and Property in Nineteenth Century New York*. Ithaca, N.Y., 1982.

Bassett, T.D. Seymour. *Vermont: A Bibliography*. Boston, 1981.

Beales, Jr., Ross W. "Studying Literacy at the Community Level: A Research Note." JIH 9 (1978):93–102.

Behrens, C.B.A. "Porn, Propaganda, and the Enlightenment." *New York Review of Books*, 29 Sept. 1977, pp. 32–33.

Belanger, Terry. "From Bookseller to Publisher: Changes in the London Book Trade, 1750–1850." In *Book Selling and Book Buying: Aspects of the Nineteenth-Century British and North American Book Trade*, 7–16. Edited by Richard Landon. Chicago, 1978.

Bellah, Robert N., et al. *Habits of the Heart: Individualism and Commitment in American Life*. New York, 1986 ed.

Benes, Peter, ed. *Annual Proceedings of the Dublin Seminar for New England Folklife*. 11 vols. Boston, 1976–1986.

Berger, Peter, and Thomas Luckmann. *The Social Construction of Reality*. Garden City, N.Y., 1966.

Berger, Jonathan, and John W. Sinton. *Water, Earth, and Fire: Land Use and Environmental Planning in the New Jersey Pine Barrens*. Baltimore, 1985.

Berkin, Carol Ruth, and Mary Beth Norton, eds. *Women of America: A History*. Boston, 1979.

Bidwell, Percy. *Rural Economy in New England at the Beginning of the Nineteenth Century*. New Haven, Conn., 1916.

Black, Cyril E., ed. *Comparative Modernization: A Reader*. New York, 1976.

Blanck, Jacob. comp. *A Bibliography of American Literature*. 6 vols. New Haven, Conn., 1955–75.

Bloch, Ruth H. "American Feminine Ideals in Transition: The Rise of the Moral Mother, 1785–1815." *Feminist Studies* 4 (1978):101–26.

Bollème, Genevieve. *Les almanachs populaires dux XVII² et XVIII² siècles*. Paris, 1969.

Bolter, W. David. *Turing's Man: Western Culture in the Computer Age*. Chapel Hill, N.C., 1984.

Boorstin, Daniel. *The Americans: The Colonial Experience*. New York, 1958.

————. *The Americans: The National Experience*. New York, 1965.

————. *The Lost World of Thomas Jefferson*. Boston, 1960.

Bowers, Fredson. *Principles of Bibliographical Description*. Princeton, N.J., 1949.

Bozeman, Theodore Dwight. *Protestants in an Age of Science: The Baconian Ideal and Antebellum American Religious Thought*. Chapel Hill, N.C., 1977.

Brainerd, Lawrence. *Epitaphs, Old South Burying Ground*. Windsor, Vt., 1914.

Braudel, Fernand. *Capitalism and Material Life, 1400–1800*. New York, 1973.

————. *Civilization and Capitalism 15th–18th Century*. 3 vols. New York, 1981–84.

Briggs, F. Allen. "The Sunday School Library." In *Readings in American Library History*, 64–71. Edited by Michael H. Harris. Washington, D.C., 1971.

Brigham, Clarence S. *The History and Bibliography of American Newspapers, 1690–1820*. 2 vols. 1947. Reprint, Hamden, Conn., 1962.

Brown, Ralph H. *Historical Geography of the United States*. New York, 1948.

Brown, Richard D. "The Emergence of Urban Society in Rural Massachusetts, 1760–1820." JAH 61 (1974):29–51.

———. *Modernization: The Transformation of American Life, 1600–1865.* New York, 1976.

———. "Modernization and the Modern Personality in Early America, 1600–1865: A Sketch of a Synthesis." JIH 2 (1972):201–28.

———. "Spreading the Word: Rural Clergymen and the Communications Network of Eighteenth Century New England." *Proceedings of the Massachusetts Historical Society* 94 (1982):1–14.

Brownlee, W. Elliot, and Mary M. Brownlee. *Women in the American Economy: A Documentary History, 1675 to 1929.* New Haven, Conn., 1976.

Brownson, Henry F. *Orestes A. Brownson's Early Life (1803–1844).* Detroit, 1898.

Bruce, Phillip. *An Institutional History of Virginia in the Seventeenth Century.* 2 vols. New York, 1910.

Bumgardner, Georgia. "American Almanac Illustration in the Eighteenth Century." In *Eighteenth Century Prints in Colonial America: To Educate and Decorate*, pp. 51–70. Edited by Joan D. Dolmetsch. Charlottesville, Va., 1979.

———. "Vignettes of the Past: American Historical Broadsides Through the War of 1812." Unpublished paper, 1980.

Burguière, André. "The Fate of the History of *Mentalités* in the *Annales.*" CSSH 24 (July 1982):424–37.

Burrows, Edwin. "The Transition Question in Early American History: A Checklist of Recent Books, Articles, and Dissertations." *Radical History Review* 18 (Fall 1978):173–90.

Bushman, Richard. *Joseph Smith and the Beginnings of Mormonism.* Urbana, Ill., 1984.

Calhoun, Craig. *The Question of Class Struggle: Social Foundations of Popular Radicalism During the Industrial Revolution.* Chicago, 1982.

Calhoun, Daniel. *The Intelligence of a People.* Princeton, N.J., 1975.

———. *Professional Lives in America, Structure and Aspiration, 1750–1850.* Cambridge, Mass., 1965.

Chartier, Roger. "Livre et espace: Circuits commerciaux et geographie culturelle de la librairie lyonnaise au XVIIIe siecle." *Revue française d'histoire du livre* 1–2 (1971):77–108.

Chartier, Roger, and Daniel Roche. "Le livre: un changement de perspective." *Faire de l'histoire III: Nouveaux objets*, pp. 115–36. Paris, 1974.

Child, Hamilton. *Gazetteer and business directory of Windsor County, Vt., for 1833–34.* Syracuse, N.Y., 1883.

Cipolla, Carlo. *Literacy and Development in the West.* Baltimore, 1969.

Clark, Christopher. "Household Economy, Market Exchange, and the Rise of Capitalism in the Connecticut River Valley, 1800–1860." *Journal of Social History* 13 (1979):168–89.

Clark, T.J. *Image of the People: Gustave Courbet and the Second French Republic, 1848–1851.* New York, 1973.

Clemmer, Robert R. "Enlightenment Church History in the United States, 1800–1850." Ph.D. diss., Univ. of Pennsylvania, 1961.

Clive, John, and Bernard Bailyn. "England's Cultural Provinces: Scotland and America." WMQ 3s 11 (1954):200–213.

Cobb, David A. "Vermont Maps Prior to 1900: An Annotated Cartobibliography." VtH 39 (1971):169–317.

Cobb, Rev. L.H. *The Old Paths: Delivered at Springfield, Vermont, May 30, 1959.* Claremont, N.H., 1869.

Cochran, Thomas C. *Frontiers of Change: Early Industrialization in the United States.* New York, 1981.

Cochrane, Warren R., and George K. Wood. *History of Francestown, N.H., 1758–1891.* Nashua, N.H., 1895.

Cohen, Patricia Cline. *A Calculating People: The Spread of Numeracy in Early America.* Chicago, 1982.

Colbourn, H. Trevor. *The Lamp of Experience: Whig History and the Intellectual Origins of the American Revolution.* New York, 1974.

Cole, Donald. *Jacksonian Democracy in New Hampshire, 1800–1851.* Cambridge, Mass., 1970.

Collins, A.S. *Authorship in the Age of Johnson.* London, 1928.

———. *The Profession of Letters, 1780–1832.* London, 1928.

Commager, Henry Steele, and Elmo Giordanetti, eds. *Was America a Mistake? An Eighteenth-Century Controversy.* New York, 1967.

Cook, Edward. *The Fathers of the Towns: Leadership and Community Structure in Eighteenth Century New England.* Baltimore, 1976.

Cott, Nancy. *The Bonds of Womanhood: Woman's Sphere in New England, 1780–1835.* New Haven, Conn., 1977.

Cremin, Lawrence. *American Education: The Colonial Experience.* New York, 1975.

———. *American Education: The National Experience.* New York, 1980.

Cross, Barbara. "Stowe, Harriet Beecher." In *Notable American Women, 1607–1950: A Biographical Dictionary.* Edited by Edward T. James, Janet Wilson James, and Paul S. Boyer. 3 vols. Cambridge, Mass., 1971.

Cross, Whitney. *The Burned-Over District: The Social and Intellectual History of Enthusiastic Religion in Western New York, 1800–1850.* Ithaca, N.Y., 1950.

Crowley, J.E. *This Sheba Self: The Conceptualization of Economic Life in Eighteenth Century America.* Baltimore, 1975.

Czitrom, Daniel. *Media and the American Mind: From Morse to McLuhan.* Chapel Hill, N.C., 1982.

Danhoff, Charles. *Change in Agriculture: The Northern United States, 1820–1870.* Cambridge, Mass., 1969.

Daniels, George H. *American Science in the Age of Jackson.* New York, 1968.

Darnton, Robert. *The Business of Enlightenment: A Publishing History of the Encyclopedie, 1775–1800.* Cambridge, Mass., 1979.

———. *The Great Cat Massacre and Other Episodes in French Cultural History.* New York, 1984.

———. *The Literary Underground of the Ancien Regime.* Cambridge, Mass., 1979.

———. "Reading, Writing, and Publishing in Eighteenth Century France." DAED 100 (1971): 14–57.

———. "What is the History of the Book?" DAED 111 (Summer 1982):65–83.

Davidson, Cathy. *Revolution and the Word: The Rise of the Novel in America.* New York, 1986.

Davis, Natalie Zemon. "Anthropology and History in the 1980s: The Possibilities of the Past." JIH 12 (1981):267–75.

———. "Interview." In *Visions of History: Interviews With [thirteen historians],* pp. 97–122. Edited by Henry Abelove et al. New York, 1984.

———. "Printing and the People." In *Society and Culture in Early Modern France,* pp. 189–226 and 326–36. Edited by Natalie Zemon Davis. Stanford, Calif., 1975.

Davis, Richard Beale. *A Colonial Southern Bookshelf: Reading in the Eighteenth Century.* Athens, Ga., 1979.

———. *Intellectual Life in Jefferson's Virginia, 1790–1840.* Knoxville, Tenn., 1964.

———. *Intellectual Life in the Colonial South, 1585–1763.* 3 vols. Knoxville, Tenn., 1978.

———. *Literature and Society in Early Virginia, 1608–1840.* Baton Rouge, La., 1973.

Davis, Stephen Roper. "From Ploughshares to Spindles: Dedham, Massachusetts, 1790–1840." Ph.D. diss., Univ. of Wisconsin, 1973.

Dawley, Alan. *Class and Community: The Industrial Revolution in Lynn.* Cambridge, Mass., 1976.

Demos, John. *A Little Commonwealth: Family Life in Plymouth Colony.* New York, 1970.

Doherty, Robert. *Society and Power: Five New England Towns, 1800–1860.* Amherst, Mass., 1977.

Donahue, Katherine Curtis. "Time is Money: Households and the Reorganization of Production in Northern New England, 1790–1900." Ph.D. diss., Boston Univ., 1981.

Draper, Theodore. "Neoconservative History." *New York Review of Books,* 16 Jan. 1986, pp. 5–15.

Dublin, Thomas, ed. *Farm to Factory: Women's Letters, 1830–1860.* New York, 1981.

———. *Women at Work: The Transformation of Work and Community in Lowell, Massachusetts, 1828–1860.* New York, 1979.

Dugger, H.H. "Reading Interests and the Book Trade in Frontier Missouri." Ph.D. diss., Univ. of Missouri, 1951.

Eckhardt, Celia Morris. *Fanny Wright: Rebel in America.* Cambridge, Mass., 1984.

Edgar, Walter B. "The Libraries of Colonial South Carolina." Ph.D. diss., Univ. of South Carolina, 1969.

Eisenstein, Elizabeth. *The Printing Press as an Agent of Change: Communications and Cultural Transformation in Early Modern Europe.* 2 vols. Cambridge, England, 1979.

Ellis, Joseph J. *After the Revolution: Profiles of Early American Culture.* New York, 1979.

Engelsing, Rolf. *Der Bürger als Leser: Lesergeschichte in Deutschland zwischen feudaler und industrieller Gesellschaft.* Stuttgart, 1974.

———. "Die Perioden der Lesergeschichte in der Neuzeit." *Zur Sozialgeschichte deutscher Mittelund Unterschichten* 4 (Gottingen, 1973):112–54.

Fabian, Bernhard. "English Books and Their Eighteenth-Century German Readers." In *The Widening Circle: Essays on the Circulation of Literature in Eighteenth-Century Europe.* Edited by Paul J. Korshin. Philadelphia, 1976.

Faler, Paul. *Mechanics and Manufacturers in the Early Industrial Revolution: Lynn, Massachusetts, 1780–1860.* Albany, N.Y., 1981.

———. "Workingmen, Mechanics, and Social Change: Lynn, Mass., 1800–1860." Ph.D. diss., Univ. of Wisconsin, 1971.

Faragher, John Mack. *Men and Women on the Overland Trail.* New Haven, Conn., 1979.

Farber, Bernard. *Guardians of Virtue: Salem Families in 1800.* New York, 1972.

Febvre, Lucien, and Henri-Jean Martin. *The Coming of the Book: The Impact of Printing, 1450–1800.* Translated by David Gerard. London, 1976.

Fenn, Mary. *Parish and Town: The History of West Windsor, Vermont.* Montpelier, Vt., 1977.

Ferguson, E.J. "Political Economy, Public Liberty, and the Formation of the Constitution." WMQ 3s 40 (1983):389–412.

Finkelstein, Barbara. "Reading, Writing, and the Acquisition of Identity in the United States: 1790–1860." In *Regulated Children, Liberated Children: Education in Psychohistorical Perspective,* pp. 114–39. Edited by Barbara Finkelstein. New York, 1979.

Fischer, David Hackett. "America, A Social History: The Main Lines of the Subject, 1650–1975." Unpublished manuscript, 1974.

———. "Federalists and Democracy." 2 vols. Ph.D. diss., Johns Hopkins Univ., 1963.

———. *The Revolution of American Conservatism: The Federalist Party in the Era of Jeffersonian Democracy.* New York, 1969.

FitzGerald, Frances. *America Revised.* New York, 1980.

Flanders, Louis W. *Simeon Ide: Yeoman, Freeman, Pioneer Printer.* Rutland, Vt., 1931.

Foster, Brian L. "Development, Modernization and Comparative Parochialism: A Review Article." CSSH 20 (1978):319–28.

Frankenstein, Alfred. *Painter of Rural America: William Sidney Mount, 1807–1868.* Stony Brook, N.Y., 1968.

Fredrickson, George. *The Inner Civil War: Northern Intellectuals in the Crisis of the Union*. New York, 1965.

Furet, François, and Jacques Ozouf. *Reading and Writing: Literacy in France from Calvin to Jules Ferry*. Cambridge, England, 1982. Partial Translation of *Lire et écrire: L'Alphabétisation des français de Calvin à Jules Ferry*. 2 vols. Paris, 1977.

Fussell, Clyde. "The Emergence of Public Education as a Function of the State of Vermont." VtH 28 (1960):179–96.

Gagliardi, Francis James. "The Babcocks of New Haven, Connecticut: Printers, Publishers, and Booksellers, with a Bibliographical Checklist of their Publications, 1764–1800." Master's thesis, Southern Connecticut State College, 1965.

Gardner, John. *The Art of Fiction*. New York, 1984.

Gastil, Raymond D. *Cultural Regions of the United States*. Seattle, Wash., 1975.

Gates, Paul. "Problems of Agricultural History, 1790–1840." AgH 46 (1972):42–44.

Geertz, Clifford. *The Interpretation of Cultures*. New York, 1973.

Geib, Susan. " 'Changing Works': Agriculture and Society in Brookfield, Mass., 1785–1820." Ph.D. diss., Boston Univ., 1981.

———. Review of *Society and Power: Five New England Towns, 1800–1860* by Robert Doherty. *New England Quarterly* 51 (1978):442–44.

Gillispie, Charles Coulton. *Genesis and Geology: The Impact of Scientific Discoveries Upon Religious Beliefs in the Decades Before Darwin*. New York, 1959.

Gilmore, William J. "The 'Annihilation of Time and Space': The Transformation of Event and Awareness in American Consciousness, 1780–1850." Paper delivered at Conference on Printing and Society, AAS, 1980.

———. "Elementary Literacy on the Eve of the Industrial Revolution: Trends in Rural New England, 1760–1830." *PAAS* 92, pt. 1 (Apr. 1982):87–178. Rptd. under separate cover, Univ. of Virginia Press, Charlottesville, 1983. [Cited as "Elementary Literacy."]

———. "Elementary Literacy on the Eve of the Industrial Revolution: Trends in Southern New Jersey, 1760–1840." Paper presented at Princeton Univ. Seminar for Historians of New Jersey, Princeton, N.J., 1982.

———. "The 'Mystic Chords of Memory': Needs and Opportunities for a History of Reading to 1876." Paper presented at Conference on the History of the Book, AAS, 3 Nov. 1984.

———. "Orestes Brownson and New England Religious Culture, 1803–27." Ph.D. diss., Univ. of Virginia, 1971.

———. "Peddlers and the Dissemination of Print Culture in Rural New England, 1780–1840." In *Annual Proceedings of the Dublin Seminar for New England Folklife*. Vol. 9: *Itinerancy*, 76–89. Edited by Peter Benes. Boston, 1986.

———. "The Process of Thought and the Circulation of Print: Event and Awareness in American Consciousness: Rural New England as a Case Study, 1780–1840." Paper delivered at the Annual Meeting of the Organization of American Historians, San Francisco, 1980.

———. "Profile of an Independent Hamlet Bookstore: Robert B. Thomas and the Book Trade in Sterling, Mass., 1790–1815." Paper presented at meeting of the Society for Massachusetts History, March 1984.

———. "Truants and Scholars: Daily Attendance in the District School, A Rural New England Case." VtH 53 (1985):95–103.

Ginzburg, Carlo. *The Cheese and the Worms: The Cosmos of a Sixteenth Century Miller*. Baltimore, 1980.

Graff, Harvey J. *The Legacies of Literacy: Continuities and Contradictions in Western Society and Culture*. Bloomington, Indiana, 1987.

————, ed. *Literacy and Social Development in the West: A Reader.* Cambridge, England, 1981.

————, ed. *Literacy in History: An Interdisciplinary Research Bibliography.* New York, 1981.

————, ed. *The Literacy Myth: Literacy and Social Structure in the Nineteenth-Century City.* New York, 1979.

Graffagnino, J. Kevin. "Representation of a Turbulent Land: Some Vermont Maps, 1755–98." Unpublished paper, 1980.

————. *The Shaping of Vermont: From the Wilderness to the Centennial, 1749–1877.* Rutland, Vt., 1983.

————. "'We Have Long Been Wishing for a Good Printer in This Vicinity': The State of Vermont, the First East Union and the Dresden Press, 1778–1779." *Vermont History* 47 (Winter 1979):21–36.

Greene, John C. *American Science in the Age of Jefferson.* Ames, Iowa, 1983.

————. "Protestantism, Science, and American Enterprise: Benjamin Silliman's Moral Universe." In *Benjamin Silliman and His Circle. Studies on the Influence of Benjamin Silliman on Science in America: Proceedings in Honor of Elizabeth H. Thomson,* pp.11–27. Edited by Leonard G. Wilson. New York, 1979.

Gross, Robert. "Culture and Cultivation: Agriculture and Society in Thoreau's Concord." JAH 69 (1982):42–61.

————. *The Minutemen and Their World.* New York, 1976.

Grubar, Francis. *Richard Caton Woodville: An Early American Genre Painter.* Washington, D.C., 1967. Exhibit catalogue.

Gutman, Herbert. Review of *Class and Community: The Industrial Revolution in Lynn* by Alan Dawley. *New York Times Book Review,* 12 June 1977, pp. 29–30.

Hacker, Andrew. "Women at Work," *New York Review of Books,* 14 Aug. 1986, pp. 26–32.

Hall, David. "The Mental World of Samuel Sewall." In *Saints and Revolutionaries.* Edited by Hall and John Murrin. New York, 1984.

————. "The Uses of Literacy in New England, 1600–1850." In *Printing and Society in Early America,* pp. 1–47. Edited by William Joyce et al. Worcester, Mass., 1983.

————. "The World of Print and Collective Mentality in Seventeenth-Century New England." In *New Directions in American Intellectual History,* pp. 166–80. Edited by John Higham and Paul K. Conkin. Baltimore, 1979.

Hanson, Charles Lane, ed. *Samuel Lane, A Journal for the Years 1739–1803.* Concord, N.H., 1937.

Harris, Michael. "Books for Sale on the Illinois Frontier." *American Book Collector* 21 (1971):15–17.

————. "Books on the Frontier: The Extent and Nature of Book Ownership in Southern Indiana, 1800–1850." *Library Quarterly* 42 (1972):416–30.

————. "Books Stocked by Six Indiana General Stores." JLH 9 (1974):66–72.

————. "Bookstores on the Southern Indiana Frontier, 1833–1850." *American Book Collector* 23 (1973):30–32.

————. *The General Store as an Outlet for Books on the Southern Indiana Frontier, 1800–1850.* Misc. pamphlet, AAS. Reprinted from JLH (1973).

————. *Readings in American Library History.* Washington, D.C., 1971.

Harrison, J.F.C. *The Quest for the New Moral World: Robert Owen and the Owenites in Britain and America.* New York, 1969.

Hart, Freeman H. *The Valley of Virginia in the American Revolution, 1763–1789.* Chapel Hill, N.C., 1942.

Harte, N.B. "Rees's *Cyclopaedia* as a Source for the History of the Textile Industries in the Early Nineteenth Century." *Textile History* 5 (1974):119–27.

Harvard Univ. *Quinquennial Catalogue of the Officers and Graduates, 1636–1925.* Cambridge, Mass., 1925.

Hatch, Nathan O. "Elias Smith and the Rise of Religious Journalism in the Early Republic." In *Printing and Society in Early America*, 250–77. Edited by William Joyce et al. Worcester, Mass., 1983.

Henretta, James A. *The Evolution of American Society, 1700–1815: An Interdisciplinary Analysis.* Lexington, Ky., 1973.

———. "Farms and Families: *Mentalités* in Pre-Industrial America." WMQ 3s 35 (1978):3–32.

———. "Wealth and Social Structure." In *Colonial British America: Essays in the New History of the Early Modern Era*, pp. 262–89. Edited by Jack P. Greene and J.R. Pole. Baltimore, 1984.

Heyrman, Christine. *Commerce and Culture: The Maritime Communities of Colonial Massachusetts, 1690–1750.* New York, 1984.

Hills, Margaret, ed. *The English Bible in America: A Bibliography of Editions of the Bible & the New Testament Published in America, 1777–1957.* New York, 1961.

Hobsbawm, E.J. *The Age of Revolution, 1789–1848.* New York, 1962.

Hoggart, Richard. *The Uses of Literacy.* New York, 1970.

Horne, Thomas A. *The Social Thought of Bernard Mandeville: Virtue and Commerce in Early Eighteenth Century England.* London, 1978.

Horwitz, Richard. *Anthropology Toward History: Culture and Work in a Nineteenth Century Maine Town.* Middletown, Conn., 1978.

Howarth, Margery D. *New Hampshire: A Study of Its Cities and Towns in Relation to Their Physical Background.* Concord, N.H., 1936.

Howe, Daniel Walker. "European Sources of Political Ideas in Jeffersonian America." RAH 10 (1982):28–44.

Hubbard, Horace, and Justus Dartt. *History of the Town of Springfield, Vermont, with a Genealogical Record, 1752–1895.* Boston, 1895.

Hudson, Winthrop. *Religion in America.* 3d ed. New York, 1981.

Hurd, John S. *Weathersfield: Century One.* Canaan, N.H. 1975.

Ide, Simeon. "Reminiscences." In *Centennial Memorial of Windsor, Vermont, July 4, 1876.* Windsor, Vt., 1876.

Irrmann, Robert H. "The Library of an Ohio Farmer [1824–25]." *Ohio Archaeological and Historical Quarterly* 42 (1948):185–93.

Isaac, Rhys. *The Transformation of Virginia, 1740–1790.* Chapel Hill, N.C., 1982.

Jacobson, Robert L. "Humanists Cheer a Call to Arms over Specialization." *Chronicle of Higher Education*, 1 May 1985.

Jauss, Robert. "Levels of Identification of Hero and Audience." *New Literary History* 5 (1974):283–317.

———. "Literary History as a Challenge to Literary Theory." *New Literary History* 2 (1970):7–37.

Jedrey, Christopher M. *The World of John Cleaveland: Family and Community in Eighteenth Century New England.* New York, 1979.

Johansson, Egil. *The History of Literacy in Sweden, in Comparison With Some Other Countries.* Umea, Sweden, 1977. Reprinted in *Literacy and Social Development in the West: A Reader*, 151–82. Edited by Harvey J. Graff. Cambridge, England, 1981.

Johnson, Paul. *Modern Times: The World from the Twenties to the Eighties.* New York, 1985.

Johnson, Paul. *A Shopkeeper's Millennium: Society and Revivals in Rochester, New York, 1815–1837.* New York, 1978.

Jones, Alice H. *American Colonial Wealth.* 3 vols. New York, 1977.

———. *The Wealth of a Nation To Be.* New York, 1980.

Jones, Howard Mumford. *O Strange New World: American Culture: The Formative Years.* New York, 1964.

Joyce, William, et al., eds. *Printing and Society in Early America.* Worcester, Mass., 1983.

Kaestle, Carl. *Pillars of the Republic: Common Schools and American Society, 1780–1860*. New York, 1983.

Kammen, Michael. "Changing Perceptions of the Life Cycle in American Thought and Culture." *Proceedings of the Massachusetts Historical Society* 91 (1979):35–66.

Kerber, Linda. "Daughters of Columbia: Educating Women for the Republic, 1787–1805." In *The Hofstadter Aegis: A Memorial*. Edited by Stanley Elkins and Eric McKitrick. New York, 1974. Reprinted in *Women's America: Refocusing the Past*, pp. 82–94. Edited by Kerber and Jane DeHart Mathews. New York, 1982.

———. *Federalists in Dissent: Imagery and Ideology in Jeffersonian America*. Ithaca, N.Y., 1970.

———. *Women of the Republic: Intellect and Ideology in Revolutionary America*. Chapel Hill, N.C., 1980.

Kerr, Clark. *The Future of Industrial Societies: Convergence or Continuing Diversity?* Cambridge, Mass., 1983.

Kett, Joseph F., and Patricia A. McClung. "Book Culture in Post-Revolutionary Virginia." PAAS 94, pt. 1 (1984):98–137.

Kinney, Charles. *Church and State: The Struggle for Separation in New Hampshire, 1630–1900*. New York, 1955.

Kirsop, Wallace. "Literary History and Book Trade History: The Lessons of L'Apparition du livre." *Australian Journal of French Studies* 16 (1979):488–535.

Kluckholm, Florence. "Variations in the Basic Values of Family Systems." In *A Modern Introduction to the Family*, pp. 304–15. Edited by Norman W. Bell and Ezra Vogel. Glencoe, Ill., 1962.

Korshin, Paul J., ed. *The Widening Circle: Essays on the Circulation of Literature in Eighteenth Century Europe*. Philadelphia, 1976.

Kousser, Morgan. "The Revivalism of Narrative." *Social Science History* 8 (1984):133–50.

Kouwenhoven, John A. *Made in America: The Arts in Modern Civilization*. New York, 1962.

Kozol, Jonathan. *Illiterate America*. New York, 1985.

Kramnick, Isaac. *Bolingbroke and His Circle: The Politics of Nostalgia in the Age of Walpole*. Cambridge, Mass., 1968.

Kraus, Michael. *The Atlantic Civilization: Eighteenth-Century Origins*. Ithaca, N.Y., 1966.

Lancaster, Edwin R. "Books Read in Virginia in [the] Early Nineteenth Century, 1806–1823." *Virginia Historical Magazine* 42 (1938):56–59.

Larkin, Jack. "Interim Center Village Report." Old Sturbridge Village. Unpublished paper, n.d.

Latham, Charles, Jr. *A Short History of Thetford, Vermont, 1761–1870*. Thetford, Vt., 1972.

Laurie, Bruce. *The Working People of Philadelphia, 1800–1850*. Philadelphia, 1980.

Lawton, Alice M. "History of Chester." Paper read at the Review Club, 28 Oct. 1930. MS 974.31 C426L, VHS.

Lehmann-Haupt, Helmut. *Bookbinding in America: Three Essays*. Portland, Me., 1941.

Lemon, James T. *The Best Poor Man's Country: A Geographical Study of Early Southeastern Pennsylvania*. New York, 1976.

LeRoy Ladurie, Emmanuel. *The Peasants of Languedoc*. Translated by John Day. Urbana, Ill., 1974.

Leventhal, Herbert. *In the Shadow of the Enlightenment: Occultism and Renaissance Science in Eighteenth Century America*. New York, 1976.

[Leverett, Charles Edward]. *A Memoir Biographical and Genealogical of Sir John Leverett, KNT. Governor of Massachusetts and of the Family Generally*. Boston, 1956.

"Leverett." *New England Historical and Genealogical Register* 2 (1848):326.

Levy, Leonard. *The Emergence of a Free Press*. New York, 1985.

Lewis, Jan. *The Pursuit of Happiness: Family Values in Jefferson's Virginia*. New York, 1983.

Lewis, Thomas R., Jr. "From Suffield to Saybrook: An Historical Geography of the Connecticut River Valley in Connecticut Before 1800." Ph.D. diss., Rutgers Univ., 1978.

Liddle, William D. "Virtue and Liberty: An Inquiry into the Role of the Agrarian Myth in the Rhetoric of the American Revolutionary Era." *South Atlantic Quarterly* 77 (1978):15–38.

Lindberg, Sten G. "The Scandinavian Book Trade in the Eighteenth Century." In *Buchund Buchhande in Europe in Achtzehnten Jahrhundert*, pp. 225–48. Edited by Giles Barber and Bernhard Fabian. Hamburg, 1981.

Lockridge, Kenneth. *Literacy in Colonial New England: An Enquiry into the Social Context of Literacy in the Early Modern West.* New York, 1974.

———. "Literacy in Early America, 1650–1800." In *Literacy and Social Development in the West: A Reader*, pp. 183–200. Edited by Harvey J. Graff. Cambridge, England, 1981.

Loehr, Rodney C. "Self-Sufficiency in the Farm." AgH 26 (1952):37–41.

Ludlow and Her Neighbors. "Chester Past and Present." Ludlow, Vt., 1899.

Ludlum, David. *Social Ferment in Vermont, 1790–1850.* New York, 1939.

Lundberg, David, and Henry May. "The Enlightened Reader in America." AQ 28 (1974):262–93.

McCarthy, William H., Jr. *An Outline of the History of the Printed Book: Being the 3rd Number of the Dolphin.* New York, 1938.

McCorison, Marcus. *Amos Taylor, a sketch and bibliography.* Worcester, Mass., 1959.

———. "Two Unrecorded American Paintings of 'Fanny Hill'." VtH 40 (1972):64–66.

———. *Vermont Imprints, 1778–1820.* Worcester, Mass., 1963.

———. [First] *Additions and Corrections.* Worcester, Mass., 1968.

———. [Second] *Additions and Corrections.* Worcester, Mass., 1973.

———. [Third] *Additions and Corrections to Vermont Imprints, 1778–1820.* Worcester, Mass., 1985.

McCoy, Drew. *The Elusive Republic: Political Economy in Jeffersonian America.* New York, 1980.

Macfarlane, Alan. *The Family Life of Ralph Josselin, a Seventeenth Century Clergyman.* Cambridge, England, 1970.

———. *The Origins of English Individualism: The Family, Property, and Social Transition.* New York, 1979.

———. *Reconstructing Historical Communities.* Cambridge, England, 1977.

McKelvey, Blake. *American Urbanization: A Comparative History.* Glencoe, Ill., 1973.

McKenzie, D.F. "The London Book Trade in the Later 17th Century." *The Library* 33 (1978):242–46.

McLoughlin, William. *Revivals, Awakenings, and Reform.* Chicago, 1979.

McLuhan, Marshall. *The Gutenberg Galaxy: The Making of Typographic Man.* Toronto, 1972.

———. *Understanding Media: The Extensions of Man.* New York, 1964.

———. *War and Peace in the Global Village.* New York, 1968.

Main, Gloria. "Probate Records as a Source for Early American History." WMQ 3s 32 (1975):88–99.

———. *Tobacco Colony: Life in Early Maryland, 1650–1720.* Princeton, N.J., 1983.

Main, Jackson T. *Society and Economy in Colonial Connecticut.* Princeton, N.J., 1985.

———. *The Social Structure of Revolutionary America.* Princeton, N.J., 1965.

Manuel, Frank. "The Use and Abuse of Psychology in History." *Daedalus* 100 (1971):187–212.

Marini, Stephen A. *Radical Sects of Revolutionary America.* Cambridge, Mass., 1982.

Martin, Henri-Jean. "Printing." In *Contact: Human Communications and Its History*, pp. 128–49. Edited by Raymond Williams. London, 1981.

Martin, Hugh. *Puritanism and Richard Baxter.* London, 1954.

Matthews, Fred. " 'Hobbesian Populism': Interpretive Paradigms and Moral Vision in American Historiography." JAH 72 (1985):92–115.

May, Henry. *The Enlightenment in America: A History.* New York, 1976.

Merrill, Michael. "Cash Is Good to Eat: Self-Sufficiency and Exchange in the Rural Economy of the United States." *Radical History Review* 4 (1977):42–71.

Merrill, Michael, and Michael Wallace. "Marxism and History." In *The Left Academy: Marxist Scholarship on American Campuses*, pp. 202–41. Edited by Bertell Ollman and Edward Verhoff. New York, 1982.

Meyers, Marvin. *The Jacksonian Persuasion: Politics and Belief*. Rev. ed. Stanford, Calif., 1960.

Miller, Douglas T. *The Birth of Modern America, 1820–1850*. New York, 1970.

Miller, Edward, and Frederic P. Wells. *History of Ryegate, Vermont*. St. Johnsbury, Vt., 1913.

Miller, Perry. *The Life of the Mind in America: From the Revolution to the Civil War. Books One Through Three*. New York, 1965.

Milstein, Barney. *Eight Eighteenth Century Reading Societies: A Sociological Contribution to the History of German Literature*. Bern, 1972.

Modelski, George. "The Long Cycle of Global Politics and the Nation-State." CSSH 20 (1978): 214–35.

Molnar, John E. "Publication and Retail Book Advertisements in the Virginia Gazette, 1736–1780." 2 vols. Ph.D. diss., Univ. of Michigan, 1978.

Monaghan, E. Jennifer. *A Common Heritage: Noah Webster's Blue Back Speller*. Hamden, Conn., 1983.

Morison, Samuel E. *The Puritan Pronaos: Studies in the Intellectual Life of New England in the 17th Century*. New York, 1936.

Mott, Frank Luther. *American Journalism: A History, 1690–1960*. 3d ed. New York, 1962.

Muir, Edward. *Civic Ritual in Renaissance Venice*. Princeton, N.J., 1981.

Muller, H. Nicholas, III. "Shifting Boundaries, Elusive Settlers, and the Population of the 'Republic of Vermont': A Review Essay on *Vermont 1771 Census*," VtH 51 (1983):179–89.

Murray, Robinson, III. "New Hampshire Imprints through 1800." Unpublished files.

Mutch, Robert E. "Yeoman and Merchant in Pre-Industrial America: Eighteenth Century Massachusetts as a Test Case." *Societas* 7 (1977):279–302.

Nash, Ray. *American Penmanship, 1800–1850: A History of Writing and a Bibliography of Copybooks from Jenkins to Spencer*. Worcester, Mass., 1969.

Nasr, Seyyed Hossein. "Islamic Conception of Intellectual Life." In Phillip P. Wiener, *Dictionary of the History of Ideas: Studies of Selected Pivotal Ideas*, pp. II:639–52. 5 vols. New York, 1973.

Nerone, John C. "The Press and Popular Culture in the Early Republic: Cincinnati, 1793–1848." Ph.D. diss., Univ. of Notre Dame, 1982.

Neustadt, Richard E., and Ernest R. May. *Thinking in Time: The Uses of History for Decision-Makers*. Glencoe, Ill., 1986.

Nichols, Charles L. "The Literary Fair in the United States." In *Bibliographical Essays: A Tribute to Wilberforce Eames*, pp. 85–92. Edited by George P. Winship. Cambridge, Mass., 1924.

North, Douglas. *The Economic Growth of the United States, 1790–1860*. New York, 1961.

Norton, Mary Beth. *Liberty's Daughters: The Revolutionary Experience of Women, 1750–1800*. Ithaca, N.Y., 1980.

Norton, Mary Beth, et al. *A People and a Nation: A History of the United States*, vol. 1. 2d ed. Boston, 1986.

Nuttall, Geoffrey. *Richard Baxter and Phillip Doddridge: A Study in a Tradition*. London, 1951.

Nye, Russell B. *Fettered Freedom: Civil Liberty and the Slavery Controversy, 1830–1860*. New York, 1972.

Obelkevich, James. *Religion and Rural Society: South Lindsey, 1825–1875*. Oxford, 1976.

Oliver, Robert T. *History of Public Speaking in America*. Boston, 1965.

Ong, Walter. *Orality and Literacy: The Technologizing of the Word*. Methuen, 1982.

————. *The Presence of the Word: Some Prolegomena for Cultural and Religious History*. Minneapolis, 1981.

————. *Ramus: Method and the Decay of Dialogue*. Cambridge, Mass., 1958.

Orians, G. Harrison. "Censure of Fiction in American Romances and Magazines, 1789–1810." PMLA 52 (1937):195–214.

Pannes, Ernestine. *Waters of the Lonely Way: A Chronicle of Weston, Vermont, 1761–1978*. Canaan, N.H., 1982.

Peladeau, Marius, ed. *The Prose of Royall Tyler*. Rutland, Vt., 1972.

Perry, Lewis. *Intellectual Life in America: A History*. New York, 1984.

Pessen, Edward. "Wealth in America Before 1865." In *Wealth and the Wealthy in the Modern World*, pp. 167–88. Edited by W.D. Rubinstein. New York, 1980.

Plant, Marjorie. *The English Book Trade: An Economic History of the Making and Sale of Books*. London, 1974.

Porter, Roy. *English Society in the Eighteenth Century*. New York, 1983.

Pred, Allan R. *Urban Growth and the Circulation of Information: The United States System of Cities, 1790–1840*. Cambridge, Mass., 1973.

Proceedings at Chester, Vermont, June, 29, 1909, on Old Home Day. Montpelier, Vt.; City of Chester, Vt., 1909.

Prothero, I.J. *Artisans and Politics in Early Nineteenth Century London: John Gast and His Times*. Baton Rouge, La., 1979.

Prude, Jonathan. *The Coming of Industrial Order: Town and Factory Life in Rural Massachusetts, 1810–1860*. Cambridge, England, 1983.

Pruitt, Bettye Hobbs. "Self-Sufficiency and the Agricultural Economy of Eighteenth-Century Massachusetts," WMQ 3s 41 (July 1984):333–64.

Read, Allen Walker. "Noah Webster's Project in 1801 for "A History of American Newspapers." *Journalism Quarterly* 11 (1934):258–75.

Ready, James K. "A Checklist of Imprints for Vermont, 1821–35." Master's thesis, Catholic Univ., 1955.

Reed, Mick. "The Peasantry of Nineteenth-Century England: A Neglected Class." HW 18 (1984):53–76.

Reilly, Elizabeth Carroll. "The Wages of Piety: The Boston Book Trade of Jeremy Condy." In *Printing and Society in Early America*, pp. 83–131. Edited by William Joyce et al. Worcester, Mass., 1983.

Rice, John L. "Dartmouth College and the State of New Connecticut, 1776–1782." In *Connecticut Valley Historical Society Papers and Proceedings, 1876–1881*, pp. 152–206. Edited by John L. Rice. Springfield, Mass., 1981.

Riesman, David. *Individualism Reconsidered*. Glencoe, Ill., 1954.

Riesman, David, Nathan Glazer, and Reuel Denney. *The Lonely Crowd: A Study of the Changing American Character*. New Haven, Conn., 1960.

Roche, Daniel. *Le Siecle des Lumières en province. Académies et académiciens provinciaux, 1680–1789*. Paris, 1978.

Rock, Howard. *Artisans of the New Republic: The Tradesmen of New York City in the Age of Jefferson*. New York, 1979.

Roth, Randolph. *The Democratic Dilemma: Religion, Reform, and the Social Order in the Connecticut River Valley of Vermont, 1791–1850*. Cambridge, England, 1987.

———. "Whence This Strange Fire? Religion and Reform in the Connecticut River Valley of Vermont, 1791–1843." 2 vols. Ph.D. diss., Yale Univ., 1981.

Rothenberg, Winifred B. "The Market and Massachusetts Farmers, 1750–1855." *Journal of Economic History* 61 (1981):281–314.

Rourke, Constance. "P.T. Barnum." In Rourke, *Trumpets of Jubilee*, pp. 276–319. New York, 1963.

Rusche, Dennis. "An Empire of Reason: A Study of the Writings of Noah Webster." Ph.D. diss., Univ. of Iowa, 1975.

Russell, Howard S. *A Long Deep Furrow: Three Centuries of New England Agriculture.* Hanover, N.H., 1976.

Rutman, Darrett. *American Puritanism: Faith and Practice.* Philadelphia, 1970.

———. "People in Process: The New Hampshire Towns of the 18th Century." *Journal of Urban History* 1 (1975):268–91.

Ryan,. Thomas R. *Orestes A. Brownson: A Definitive Biography.* Huntington, Ind., 1976.

Salmon, Marylynn. "Equality or Submersion? Feme Covert Status in Early Pennsylvania." In *Women of America: A History,* pp. 92–113. Edited by Carol Ruth Berkin and Mary Beth Norton. Boston, 1979.

Samuel, Ralph, and Gareth Stedman Jones. "Editorial: Ten Years After." HW 20 (Autumn 1985): 1–4.

Sanford, Charles L. "The Intellectual Origins and New-Worldliness of American Industry." *Journal of Economic History* 18 (1958):1–16.

Schlatter, Richard. *Richard Baxter and Puritan Politics.* New Brunswick, N.J., 1957.

Schlesinger, Arthur M., Jr. *The Cycles of American History.* Boston, 1986.

———. *Orestes A. Brownson: A Pilgrim's Progress.* Boston, 1939.

———. "Orestes Brownson, An American Marxist Before Marx." *Sewanee Review* 47 (1939):317–23.

Schutz, Alfred. *The Phenomenology of the Social World.* Translated by George Walsh and Frederick Lehnert. Evanston, Ill., 1967.

———. *Reflections of the Problem of Relevance.* Edited and translated by Richard M. Zaner. New Haven, Conn., 1970.

———. "Some Structures of the Life-World." In *Studies in Phenomenological Philosophy.* Edited by I. Schutz. Vol. 3, *Alfred Schutz – Collected Papers.* The Hague, 1970.

———. "The Stranger: An Essay in Social Psychology." In *Alfred Schutz on Phenomenology and Social Relations: Selected Writings,* pp. 74–75. Edited by Helmuth Wagner. Chicago, 1970.

———. "Tiresias, or Our Knowledge of Future Events." In *Alfred Schutz on Phenomenology and Social Relations: Selected Writings,* pp. 75–76. Edited by Helmuth Wagner. Chicago, 1970.

Schutz, Alfred, and Thomas Luckmann. *The Structures of the Life-World.* Translated by Richard M. Zaner and H. Tristram Engelhardt, Jr. Evanston, Ill., 1973.

Scott, Donald. "The Popular Lecture and the Creation of a Public in Mid-Nineteenth Century America." JAH 66 (1980):791–809.

———. "Print and the Public Lecture System, 1840–1860." In *Printing and Society in Early America,* pp. 278–99. Edited by William Joyce et al. Worcester, Mass., 1983.

Seaver, Paul. *Wallington's World: A Puritan Artisan in 17th-Century London.* Methuen, 1985.

Sellers, Charles; Henry May; and Neil R. McMillen. *A Synopsis of American History.* 6th ed. Boston, 1985.

Shaw, Ralph; Richard Shoemaker; et al. *American Bibliography.* New York, 1958–.

Silver, Rollo. *The American Printer, 1787–1825.* Charlottesville, Va., 1967.

———. *The Boston Book Trade, 1800–1825.* New York, 1949.

Simpson, Lowell. "The Development and Scope of Undergraduate Literary Society Libraries at Columbia, Dartmouth, Princeton, and Yale, 1783–1830." JLH 12 (1977):211–21.

Siracusa, Carl. *A Mechanical People: Perceptions of the Industrial Order in Massachusetts, 1815–1860.* Middletown, Conn., 1979.

Skillen, Glenn B. "Additional Vermont Imprints, 1821–1835." Master's thesis, Catholic Univ., 1964.

Sklar, Kathryn Kish. "The Founding of Mount Holyoke College." In *Women of America: A History,* pp. 177–201. Edited by Carol Ruth Berkin and Mary Beth Norton. Boston, 1979.

Slawson, George Clarke. *The Postal History of Vermont.* New York, 1969.

Sloane, Eric. *A Museum of Early American Tools.* New York, 1973.

Smart, George K. "Private Libraries in Colonial Virginia." *American Literature* 10 (1938):24–52.

Smith, Daniel Scott. "Population, Family, and Society in Hingham, Massachusetts, 1635–1880." Ph.D. diss., Univ. of California at Berkeley, 1973.

——. "Underregistration and Bias in Probate Records: An Analysis of Data from Eighteenth Century Hingham, Massachusetts." WMQ 3s 32 (1975):100–112.

Smith, Donald Alan. "Legacy of Dissent: Religion and Politics in Revolutionary Vermont, 1749 to 1784." 3 vols. Ph.D. diss., Clark Univ., 1981.

Soltow, Lee, and Edward Stevens. *The Rise of Literacy and the Common School in the United States: A Socioeconomic Analysis to 1870.* Chicago, 1981.

Stebbins, Theodore E., Jr., et al. *A New World: Masterpieces of American Painting, 1760–1910.* Boston, 1983.

Stilwell, Lewis D. *Migration From Vermont.* Montpelier, Vt., 1937.

Stiverson, Gregory A. "Books Both Useful and Entertaining: Reading Habits in Mid Eighteenth Century Virginia." *Southern Librarian* 24 (1975):52–58.

Stone, Lawrence. *The Family, Sex and Marriage in England, 1500–1800.* London, 1977.

——. *The Past and the Present.* Boston, 1981.

Taft, Russell S. "Windsor." *Windsor Journal,* 16 Jan. 1892.

Tanselle, G. Thomas. "The Bibliographical Concepts of Issue and State." PBSA 69 (1975):17–66.

——. "The Concept of Ideal State." SB 33 (1980):18–53.

——. "Copyright Records and the Bibliographer." SB 22 (1969):77–124.

——. *The History of Books as a Field of Study.* [Chapel Hill, N.C.], 1981.

——. *Royall Tyler.* Cambridge, Mass., 1967.

——. "Title-Page Transcription and Signature Collation Reconsidered." SB 38 (1985):45–81.

Taylor, George Rogers. "Comment." In *The Growth of the Seaport Cities, 1790–1825,* pp. 26–53. Edited by David T. Gilchrist. Charlottesville, Va., 1967.

Thistlethwaite, Frank. *America and Atlantic Community: Anglo-American Aspects, 1790–1850.* New York, 1959.

Thompson, E.P. "Eighteenth Century English Society: Class Struggle Without Class?" *Social History* 3 (1978):133–50.

Tiffany, N. *The Tiffanys of America.* N.p., n.d.

Trewartha, Glenn T. "The Unincorporated Hamlet: One Element of the American Settlement Fabric." *Association of American Geographers Annals* 33 (1943):32–81.

Tuchman, Barbara. *The March of Folly: From Troy to Vietnam.* New York, 1984.

Ullery, Jacob G. *Men of Vermont: An Illustrated Biographical History of Vermonters and Sons of Vermont.* Brattleboro, Vt., 1894.

Ulrich, Laurel Thatcher. *Good Wives: Image and Reality in the Lives of Women in Northern New England, 1650–1750.* New York, 1982.

Vermont's Susquicentennial: The Celebration at Windsor, July 8, 1927. Windsor, Vt., 1927.

Veysey, Laurence. "Intellectual History and the New Social History." In *New Directions in American Intellectual History,* pp. 3–26. Edited by John Higham and Paul K. Conkin. Baltimore, 1979.

Wallace, Anthony F.C. *Rockdale: The growth of an American village in the early Industrial Revolution.* New York, 1978.

Wallerstein, Immanuel. *The Modern World-System.* 2 vols. New York, 1974 and 1980.

Ward, Albert. *Book Production, Fiction, and the German Reading Public, 1740–1800.* Oxford, 1974.

Ward, Donal. "Religious Enthusiasm in Vermont, 1761–1847." Ph.D. diss., Univ. of Notre Dame, 1980.

Ward, Nicholas Hayes. "Pianos, Parasols, and Poppa: The Migration of Vermont Farm Girls to the Massachusetts Mill Towns." Master's thesis, Brown Univ., 1974.

Wardner, Henry Steele. *The Birthplace of Vermont: The History of Windsor to 1781*. New York, 1927.

———. *Historical Address Delivered at the Recent Dedication of the Old South Meeting House*. Windsor, Vt., 1923.

———. "Judge Jacob and Dinah," *Vermonter* 19, nos. 5–6 (May-June 1914):1–7.

Wellman, Rev. Joshua Wyman. *Descendants of Thomas Wellman of Lynn, Massachusetts*. Boston, 1918.

Wenrick, Jon. "For Education and Entertainment: Almanacs in the Early American Republic, 1783–1815." Ph.D. diss., Claremont Graduate School, 1974.

Wheeler, Joseph T. "Literary Culture and 18th Century Maryland: Summary of Findings." *Maryland Historical Magazine* 34 (1943):273–76.

Wiebe, Robert. *The Opening of American Society: From the Adoption of the Constitution to the Eve of Disunion*. New York, 1984.

———. *The Segmented Society*. New York, 1975.

Wiener, Philip P. *Dictionary of the History of Ideas: Studies of Selected Pivotal Ideas*. 5 vols. New York, 1973.

Wilentz, Sean. *Chants Democratic: New York City and the Rise of the American Working Class*. New York, 1983.

———. "On Class and Politics in Jacksonian America." RAH 10 (1982):45–63.

Wiles, Roy. "The Relish for Reading in Provincial England Two Centuries Ago." In *The Widening Circle: Essays on the Circulation of Literature in Eighteenth Century Europe*, pp. 85–115. Edited by Paul J. Korshin. Philadelphia, 1976.

Wilgus, William. *The Role of Transportation in the Development of Vermont*. Montpelier, Vt., 1945.

Willey, Basil. *The Eighteenth Century Background: Studies on the Idea of Nature in the Thought of the Period*. Boston, 1961.

Williams, Raymond, ed. *Contact: Human Communications and Its History*. London, 1981.

———. *Marxism and Literature*. Oxford, 1977.

———, ed. *Problems in Materialism and Culture: Selected Essays*. London, 1980.

Willingham, William. "Windham, Connecticut: Profile of a Revolutionary Community, 1775–1818." Ph.D. diss., Northwestern Univ., 1972.

Wills, Gary. *Inventing America*. New York, 1976.

Winans, Robert. *A Descriptive Checklist of Book Catalogues Separately Printed in America, 1693–1800*. Charlottesville, Va., 1981.

———. "The Growth of a Novel-Reading Public in Late-Eighteenth-Century America." *Early American Literature* 9 (1975):267–75.

Winters, Donald L. *Farmers Without Farms: Agricultural Tenancy in 19th Century Iowa*. Westport, Conn., 1978.

Wise, Gene. "The Decline of American Intellectual History: A Diagnosis and a Possible Reprieve." Unpublished paper, Case Western Reserve Univ., 1975.

Wolf, Edwin 2nd. "Great American Book Collectors to 1800." *Gazetteer of the Grolier Club* 16 (1971):3–25.

———. "Introduction," *The Books of Isaac Norris (1701-1766) at Dickinson College*. Edited by Marie Korey. Carlisle, Pa., 1976.

———. *The Library of James Logan of Philadelphia, 1674-1791*. Philadelphia, 1974.

———. "The Library of Ralph Assheton: The Book Background of a Colonial Philadelphia Lawyer." PBSA 58 (1964):345–79.

Wolf, Stephanie. *Urban Village: Population, Community, and Family Structure in Germantown, Pennsylvania, 1683–1800*. Princeton, N.J., 1976.

Wood, Gordon. *The Creation of the American Republic, 1776–1787*. Chapel Hill, N.C., 1969.

———. "The Democratization of Mind in the American Revolution." In *The Moral Foundations of the American Republic*, pp. 102–28. Edited by Robert H. Horwitz. Charlottesville, Va., 1977.

———. "Social Radicalism and Equality in the American Revolution." In *B.K. Smith Lectures in History: Univ. of St. Thomas*, pp. 5–14. Houston, Texas, 1976.

Wood, Joseph S. "The Origins of the New England Village." Ph.D. diss., Pennsylvania State Univ., 1978.

Worst, Jonathan. "New England Psalmody, 1760–1810: Analysis of an American Idiom." Ph.D. diss., Univ. of Michigan, 1974.

Wright, Louis. "The Purposeful Reading of Our Colonial Ancestors." *ELH: A Journal of English Literary History* 4 (1937):85–111.

———. *Cultural Life on the Moving Frontier*. Bloomington, Ind., 1955.

Wroth, Lawrence, and Rollo Silver. "Book Production and Distribution from the American Revolution to the War Between the States." In *The Book in America: A History of the Making and Selling of Books in the United States*, pp. 63–136. Edited by Hellmut Lehmann-Haupt. 2d. ed. New York, 1952.

Index

Abell, Truman: *New England Farmer's Diary and Almanac*, 295

academies, 357; academy education, 40, 219; academy library, 161; attendance, 289; at Windsor supported by newspaper, 45

access zone. *See* transportation and communications network

account books, 55; and use of money equivalents, 59 n.11

Adams, Daniel: *Scholar's Arithmetic*, 57, 297

Adams, George: *Natural Philosophy*, 341

Adams, Hannah: *View of Religions*, 338

Addison and Steele: *Spectator*, 316–17, 334

adult education, 123

adulthood. *See* life cycle

advertising. *See* newspapers, advertising

affiliative behavior, 106

Afflicted Man's Companion, 298

African Americans: Aaron Burdow, Reading, Vt., tenant farm family, 295, 301

"age of benevolence," explained by Rev. Asa Burton, 200

"age of knowledge," explained by Daniel Webster, 18–20

Age of Reason, 340

age of reading, emergence of, 354–59; transition to in New England, 263

agricultural life, 56, 97; activities in Windsor District, 73; "changing works," 56, 73, 77, 82–83, 302, 352; commercial agriculture, 68 n.28; cycle of and book trade, 169, 175, 202; difficulties of existence, 12; household, minimum viable, 397; "middling sort" ideal, 302; production and products, 95, 231; tasks, 302; works, 324, ch. 2:53–113; *see also* commercial exchange; science and technology

Aikin, John: *Life of Howard*, 317, 342

Alba, proposed name for new county, 332 n.75

Albany, 13, 31, 59

Algerine Captive, 317

alienation, roots of, 15

Allen, Ethan: *Narrative of Captivity*, 327–28; *Reason the Only Oracle of Man*, 196

Allen, Ira, 80

Allestree, Richard: *Whole Duty of Man*, 61

almanacs, 21, 26, 35, 80, 158, 160, 162, 165, 167, 169, 171–73, 175, 184, 190–93 and n.4, 196, 198–99, 201–2, 205, 216, 221–22, 248, 253, 265, 278–79, 280, 288–89, 294–97, 304, 307, 313, 318, 323–26, 332, 334–35, 346, 358; share in Windsor District libraries, 407

Alphonso and Dalinda, 340

America as republic of knowledge, 355

American authored works as majority retained, 339

American Dictionary, 82

American Gazetteer, 297, 299, 327, 334

American Preceptor, 327

American Selection, 327

American Speller, 53

American State Papers, 324

American Universal Geography, 308, 324, 327, 334

Americanization of knowledge, 341

Amsden, Abel, family, 239

Ancient History, 310

Andover, Vt., 63, 93, 100, 140, 146, 184–85, 187, 238, 292–94, 312, 316, 358, 388, 401

Anglo-American civilization, fascination with, 132

Annalistes, 205

Anson, Commodore George: *Voyage to the South Sea*, 327

antebellum reform, 103

Antimasons, 103–4, 294, 358

Appeal from the Judgments, 68

appendices: referred to, 1, 115; 2, 141; 3, 228; 4, 255, 270; 5, 252, 326

apprenticeships, 122

Arabian Nights, 266

arithmetic, works, 68, 208, 219, 297, 314, 325, 333; in district school education, 124; and intellectual arithmetic, 42; and mathematics works, 411; as part of basic stock of knowledge, 127; *see also* numerical skills

Arminianism, 296

artisans and artisan families, 57, 73, 77–78, 109, 138, 143, 145–47, 152, 234–36, 242, 244, 263, 275, 288, 291, 294, 298, 300–2, 304, 306–7, 309, 312, 315–16, 319, 322–23, 330, 333, 390, 392–93; as forerunners of "modern" attitudes to knowledge, 298; and new communications environment, 349–50; and reading matter, 236; and wealth, table N–2, 453; *see also* family life; family libraries, by library types

artisan shops, 79, 81, 85, 88–89, 93–94, 101; seeking customers in Windsor District, 79, 81, 92–95, 102

arts, works, 221; *see also* visual expression

Ascutney Mountain, 320

Atlas, 337

audiences of culture, 289 n.6, 377; *see also* reading and readers

Augustan age, 265; writers, 69–70; perspectives, 309; thought, 340

Austria, 22

author and publisher. *See* book trade

authority of printed word, too readily accepted, 39

auxiliary print centers. *See* printing and publishing: print centers

Axtell, James: quoted, 378

Babylon the Great, 299

ballad sellers. *See* peddlers

Ballou, Hosea: *Treatise on Atonement*, 338

Baltimore, Md., 22, 59, 100

Baltimore, Vt., 63, 93, 100, 140, 145, 185, 301

Bank of Windsor, 102

Banks, John: *Life of Peter the Great*, 324, 328, 334, 402

baptism, infant, in Leverett family library, 411

Baptist Missionary Magazine, 200

Baptist works, 199–200, 202, 307, 316, 326, 331; denominational reports, 198; hymnals, 198

Baptists, 62, 303, 318, 323, 358, 411; meetinghouse, 410

Barlow, Joel: *Columbiad*, 334; *Vision of Columbus*, 334

Barnet, Vt., 107

Barron, Hal, 368

Baxter, Richard, 61–62; *Saints' Everlasting Rest*, 13, 259, 290–91, 298, 327, 337

Beattie, James: *Minstrel*, 316

Beecher, Lyman, 363, 371

Beers' Almanac, 190

Belgium, 22

belief: importance of in history, xxi

Bellah, Robert: *Habits of the Heart*, 373

Bellows Falls, Vt., 187 n.41, 303 n.24, 322

benevolent reform organizations, 103 n.105, 262, 343; moral reform, 200, 210–11, 357; *see also* social reform organizations

Bennett, John: *Letters to a Young Lady*, 262; quoted, 47 n.64

Bennington Gazette, 160

Bible and New Testaments, 13, 21, 26–27, 35, 62, 80, 115, 146, 152, 192, 199–200, 208, 221, 248, 251, 259, 265–66, 277, 279–81, 286, 293–96, 300, 303–4, 306–10, 314, 316, 319, 323, 325–27, 329, 334, 337, 358, 378; "Bible, Great," 323; Bible, "large," 324; "Bible, old large," 324; Brattleboro Bible, 211 pl., 259; and family reading, 1780–1835, 257–60; "Family Record," 259; as a "sacred encyclopedia," 257–60; Windsor Bible, frontispiece, 259

Bible, plates from: frontispiece, 211

Bidwell, Percy, 59, 235, 398, 400

Bigland, John: *Geographical and Historical View*, 308; *Letters on the Study*, 310

bindery, 167 and n.20

Bingham, Caleb: *American Preceptor*, 327

biographies, works, 261, 267

Birmingham, England, 22

Bixby, Levi, Ludlow yeoman farm family, 294, 301

Black River Academy, 45, 312

Black River Turnpike, 182

Blackstone, William: *Commentaries on the Laws of England*, 68, 327; quoted, 43, 233

Blair, Hugh: *Lectures on Rhetoric*, 40, 310

Bolingbroke circle, 61, 69

book carters, 162, 190, 408

Book of Common Prayer, 337

book reviews, as evidence about texts, 205 and n.35

books, excerpts from, 162 n.17, 221

books generally, as vehicle of printed matter, 20–21, 26, 35, 45, 190, 192–93, 205, 216, 264, 303, 309, 319, 408

books, number of and amount of reading, 348

booksellers, private. *See* book trade

bookstore, 24, 80, 88, 93–94, 97, 103, 152, 160, 162, 166–67, 169–84 and n.23, 322, 332; Robert Thomas's, Sterling, Mass. bookstore, 171–73; Walpole, N.H., 59; *see also* circulation system for print culture—formal circuit; Brattleboro; Chester; Hanover; Keene; Walpole; Windsor book trade in rural New England, 1778–1835, 29, 157–88; areas of sales and local publishing, 201–3; bookbinders, 167 and n.20; catalogues, 205 n.35; contact points through which all printed matter passed, 159–63; defined, 158; exchanges of stock, 197; imported works, 173, 195, 198, 200, 203, 222; patent medicines, 169; popular sellers, 173; role of newspaper advertisements, 205; steady sellers, 173; subscription pattern and human habitats, 363; wholesaling, 102 n.99; *see also* popular sellers in Upper Valley

borrowing and lending of printed matter. *See* reading and readers; book trade

Boston, Thomas: *Human Nature*, 304, 337; *The Crook in the Lot*, 327

Boston, 13, 22, 31, 59, 85, 107, 173, 203, 207, 274, 318, 342

Bowden, John: mentioned, 338

Bowen, Abel: quoted, 339

Bozeman, Theodore, 342

Bradford, Vt., 79

Brainerd, Rev. David, 343

Brattleboro, Vt., 74, 85, 167, 200

Braudel, Fernand: quoted, 240, 353

Brief Concordance, 259

Bristol, England, 22

British authorship, 25; cultural perspective, 8, 351; literary heritage, 316; periodicals, 407; *see also* England

broadsides, 21, 26, 160, 162, 165, 167, 169, 171, 190, 192, 222, 279, 332

Brookfield, Mass., 77

Brown, John, 363; *Brief Concordance*, 259

Brownson, Orestes A., 12, 14–15, 27, 115, 226, 262, 276, 309, 351, 369; quoted, 1; career discussed, 352–53; earliest attitudes toward "the laboring classes," 108–9 and nn.120–21; Sylvester, father, 233

Brydon, Patrick: *Tour through Sicily*, 334

Buchan, William: *Domestic Medicine*, 316

Buchanan, Claudius: *Christian Researches in Asia*, 308

Buckingham, Joseph: quoted, 226

Buffalo, N.Y., 100

Bullard, Isaac, 309

Bunyan, John: *Pilgrim's Progress*, 13, 176, 327, 338; quoted, 344

Burder, George, 371

Burdow, Aaron, Reading free black tenant farm family, 295, 301

Burlington, Vt., 59, 100

burned-over districts, 12, 158, 241

Burroughs, Eden: *The Profession and Practice of Christians*, 304

Burrows, Edwin: quoted, 55 nn.6–7

Burton, Rev. Asa: quoted, 200

business. *See* commercial exchange; economic life; stores

Byron, George Gordon: *Works*, 316, 340–41

Cadwell and Hubbards' general store, 96

calculating mentality, 341

Caledonia County, Vt., 29

Calhoun, Craig: quoted, 61 n.21

California News, 378

Calvinism Improved, 338

Calvinist: and evangelical theology and morality, 203, 210, 306–7, 316, 326–27, 338, 411; Calvinist works, 296

Canada, 100

canal development, 107

capital formation, rural, and retention of printed matter, 409

capitalism, 6; *see also* commercial exchange; commercialization; economic life

Carey, Mathew, 61, 68; *Atlas*, 337; *Olive Branch*, 327

Carleton, Captain Henry, family, 238

Carp, Alvah, Chelsea, Vt., family, 302

Carver, John: *Travels through the Interior Parts of North America, 1766–1768*, 295

cash, 57, 59, 80–82, 88, 95–96; contemporary meaning, 80–82 and n.55, 95–96 and n.84; *see also* economic life

Cavendish, Vt., 18, 41, 44, 49, 68, 71–72, 89, 93, 100, 119, 129, 140, 144–45, 184–85, 233, 238, 289, 301–2, 308, 311–12, 318–19, 358, 401, 406; Academy, 312; Proctorsville [Cavendish] Reading Club, 49; Social Library, 308; records, 1815–37, 289, 318–19, 323 n.61

Cecil's Remains, 254

Chalmers, Thomas, and relationship between science and religion, 411

Chandler, Thomas II, 81

change: awareness of, 9, 138; and permanence, relationship between, 300; *see also* mending; rebirth

"changing works," 56, 73, 77, 82–83, 302, 352

chapbooks, works, 21, 80, 146, 176–77, 220, 279, 295–96, 346, 408

Charles the Twelfth, 308

Charlestown, N.H., 187 n.41

Chase, Jonathan, 97

Chelsea, Vt., 302, 368

chemistry, works, 107

Cheshire Bridge, 182

Cheshire County, N.H., 32

Chester, Vt., 45–46, 49, 68, 71–72, 76, 78–81,

Chester, VT. (*continued*)
83–84, 88–89, 93–95, 100, 102–3, 139, 142, 144, 148, 152, 182, 184, 187, 235, 238, 240, 255, 270, 295, 300–2, 305, 307, 322–24, 330–32 and n.75, 357–58, 401, 406; Academy, 45–46; Congregational meetinghouse, 324; Union meetinghouse, 323

Chetwood, William Rufus: *Voyages and Adventures*, 327

Child's Arithmetic: quoted, 4

childhood, and early youth, 266; goal of, 44; *see also* life cycle

Children of the Abbey, 340

children's books, 193, 208, 358, 408; and toy books, 219

Chipman, Nathaniel: *Reports and Dissertations*, 327

cholera epidemics, 320

Christian morality. *See* popular sellers

Christian Oeconomy, The, 80

Christian Researches in Asia, 308

Christian republicanism, 325, 359; rural version of, 115; values inculcated, 35; *see also* wisdom of the ages

Christian sect, 62, 293, 358

Chronology, 308, 310

church history, works, part of stock of knowledge, 127; *see also* theology

Churchmen's Magazine, 338

Cicero, 69

circulating libraries, 118, 161, 205, 255, 270, 295, 302, 322–23, 325, 332–33, 358; in Europe, 255–56

circulation system for print culture, 1778–1835: generally, 163–78; *see also* peddlers; transportation and communications network

—formal circuit: 165–75; bookstore, 171–75; newspapers, 175; printing office, 170–71; rivers, bridges, and roads, 165, 169–70; *see also* bookstore; book trade; newspapers, printing and publishing

—informal circuit: 165, 175–78; clandestine works, 175, 177–78; itinerant authors, 175; local authors, 175; paper mill owners, 175; *see also* clandestine works; itinerant authors

cities: of American Northeast, 354; lack of in Upper Valley, 31; seen as fascinating yet dangerous places, 342

Citizen, The, 317

Citizen of the World, 334

clandestine works, 26, 35, 177–78; *see also* circulation system for print culture: informal circuit

Claremont, N.H., 79–80

Clark, Christopher, 80, 292; quoted, 81

Clark, Jefferson: quoted, 42 n.55

Clarke, Edward D.: *Travels in Various Countries*, 308, 319

class structure: re American Northeast, 1760–1830, 240–47; and class based action, 106 n.107; and class relations, 83–84, 93, 107–9; economic and social, 1780–1830, 396–401; economic class structure of Windsor District, 245–47; in rural New England, 226; *see also* intellectual debate; Brownson, Orestes

classical writers, works, 69, 193, 208, 212, 221, 265, 279, 281, 316, 323, 334, 340, 358, 411

Cleland, John: *Memoirs of a Woman of Pleasure*, 177

Clerk's Magazine, 304, 308

Clerke, Francis: *Young Clerk's Companion*, 308

Cobb, Samuel, 240

Cochran, Thomas: quoted, 285

Colburn, Warren: quoted, 42

Colchester, Vt., 80

Cole, Donald, 398

Cole, Thomas, 216–17

Collected Poems, 69

Collection of Poems, 334

college education, 219; graduates, 289; students, 263; colleges, 357

Columbiad, 334

Columbian Academy, 45

Commentaries on the Laws of England, 68, 327; quoted, 43, 233

commentaries, works. *See* Bible

commerce and trading families, 143, 146–47, 152, 236–38, 242, 244, 247, 263, 265, 275, 280 and n.35, 291, 302, 306–7, 312, 314–15, 322, 330, 333, 337, 390, 392; *see also* family life; family libraries, by library types

commerce, forms of inequality fostered by its spread, 93, 102

commercial exchange, 73, 77, 99, 138, 153; attitudes toward, 97; business connections in 1780s, 74; businesses seeking customers in Windsor District, 79, 81, 92–95, 102; and economic advancement, 110, 112; and material accumulation, 110, 112; from mending to acquisitiveness, 110, 112

—share of families involved: in general, see table N–1, 434; share of families involved in 1790, 83; share of families involved in 1790–1800, 88; share of families involved in 1810, 96–97; share of families involved in 1830, 102; sources, 55 n.5; transition in, 1760–1835, 55, 59; and Windsor District family life, 227–40; *see also* commerce; currency; economic life; stores

commercial society, widespread advocacy of, 68

commercialization and elementary literacy, interaction, 54

commercialization and knowledge of lifestyles of wealthier groups, 362

commercialization and rural infrastructure, 352–54
commercialization of rural life in Upper Valley, 1,
    3, 18, ch.2:53–113, 132, 134, 256, 292, 332, 349;
    affiliative behavior, 103–4; defined, 127; levels of
    participation in, 54; society and economy,
    90–93; see also commercial exchange; economic
    life
— stages: stage one, settlement era, 1760–1795,
    70–84; stage two, rise of commercial society
    and economy, 1795–1815, 84–98; stage three,
    commercialization of daily life, 1815–35, 98–110
— variety of understandings of economic life in
    Windsor District, 1760–1835, 60–70
commonplace books, 47
communication system: adequacy of supply, 200;
    contact points through which all printed mat-
    ter passed, 159–63; and contemporary life,
    364–74; creation of, 1; and economy, relation-
    ship between, 368; in rural New England,
    1778–1835, 157–88
communications environment, 89, 112, 157, 169,
    181, 186, 355; in American Northeast, 17–18;
    cultural and material history of, 35; decentrali-
    zation of, 148; and formation of new rural
    mass society, 98; importance of oral modes of,
    37–41; as limiting cultural change, 301; in past
    societies, technology and, xx; underestimating
    extent of, 114
communications network, 298; see also transporta-
    tion network
communications revolution: contemporary, xx;
    and Early Republic, 366; and process of cul-
    tural change, 371
communicative economy, fundamental shift in,
    377
community life: economic dimension, 74; tradi-
    tional web of, xx; see also cultural values and be-
    liefs; economic life; economic thinking; human
    habitats; intellectual traditions and themes; men-
    talités; reading; voluntary organizations
Compendious Dictionary, 82
Compendium to the Bible, 324
Complete Duty of Man, 337
Concord, N.H., 31, 59, 85
concordances, works, 279–80; see also Bible
Congregationalism, 200, 293, 338, 358, 411; Con-
    gregationalist Calvinists, 62; Old South
    meetinghouse, 410
Connecticut, 72, 74, 128
contact points. See book trade; communication
    system
contemporary civilization: historical parallel with,
    2, 364–74; origins of, xx; in relation to Early
    Republic, implications, 364–74

contemporary meaning of: "age of benevolence,"
    explained by Rev. Asa Burton, 200; "age of
    reading," 19; "age of knowledge," explained by
    Daniel Webster, 18–20; "cash," 80–82, 95–96;
    "changing works," 56, 73, 77, 82–83, 302, 352;
    "currency," 81–82, 89, 95, 175; "employment,"
    228; "family library," 257, 280, 404; "knowledge
    from distant climes," 8, 12–15, 25, 39, 353; "li-
    brary," 257; "mechanick question," attitudes re
    107; "middle station" as rural ideal, 14, 342, 364;
    "modern" age, 346; "modern intelligence" as
    cultural ideal, e.g., of, 267, 350; "modernness"
    as contemporary ideal, 13; "money," 81; "occu-
    pation," 227–28; "private library," 257; "profes-
    sional library," 240, 280; "ready money," 96
    n.85; "real property," 233; "Republic of Letters,"
    19; "spirit of fact," 107, 299; "white heat of vital
    piety," 1, 296, 337–38; "wisdom of the ages," 37,
    39; "Work," 227
contemporary world, growing fascination with,
    132
continuity and change in Upper Valley network
    of human habitats, 285–88; continuity insured
    by ideology and social institutions, 372
Cook, Edward, 127, 400; quoted, from 1978 letter
    to author, 407 n.13
Cooper, Anthony Ashley (Earl of Shaftesbury),
    61
Cooper, James Fenimore: Notions of the Ameri-
    cans; quoted, 351 and n.6
copyright, 161 and n.10; see also printing and
    publishing
Cornish Bridge, 85, 97, 182
cosmopolitanism and British connection, 212, 214
    pl., 299, 339–40; see also British
Cott, Nancy: quoted, 47, 50
Cowper, William: Collected Poems, 69, 316, 340
Coxe, Tench, 61, 68
crafted items and visual expression, 379
Cremin, Lawrence. quoted, 115
Cressy, David, 9
Critical and Candid Examination, 338
Critical Pronouncing Dictionary, 341
Crook in the Lot, 327
Cross, Whitney, 13
Crowley, J. E.: quoted, 60 n.17; 61 and n.20
Culpeper, Nicholas: English Physician, 314
cult of domesticity, 221; and family, 343
cultural analysis, regional approach, 27, 29
cultural change and communications revolution,
    371
cultural diffusion, layers of, 358
cultural expression, forms other than print cul-
    ture: in general, app. 1:377–83; dance and

cultural expression (*continued*)
theater, 114; modes of described, 114; music and singing, 114; oral expression, 114; place of print communications in Upper Valley, 114–18; visual expression, 114; written forms, 114

cultural expression, print culture: changes with spread of reading, 104; interaction with voluntary organizations, 103–4, 106; mix of media, 37, 41, 115; modes of interpenetration, 41–42; partial media-blindness in Early Republic, 37; vehicles of, 34

cultural geography of print communications, 188 and n.42, 207; of rural New England *mentalités*, 286

cultural and material factors. *See* material and cultural conditions of life

cultural participation, xx–xxi, 6, 33, 122 n.17, 136, 138, 205, 207, 287, 292, 301; expanding access to knowledge and diversity, 353; intellectual foundations for, 269; minimum threshold of, 248; patterns, 385; and poverty level defined, 384; in print communications, levels of, 116; rural New England foundations, 1760–1835, ch. 3:114–34; and wealth, 248–49; *see* transportation and communications network, varying access to

cultural pluralism in America, 1780–1835, 366, 373

cultural poverty level, 249; connection between poverty and reading, 251

cultural turmoil between 1815 and the 1850s, 362; *see also* disillusionment

cultural values and beliefs: collective trends, 1805–30, 204–17; diversity among habitats, 116; fortunate farmstead human habitat, 320–29; fortunate village human habitat, 329–43; hardscrabble human habitat, 292–301; self-sufficient farmstead human habitat, 301–11; self-sufficient hamlet human habitat, 311–20

culture and communications, 158

Cummings, Jacob: *Introduction to Ancient and Modern Geography*, 68, 308

"currency," 81–82, 89, 95, 175; *see also* commercial exchange; economic life

Cutting, Sewall, 267; quoted, 17

dance, 305, 377–79
Dance of the Haymakers, 379
Dancing on the Barn Floor, 379
Danhoff, Charles, 232
Daniels, George H.: quoted, 342
Darnton, Robert, 9, 301; quoted, 204–5
Dartmouth College, 97, 201, 358, 363
Davidson, Cathy, 40
Davis, Natalie Zemon, 9; quoted, 226
Davis, Richard Beale, 189

Davison, Phineas: *Evangelical Poems*, 327
Dawley, Alan, 341
Dean, Parnell, Windsor yeoman farm family, 323–24
Death of Abel, 310
death rates, difficulties of evidence, 270 n.22
decline, perceptions of in 1830s. *See* disillusionment
Defoe, Daniel: *Robinson Crusoe*, 13, 176, 241, 266, 364; *Moll Flanders*, 176
democratization of access to knowledge, 133, 360
Denmark, 22
development, ideas re true sources of national wealth, 10; rural cycle of, 14, 54; *see also* circulation system for print culture; commercial exchange; commercialization; communication system; cultural participation; economic life; family; human habitats; infrastructure; market economy; *mentalités*; rural life; transportation and communications network; women
devotional works, 13, 21, 26, 115, 146, 152, 172, 192, 198–99, 208, 220–21, 251, 259, 262, 265, 277–81, 291, 294, 296–98, 304, 306, 309–10, 313–14, 316, 319, 323–24, 326–27, 329, 334, 337–38, 342–43, 358, 411; major types of, 307
Devout Exercises, 337
Dickinson, Rodolphus: *Compendium to the Bible*, 324
dictionaries, works, 172, 175, 192, 208, 220, 251, 265, 267, 278–79, 297, 306, 310, 314, 319, 324–25, 327, 329, 337, 341, 358
Dilworth, Thomas: *Speller*, 124
disillusionment in 1830s, xvii–xviii, 9–15, 345, 359, 362
Dissertations on the Prophecies, 338
distance, complex relationship with isolation, 25
distant world, 23; *see also* knowledge of the world
distribution systems, 24; *see also* circulation system
district schools. *See* schools, district
doctors, familiy libraries, 281; *see also* occupations
Doddridge, Philip: *Rise and Progress of Religion*, 259, 298, 337; *Family Expositor*, 327; *Religious Education of Children*, 319
Doherty, Robert, 400
Domestic Encyclopedia, 343
Domestic Medicine, 316
domesticity, works re, 221, 280
Dorrilites, 115
Dresden, N.H./Vt., 196
Dryden, John: *Poetical Works*, 334
Dunham, John M.: *Masonic Register*, 324
Dutton, Salmon, Cavendish family, 319; and lending library borrowing, 318
Dwight, Timothy: *Sermons*, quoted, 106; *Travels in New England*, quoted, 329–30, 351

Easy Lessons in Reading, 41
economic class structure of Windsor District,
  245–47; re American Northeast, 1760–1830,
  240–47; class relations, 83–84, 93, 107–9;
  economic and social, 1780–1830, 396–401; in
  rural New England, 226; *see also* intellectual
  debate; Brownson, Orestes
economic growth: access and spread of reading,
  274; arrested after 1825, 13
economic and intellectual life, belief in integration of, 10–15
economic interdependence, 228; local, 77; *see also*
  changing works
economic life: class based relations and conflict,
  83–84; exchange-value commodity relations, 77,
  80–82, 315; household production and market
  economy, 82, 89; North-Callender thesis, 59;
  Percy Bidwell's analysis of rural economy, 59;
  relationship among production, distribution,
  and consumption, 55–57, 59, 99; rural forms of
  payment, 80–82, 88, 95–96, 102, 175; and "simple commodity production," 55; and subsistence production, 55; *see also* commercial exchange; economic thinking; market economy
economic locale, 75–78, 148; as basic geographical
  unit, defined, 75; Chester, 76 and n.44, 78;
  Windsor, 76 and n.44, 78, 85 n.68, 87
economic thinking in Windsor District, 1760–
  1835, 60–70; active embrace of commerce, 63,
  68–69; agrarianism, 63, 69; ambivalent acceptance of commerce, 63, 69; benevolist
  ethics, 60–61; broad transatlantic intellectual
  viewpoints, 60–62; cash defined in contemporary usage, 80–82; Christian pietistic moralism,
  60–62; entrepreneurial ethos, 112; major positions re prosperity, 63, 68; Mandevillian social
  theory, 60–62; mercantilist and Modern Whig
  political economy, 60–61; money defined in
  contemporary usage, 81; Tory and radical
  strains of opposition political economy, 60–61
economic ties beyond family unit, 75
economics, works, 193, 267, 297–99
economies and communication systems, relationship between, 368
economy, local: five interrelated levels defined, 77
Eddy, Isaac: *Chronology*, 308, 310
Edinburgh, 22–23, 31, 178, 205
education: contemporary attention to in New
  England, 118; formation of conscience and
  world view as goal of childhood, 37, 356; most
  widely discussed aspect of childhood, 123
educational works, 201–2, 208, 219, 310, 323; *see
  also* schoolbooks
Eisenstein, Elizabeth: quoted, 289 n.6

elderly. *See* life cycle
electronic media and study of print media, 255
Elements of Criticism, 340
Elements of the Philosophy of Human Mind, 340
Elizabethan: cosmology, 318; view of nature, 314
Ellicott, Andrew: quoted, 191
elocutionists and practice of reading, 40
Encyclopedia library, 152, 302, 342
encyclopedias, works, 267, 341
Engelsing, Rolf, 39, 152
England, 20, 22, 26–27, 59; *see also* British; Great
  Britain; London
English Physician, 314
English Reader, 297
Enlightenment, 196, 203, 211, 267, 285, 304, 316,
  338, 411; Christian history, 308; Christian ra-
  tionalism, 319, 335; Skeptical, 412; *see also* Scot-
  tish Enlightenment
entrepreneurial ethos, 112; *see also* economic
  thinking in Windsor District
environmentalism, 317
Episcopalianism, 327, 331, 338, 358; works, 200, 211
Essay on Civil Society, 319
Essay on Human Species, 340
Essay on Human Understanding, 340
Essay on Man, 317, 328, 342
Essex County, Vt., 29
estate inventories. *See* inventories
evangelical theology and morality. *See* Calvinist
  and evangelical theology and morality
Evangelical Poems, 327
expanding holdings, defined, 251
Explanation of the Types, 338
extensive reading: matter and reading styles, 295,
  300, 313, 315–16, 326, 328; *see also* reading matter
  and styles

Fabian, Bernhard, 268
Fable of the Bees, 60–62
Fables, 316–17
factories, 33 n.36, 77, 80, 94–95, 102, 107, 292; expansion of, 89; factory villages, 31; factory villages and habitats, 149 n.16; impact of, 56;
  manufacturing, seen as desirable by contemporaries, 27; relationship to lifelong learning, 21;
  see also artisan families; Industrial Revolution,
  rural; manufacturing families
Faler, Paul, 341
families in study group: issue of representativeness, 227
family: as agent of literacy, 121–27; as basic unit
  of agricultural production, 74; as center of
  reading activity in Windsor District, 1780–1835,
  254–64; circle, and transmission of knowledge

family (*continued*)

into, 104; and five major dimensions of involvement in print culture, 261–63; as foundation of collective existence, 225–27; and household, as basic unit of collective experience, 7; powerful ideology of, 261

Family Bible, 295, 325, 327; *see also* Bible

Family Expositor, 327

family libraries, 4, 25, 125, 130, 151, 160–62, 187, 253, 256, 263, 346, 369, 379, 404; catalogues, 205 n.35; "family library" in contemporary usage, 257, 280, 404; expanding and noteworthy holdings defined, 251; incidence and size, 269–73; and inclusion of women, 49; intergenerational accumulation and transmission of, 404; inventories, and spine titles, 1787–1835, xxi n.5, 402–9; kinds of works retained and reading habits, 264–69; nature of, 289; and placement or works on shelves, 295; relationship of length of retention, pace of change in knowledge and publication, 409; share of families, 26 n.20, 116; and wealth, 142–47, 150; single-volume collections, 248; and texts, interests, and meanings, 288–91; Windsor District and rural America, 1700–1850, 273–76; Windsor District compared with less settled Upper Valley areas, 274

—by human habitats: discussed generally for human habitats, 1780–1830, 141–48, 285–343; fortunate farmstead, 320–29, tables N–7, N–8, and N–9, 467–69; fortunate village, 329–43, table N–10 and N–11, 470–71; hardscrabble, 31, 292–301, 300 n.19; table N–3, 462; self-sufficient farmstead, 301–11, tables N–4 and N–5, 463–64; self-sufficient hamlet, 311–20, table N–6, 465

—by library types in Windsor District, 1780–1830, 277–82; mixed-extensive, 277, 279, 297, 306, 335; mixed-intensive, 277; and mix of intensive/extensive works, 277, 282; professional libraries, 277, 280; sacred combined, 277, 278; sacred intensive-reading libraries, 277; secular extensive reading libraries, 277, 280 and n.35

family library of John Leverett household, 410–13

family life: household, wealth, work, and public positions, 1780–1830 (general), 227–40; variety in economic and social conditions, 1780–1835, 225–53

—by primary occupation: artisan families, 234–36; commerce and trading families, 236–38; gentleman farm families, 228–31; manufacturing families, 238–39; professional families, 239–40; semi-skilled laborer families, 233–34; tenant farm families, 232–33; yeoman farm families, 231–32

Fanny Hill. See Memoirs of a Woman of Pleasure

Farmer's Almanac, 295

Farmer's Library, 334; essay by "Viator," quoted, 74 and n.42

Farwell, Oliver, Reading, Vt., commerce and trading family, 313–14

Febvre, Lucien: quoted, 269

federal censuses, 1790–1830, occupational listings, 396–98

Federal Constitutional Convention, 26

Federalism, 61, 316; Federalists, 294, 357; Hamiltonian, 63, 68, 412; moderate, 68; strongholds, 68, 331; works, 199, 339 n.86; *see also* Hamilton, Alexander

female(s). *See* women

Ferguson, Adam: *Essay on Civil Society*, 319

Ferguson, E. James: quoted, 63

Fessenden, Thomas G.: *Terrible Tractoration*, 334; quoted, 41–42

fiction. *See* novels

Fielding, Henry: *Tom Jones*, 334

figures, referred to: 1–1, 29; 1–2, 63, 406; 2–1, 70, 85; 2–2a, 74; 2–2b, 88; 2–3, 76; 2–4, 85; 2–5, 85; 2–6, 89, 100; 2–7, 89; 2–8, 92; 2–9, 101; 4–1, 139, 142, 292; 5–1, 167; 5–2, 167–68; 5–3, 171, 180; 5–4, 175; 5–5, 179–80; 5–6, 179, 181; 5–7, 182; 5–8, 146, 184, 186, 268, 385, 388; 5–9, 146, 184, 186, 268, 270, 385–86, 388; 6–1, 203, 205

"Flying stationers." *See* peddlers

Finland, 27

Firman, Giles: *Real Christian*, 304

Fischer, David Hackett, 398, 400; quoted, 17 n.2

Fisher, George: *Instructor or The Young Man's Best Companion*, 123, 304, 310; quoted, 157

Fisk, Ebenezer Sr., Chester lawyer family, 324

Flavel, John: *Two Select Works*, 62, 298, 327

Forbes, General, of Windsor: quoted, 350

Foster, Dan: *Critical and Candid Examination*, 338

Foundlings of Belgrade, 340

France, 20, 22, 26; *see also* Paris

Franklin, Benjamin: *Way to Wealth*, 201

Franklin Typographical Society, 41

Frederick the Great, 334

Free Mason Constitutions, 304; *see also* Masonic order

Freewill Baptists, 293, 358; works, 211

French, Latin, and Greek language works, 411

Freneau, Phillip: *Poems*, 334; *Works*, 334

Fullerton, Thomas, family, 238

Gallatin, Albert, 97

Gallup, Joseph, 97

Gardner, John: quoted, 285

Garrison, William Lloyd, 369

Gastil, Raymond: quoted, 27

Gay, John: *Fables*, 316–17
Gazetteer of New York, 316
gazetteers. *See* geographies and atlases
Geib, Susan, 77, 292; quoted, 226
Geldof, Bob, 369
gender: differences, approach to discussed, 33; and reading, 217–22; and work, 228; *see also* women
general stores: building materials, 80; clothing, 80; emerge in unison with district schools, 22; operating procedures, 79; and printed items, 80, 185 n.40; range of products, 79; role of, 56–57, 59, 79, 81, 86, 88, 92, 94–96, 101, and ch. 2:53–113 passim; 160, 171, 174–77, 292, 312; *see also* stores; book trade
generations, two living as adults, 1780–1835, xxi, 5–7, 34
Genlis, Stéphanie: *Alphonso and Dalinda*, 340
gentleman farm families, 144–46, 152, 228–31, 242, 263, 275, 291, 303, 306–8, 322, 390, 395, 410; *see also* family life; family libraries, by library types
Geographical and Historical View, 308
geographies and atlases, works, 26, 68, 192, 198, 202, 216, 219–20, 251, 261, 267, 278–79, 281, 297–99, 301, 304, 306, 308–9, 313, 316–17, 319–20, 323–27, 329, 333–34, 339, 341, 358, 411
geography: and basic stock of knowledge, 127; in district school education, 124
German treatises, 411
Germany, 20, 26–27, 39, 354; book trade and reading, 408; reading habits, 268
Gessner, Salomon: *Death of Abel*, 310
gifts of printed matter. *See* reading
Gilmore, Asa, family, 239
Glasgow, 22
Glazier, Z. B., 106
Gleaner, The, 317
global perspectives, 372
golden age of possibility, to Upper Valley residents, 12
Goldsmith, Oliver, 69; *Vicar of Wakefield*, 13, 241, 324, 328; *Citizen of the World*, 334
Goodrich, Samuel: *Child's Arithmetic*, quoted, 42
government: specialization in local, 232; *see also* politics and government
Grafton County, N.H., 29, 32
grammars, works, 219, 280, 282; in district school education, 124, 126; Latin and Greek, 220
Grant, Charles, 72
graphs, referred to, 3–1, 121; 3–2, 121; 6–1, 196; 8–1, 270; 8–2, 271
Great Britain, 20, 23–24, 26, 355; *see also* British; England; London
great leaders, uniqueness of as theme, 340

Great Transformation, xxi, 5, 33, 247, 367; historiography re, 17; study of inner transformation, 34; study of outer transformation, 34; system-wide changes, 21, 112
Greek, French, and Latin language works, 411
Greeley, Horace, 27
Green Mountain Turnpike, 182
Greene, John C.: quoted, 348
Grout, Seth Jr., Weathersfield storekeeper family, 333–34
Guthrie, William: *New Geographical Grammar*, 68, 304, 334
Gutman, Herbert, 34

Habits of the Heart, 373
Hall, David, 39
Hamilton, Alexander, 61, 68; *see also* Federalism
hamlets, 23, 77, 89; defined, 311, 313; *see also* human habitats
Hanover, N.H., 44, 47, 79, 84, 167, 198
happiness: complexities re, xviii, 112, 134; material and spiritual aspects, xviii–xix; and material prosperity, 361; shift in meanings of, 361–64
Harris, Michael, 273–74 and n.25, 407
Hartford, Conn., 31, 107
Harwood, Edward: *Life of Jesus*, 338
Hatch, Nathan: quoted, 359
Haverhill, N.H., 74, 167, 198
Hawkesworth, John: *New Voyage Round the World*, 304
Hawthorne, Nathaniel: *Twice Told Tales*, 49
Heaton, Nathaniel: *Pleasing Library*, 327
Hebrew treatises, 411
Henretta, James, 33, 137, 292; quoted, 74–75 and n.43
Hervey, James: *Meditations and Contemplations*, 69, 298, 323, 327, 338
Hints for the Improvement of Early Education and Nursery Discipline, 201
historical conclusions, major: 344–64; commercialization and rural infrastructure, 352–54; dawn of a "modern" age in rural New England, 346–52; emergence of an age of reading, 354–59; era of rural pluralism and cultural diversity, 359–61; shift in meanings of human happiness, 361–64
historical novels, 212
histories. *See* history works
history: and contemporary implications, 364–74; as morally instructive, xix; need for realism, xix; need for wisdom, xix–xx; parallel between Early Republic and contemporary America, 366–74; perspective and public policy formation, xix–xx, 137, 364–66; radical history, xxi;

history (*continued*)
scale of generalization, 137; theory, materialist
approaches, 98, 110, 112–13
— intellectual history, 133, 137; trickle-down model
of diffusion, 163, 187, 288
— new cultural history, 118; recent impact of anthropology on, 115
— new history of 1910–40 era, 137
— new social history, 27; 133; 137
History of America, 308, 310, 340
History of communications, 158
History of the Indian Wars, 308, 310, 324
History of New England, 295
History of Scotland, 304, 308, 310, 340
history, works, 26, 192, 199, 201, 203, 208, 212,
216, 220–21, 251, 261, 265, 267, 279, 295, 298–99,
304, 306, 308–10, 313, 316, 319, 324–29, 333–35,
339–40, 358, 411; history as part of basic stock
of knowledge, 127; sacred history, 260; *see also*
schoolbooks
Hoare, Louisa: *Hints for the Improvement of Early
Education and Nursery Discipline*, 201
Hobbes, Thomas, 68
"Hobbesian populism," 367
Hobsbawn, E. J.: quoted, 27 n.24, 55
Hofland, Barbara: *Says She to Her Neighbor,
What*, 201
Holmes, Oliver Wendell Sr.: quoted, 266
Homerus: *Iliad*, 316; *Odyssey*, 316
Hopkins, Samuel, 61
Horace: *Opera Interpretation*, 69
household size. *See* family life in Windsor
District
Hubbard, Horace: quoted, 301
Hubbard, Watts, family, 237
human habitats, 4, 109, 128–29, 134, ch.4:135–53,
384; all types represented in Windsor District,
33; and commercial and cultural integration,
138–39; and contemporary civilization, 371;
defined, 8, 139–40, 287–89; and factory villages,
149 n.16; family and, 136; as organizing conception, 135; purpose of conception, 359–63; and
rural infrastructure, 371; and social milieu, 137
n.6; tests of usefulness, 150 n.18, 362–63; and
varieties of collective consciousness, 140
— cultural life in: fortunate farmstead, 320–29;
fortunate village, 329–43; hardscrabble, 31, 148
n.44, 292–301; self-sufficient farmstead, 301–11;
self-sufficient hamlet, 311–20
— described: fortunate farmstead, 140, 144, 152,
346–49, 352, 363; fortunate village, 139, 141,
143–44, 152, 346–49, 352, 363, 369; hardscrabble,
140, 146–48, 151, 346–49, 352, 360–61, 369,
385–86, 392; self-sufficient farmstead, 140,

human habitats (*continued*)
145–46, 151, 276, 346–49, 352, 360–61; self-
sufficient hamlet, 140, 144–45, 151, 346–49, 352,
363
— interrelationships among primary factors comprising habitats, app. 2: 384–95; access within
communications network, app. 2: 385; community, type of, and communication system,
app. 2: 384–88; household placement in network of human habitats, app. 2: 392–95; primary occupation of households, app. 2:385,
390–92; wealth, app. 2: 384, 388–89
— network of, 137–38; construction of conception,
app. 2: 384–95; decline of network, 149; described, 1760–1835, 141–48; 1830s basic change in
network, 354; key characteristics of network,
149–53; as organizing conception, 137–41; thirty
separate entities in Windsory District, 140;
three stages in history of, 148–49
Human Nature, 304, 337
Hume, David, 68
Hunter, Henry: *Sacred Biography*, 338
Hunter, John B.: *Manners and Customs*, 317
Huntington, Joseph: *Calvinism Improved*, 338
hymnals, 13, 21, 26, 41, 115, 146, 152, 172, 175, 192,
199, 208, 211, 221, 251, 265, 277–79, 281, 288,
294, 296, 306–7, 314, 316, 319, 323, 325–27, 329,
337, 358; and hymn singing, 378–79
Hymns and Spiritual Songs, 62

Ide, Simeon, 109 n.123, 410; quoted, 10–15, 191
ideal of political involvement, 355
ideology of literacy. *See* literacy
Iliad, 316
illiteracy. *See* literacy
Imitation of Christ, 337
imprints, defined, 196; *see also* printing and publishing in Upper Valley, 1778–1830
Improvement of the Mind, 262
Indiana, Southern, family library incidence and
size, 273–74
individualism, 14, 131, 340
Industrial Revolution, rural, xx, 18, 33, 88, 98,
127, 344; impact of, 56; railroad route through
Windsor District, 107, 363; relationship to lifelong learning, 21; steamboats, 107; and Windsor District family life, 227–40; *see also* artisan
families; factories; manufacturing families
industry, belief in a spirit of, 12
infrastructure, xx, 6, 23, 33 n.33, 89, 135, 163;
changes in, 7; creation of an early modern
rural, overview, 344–64; defined, 7; eight dimensions, 7, 137–38, 140, 150; new rural, difficulties in adjusting to, 359

Instructor or The Young Man's Best Companion,
123, 304, 310
intellectual change and instability, 359
intellectual currency, 25, 112, 138; as contemporary
ideal, 13, 27, 84, 134, 349–50; and human habitats, 412; ideology of, 337; keeping up with
newer versions of intellectual traditions, 311;
and Leverett family library, 412
intellectual debate about nature of America,
1825–50, 112; laboring classes defined, 107 n.115;
role of mechanics and laboring classes, 107–8
and n.118
intellectual foundations of early modern thought,
346
intellectual history. *See* history
intellectual orientations to life: three different,
346
intellectual traditions and themes. *See also* contemporary meaning of; economic thinking in
Windsor District; knowledge of the world
—general overview, 204–10, 217; British connection and cosmopolitanism, 212, 214 pl.; Calvinist and evangelical theology and morality,
210–11, 211 pl., 317, 343; fresh fabric of nineteenth-
century thought, 203, 217, 286, 297, 309, 311,
320, 337–43, 351; nationalism and neoclassical
republicanism, 211–12, 213 pl., 298–99, 317, 325,
339 and n.86; "spirit of fact," 107, 215 pl., 216,
299, 310, 341; understandings of economic life
in Windsor District, 1760–1835, 60–70; Voyage-
of-Life tradition, 216–17, 218 pl., 310
—among: fortunate farmstead reading community, 320–29; fortunate village reading community, 329–43; hardscrabble reading community, 292–301, 310; self-sufficient farmstead
reading community, 301–11; self-sufficient
hamlet reading community, 311–20; self-sufficient
hamlet compared with hardscrabble and self-
sufficient farmstead reading communities,
319–20
—specific themes: Americanizing of knowledge,
341, 351; commercialization and links with
cities, trade, and business, 317; competing
political allegiances beyond Windsor District,
310, 317, 339; cult of representative historical
leader, 340; in economic life, 60–70; Enlightenment, 310, 317, 340; entrepreneurial ethos, 311,
339, 341; patriotism, 299, 317; practicality and
technique, 342; rational organization, planning,
and bureaucracy, 317, 341; Romanticism, 310,
317, 340; rural felicity, 316; sacred and secular,
volatile interaction of, 348; science, mathematics, medicine, and technology, 310, 342; technological sublime, 349; vital piety, 296, 315,

intellectual traditions and themes (*continued*)
337–38, 361; Voyage-of-Life tradition of personality
theory, 342
"intelligence," contemporary meaning of, 267, 350;
unintended consequence of access to, 345; *see
also* modern
intensive reading matter and styles, 294, 297, 300,
314, 316, 325, 333, 351, 361; persistence of, 348; *see
also* reading matter and styles
international electronic based civilization, 366–74
Introduction to Ancient and Modern Geography, 68, 308
inventories, estate: 227, 260–61, 270, 272; and
representation of Windsor District population,
407; spine titles, and family libraries, 1787–1835,
270 n.23, 402–9; strengths and weaknesses,
161–62, 404–9
Ireland, 22
Irving, Washington: *Sketch Book*, 308, 310, 319
Isaac, Rhys, 9, 137, 153
isolation: complex relationship with distance, 25;
see also transportation and communications
network
itinerant authors, 312; *see also* circulation system
for print culture: informal circuit

Jacksonian society, 108
Jacksonians, 103, 358; Jackson administration, 10;
policies, 10–11
Jacob, Stephen, Windsor lawyer family, 334–35
Jefferson, Thomas: *Notes on Virginia*, 69
Jeffersonian republicanism, 294, 299, 357
Jennings, W.: *Foundlings of Belgrade*, 340
Johansson, Egil: quoted, 37 n.45, 127
John, Andover, family owns Koran, 316
Johnson, Paul, 137, 153
Josephus, Flavius: *Genuine Works*, 338

Kcate, George: *Sketches From Nature*, 268
Keene, N.H., 85, 167, 198
Kent, Conn., 72
Kentucky frontier, family library incidence and
size, 274
Kerber, Linda: quoted, 43, 130
Kerr, Clark, 371 and n.45
Kett, Joseph, and McClung, Patricia, 274
Khadafy, Moammar, 369
Kinne, Aaron: *Explanation of the Types*, 338
kinship, role of, 29
Kluckholm, Florence: quoted, 75 n.4
knowledge, diffusion of, 18–20
"knowledge from distant climes," 8, 12–15, 25, 39,
353, and n.11
knowledge of the world, 8, 18; Americanization
of, 341, 351; basic stock of, 5, 35, 126; contem-

knowledge of the world (*continued*)
porary ideas re diffusion of, 18–20, 112; core of
ideas reaching all families, 115–16; defined, 133
and n.37; and democratization of access, 133;
implications of reading instruction for, 38–42;
and intellectual reservoirs, 269; kinds of, 15;
material determinants of defined, 225; mind as
a repository for, 133; need for a new history
of, 122 n.17, 133; power of discussed by contemporaries, 19; reception, integration, and uses of,
137; role of, xx; struggle over kinds of acceptable knowledge, 41; Upper Valley history of,
130–34; *see also* sacred and secular knowledge
—in relation to change: and decline of localism,
350–51; developing vocabulary for understanding change, 134, 346; expansion in re many
aspects of world, 264–65; greater acceptance of
change, 349–50; modernizing attitudes toward,
344–52; modernizing of substantive knowledge,
346–49; opposition to diffusion, 39; secular information in schooling, 127; shift, intensive to
mix of reading styles and subject matter, 124,
349
Koran, Commonly called the Alcoran of Mahomet,
316, 318

Lafayette, Marquis de: visits Windsor, 350
Lane, Samuel: directing his children's reading,
319–20
Langdon, Samuel: *Observations on the Revelation*,
338
Lathrop, Leonard: *Farmer's Library*, 74, 334
Latin, French, and Greek language works, 411
Law, William: *Serious Call*, 298, 337
law works, 198, 201, 208, 212, 220, 279–81, 298–
99, 304, 306, 308–9, 313, 316–17, 319, 324, 327–
29, 332, 334, 338, 341, 358, 411; law library, 334
lawyer households, 280
Leavitt, Joshua: *Easy Lessons in Reading*; quoted,
41
Lebanon, N.H., 79
Lectures on Rhetoric, 40, 310
Lee, Richard Henry, 299
Leeds, England, 22; invention, 31
Lemon, James, 312
lending libraries, 77, 130, 144–45, 147, 150, 152 and
n.22, 161–62, 195, 201, 205, 248 n.47, 251, 256,
270, 279–81, 294–95, 300, 302, 307–9, 312, 314,
316, 318–19, 322–26, 332–33, 346, 357–58, 388;
Cavendish Social Library, 289, 308, 318–19
LeRoy Ladurie, Emmanuel, 226, 398
Lessons in Elocution, 40, 333
letter writing manuals, 383
letters. *See* writing

Letters from England, 340
Letters on the Study, 310
Letters to a Young Lady, 262
*Letters written by the Late Earl of Chatham to His
Nephew, Thomas Pitt, Esq.*, 262, 402
Leventhal, Herbert: *In the Shadows of the Enlightenment*, 318
Leverett, John, Windsor gentleman farm family,
231, 252, 326, 328–29, 410–13; family library, 280
and n.35, 410–13
Leverett, William, family, 239; general store, 88
liberalism, 339
libraries, circulating. *See* circulating libraries
libraries, family. *See* family libraries
libraries, lending. *See* lending libraries
libraries, texts, interests, and meanings, 288–91
library at Chester Academy, 45
"library," 257 and n.6
Liddle, William: quoted, 69
life cycle: and popular sellers, 217–22; of printed
objects, 4, 157–63; *see also* stage of life
life goals: prosperity on earth, 62–63, 68–70;
salvation, 62–63
Life of Alexander, 308
Life of Baron Fredrich Trenck, 298
Life of Elizabeth Cady Stanton, 49
Life of Howard, 317, 342
Life of Jesus, 338
Life of Joseph, 338
Life of Mrs. John Adams, 49
Life of Peter the Great, 324, 328, 334, 402
Life of Washington, 308
Life, Conversion, 314
lifelong learning, emergence of, 5, 18, 21–22, 35,
83, 287, 303; emergence of first two widely literate rural generations, 23; institutional encouragements to reading, 356
Lights and Shadows of Scottish Life, 340
Lincoln, Micah, family, 237
literacy, 271; acquisition and maintenance, 119;
pace and motives, 127–30; skills, 3, 20, 133; *see
also* women; numerical skills
—effects, 31; content of home instruction, 122;
content of Sunday school instruction, 123; family and district school as agents of, 121–27; first
age of mass, 20; ideology of, 355; and individualism, 14, 131, 340; interlocking developments accounting for higher levels, 127; issue
of standards, 354; literacy's interaction with
commercialization, 54; and national goals, 129;
not universal, 121; private uses of, 131–32; pro-
moting of, 35; public uses of in preservation
and dissemination of knowledge, 131; sacred
push for, 129–30; and Sunday schools, 122; two

literacy (*continued*)
widely literate rural generations of males and females, 356; uses of in Upper Valley, 130–34
—sources, 121 n.16, 133; account books as sources, 119; deeds as sources, 119; multiple-moment life-stage research design, 119; township petitions as sources, 119; ways to acquire, 121; wills as sources, 119
—trends in, 1760–1830, xx, 5, 21–23, 116; 118–21, 136; adjusted rates, 127; defined, 118; female rates, 318; general levels, 128, 132, 322; male rates, 129; minimum total female/male rates, 120; teacher/inhabitant ratio, 124
literate obsession, 2
literature. *See* modern literature
Liverpool, England, 22
living arrangements, distinct types of, 31
living situations and audiences of print communications. *See* human habitats
local authors. *See* circulation system for print culture: informal circuit
localism: decline of, 15, 18, 149, 345; and cultural isolation, 9
Locke, John: *Essay on Human Understanding,* 340
Lockridge, Kenneth, 398
Loehr, Rodney: quoted, 302
London, 22, 31, 59, 178, 205, 212, 299, 342
Longfellow, 49
Lord Bacon, 19
lottery office at Windsor, "The People's Mint," 106
Loveland, Rev. Samuel, ministerial training center, 45
lower classes: and habit of reading, 35; and literacy, 119, 132; lower middle class, 249, 251
Ludlow, Vt., 45–46, 63, 89, 93, 100, 140, 145–46, 149, 184–85, 293–95, 301, 311–12, 397, 401
Ludlum, David, 367
luxury and vice, 299

McCorison, Marcus, quoting Concord bookseller, 178
McCoy, Drew, 69
Macgowan, Joseph: *Life of Joseph,* 338
machine civilization in mid-nineteenth century, 344
McLuhan, Marshall, 374
Madison, James, 69
M'Fingal, 317
Main, Gloria, 246
Main, Jackson Turner, 245–47, 249, 398, 400; quoted, 242
Manchester, England, 22
Mandeville, Bernard: *Fable of the Bees,* 60–62;

Mandeville, Bernard (*continued*)
quoted, 60 n.17; Mandevillian decay, 69–70; Mandevillian paradise, 63
Manners and Customs, 317
Manuel, Frank: quoted, 7
manufacturing. *See* factories
manufacturing families, 143, 145, 238–39, 244, 263, 275, 302, 306–7, 312, 315, 330, 350, 390, 392, 395; *see also* family life; family libraries, by library types
maps, 68; *see also* Whitelaw, James
market economy, 9, 14, 18, 21, ch. 2:53–113; beginning of market sector, 73; exchange system, 57, 59; expansion of, 355; and household production, 82; and literacy, 127; local and international markets, 57, 59; newspaper information about, 54, 57, 261–62; perceptions of integrated regional, 12
market exchange. *See* commercial exchange; commercialization; economic life
Martin, Henri-Jean: quoted, 53
Martin, James Jr., Springfield artisan family, 304
Marx, Karl, 81; Marxist formulations, 55 n.6, 109–10 and n.126
Maryland, family library incidence and size, 274
Mason, Daniel, Cavendish gentleman farmer family, 308, 318; quoted, 41
Mason, John: *Treatise on Self Knowledge,* 328, 337
Masonic Order, 104, 317 and n.50, 340; orations, 198; works, 333
Masonic Register, 324
mass culture: defined, 23, 25; emergence of, 33; of printed and written word, xx, 2, 6, 27, 133
mass media, impact in Early Republic underestimated by historians, 98
Massachusetts, 72–74, 128, 268; family library incidence and size, 274; Suffolk County, family library incidence and size, 274; Worcester County, family library incidence and size, 274
material and cultural change, 17–18, 110; acquired resistance to, 53
material and cultural conditions of life, xx–xxi, 6–7, 109, 128–29, 134, 138; defined, 8
mathematics. *See* arithmetic
Matthews, Fred: quoted, 367
May, Henry, 317, 340, 412
meaning making: active process of, 299–300; field of delivery (Jauss), 160–61 and n.7; field of intentionality (Jauss), 160 and n.7; framework of relationships employed, 289–90; and general social class of owner, 289–90
"mechanick question," differing attitudes, 107
media. *See* communication; cultural expression
Medical Repository, 314
medical society in Vermont, 95

medical works, 198, 208, 212, 220, 279, 281, 314, 317, 358, 411
Meditations and Contemplations, 69, 298, 323, 327, 338
Melville, Herman, xxi
Memoirs of a Woman of Pleasure, 177
memory, perceived as first faculty developing in children, 378
mending, concept of, and slow change defined, 286–87, 301; see also change, awareness of
mentalités, 140, 210, 353, 360, 363, 369; defined, xxi, 4, 7; and family reading, 1780–1835, 254–82; five different settings delineated, 285–343; fortunate farmstead human habitat, 320–29; fortunate village human habitat, 329–43; hardscrabble human habitat, 292–301; self-sufficient farmstead human habitat, 301–11; self-sufficient hamlet, 311–20
mentalités, contemporary American, 370
Merrill, Michael, 80, 292; quoted, 81 and n.53
"The Metabasist": quoted, 263–64
"method," importance of, 341
Methodism, 62, 293, 298, 323, 327, 338, 358, 361; theology, 411; works, 200, 202, 211, 296, 307, 316, 326, 331
"middle station": as rural ideal, 14, 342, 364; middling sort, 249, 251, 264
Middlebury College, 358
migration, 96; and livelihood, role of transients, 233, 235, 241–42, 244
military affairs, works, 192, 221, 298–99, 308, 324, 328, 339; and heroism, 299, 339 n.86; militarism, 339
Miller, Perry, 216; quoted, 344
Miller, Rev. Samuel: quoted, 40
Miller, William, 27, 309, 351; Millerites, 301, 362
Mills, Nathan, family, 238
Milton, John: *Poetical Works*, 316; *Paradise Lost*, 13, 328
Mineral Waters, 324
ministers and deacons, 280–81; see also Protestant Christianity; religion
Minstrel, 316
Missouri frontier, family library incidence and size, 274
modern (and variants): defined, 346; "Modern" age, emergence of in rural New England, xx, 2, 18, 346–52; "modern intelligence" as cultural ideal, e.g., of, 350; "modernness" as contemporary ideal, 13
Modern Europe, 324
modern literature, 172, 192, 198–99, 201–3, 208, 212, 220–21, 251, 265, 267, 279, 298, 308–9, 313, 316, 319, 326, 328, 334–35, 338–40, 358, 408, 411;

modern literature (*continued*)
British and European literary classics and stock of knowledge, 127; see also novels; plays; poetry
"Modern Whigs," 68
modernization theory, xx–xxi, 18, 23, 34, 136, 344–45; materialist versions, 98
Moll Flanders, 176
Monaghan, Jennifer: quoted, 38
money: instruction in uses of, 57; means of exchange and standard of equivalence, 57; "ready money," contemporary meaning, 96 n. 85; see also currency
Montpelier Lyceum, 49
Moor's Academy, 44
Moore, John: *Voyage to Georgia*, 334
moral libraries. *See* lending libraries
Mormonism, 301; cultural and material roots, 360–61
Morse, Jedidiah: *American Gazetteer*, 68, 297, 299, 327, 334; *American Universal Geography*, 68, 308, 324, 327, 334; geographies, 68, 297, 299, 308, 327, 334
Mount, William Sidney, 132; *California News*, 378; *Dance of the Haymakers*, 379; *Dancing on the Barn Floor*, 379; *Rustic Dance After a Sleigh Ride*, 379
Mudie, Robert: *Babylon the Great*, 299
Muhammad: *Koran, Commonly called the Alcoran of Mahomet*, 316, 318
Murphy, Arthur: *Citizen*, 317
Murray, Judith Sargent: *Gleaner, The*, 317
Murray, Lindley: *English Reader*, 297; *Sequel to English Reader*, 297
music, 305; as popular selling works, and strength in family libraries, 379; sacred works, 310; secular works, 193, 198–99, 202, 265, 278, 307, 316, 378–79; and singing, 377–78

Napoleon in Exile, 308
Narrative of Campaign in Russia, 324, 328, 403
Narrative of Captivity, 327–28
Narrative of the Captivity and Sufferings, 334
National Republicans, 103, 294, 358
nationalism. *See* intellectual traditions and themes
Native Americans, 299, 343
Natural and Civil History, 308, 310, 316, 338
Natural Philosophy, 341
navigation of Connecticut River, 363
neighboring and visiting, 300
Netherlands, 22
New Cyclopaedia, 411
New England: belief re geographical position, 11; characteristics, 1780–1835, 287, 352, 363; contemporary view of intelligence and enterprise in, 118

New England Farmer's Diary and Almanac, 295
New England Primer, 115, 124, 286
New Geographical, Historical, and Commercial Grammar, 68, 304, 334
New Hampshire, 27, 29, 32, 41, 59, 124; Cheshire Bridge, 182; Cheshire County, 32; Grafton County, 29, 32; imprints, 197, 201 n.28; Samuel Lane directing his children's reading, 319–20; Sullivan County, 29, 32; Walpole bookstores, 59, 162, 200; *Walpole Farmer's Museum*, 167; *see also* Charlestown; Claremont; Concord; Dresden; Hanover; Haverhill; Keene; Lebanon; Orford; Stratham; Walpole
New Harmony, 361
New Haven, 31
New Jersey, southern, and literacy levels, 23 n.16, 127
New Testament. *See* Bible
New Voyage Round the World, 304
New York City, 22, 31, 59, 173, 203, 207, 342; State, 31
Newbury, Vt., 198
Newell, Harriet, 343
newspaper editors: role in disillusionment, 10; *see also* disillusionment
newspapers, 21, 24, 26, 91, 96–97, 117, 128, 160–62, 165–69, 171–72, 175, 177, 180–82, 184, 190, 193–94, 198–202, 210, 216, 221, 248, 253, 261–63, 267–68, 276, 278–80, 282, 288–89, 294–95, 304–5, 307, 312, 322–24, 326, 329–30, 332, 334–35, 337, 342, 346, 349, 357–58, 362; advertising, 24, 78, 83, 88, 161, 168–70, 175; as book catalogues, 175; and capitalism, 53; contents of, 26; conventions in advertising printed matter, 205; impact of, 185 n.40, 350; interest in, 26; and nonlocal news, 212; proliferation, 1790–1800, 85; reading, 149; reading in public, 378; and role in market economy, 54, 57, 103; role in shaping consumption habits, 57; share among Windsor District libraries, 407; size of edition, 193 n.11; sources, 70 n.35, and spread of knowledge about commerce, 68, 78; and spread of participation in public life, 84; subscriptions, 79, 150; supports local academy, 45; and visibility of disparities in wealth, 241; *see also* specific titles
Newton, Bishop Thomas: *Dissertations on the Prophecies*, 338
Nichols, Levi, family, 238
Night Thoughts, 69, 324, 327, 338
nineteenth-century thought: European origins of, 351; fresh fabric of, 203, 217, 286, 297, 309, 311, 320, 337–43
nonlocal world, interest in, 350–51
nonreaders sharing in print culture, 132 n.36, 378

North Atlantic: context of spread of literacy and reading, 17–23, 25–27, 33, 121; trading community, 74
North-Callender thesis, 59
Northeast American, 26, 29, 42, 50, 74, 82, 100, 116, 118; ties with Upper Valley, 30
Northfield, Mass., Academy of Useful Knowledge, 46
Norton, Mary Beth: quoted, 43, 50
Norway, 27
Norwich, Vt., 79, 81
Notes on Virginia, 69
noteworthy holdings, defined, 251
Notions of the Americans, 351
novel reading, 35, 134, 261; and critics of, 39–40
novels, 21, 26, 39–40, 49, 172, 208, 212, 220–21, 251, 261, 267, 288, 298, 307, 309, 313, 317, 319, 334, 408, 411; *see also* modern literature
Noyes, John Humphrey, 115
numerical skills, as dimension of elementary literacy, 126, 130 and n.33

Observations on the Revelation, 338
occult works, 314
occupational systems: construction of, 1780–1835, 396–401; "Employment," 228; and inventories, 227; "occupation," 227–28; occupational designations as cultural symbols, 397; in previous scholarship, 398
occupations: artisan families, 234–36; commerce and trading families, 236–38; gentleman farm families, 228–31; manufacturing families, 238–39; professional families, 239–40; semiskilled laborer families, 233–34; tenant farm families, 232–33; yeoman farm families, 231–32; *see also* artisan, etc.
Odyssey, 316
Ohio, Athens County, family library incidence and size, 274
Ohio, Washington County, family library incidence and size, 274
old age. *See* life cycle
Olive Branch, 327
O'Meara, Barry: *Napoleon in Exile*, 308
Opera Interpretation, 69
Opinions on the Revolution in America, 304, 308, 310
oral discourse, 115 n.4, 300, 377–78 and n.6
Orange County, Vt., 32, 85
"Oratory, Golden Age of," 377
Orford, N.H., 79

Paine, Thomas: *Age of Reason*, 340
Paley, William: *Principles of Moral and Political Philosophy*, 340–41

Palmer, Elihu: *Principles of Nature*, 340

pamphlets, 21, 26, 160, 162, 165, 167, 169, 171–73, 182, 264, 267, 288, 299, 302, 309, 318–19, 325, 343, 408

paper mill owners. *See* circulation system for print culture: informal circuit

Paradise Lost, 13, 328

Paris, 31, 178

Parker, Joseph, Chester artisan family, 323

Parnell, Thomas: *Collection of Poems*, 334

passions, control of, 310

patentees, Windsor District, and human habitats, 363

patriotism, 299, 317

peddlers, 169, 175–78 and n.29, 181–82, 185, 312; *see also* book trade

Pennsylvania, rural literacy levels, 127

periodicals, 21, 24, 26, 150, 152, 160, 162, 165, 167, 169, 171, 182, 190, 194–95, 201, 205, 216, 222, 262–64, 267, 278–81, 288, 295, 302, 309, 312, 317–18, 332–33, 342; British, 407; in Windsor District libraries, 407–8

Perry, William: *Royal Standard English Dictionary*, 297, 327, 341; quoted, 57 n.10

Philadelphia, 22, 31, 59, 173, 203, 207, 342

Philadelphia Analectic Magazine, "Systems of Elementary Education," quoted, 114, 118

Philadelphia Repository and Weekly Register, 328

philosophy, works, 192, 196, 199, 221, 251, 279, 281, 304, 310, 316, 319, 326–29, 333–34, 338, 341, 358, 411

physics, works, 107

piety, vital as theme in reading matter, 296, 315, 337–38, 361

Pike, Nicholas: *System of Arithmetic*, 297

Pilgrims, The, group, 115

Pilgrim's Progress, 13, 176, 327, 338

Pitt, William: *Letters Written by the Late Earl of Chatham to His Nephew, Thomas Pitt, Esq.*, 262, 402

plays, works, 221, 305, 309, 319, 334

Pleasing Library, 327

Pleasures of Memory, 316

Plutarch's Lives, 316

Plymouth, Vt., 31, 63, 89, 93, 96, 100, 119, 128–29, 140, 145–46, 149, 181, 185, 293–94, 297, 311, 314, 316, 401

Poems (Ramsay), 304

Poetical Works, 316, 334

poetry, works, 41, 172, 198, 220–21, 267, 288, 298, 309, 313, 319, 334

Polanyi, Karl, 247

political economy, and basic stock of knowledge, 127

politics, local Windsor District, 294, 362 n.28; backcountry Jeffersonian in 1800–24, 294; 1808 gubernatorial election, 294; 1813 gubernatorial election, 294; 1834 gubernatorial election, 294

politics and government, works: 68, 193, 196, 198–99, 201–3, 221, 251, 267, 281, 297–99, 304, 307, 313, 316, 318–19, 324, 327–29, 339, 358, 411

poor families. *See* poverty

Pope, Alexander: *Essay on Man*, 317, 328, 342; translation of Homer, 316

popular sellers in Upper Valley: 203, 205, 207–8, 212, 265, 408; British connection, 212, 214 pl.; Calvinist and evangelical theology and morality, 210–11, 211 pl.; collective cultural trends, 1805–30, 204–17, 191 pl.; evidence for, 205 n.37; general overview, 204–10, 217; and life cycle, 217–22; neoclassical republicanism, 211–12, 213 pl.; "spirit of fact," 107, 215 pl., 216, 299, 310, 341; Voyage-of-Life tradition, 216–217, 218 pl.

population: comparative North Atlantic, 22–23; Upper Valley, 1790–1800, 85; Windsor District, table 1-1, 32; Windsor District in 1790, 70, 72; Windsor District in 1810, 89; Windsor District, 1810–30, 100–1; Windsor District peak reached by 1830, 31

Porter, Jane, *Thaddeus of Warsaw*, 340

Porter, Samuel, Chester, Vt., general store, 79–81

Porter, Sir Robert: *Narrative of Campaign in Russia*, 324, 328, 403

Portland, Maine, 59, 100

Portugal, 22

post office, 24, 73, 103, 146, 332, 358

post rider routes, 79, 88, 193–94; of *Windsor Vermont Journal* in 1800, 85

postmillennialism, 296, 338

poverty in Windsor District, 245, 248, 252, 354, 386; and family life, 148, 227–40; human habitats and, 144 n.11; level of cultural poverty, 142, 249, 292 n.9; meaning for cultural participation, 251, 384 (defined); poorest households and inventory evidence, 405

prayer books. *See* devotional works

premillennialism, 296, 309, 316, 323, 338

Presbyterians, 62

primers, 39, 123–24 and n.19, 152, 193, 196, 219, 261, 265, 282, 286, 358, 408

Primitive Physic, 314

Principles of Moral and Political Philosophy, 340–41

Principles of Nature, 340

print and written culture and other forms of cultural expression: app. 1: 377–83; defined, 20, 114 n.1; diffusion of, 288; ideology of, 162; indissolubly linked to oral culture, 39; relation to a history of knowledge, 133 print communications, in context of Upper Valley cultural expression, 114–18

printed matter: placement within home, 257; and wealth in Windsor District, 247–53

printing and publishing, 24, 103, 108; bindery, 167 and n.20; copyright, 161; decentralization of, 353–55; facilities in Windsor County, 73, 79, 81, 92–94; and general store, 80; local production, 204; low cost of printed matter, 253; printing press, 171; see also book trade; Spooner, Alden

—books published in Upper Valley, 1778–1830: generally, 161 n.9; 196–203; 1778 sample year, 196; 1784 sample year, 196–97; 1796 sample year, 197–99; 1812 sample year, 199–200; 1826 sample year, 200–1

—other printed matter published in Upper Valley, 1778–1830, 26, 195–203; almanacs, 196–203; broadsides, 196–203; generally, 1780–1830, 190–95; pamphlets, 196–203; varying rates of enumeration, 405

—print center (defined, 24), 103, 109 n.125; 132, 166–71, 173, 175–78, 181, 198–200; auxiliary (defined, 167), 168–69, 171, 181, 332; competition among, 174; permanent (defined, 167), 167–69, 171, 178, 332

—printing office, 73, 161, 168, 170–71, 175; see also circulation system for print culture—formal circuit

private libraries. See family libraries

"private library," contemporary meaning, 257

probate court, Windsor District, 245; relationship between sites and number of estates inventoried, 270; travel patterns, 406–7

Proctorsville. See Cavendish

production, modes of: complications in understanding, 55–56; household/domestic, 73, 81

Profession and Practice of Christians, 304

professional families, 143, 145–46, 152, 242, 244, 247, 263, 265, 302, 306–7, 309, 312, 315–17, 330, 333, 335, 350, 390, 392, 395; see also family life; family libraries, by library types

"professional library," contemporary meaning, 240, 280

professions, and works in art, architecture, law, medicine, and theology, 193, 267, 408

pronouncing-form method. See reading instruction

Protestant Christianity, 347; Calvinist versions of, 129; emphasis on printed word, 127 n.24, 355; religious beliefs as part of basic stock of knowledge, 127; see also ministers and deacons; religion; sacred and secular knowledge

Protestant Confession of Faith, 319–20

proto-industrialization, 18; and Christian work ethic, 341

provincialism, 15

Prude, Jonathan, 312; quoted, 241 n.34

Prussia, 22

psalm books, 13, 21, 26, 41, 115, 146, 152, 172, 175, 199, 208, 221, 251, 277–79, 281, 288, 294, 296, 303, 306–7, 314, 319, 323, 325–27, 329, 337, 358, 378–79; see also Watts, Isaac

Psalms of David, 62, 327, 337

public opinion, concept of and reading publics, 360; discussed by Webster and Story, 19–20

public policy, 2, 6; implications, 364–74

public position. See family life in Windsor District

publishing. See book trade; printing and publishing

railroad route through Windsor District, 107, 363

Ramsay, Allen: *Poems*, 304

Randolph, Vt., 85

Raynal, Abbe: *Opinion on the Revolution in America*, 304, 308, 310

Reading, Vt., 45, 63, 71–72, 89, 93, 95, 100, 129, 140, 144, 146, 185, 187, 292–95, 297, 301, 311–14, 358, 401

reading and readers: and advertising, 268; control over, 261; differences between measures of incidence and influence, 62; diffusion of, 25; factors inhibiting spread of, 274; first rural age of, 25, 41, 132; general causes for rise of, 355–56; history of in Windsor District, 34, 189–222, 285–343; as a necessity of life, xxi, 3, 18, 25, 133, 253; North Atlantic context, 18–27; and ostentatious display, 264; "reading, age of oral," 378; as reception, assimilation, and use, 161; "relish for reading," 18, 22; role of, 2, 15, 31, 34–35, 37–42; spread of regular reading, 20, 354; traditional task of, 265; and writing as adjuncts to talking and listening, 116; see also age of reading

—contemporary ideas about, 20, 34–35, 37–42; anxiety re, 35; contemporary usage, 20; cultural battle over, 41; preserving traditional values, 27; role of passions and emotions in, 40

—readers, female, 25; issue of correlation between volumes retained and reading activity, 260; layers of diffusion and share of readership, 358; share of active readers, 127; types of listed, 268

—reading public: adult male farmers and craftsmen, 221; adult women, 221; children, 219–20; eight audiences, 219–22; and human habitats, 1780–1830, 285–343; leisure reading, 221; old age, 220; readers of professional works, 220–21; reading communities, 8, 152; reading publics and public opinion, 360; rural in 1760s, 263; utilitarian reading, 221; youth, 220 reading matter and style: extensive alternatives, 267, 271 (defined, 265); guides to, 262; intensive, 39, 146, 151–52, 266–67, 271, 282 (defined, 265); reading habits, 254–82; reading habits reconstructed, 4; role of prefaces and advertisements, 217, 221; shift away from intensive, 117; in Sweden, 116; universe of available reading matter (defined, 195), 196, 198, 205, 403; and unread works, 264; *see also* almanacs; Bible; books; broadsides; children's books; clandestine publications; classical writings; devotional works; dictionaries; economics; geographies; histories; hymnals; law works; medical works; military affairs; modern literature; newspapers; novels; pamphlets; periodicals; philosophy; politics and government; prayer books; psalm books; schoolbooks; science and technology; secular music; sermons; stages-of-life works; theology; travel accounts

—instruction: oral recitation, 37; prevailing methods, 1780–1830, 34–42; "pronouncing-form method," 37–40; "reading-for-comprehension method," 42; Samuel Lane directs his children's reading, 319–20

—reading experience, 297; amount and number of books, 348; complexity in, 288–91; control over, 257; in district school education, 124, 126; field of delivery (Jauss), 160–61 and n.7; field of intentionality (Jauss), 160 and n.7; habit of, 226; increase in variety, 275; institutional encouragements to lifelong learning, 356; private, 378; public, 132, 256 n.2; reading at home, 132; reading period in Upper Valley, late November through early April, 351; reading rooms, 256 n.2, 262, 358; silent, 378

—substance of: complexity of reading interests seen in Baxter, *Saints' Everlasting Rest*, 290–91; family library and core or reading, 263; popular fictional works, 13; popular works re economic life, 62–63, 68–70; reading patterns in human habitats, 1780–1830, 285–343; relationship between sacred and secular, 25, 117; *see also* popular sellers in Upper Valley: collective cultural trends, 1805–30

—ways to obtain reading matter: borrowing and lending of printed matter, 128, 160, 248, 256, 407; circulating libraries, 255; printed matter as gifts, 160–61, 245, 255–56; purchases for family libraries, 256; reading matter not usually retained in family libraries, 117; social libraries, 256; war of lists, 47

Real Christian, 304

"real property," contemporary meaning, 233

Reason the Only Oracle of Man, 196

rebirth, concept of, and radical change, 286–87, 301; *see also* change: awareness of

Redeemed Captive Returning to Zion, 324

Reed, Mick, 59

Rees, Abraham: *New Cyclopaedia*, 411

reform, 153; and cultural ferment, 362; organizations, 358

region: importance of in research, 29; subregional geographical unit, 29

religion, 153, 292–93, 331; and controversy, 103 n.105; and theology, 196; religious works, 198–200, 203, 208; *see also* Bible; devotional works; hymnals; psalm books; sacred and secular knowledge; theology

Religious Education of Children, 319

representativeness, of Windsor District study group, 270

republic of knowledge, as defining characteristic, 355, 371

Republic of Letters, 205, 304, 410; sophisticated knowledge possible outside of, 115; use by Webster, 19

republican aesthetic, 317

republican ideology, 110; bases of, 10; citizenship, 355; political economy, 74, 211; relations between commerce and luxury, 10; republicanism, 294, 339; Republicans, Madisonian and Jeffersonian, 68

research design: general, ch.1:27–34; ch.4:135–53; app. 2:384–95; multiple-moment life-stage approach to literacy, 119; northwestern New England laboratory, 18; unit of analysis, 27 n.23

retail sales. *See* book trade

Retrospect of the Eighteenth Century, 40

rhetoric and oratory, works, 220

Richmond, 274

Riedesel, Johann: *Travels through Sicily*, 334

Rinald Rinaldini, 298

Rise and Progress of Religion, 259, 298, 337

ritual and festive occasions, 292

Robert Thomas's, Sterling, Mass. bookstore, 171–73

Robertson, William: *History of America*, 308, 310, 340; *History of Scotland*, 304, 308, 310, 340

Robinson Crusoe, 13, 176, 241, 266, 364

Roche, Regina: *Children of the Abbey*, 340

Roderick Random, 334

Rogers, Samuel: *Pleasures of Memory*, 316

Rollin, Charles: *Ancient History*, 310; *Life of Alexander*, 308

Romantic approach to human personality, 130, 216

Romanticism, 310–11, 317, 319, 343

Roth, Randolph, work of discussed, 103 n.101,

Roth, Randolph (*continued*)
  153, 203, 229, 244–45 and nn.38–40, 359, 362,
  367, 401
Rowe, Elizabeth: *Devout Exercises*, 337
Royal Standard English Dictionary, 297, 327, 341
Royall, Anne: quoted, 329–30
Royalton, Vt., 262, 352–53
rural infrastructure. *See* infrastructure, rural
rural life: building blocks of, 360; complete cycle
  of rural civilization, xx; diversity, 33, 110, 112,
  136, 140; dominant pattern in rural economy,
  31; emergence of first two widely literate rural
  generations, xxi, 5–7, 23, 27; new order of, 98,
  103, 107; pluralism and cultural diversity,
  359–61; rural development, full cycle of, defined, 9; rural industrialization, 98, 344; rural
  industry and Windsor District family life,
  227–40; structures of, 8; transformation, 135–36;
  variety in, 8, 31; *see also* economic life; human
  habitats; Industrial Revolution; knowledge of
  the world; women
  —ideas about: entrepreneurial ethos, 107; positive
  and negative attitudes toward, 107; rural critique of commercial society, 107; rural felicity,
  traditional image transformed, 350; rural ideal
  of "middle station" in Windsor District, 14,
  342, 364
  —major developments, 1780–1835: commercialization and rural infrastructure, 352–54; dawn of a
  "modern" age in rural New England, 346–52;
  emergence of an age of reading, 354–59; era of
  rural pluralism and cultural diversity, 359–61;
  shift in meanings of human happiness, 361–64
Rural Magazine, 298
rural printing, urban influence on, 203
rurality of Upper Valley, extreme in North Atlantic context, 22
Rusche, Dennis, 38, 265–66; quoted, 37, 378;
  "reading, age of oral," 378
Rush, Benjamin: quoted, 43
Russell, Howard, 398
Russell, John: *Vermont State Prison*, 310
Russia, 22
Rustic Dance After a Sleigh Ride, 379
Rutland, Vt., 31, 74, 182, 198, 200, 298
Rutman, Darrett B., 398; quoted, 226
Ryegate, Vt., boarding school at, 46

Sabbath schools, 357
Sacred Biography, 338
sacred history, 260; *see also* history, works
sacred knowledge and works. *See* Protestant
  Christianity
sacred and secular knowledge, combination of,

sacred and secular knowledge (*continued*)
  21, 134, 138, 193, 197–98, 347; evidence for distinction, 277 n.31; sacred and secular works,
  222, 275, 300, 324; *see also* ministers and deacons; Protestant Christianity; religion
Saints' Everlasting Rest, 13, 259, 290–91, 298, 327,
  337
Salisbury, Elizabeth, 411
Sanders, Daniel: *History of the Indian Wars*, 308,
  310, 324
Sargeant, Rev. Samuel, family library, 280–81
Says She to Her Neighbor, What, 201
scale of generalization, problem discussed, 27–34
Schofield, Roger, 124
Scholar's Arithmetic, 57, 297
schools, district, 121, 148, 200, 256, 287; as agent
  of literacy, 121–27; attendance rates in 1827–28,
  124; content of district school education, 6,
  124, 126–27; in diffusion of knowledge, 19;
  district committees, 261; emerge in unison with
  general stores, 22; enrollment, 21–22; lack of,
  and spread of reading, 274; neighborhood
  district system, 355; numbers of, 357; and relationship to market activity, 128; and relation to
  Protestantism, 127 n.24; school environment,
  21–22; schooling, 273; sequence of skills development, 41, 124; summer and winter district
  schools, 124; and women, 44; *see also* academies; reading instruction
schoolbooks, 5, 21, 26, 146, 152, 172, 175, 192,
  198–99, 201, 208, 216, 219, 251, 261–62, 265–67,
  277–79, 281, 288, 297–98, 306, 308–10, 314, 316,
  323–26, 329, 334, 337, 339, 341, 358, 408, 411;
  arithmetics, 115; geographies and atlases, 115,
  220, 408; grammars, 314; histories, 220; in
  district school education, 125; readers, 39, 115,
  124, 209, 219, 282, 308, 325, 333, 408; readers as
  introductions to Western intellectual tradition,
  408; readers, newer types, 298; spellers, 39, 123,
  124 n.19, 146, 219, 282, 333
Schutz, Alfred, 140, 153; quoted, 135, 285
science, 97, 107
science and religion, as staunch allies, 299; relationship between, 411
science and technology, works, 193, 200–3, 208,
  216, 221, 251, 267, 281, 310, 314, 316, 318, 328–29,
  334, 340–42 and n.96, 358, 411
scientific farming, 411
Scotland, 20, 22, 25, 27, 132, 354–55; literacy rate,
  276; *see also* Edinburgh; Glasgow; Scottish
Scott, Donald, 378
Scott, Thomas: *Family Bible*, 295, 325, 327
Scott, Sir Walter, 267; *Works*, 316, 340–41
Scott, William: *Lessons in Elocution*, 40, 333

Scottish: Common Sense philosophy, 310, 340; Enlightenment, 312, 338, 412; perspectives, 299
Seaman, Valentine: *Mineral Waters*, 324
Seasons, 316, 334
secular knowledge and works, 196, 198–99, 201, 208, 275, 281–82, 286, 347, 411; *see also* almanacs; books; broadsides; children's books; clandestine publications; classical writings; dictionaries; economics; geographies; histories; law works; medical works; military affairs; modern literature; newspapers; novels; pamphlets; periodicals; philosophy; politics and government; schoolbooks; science and technology; secular music; stages-of-life works; travel accounts
secularization, 337, 346, 349
self-sufficiency, defined as relative dependence and not isolation, 302
Sellers, May, and McMillen: quoted, 367
semiskilled laboring families, 143, 147, 233–34, 244–45, 302, 330, 390, 393; *see also* family life; family libraries, by library types
Sentiments Concerning the Coming and Kingdom of Christ, 323, 338
Sequel to English Reader, 297
Serious Call, 298, 337
sermons. *See* theology
settlement, 85, 100; pioneer stage, 301; proximity to transportation routes as key determinant, 72
Shaftesbury, 61
Shay's Rebellion, 26
shipping routes, 24; *see also* book trade
short title system of transcription, 402
singing: and music, 377–78; schools, 379
Sketch Book, The, 308, 310, 319
Sketches From Nature, 268
Smart, George: quoted, 269
Smith, Adam: *Wealth of Nations*, 61, 340
Smith, Asa: quoted, 352
Smith, Donald, 72
Smith, Elias, 309, *Life, Conversion*, 314
Smith, Ethan: *View of the Hebrews*, 308
Smith, Joseph, 27, 115, 226, 309, 351, 369; family, 360–61
Smith, Rev. Roswell, family, 239
Smith, Samuel Stanhope: *Essay on Human Species*, 340
Smollett, Tobias: *Roderick Random*, 334
snuff boxes and "an Electrikl Machine," symbols of continuity and change, 410
social development. *See* development
social libraries. *See* lending libraries
social reform organizations, 103 n.105; 262, 411; *see also* benevolent reform organizations

society, nature of American as central cultural question, 359
Soltow, Leo, and Stevens, Edward: quoted, 130
South, of U.S., 27
South Carolina, 405; family library incidence and size, 275
Southey, Robert: *Letters from England*, 340
Spafford, Horatio Gates: *Gazetteer of New York*, 316
Spain, 22
Spalding, Joshua: *Sentiments Concerning the Coming and Kingdom of Christ*, 323, 338
Spaulding household, 239; intergenerational accumulation and transmission of libraries, e.g. of, 404
Spectator, 316–17, 334
Speller, 115, 124, 297
spelling in district school education, 124; *see also* reading instruction; schools, district; Webster, Noah
spine titles, defined, 402–3; and family libraries, 1787–1835, xxi n.5, 270 n.23, 402–9
"spirit of fact," 215 pl., 216, 310, 341; contemporary meaning, 107, 299; and mensuration, 310
Spiritual Songs, 327, 337
Spooner, Alden, 80, 88, 97, 239, 256, 280, 353; quoted, 193
Springfield, Mass., 59
Springfield, Vt., 68, 71–72, 88–89, 100, 103–4, 139–40, 142, 144–45, 176, 182, 184, 235, 238, 275, 301–2, 304, 330–32 and n.75, 344, 357, 401; Baptist society, 303; Fire Insurance Company, 104
St. Louis, 274
stage of life works, 172, 193, 199–202, 208, 216, 220–21, 265, 267, 282, 298, 307, 310, 313, 316–19, 326–29, 334–35, 340–43, 358, 411; *see also* life cycle
stagecoach line: Boston and Keene Telegraph and Dispatch Line, 100; Pioneer Line, 100
stationery, 80, 169; *see also* bookstore; book trade; printing and publishing
steady sellers, 127 n.23, 383; *see also* popular sellers
steamboats, 107
Steele, Zadock: *Narrative of the Captivity and Sufferings*, 334
Sterne, Laurence: *Works*, 334, 340
Stewart, Dugald: *Elements of the Philosophy of the Human Mind*, 340
Stilwell, Lewis, 362
Stockbridge, Vt., 181, 233, 262, 352
stores, 76–79, 81–82, 84–85, 88–90, 92–98, 100, 102; *see also* commercial exchange; economic life
Story, Joseph: quoted, 19–20

Stowe, Harriet Beecher: quoted, 266
Stratham, N.H., 319
Sullivan County, N.H., 29, 32
Sunday schools, 378; libraries, 161; Sunday School Union, 104; in relation to literacy training, 122
supernatural world of magic and spirits and Mormonism, 361; secular supernatural world, 299
Sweden, 20–21, 25, 27, 116, 121, 354–56; literacy rate, 276
Swedenborg, Emmanuel: *Miscellaneous Works*, 340
System of Arithmetic, 297

tables, referred to: 1–1, 31, 72, 100; 2–1, 62, 257, 297; 3–1, 119; 3–2, 119, 128; 4–1, 150, 152, 386, 393; 4–2, 143, 389, 393; 4–3, 150; 5–1, 165, 171; 5–2, 165, 171; 5–3, 169; 6–1, 193; 6–2, 205, 219; 6–3, 205, 208, 219, 409; 7–1, 228, 240, 390, 393; 7–2, 242, 244, 401; 7–3, 246–47; 7–4, 249, 251; 8–1, 271; 8–2, 275; 8–3, 277; 9–1, 296; 9–2, 305; 9–3, 314; 9–4, 324; 9–5, 335; 9–6, 337; app. 1–1, 380; app 2–1, 187, 386, 388–89, 392–93; app. 2–2, 388; app. 2–3, 187, 390, 392–93; app. 2–4, 187, 392–93; app. 3–1, 398; app. 4–1, 406; app. 5–1, 410–11; *see also* family libraries–by human habitat for tables N–I to N–II
Tale of the times, 340
Tales, 21
tax records, 244; *see also* Roth, Randolph
Taylor, John, of Caroline, 69
technology, 107, 342; *see also* science and technology
telegraph, 149, 349
temperance, 107–8
tenant farm families, 147, 233–34, 244–45, 295, 301–2, 306–7, 390, 392–93; *see also* family life; family libraries, by library types
Terrible Tractoration, 334
texts and meanings, 288–291 and n.6; complexity of seen in Baxter, *Saints' Everlasting Rest*, 290
Thaddeus of Warsaw, 340
theaters, Windsor District, 358
theology, 21, 172, 192, 198–202, 208, 211–12, 220–21, 251, 265, 278–81, 296, 298, 304, 306–10, 313, 316, 318, 326–27, 329, 331, 334, 338, 342, 358, 411
Thiebault, Dieudonne: *Frederick the Great*, 334
Thomas á Kempis: *Imitation of Christ*, 337
Thomas, Isaiah, 200
Thomas, Robert: *Farmer's Almanac*, 295
Thompson, E. P.: quoted, 83
Thomson, James, 69: *Seasons*, 316, 334
Thoreau, Henry David: quoted, 117
Tillotson, John: *Works*, 338
Tilton, Theodore: *Life of Elizabeth Cady Stanton*, 49

Tinkham, Amos, Windsor artisan family, 294, 301
Tom Jones, 334
Tomkins, Abel: quoted, 11, 359
Tour through Sicily, 334
townships: defined, 32 n.30; diversity in Windsor District, 400–1
tradition, reading as strong defender of, 34–35, 37–40, 42
tragedy, unfolding of from perspective of contemporaries, 11–15; *see also* disillusionment
transatlantic intellectual traditions, 189; European-authored works, 193
transportation and communications network, 21, 24, 29, 73–75, 89, 100, 163; access zones, 178–88 and n.39; full-access zone, 93, 128, 179–80, 182, 184, 187, 268, 388–90, 392–93, 395; minimum-access zone, 93, 129, 144, 146–47, 181 and n.33, 184–85, 207, 297, 388–90, 393, 395; partial-access zone, 93, 128, 144, 181, 184–86, 268, 305, 388–90, 393, 395; transportation revolution, 148; travel conditions, 178, 180; travel distances, 183; varying access to, 96, 102, 127, 136, 138–39, 181–82; *see also* circulation system for print culture
travel accounts, 21, 26, 172, 192, 199–200, 208, 212, 216, 220–21, 251, 261, 267, 279, 295, 298–99, 308, 311, 319, 327, 329, 334–35, 339–40, 358, 411
travel distances and access to print, 386
Travels in New England, 351
Travels in Various Countries, 308, 319
Travels through the Interior Parts of North America, 1766–1768, 295
Travels through Sicily, 334
Treatise on Atonement, 338
Treatise on Self Knowledge, 328, 337
Trenck, Fredrich von der: *Life of*, 298
Trewartha, Glenn T.: quoted, 313
Trumbull, John: *M'Fingal*, 317
Tutu, Bishop Desmond, 369
Twice Told Tales, 49
Two Select Works, 62, 298, 327
Tyler, Royall: *Algerine Captive*, 317

Unitarianism and Unitarians, 331, 358; theology, 411; works, 211
Universalism and Universalists, 62, 293, 296, 298, 307, 318, 323, 327, 338, 358, 361; hymnals, 198; ministerial training school at Reading, 358; theology, 411; works, 202, 211, 296, 316, 319, 326, 331, 338
University of Vermont, 358
Upper Valley: as representative subregioal unit, 2 (defined, 27–34); communication system and

Upper Valley (*continued*)
    book trade, 1778–1835, 157–88; population, 2;
        settlement, 29; variety in, 31
urbanization, xx, 18; difference vs. change in
    rural society, 353; relationship to lifelong learn-
    ing, 21
utilitarianism, Christian, 340

values: contemporary diffusion by electronic
    media, 372; entrepreneurial, 106–8; manufactur-
    ing and marketplace, 97; *see also* cultural values
    and beliefs; intellectual traditions and beliefs
Venn, Henry: *Complete Duty of Man*, 337
Vergilius Maro, Publius: *Works*, 69
Vermont Laws and Statutes, 80, 299, 327
Vermont maps, 310, 316, 327; *see also* Whitelaw,
    James
Vermont State Bank, 102
Vermont State Prison, 310
"Viator," essay by: quoted in [Rutland] *Farmer's
    Library*, 74
Vicar of Wakefield, 13, 241, 324, 328
View of the Hebrews, 308
View of the Religions, 338
Village Harmony, 316
Village Magazine, 167, 357
villages: major rural, 23–24; population in Wind-
    sor District, 1810–30, 100–1; sharply distin-
    guished from cities, 74; *see also* Chester;
    Springfield; Weathersfield; Windsor
Virginia: family library incidence and size,
    274–75; and in Shenandoah Valley, 274
Vision of Columbus, 334
visual expression, 377, 379–80
visual objects, proportion of population engaged
    in making, 380
Voltaire, Jean François-Marie Arouet de: *Charles
    the Twelfth*, 308
voluntary organizations, 103–4, 106, 109 n.125,
    353; and villages, 333
Voyage to Georgia, 334
Voyage to the South Sea, 327
Voyages and Adventures, 327
Vulpius, Christian: *Rinald Rinaldini*, 298

Wales, 22
Walker, 310
Walker, John: *Critical Pronouncing Dictionary*, 341
Wallace, Anthony, 153, 312, 341
Walpole, N.H., 41, 160, 162, 167, 177, 198, 200
Walpole: bookstores, 59, 162, 200; printing
    office, 57 n.9
Walpole Farmer's Museum, 167
Walsh, Robert: *Appeal from the Judgments*, 68

*Walton's Vermont Register and Farmer's Almanac
    for 1828*: quoted, 189
War News from Mexico, 378
Ward, Donal, 368
Warville, Brissot de: quoted, 73
Washington, George, 299
Watts, Isaac: *Improvement of the Mind*, 262;
    Hymns and Spiritual Songs, 62, 327, 337; *Psalms
    of David*, 62, 327, 337; *see also* hymnals; psalm
    books
Way to Wealth, 201
wealth: and cultural participation, 248–49; and
    holdings of printed matter in Windsor District,
    247–53; and incidence of family libraries, 249;
    and lending library shares, 249; levels of
    among families, 249; and print retention, 389;
    and relationship to printed matter, 249, 252;
    role of newspaper in making disparities visible,
    241; and size of holdings, 249; among wealthy,
    249, 251–52, 264; and Windsor District family
    life, 227–40; *see also* economic class structure of
    Windsor District
Wealth of Nations, 61, 340
weather, Upper Valley, 1, 13
Weathersfield, Vt., 68, 71–72, 80, 84, 89, 95, 103,
    140, 142, 145, 184–85, 187, 301–2, 318, 330–34 and
    n.75, 401
Webster, Charles and George: *Clerk's Magazine*,
    304, 308
Webster, Daniel, 20; quoted, 18–19, 54
Webster, Noah, 40, 265; *American Dictionary*, 82
    and n.58, 96 nn.84–85; *American Selection*, 327;
    American Speller, 53; beliefs re goal of educa-
    tion, 37; *Compendious Dictionary*, 82; quoted,
    37–38, 158, 225, 228; *Speller*, 115, 124, 297
Weems, Mason Locke; *Life of Washington*, 308
Wells, Mrs. A. M., Academy for Young Ladies,
    45
Wesley, John: *Primitive Physic*, 314; *Sermons*, 62
West, Jane: *Tale of the Times*, 340
West, of U.S., 27
West Windsor, Vt., 140, 144, 311–12, 358, 407;
    moral library, 322; *see also* Windsor
Western World: comparative framework, 6, 20,
    23–24, 26; cultural tradition, 351
Weston, Vt., 63, 93, 100, 128–29, 140–41, 144,
    146, 149, 185, 292–94, 297, 311–12, 358, 388, 401,
    407
Wheelock, Rev. Eleazer, 343
White, Henry Kirk: *Remains*, 340
Whitelaw, James, maps, 68; Vermont maps, 310,
    316, 327
Whole Duty of Man, 61
wholesaling. *See* book trade

Wife, The, Interspersed with a Variety of Anecdotes and Observations, 343
Wiles, Roy: quoted, 18
Williams, John, family, 326
Williams, John: *Redeemed Captive Returning to Zion*, 324
Williams, Nicholas, Springfield gentleman farmer family, 303
Williams, Samuel, 298; *Natural and Civil History* 308, 310, 316, 338
Williams River, 182
Willich, Anthony: *Domestic Encyclopedia*, 343
Willingham, William, 247
Willis, Dr. James, Plymouth Union physician family, 314, 316
Willison, John: *Afflicted Man's Companion*, 298
Wilson, John: *Lights and Shadows of Scottish Life*, 340
Windham, Conn., economic class structure, 246
Windham County, Vt., 32
Windsor, Vt., 46, 49, 68, 71–73, 76, 78–80, 83–89, 92–96, 100, 102–3, 106, 128, 139, 142, 144, 148, 152, 163, 167, 169, 181–85, 187, 198–200, 207–8, 226, 235, 239–40, 255, 268, 270, 275, 294–95, 300–2, 305, 307, 311, 318, 320, 322–24, 330–35 and n.75, 344, 350, 357–58, 388, 401, 406, 410; academies at 44–45, 47; population, 31, 184; *see also* West Windsor
—organizations, Windsor: Bank, 104; Circulating Library, 150; County Bible Society, 104; County Temperance Society, 104; County Farmers' and Mechanics' Association, 104; Dancing Academy, 45; Debating Society, 45, 256; Encyclopedia Library, 152; Female Academy, 45; Grammar School, 44, 46; High School, 44; Lyceum, 49, 358; Mechanics Association, 256; Mrs. A. M. Wells Academy for Young Ladies, 45; Old South Congregational Church, 323; Scientific and Literary Institution, 44; Stenography School, 45
Windsor County, Vt., 32
Windsor District, as unit for intensive analysis, 400–1; defined, 2, 29; rationale for focus on, 31–34
Windsor Federal Gazette, 85 n.66
Windsor Morning Ray, 148
Windsor Post Boy, 85 n.66
Windsor Vermont Chronicle, 107, 254
Windsor Vermont Journal, 26, 73, 78–81, 83–86, 97, 107, 148, 160, 167, 193, 212, 313
Windsor Vermont Republican and Journal, 10–11, 45, 107
Windsor Washingtonian, 199
wisdom of the ages, 8, 35, 37, 39, 124, 126, 133,

wisdom of the ages (*continued*)
140, 265, 268, 297, 309, 325, 359, 361, 369, 372; in contemporary usage, 37, 39
Witherspoon, John: *Works*, 340
women and Upper Valley life: and domestic sphere, 43–44; and estate inventories, 229 n.8, 260–61, 407; as family members, aspects studied, 33; female headed households, 229, 232, 234, 236, 326; females and "occupation," 228; greater visibility and diversity of female participation in hamlet habitat, 318; and occupational designation system, 396–97; and property, wife's dower and personal property, 229 n.8, 245; scarcity of in mountainous townships during settlement era, 72 and n.37, 85 n.65; women's roles, conservative attitude toward, 44; *see also* commercial exchage; family life; gender differences; human habitats
—cultural participation by, 49; and academy education, gender segregated, 43–47, 49 (mixed, 46); appeals to, 318 (and in newspapers, 221); and cultural transformation, 35, 37, 44–47, 49; and district school education in Windsor District, 42–47, 49; graduate of Susannah Rowson's academy, quoted on participation, 43; ideology of republican motherhood and, 37, 42–44, 49, 130, 261; increasing newspaper reading and rising literacy rates, 305; intellectual emancipation, progress toward and limits on, 42–50; in lyceums, 49; new cultural role for, 43; and Sunday schools, 44; and writing to preserve knowledge, 382; *see also* cultural participation; cultural values and beliefs; economic thinking in Windsor District; human habitats; intellectual traditions and themes; knowledge of the world; *mentalités*
—and literacy: adjusted literacy rates, 127; changing uses of literacy and shifts in reading habits, 117; expansion in literacy, 116–17, 119, 128–29; increasing newspaper reading and rising female literacy rates, 305; minimum total female literacy rate, 120; sources for study of literacy trends, 119; *see also* literacy; schools, district
—and reading, 25, 35; achievement in lifelong learning, 118; adult women, 221; appeals to, 318 (and in newspapers, 221); and Blackstone's *Commentaries*, 43; changing uses of literacy in shifts in reading habits, 117; and informal enlargement of reading circle, 47; reading communities shaped by human habitats, 47; war of lists of appropriate works, 47; *see also* family library types; intellectual traditions and themes; reading
Wood, Gordon: quoted, 316

Woodstock, Vt., 11 n.10, 93, 167, 187, and n.41
Woodstock Working Man's Gazette, 109
Woodstock Workingmen's Society 108
Woodville, Richard Caton, 132; *War News from Mexico*, 132 n.36, 378
Worcester, 13
Worcester, Mass., 31, 59
work: and gender, 228; contemporary meaning, 227; greater specialization in, 110 n.132, 228; *see also* family life; occupations
workingmen, 103, 358; Workingmen's movement, 349
Works of Rev. E. Young, 363
Worst, Jonathan, 337, 379
Wright, Frances, 50
writing, 20–21, 37, 41, 45, 47, 115, 118, 123–24, 126, 377, 380, 382–83 and n.13; cultural context of,

writing (*continued*)
380; in district school education, 124; evidence for share of households, 127 n.23; letter writing, 73, 132, 382–83; lists of letters, 357; signs of in inventories, 325; types of written matter preserved, 382 and n.16; writing school, 357; writing skills, 131

yeoman farm families, 138, 144–45, 147, 231–32, 244, 275, 291, 294, 301, 306–7, 322–23, 325, 390, 392–93; *see also* family life; family libraries, by library types
yeomanry, ideal of rural Christian, 11
Young, Edward: *Night Thoughts*, 69, 324, 327, 338
Young Clerk's Companion, 308
Young Men's County Convention, Woodstock, Vt., 11 n.10
youth. *See* life cycle